Art and Society

SUNY Series in the Sociology of Culture
Charles R. Simpson, editor

Art and Society

Readings in the Sociology of the Arts

edited by

Arnold W. Foster
and
Judith R. Blau

State University of New York Press

Published by
State University of New York Press, Albany

© 1989   State University of New York

For information, address State University of New York
Press, State University Plaza, Albany, N.Y., 12246

Library of Congress Cataloging in Publication Data

Art and society: readings in the sociology of the arts / edited by
    Arnold W. Foster and Judith R. Blau.
        p.   cm. — (SUNY series in the sociology of culture)
    Bibliography: P.
    Includes index.
    ISBN 0–7914–0117–0 (pbk.).—ISBN 0–7914—0116–2
    1. Arts and society—United States. 2. Arts and society.
I. Foster, Arnold W., 1919–. II. Blau, Judith R., 1942–
III. Series.
NX180.S6A684   1989
306′.47—dc19   88–38446
                                                                          CIP

10 9 8 7 6 5 4 3 2 1

To Janet, Ruth, and David and their continuing encounters with the arts.

And, to the memory of a student of culture, William E. Hall.

Contents

Preface

We estimate that if we would pool the numbers of students in our classes in the Sociology of the Arts and the Sociology of Culture, together we have taught over 2500 students. This collection is based on our experiences with these students over the years. We have included selections that deal with the "elite arts" and also with the commercial and folk arts, and because it is our conviction that other disciplines have much to contribute to a sociological perspective on the problems in this field, we have included selections by anthropologists and musicologists.

Introduction

Art is Old and Ubiquitous

Attuned to our own place and time, we sometimes forget that art is universal and has existed since the Paleolithic Age. It also is a truism that all peoples have art, but not all peoples have all of the arts. Sometimes aesthetic activity is not recognized because it is merged with something else such as the music and dance of a military parade or the architecture of a building used by a religious organization. Much of the earliest art known is thought to have been used for magical purposes such as to insure fertility or guarantee success on the hunt.

Certainly art is old. The elaboration of the cave paintings, the care in the carving of some of the "Venuses" and animal forms, and the balance and grace of many stone tools, from different periods and cultures of the earliest humans, attest to the age of the aesthetic impulse, even if these objects were designed for other uses. Folktales and myths, the most ancient forms of literature, were used to teach the young as histories of heroic events, as explanations of the world and as hymns to the deities (Thompson, 1946), yet many myths still survive because they have literary interest. Franz Boas (1955) believed that art resulted from the practice of making utilitarian objects. The developed skills became devices for playing with form and creating beauty. Boas' thesis is supported by a recent study of a "factory" in Nairobi which produces "tourist" art, where carvers, hired to produce crude "Masai" figures (those slender, rough, black figures of an animal or a person), began to refine their work, produce creative innovations and apply aesthetic judgment (Jules-Rosette, 1984).

Certainly art as a universal activity has special value for humankind. Yet we have not to this point in time learned enough about its connections to social behavior to speak easily and with authority about them. The articles contained within this book should help our understanding about the relationships between art and society.

1

Sociologists and Art

Because of the ubiquity of the arts, one might expect that a great deal of attention would have been given them by sociologists. Anthropologists have written extensively about the arts as cultural artifacts and have showed how they attach to the cultural core in many places. Ethnomusicology is an active field of study. Psychologists have tested people for taste, for the development of skills in the arts and for the emotional parallels to color and sound. But in recent years, sociologists have paid little attention to the arts.

The early sociologists in Europe and the United States thought that art was important. Karl Marx argued that art was a social product. He wrote,

> "The senses of social man are different from those of non-social man. It is only through the objectively deployed wealth of the human being that the wealth of subjective human sensibility (a musical ear, an eye that is sensitive to beauty of form, in short, senses which are capable of human satisfaction and which confirm themselves as human faculties) is cultivated or created. . . . The cultivation of the five senses is the work of all previous history" (1963).

Simmel wrote about the place of the arts in social interaction. Max Weber wrote on "ethics" as congeries of beliefs and values centering on religion or art or some other institutional value, which gave direction to social behavior. He contended that the religious ethic and art ethic were nonrational rivals and that one had to dominate or conflict with the other (1946). Weber's major work on the arts has a different theme. It examined music as an example of the process of rationalization which changed this essentially nonrational activity in the modern world (1958).

Many of the first generation of American sociologists also thought that art was important. Dealey and Ward placed it with the "spiritual forces" which marked human society. They wrote that

> "Art is a socializing agency. It is an agency of civilization as distinguished from preservation and perpetration" (1907).

E. A. Ross treated art as a major form of social control (1897). In the last chapter of his *Social Process*, Cooley tells us that art

> " . . . takes the confused and distracting reality, and by omitting the irrelevant and giving life and color to the significant, enables us to see the real as the ideal" (1966).

Most of the early American sociologists agreed with Cooley that art had a moral function—that beauty and the ideal were related.

Despite the early interest, things changed. From the middle 1920s to recently, sociologists have neglected art. Mention of art disappeared from introductory textbooks, a condition that is generally true today.

Why was art neglected during this period? There appear to be a variety of reasons. First, sociologists, like plumbers, fishermen and bankers, are products of their own culture. American culture has strong components of pragmatism, materialism and puritanical ideology, all of which devalue the arts. As the "art for art's sake" doctrine became more popular, it became more difficult to maintain the stance that art had a moral function, that it was useful to the good society as Cooley, Ward and others had argued.

In general, sociologists in the United States have been reform minded. For example, studies of stratification deal with questions of stratification; questions of distributive justice; studies of prisons deal with the deprivation of prisoners; research on work often examines the working conditions of the workers. That is, sociologists—though they try to remain unbiased—are more often interested in issues that will improve the world or benefit the disadvantaged. The arts are considered good in and of themselves, and of little importance to solution of social problems.

The development of a rigorous methodology patterned after the natural sciences may be another factor that explains the neglect of art. The Columbian trained school of methodologists, Rice, Chapin and Ogburn[1] and Chapin's student Lundberg, had great influence in limiting sociology to phenomena which could be studied directly with quantitative techniques.[2]

A final reason why American sociologists have paid little attention to art is somewhat more complex. Judith Kramer has written, "Sociologists acknowledge the universality of art while they ignore its uniqueness" (1965). And later she writes,

> "And if art is indistinguishable from anything else, then there is nothing distinctive about the role of artists or the institutions of art. There is therefore no sociological basis for attributing any special social function to art." (Kramer).

The distinctiveness of art has been ignored, and many sociologists have treated art as a derivative of an other activity such as recreation, as communication, as occupation or as an instrument of something else.

However, in the past twenty years there has been renewed interest in the sociology of the arts. More research is taking place, as can be judged by the number of recent articles and books in the bibliography at the end of the book. An annual Social Theory, Politics and the Arts Conference is held in the United States, and many American sociologists belong to the Sociology of Art Research Council of the International Sociological Association. The new Cultural Sociology Section of the American Sociological Association has grown rapidly, and sociologists of the arts mingle happily with sociologists of science, of religion and those interested in leisure studies. What are the reasons for this turn-around?

Since World War II there has been greater contact with sociologists in countries where art is considered an important social institution. Second, art has become a major part of ethnic and racial identity. Third, government—federal, state and local—through arts councils has underscored the significance of arts in American society. A major goal of the National Endowment for the Arts was to support grass roots arts. Even before government took note, the arts were made visible through their use in support of equal rights for Blacks and as part of the youth culture in the 1960s.

Finally, due to the youth movement of the late sixties, and its use of folk and popular music and art in promoting concern for social problems, a new generation of sociologists turned their attention to popular culture. Supported by a populist ideology, the argument was made that the popular arts, as arts of the working classes, were as important as the "fine" arts. A dialogue that developed around this issue, turned the attention of many young sociologists to the arts, popular and fine. Today, the line between elite and popular art is not as clear as it once seemed to be. As the arts are defined more broadly now, we recognize the consequence that an increase in leisure time has fostered participation in the arts, as well as in sports and hobbies. Because we have defined the arts more broadly, there is a growing recognition that art is involved in the quality of life, not just by solving social problems, but by making this increasingly urbanized and rationalized world more attractive and humane.

Social Theories of Art

As one might expect, there are a variety of theories about the relationships between society and art. Although they all deal with the social nature of art, some of them use psychological and biological explanations. Some emphasize certain aspects of culture at the expense of others, such as those that focus on communication and/or symbols while neglecting other dimensions of culture. The social theories of art have been created by scholars in the fields of aesthetics as well as the social sciences. In a review of the approaches, five major emphases can be found (Foster, 1979).

Biological and Psychological Emphases

The first emphasis stems from biology and psychology and assumes a variety of forms.

A. In the Nineteenth Century when sociology was forming, *biologically based theories* of society and art were predominant and their influence is still with us. Art was considered part of the evolutionary force by Herbert Spencer (1900). It was called an ''impulse'' by Hirn (1900), a ''need'' by others.

B. *Psychological theories* are still popular. There are three major approaches. One is the freudian in which art is regarded as fantasy providing catharsis (Freud, 1943; 1956; 1958). Another approach is employed by art and music therapists who legitimate their work by affirming the efficacy of the use of art in dealing with mental illness. Finally, from Friedrich Schiller's time to the present, many writers have treated art as a form of play and explained it psychologically. Art has certainly been used as entertainment, and the play notion today is mostly held by those who study the popular arts.

There are a number of ways these theories are similar which relate to their biological and/or psychological slant. First, they are all theories of motivation. They imply that internal energy sets the conditions for art. Second, they emphasize the common-human nature of the aesthetic impulse of need. Finally, there is the further hidden assumption that since we all have the capacity for the same response to any art object, art transcends culture and there are objective standards of quality which can be discovered. Support for this assumption comes from the work of the psychologist Irvin Child (1968; 1972; Child & Spiroto, 1965) who has been conducting cross-cultural studies on aesthetic judgment. He has found remarkable concurrence about the quality of works of art between artists and craftsmen of diverse cultures. Not only do his findings support the notion that art is universal, but they indicate that quality or evaluation of art is not simply relative to a specific culture. Child's research indicates that, although cultural styles differ, quality appears to be based on common-human perception and appreciation. He also found that artists and untrained members of the public in the same society agree less about quality than do artists from different cultures. This indicates that awareness of quality requires learning, that whatever common-human biological basis for understanding art exists, it needs cultural experience to bring it out.

But when Morse Peckham (1967), a literary scholar, writes that ''creating works of art and looking at them serves some physiological need,'' the sociologists shrugs and says, ''Alright, but how does that apply?'' It is the old instinct theory that was very popular in the early part of this century that explained everything and explained nothing. Like much of current socio-biology theory, a certain kind of human behavior (such as aggressiveness) is observed, and because it is so widespread, an assumption is made that it must be biological at its base.

Other than emphasizing its common-human nature, biological and psychological explanations are not sufficient to explain the existence of art. A need for aesthetic experience can be satisfied without creating art, such as in the appreciation of nature. Another shortcoming of these explanations is that cultural diversity in creating art is not demonstrated. Why have African peoples advanced the dance while ignoring painting? Why have some cultures specialized in music, others literature? Cultural diversity is not explained by biology except through the questionable argument that in different gene pools (read races) different talents are more common. Also, despite occasional discussion of the elements of form, the art work is seldom treated in any way except as a complex of stimuli. In this approach the search for the appeal of art is in the stimuli cue response in the individual, not in the individual's relationship to specific and concrete aspects of the art work. Bio-psychological approaches have little use for anyone who wants to understand art as something which acts in society and, in turn, is influenced and shaped by society.

Yet such reductionistic theories continue today. The psychological theories satisfy the great emphasis on individualism shared by many Americans. The biological imagery also satisfies those who accept mass and weight as more real than behavior and relationships.

Broad Social and Cultural Emphases

An alternative to the bio-psychological approaches are emphases that are called "cultural." But social and cultural conditions are usually mixed, they are each dependent on the other. There are different aspects of a socio-cultural theme also. Art might be viewed as knowledge, or value expression, or as the visible component of socio-cultural beliefs. Art might express religious, or political, or economic beliefs.

A. One approach is the treatment of art as *an aspect of spiritual production or culture*. For example, Karl Mannheim (1971) finds a basic intention (*Kunstwollen*), an aspect of the orientation of social values, behind each style of art.

The work of Vytautas Kavolis represented by a paper in this book, follows well this mode of analysis. Kavolis is careful to note that culture should not simply be considered a determinant of art style, because the development of style has a logic of its own which must be taken into account. In one of Kavolis' most interesting analyses, he finds that abstract expressionism became influential in the United States because it fit in well with Puritan value orientations (1968). In his second book (1972) he pushed his mode of analysis even further. Using data from Sorokin's, **Social and Cultural Dynamics** (1937) and applying interpretations from Bales' and Parsons' phase-cycle theory, he attempts to identify the social conditions which provide the seedbed for outbreaks of artistic creativity in history. His conclusion is that

> . . . . artistic creativity tends to be stimulated by a disturbance of a condition of relative equilibrium; reduced during the period of intense goal-directed action; increased during the normally following integrative phase, when the social system is settling down to a new equilibrium; and again reduced when the new equilibrium is taken for granted (1972).

Kavolis uses both social and cultural explanations in his work.

James Fernandez, an anthropologist, also uses a socio-cultural explanation. In an early article he found the impetus for art in a duality of opposition running through the Fang culture (1966). Reconsideration of the early thesis led him to the Durkheimian notion that Fang art really supported moral law and harmony (1973). The orientation of the English critic, Edward Lucie-Smith is in opposition to Fernandez' when he argues that art fills a gap in society—that it "supplies whatever elements are missing" (1970).

B. The very influential anthropologist, Franz Boas, started where the evolutionists and psychologists ended. By assuming the common-human nature of the aesthetic drive, he was able to get to the specifics of the development of art which he found in the technical advances made by primitive humans. His interpretation depended on the assumption that "there must be an intimate relation between *technique and a feeling for beauty*" (1955). The assumption was based on "the very fact that the manufacturers of man in each and every part of the world have a pronounced style proves that a feeling for form develops with technical activities" (1955). Although Boas might fit under the psychological and biological rubric, those factors are latent. His emphasis is on the activity involved in the production of the aesthetic object in which the interaction between the artist and the work is the precipitating or dynamic factor.[3]

C. Arthur Child (1944), a philosopher, took a *cultural deterministic* position and argued that art is simply *relative* to the values of a people. Anything can thus be designated as art. Child has gone too far in his rejection of the contribution of biologists and psychologists. Perhaps owing to Child's work, but more sophisticated and less deterministic, because other possible factors are mentioned, is the view suggested by Arthur Danto (1973) and developed by George Dickie (1974). Dickie tells us that a work of art is an artifact presented as a candidate for appreciation by someone called an artist. How does one know if the art is appreciated? Dickie answers that "An artifact's hanging in an art museum as part of a show and performance at a theater are sure signs" (Dickie: 37). But such presentation is not necessary, because status " . . . is usually conferred by a single person, the artist who creates the artifact" (p. 39). His definition seems like labelling theory, but the labelling comes from one person, the artist. It diminishes the importance of support from the art world that the sociologist would insist is necessary.

D. The *social structural* approach is very popular today. There are several variants. Perhaps best known is the Marxist. In general, it sees the class position of the artist and the public as determinants of the style of art produced. The notion that "fine art" is upper class art and "popular" or perhaps "folk art" is working class fits this approach. Indeed, it goes even deeper. Art supported by the upper classes serves to enhance and protect the power of the members of the upper class. A. L. Lloyd, for example, looks at the history of the working class and credits the conditions under which it lives for the shifts and turns of the creation of English folk music (1967). But Marxist writers so often admit other factors into their analyses that one might dub them "Marxist pluralists".

E. As with many of the Marxist writings, some of the cultural emphases are *pluralistic* in that they designate differences resulting from the variety of ethnic communities, classes, taste publics or value orientations in history as bases for understanding the operation of the arts in society (Foster, 1979b). For example, art is used to support cultural uniqueness in the writings of LeRoi Jones (1963; 1968); political orientation (1970); or national identity (1955). Adolph Tomars (1940) demonstrated that the community, class, the association and the ephemeral group provided publics which required different types of art. The Marxists make much of the class differences in art. Another dimension of pluralism is found in the different taste publics most recently documented by Herbert Gans (1974). Sorokin (1937) described different cultural orientations each with their own art styles, which existed in each society. To him, *Ideational* and *Sensate* tendencies (and the intermediate, *Idealistic*) are found in all cultures. Sometimes one or the other is in the ascendency. Sometimes they become synthesized and the society is called *Idealistic*. The qualitatively different styles of art are always found in any culture. Pluralism in art always exists. Art and other aspects of social life are bound up with a value orientation of a culture or an age. The three orientations are found in all societies, but usually not in equal proportions. *Sensate* obtains when values of the flesh are dominant. *Ideational* societies exist where ideas, ideals and beliefs are more important then physical needs or desires. *Idealistic* periods exist when there is an attempt to satisfy both physical and spiritual values. Change is understood as fluctuation between these different orientations. Thus art is seen as an expression of sensate or ideational values and can be used as a measure of social change and dominant values in society.

In sum, characteristics of the socio-cultural theme are fairly clear. They show well the complexity of art and its relationship to socio-cultural values. They make art an integral part of culture, as Fernandez demonstrates. Mannheim, Tomars, Sorokin and Marx are especially anti-reductionist. In addition, this approach makes it easy to relate the institutions of art to other social institutions, as Marx and Kavolis in an article in this book so well demonstrate.

Some features of this approach might indicate that a special sociology of the arts is not necessary. It can lead to the treatment of art as a simple derivative of culture like any other culture complex. That is the theory of cultural determinism. Under its influence the innovative or creative nature of art is neglected. Art becomes only a dependent factor, never an independent factor. It can take a different forms. In Arthur Child's hands it becomes cultural relativism. It almost does so in Dickie's work, except that he admits that "I am saying that every work of art must have some minimal *potential* value or worthiness" (1974: 42–43). With Fernandez, art is an aspect of the culture. Fernandez, studying a traditional society, may leave the impression that art is is merely supportive of a culture everywhere. Cultural determinist theories mask the common-human appeal of art. In its extreme form, art becomes anything that is so labelled. Followers of this approach miss the special nature of art.

Countering cultural determinism is the argument that if art is at the core of culture, its influence must thereby be strong and changes in art will effect more widespread change.

Art as an Aspect of Communication

Communication is cultural activity, but because so much attention is given it exclusive of other factors, it is treated as a separate category.

A. Wilhelm Wundt, a very influential early German psychologist, suggested that art was a form of gesture (1919). Today, there are a number of *communication theories*. One version focuses on the medium. By turning attention to the new modes of reproduction and dissemination of images, artistic and other, Marshall McLuhan helped to give an identity and a rationale for their profession top the craftspeople of the mass media (McLuhan, 1964). His phrase, "the medium is the message", helped popularize an idea which was earlier stated by Walter Benjamin (1936) and Arnold Hauser (1951) among others, that the machine, mass production of art objects and the organization oaf labor around new means of communication have had strong influence on the way in which we perceive the world. McLuhan's formula came in about the time when the discussion of the place and value of the mass arts in society became heated. As a formula it helped to bypass the old tedious arguments about quality and purpose of the arts. It found support from populist thinkers who had their faith in whatever was liked by ''the people'' and from those intellectuals who wanted to admit film, photography and television to the realm of the arts. It brought back support for a new form of craft activity which the mechanically, electronically, technologically oriented modern person could understand. It did turn attention to the exchange of meaning and feeling and promised that one could learn how to do this through technical know-how. This orientation is common today in the work of many sociologists who study the mass or popular arts.[4]

B. *Symbolic interactionism* identified with George Herbert Mead and others has similarities to communications theory, but is more analytical and probing, deals with a broader realm of social behavior. It has some similarities to the cultural structuralist approach to be discussed below, but focuses on the creation of meaning in social interaction rather than on interaction with the larger total world and its ''deep structures''. The symbolic interactionist emphasis, in extreme form considered a *dramatistic approach*, was used by H. D. Duncan (1953; 1957; 1962; 1964) a sociologist and Kenneth Burke (1945) a critic, to study social influences on literature. It appears to be more useful for the understanding of the graphic arts which use explicit symbols, rather than for the study of music or dance where the symbols may be more ambiguous. Some symbolic interactionists regard art as a product of consensus and symbolic identification. McCall writes

> ''Things like rectangles of canvas which have been stretched over wooden frames and painted on become art when they are treated as art by the people and collectivities who constitute an art world'' (1977: 32).

Expressed in this way, there is a relativism in this approach. George Dickie's thesis discussed above also has some similarities, but it diminishes awareness of the interactional nature of labelling.

The virtue of the symbolic interactionist approach is that it permits the explanation of the treatment of anti-art as art. It also helps one to understand the process by which objects are ''sold'' to a public as art. Advertising and other means of forming public opinion are very much a part of the legitimatization of art today. It is most useful in literature which depends on the understanding of verbal symbols. Above all, symbolic interaction-ism, in line with its title, reminds us that art conveys meaning in a social setting.

On the other hand, symbolic interactionism tends to direct attention away from the properties of objects which psychologists and aestheticians have found to be of importance. The symbolic interactionists may be lead-ing us to study only the relative and transitory dimensions of the art world, the fads and fashions, the culture-bound and voluntaristic. The sociologist must do this, but we can hope that he or she would also be concerned with the more universal aesthetic dimensions found in the properties of the art objects. The emphasis on the social nature of symbols, while neglecting the objects to which symbols are attached, makes for a narrow sociology (Foster, 1985).

However, symbolic interactionists do not have to ignore the value inherent in the objects. Charles Morris (1956), a student of and successor to George Herbert Mead, has given some suggestions as to how this can be done. He argues that value stems not only a from social definitions, but *also* from individuals' preferences, and from the properties of objects them-selves.

C. Jane Harrison (n.d.) wrote that art developed from religious ritual which bound the community together by communicating beliefs and values. She thought of art as a factor supporting the moral core of society. The moral dimension is recognized in her statement that

"We feel . . . a certain 'ought' which always spells social obligation" (240–241).[5]

D. Claude Lévi-Strauss links art, communication and *social structure*. Lévi-Strauss' method is to search for similarities or analogies in culture. If the similarities cannot be explained by diffusion, then there is an attempt to explain them by relating them to common conceptual themes. But it is not the themes that fully explain the similarities. The themes give a clue to a pattern of nature which underlies society and gives meaning and unity to that society. It seems that Lévi-Strauss is using a method much like that used by art historians when they bind the similarities between works of art into an explanation of the unity through the concept of style. However, he goes one step beyond and looks at the iconographic meaning of the style as revealed in a deeper time-defying pattern. Art contains meaning which helps like the structures of language to get through into the deep structures. "We can also find in society other kinds of languages . . . art, myth, ritual and religion" (1963: 84).

Like Sorokin, Lévi-Strauss is using art as an indicator of an ethos which is considered to be more basic and fundamental than the art itself. Unlike Sorokin, he has no predetermined value system in mind, although the kinship and economic structures are not simply relative since only a finite number of variations can work. Lévi-Strauss has helped us to understand more about the nature of art. He has linked it to dominant myths in a culture. In turn, he shows the importance of art in maintaining the myths and through them the stability of society. Art is not merely a commodity. Essentially used as communication, it is an important factor in the maintenance of society. Lévi-Strauss had a strong influence on scholars and critics in literature. Today many have become critical of his approach, yet their focus is still on communication.

The shortcomings of the communications approach are several. To begin, there is the tendency to be rationalistic and to neglect the expressive and the affective attributes. There is also the tendency to focus on the message and to neglect the formal dimensions of art. In its extreme Zhdanovite form, Socialist Realism only supports art which has a message, and proscribes art that has as its primary purpose the exploration of form. Those who emphasize the exchange of ideas often relegate art to merely being a vehicle for something else. The something else is, of course, the message. The further extension of this tendency is to equate art with other media, thus blurring the distinction between it and propaganda, advertising or education. Communications theories also tend to show only one side of a relationship. It helps explain art's influence on society, but not the influence of society on art.

Art as Ideal, Metaphysical Entity, Spiritual or Moral Force

There are a number of authors who write about the arts as not simply rooted in the material or cultural world, but in an idea or an abstract force.

A. Lester Ward, an early American sociologist classified art as one of the *spiritual forces* (1896: 623). Moving from one level, where exist the biological, the reproductive and nutritive, up the ladder to the aesthetic, emotional, moral and intellectual, the forces become progressively more spiritual. It is his theory of emergent evolution. Later on it became popular for psychologists and sociologists to consider such spiritual forces as biological in nature. They were named instincts, and more recently, drives and appetites. But Ward was not a simple materialist and he placed the emphasis on the forces rather than on their origins which he believed to be mixed.

B. Max Weber, in addition to his well known discussions of different religious ethics, gave us a few notions about the *aesthetic ethic* (1946: 343). A shared ethic provides a basis for the organization of social behavior. People can accept as real and basic, certain religious, business, political or aesthetic beliefs and use them to make judgments about other peoples' behavior, to set up priorities and to organize their own activity. The aesthetic ethic was paralleled, and sometimes dominated, by other ethics such as the religious. At other times it dominated. As expressed by Martindale and Riedel

> "An artist might take some ideal of beauty as an absolute end and sacrifice fame, fortune, and perhaps even his family and health to it." (1958: xvi).

It is an aspect of Weber's voluntarism that one seems to be able to choose an ethic. However, at any historical period and in any culture there is not much choice because of limitations imposed by socialization, social controls and the fact that alternative ethics are not presented equally to any individual. In its extreme form, allegiance to the aesthetic ethic becomes "Æstheticism" (Green, 1966: vii–viii). Recognition of the existence of the aesthetic ethic is not the same as accepting it as an operating principle. In their writings, sociologists have tended to treat the doctrine as a social fact.

The aesthetic ethic continues to be recognized in the works of several recent sociologists. In some it is a first principle. Jose Ortega y Gasset (1948) and Theodor Adorno (1973; 1976) accept it without question. Others see it as a social fact, simply the name for the collective values of artists and other art lovers (Bensman & Gerver, 1958; Becker, 1951; Rosenberg & Fliegel, 1965).[6]

D. There are also several strongly *psychic* but not psychological emphases, because they treat art as a function of or as coming from inspiration. The idea that art as comes from a creative impulse is a simplification of John Dewey's ideal, and in its extreme form called the "cult of creativity," this approach still attracts sociologists. Recent American studies by Miller (1974), Garaudy (1970), Wilson (1986) and Siegman (1975) have been supplemented by a similarity of interest elsewhere. The social value of creativity is increasingly recognized by Eastern Bloc writers (Nikolov, 1982; Vitányi, 1982; Sági, 1982; Iovchuk & Kogan, 1975; Morawski, 1972) and by western Marxists such as Goldmann (1977).

One criticism of this quasimetaphysical approach is that we may not all agree with its assumptions. Many sociologists may not see the aesthetic ethic as anything but a "definition of the situation." It may be considered merely ideal in a world which is real. Secondly, in its Hegelian form, it supports what Popper calls *historicism*. As with earlier evolutionary theories, art and society become a derivative of determined change. The possibility of any degree of volunterism is denied. As a third consideration there is a strong and underlying assumption that art is separate from society or the physical world. Where art is treated as inspiration, as creativity, the belief that there are meta-physical sources, denies other influences. And fourth, art is often deemed sacred by people who find metaphysical origins for it. A mysticism—an æstheticism can ensue and provide a strong bias for sociologists who wish to study art. Such a bias shows up in Adorno's writings on music and weakens acceptance of his findings.

Non-aesthetic Aspects of Art

Probably most studies made by sociologists are of the organization of the arts, or of the artists, middlemen and public roles in the art world without attention given to the art product. For some, problems the sociology of art are used to illustrate or clarify social phenomena or processes.

A. The most common type of study is of *art as a commodity* to be produced, exchanged and consumed. Economic studies of the art market necessarily take this approach (*Arts and the People*, 1973; Baumol & Baumol, 1984; Baumol & Bowen, 1966; Blaug, 1976; Hendon, Shanahan & MacDonald, 1980; Keen, 1971; Throsby & Withers, 1979; Toffler, 1965). The antecedent to this approach is found in some of the writings of Karl Marx, although he, it must be admitted, was not consistent in regarding art as simply as product of the economic system. J. O. Hertzler (1946) described aesthetic institutions as existing to regulate and distribute art.

B. The more recent *production of culture* approach belongs here rather than under the cultural emphasis, because the focus is on production, while neglecting the meaning of the cultural objects. In his definition of the production of culture approach, Peterson (1976) includes cultural institutions which produce symbols—art, science and religion. The production of symbols places emphasis on the dynamic activity of these institutions. It leaves the impression that cultural institutions *support* the production of new symbols when many, such as orchestras, opera companies and art museums, simply maintain old symbols and innovation is squelched. The approach is most useful in clarifying the rapid changes in popular culture where "production" is out front and where the explanation of novelty and change is more pertinent than the explanation of stasis. Yet Peterson writes that a shortcoming of the approach is that it cannot predict or identify cultural revolutions. One would think the opposite.

A benefit of the production of culture approach is that it fits the contemporary mode of sociological research. As claimed, the scope is circumscribed so that the findings of studies can accumulate. Concepts and methods can be adapted from studies with a similar focus in other established fields of sociology. Comparisons can be made with studies in religion and science.

These are important considerations and have made this approach one of the most popular today. It is worth while to be reminded again of the similarities between what Znaniecki called the cultural sociologies. Sociologists studying art activity can learn much from sociologists studying the other cultural institutions. Peterson also avoids Weber's tendency to view the "ethics" of these institutions as contenders.

It might be possible to balance the dynamic bias by introducing a *maintenance of culture* dimension. To do so would not unduly affect the usefulness of the approach for research, but it would correct the tendency to neglect the institutionalized barriers to change. A further consideration is that there is room for the cultural influence on society implicit in Peterson's approach. Although he makes the cultural dimension, i.e. symbols, the dependent factor, at least a connection between society and the meaning of art, or religion, or science is established. Might it not be possible to recognize the feedback of that meaning and its effect on society?

C. The *instrumental uses of art* are many. Art is sometimes studied as an agent of propaganda (Leith, 1965; Denisoff, 1971). The *socialist realists*, claiming to follow Marx, have stated that the major utility of art is propaganda. Socialist realism had been narrowly defined at one time in the Soviet Union as "a truthful, historically concrete representation of reality in its revolutionary development", and had as its goal "ideological education of the toiling masses in the spirit of socialism" (Sjeklocha & Mead, 1967). It was from this orientation that Lenin stated "of all the arts, for us the cinema is most important" (Leyda, 1960: 161). In another direction, there are studies of art as hobby, as recreation. Art for investment or as a hedge against inflation is also a popular topic of some "how to do it" books (Rush, 1961). In all of these orientations is the idea that art is valuable for something else. The meaning of art in itself is neglected and so it is impossible to deal with the influence of art on society. Art is treated as a passive link in a chain—a means to some other desired end.

E. A. Ross (1897) wrote of art as an instrument of *social control*. He also recognized that, in turn, art is socially controlled. Art is used by the religious, political, economic, military, educational and other institutions to garner support and for their special purposes. That its utility for education is accepted can be shown by John Dewey's influence on American education. Rather than supporting the view that the importance of the arts lies in their consummatory function, he points out that they have instrumental value for the growth of perception and creativity.

Studies of advertising, the mass media and the formation of public opinion are other examples of the treatment of art as instrument to some further end.

D. Art has also been used by some social scientists as *measures* of social phenomena or as *social indicators*. Social change, for example, has been seen to vary with historic conditions and with social values. Kroeber (1963), Sorokin (1937) and Kubler (1962) among others have assumed that style or morphologies are deeply connected to other aspects of cultural development. Sorokin asserted that "each form of art expresses a certain mentality of 'soul' and is inseparably connected in each instance with a specific type of personality and culture'' (1963: 47).

The use of art as a measurement is based on several assumptions. The major one is that art and culture are integrated and therefore change together. A second methodological assumption is that one can pick out the significant themes and forms in art which most mark the culture. To be able to do this for other cultures and other times is a strong presumption.

Re-evaluation of the Social Theories of Art

As we review the various emphases made by writers on the sociology of the arts, we find that it is possible to construct guidelines for a theory. From the biological and psychological approaches we can accept the common-human nature of aesthetic awareness. Although there are societies where people may not have opportunity to come into contact with all of the arts, there is potential to learn to appreciate. Standards of quality in art may also have a biological basis. Recognition of the norms of quality, however, requires learning (Child, 1972). Biology and psychology also present a theory of motivation. They tell us that something innate is the reason art is found in all cultures and that we search for the aesthetically pleasing.

The theories of cultural influence bring us to consideration of art as part of the human endeavor, related to and influenced by other material and non-material inventions. Art has become entangled with other human values as Lukács and Mannheim have argued. In its development, art has depended on technical invention according to Boas. Art has also been used to symbolize and support nations, classes, and other self-conscious social communities. Anthropology has contributed much to the understanding of the cultural factors.

A special part of culture is the communication system. Art provides a special kind of communication and the analysis of how it works leads us to consideration of social relationships. It also leads us to a consideration of the meaning in art and the ways in which it influences human behavior. Art is used to educate to propagandize and to advertise. It may even lead us to a consideration of the deeper structures influencing human experience. Marx, Lévi-Strauss, Dewey, Wundt, Harrison and Burke are all necessary for a full sociology of aesthetic activity.

What I have labelled the metaphysical or spiritual forces approach points up the qualitative aspect of art. Writers taking this position emphasize the importance of art in affecting human values. If Adorno is correct, quality in art is important to the development of a good society. Max Weber directs us to another insight. Since humans are evaluating creatures, they share *ethics* or systems of belief that some things are right in themselves. The aesthetic ethic is a value which sometimes clashes with other ethics in society and may explain the sacrifices of individuals and societies to further art. For example, some artists decry "commercialism" on the basis of the belief that art is good in itself and should not be dominated by the business ethic.

With the focus of sociologists on social structure and process, it is not strange that most of the writing on the sociology of the arts deals with the structure and activity of groups and institutions that handle art. We study the organization of production and distribution of art. We are interested in the uses to which art is put, whether it be to enhance ideas, products or events. We use art to measure social phenomena as Sorokin did. We are interested in describing the artist, the patron, the critic and the public. All of this is important in reminding us of the influence of social organization on art. Even though the connection is seldom clear in our studies, by implication we learn something about the distinctiveness of art when compared to other cultural artifacts.

The Sociology of the Arts Today

Most of the early sociologists in the United States included in their works discussion of the place of art in society. In a survey Foster conducted in 1968 of introductory sociology textbooks, it was found that the arts were given a prominent place in the earliest period of American sociology [1890 to 1929]. The earliest sociologists agreed that art's function was moral in the sense that art influenced social values. As noted earlier, mention of art disappeared from almost all of the textbooks from 1930 until recently.

Europeans and ex-Europeans provided most of the available sociology of art publications during this period. Paul Honigsheim, a refugee scholar and one of the very few students of Weber, introduced his teacher's ideas to American sociologists. Honigsheim taught one of the first courses in the sociology of the arts given in the United States at Michigan State University. Another European emigrant who treated the arts seriously was Pitirim Sorokin. Also refugees, Adorno, Horkheimer, Lowenthal and others of the "Frankfort School" fleeing Hitler introduced consideration of the differences between art which humanizes and art which dehumanizes. Lowenthal wrote about literature. Adorno, a skilled composer wrote about music. Schücking's, **The Sociology of Literary Taste** was translated into English (1944). A few Americans continued interest—Don Martindale at Minnesota; John Mueller at Indiana; Anselm Strauss at Chicago; Adolph Tomars at CCNY.

But there is much more activity today. A contemporary survey would need to review the work of Becker and his students, the influence of the French, especially Moulin and Bourdieu, the much neglected work of Kavolis who is indebted to Parsons and Sorokin, the development of "working theories" specific to the sociology of the arts such as Peterson's "production of culture" approach (1976), the use of structuralist theory and techniques, and the controversy and then merging of the sociology of the arts with aspects of the sociology of popular culture and the sociology of the mass media.

Around the world, there is much activity in the sociology of the arts, although the emphases and modes of research may differ.

England produces a great many publications on the relationships between political power and the arts, especially the popular arts and literature.[7] France treats the sociology of the arts as a core speciality and publications are found in all areas of the field—from Hennion's writings on popular music (Hennion & Meadel, 1986)[8] to Bourdieu's (1984) attempts to outline and describe the organization and importance of taste to Moulin's (1987) analysis of the art market. In much of Europe, sociologists are enlisted in government planning and many of the topics studied are geared to policy. Pim Fenger (1985) in the Netherlands has developed much data about art activities in that nation which is useful for public policy. The sociology of music is alive and well in Austria with the much esteemed Kurt Blankopf and his colleagues in the International Institute for Audio-Visual Communication and Cultural Development. Irmgard Bontinck is Secretary General of the Institute. Dimitrij Rupel in Yugoslavia has written insightful papers on alienation and art (Herek & Rupel, 1985). In Eastern Europe, there is much interest in the utility of art for individuals. This is an area which had been neglected for some time in the socialist nations. For example, in Russia, there is interest in the humanistic dimensions of art as well as in policy issues (Zimenko, 1976). In Hungary, creativity has been studied by Ivan Vitányi, Mária Sági and Gideon Dienes mentioned above. Elit Nikolov (1981) in Bulgaria has written about the importance of art in the development of a harmonious personality. Discussion of important work in Poland requires attention to the work of Antonina Kloskowska (1983), a sociologist who has done research on individual and social values about art, and Stefan Morawski (1974), a philosopher who has attempted to wed the individualistic theories of Mead, Dewey, and Cooley with the collective theories of Marx followers. Interest in the sociology of art in India goes back at least forty years to the work of Radhakamal Mukerjee (1954). Very active is V. Subramanian, who is currently teaching in Canada. He has many publications on dance and music.[9] The sociology of literature is also active in India (Raghava, 1987).

In This Book

The art world, like any other behavioral institution, consists of many topical subfields. We believe that we have selected articles that best demonstrate the work done in these areas. Our reason for doing the book was to provide readings for a course in the sociology of the arts that we both teach. The papers have been selected because they are readable, of general interest and present a good sampling of the work of social scientists in this field today. All contribute to an understanding of the relationship between the arts and social behavior.

There are six sections. The first, titled Orientation, consists of papers which provide an introduction to the field of the sociology of the arts. They provide empirical evidence by sociologists that the taste for beauty is widespread and that activity centering on such an impulse is organized. A discussion of the popular arts is also included in Part I to demonstrate the scope of sociologists' investigations of art organization.

The primary roles in the art world are those of the artist and the public. All other roles are supportive of these. The creation of, and response to, art can take place through these roles alone as might be found in some of the smaller and less differentiated societies. Part II contains papers which analyze these roles and their relationship.

Part III focuses on patrons, gatekeepers and critics—what might be called secondary roles in the art world. In complex mass society these roles are necessary to maintain the organization of art activity. Patrons are needed to provide economic support. Gatekeepers are important today to insure that standards be maintained in the art work that is offered to the large and dispersed public. Critics provide information and education to the public.

Amateur and professional, popular and high culture artists are all bound up in networks which influence the way in which art is presented. To understand the process of "arting," attention needs to be given to the social dimensions of creating art. Part IV deals with the networking process among artists.

In Part V, Art Organizations, what Max Weber and Hans Gerth called the economic and political spheres in the arts are in view. Two papers in this section regard the influence of authority, the political sphere, on art activity. Again, in another paper the relationship between the economic and aesthetic demands on social behavior are discussed—this time in a specific art form, opera.

A broader view of the relationship between art and society is the topic of Part VI. These papers clarify the way in which art can be used as an instrument to some further end such as to sway people to support a cause.

The relationship between art and the economy is important and art may also be used as a means to gain further understanding of the nature of the ethos of a people.

Because the published work in the sociology of the arts is spread around in so many different journals we have included an extensive bibliography. Anticipating that the needs of students who use the bibliography for term papers will evolve around specific issues (e.g., sociology of literature; performing arts), it has been organized topically to meet those needs.

Notes

1. Ogburn, using Freud as his authority, was concerned about unconscious bias in research. It is amusing to note that he rejected Freud's analytic approach on Freud's authority (1922).

2. Art, a nonrational activity seemed inaccessible to quantitative analysis until Mueller (1951) did his study of the symphony orchestra.

3. Howard S. Becker points out the inadequacy of Dickie's approach for sociologists in his *Art Worlds*. (1982: 148–158).

4. A concern held by Benjamin and Hauser as well as Adorno (1941; 1954) and Horkheimer (1941), other members of the *critical school*, was that the popular arts, in order to sell were reduced to a brutal level which further alienated the members of the public.

5. To Harrison, the sin of individualism in art seems to be the sin of not communicating and thereby not building community. Harrison stands in opposition to John Dewey (19—) who thought of art as developing reliance on oneself as an individual. Could art do both of these things?

6. Hegel's notion of the *dialectical development* of ideas in history is sometimes sensed in the writings of Northern European sociologists. Adorno's (1976) treatise on Stravinsky and Schoenberg views the development of music in this way.

7. A small sample of the writers might include Terry Eagleton (1976), Richard Hoggart (1957), John Orr (1977), Alan Swingewood (1977), Raymond Williams (1961) and Janet Wolff (1975; 1981). There is also much from Britain on jazz and the blues.

8. Volume XXVII, no. 3 of the *Revue française de sociologie*, contains many interesting papers on the arts.

9. In addition to his writing, Professor Subramanian creates dance dramas in traditional modes.

References

———— 1973. *Arts and the People*. New York: Publishing Center for Cultural Resources.

Adorno, Theodor W. 1941 "On popular music," *Studies in Philosophy and Social Science* 9: 17–48.

Adorno, Theodor W. 1954 "Television and the patterns of mass culture," *Quarterly of Film, Radio and Television* 8: 213–325. [Reprinted in Bernard C. Rosenberg & David Manning White, eds. 1957 *Mass Culture*. Glenco: Free Press.

Adorno, Theodor W. 1973. *Philosophy of Modern Music*. New York: Seabury.

Adorno, Theodor W. 1976. *Introduction to the Sociology of Music*. New York: Seabury.

d'Azevedo, Warren L., ed. *The Traditional Artist in African Societies*. Bloomington: Indiana U. Press.

Baumol, Hilda & William J. Baumol, eds. 1984. *Inflation and the Performing Arts*. New York: New York U. Press.

Baumol, William J. & William G. Bowen. 1966. *Performing Arts: The Economic Dilemma*. Cambridge: M.I.T. Press.

Becker, Howard P. & Alvin Boskoff, eds. *Modern Sociological Theory*. New York: Dryden; 1962.

Becker, Howard S. 1951. "The professional dance musician and his audience," *American Journal of Sociology* 57: 136–44.

Becker, Howard S. 1982. *Art Worlds*. Berkeley: U. of California Press, pp. 148–158.

Benjamin, Walter. 1936. "The work of art in the age of mechanical reproduction," *Zeitschrift für Sozialforschung* V. [Reprinted 1960. *Studies on the Left* I: 28–46; and 1969. pp. 217–51 in his *Illuminations*. New York: Schocken Books.]

Bensman, Joseph & Israel Gerver. 1958. "Art and the mass society." *Social Problems* 6: 4–10.

Blaug, Mark, ed. 1976. *The Economics of the Arts*. Boulder: Westview Press.

Boas, Franz. 1955 [1st pub. 1927]. *Primitive Art*. New York: Dover Publications.

Bourdieu, Pierre. 1984. *Distinction: A Social Critique of the Judgement of Taste*. Cambridge: Harvard U. Press.

Burke, Kenneth. 1945. *A Grammar of Motives*. New York: Prentice-Hall.

Child, Arthur 1944. "The social-historical relativity of esthetic value." *The Philosophical Review* 53: 1–22.

Child, Irvin L. 1968. "Esthetics" in Gardiner Lindzey and Elliot Aronson (eds.) *Handbook of Social Psychology, III.* Reading: Addison-Wesley.

Child, Irvin L. 1972. "The experts and the bridge of judgment that crosses every cultural gap," pp. 17–21 in *Change: Readings in Society and Human Behavior.* Del Mar: CRM Books.

Child, Irvin L. & Leon Spiroto. 1965. "Bakwele and American esthetic evaluations compared, *Ethnology* 4: 349–60.

Cooley, Charles Horton. 1966. *Social Process.* Carbondale: Southern Illinois U. Press, p. 411.

Creedy, Jean, ed. 1970. *The Social Context of Art.* London: Tavistock.

Danto, Arthur. 1973. "Art works and real things." *Theoria* 1–3: 1–17.

Dealey, James Q. & Lester F. Ward. 1907. *A Textbook for Sociology.* New York: Macmillan, p. 32.

Denisoff, R. Serge. 1971. *Great Day Coming.* Baltimore: Penguin Books.

Dewey, John. 1934. *Art as Experience.* New York: G. P. Putnam's Sons.

Dickie, George. 1974. *Art and the Aesthetic: An Institutional Analysis.* Ithaca: Cornell U. Press.

Duncan, Hugh Dalziel. 1953. *Language and Literature in Society.* New York: Bedminster.

Duncan, Hugh Dalziel. 1957. "Sociology of art, literature and music: social contexts of symbolic experience," in Howard P. Becker & Alvin Boskoff, eds. *Modern Sociological Theory.* New York: Dryden.

Duncan, Hugh Dalziel. 1962. *Communication and Social Order.* New York: Bedminster.

Duncan, Hugh Dalziel. 1964. *The Rise of Chicago as a Literary Center from 1885 to 1920.* Totowa: Bedminster.

Eagleton, Terry. 1976. *Criticism and Ideology.* London: NLB.

Egbert, Donald Drew. 1970. *Social Radicalism and the Arts.* New York: Alfred A. Knoph, p. 737.

Fenger, Pim. 1985. "Development and Issues in the Arts Policy of the Netherlands, 1945–1983," in L. Herek & D. Rupel, eds., *Alienation and Participation in Culture.* Ljubljana: U. Edvard Kardelj, pp. 64–78.

Fernandez, James W. 1966. "Principles of opposition and vitality in Fang aesthetics." *Journal of Aesthetics and Art Criticism* 25: 53–64.

Fernandez, James W. 1973. "The exposition and imposition of order: artistic expression in Fang culture." In Warren L. d'Azevedo, ed. *The Traditional Artist in African Societies.* Bloomington: Indiana U. Press.

Foster, Arnold W. 1979. "Dominant themes in interpreting the arts: materials for a sociological model," *European Journal of Sociology* 20: 301–332.

Foster, Arnold W. 1979b. "Marxist pluralism and the sociology of the arts; some theoretical issues," paper read at the Conference on Social Theory, Politics and the Arts. Wayne, N.J., William Paterson College April 22.

Foster, Arnold W. 1985. "The art object: its socially important attributes," paper read at the International Sociological Association Research Committee #37 [Sociology of the Arts] conference, Marseilles, France, June 16.

Foster, Arnold W. & Jiri Kolaja. 1966. "Príspevek k teorii soukromého chováni. Opomíjeny aspekt modelu chováni," *Avástní otisk ze Sociologického casopisu* 5: 686–90.

Freud, Sigmund. 1943. *A General Introduction to Psychoanalysis.* Garden City: Doubleday.

Freud, Sigmund, 1956. *Delusion and Dream.* Boston: Beacon Press.

Freud, Sigmund. 1958. *On Creativity and the Unconscious.* New York: Harper & Row.

Gans, Herbert. 1974. *Popular Culture and High Culture.* New York: Basic Books.

Garaudy, Roger. 1970. *Marxism in the Twentieth Century.* New York: Charles Scribner's Sons.

Goldman, Lucien. 1977. *Cultural Creation.* Oxford: Basil Blackwell.

Green, Martin. 1966. *The Problem of Boston.* London: Longmans, Green, pp. vii–viii.

Harrison, Jane Ellen. n.d. *Ancient Art and Ritual.* London: Williams & Norgate, pp. 240–241.

Hauser, Arnold. 1951. *The Social History of Art, II.* London: Routledge and Kegan Paul.

Hendon, William S., James L. Shanahan & Alice J. MacDonald, eds. 1980. *Economic Policy for the Arts.* Cambridge: Abt Books.

Hennion, Antoine & Cecile Meadel. 1986. "Programming Music: Radio as Mediator." *Media, Culture & Society* 8: 281–303.

Herek, L. & D. Rupel, eds., 1985. *Alienation and Participation in Culture.* Ljubljana: U. Edvard Kardelj, pp. 64–78.

Hertzler, J. O. 1946. *Social Institutions.* Lincoln: U. of Nebraska Press.

Hertzler, J. O. 1961. "Art Institutions" in his *American Social Institutions.* Boston: Allyn & Bacon.

Hirn, Yrjö. 1900. *The Origins of Art.* London: Macmillan.

Hoggart, R. 1957. *The Uses of Literacy: Changing Patterns in English Mass Culture*. Boston: Beacon Press.

Horkheimer, Max. 1941. "Art and mass culture," *Studies in Philosophy and Social Science*. 9: 290–304.

Iovchuk, M. T. & L. N. Kogan, eds. 1975; *The Cultural Life of the Soviet Worker: a Sociological Study*. Moscow: Progress Publishers. chapt. 7.

Jones, LeRoi. 1963. *Blues People*. New York: William Morrow.

Jones, LeRoi. 1968. *Black Music*. New York: William Morrow.

Jules-Rosette, Bennetta. 1984. *The Messages of Tourist Art*. New York: Plenum Press.

Kavolis, Vytautas. 1968. *Artistic Expression. A Sociological Analysis*. Ithaca: Cornell U. Press.

Kavolis, Vytautas. 1972. *History on Art's Side*. Ithaca: Cornell U. Press.

Keen, Geraldine 1971. *Money and Art*. New York: G. P. Putnam's Sons.

Kloskowska, Antonina. 1983. "Popular Culture and the Hierarchy of Cultural Values." In Elit Nikolov, ed. *Contribution to the Sociology of the Arts*. Sofia: Research Institute for Culture, pp. 381–386.

Kofsky, Frank. 1970. *Black Nationalism and the Revolution in Music*. New York: Pathfinder.

Kramer, Judith. 1965. "The sociology of art and the art of sociology." Paper read at the American Sociological Association annual meeting, Chicago, p. 3.

Kroeber, Alfred L. 1963. *Style and Civilizations*. Berkeley: U. of California Press.

Kubler, George. 1962. *The Shape of Time*. New Haven: Yale U. Press.

Leith, James. 1965. *The Idea of Art as Propaganda in France, 1750–1799*. Toronto: U. of Toronto Press.

Lévi-Strauss, Claude. 1963. *Structural Anthropology*. New York: Basic Books, p. 84.

Leyda, Jay. 1960. *Kino: a History of the Russian and Soviet Film*. New York: Macmillan, p. 161. [Quoted in Egbert, Donald Drew. 1970. *Social Radicalism and the Arts*. New York: Alfred A. Knopf, p. 737].

Lloyd, A. L. 1967. *Folk Song in England*. New York: International Publishers.

Lucie-Smith Edward. 1970. "Manifestations of current social trends in contemporary art," pp. 27–44 in Jean Creedy, ed. *The Social Context of Art*. London: Tavistock.

Mannheim, Karl. 1971. Kurt Wolff, ed. *From Karl Mannheim*. New York: Oxford U. Press.

Marx, Karl. 1963. *The Grundrisse*. Harmondsworth: Penguin Books, pp. 160–161.

Marx, Karl. 1963b. *Theories of Surplus Value, I*. Moscow: Progress Publishers.

McCall, Michal M. 1977. "Art without a market: creating artistic value in a provincial art world," *Symbolic Interaction* I: 32.

McLuhan, Marshall. 1964. *Understanding Media: The Extensions of Man*. New York: McGraw-Hill.

Miller, D. Paul. 1974. "Toward a sociology of creativity." Paper read at the American Sociological Association meeting in Montreal.

Morawski, Stefan. 1972. "Three functions of art," *Arts in Society*. 8: 290–305.

Morawski, Stefan. 1974. *Inquiries into the Fundamentals of Aesthetics*. Cambridge: MIT Press.

Morris, Charles. 1956. *Varieties of Human Value*. Chicago U. of Chicago Press.

Moulin, Raymonde. 1987. *The French Art Market: A Sociological View*. New Brunswick: Rutgers U. Press.

Mukerjee, Radhakamal. 1954. *The Social Function of Art*. Westport: Greenwood Press.

Nikolov, Elit. 1981. "On the conception 'Harmoniously Developed Personality'." In his Problems of Culture. Sofia: Committee for Culture, pp. 129.

Nikolov, Elit. 1982. "The creative beginning and its social basis," pp. 14–16 in his, ed. *Contribution to the Sociology of the Arts*. Sofia: Balkan State Printing House.

Nikolov, Elit., ed. 1982. *Contribution to the Sociology of the Arts*. Sofia: Balkan State Printing House.

Ogburn, William F. 1922. "Bias, psychoanalysis, and the subjective in relation to the social sciences." *Publications of the American Sociological Society* 17: 62–74.

Orr, John. 1977. *Tragic Realism & Modern Society: Studies in the sociology of the Modern Novel*. London: Macmillan.

Ortega y Gasset, Jose. 1948. *The Dehumanization of Art*. Princeton: Princeton U. Press.

Peckham, Morse. 1967. *Man's Rage for Chaos*. New York: Schocken Books.

Peterson, Richard A., ed. 1976. *The Production of Culture*. Beverly Hills: Sage.

Raghava, Sulochana Rangeya. 1987. *Sociology of Indian Literature*. Jaipur: Rawat Publications.

Rosenberg, Bernard & Morris Fliegel. 1965. *The Vanguard Artist*. Chicago: Quadrangle Books.

Rosenberg, Bernard C. & David Manning White, eds. 1957. *Mass Culture*. Glencoe: Free Press.

Ross, Edward Alsworth. 1897. "Social Control, VIII," *American Journal of Sociology* 3: 64–78.

Rush, Richard H. 1961. *Art as an Investment*. New York: Bonanza Books.

Sági, Mária. 1982. "Creativity and the sociology of art," pp. 22–25 in Elit Nikolov, ed. *Contribution to the Sociology of the Arts*. Sofia: Balkan State Printing House.

Schücking, Levin L. 1944. London: Kegan Paul, Trench, Trubner.

Siegman, Jack. 1975. "Alienation and creativity." Paper read at the Second Annual Conference on Social Theory and Art, Fredonia.

Sjeklocha, Paul & Igor Mead. 1967. *Unofficial Art in the Soviet Union*. Berkeley: U. of California Press.

Sorokin, Pitirim A. 1937. *Social and Cultural Dynamics, I: Fluctuation of Forms of Art*, New York: American Book.

Sorokin, Pitirim A. 1963. *Modern Historical and Social Philosophies*. New York: Dover.

Spencer, Herbert. 1900. *First Principles*. New York: P. F. Collier.

Swingewood, A. 1977. *The Myth of Mass Culture*. London: Macmillan.

Thompson, Stith. 1946. *The Folktale*. New York: Dryden Press.

Throsby, C. D. & G. A. Withers. 1979. *The Economics of the Performing Arts*. New York: St. Martin's Press.

Toffler, Alvin. 1965. *The Culture Consumers*. Baltimore: Penguin Books.

Tomars, Adolph S. 1940. *Introduction to the Sociology of Art*. Mexico City: privately printed.

Vaughan Williams, Ralph. 1955. *The Making of Music*. Ithaca: Cornell U. Press, pp. 49–61.

Vitányi, Ivan. 1982. "Patterns of Creativity in Society," in Elit Nikolov, ed. *Contribution to the Sociology of the Arts*. Sofia: Research Institute for Culture, pp. 17–21.

Ward, Lester, 1896. "Sociology and psychology. Contributions to social philosophy," *American Journal of Sociology* 1: 623.

Weber, Max. 1946. Tr. & Ed. by H. H. Gerth & C. Wright Mills. *From Max Weber*. New York: Oxford U. Press, p. 343.

Weber, Max. 1958. Tr. & Ed. by Don Martindale, Johannes Riedel & Gertrude Neuwirth. *The Rational & Social Foundations of Music*. Carbondale: Southern Illinois U. Press.

Williams, Raymond. 1961. *The Long Revolution, rev. ed.* New York: Harper & Row (Torchbooks).

Wilson, Robert N. 1986. *Experiencing Creativity.* New Brunswick: Transaction Books.

Wolff, Janet. 1975. *Hermeneutic Philosophy and the Sociology of Art.* London: Routledge & Kegan Paul.

Wolff, Janet. 1981. *The Social Production of Art.* New York: St. Martin's Press.

Wundt, Wilhelm, 1919. *Völkerpsychologie, II* (3rd ed.). Leipzig.

Zimenko, Vladislav. 1976. *The Humanism of Art.* Moscow: Progress Publishers.

Part I

Orientation

Introduction

In the first section of the book we are concerned with developing a framework within which the social nature of art activity can be investigated.

Questions about beauty appear in discussions of art and documentation of the human activity of making art or of maintaining certain norms of beauty is a proper task for sociologists. Iwanska has presented cross-cultural evidence of social behavior to establish that there is common-human concern for attractive form or behavior. The man who used his welding torch to "create" beauty followed an aesthetic standard because there was "intentionality" in his activity. In El Nopal, norms of beauty different from ours had developed. They had not been formed through the work of artists, critics and scholars, but were in Giddings' term "crescive", they grew out of the conditions of living. The paper also illustrates that in El Nopal norms of beauty have been developed and that there are informal social controls to enforce them.

The second paper takes us one step further. Production and distribution of art is clearly seen to be social activity. Becker's account of the collective action of artists and others demonstrates the complexity of the art world. Although art can be done by individuals, it cannot be known in the larger society without collective cooperation. The process of "arting" is aided by conventions, a common set of perceptions and understandings. But conventions also limit the artist because to break them requires adjustments throughout the supportive network.

The collective activity of popular culture serves as a buffer to the instability of modern society. Collective artistic action does not exist in a vacuum, but is tied to the larger organization of society. Simpson leads us a step further into the realm of sociological interpretation. He tells us that popular culture allows us to escape into childhood, but only gives us affective relief rather than helping us to understand our plight.

No, dear, it looks. We see!

——— 1 ———

Without Art[1]

ALICJA IWÁNSKA

Since the invention of sociology by August Comte it has been generally recognized that the function of the sociologist is 'to know', 'to predict' and eventually 'to act' on the basis of his predictions, and it has been constantly repeated that the sociologist should abstain from judging the human groups he studies in terms of his personal and cultural values. In spite of this commitment to objectivity sociologists have been rather abundantly evaluating their 'human data', passing judgements on their morality, efficiency, taste. Ethnocentrism—a tendency to judge other peoples in terms of one's ethnic (or national) values—was identified as the source of dangerous biases in sociology. American sociologist Robert Bierstedt (1948) invented a supplementary term 'temporocentrism', meaning a tendency to judge other people in terms of 'one's own century, one's own era or one's own lifetime'. But even these two concepts are not sufficient to describe all types of biases resulting from investigators' unconscious involvements. Sociologists of art and science, for instance, are most likely to judge cognitive and artistic pursuits of non-professionals in terms of the criteria developed by professional artists and scholars with whose ideas they happened to be familiar.

In this paper I would like to identify and examine some of my own biases which led me to mistaken conclusions that there was 'no art whatsoever' in the two communities where I conducted intensive investigations: in 'Good Fortune' (Iwanska, 1971), a community of American farmers from the state of Washington, and in 'El Nopal' a community of Mazahua Indians from Central Mexico. Let me introduce a few distinctions necessary for this analysis.

The main assumption of this study is that there exist in all human societies four basic orientations towards the environment: cognitive orientation, moral orientation, activistic orientation and aesthetic orientation. In all human societies there is something which people try to learn about. Sometimes their curiosities are directed towards their natural environment, sometimes towards their inner life or towards supernatural forces; but always they have some standards by which they judge the correctness or truthfulness of their observations. In all human societies certain things and activities are and some others are not a target of moral evaluations. In some cultures it is customary to evaluate morally mainly the behavior of a man towards his fellowmen; in others the behavior and attitude of a man towards his fields and his animals is a target of moral evaluation. In all human societies there exist some standards of good work or efficiency, though in some societies saints and devils are classified in terms of efficiency while in others factory workers or administrators are so classified. And in all human societies certain activities and objects are evaluated in terms of their beauty and ugliness: furniture, food, scientific theories, the human body or conversation may or may not be evaluated aesthetically.

It has to be emphasized at this point that there is nothing exclusive about these evaluations. Objects and activities are constantly evaluated from all points of view: an aeroplane may be evaluated from the point of view of its efficiency and from the aesthetic point of view as well. In some human groups elegance is deeply associated with character; in some others efficiency is considered a moral virtue. It would be harmful for the sociologist of art to be too specialized. They study of aesthetic orientations without their larger sociocultural context could lead him to great errors.

The distinction between 'aesthetic evaluation' and 'artistic activity' should be made at the start of any empirical investigation in the sociology of art. The term 'aesthetic evaluation' may be defined as an assessment of an object predominantly in terms of its exterior qualities, i.e. the characteristics which present themselves directly or indirectly to our senses. We may evaluate aesthetically practically anything and the differences in objects singled out for aesthetic evaluation by different human groups have been studied by sociologists of art ever since this branch of sociology was recognized. There are two broad categories of objects which have been customarily evaluated aesthetically: (1) natural objects found in our natural environment or those created by man not specifically for the purpose of aesthetic enjoyment, and (2) art objects created for the purpose of aesthetic enjoyment.

There exist many popular and scientific hypotheses stressing relationships between the characteristics of a sociocultural system and the tendency towards aesthetic evaluations of one or another type of objects. It has been, for instance, often erroneously assumed that agricultural groups, particularly those with simple technologies, tend to be more sensitive to the 'beauties of nature' than towards man-made objects.

The term 'artistic activity' may be defined as any manipulation of an object in order to make it aesthetically valuable according to some specific criteria current in a given society or group. Harmony of parts, external unity or autonomy, juxtaposition of contrasting characteristics may serve as examples of such criteria. Artistic activity defined in this way may but does not have to produce works of art either of 'popular' or of 'great art' type. Some artistic activities never go beyond the stage of improvisation for a variety of reasons. Sometimes a given group may value above all improvisation *per se*. Sometimes the lack of cultural, economic or political support of social milieu may prevent a full development of a given type of art.

A great deal of misunderstanding and confusion results from the fact that identification of the products of artistic activities as being or not being 'art', and sometimes even assigning them to respective art categories, is done from many different and often contradictory perspectives. It is done by persons claiming to represent the model taste of a given social group, by the producer of a given object himself, by persons enjoying prestige within the producer's social group, or by outside 'experts': by administrators, by famous artists representing different artistic schools, by art critics and even by sociologists or anthropologists. In order to clarify some of these misunderstandings I decided to concentrate mainly on a relatively simple concept, that of 'artistic activity', and the analyse some artistic activities in two very different communities: that of American farmers and that of Mexican Indians about whom I have an abundance of first-hand observations.

If we make a distinction between non-professional and professional artistic activities, it would be easy to conclude that there were not even part-time professional artists of any sort in Good Fortune, a community of American farmers from the western part of the State of Washington. Nobody in this community was even supplementing his income through music, painting, dancing, acting or the writing of fiction. And, as it appeared to me during the period of my field work, nobody in Good Fortune was involved in any non-professional artistic activities either. I did not notice any artistic hobbies in this community; I did not hear of any community poet, painter or story teller. In the first report from my field work I concluded that there was 'no art whatsoever' among Good Fortune farmers, and my conclusions seemed to be supported by the observation on the relative non-importance of aesthetic evaluations in this community.

Since the inhabitants of Good Fortune were farmers by choice (some of them of urban origin), and talked constantly about the superiority of the rural life which they chose to live, I expected from them at least some appreciation of the beauties of nature, for which this part of the country was famous. In spite of this strong assertion of their preference for rural life, inhabitants of Good Fortune almost never emphasized the beauties of their environment, stressing only the good healthy air and the 'scenic value' of nice views recognized apparently by some tourist agencies—scenic value which might eventually bring profits to the community. In spite of the fact that the climate of Good Fortune was perfect for round-the-year gardening, there were practically no gardens around farmhouses and a Garden Club with small membership consisting chiefly of women living in the commercial center of Good Fortune was ridiculed by most inhabitants, who considered preoccupation with flowers as an unserious and rather frivolous concern.

Years later when I went again through my notes from Good Fortune, I realized that I did miss some important data on the aesthetic orientations of these American farmers, owing probably to my own cultural biases, since even if they did not evaluate nature aesthetically in any direct way, and had the most commercial and matter-of-fact approach to what they called 'scenery', Good Fortune farmers did travel a great deal through their hilly forests, took many photographs and some of them even made movies of these trips. It was very surprising to me to realize that on these trips they would stop only for the time necessary to take photographs of those very lovely views. They would never make any comment about how anything looked and they would never relax to enjoy it. It was only later, when the slides or movies were shown in their homes, they would comment about the shape of lakes, about trees or roads, about colors of sunsets and clouds. Their aesthetic evaluation of nature was not direct but mediated through technology, so to say. And when viewing these movies and slides they would always discuss the qualities of the cameras and the talents of their owners, very much as painters discuss the characteristics of their canvas and brushes and their painting techniques. Taking pictures and making movies should, then, be identified as one of their typical artistic activities and their products—movies and photographs—as art objects of their favorite type. If we further subdivide professional and non-professional artistic activities into traditional and non-traditional, the picture-taking and movie-making by Good Fortune farmers should be identified as non-professional and non-traditional since they were not supplementing their incomes through these activities and there was no tradition of picture-taking and movie-taking in Good Fortune. If we further subdivide traditional and non-traditional artistic activities into creative activities and routine activities, taking pictures and making movies would be somewhere in between these two categories: a great deal of routine was definitely involved but some variations in the manipulation of cameras, use of filters and selection of scenery was introduced by Good Fortune farmers. As an example of non-traditional and completely or almost completely routinized artistic activity which I did not notice in Good Fortune during my field work, I should mention making of decorative lamps and various other decorative objects such as little paper dolls from prefabricated materials. Since these objects were made either partially or completely for the purpose of aesthetic enjoyment, they definitely belong to the category of non-professional artistic activities. I certainly did not consider them to be 'artistic' during my field work, because the offended my personal taste too much. There was another reason as well for my blindness, it seems to me now: I had a tendency to consider only highly creative artistic activity as being artistic, a definition much too narrow, as it seems to me at present.

But the most striking example of a creative artistic activity which was not identified by me as artistic during the field work in Good Fortune, but entered into my notebooks, was welding for fun done by one of the farmers. The welding done by this farmer was completely non-utilitarian since he did not weld anything useful. He did not do it for prestige either, to show for instance that he owned a welding machine. From time to time he would go to his old barn, put on a mask and start welding anything, concentrating mainly on bright sparks produced through this welding. He would move the machine skilfully so to produce nicer and nicer sparks, and various compositions made out of them. I found in my field notes a record of his monologue from one of those welding sessions at which I was present 'Look at these sparks,' he would say, 'Isn't this like in Hollywood? . . . and this is me who is doing it all . . . sparks like fireworks, like stars, like aeroplanes . . . I feel really like God creating the world . . . see how the lights move while I am moving the machine. . . . Isn't this wonderful!' I do not hesitate today to call this non-utilitarian welding of the Good Fortune farmer a non-professional artistic activity of creative type. He used the machine in order to produce sparks which he considered very beautiful. This was done for no other but purely aesthetic reasons and the various constellations of sparks he was producing, though they did not have the durability of a decorated basket or painted pitcher, certainly had the durability of a song or a musical composition. This was an improvisation, we may say, spontaneous experimentation with a new medium. under favorable social conditions this type of improvisation by a non-professional could have probably developed into a new type of professional art: he had discovered for himself the art of the 'happening'.

I was even more surprised and distressed not to find any art in El Nopal, a village of Mazahua Indians from Central Mexico situated in a green valley between mild hills cut by a large river and surrounded by spectacular dark mountains. Little *adobe* huts were dispersed between large century plants (*magueyes*) and tall cactuses (*los nopales*). The beauty of this scenery was striking to any outsider.

In this case too, I assumed that an agricultural people would be very sensitive to the beauties of their natural environment, and I was very surprised not to see such sensitivity at all. Instead of the aesthetic orientation towards nature which I expected the Mazahuas from El Nopal had a strongly cognitive orientation towards their natural environment. They displayed a great curiosity about practically all natural phenomena and they wanted to learn about 'laws of nature' quite independently of any utilitarian concerns (Iwanska, 1963). And there was almost no folk art left in El Nopal. A few women who still knew how to make the traditional embroideries on their skirts were rather apologetic about this and most of the Indians from the area preferred to buy factory-made clothes or to imitate them as closely as possible if they couldn't afford to buy them.

It was only after a few months of living in El Nopal that I realized that these Mazahua Indians were in fact judging certain things from an aesthetic point of view and were involved in some artistic activities at first invisible to me. I learned about some of their aesthetic concepts only when I started decorating a little hut in which I lived in El Nopal. Since I do not accept the idea that 'living as everybody else around does' is 'the best technique of relating to people whom you study', I had some rudimentary furniture in my hut, though in this village furniture was not used, and I even had a window made in this windowless community. On the walls I hung many prints of my favorite paintings, some figurative, some abstract, a few old engravings from Poland, some Mexican straw figures, some plates and pots. Neither furniture nor the window evoked much comment from my Indian friends. They expected me to sleep in a bed, not on the floor as they do themselves, and they expected me to have a table and some chairs as well. My wall decorations, however, provoked a great deal of comment of a definitely aesthetic character. Though many Indians liked individual objects and paintings hanging on my walls, they strongly disapproved of the multiplicity of these objects. 'This thing is nice, and this one too,' they used to tell me, 'but they are too many . . . your place is crowded with objects!' They themselves, if they owned any objects, would hide them behind the logs of the ceiling. Only those objects which were 'sanctified' by some cherished association, as often were photographs and alarm clocks given to them by friends or relatives, were placed on their home altars. Unlike their rooms these home altars were supposed to be crowded. Some useful objects they owned (pocket knives, mirrors and such) were usually hidden in the pockets of their dresses and suits. In their rooms they had practically nothing: no furniture, no decoration of any sort. Only after some time in El Nopal I realized that this striking emptiness of their interiors was neither a result of their poverty nor was it purely accidental. I noticed that these almost empty interiors were in fact carefully planned. A few pots which hung on the walls were carefully spaced, ropes on which they hung their clothes and blankets were also carefully spaced in such a way as to make the whole interior look 'nice' which, as I later realized listening to their comments, meant to them mainly three characteristics: 'spaciousness', 'symmetry' and 'order'. If pots were hanging on one side of the room, for instance, the rope with clothes was placed on the other side. The continuous sweeping of their dirt floors and of the whole large area around the huts had also the same purpose: to acquire more orderly space. The years around Mazahua huts were swept, in fact, more carefully than any of the most elegant European parlors, more carefully than any of the most antiseptic American apartments. And I have never heard Mazahuas from El Nopal talking about the relationship between health and cleanliness or defining the concern with daily cleaning as a moral characteristic, as it is often done in the United States. Their concern with sweeping was, I am convinced, a part of their aesthetic concern with 'spaciousness' and 'order'.

Decoration of interiors and what is called today 'landscaping of the exterior area around a house' would be called without hesitation an 'artistic concern' by modern urban people used to professional interior decorators and landscapers. And according to my definition of 'artistic activity' both interior decoration and landscaping are particular types of artistic activities. In the case of non-professional interior decoration or landscaping it often happens that only more conventional or more familiar artistic efforts of this type are noticed by an outside observer, while the less conventional and less familiar pass altogether unnoticed. Concern with the distribution of empty spaces, with simplicity and symmetry, so traditional in Japanese interiors, has only relatively recently entered into the aesthetic theories of Europeans and Americans. We occidentals have probably been as often blind to the aesthetic orientations of other peoples as we have been blind to the refinements of their moral concepts. A Japanese investigator would very likely have noticed and understood much sooner than I did the aesthetic orientation and artistic activities of the Mazahua Indians from El Nopal.

The American farmer from 'Good Fortune' who was doing non-utilitarian welding resulting in fascinating showers of sparks was according to my distinctions involved in non-professional artistic activity of a highly creative type. Mazahua Indians from El Nopal placing their meagre possessions on the walls of their almost empty huts, with special attention to spaciousness and symmetry, were involved in non-professional artistic activities of a traditional type. Neither the artistic activity of the American farmer from Good Fortune nor the artistic activities of the Mazahuas from El Nopal were identified by them as being artistic simply because, belonging to a 'nonsophisticated part of the world', they did not categorize their activities in this way.

Comtean emphasis on objectivity has been today supplemented with the idea that every student of society should understand his own cultural, professional and personal values in order to be able to study any group objectively. Though often professed, this principle is rarely practiced and we have been continuously committing many errors of this type harmful for the development of social sciences and sometimes harmful for society as well. The relationship between what Robert Redfield (1953) named respectively 'Little Tradition' and 'Great Tradition' is far from being truly explored. We do not know much, for instance, about what an educated doctor of medicine can learn from folk medicine of various areas or how a professional philosopher may profit from various concepts of inference or empirical evidence elaborated by so-called 'primitive peoples'. The relationship between 'folk art' and 'great art' is usually much more thoroughly explored than is the relationship between great economic, political or scientific systems and their primitive counterparts. It is generally assumed, not only by great artists and investigators of art but often by people from literate populations as well, that not only can the primitive artist learn something from the 'civilized artist', but also the other way around: primitive art is a great inspiration for so-called 'great art'.

In spite of the fact that a reciprocal relation between Little Tradition and Great Tradition is better established in the area of art than probably in any other area of human effort, a great deal of non-professional artistic activity in both primitive and civilized societies still passes unnoticed by professional artists and students of art as well. Such blindness may have serious consequences both for potential artists and for the societies in which they live. If never noticed by people professionally concerned about art, some of the valuable artistic activities may never get a chance to go beyond the stage of improvisation; professional artists may miss an important source of inspiration which so often comes from the confrontation with new artistic activities; and finally the population at large may miss a possible source of aesthetic enjoyment. Utopian thinking of both ideological and satirical character is probably necessary for the functioning of any society and particularly important for the functioning of highly complex modern nations. In comparison with utopian thinking in the area of economics, politics and science, utopian thinking in the area of art has been rather poorly developed. We have very few major works in which a hypothetical or visionary development of various types of art, and the consequences of such development for society, are described. I recently read an interview with an excellent American sculptress, Louise Nevelson, who makes tall wooden or glass reliefs which looked to me like possible walls of some *avant-garde* cathedral. She certainly presented at least a part of her artistic utopia in this interview. She would like to see people living inside big sculptures, in apartments where every piece of furniture would be both functional and artistic. In fact, every room would be a sculptural composition. She had also something to say about the type of people who would enjoy living in such utopian apartments: these people would be highly creative (though not necessarily creative in the plastic arts) and after work they would not have to relax in overstuffed armchairs since their work would be enjoyable, of the type from which one does not have to relax.

Giovanni Papini in his collection of short stories entitled *Gog* also gives a little of his utopian thinking connected with art and its place in society. In one of these stories he describes a sculptor who makes sculptures of smoke within a tent to which selected people are invited for these improvisations. He is described by Papini as an established professional artist, to whose tent travel many people from all over the world. I was remembering, of course, Papini's story while re-reading my field notes from Good Fortune . . . If the welder from Good Fortune—I realized—began inviting people to his welding shows, his sessions would probably start being perceived as the kind of art we now call 'happenings'.

Artistic activity of a non-professional character may change into professional artistic activity as a result of many factors, some of them economic, some cultural, some social. The diagnosis of a non-professional artistic activity as 'art' by a person of sufficient prestige and standing is only one of such conditions. The sociologist of art may contribute to the development of new types of art through such diagnoses; but in order to do it well he should formulate his own frame of reference for the study of art and he must first understand his own professional, cultural and personal values, which may inhibit his insights into a variety of aesthetic evaluations and artistic activities.

Notes

1. Reprinted with the permission of the author and the publisher from the *British Journal of Aesthetics* (vol. 11, 1971).

References

Bierstedt, Robert, 1948. "The Limitations of Anthropological Method in Sociology," *American Journal of Sociology* 54, no. 1 (July): 27–28.

Iwanska, Alicja. 1963. "New Knowledge, the Impact of School Upon the Traditional Structure of a Mexican Village," *Sociologus* 15, no. 1.

Iwanska, Alicja. 1971. *Purgatory and Utopia*. Cambridge: Schenkman.

Redfield, Robert. 1953. *The Primitive World and Its Transformation*. Ithaca: Cornell U. Press.

2

Art as Collective Action[1]

HOWARD S. BECKER

A distinguished sociological tradition holds that art is social in character, this being a specific instance of the more general proposition that knowledge and cultural products are social in character or have a social base. A variety of language has been used to describe the relations between art works and their social context. Studies have ranged from those that attempted to correlate various artistic styles and the cultural emphases of the societies they were found in to those that investigated the circumstances surrounding the production of particular works. Both social scientists and humanistic scholars have contributed to this literature. (A representative sample of work can be found in Albrecht, Barnett and Griff, 1970).

Much sociological writing speaks of organizations or systems without reference to the people whose collective actions constitute the organization or system. Much of the literature on art as a social product does the same, demonstrating correlations or congruences without reference to the collective activities by which they came about, or speaking of social structures without reference to the actions of people doing things together which create those structures. My admittedly scattered reading of materials on the arts, the available sociological literature, (especially Blumer, 1966, and Strauss et al., 1964) and personal experience and participation in several art worlds have led me to a conception of art as a form of collective action.

Cooperation and Cooperative Links

Think, with respect to any work of art, of all the activities that must be carried on for that work that must be carried on for that work to appear as it finally does. For a symphony orchestra to give a concert, for instance, instruments must have been invented, manufactured and maintained, a notation must have been devised and music composed using that notation, people must have learned to play the notated notes on the instruments, times and places for rehearsal must have been provided, ads for the concert must have been placed, publicity arranged and tickets sold, and an audience capable of listening to and in some way understanding and responding to the performance must have been recruited. A similar list can be compiled for any of the performing arts. With minor variations (substitute materials for instruments and exhibition for performance), the list applies to the visual and (substituting language and print for materials and publication for exhibition) literary arts. Generally speaking, the necessary activities typically include conceiving the idea for the work, making the necessary physical artifacts, creating a conventional language of expression, training artistic personnel and audiences to use the conventional language to create and experience, and providing the necessary mixture of those ingredients for a particular work or performance.

Imagine, as an extreme case, one person who did all these things: made everything, invented everything, performed, created and experienced the result, all without the assistance or cooperation of anyone else. In fact, we can barely imagine such a thing, for all the arts we know about involve elaborate networks of cooperation. A division of the labor required takes place. Typically, many people participate in the work without which the performance or artifact could not be produced. A sociological analysis of any art therefore looks for that division of labor. How are the various tasks divided among the people who do them?

Nothing in the technology of any art makes one division of tasks more "natural" than another. Consider the relations between the composition and performance of music. In conventional symphonic and chamber music, the two activities occur separately; although many composers perform, and many performers compose, we recognize no necessary connection between the two and see them as two separate roles which may occasionally coincide in one person. In jazz, composition is not important, the standard tune merely furnishing a framework on which the performer builds the improvisation listeners consider important. In contemporary rock music, the performer ideally composes his own music; rock groups who play other people's music (Bennett, 1972) carry the derogatory title of "copy bands." Similarly, some art photographers always make their own prints; others seldom do. Poets writing in the Western tradition do not think it necessary to incorporate their handwriting into the work, leaving it to printers to put the material in readable form, but Oriental calligraphers count the actual writing an integral part of the poetry. In no case does the character of the art impose a natural division of labor; the division always results from a consensual definition of the situation. Once that has been achieved, of course, participants in the world of art regard it as natural and resist attempts to change it as unnatural, unwise or immoral.

Participants in an art world regard some of the activities necessary to the production of that form of art as "artistic," requiring the special gift or sensibility of an artist. The remaining activities seem to them a matter of craft, business acumen or some other ability less rare, less characteristic of art, less necessary to the success of the work, and less worthy of respect. They define the people who perform these special activities as artists, and everyone else as (to borrow a military term) support personnel. Art worlds differ in how they allocate the honorific title of artist and in the mechanisms by which they choose who gets it and who doesn't. At one extreme, a guild or academy (Pevsner, 1940) may require long apprenticeship and prevent those it does not license from practicing. At the other, the choice may be left to the lay public that consumes the work, whoever they accept being ipso facto an artist. An activity's status as art or non-art may change, in either direction. Kealy (1974) notes that the recording engineer has, when new technical possibilities arose that artists could use expressively, been regarded as something of an artist. When the effects he can produce become commonplace, capable of being produced on demand by any competent worker, he loses that status.

How little of the activity necessary for the art can a person do and still claim the title of artist? The amount the composer contributes to the material contained in the final work has varied greatly. Virtuoso performers from the Renaissance through the nineteenth century embellished and improvised on the score the composer provided (Dart, 1967, and Reese, 1959), so it is not unprecedented for contemporary composers to prepare scores which give only the sketchiest directions to the performer (thought the counter-tendency, for composers to restrict the interpretative freedom of the performer by giving increasingly detailed directions, has until recently been more prominent). John Cage and Karlheinz Stockhausen (Wörner, 1973) are regarded as composers in the world of contemporary music, though many of their scores leave much of the material to be played to the decision of the player. Artists need not handle the materials from which the art work is made to remain artists; architects seldom build what they design. The same practice raises questions, however, when sculptors construct a piece by sending a set of specifications to a machine shop; and many people balk at awarding the title of artist to authors of conceptual works consisting of specifications which are never actually embodied in an artifact. Marcel Duchamp outraged many people by insisting that he created a valid work of art when he signed a commercially produced snowshovel or signed a reproduction of the Mona Lisa on which he had drawn a mustache, thus classifying Leonardo as support personnel along with the snowshovel's designer and manufacturer. Outrageous as that idea may seem, something like it is standard in making collages, in which the entire work may be

constructed of things made by other people. The point of these examples is
that what is taken, in any world of art, to be the quintessential artistic act,
the act whose performance marks one as an artist, is a matter of consensual
definition.

Whatever the artist, so defined, does not do himself must be done by
someone else. The artist thus works in the center of a large network of
cooperating people, all of whose work is essential to the final outcome.
Wherever he depends on others, a cooperative link exists. The people with
whom he cooperates may share in every particular his idea of how their
work is to be done. This consensus is likely when everyone involved can
perform any of the necessary activities, so that while a division of labor
exists, no specialized functional groups develop. This situation might occur
in simple communally shared art forms like the square dance or in segments of a society whose ordinary members are trained in artistic activities.
A well-bred nineteenth century American, for instance, knew enough music
to take part in performing the parlor songs of Stephen Foster just as his
Renaissance counterpart could participate in performing madrigal. In such
cases, cooperation occurs simply and readily.

When specialized professional groups take over the performance of the
activities necessary to an art work's production, however, their members
tend to develop specialized aesthetic, financial and career interests which
differ substantially from the artist's. Orchestral musicians, for instance, are
notoriously more concerned with how they sound in performance than with
the success of a particular work; with good reason, for their own success
depends in part on impressing those who hire them with their competence
(Faulkner, 1973a, 1973b). They may sabotage a new work which can make
them sound bad because of its difficulty, their career interests lying at
cross-purposes to the composer's.

Aesthetic conflicts between support personnel and the artist also occur.
A sculptor friend of mine was invited to use the services of a group of
master lithographic printers. Knowing little of the technique of lithography,
he was glad to have these master craftsmen do the actual printing, this
division of labor being customary and having generated a highly specialized
craft of printing. He drew designs containing large areas of solid colors,
thinking to simplify the printer's job. Instead, he made it more difficult.
When the printer rolls ink onto the stone, a large area will require more
than one rolling to be fully inked and may thus exhibit roller marks. The
printers, who prided themselves on being the greatest in the world, explained to my friend that while they could print his designs, the areas of
solid color could cause difficulty with roller marks. He had not known
about roller marks and talked of using them as part of his design. The
printers said, no, he could not do that, because roller marks were an obvi-

ous sign (to other printers) of poor craftsmanship and no print exhibiting roller marks was allowed to leave their shop. His artistic curiosity fell victim to the printers' craft standards, a neat example of how specialized support groups develop their own standards and interests.

My friend was at the mercy of the printers because he did not know how to print lithographs himself. His experience exemplified the choice that faces the artist at every cooperative link. He can do things the way established groups of support personnel are prepared to do them; he can try to make them do it his way: he can train others to do it his way; or he can do it himself. Any choice but the first requires an additional investment of time and energy to do what could be done less expensively if done the standard way. The artist's involvement with and dependence on cooperative links thus constrains the kind of art he can produce.

To say that the artist must have the cooperation of others *for the art work to occur as it finally does* does not mean that he cannot work without that cooperation. The art work, after all, need not occur as it does, but can take many other forms, including those which allow it to be done without others' help. Thus, though poets do depend on printers and publishers, one can produce poetry without them. Russian poets whose work circulates in privately copied typescripts do that, as did Emily Dickinson (Johnson, 1955). In both cases, the poetry does not circulate in conventional print because the artist would not accept the censorship or rewriting imposed by those who would publish the work. The poet either has to reproduce and circulate his work himself or not have it circulated. But he can still write poetry. My argument thus differs from a functionalism that asserts that the artist must have cooperation, ignoring the possibility that the cooperation can be foregone, though at a price.

The examples given so far emphasize matters more or less external to the art work-exhibition space, printing or musical notation. Relations of cooperation and constraint, however, penetrate the entire process of artistic creation and composition, as will become clear in looking at the nature and function of artistic conventions.

Conventions

People who cooperate to produce a work of art usually do not decide things afresh. Instead, they rely on earlier agreements now become customary, agreements that have become part of the conventional way of doing things in that art. Artistic conventions cover all the decisions that must be made with respect to works produced in a given art world, even though a particular convention may be revised for a given work. Thus, conventions dictate the materials to be used, as when musicians agree to base their music on the notes contained in a set of modes, or on the diatonic, pentatonic or chromatic scales with their associated harmonies. Conventions dictate the abstractions to be used to convey particular ideas or experiences, as when painters use the laws of perspective to convey the illusion of three dimensions or photographers use black, white and shades of gray to convey the interplay of light and color. Conventions dictate the form in which materials and abstractions will be combined, as in the musical use of the sonata form or the poetic use of the sonnet. Conventions suggest the appropriate dimensions of a work, the proper length for a musical or dramatic event, the proper size and shape of a painting or sculpture. Conventions regulate the relations between artists and audience, specifying the rights and obligations of both.

Humanistic scholars—art historians, musicologists and literary critics—have found the concept of the artistic convention useful in accounting for artists' ability to produce art works which produce an emotional response in audiences. By using such a conventional organization of tones as a scale, the composer can create and manipulate the listener's expectations as to what sounds will follow. He can then delay and frustrate the satisfaction of those expectations, generating tension and release as the expectation is ultimately satisfied (Meyer, 1956, 1973; Cooper and Meyer, 1960). Only because artist and audience share knowledge of and experience with the conventions invoked does the art work produce an emotional effect.

Conventions make art possible in another sense. Because decisions can be made quickly, because plans can be made simply by referring to a conventional way of doing things, artists can devote more time to actually doing their work. Conventions thus make possible the easy and efficient coordination of activity among artists and support personnel. Ivins (1953), for instance, shows how, by using a conventionalized scheme for rendering shadows, modeling and other effects, several graphic artists could collaborate in producing a single plate. The same conventions made it possible for viewers to read what were essentially arbitrary marks as shadows and modeling. Seen this way, the concept of convention provides a point of contact between humanists and sociologists, being interchangeable with such familiar sociological ideas as norm, rule, shared understanding, custom or folkway, all referring in one way or another to the ideas and understandings people hold in common and through which they effect cooperative activity.

Though standardized, conventions are seldom rigid and unchanging. They do not specify an inviolate set of rules everyone must refer to in settling questions of what to do. Even where the directions seem quite specific, they leave much unsettled which gets resolved by reference to customary modes of interpretation on the one hand and by negotiation on the other. A tradition of performance practice, often codified in book form, tells performers how to interpret the musical scores or dramatic scripts they perform. Seventeenth century scores, for instance, contained relatively little information; but contemporary books explained how to deal with questions of instrumentation, note values, extemporization and the realization of embellishments and ornaments. Performers read their music in the light of all these customary styles of interpretation and thus were able to coordinate their activities (Dart, 1967). The same thing occurs in the visual arts. Much of the content, symbolism and coloring of Italian Renaissance religious painting was conventionally given; but a multitude of decisions remained for the artist, so that even within those strict conventions different works could be produced. Adhering to the conventional materials, however, allowed viewers to read much emotion and meaning into the picture. Even where customary interpretations of conventions exist, having become conventions themselves, artists can agree to do things differently, negotiation making change possible.

Conventions place strong constraints on the artist. They are particularly constraining because they do not exist in isolation, but come in complexly interdependent systems, so that making one small change often requires making changes in a variety of other activities. A system of conventions gets embodied in equipment, materials, training, available facilities and sites, systems of notation and the like, all of which must be changed if any one segment is.

Consider what a change from the conventional western chromatic musical scale of twelve tones to one including forty-two tones between the octaves entails. Such a change characterizes the compositions of Harry Partch (1949). Western musical instruments cannot produce these microtones easily and some cannot produce them at all, so conventional instruments must be reconstructed (as Partch does) or new instruments must be invented and built. Since the instruments are new, no one knows how to play them, and players must train themselves. Conventional Western notation is inadequate to score forty-two tone music, so a new notation must be devised, and players must learn to read it. (Comparable resources can be taken as given by anyone who writes for the conventional twelve chromatic tones). Consequently, whereas a performance of music scored for the conventional set of tones can be performed adequately after relatively few hours of rehearsal, forty-two tone music requires much more work, time, effort and resources. Partch's music has typically come to be performed in the following way: a university invites him to spend a year. In the fall, he recruits a group of interested students, who build the instruments (which he has already invented) under his direction. In the winter, they learn to play the instruments and read the notation he has devised. In the spring, they rehearse several works and finally give a performance. Seven or eight months of work finally result in two hours of music, hours which could have been filled with other music after eight to ten hours of rehearsal by trained symphonic musicians playing the standard repertoire. The difference in the resources required measures the strength of the constraint imposed by the conventional system.

The limitations of conventional practice, clearly, are not total. One can always do things differently if one is prepared to pay the price in increased effort or decreased circulation of one's work. The experience of composer Charles Ives exemplifies the latter possibility. He experimented with polytonality and polyrhythms before they became part of the ordinary performer's competence. The New York players who tried to play his chamber and orchestral music told him that it was unplayable, that their instruments could not make those sounds, that the scores could not be played in any practical way. Ives finally accepted their judgment, but continued to compose such music. What makes his case interesting is that, according to his biographers (Cowell and Cowell, 1954), though he was also bitter about it, he experienced this as a great liberation. If no one could play his music, then he no longer had to write music that musicians could play, no longer had to accept the constraints imposed by the conventions that regulated cooperation between contemporary composer and player. Since, for instance, his music would not be played, he never needed to finish it; he was quite unwilling to confirm John Kirkpatrick's pioneer reading of the *Concord Sonata* as a correct one because that would mean that he could no longer change it. Nor did he have to accommodate his writing to the practical constraints of what could be financed by conventional means, and so he wrote his Fourth Symphony for three orchestras. (That impracticality lessened with time; Leonard Bernstein premiered the work in 1958 and it has been played many times since.)

In general, breaking with existing conventions and their manifestations in social structure and material artifacts increases the artist's trouble and decreases the circulation of his work, on the one hand, but at the same time increases his freedom to choose unconventional alternatives and to depart substantially from customary practice. If that is true, we can understand any work as the product of a choice between conventional ease and success and unconventional trouble and lack of recognition, looking for the experiences and situational and structural elements that dispose artists in one direction or the other.

Interdependent systems of conventions and structures of cooperative links appear very stable and difficult to change. In fact, though arts sometimes experience periods of stasis, that does not mean that no change or innovation occurs (Meyer, 1967). Small innovations occur constantly, as conventional means of creating expectations and delaying their satisfaction become so well-known as to become conventional expectations in their own right. Meyer (1956) analyzes this process and gives a nice example in the use of vibrato by string instrument players. At one time, string players used no vibrato, introducing it on rare occasions as a deviation from convention which heightened tension and created emotional response by virtue of its rarity. String players who wished to excite such an emotional response began using vibrato more and more often until the way to excite the emotional response it had once produced was to play without vibrato, a device that Bartok and other composers exploited. Meyer describes the process by which deviations from convention become accepted conventions in their own right as a common one.

Such changes are a kind of gradualist reform in a persisting artistic tradition. Broader, more disruptive changes also occur, bearing a marked resemblance to political and scientific revolutions (Kuhn, 1962). Any major change necessarily attacks some of the existing conventions of the art directly, as when the Impressionists or Cubists changed the existing visual language of painting, the way one read paint on canvas as a representation of something. An attack on convention does not merely mean an attack on the particular item to be changed. Every convention carries with it an aesthetic, according to which what is conventional becomes the standard by which artistic beauty and effectiveness is judged. A play which violates the classical unities is not merely different, it is distasteful, barbaric and ugly to those for whom the classical unities represent a fixed criterion of dramatic worth. An attack on a convention becomes an attack on the aesthetic related to it. But people do not experience their aesthetic beliefs as merely arbitrary and conventional; they feel that they are natural, proper and moral. An attack on a convention and an aesthetic is also an attack on a morality. The regularity with which audiences greet major changes in dramatic, musical and visual conventions with vituperative hostility indicates the close relation between aesthetic and moral belief (Kubler, 1962).

An attack on sacred aesthetic beliefs as embodied in particular conventions is, finally, an attack on an existing arrangement of ranked statuses, a stratification system. Remember that the conventional way of doing things in any art utilizes an existing cooperative network, an organized art world which rewards those who manipulate the existing conventions appropriately in light of the associated sacred aesthetic. Suppose that a dance world is organized around the conventions and skills embodied in classical ballet. If I then learn those conventions and skills, I become eligible for positions in the best ballet companies; the finest choreographers will create ballets for me that are just the kind I know how to dance and will look good in; the best composers will write scores for me; theaters will be available; I will earn as good a living as a dancer can earn; audiences will love me and I will be famous. Anyone who successfully promotes a new convention in which he is skilled and I am not attacks not only my aesthetic but also my high position in the world of dance. So the resistance to the new expresses the anger of those who will lose materially by the change, in the form of aesthetic outrage.

Others than the artist have something invested in the status quo which a change in accepted conventions will lose them. Consider earthworks made, for instance, by a bulldozer in a square mile of pasture. Such a sculpture cannot be collected (though a patron can pay for its construction and receive signed plans or photographs as a document of his patronage), or put in museums (though the mementos the collector receives can be displayed). If earthworks become an important art form, the museum personnel whose evaluations of museum-collectable art have had important consequences for the careers of artists and art movements lose the power to choose which works will be displayed, for their museums are unnecessary for displaying those works. Everyone involved in the museum-collectable kind of art (collectors, museum curators, galleries, dealers, artists) loses something. We might say that every cooperative network that constitutes an art world creates value by the agreement of its members as to what is valuable (Levine, 1972; Christopherson, 1974). When new people successfully create a new world which defines other conventions as embodying artistic value, all the participants in the old world who cannot make a place in the new one lose out.

Every art world develops standardized modes of support and artists who support their work through those conventional means develop an aesthetic which accepts the constraints embedded in those forms of cooperation. Rosenblum (1973) has shown that the aesthetic of photographers varies with the economic channels through which their work is distributed in the same way that their customary work styles do, and Lyon (1974) has analyzed the interdependence of aesthetic decisions and the means by which resources are gathered in a semi-professional theater group. One example will illustrate the nature of the dependence. The group depended on volunteer help to get necessary work done. But people volunteered for nonartistic kinds of work largely because they hoped eventually to get a part in a play and gain some acting experience. The people who ran the company soon accumulated many such debts and were constrained to choose plays with relatively large casts to pay them off.

Conclusion

If we focus on a specific art work, it proves useful to think of social organization as a network of people who cooperate to produce that work.

We see that the same people often cooperate repeatedly, even routinely, in similar ways to produce similar works. They organize their cooperation by referring to the conventions current among those who participate in the production and consumption of such works. If the same people do not actually act together in every case, their replacements are also familiar with and proficient in the use of the same conventions, so that the cooperation can go on without difficulty. Conventions make collective action simpler and less costly in time, energy and other resources; but they do not make unconventional work impossible, only more costly and more difficult. Change can occur, as it often does, whenever someone devises a way to gather the greater resources required. Thus, the conventional modes of cooperation and collective action need not recur because people constantly devise new modes of action and discover the resources necessary to put them into practice.

To say all this goes beyond the assertion that art is social and beyond demonstrations of the congruence between forms of social organization and artistic styles or subjects. It shows that art is social in the sense that it is created by networks of people acting together, and proposes a framework in which differing modes of collective action, mediated by accepted or newly developed conventions, can be studied. It places a number of traditional questions in the field in a context in which their similarity to other forms of collective action can be used for comparative theoretical work.

The discussion of art as collective action suggests a general approach to the analysis of social organization. We can focus on any event (the more general term which encompasses the production of an art work as a special case) and look for the network of people however large or extended, whose collective activity made it possible for the event to occur as it did. We can look for networks whose cooperative activity recurs or has become routine and specify the conventions by which their constituent members coordinate their separate line of action.

We might want to use terms as social organization or social structure as a metaphorical way of referring to those recurring networks and their activities. In doing so, however, we should not forget their metaphorical character and inadvertently assert as a fact implied in the metaphor what can only be discovered through research. When sociologists speak of social structure or social systems, the metaphor implies (though its user neither proves nor argues the point) that the collective action involved occurs "regularly" or "often" (the quantifier, being implicit, is non-specific) and, further, that the people involved act together to produce a large variety of events. But we should recognize generally, as the empirical materials require us to do in the study of the arts, that whether a mode of collective action is recurrent or routine enough to warrant such description must be decided by investigation, not by definition. Some forms of collective action recur often, others occasionally, some very seldom. Similarly, people who participate in the network that produces one event or kind of event may not act together in art works producing other events. That question, too, must be decided by investigation.

Collective actions and the events they produce are the basic unit of sociological investigation. Social organization consist of the special case in which the same people act together to produce a variety of different events in a recurring way. Social organization (and its cognates) are not only concepts, then, but also empirical findings. Whether we speak of the collective acts of a few people—a family or a friendship—or of a much larger number—a profession or a class system—we need always to ask exactly who is joining together to produce what events. To pursue the generalization form the theory developed for artistic activities, we can study social organizations of all kinds by looking for the networks responsible for producing specific events, the overlaps among such cooperative networks, the way participants use conventions to coordinate their activities, how existing conventions simultaneously make coordinated action possible and limit the forms it can take, and how the development of new forms of acquiring resources makes change possible. (I should point out that, while this point of view is not exactly commonplace, neither is it novel. It can be found in the writings of, among others, Simmel [1898], Park [1950, 1952, 1955 passim], Blumer [1966] and Hughes [1971, esp. pp. 5–13 and 52–64]).

Notes

1. Reprinted with the permission of the author and the publisher from the *American Sociological Review* (vol. 39, 1974).

References

Albrecht, Milton C., James H. Barnett & Mason Griff (eds.). 1970. *The Sociology of Art and Literature: A Reader.* New York: Praeger.

Bennett, H. S. 1972. "Other People's Music." Unpublished doctoral dissertation, Northwestern U.

Blumer, Herbert. 1966. "Sociological Implications of the Thought of George Herbert Mead," *American Journal of Sociology* 71: 535–544.

Christopherson, Richard. 1974. "Making Art with Machines: Photography's Institutional Inadequacies," *Urban Life and Culture* 3, no. 1: 3–34.

Cooper, Grosvenor W. & Leonard B. Meyer. 1960. *The Rhythmic Structure of Music*. Chicago: U. of Chicago Press.

Cowell, Henry & Sidney Cowell. 1954. *Charles Ives and His Music*. New York: Oxford U. Press.

Dart, Thurston. 1967. *The Interpretation of Music*, (4th ed.). London: Hutchinson.

Faulkner, Robert R. 1973a. "Orchestra Interaction: Some Features of Communication and Authority in an Artistic Organization," *Sociological Quarterly* 14: 147–157.

Faulkner, Robert R. 1973b. "Career Concerns and Mobility Motivations of Orchestra Musicians," *Sociological Quarterly* 14: 334–349.

Ivins, W. 1953. *Prints and Visual Communication*. Cambridge: M.I.T. Press.

Johnson, Thomas. 1955. *Emily Dickinson*. Cambridge: Harvard U. Press.

Kase, Thelma. 1973. "The Artist, the Printer and the Publisher." Unpublished master's thesis. U. of Missouri-Kansas City.

Kealy, Edward. 1974. "The Real Rock Revolution: Sound Mixers, their Work, and the Aesthetics of Popular Music Production." Unpublished doctorial dissertation, Northwestern U.

Kealy, Edward. 1974b. "The Recording Engineer." Doctoral dissertation in progress, Northwestern U.

Kubler, George. 1962. *The Shape of Time*. New Haven: Yale U. Press.

Kuhn, Thomas. 1962. *The Structure of Scientific Revolution*. Chicago: U. of Chicago Press.

Levine, Edward M. 1972. "Chicago's Art World," *Urban Life and Culture* 1: 292–322.

Lyon, Eleanor. 1974. "Work and Play: Resource Constraints in a Small Theater," *Urban Life and Culture* 3, no. 1: 71–97.

Meyer, L. B. 1956. *Emotion and Meaning in Music*. Chicago: U. of Chicago Press.

Meyer, L. B. 1967. *Music, the Arts and Ideas*. Chicago: U. of Chicago Press.

Meyer, L. B. 1973. *Explaining Music*. Berkeley: U. of California Press.

Park, Robert E. 1950. *Race and Culture*. New York: The Free Press.

Park, Robert E. 1952. *Human Communities*. New York: The Free Press.

Park, Robert E. 1955. *Society*. New York: The Free Press.

Partch, Harry. 1949. *Genesis of a Music*. Madison: U. of Wisconsin Press.

Pevsner, Nikolaus. 1940. *Academies of Art: Past and Present*. Cambridge: Cambridge U. Press.

Reese, Gustave. 1959. *Music in the Renaissance*, rev. ed. New York: W. W. Norton.

Rosenblum, Barbara. 1973. "Photographers." Ph.D. dissertation, Evanston, Northwestern University.

Simmel, Georg. 1898. "The Persistence of Social Groups," *American Journal of Sociology* 3: 662–669 & 829–836; 4: 35–50.

Strauss, Anselm L. et al. 1964. *Psychiatric Ideologies and Institutions.* New York: The Free Press.

Wörner, Karl H. 1973. *Stockhausen: Life and Work.* Berkeley: U. of California Press.

3

Shadows of Anxiety:
Popular Culture in Modern Society

CHARLES SIMPSON

A sociology of popular culture should locate the mass production, distribution, and consumption of experience with the processes of modernization. The technology of popular culture began only with the 19th-century penny press, the mass circulation weekly, and the magazine (Schudson, 1967). In the 20th-century, popular culture has rooted itself more deeply with each new means of mass communications. With television and radio, it now comprises a continuous alternative stream of experience. This stream of experience is the shadow of intersubjective social interaction, the dream-mode of modern society.

The character of modernization in the West appears to require a non-rational component of enchantment which the dominant institutions, with the exception of politics, cannot provide. Modernization has come to mean an urbanized life channeled through bureaucratic organizations. The market and increasingly government coordinate production. Positive legislation rather than moral tradition or conviction is the basis of social regulation. The cohesion that flows from the capacity of individuals to emotively participate in the pain and happiness of others has found itself assaulted by modernization. Technological changes, government policy, and the business cycle have joined disease and the weather in producing erratic and differential effects, enriching some and impoverishing others beyond any moral logic. For the average person, powerless to shape the conditions of life, the social world has taken on a provisional tone unsanctioned by any deeper metaphysical meaning and thus unknown to previous eras. The desire for national security has come to necessitate the preparation for global annihilation (Schell, 1982). On a more modest scale, old formulas of self-discipline and satisfaction no longer function. Robotic production at home and abroad threatens to make the lifetime skills of workers meaningless. Engineering graduates can anticipate a half-life of five years for the marketability of their knowledge. Third-generation farm owners are increasingly seeing their life's work liquidated under the auctioneer's gavel as machinery costs, soft markets, and high interest rates drag their enterprises under. The routines by which life is organized have taken on an iridescent insubstantiality. Few cognitive, moral, or psychological props are available within the structures of work or locality; like psychoanalysis and support groups for alcoholics, these are organized on an institutionally independent basis and comprise asylums of respite and repair rather than a redesign of work and community. Modernization has transformed the collectivities of family and local community, sharpening the edges of contending interest groups and widening the gaps into which isolated individuals free-fall into social oblivion (Lasch, 1977).

This essay seeks to demonstrate that the mass entertainment media made possible by 20th-century technology is best understood as a means through which individuals cope with the dislocations of modernization. Imaginative popular entertainment acknowledges our existential precariousness. It gives imagery to our dread that human character and the social order are becoming detached from any transcending meaning. But this apprehension is projected into a surreal space where dread can be simultaneously expressed and contained. This space—the social order within film, television, the tabloid—acts as a foil to the practical world. Like dream space, mass entertainment provides for the safe expression of hungers and fears that otherwise would haunt and obstruct everyday life.

While the content of mass entertainment is frequently a glimpse into the void of social collapse, its form as ubiquitous imagery comprises a classless landscape with frequent and inexpensive points of audience access and interaction. The iconography of film and television is as available as toys, tee shirt insignia, electronic game format, posters, and fashion accessories. Cartoon characters, film personalities, and popular music supply the public with an array of symbols useful essentially for mutual recognition by their adherents. These images are claimed as objects of identification by various cultural and generational subgroups. As these cultural touch-stones move through the spotlight of currency and later of nostalgia they layer into a complex stratification of icons. Each objectifies, accumulates, and encodes the collective experience of national subgroups.

News as Catastrophe

The instability of the world's ecological, political, and economic systems has become increasingly apparent to the general public in the industrial nations because they have the greatest access to modern communication equipment. Beginning with movie-house newsreels in the 1920s and now including instantaneous reception of video transmissions, mass media innovations have brought the events of all regions into focus. But the topics eliciting this communication have not been the normal functioning of diverse social systems and cultures; instead it has been the immediately obvious and visually communicable catastrophy. Flood, military invasion, famine, and terrorism constitute the texture of this news, presented in close-up detail without assessment of social context or broader implications. Crime reporting is nearly as old as newspapers. *The New York Sun*, founded in 1833 as the first penny press, hired reporters to cover the police court proceedings on a regular basis, and carried accounts of rape, mail robbery, and child abandonment along with the political and commercial news (Schudson, 1967; 14–31). One hundred and fifty years later the media continues to capitalize on the popular premise that the truth about the world is that it is not merely dangerous but abhorrent. But now not merely the city streets but the globe can be gleaned for confirmation of this suspicion.

As consciousness of the power of imagery has grown, political leaders have increasingly staged events specifically for the camera and its audience: parading storm-troopers and athletes imbued with the national spirit; tanks and missiles rumbling through Red Square; the televised American moon landings. These events at their most epic are spectacles of national power which promote identification with the nation and its leadership. Potential opponents are implicitly crushed. But such spectors of social mobilization affect the private spheres of citizens; the security to be found in the familiar and the personally satisfying is dislocated. But at the same time that the private sphere is destabilized, the public increasingly distrusts established leadership, if only as a means to regain some semblance of personal autonomy. The moonlandings were witnessed, yet widely believed to have been staged in some obscure Arizona sandpit. The public saw John F. Kennedy shot and, in turn, Lee Harvey Oswald killed; yet an industry has developed which impugns the integrity of Chief Justice Earl Warren and his commission and which persists in believing that the assassination of a President was a political plot and its investigation cooked.

News accounts, but particularly the camera, distance the audience from the event, even in its descriptive immediacy. Whether looking at Nazi death camp footage or the methodical digging of a backhoe as it unearths the victims of another New Jersey mass murderer, the audience and its surroundings are not physically touched. Their separateness from the events are emphasized. Hence the ritual of normal people watching the aberrant is possible. Yet the audience is not undamaged when victims proliferate. From the Vietnam War onward, a trail of refugees has wandered without evident purpose or hope, across American television screens. The immediate empathetic response of the viewer has been blunted, replaced by a blasé or even hostile reaction to those who present us with tragedy on such a continuous scale that we cannot effectively respond (Simmel, 1969). Our prudent denial of the emotional meaning of what we see and read about increases our alienation and unease within the world. In the midst of our electronic detachment, our existential security crumbles.

Popular Entertainment and the Emotional Apprehension of Reality

The defining characteristic of popular culture in the modern world is that it seeks to overcome the experience of social fragmentation without being critical. It neither seriously explores the contradiction between the individual and social institutions nor does it treat its products as aesthetic compositions. Commercially produced popular culture in the 20th-century provides the public with emotional and expressive social integration which is otherwise largely absent from the narrowly functional arrangements of industrial capitalism. It provides a plane of common experience and nationally enacted drama which appears to transcend economic conflict and occupational frustration. It supplies scripts and the background music, the diversion by which social engagement is temporarily evaded. A semblance of affective participation in a social whole is thus achieved.

Unlike fine art, popular culture has not generated a critical audience. Its mode of apprehension precludes this. Commercially produced entertainment is able to attract a broadly-based audience only to the extent that it can offer an escape to a mass population contending with complex social constraints. Whether as electronic games at which adolescents purchase illusions of power or soap opera from which viewers borrow a substitute life of exaggerated sexuality, evil, and pain, popular entertainment does not analyze the situation of its audience nor generate complex genera standards. Presenting little conceptual challenge to the audience, popular entertainment cannot support critical discussion. Few commentators earn a living from holding television shows, popular movies, or mass market paperback books to literary or technical standards. With the exception of a few journals such as *The New Yorker* which present their movie reviews as exercises in journalistic wit (Simon, 1982)—disguising the fact that intellectuals, too, dip into escapist popular culture but are not comfortable doing this plainly—accounts of popular culture items are previews. They are trailers which entice without spoiling the surprises of the plot. Coverage of mass culture from within mass culture, usually taking the form of magazines which cover the private troubles of actors, is synonymous with publicity. Such articles are not criticism but touts.

Critical evaluation would require that the audience treat the work as a created object and so improvable, and not merely as an affect within which to lose oneself for a time. When an audience is not moved to assume the perspective of the author, actor, or artist, and is unable to discuss how an affect is achieved, enthusiastic recognition and identification with a work are all that remains.

The aesthetic object, if it is to be treated as an object of art, must be able to sustain analysis. But the market process affecting popular entertainment inhibits subtlety. Aesthetic complications have the effect of stratifying the audience by taste and knowledgeability. Important segments of the general audience are thus lost, and with them sales or a favorable advertising rate structure. To avoid this, television, movies, and novels for the general public exist in a perceptual space which is at once emotionally direct and without intellectual seriousness. Symbols in this space are without complex references to broader reality or truth. It is a region of graphically crafted stereotypes, signs whose messages are instantly obvious and quickly exhausted.

In television and popular movies, information is conveyed through a montage of images focused on concrete objects. The reference matrix through which these objects gain connotative depth is the genre tradition itself, its format of expectations and history of enactments. Those in the audience who can point out these references are rewarded with a sense of cultural mastery. Rummaging for trivia amid the fragments of accumulating popular culture functions as a substitute for analysis. Due to its capacity to cling by association to the historic and personal context of the audience, year by year popular culture refines a series of stereotypical situations, images, characters and dilemmas, the best of which contain the emotional energy of our collective past. They distill our fears and express our hopes with a borrowed intensity, an intimacy by association.

In popular entertainment, language is secondary to plot action and the self explanatory character of image. This deemphasis on words originated when films lacked sound and were able to appeal to diverse immigrant audiences on the basis of melodramatic techniques (Ewen and Ewen, 1982; 81–105). In the present era, soundtracks have facilitated a standardization and heightening of the mood-altering potential of music, and conversation is still avoided. The television comedy monologue is typically two sentences in length. Simplified dialogue neatly coincides with the need of production studios to sell their products to an international and multilingual audience.

Apart from soundtracks, the central place of music in popular culture is due to the fact that it can be combined with other activities: dancing, driving, working and beachgoing. It has the potential for an intimate involvement with emotionally charged moments in the life cycle—romance and the failure of romance, adolescence and infidelity. It can focus and stabilize the emotional coloration of historical eras and events, combining with them in the experience of the listener. The music of Glenn Miller and his fellow band leaders are the sound of World War II. As highway construction transforms the scale and geography of localities into an historic sameness, the vitality and specificity of the remembered past—its solidarity—becomes composed largely of its associated music. Popular music reflects collective experience because it is both temporally specific and widely distributed, it is a peg for individual memory because it permeates personal experience.

By contrast, television entertainment demands too exclusive visual preoccupation, thus separating the program experience from the context of daily life. At the same time cost considerations, the interest in attracting a general audience, and the uneventful nature of a medium that broadcasts continuously, all tend to erode program quality standards to the point where the programming is not memorable in itself. Television has become an eternal present whose program content phenomenologically dissolves into streams of continuous but non-indexical time. While the technology of home video storage has recently allowed select bits of the stream to be preserved and retrieved by viewers, the vast bulk of programming has not continuing life. It is merely a present, impossible to reference within collective or personal history, and pointless to remember. Its phenomenological existence lies in its power to temporarily annihilate simultaneous streams of personal and collective life. Its lack of intrinsic vitality is exposed in the dead time of the rerun.

Divisions within and between specific units of television programming are weak, impinged upon by commercial breaks and annihilated by a simple change of channel. By contrast, film and conventional theater disciplines the spectator as part of a co-present audience to accept intact the period required for a complete performance and to refrain from ignoring that performance. Theater's proscenium—the architecture and conventions that focus attention on a single complete performance—is strong. Video morphology—its private viewing locale, multiplicity of channel choice, and commercial interruption undermine the integrity of its program boundaries.

The most prevalent form of rating and criticizing popular culture content takes place outside the realm of aesthetic consideration; it is the general public's reaction to sexual explicitness, vulgarity and violence as openly available entertainment. Discussion of popular culture from the perspective of moral offensiveness is not an anesthetic debate. Popular film, television drama, and mass market fiction constantly encounter moral objections because they are materialized dreams. As such, they are both appealing and censorable. The surreal landscape of the media, because it emphasizes emotional encounter rather than aesthetic or cognitive distance, allows members of modern society to formulate and displace their fears through the evocation of systematic experiences of horror, to achieve sexual release in a manner that does not require or endanger social success, and to banish isolation through a kind of solidarity with strangers.

The Celluloid Dream

Building on the insights of Fritz Lang and other directors of the surrealist school of German film in the 1920's, moviemakers have achieved their most compelling effects through creating dream-like emotional experiences which purge their audiences. Alfred Hitchcock and his students such as Brian DePalma brought this technique into American film and television. Mass market authors of fiction from H. G. Wells to Peter Benchley and Stephen King have made the emotive technique a cornerstone of popular literature. Why does the mass produced dream have appeal?

In ordinary dreaming, modern man is able to transmogrify the anxieties of wakeful life into images which give shape to and thus externalize disruptive emotions. In this form, anxieties become concretized antagonists who can be confronted and at least temporarily mastered. The absence of primitive mythic integration with the cosmos and the passing of medieval ideals of religiously integrated social solidarity has left modern man existentially exposed (Eliade, 1957). The pervasive insecurity of modern life, a function of its diminished emotional and moral coherence which enhances our vulnerability to its physical danger, has heightened this need for the safe discharge of anxiety. The perception of our individual existence uprooted from mythic past and paradisaical future makes the precariousness of life and the frustration of desire difficult to bear. Mass media dreams allow us to depict the insufficiencies of our lives and momentarily escape them. In media dreams, the menace of the dark staircase is ultimately shown to obscure a very specific if horrible opponent; we conquer that opponent or, if not, as spectators we survive our own death. If existential self-consciousness takes the form of a diffuse sexual want, mass entertainment channels this to a specific object of desire and attainment of proxy. Media dream encounters suspend the routine limits to life.

The appeal of popular culture as entertainment is that it provides escape into childhood, a childhood that Freud described as co-present in adults as a substratum of resistance to socialization. Its manifestations are recognizable in our longing for release from the censorship of thought and act which is imposed by society or by our adult selves. As adults, however, we realize that a life of surrender to impulse gratification is self-defeating. We compromise. We allow ourselves to play at disregarding the consequences of impulse gratification in a manner that makes it clear to others and to ourselves that we don't intend to be taken seriously. This zone of play, joking, feinting, and spontaneous theater balances out the repression of impulse that ordinarily characterizes our lives. This zone of play includes the dream, a theater of the mind. Freud writes (1963: 587–8).

> Dreaming is on the whole an example of regression to the dreamer's earliest condition, a revival of his childhood, or the instinctual impulses which dominated it and of the methods of expression which were then available to him. Behind this childhood of the individual we are promised a picture of a phylogenetic childhood—a picture of the development of the human race, of which the individual's own development is in fact an abbreviated recapitulation influenced by the chance circumstances of life.

According to Freud, "A conscious wish can only become a dream-instigator if it succeeds in awakening an unconscious wish with the same tenor and in obtaining reinforcement from it . . . A wish which is represented in a dream must be an infantilization" (1963: 541–2).

It is not necessary, however, to depict the subconscious as radically different from and unavailable to conscious thought. A continuum of degrees of consciousness is a sufficient assumption to account for suspension of disbelief and conditional self-deception. Individuals employ a variety of expressive techniques which circumvent self-censorship. These may be called modes of expressive deception, in which message content is denied social weight by the form or circumstances of the message. Such modes of expressive deception include the risque narrative and off-color joke, double entendres, and declarations made in a state of manifest drunkenness. Selective inattention and convenient forgetting are more passive forms of expressive deception. Where the audience is limited to the self, expressive deception includes fantasizing, daydreaming, and the sleeping dream. In each of these modes, an impulse is both affirmed and denied. Or, rather, the impulse is affirmed in a responsible, non-disruptive manner. Mass entertainment is a commercialized mode of expressive deception. Because such experiences as reading and watching movies and television, while being interruptable, preclude simultaneous group mediation, they come closest to the form of solitary expressive deception—the fantasy or dream. Popular entertainment capitalizes on this immediacy of apprehension. The commercial dream is tailored from materials appropriated from and resembling the personal dream. In adopting an established vocabulary of expressive deception, it more easily instigates in the audience a dream-like suspension of reality and an affective rather than a cognitive or critical response. Commercial technology has, thus, added new forms of expressive deception and facilitated a standardized form of dream-release.

The hiatus provided by the media dream is functional. Besides being profitable to its manufacturers, it does not ordinarily disrupt the economic lives of audiences or threaten their attention to social responsibilities. It is a magic theater in a secular world.

Composing dream-fiction for the general audience so that it releases individuals from the constraints of social reality and their own sense of responsibility, without at the same time triggering their self-censorship, is the script-design problem for writers and directors. While standards change over time, it is always possible to be too overt in the portrayal of sexuality and violence or too cavalier in suspending natural laws and ordinary social dynamics. While the licentious and the fantastic are appealing to many adults and children, it makes others feel self-conscious when seen in public enjoying such fare. Furthermore, parents and community pressure are likely to deny children access to sexually explicit or morbid entertainment, diminishing the market.

Steven Spielberg's recent film ''E. T.'' which has set a world record in ticket sales, is an instance of a successful solution to the media-dream design problem. ''E. T.'' appeals to children because it allows them to vicariously defeat the adult world through magic flights on bicycles, the employment of extraordinary powers, and gumption. The film appeals to the children in adults because most adults would like to believe that love can revoke the finality of death, that existential abandonment is only momentary, and that individual friendship can overcome the most extreme differences in social origin. Children and adults would like to believe that tragedy is the equivalent of the child lost in a supermarket. Spielberg's images allow us to indulge this wish without incapacitating ourselves with confusion between the wish and the contrary reality.

Mystery Stories and Existential Anxiety

A portion or mass market fiction and film do retain a critical edge and merit separate consideration. These works utilize a tough realism to describe society's more coercive institutions. The dramatic tension in these works stems from the difficulties which the characters have in remaining loyal to others in the face of institutional pressures. Organized society is portrayed as striving to corrupt personal bonds and so gain unimpeded access to an isolated self. Usually marked by cliche and stereotyped character, these works are not ranked by scholars as literature. But as dramas of little

people and underlife, they have become staple expressions of popular alienation from organized society. The reveal the arrogance of petty position
and elevated office and depict the odor of indifference in the corridors of
public life.

The best of this popular fiction are mysteries, a genre which emphasizes our awareness that appearance and reality do not coincide, and that
life in society disrupted by modernization is strewn with casualties. Reader
and hero alike achieve insights into the world through having to evade a
system of social constraints which ignores their values and threatens their
purposes. Gradually, the social system is shown to be too broad and too
deep to be beaten by the individual, yet too corrosive of self, family, and
friendship to permit capitulation. What is left to the hero, however tainted,
are moments when personal effort affirms private loyalties and integrity,
while fatal, nevertheless redeems. The bureaucratic and economic system is
shown as a haphazard conspiracy: officials are corrupt, crooks are inform-
ers. In its midst, heroism takes the form of exemplary opposition by society's loners to the supremacy of market values and the carelessness of
power (LaFarge, 1950).

The perception of the world as off its moral and logical center is nowhere as apparent as in the mystery story. The name "mystery" is both
suggestive and misleading. Where the Mystery pageant was also a drama, it
depicted with folk-regularity the presence of a cosmic order in this world.
Jesus, an inexplicable fusion of human and divine qualities, underwent on
the medieval stage the cycle of betrayal, suffering and death. With his as-
cension into heaven, the grieving followers on stage and in the audience
were shown the possibility of a place in paradise (Burkhardt, 1954; Pirenne,
1925; Gimpel, 1961).

The contemporary mystery is without a savior and without salvation.
A cosmic design for human life is wanting, longed for but not believed
possible. The hidden truth of the popular mystery is not god's presence on
earth but man's bewilderment in a purposeless landscape. The cause of
events is obscure, revealed only partially by the floundering of characters
in a present unrelieved by hope for improvement. Off-balance, they collide
with events against which they struggle for understanding and mastery.
Their reactions give them their only knowledge of the other mystery, that
is, themselves.

Mystery stories involve a crime, and that crime is nearly always murder. The smaller point is the uncovering of the guilty individual. But in a
universe of suspects, no one is beyond the capacity for murder, and that is
the larger point in the mystery story. This murder may be solved; murder,
as such, remains baffling.

The Detective Drama

In the late 1800's, weekly newspapers and magazines in European cities began to serialize fiction, much of it involving criminal acts and their detection, and enlisting writers such as Dickens and Dostoyevski. In the 1890's the Strand magazine in England was successful in increasing its circulation through commissioned serial stories about Sherlock Holmes, establishing the continuous character as a feature of crime stories (Doyle, 1980). *Lippincott's* magazine brought the London detective to America in serial form shortly after, and before 1914 introduced full length fictional crime stories (Tebbel, 1974: p. 260). After the war, weekly and monthly magazines, cheaply printed on wood fiber and so known as "pulps," began to specialize in crime stories. Magazines such as *Black Mask, Detective Fiction Weekly,* and *Dime Detective* provided a market for a new generation of writers who came to specialize in mysteries involving a crime and its solution.

Former Pinkerton Detective Agency operative Dashiell Hammett (1894–1961), who began writing for the pulp crime magazines in the early 1920's, created work that has been frequently reprinted and remains continuously popular. In the late 1920's, Hammett turned to full length novels, many subsequently adapted as movie scripts (Wolfenstein and Leites, 1971; 175–242). These established the cynical detective in the big city as a standard character in American fiction and in the American moral imagination. The well-known *Maltese Falcon* (1929) is an exemplary instance of the hard-boiled style in crime mysteries and the foundation for a style which has persisted for fifty years as a central iconography in popular culture.

In the *Maltese Falcon*, a beautiful and seemingly vulnerable client hires the detective agency of Spade and Archer to find her sister, a small-town girl who ran off to San Francisco with a dangerous character. Archer, lusting for the client herself as well as for her money, snatches the case away from Spade and sets off to meet the sister's lover. Archer is found shot dead in the street. Spade, the surviving partner, has a double reason to try to solve the crime. Because he has been carrying on an affair with Archer's wife, the police suspect him of the murder. Because he has professional pride he feels an obligation to defend his agency.

Nothing in the case is as it first appears to be. The client lies about her name and the specifics of her story; she has no sister. In fact, she is one of a gang of thieves who have snatched a medieval gold statue made in the shape of a falcon and encrusted with jewels. Each of the gang maneuvers to monopolize possession of the bird and claim its entire cash value. As thieves, they lack the necessary modicum of honor that would allow their shifting partnership to hold together and their venture succeed. Spade gradually learns that he has really been hired to support Brigid O'Shaughnessy's chances of getting and keeping the bird. Through lie after lie, he gropes toward the truth about the location of the statue and the death of Archer.

Spade moves through a dream-like San Francisco. It is a marketplace with cash as its truth and love as its illusion. The characters in the story are vivid but generally one dimensional. They are parodies or exaggerated cliches of existing media characters. Dope-addicted and psychopathic young Wilmer satirizes the image of the wholesome American adolescent; the oily Levantine gangster Cairo is Hollywood's generalized Middle Easterner; the master criminal, the "bulbously" fat Gutman, is the over-polite and hence doubly-devious Anglo-Saxon businessman. The crew is a criminal sideshow, and the novel a satire both of American society and of its own pretensions.

Spade's clients—and he has two of them competing for his loyalty—are subject to sudden appearances and disappearances. They don't seem to exist in a spatially contiguous world, and they continuously challenge the reader's emotional assumption that the world is coherent. The leads which Spade follows usually originate outside of his control rather than through his methodical sleuthing. And then they fit together poorly or not at all. He is kept moving more than he is enlightened.

When he does get the statue, it is delivered to him unexpectedly by a spectoral stranger.

> The corridor door opened . . . He stood in the doorway with his soft hat crushed between his head and the top of the door-frame: he was nearly seven feet tall. A black overcoat cut long and straight like a sheath, buttoned from throat to knees, exaggerated his leanness. His eyes were dark and bloodshot and mad above lower lids that hung down to show pink inner membrane. Held tight against the left side of his chest by a black-sleeved arm that ended in a yellowish claw was a brown-paper-wrapped parcel . . . Holding himself stiffly straight, not putting his hands out to break his fall, he fell forward as a tree falls (Hammett, 1929: 162–3).

Spade himself is Hammett's most interesting character. He is a "blond satan" who at any point may or may not impose ethical restraints upon himself. He is sequentially defined by the choices he makes, not by his character. As a detective in business for himself, he is marginal to the criminal justice system, and that's the way he wants it. He is willing to break the law for his clients, and expects his attorney to protect him in the same way. He has an affair with Archer's beautiful wife, yet is morally stunned when she asks him, while they kiss, if he killed her husband; under the toughness, he remains a romantic. He responds protectively to the apparent vulnerability of his client, and yet can punch a disarmed man in the face. Spade is ambiguous. He wants to right the wrongs done to him and to those he protects, but he reserves the right to decide just who he will protect and just how he will do it. No saint, he can relish the feeling of greed and the stirrings of self-interest. They help him savor the sense of his own ego.

Like Sherlock Holmes, Spade works outside the law so as to avoid its organizational restrictions. Unlike Holmes, Spade sees the legal system as corrupt and inefficient, and holds it in contempt. With his lawyer delaying his arrest, Spade knows that his freedom to operate is temporary. He is permitted the space to run. For political reasons, murders must be solved. He is an informal part of the system: if he fails to use his freedom to unearth a suspect, he becomes the suspect himself. "Listen, Gutman, we've absolutely got to give them a victim", he says as the case draws to a close. "There's no way out of it. Let's give them the punk." Spade indicates Gutman's homocidal associate, and smiles pleasantly. "He actually did shoot both of them . . . Let's pin the necessary evidence on him and turn him over to them." (Hammett, 1929: 186). The police require a closed case. Spade explains the system of criminal justice in San Francisco:

> "Bryan is like most district attorneys. He's more interested in how his record will look on paper than in anything else. He'd rather drop a doubtful case than try it and have it go against him. I don't know that he ever deliberately framed anybody he believed innocent, but I can't imagine him letting himself believe them innocent if he could scrape up, or twist into shape, proof of their guilt. To be sure of convicting one man he'll let half a dozen equally guilty accomplices go free—if trying to convict them all might confuse his case. That's the choice we'll give him and he'll boggle it up (Hammett, 1929: 186–189).

Prudent people are never candid in this San Francisco. Conversations take the form of negotiations for scraps of usually tainted information. The conversants strive never to show fear, curiosity, or eagerness least they weaken their bargaining positions or give something away from nothing. A gulf of mistrust isolates everyone in this city except the naive.

If trust in others is foolish, passion is dangerous. It incites improbably relationships, flaunts reason, and will not dutifully accompany love. Love in this world is rare enough. Archer dead is not a man mourned by his wife but ten thousand dollars of insurance money. Gutman, who tells Wilmer he loves him like a son, sets this son up for the fall guy. Cairo's love is a foppish parody.

But love can exist. Effie, Spade's secretary, loves him. She mothers him and eagerly takes risks for him. But if Spade loves her, he has no passion for her. Instead he is illogically drawn to the more sexually magnetic Miss O'Shaughnessy. He sees she is manipulating him and laughs at her to defend himself. He knows she is lying to him, and tells her so. But still he pursues her. He feels a passion for her that is without trust. When his distrust becomes aggressive, she makes love with him. Later, awakening, he methodically searches her apartment.

Love, passion, and trust never unite the same two people. Sexual attraction is inexplicable, neither instigated nor extinguished at will. The prudent man guards against passion. The pursuit of O'Shaughnessy killed two men, or rather disarmed them so that she herself could kill them. But even knowing that, Spade does not cease feeling drawn to her. Since what he knows and what he feels cannot be reconciled, Spade is alienated from his emotions. They make him feels cannot be reconciled, Spade is alienated from his emotions. They make him feel insecure and off-center; they threaten to make him vulnerable. At times he resists passion and at times he does not, but he cannot shape his emotions. So he does the best he can; on the crucial issue of deciding who will face the police to take the blame for Archer's murder, Spade will not let his emotions decide his choice.

Spade's final confrontation with O'Shaughnessy is Hammett's exposition of the existentialist dilemma that characters in his world face. Spade lists all the reasons why he should allow O'Shaughnessy to escape, these include the fact that he desires her and perhaps loves her; then he lists the reasons why he should hand her over to the police. Not logic, morality, or basic self-interest is sufficient to force his decision, once he has made himself aware that it is his decision to make. He is free, and the realization is excruciating. He will be able to cite no other source but his own decision, no matter what he does.

Worse, the choice will not compose his emotions, his knowledge, and his moral perceptions into a harmonious whole. In Spade's world, one cannot be aware and remain a wholly integrated self. Self-respect lies in being tough enough not to hide from the realization that passion or morality or conventional routine are false courts of appeal; one's acts are one's own.

Mysteries work as entertainment because they created a world of expressive emotion which is not random fantasy; it is congruent with the inchoate dread of the modern world which audiences ordinarily repress least they risk dysfunctional demoralization. The twentieth-century has been a period when the reformist and utopian assumptions about the direction of social change (Mannheim, 1936)—the optimism that has enabled Western men and women to welcome modernization and excuse its costs—has come into question (Sartre, 1956; Douglas and Johnson, 1977).

The Popular Arts and Generational Stratification

While the forms or themes underlying popular art endure, for they appeal to an unfulfillment in modern society, the ways in which these themes are elaborated quickly become stale. Media-produced entertainment formula characteristically lack complexity and cannot sustain re-viewing or re-reading. Their very accessibility as alternative worlds of objectified emotion makes them boring in their predictability. The surface texture of characterization-running-to-stereotype is quickly exhausted. Music and film have the additional problem of being quickly exhausted by the ubiquity of their distribution. What results is a rhythm of fashion in entertainment, a movement from omnipresence to obsolescence and replacement. The new fashion is not an aesthetic improvement over the old, nor does the old remain popular even when it is an artistic accomplishment. The new item or, at the broader level, the new style, has appeal because it is fresh. Its emotional implications are historically unfocused while being affectively immediate, making it serve as a container for the personal feelings of a diverse audience. Audience members project themselves into the work, becoming emotional co-participants. Each work is an emotional mirror of those who behold it. Whether as song, movie or popular fiction, few items of mass culture can long sustain consumption on such an intimate and intense level. Familiarity soon reduces a work and its style to affective neutrality, and the audience seeks new material.

Because particular products of commercial culture are quickly exhausted by the emotional demands of their audience, the market for new products can be misjudged but it cannot be saturated. Recorded songs, the succession of bands and vocalists identified with these songs, films and their star performers, characters and theme music in television serials— these over time comprise a chronology of American popular culture through which the general population arranges itself and its memories by age and preference (Vidich and Bensman, 1968: 86–88).

Mannheim has noted the importance of generation in social stratification. Generational place is particularly important in the formation of cultural boundaries. The emphasis on the new in popular culture is particularly appealing to youth. New styles offer them an avenue for collective identification with symbols of emancipation, symbols whose appeal lies in no small part to their not being shared with the established adult audience. Popular culture is thus able to act as a major force for the displacement of potential rebellion by those whom the economy has yet to absorb or the political system endow with legitimate power. Emergent identities can be attached to popular culture styles rather than asserted through delinquency or politicized alienation.

New waves of culture in any period of the modern era provide for the social integration of youth as a group, both reflecting and deflecting their estrangement from adult society. For this reason, the newest cultural commodities, particularly movies, music, and clothing, frequently incorporate postures of defiance, vulgarity, reckless hedonism, morbidity, and the germ of political protest. But this symbolic rejection of existing culture is essentially a posture, an attitude which serves a transient need. Rock bands with names such as "The Nuclear Accidents", "Spinal Tap" and "The Dead Boys", while suggesting a social critique, engage in the alienation of adults to reassure youth that, despite their economic and political marginality, they possess some bounded territory, if only that of taste. It is for this reason that excursions by adults into teenage fashion in clothes, dance or intoxicants is a violation of intergenerational etiquette, an aesthetic if not a mental disorientation.

While popular culture stratifies society by giving each generation a sound and a set of cultural icons which are uniquely its own, popular culture also weaves these generational layers together. The most over-exposed song or film, once lived through in the enthusiasm of youth, can be re-endowed with appeal as a peg for nostalgia. The mass media continually return to the music and movies of generations no longer young, mining these cultural strata for artifacts which retain, through association, an emotion aura. The music we danced to in high school remains the sound of our youth; the movie stars we watched on first dates remain exemplars of sexual mastery. Our youthful expectations still linger in these images and sounds, untarnished by experience. As an audience ages in a rapidly changing society, a thread of continuity is strung out, marking a path through mass culture. The personal past, objectified and linked to a generational past, can be revisited as a place of refuge from the present. Transported by emotional association, recycled mass culture lets us stand within the landscape of our youth.

Other collectives crises in society, war and economic depression principally, may similarly establish settings of emotional intensity, made re-accessible through the items of commercial culture with which they have become associated.

Conclusion

Amid the erosion of meaning structures and the clash of group purposes that marks the modern period, popular culture constitutes a society-wide net which catches the individual who fails to construct sufficient personal coherence of purpose. Like stage scenery, the surface of popular culture is intended for viewing from one dimension. It is a weave of apparent dialogue, a realm of vicarious emotional encounter and the facade of collectivity. Radio music, motel chains and fast food outlets lend society a look of uniformity and coherence; in this sense America is a Potemkin village. Yet this appearance of social solidarity is a modern necessity. It is our broadest landscape, its boundaries delineate public arenas where some common definition of purpose and moments of affective sharing can occur. In mass culture, electronic omnipresence passes for the inter-subjective verification of experience, and repetition substitutes for complexity of cultural reference.

Despite being a paper skyline, popular culture lays a strong claim to our attention. It is constructed from the primary colors of existential anxiety. These emotions are the elemental concerns that preoccupy us throughout life, concerns with security, affection, intellectual coherence, sexual expressiveness, and the desire to imprint the world with our ego. Popular culture magnifies these affective states, removing them from the restraining particularities of setting that give individuated and prudent structure to these feelings. The description of these emotions in popular culture takes place in a space from which definite historical location, the political economy, and self-imposed constraints have been boiled into stereotype. Unlike primeval myth honed by group purpose and experience, these emotional dramas are, in fact, prefabricated dream experiences, a blend of the desires and nightmares of childhood.

The rituals of primitive and feudal societies were instruments of revelation; they directed the viewer toward an encompassing cosmic whole whose secrets and power they revealed. The fine art of the modern period was created in the absence of this cosmic dimension. Modern art proceeds from existentialist assumptions: human demands for meaning, purpose, coherence evoke only silence from the universe. In the absence of a transcendent realm, it becomes necessary for man to act as god, creating aesthetic or other significance and coherence in a heroic response to cosmic alienation.

Popular culture deals only indirectly with the tension between unfulfilled man and an indifferent world, the area that is the creative field for art. Instead, popular culture softens the constraints of the world by the substitution of a surreal world as its stage. Here, the emotional projections of the audience are objectified and made the stuff of drama. These emotions are the primal fears we all harbor, most vivid in the dependency of childhood but never completely allayed because we know that our mastery of the world is incomplete and temporary. When King Kong looks in through the

window, half way up the Empire State Building, he is looking at our childhood selves through our bedroom windows. And at the same time we are
the gorilla, looking at a beautiful and helpless Fay Ray.

The projection and resolution of primary emotional tensions, the sub-
stance of popular culture, frequently requires the intervention of a hero.
This hero is a larger-than-life mask for the ego of the viewer or audience
member, and he transcends the difficulties through a magical suspension of
natural laws. He is us as we would like ourselves to be, but know we cannot
be in the ordinary world. Butch Cassidy and the Sundance Kid, hopelessly
surrounded by their pursuers, smile and charge out into a hail of bullets.
The slow-motion camera prolongs the moment into a final freeze-frame, the
friends still on their feet, firing. Death has solved for them the more complex problems of living, while the freeze-frame has spared them and us the
vulgarity of death. For a surreal interval, friendship and heroic gesture are
all that matter. The film gives objectivity to our wish that it were true.

References

Burckhardt, Jacob 1954. *The [1878] Civilization of the Renaissance in Italy.* Tr.
S. G. C. Middlemore, New York: Random House.

Douglas, Jack and Johnson, John M. 1977. *Existential Sociology.* London: Cambridge University Press.

Doyle, Arthur Conan 1980. *The Original Illustrated Sherlock Holmes.* Secaucus,
N.J.: Castle.

Eliade, Mircea 1957. *Myths, Dreams, Mysteries: An Encounter Between Contemporary Faiths and Archaic Realities.* Tr. Phillip Mairet. New York: Harper and
Row.

———— 1963. *Myth and Reality.* Tr. W. R. Trask. New York: Harper and Row.

Ewen, Steward and Ewen, Elizabeth 1982. *Channels of Desire: Mass Images and
the Shaping of American Consciousness.* New York: McGraw-Hill.

Freud, Sigmund 1963. *The Interpretation of Dreams.* Tr. J. Strachey. New York:
Basic.

Gimpel, Jean 1961. *The Cathedral Builders.* New York: Grove Press.

Hammett, Dashiell 1972 [1929]. *The Maltese Falcon.* New York: Vintage.

LaFarge, Christopher 1957. ''Mickey Spillane and His Bloody Hammer.'' Pp. 176–
85 in Bernard Rosenberg and David Manning White (eds.), *Mass Culture:
The Popular Arts in America.* Glencoe: Free Press.

Lasch, Christopher 1977. *Haven in a Heartless World.* New York: Basic Books.

Mannheim, Karl 1936 [1929]. *Ideology and Utopia*. Tr. Louis Wirth and Edward Shils. New York: Harcourt, Brace and World.

Pirenne, Henri 1925. *Medieval Cities*. Tr. F. H. Halsey. Princeton: Princeton University Press.

Sartre, Jean-Paul 1956. *No Exit and Three Other Plays*. New York: Vintage.

Schudson, Michael 1967. *Discovering the News: A Social History of American Newspapers*. New York: Basic Books.

Schell, Jonathan 1982. *The Fate of the Earth*. New York: Alfred A. Knopf.

Simpson, Charles R. 1981. *SoHo: The Artist in the City*. Chicago: University of Chicago Press.

Simmel, Georg 1969. ''The Metropolis and Mental Life.'' Pp. 47–60 in Richard Sennett (ed.), *Classic Essays on the Culture of Cities*. New York: Appleton, Century-Crofts.

Simon, John 1971. *Movies into Film: Film Criticism, 1967–1970*. New York: Dial Press.

Trebbel, John 1974. *The Media in America*. New York: New American Library.

Vidich, Arthur J. and Bensman, Joseph 1968. *Small Town in Mass Society*. Princeton: Princeton University Press.

Weber, Max 1930. *The Protestant Ethic and the Spirit of Capitalism*. London: G. Allen and Unwin.

Wolfenstein, Martha and Leites, Nathan 1971 [1950]. *Movies: A Psychological Study*. New York: Hafner Publishing Co.

Part II

Artist and Public

The Artist

The two primary roles in the world of art are the artist's and the public's. Without the artist, art, of course, would not exist; and, without the public, art would be little more than idiosyncratic expressions. Owing to the personal commitment artists typically have, and the considerable autonomy they enjoy in their work, they are often considered to be professionals. On the other hand, because artists have highly variable training and are not often licensed to practice—as doctors, dentists, and lawyers are—they are considered by many to be simply members of a variety of occupational groups, albeit with special recognition often accorded them for creativity and talent.

The U.S. Bureau of the Census (National Endowment for the Arts, 1982) defines artist quite generally. The category includes the following: actors, architects, authors, dancers, designers, musicians and composers, painters and sculptors, photographers, radio and TV announcers, and teachers of art, drama and music in higher education. In the 1980 federal census, the number of people who defined themselves as being a member of one of these occupational groups was about 1,020,000, which represented an increase of about 46% over the total reported in the 1970 census. While it is widely known that the professional and technical occupations are increasing dramatically, artist occupations are increasing at an even faster rate. Specifically, the growth of the labor force for all professional and technical workers was 40% in the decade of the seventies, while the growth in artists' occupations was 46%.

Artists differ from professionals in other ways. Their annual earnings tend to lag considerably behind those of professionals, and any recession results in higher unemployment rates for artists compared with professionals and most other occupational groups. Artists are relatively young and predominantly male. More precisely, the median age of artists in 1980 was 34 years and 67% were male.

The Variety of Artists' Roles

A traditional distinction is between the creative and the interpretive roles in art. In some fields these roles are distinct. In most forms of music the composer creates and the musicians interpret, but folk musicians both create and interpret. In film making, because so many specialists are involved, it is difficult to know who is the creator and who is the interpreter, especially when many actors produce their own films.

Another distinction is made between the nonperforming and the performing artist (Bensman, 1983). Of course, we must recognize that some of the people in the performing arts do not appear in front of an audience; the scene designer or composer provide examples. However, this difference is useful and is usually understood in context.

A third distinction is between the artist and the craftsperson. This is a distinction which began in the late Renaissance and was related to a change in patronage and a greater division of labor. In contemporary times these two roles overlap (Becker, 1978; Neapolitan & Ethridge, 1985).

Getzels and Csikszentmihalyi (1968) point out that within the visual arts it is possible to distinguish between industrial artists, advertising artists, fine artists and art educators. Howard S. Becker, who is interested in artists' orientations, classifies cultural workers in the following way; the professional (or canonical) artist who is fully in consonance with the standards and conventions of the time: the maverick, who creatively breaks loose from some of the conventions: the naive artist, sometimes called the primitive or grass roots artist: and the folk artist, who is guided more by community norms than by artist conventions (1976: 41–56; 1982: 226–271).

In Foster's frame of reference (1974), a tripartite division is made between the artist-craftsperson, the amateur and the committed (or pure, or serious) artist. The division is based on the different values held by artists and the different publics to which they appeal. The craftsperson has a work ethic and the primary goal it to produce a good, serviceable product (or a reasonable imitation) for a client. Techniques are of greater concern than "creativity" to the craftsperson, who may simply copy earlier productions. Most commercial artists fit the craft mold. The amateur is motivated by what has been called "fun morality". The amateur wants personal satisfaction and is usually reluctant to continue if "arting" becomes work. Amateurs provide a good audience for the third type, the committed artist. The committed artist subordinates virtually all other concerns to the role of art worker and usually endorses a set of values which Max Weber called the "aesthetic ethic" (1946). Art to this person is something to be deeply involved in, and in the extreme, this role takes on the cast of a super-romantic, tragic and alienated aestheticism, a version of the artist's role that owes much to the Romantic movement of the 19th century.

Recruitment and Career of the Artist

Although there is variation among the different arts, some broad generalizations can be made. Most American artists come from middle-class homes, more from professionals' than from businessmen's homes. Talent is recognized early in children heading for the arts. For music and dance this is especially important because training must start in childhood. On the whole, the careers of performing artists start earlier and end earlier than the non-performing artists' careers.

As patronage has moved since the Middle Ages from royalty and the Church to the broader public, the status of the artist has gone up. Haydn was forced to appear before his duke properly shaved and with his hands washed. By the end of his career he was supported by the general public from the concerts of his music in Paris and London. The image of the artist as someone with special talents, perhaps akin to genius, raised the creator's status. In modern times, especially for popular artists, public relations experts are hired to enhance visibility and sales through promotions in newspapers and magazines. As a commodity, the popular artist can be cleverly sold these days.

The image of the artist has varied in different times and places. To the 19th century American (and to the 20th century communist), the artist was considered a worker. But contradictory images have been maintained at the same time. The 19th century American also thought of the artist as a moralist and a critic with a superior sense of truth (Harris, 1970). The first view is populist or democratic in nature; the second view is elitist or aristocratic. Artists are sometimes considered to be free spirits and sometimes as eccentric and alienated from society. Both are elements of the romantic ideology. The artist as deviant—as bohemian—has been popular for more than a century. Freud suggested that it is not the artist who becomes a deviant, but it is the psychologically deviant who becomes the artist. The artist is sometimes viewed as a rebel, sometimes as maintainer of the sacred—as "keeper of the flame". Writers are treated as intellectuals (Coser, 1965). Often actors and popular singers are attributed with extraordinary sexuality, quite out of synch with other stereotypes of artists as effeminate, or as moralists.

Artists' images of themselves tend to emphasize the importance of the work they do. The aesthetic ethic is often mentioned (Rosenberg & Fliegel, 1965). The bohemian image is often mentioned, but more often by unsuccessful artists than by those who have "made it". The images held by the public are translated into expectations which artists often feel are constraining. But one could argue that some aspects of the many images held by the public, free the artists in other ways. For example, the expectation that artists will live a deviant life style permits the artist to live quite freely without censure.

Publics

When we use the collective term "public", we must remember that there are plural publics subsumed under the term and different publics for different art forms and different artists. The whole of the population that comes into contact with any art form may be called the general public. It contains those who have little technical training or knowledge about art, but "know what they like". The general public also includes sophisticated respondents who have training in and/or knowledge about art, but these are in the minority. It is the general public that supports art productions, visits art museums and pays the taxes for the support of them. The general public listens to radio, views television and attends the movies. The general public is conservative. A survey Foster made in 1949 and repeated in 1964, showed no discernable shift in preference for painting reproductions over the fifteen year period. The older, traditional paintings continued to be favored despite the fact that during the period between the surveys, *Life*, *Time* and other popular magazines had continued to report on and laud modern art.

Within the general public is a smaller public which we can call the art-conscious public. This public gives active support to the art organizations and upholds high standards of production and performance. One writer called it the "taste-upholding public" (Schücking, 1944). An art-conscious member of the jazz public would probably know the history of jazz; might collect records; upon hearing a record would be able to identify the style of jazz and the band playing; and would be able to discuss the technical points of the music using the proper terminology or jargon. Members of the art-conscious public share the aesthetic ethic with serious artists, and may be labelled "elitist" by members of the general public. This minority provides the core membership of volunteer organizations which support the arts, of boards and committees of the institutions of art. They buy paintings, statues, recordings and tickets for all sorts of performances, and might be considered modern day patrons.

The art-conscious public, like the general public, is plural. Some support the traditional arts and play a great role in the preservation of them. Some support new styles and current movements in the art world and are collectively called the avant-garde. The avant-garde provides support for artists who present new metaphors, symbols, images; and in so doing, provide support for change (Poggioli, 1968).

There are also special interest publics that actively support one or several artists or works of art but are indifferent to the larger field. Van Cliburn, who became a media "star", because he won a competition in Russia, once had such a public, and his record sales were said to be much higher that other pianists of equal ability. Many performers in the popular arts have cult followers. Extra aesthetic explanations are needed to understand the development of these publics. Another variant of the special interest public is the one which supports the home town boy or girl. Local pride is important here. The organization which develops from the special interest public is the fan club.

Recruitment of Publics

People sharing the same backgrounds are more likely to prefer the same art forms. For example, young people rebelling against their elders are open to novelty. The public of young people in its time supported the Romantic Movement, jazz in the 1920s and rock in recent times. To be accurate, we must point out that the youth public is recruited from the much larger category of youth.

Social factors are related to the support of different styles within the same art form. Francis Newton reported in the late 1950s that "cool" jazz attracted white intellectuals, the Dixieland revival was for white youths and intellectuals, and the blues still attracted black people (Hobsbaum, 1961). But publics shift and many young whites today are attracted to the blues.

Age is one basis for the recruitment of the public. Gender is another. More men report interest in marches and jazz; more women report interest in lush string arrangements of popular and traditional music. Rural radio stations play more country and western music than do urban stations. One suspects that with the narrowing of the gender gap and with greater residential mobility the difference between the social characteristics of the different publics will decrease.

The Audience

When a portion of a public comes together in one place it is called an audience. Audience behavior varies with the type of art presented, with the location and with the composition of the public. Listening to folk music or attending an outdoor public park exhibition of painting are informal affairs. The folk musician tries to decrease social distance between him- or herself and the public. Folk music is communal music and community is enhanced through group participation in some of the songs. At the other extreme is opera, ballet or behavior in a great national museum. The older elite arts require much more formal behavior from the audience and the social distance between performer and audience is great. At the same time such an audience is often distinguished by upper class origins.

The Papers

To explain the recruitment of the American composer or student of composition, Nash looks to early socialization. A small part of his study which was not played up at the time of its publication has to do with the lack of recruitment of women (only two in his sample). His statements that

> "If a woman is to succeed as a composer, she must have strong and consistent support . . . by her family of orientation."

and

> "the factor of family support . . . is more selective for females than for males."

considers the early period of socialization while still in the family as most important in the choosing of the artistic career. While this may still be the case, it should be noted that more women are entering the field now.

Ballet, a traditional art form, was structured around a distinction between male and female roles. And perhaps because more men than women have the strength to lift another dancer, and because male and female roles in classical ballet still remain distinct, the result is a different training in dance for the sexes. Sutherland has taken data from an earlier study by Federico and has compared male to female recruitment and some of the differences that he finds helps clarify male and female roles in the larger society as well as in the structure of the ballet world.

While the first two studies use survey methods, the study by Emmanuel Levy employs biographical and auto-biographical sources and other documents. The sample is large—564 players nominated for the Oscar. Levy finds a wider class background for film actors, perhaps due to the greater contact of children of all classes with the movies. Many ethnic minorities are represented. Levy also finds more family connections in the same occupation than one might expect in the arts. All of these papers—Nash's, Sutherland's and Levy's—show that recruitment and socialization into the arts is complex, reflecting a combination of influences from society at

When I'm 18 I think I'll be a ballet dancer, and when I'm 20 a rock star, and when I'm 25 a famous actress, and when I'm 30 . . . I guess I'll just have to be an arts administrator.

large, from the family and from the artist's own personality (which is, of course, socially developed).

The last two papers in this section are about publics. Two hundred years ago, publics adored some of the singers in ways similar to the adoration of Sinatra in the late 1930s and early 1940s, and Presley and the Beatles more recently. But Hughes shows us that there were national differences between Italy and France in taste. The peek into history can help us to place current public behavior in a larger context.

The last paper in this section is part of a survey of many small research studies made of art publics all over the United States. An important finding is that, despite attempts to develop a broader public for the arts by drawing in all segments of the population, those who attend concerts, plays and museums continue to be people from a higher class position than the general population.

References

———— National Endowment for the Arts. 1982 *Artist Employment and Unemployment*. Research Report 16. Washington: NEA.

Becker, Howard S. 1976. "Art worlds and social types." Pp. 41–56 in Richard A. Peterson (ed.), *The Production of Culture* Beverly Hills: Sage.

Becker, Howard S. 1978. "Arts and crafts." *American Journal of Sociology* 83 no. 4: 862–889.

Becker, Howard S. 1982. "Integrated professionals, mavericks, folk artists and naive artists." In his *Art Worlds.* Berkeley: U. of California Press, pp. 226–271.

Bensman, Joseph. 1983. "Introduction: the phenomenology and sociology of the performing arts." In Jack B. Kamerman & Rosanne Martorella (eds.), *Performers and Performances.* New York: Praeger, pp. 1–37.

Coser, Lewis, 1965. *Men of Ideas.* New York: The Free Press.

Foster, Arnold W. 1974. "The dissident trinity: the three roles of the artist." Paper presented at the 44th Annual Meeting of the Eastern Sociological Society, Philadelphia.

Getzels, J. W. & M. Csikszentmihalyi. 1968. "On the roles, values and performance of future artists: a conceptual and empirical exploration," *The Sociological Quarterly* 9: 516–530.

Harris, Neil. 1970. *The Artist in American Society.* New York: Simon and Schuster (Clarion).

Hobsbaum, Eric (Francis Newton, pseud.). 1961. *The Jazz Scene*. Harmondsworth: Penguin Books.

Kamerman, Jack B. & Rosanne Martorella (eds.), *Performer and Performances*. New York: Praeger.

Neapolitan, Jerry & Maurice Ethridge, 1985, "An Empirical Examination of the Existence of Art. Art/Craft, and Craft Segment among Craft Media Workers," *Mid-American Review of Sociology* 10: 45–64.

Peterson, Richard A., ed., *The Production of Culture*. Beverly Hills: Sage.

Poggioli, Renato. 1968. *The Theory of the Avant Garde*. Cambridge: Belknap Press.

Rosenberg, Bernard & Norris Fliegel, 1965. *The Vanguard Artist*. Chicago: Quadrangle Books.

Schücking, Levin L. 1944. *The Sociology of Literary Taste*. London: Kegan Paul, Trench, Trubner.

Weber, Max. 1946. *From Max Weber* (H. H. Gerth & C. Wright Mills, trs. & eds.). New York: Oxford U. Press.

4

The Socialization of an Artist: The American Composer[1]

DENNISON J. NASH

Any society may be thought of as a network of roles which must be manned continuously if the work of the society is to get done. But some of these roles are more necessary or important to the society than others. If the society is to survive, these more necessary, or important, roles must receive a sufficient supply of adequate recruits from every generation. In some societies, as has been pointed out by Linton (1936), such a supply is ensured by ascribing roles (or statuses) on the basis of cultural patterns or biological facts. Thus, the fact that one is born the first son of a king may mean that he gets to be king in the next generation. Other societies leave the supplying of recruits for even the more necessary roles to the individual's conscious choice and successful effort. This emphasis upon achieving roles is characteristic of our own society.

But the emphasis upon achievement in a society does not seem to mean that selective processes do not operate to train individuals for, and direct them to, necessary roles. For example, Merton (1953), has pointed out that certain selective processes may be operative before the individual makes the conscious choice and successful effort to achieve a bureaucratic role. Thus, in a sort of backhanded way, a society still may guarantee enough recruits to get its work done. This paper attempts to show that even in one of the least necessary vocational rules in our society—the composition of serious music—such forces operate in recruiting personnel.

Two aggregates of interviewed individuals have provided primary data for this paper: (1) 23 jury-determined "most successful" American-born composers of serious music; (2) 24 advanced students of musical composition selected by the heads of three outstanding American schools of music (see Nash, 1954; 1955). The mean age of the composers is 51; the students, 31. There is one female in each aggregate—a representation which does not seem disproportionate when compared, impressionistically, with the respective universes.

The two aggregates under study obviously represent two stages of achievement. The students are on the verge of entering the vocation of composition. Probably, their ranks will thin in the process of becoming professionals. And it would seem that only a fraction of the professionals will be termed "most successful" (the jury determination of the composers under study). But to see these two aggregates as representing different stages of success in achievement of the compositional role, it must be assumed that the situational characteristics of the role are the same for both despite the difference of one "professional generation" (in this case, 20 years). An analysis of all available materials indicates that though there are some slight differences (the amount of public funds available to finance musical training is one), the broad characteristics of the compositional role outlined below apply to both aggregates.

Other reservations to the study concern the techniques of observation, the representativeness of data, and the method of experiment. The techniques of observation are, admittedly, crude, but this was made necessary by the exploratory nature of the project and the desire to secure reliable data. There is no way of determining how representative these aggregates are of their universes. Consequently, the term American composer, when used here, can apply only to those composers in the aggregate under study. Finally, the experimental Method of Agreement used cannot hope to delineate, precisely, selective or causal factors. Additional work with control and experimental groups will be necessary to give scientific weight to the conclusions of this paper, even though some tentative comparisons with other aggregates have been attempted.

In view of these reservations, the conclusions of this study must be tentative and limited. I hope that they may constitute stimulating hypotheses for additional work in the field of personality and culture in general and the social psychology of the arts in particular.

The Role Situation of the American Composer

In general, the role situation of the American composer may be said to be relatively nonsupporting of his musical aspirations (which include the desire for performance of his works to an audience). Though the contemporary American composer works hard and long at the solitary activity of putting musical notes on paper, the evidence indicates that most members of the American serious-music audience (which numbers only a small fraction of the total American music audience) can get along quite happily without hearing any of his music. And, in general, the attitudes of those who cooperate with the composers to produce and perform their music (i.e.

the musical businessman, conductor, and instrumentalist) reflect the attitude of his audience.

One indication of the relatively dispensable nature of the American composers (judged "most successful" by a jury of musical experts) is given by their mean annual income from composition for 1951: $2,640. Almost no composer can live as he would like on his income from serious composition alone. But he can, and does, turn to other jobs which fatten his income. He may play (at the same time) additional roles such as musical businessman, conductor, critic-author, instrumentalist, and teacher. Such *role versatility* tends to increase his control over the performance-destiny of his own works as well as to enhance his socio-economic status. But when the composer is ranked as a composer (his favorite self-conception), his social standing is relatively low (as compared with other vocations requiring an equivalent amount of training and intelligence) in the total society.

In addition to the obvious criterion of the ability to compose serious music, then, recruits for the role of serious composer in American society must meet the following criteria: (1) ability to work in the face of social non-support; (2) ability to assume certain other vocational roles at the same time; (3) ability to pursue considerable solitary activity. This research seeks to set down and explain those factors which, acting through the socialization process, select or prepare a person for this kind of role. That the results of this investigation may have broader application is suggested by Wilson's analysis of the American poet's role the criteria for which are similar to those listed above. Therefore, we might expect to find similar selective factors operating in the poet's background.

Selective Factors in the Socialization of the Composer

1. Heredity

Any simple explanation of the achievement of the composing role does not, apparently, lie in the realm of heredity. If professional compositional ability is taken as the inherited trait, there appears to be almost no connection between the student and successful composers and their primary relatives. Only one primary relative of the subjects showed professional compositional ability (a brother). Professional instrumental ability in primary relatives seems to be more closely connected with compositional ability, yet the fact that 14 composers and 16 students had pairs of parents who were not instrumentalists suggests that, although some general inherited trait such as "musicality" may be operative as a selective factor, the investigation of environmental factors cannot be ignored.

2. Sex

The infrequent appearance of top female composers has been explained on constitutional (hereditary) grounds (Pannenborg and Pannenborg, 1915). The data of this study do not lay to rest this contention one way or the other, but they do suggest that, if a woman is to succeed as a composer, she must have strong and consistent support of her musical aspirations by her family of orientation. The single female in each aggregate and all other female composers known to me received this kind of support. On the other hand, though most of the men said that their musicality was valued until age 12, eight of the composers and 11 of the students ran into family objections during the age period 12–25 (judged to be the career-deciding period). Therefore, it can be concluded that the factor of family support of musical aspirations facilitates the achievement of the compositional role, but it is more selective for females than for males. The female drive to achieve the compositional roles appears to be more easily blunted, or redirected, by her family environment.

3. Ethnic Group Membership

> It was an extremely sensitive and intelligent family, as such. And they were most anxious that I should not be put upon in terms of my talent. But at the same time they were wildly encouraging. . . . To have an artist in the family was considered a great boon.

This statement by one of the Jewish composers in the aggregate about his family's attitude toward his musicality gives some insight into the workings of family social support and may help to explain why Jews appear more frequently in the aggregate of successful composers than would be expected from their representation in the total population. The various ethnic groups (Jewish, Italian, German, and French) contributed nearly half of the successful composers, and the data for the career-deciding period indicate that they met less resistance in their choice of a musical career than the native Americans. It can be tentatively concluded, therefore, that the impress of certain "Old World ethnic intellectual and artistic traditions, acting through the medium of parental support of compositional aspirations, have contributed considerably to the development of musical composition in America.

4. Social Status

That the factor of rather high social status facilitates achievement of the compositional role seems to be indicated in Table 1, which enumerates

Table 1
Vocations of Heads of 23 Composers' and 24 Students'
Families of Orientation

Vocation	Composers*	Students'
Total	22	24
Professional	10	9
Business	9	9
Farmer	1	3
Skilled Labor	2	3
Unskilled Labor	0	0

*No evidence for one composer.

the principal vocations of the heads of the composers' and students' families of orientation.

The professional and business categories, it is clear, contribute most of the recruits to the composing role. But this predominance does not distinguish musical composition from other intellectual vocations. Anne Roe (1952) found that the same categories contributed nearly all of her eminent biologists, physicists, psychologists, and anthropologists. The specific selective factor operating in all of these cases may be economic; it permits, or prevents, the extensive formal education necessary to achieve an intellectual or artistic vocational role.

5. Family of Orientation

A. SIZE. The mean size of the families in which the composers grew up (4.3) was close to the national mean (4.4) for the age period of their childhood. This suggests that, insofar as family size acts as a determinant of role-taking ability, the typical composer received training not unlike the average American. The significance of the markedly larger student mean family size (5.3) and its greater divergence from the national average (4.0) will be discussed below.

B. STABILITY. Approximately two-thirds of the composers' families of orientation remained unbroken (i.e., neither death, divorce, nor separation intervened) until the subjects were 18 years old. This compares with the four-fifths "unbroken" in the student—and the three-fourths "unbroken" in Roe's biologist—aggregate. How these proportions compare with the

Table 2
Position of 23 Composers and 24 Students
in the Birth Order of Their Families
of Orientation

Position	Composers' Families	Students' Families
Total	23	24
Only Child	5	5
Youngest Child	9	7
Middle Child	3	4
Oldest Child	5	8
Undetermined	1	0

United States mean is impossible to determine. But most of the composers and students were subject to the stabilizing influence of an unbroken family during their childhood and adolescence.

C. CHARACTER OF FAMILY RELATIONSHIPS. What about the nature of interaction within the family? Unfortunately, adequate data do not exist for the composer aggregate (there is a large number in the "undetermined" category), but in those cases for which there is sufficient evidence 40 percent reveal conflict as the characteristic mode of interaction of parents during the subjects' childhood (age 0–12); and about half of the "determined" cases show conflict between the subject and one parent, usually the father (Graf, 1947). Further investigations may support my hunch that family conflict is a necessary factor in composer-etiology.

The data for the relative social distance of parents from the subjects tend to support Graf's contention that musical fantasy displays many feminine traits and is mysteriously bound to the emotional life of the mother. In the model cases, both students and composers felt that their mother had been closer than their father to them during their childhood (age 0–12). Of course it may be argued that this factor could hardly be selectively of composers since this type of relationship may be characteristic of most American families. But, until adequate comparative data are available in this regard, it seems legitimate to list this factor in the background of the composing role.

D. POSITION IN THE BIRTH ORDER. The subject position in the birth order of their families of orientation seems, according to Table 2, to be of crucial importance as a selective factor. The large numbers in the only and youngest-child categories, plus the fact that 3 composers and 5 students who were oldest or middle-children were separated from the next (or later)

Table 3
Principal Role Composers and Students
Played with Peers, Age 0–12

Role	Composers	Students
Total	23	24
Considered peculiar; tended to conform	6	5
Considered peculiar; tended towards passivity or withdrawal	10	11
Considered normal; conformed	4	3
Undetermined	3	5

born by at least four years, indicates that the majority of the subjects came from family roles associated with an indulged and precocious personality, if Bossard's (1954) outline of the characteristics of these sibling positions is accepted as authoritative. Additional evidence for another art (drama) is provided by a study of drama majors at Middlebury College. (Tuttle, 1955) It was found that *all* of these subjects were only children. It can be said, therefore, that this aspect of the family environment of these artists-to-be encouraged the development of the personal autonomy which later would be necessary to deal with a hostile or indifferent social world.

6. Peer Relationships

   Although the data of Table 4 are unsatisfactory, statistically, the general impression gained from Tables 3 and 4 is that most of the subjects early fitted themselves into roles which, like musical composition, are at variance with the dominant themes of their society. In other words, their training in the extra-musical aspects of the composer's roles began early. A possible explanation for the relatively great numbers of participants in "social activities" is given by one composer who said that he went through the motions, but wasn't very interested. By playing a musical instrument or dreaming up new melodies one is not necessarily disqualified from the youth society. Indeed, the musical ability of some of the subjects made them very acceptable on "social occasions."

7. Musical Development

   The musical drives of the subjects were manifested prior to formal teaching cues. It would seem that this manner of beginning would be a rewarding experience generally. Ten of the composer-subjects and 12 of the

Table 4
General Role Played by Composers and Students in Peer "Social Activities" (Dates, Parties, Etc.), Age 12–18

Role	Composers	Students
Total	23	24
Participant	7	7
Non-Participant	10	13
Undetermined	6	4

students began formal musical training before age 6, and almost all of the remainder started between the ages of 6 and 12. In general, first training (and the first manifestations of talent) was instrumental, with compositional efforts following later. One of the more precocious of these generally precocious subjects illustrates his early course of musical development as follows:

> I can remember waiting from—well, certainly three anyway, to five—waiting for my piano lessons. And I wanted to play the organ when I was six and I couldn't reach the pedals to play the organ. . . . And waiting to study composition. They wouldn't let me study composition at the school until I was college age, which was ridiculous.

In his musical development, therefore, the composer is generally in the van, with his social environment lagging behind, musically speaking. Such a picture contrasts sharply with the stereotype of the American boy who is forced to take music lessons—usually against his will.

Summary

So far, in this tentative presentation of selective factors which operate in the recruitment of American composers, the similarities in the backgrounds of students and successful composers have been stressed. But it would seem that differences should be examined too, since not all students become professional composers and not all professional composers become highly successful. What factors seem to enable the individual to survive this thinning of the ranks? Analysis of the differences in the central tendencies of the various selective variables shows that the two aggregates differ markedly in three instances: inheritance (the "trait" of musicality), family valuation of musicality (age 12–25), and family size. More of the composers had primary relatives who were professionally musical, more had families who supported their serious interest in music during the crucial career-deciding period, and the average composer family was smaller (by 1.0 persons) than the student.

The significance of inheritance and environmental support (familial) for the achievement of success seems obvious. Less clear is the function of family size. Probably, the smaller family is better able to assist the aspirations of its children. This conclusion is supported by a rough estimate of the mean social status of the student and composer families. The former were four points lower on the North-Hatt scale (1947), which means that there probably were less family resources available to the child growing up in them. The advantage is to the successful composers here.

In addition, the complex of selective factors which, in general, tend to be associated with achievement of the compositional role may be summarized briefly: (1) inheritance of some general trait such as "musicality," (2) male sex; (3) membership in some "Old World" ethnic group; (4) relatively high social status; (5) family valuation of musicality, especially in the age period 0–12; (6) structural stability of the family of orientation; (7) subject closer to mother than father during childhood years; (8) subject plays a role in the family associated with an indulged and precocious personality; (9) subject plays a role on the fringe of his youth society (he is considered peculiar, does not participate in "social" activities); (10) subject is precocious in musical development, his first musical activities being instrumental.

These factors, determined by the experimental Method of Agreement, tend to be selective of composers; how many of them are also selective of recruits to other vocations will have to be determined by further investigation.

Discussion

The composer, it is clear, needs more than compositional talent to function professionally in our society. Additional qualities which enable him to carry out the compositional role are the ability to stand up to a hostile or indifferent social environment and the traits which facilitate role versatility. Speaking in terms of learning theory (Miller and Dollard, 1941), how are these qualities "built in" to our composer-recruits through the process of socialization?

None of the selective factors outlined in the summary above seem to account for the development of personality traits which facilitate considerable role versatility. In fact, Rorschach evidence for the most versatile of the composers indicates considerable personality rigidity, if thinking method and strength of ego are taken as indications (Nash, 1954). This is opposed to the quality of personality flexibility which common sense might suppose and suggests that the different roles played by the American composer do not require very different personality sets for their performance. The behaviors required of the composer, instrumentalist, conductor, music teacher (composition), etc., can be provided (without too much difficulty) by a personality which is not extra-ordinarily flexible.

The ability to stand up to a hostile or indifferent social environment and to pursue a largely solitary activity seems to be connected with the following selective factors: the sex of the person, his role in the birth order of his family and in his childhood peer groups, and perhaps the precocity of his musical development. Though it is not clear whether the determinant is environmental or constitutional, it is clear that a man's musical ambitions are less easily blunted by social opposition in our society. The "rugged individualism" which may be facilitated by maleness also is encouraged (according to Bossard's theory) by the role played by the composer in the birth order of his family of orientation. In addition, this last factor may be responsible for assisting the precocious musical development of the composers, and this in turn may be the factor which helps to set the composer off from his age-mates—in part accounting for his position on the fringe of his youth-society and consequent training for the compositional role which has very similar characteristics.

Manifest compositional talent and general compositional activity seem to be products of the hereditary factor, the explicit valuation of musicality in the subject's family of orientation, his attachment to mother (which may be determined by a variety of constitutional and environmental factors), and the musical training made possible by a relatively high social status (and the accompanying valuation of musicality by the family). The selective process here may be explained in terms of learning theory. Give a person the necessary inherited trait ("musicality," perhaps) which he expresses in random fashion (along with other traits), reward one aspect of his response through the valuation of "musicality" in general and composing in particular by his family—especially by his mother—music training, and the intrinsic pleasure of composing, and he will acquire the composing drive which will be manifested at the presentation of appropriate cues.

Is It "Accidental" Or "Design"? Does the process by which our society obtains recruits for the compositional role appear to be a matter of "accident" or "design"? If "design" is taken to refer to the explicit valuation of musical composition and reward for learning it, then obviously a part of the recruiting process is not "accidental." The families of the composers-to-be approved their musical activities (at least in the formative years), and the existence of institutions which teach composition provided an implicit sanction of the activity. Composition may be lowly valued, but it is valued nevertheless. Probably no recruitment for any social role could take place without such "design."

On the other hand, there are two kinds of "accidental" factors which take a part in selecting personnel for musical composition in our society. First, there is the base provided by the inherited constitutions of the members of a given generation. Some people may have more native talent than others and the populations of some societies may be more talented at birth than others (though we are not sure about this), but no society can predict the quantity and quality of the musical talents it will get in one generation. It is a matter of chance or "accidents." The second kind of "accidental" factor is inherent in the very nature of a society. It cannot be perfectly homogeneous, and this means that there is bound to be a heterogeneity of experience in the socialization process (e.g. different positions in the birth order, families of differing degrees of stability, status differences, etc.). Thus, any society, because it is a society, may direct individuals toward a variety of roles—one of which may be musical composition.

By "design," "accident," and through the competitive process involved in the achievement of roles, our society gains recruits for one of its less necessary roles—the composition of serious music. Mead outlines the place of this role in the value system of the society as follows:

> Each society approximates in its chief emphasis one of the many possible types of human behavior. Those individuals who show this type of personality will be its leaders and saints; . . . those who have perversely seized upon some perfectly alien point of view, it will sometimes lock up in asylums, . . . burn as heretics, or possibly permit to live out a starveling existence as an artist.

Now, although Mead (1939: 227), includes both in the same category, it is obvious that the role of patient in a mental hospital is assigned a different order of value than composer of serious music. But a Rorschach investigation of the successful composer-personalities reveals a rather high incidence of pathology as defined by conventional clinical diagnosis. (Nash, 1954) This suggests that the two roles have a common denominator on the personality level. The difference in order of values seems to mean that some individuals with trends towards mental disorder find a constructive and dignified outlet for their energies while others are condemned to a life of ignominy. But for the existence of the composer's role (and others like it) there might be many more recruits for the role of patient in mental hospitals. This, rather than the writing of serious music for performance, may be the primary function of the composing role in our society.

Notes

1. Reprinted with the permission of the author and the publisher from *Social Forces* (vol. 35, 1957).

References

Bossard, J. 1954. *The Sociology of Child Development* (rev. ed.). New York: Harper & Bros.

Graf, M. 1947. *From Beethoven to Shostakovich*. New York: Philosophical Library.

Linton, R. 1936. *The Study of Man*. New York: Appleton-Century-Crofts.

Mead, M. 1939. "Growing Up in New Guinea." In *From the South Seas*. New York: William Morrow.

Merton, R. 1953. "Bureaucratic Structure and Personality." Pp. 376–385 in Clyde Kluckhohn et al (eds.), *Personality in Nature, Society and Culture*. New York: Alfred A. Knopf.

Miller, N. & J. Dollard. 1941. *Social Learning and Imitation*. New Haven: Yale U. Press.

Nash, D. 1954. "The American Composer: A Study in Social Psychology." Ph.D. thesis, U. of Pennsylvania.

Nash, D. 1955. "Challenge and Response in the American Composer's Career," *Journal of Aesthetics and Art Criticism* (Sept.): 116–122.

North, C. & P. Hatt. 1947. "Jobs and Occupations: A Popular Evaluation," *Opinion News* 9 (Sept.): 3–13.

Pannenborg, W. & H. Pannenborg. 1915. "Die Psychologie des Musikers," *Zeitschrift für Psychologie* 73: 130.

Roe, A. 1952. "A Psychologist Examines 64 Eminent Scientists," *Scientific American* (Nov.): 21–25.

Tuttle, G. 1955. "The Drama Major at Middlebury College." Unpublished term paper, Middlebury College.

Wilson, R. 1952. "The American Poet: A Role Investigation." Ph.D. thesis, Harvard U.

─── 5 ───

Ballet as a Career[1]

DAVID EARL SUTHERLAND

Ronald Charles Federico (1968) interviewed 146 dancers belonging to twelve ballet companies in the United States; and while other sources of information based on his own training as a dancer and participant-observations infuse his analysis, the empirical thrust of his work stems from these interviews. His interpretation depends on the patterns of total distributions over pertinent characteristics for these 146 professional ballet dancers. However, an alternative way of analyzing these data exists that magnifies relevant structural features of ballet as a profession.

The twelve companies represented in his 146 dancers constitute two classes of companies: those representing the pinnacle for a dancer's career and defining an elite set of companies, and those companies which—while employing dancers full time—nevertheless are not the most prestigious companies. Collapsing Federico's data into two sets—prestigious companies and dancers (the American Ballet Theater, New York City Ballet, City Center-Joffrey Ballet, and Harkness Ballet) and less prestigious companies and dancers (the Metropolitan Opera Ballet, Manhattan Festival Ballet, Boston Ballet, Pennsylvania Ballet, Chicago Opera Ballet, San Francisco Ballet, National Ballet, and Atlanta Civic Ballet)—yields findings and patterns not ascertained in his original discussion. His data can be reorganized and reanalyzed to investigate the structural features of ballet as a profession.

Age of Entry

The discipline, technique, and skills of the art necessitate very early exposure to ballet training. This situation is particularly true for female dancers compared to male dancers, and constitutes the first instance of definitive sex role differences that permeate the careers of ballet performers. The tenacity of sexual differentiation in the ballet world constitutes a major

DAVID EARL SUTHERLAND

Table 1
Age Began Ballet Lessons (by Sex and Age)

Sex	Under 5	6–10	11–16	17–20	Over 20
Male	0.0	22.2	31.5	40.7	5.6
Female	28.3	59.8	10.9	1.1	0.0
Total	17.8	45.9	18.5	15.8	2.1

Note: Numbers represent percent of respondents.
Source. Adapted from Ronald Charles Federico, *Ballet as an Occupation (unpublished Ph.D. dissertation, Northwestern University, 1968).*

structural features of ballet as a profession and style of life. Nevertheless, because of physiological demands required for technical mastery of ballet (not to mention other aspects, such artistic and emotional expression in the dance), both male and female candidates for ballet must obtain early training at an age not required by any other profession.

Table 1 contains information about the age when dancers began ballet lessons; obviously females started lessons earlier than males. Indeed, whereas some 46 percent of the males were "old" in beginning lessons after age 17, only 1 percent of the females began at such an advanced age.

However, Table 2 shows an interesting pattern only revealed by controlling for company prestige. Females start earlier than males and, more importantly, there is no difference between age of beginning lessons for

Table 2
Age Began Ballet Lessons
(by Company Prestige, Sex, and Age)

Company	Under 5	6–10	11–16	17–20	Over 20
Prestigious					
Male	0.0	35.7	35.7	28.6	0.0
Female	33.3	58.3	8.3	0.0	0.0
Total	21.1	50.0	18.4	10.5	0.0
Less Prestigious					
Male	0.0	17.5	30.0	45.0	7.5
Female	26.5	60.3	11.8	1.5	0.0
Total	16.7	44.4	18.5	17.6	2.8

Note: Numbers represent percent of respondents.
Source: Ibid.

prestigious dancers compared to less prestigious dancers. Simply put, for any female to dance anywhere she must begin early (before the age of 10).

On the other hand, males in prestigious ballet companies clearly began their lessons earlier than males who belonged to a less prestigious company. Only 29 percent of prestigious male dancers began as late as age 17 to 20, and none started over 20; slightly more than half the less prestigious male dancers (52 percent) began after age 17.

Age of Commitment

Unlike other occupations and professions, ballet requires that dancers in their teens reach a conscious decision that raises the possibility of being "serious" about the dance. This commitment in turn exemplifies itself in the kind of intensive study, practice, and concentration on the dance that results in significant shifts in adolescent behavior markedly different from the bast majority of non-dancing peers. This pattern likewise applies in comparison to their peers who engage in dance lessons, but not seriously. More particularly, differentiation by sex occurs as well at this point as a significant social role differention above and apart from the obvious technical differences between female and male ballet dancers, and this occurrence of early sex role differentiation is only one of a series extending throughout the life and career cycle of ballet dancers.

Obviously, both male and female dancers undergo some kind of adolescent peer experiences, but sex role differences distinguish dancers here too. For females this early teen commitment entails a withdrawal from the usual American adolescent high school experiences. The requirements of mastering very difficult techniques in ballet demand an intense concern with physique; especially health conditions (e.g., diet, weight, sleep), and the devotion of increasing numbers of hours to practice. Consequently, time

Table 3
Age Decided to be Professional (by Sex)

Sex	Under 10	11–16	17–20	Over 20
Male	5.6	37.0	48.1	9.3
Female	32.6	61.1	13.0	3.3
Total	22.6	45.9	26.0	5.5

Note: Numbers represent percent of respondents.
Source: Ibid.

Table 4
Age Decided to be Professional
(by Company Prestige, Sex and Age)

Company	Under 10	11–16	17–20	Over 20
Prestigious				
Male	14.3	42.9	42.9	0.0
Female	41.7	45.8	4.2	8.3
Total	31.6	44.7	18.4	5.3
Less Prestigious				
Male	2.5	35.0	50.0	12.5
Female	29.4	52.9	16.2	1.5
Total	19.4	46.3	28.7	5.5

Note: Numbers represent percent of respondents.
Source: Ibid.

for normal teen activities decreases. Potential ballerinas begin early to separate themselves from their nondance peers—a trend that will be intensified
throughout the professional career of a ballerina.

For males, in addition to the increasing absorption into dance training,
they must also overcome normative definitions of appropriate behavior and
occupational goals for men. This necessity entails a double bind for men
that does not apply to females. On the one hand, family support for this
occupational choice must pertain; on the other hand, the male must (1) be
willing to withstand non-dancing male pressures and (2) begin acquiring a
changed definition of self that acquires dancers as his appropriate reference
group (though this latter event cannot become truly significant until he becomes caught up in more intensified schooling that must occur roughly at
high school graduation).

Unfortunately very little literature exists studying the process by which
dancers arrive at these decisions. In any event, it is plausible that male
dancers encounter more obstacles in this development of occupational identity than female dancers.

Sex differences in decision making can be analyzed in general terms by
examining the date in Tables, 3, 4, and 5. Given earlier patterns, it is not
surprising that female dancers decided at an earlier age than males that they
wanted to become professional dancers: 84 percent of the females decided
before age 16 compared to 43 percent of the males deciding before 16 (see
Table 3). Obviously something is occurring in the young teens for these
people.

Table 5
Reason for Beginning Ballet Lessons
(by Company Prestige and Sex)

Company	Mother's Influence	Peer Influence	Own Desire	Exposure	Other*
Prestigious					
Male	28.6	0.0	7.1	21.4	42.9
Female	70.8	12.5	0.0	4.2	12.5
Total	55.3	7.9	2.6	10.5	23.7
Less Prestigious					
Male	5.1	20.5	17.9	12.8	43.6
Female	48.5	14.7	19.1	7.4	10.3
Total	32.7	16.8	18.7	9.3	22.4

*The major components of this category are medical reasons (especially for women), being motivated by someone outside the field, and taking ballet to complement some other dance or athletic activity (the latter two especially for males).

Note: Numbers represent percent of respondents.

Source: Ibid.

However, this age-intensity decision-making process becomes accentuated when we compare the pattern for prestigious against less prestigious dancers (see Table 4). Prestigious female dancers tend to decide earlier than their counterparts in the less prestigious companies. Indeed, 42 percent of the former decided under age 10 to become professional, compared to 29 percent of the less prestigious females. This pattern is intensified more obviously for prestigious males. Over half the prestigious males decided before age 16 (57 percent), compared to more than one-third of the less prestigious dancers (38 percent). No prestigious male dancer reached his professional decision to dance over the age of 20!

Although information about the nature of decision rules appropriate for this pattern is not readily available, data in Table 5 indicate suggestive lines of inquiry. Clearly female dancers acquired more social support in their reasons for beginning ballet lessons than did males. Mothers and peer influences provided approval for women taking such lessons that was generally lacking for male dancers.

Again, however, the prestige levels of ballet companies indicate a discrete patterning of social support. Prestigious female dancers acquired far more parental influence than did women in less prestigious companies (71 percent compared to 49 percent). Indeed, over four-fifths of the women be-

longing to prestigious companies acquired parental and peer bases supporting decisions to begin lessons, compared to slightly less than two-thirds of
the females in less prestigious companies.

Males indicated a different process. Slightly more than one-fourth of
prestigious male dancers indicated parental influence through the mother in
taking up the dance, compared to only 5 percent of males in less prestigious
companies. Indeed, the latter acquired more peer influence for lessons than
did the former. It is clear that the direct exposure to performance (either
live or televised) played a more significant factor in inspiring males who
eventually achieved membership in the most prestigious companies in the
United States to begin lessons.

This pattern indicates that males indeed encounter a double bind in
acquiring their occupational identities—the best dancers have some family
support but definitely must ignore or disavow any chance of meaning ful
peer support and (presumably early) experience example by performance of
inspiration. And note the time dimension of such a decision, that is, the
necessity of acquiring exposure in the teens to the end product of a performer—although the performer himself will be between 20 and 30.

While it is not possible to relate sex differences (if any) in educational
attainment for dancers in companies, there is a slight indication of a general
difference. The percentage of prestigious dancers and less prestigious dancers with some college education or more was virtually identical; however,
there was a slight difference at the other end of the educational scale. Some
16 percent of the prestigious dancers had less than twelfth grade compared
to only 6 percent of dancers in less prestigious companies. This finding
suggests a willingness on the part of the most professional dancers to abandon high school under appropriate circumstances of gaining entry into a
route that leads to membership in a top ballet company. In other words,
public schools do not provide the opportunity required to enter the more
prestigious levels of the dance.

First Stage of Professional Entry

Provided that candidates for ballet successfully transverse the above
two stages, dancers—again unlike other professions and occupations—must
acquire early exposure to top-notch "professional" teachers to gain necessary expertise. Females need earlier exposure than males (e.g., 15–16 versus 18 or so). These conditions do not easily pertain throughout the United
States.

None of the prestigious dancers indicated the location of professional
training in a rural setting (defined as a city under 50,000 population), and
only some 6 percent of dancers from less prestigious dancers apparently

Table 6
Job Experience before Present Position
(by Company Prestige)

Company	*No Previous Experience*	*Previous Ballet Experience*	*Ballet and Other Dance Experience*	*Other Nonballet Experience*
Prestigious	23.7	42.1	26.2	7.9
Less Prestigious	42.6	24.1	24.1	9.3
Total	37.7	28.8	24.7	8.9

Note: Numbers represent percent of respondents.
Source: Ibid.

acquired training in small towns. A very slight tendency existed for prestigious dancers to have acquired training in a city different from the location of their present company (58 percent versus 53 percent), but some 43 percent of prestigious and less prestigious dancers trained in the same city in which their company was located. However, these data do not allow consideration of necessary migration from location of first ballet lessons to location of studios for advanced training. Even then, a few companies (especially one prestige company) started developing company schools for recruitment and training.

It would be surprising if the findings characteristic of other arts do not also pertain to dancers. Professional ballet dancers who obtain membership in the top companies in the country do not emerge from places like Interlochen or university dance departments, but must make the decision and commitment to attend professional dance schools (preferably in New York). The structural characteristic here is the age at which this professional training must occur, and it must be in the late teens at the latest.

Second Stage of Professional Entry

At this point in the career of a dancer the professional identity officially emerges: acceptance into a major ballet company as a member, even if only at the corps level. The dancer is surrounded by others equally intensely involved with dancing. Indeed, it is the intensity—better, the density—of the dance environment that clearly distinguishes ballet from other professions: and this environment is clearly the dominant pattern that infuses and structures the entire life-style of the dancer.

Tables 6 and 7 shed some insight on the nature of this move. Clearly for dancers in the prestigious companies, acquiring that entry demands pre-

Table 7
Reasons for Choosing Company
(by Company Prestige)

Company	Availability of Roles	Working Conditions
Prestigious	72.7	27.3
Less Prestigious	45.9	54.1
Total	53.4	46.6

Note: Numbers represent percent of respondents.
Source: Ibid.

vious work experience in ballet per se in its purest (e.g., not contaminated by other dance experiences). Twice as many less prestigious as prestigious dancers belonged to their companies as a first job; twice as many prestigious as less prestigious dancers acquired their current position only after previous ballet experience (see Table 6).

Reasons for company choice differed between prestigious and less prestigious dancers, with the former emphasizing opportunity for acquiring roles in a company more than general working conditions (see Table 7). This finding could no doubt reflect the greater dance experience for prestige dancers and, hence, their having appropriate skill levels for mastering offered roles. But it also indicates the greater professionalism of dancers in high-prestige companies. But above and beyond initial grounds for entering a company, several dimensions of this career stage that bear on the larger-issue of the life-style of a dancer can be delineated.

Table 8
Most Preferred Company
(by Company Prestige)

Company	Own Prestige Company	Own Less Prestige Company	Other Prestige Company	European/ Russian Company
Prestigious	88.2	0.0	8.8	2.9
Less Prestigious	0.0	40.7	33.0	26.4
Total	24.0	29.6	26.4	20.0

Note: Numbers represent percent of respondents.
Source: Ibid.

Table 9
Professional Dislikes
(by Company Prestige)

Company	Nature of Work	Art's Social Position	Company Operation
Prestigious	60.0	28.6	11.4
Less Prestigious	45.9	17.3	36.7
Total	49.6	20.3	30.1

Note: Numbers represent percent of respondents.
Source: Ibid.

Competition, Employment, Salaries

While general studies in the sociology of professions and occupations deal with implications for career advancement, generally on the part of males, the competitive features of ballet (acquiring parts, recognition, advancement, technique) apply strongly to *both* males and females. This competitive situation obviously entails failure—and note the youthfulness of such potential failure.

Some mobility exists among the four prestigious companies. But mobility patterns are obviously restrictive here, a feature not characteristic of the usual professions examined by social scientists. Not surprisingly, the data in Table 8 indicate that almost 90 percent of dancers already in a prestigious company preferred their own company. But no data exist that carefully explore the precise pattern of movement between and among companies—its extent, direction, and frequency.

None of this evidence denies that dancers do not have complaints. From Table 9 we learn that these complaints are patterned in terms of company prestige, with the nature of work and social position of the arts of more concern to dancers belonging to the prestigious companies.

A second unique feature of this stage of the dancer's career concerns actual employment patterns after the attainment of "professional" status. With minor exceptions for superstar status, ballet dancers are not guaranteed a full year of employment. Census data indicate that male dancers (including ballet dancers) have 42.7 median weeks worked, while females dancers have only 36.9 median weeks worked. Yet the necessity of maintaining technical skills and body tone throughout the year severely restricts "moonlighting," a phenomenon characteristic of some professions (e.g., musicians). Ballet is simply not a part-time activity.

Table 10
Salary of Dancers
(by Company)

Company	Under $3,000	$3,001– 5,000	$5,001– 7,000	Above $7,001
Prestigious	0.0	44.4	33.3	22.2
Less Prestigious	25.5	50.0	18.1	6.4
Total	18.5	48.5	22.3	10.8

Note: Numbers represent percent of respondents.
Source: Ibid.

Dancers can also expect to encounter downward mobility as indexed by salary levels. Prestigious dancers do earn more money than less prestigious dancers (see Table 10); however, comparing their earnings with the income of their parents shows that dancers promote themselves downward. For example, while 60 percent of prestigious dancers came from families with income in the $10,000–$20,000 range, Table 10 shows that almost 80 percent of these dancers will earn below $7,000 (the comparable figures for less prestigious dancers were 45 and 94 percent).

Active Professional Age Span

Assuming a steady progression in the professional ranks of ballet, an additional unique feature of this profession concerns the relatively brief span of peak performance. While individual exceptions exist, male dancers generally begin to descend in their professional skills in their mid-thirties, precisely at the time that characterizes ascendancy in other professions. Indeed, only 5 percent of prestigious dancers are over 30 compared to some 16 percent of dancers from less prestigious companies. The median age for all dancers in the 1970 census was 29 for males and 23.7 for females.

Moreover, the active dancing period extends longer for females than males. Clearly the sex differentiation noted in the early stages of a dancer's career persists even to the end. One indication of this phase for a dancer is his or her role specialization for specific parts and ballets, causing the dancer to adjust and limit his or her repertoire. In addition, the more extended the active period of dancing, the higher the prestige and recognition granted to the dancer by audiences (significantly, non-dancers).

Retirement from the Dance

Nothing is known of what happens to ballet dancers who end careers either at this point of aging or at any other stage past admittance to a company. Some obvious possibilities come to mind that allow for the transference of ballet skills from active performance to activities such as ballet directors, company directors, choreography, teaching, establishing dance studios, and joining the faculty of dance schools in universities.

Federico's dancers—whether prestigious or less prestigious—displayed a general pattern of avoidance when questioned about retirement plans. About 20 percent of prestigious dancers (15 percent for less prestigious) expected to retire over 40, and almost 30 percent of them (21 percent for less prestigious dancers) indicated no plans at all. Both these options seem equally unreal, though we must keep in mind that Federico was asking 20- to 30-year-olds about old age plans.

Nevertheless, the fact remains that the nature of ballet as a skill offers restricted skill transference. The question is what happens to dancers who must enter non-dance-related occupations? Federico argues that for females that non-dance occupation is marriage, and that for males there is no evidence available. Thus, any occupational transference strain will be more severe for males than females given general expectations in American society that adult males must work. As at other times, this phase constitutes a significant crisis in the careers of male dancers.

One-dimensional Life-styles

Ballet companies constitute a colonial plantation system in which remarkably little interorganizational mobility occurs in the lifetime of a dancer. Furthermore, a critical issue concerns the life-style possible under such demanding occupational constraints. For example, with respect to male dancers it is clear that their entry into first professional training and acceptance into a company marks a significant phase in their acquiring a definition of self-image in which dancing is acceptable for males. This result occurs largely by surrounding oneself with other males likewise engaged in the pursuit of ballet. But the other side of this situation is to recognize what this social construction of reality constitutes—a special kind of intense separation from the non-dance world. Female dancers do not need as sharp a role-image definition to enter ballet, but they too eventually enter a dance-dominated world.

The result for both male and female dancers is a one-dimensional condition. Ballet per se becomes the core concern around which the life of a dancer pivots. In terms of peer-association, friends, acquaintances, room-mates, and spouses, we could hypothesize a linear progression moving out-ward from the dance. These people have the highest probability of being dancers; they have a lower probability of being people associated with the company who are not dancers (musicians); they have the least probability of being people peripheral to dance (audience, interested lay persons, spon-sors). For example, only 8 percent of the prestigious dancers reported that none of their three closest friends were dancers, compared to about 18 per-cent of less prestigious dancers. Company prestige made no difference in the percentage distributions when two and three closest friends were danc-ers. Or, while fewer prestigious dancers are married than less prestigious dancers (18 percent versus 28 percent), marital spouses nevertheless tended in the majority of cases to be a dancer in the same company.

Such data barely begin to tap the one-dimensionality characteristic of the dance world which extends beyond circles of people for social relation-ships. What about the general social and political values of dancers? These people easily spend half the year traveling domestically and abroad and are thus exposed to a variety of cultural environments. Yet the insularity of the dance as a profession acts to restrict the ethos of dancers. Like colonial plantations, ballet companies operate in terms of restricted world views.

An analytical tool completely missing from limited dance research is that of cohort. Informal conversations with dancers suggest that some feel sharp differences between themselves as "elders" and the new generation of dancers in terms of attitudes toward dance and such relatively unheard of activities as union practices. With a rather narrow time base (20 to 30), generational phenomena can occur rapidly and dance could be an occupa-tional world with time-series data for studies in social change.

Ballet as a Profession

Several possibilities exist for a more general interpretive scheme for understanding ballet. The first is a structural approach focusing on conse-quences of the unique occupational features of ballet for the dancer. Feder-ico's recent discussion of his study, published in *Varieties of Work Experience* (1974), an anthology edited by Phyllis L. Stewart and Muriel G. Cantor, takes exactly this approach in arguing that the informal recruitment and training procedures ballet in fact integrate poorly with the performing needs of dancers. The structural features of ballet as an occupation result in dysfunctional consequences for its practitioners.

Second, a phenomenonological approach remains possible. In direct response to this paper (personal communication), Federico argues that a key to making sense of the dance world is the dance class. Through lifelong exposure to the controlled and disciplinarian (totalitarian?) demands of those teachers conducting the classes, the dancer acquires an occupational world view. An occupation is equally able to develop world images for its members in the arts as it is in other fields.

A third approach—social networks—is implicit in the general discussion of art by Howard Becker in the *American Sociological Review* (1974), although it is not inconsistent with the first approach. Becker argues for the examination of social networks involved in the production of any art form. The empirical reality of people cooperating to produce art is important. But Becker clearly does not touch on the totality of social networks involved in producing a dance performance.

However, a fourth approach—critical theory—holds more promise, and its application here is a new one. Three processes operate in all societies and each is inherently social: work, language (speech), and "steering." The idea of work and language present no special problems here, but steering means the ability of people to seek to change and alter their social world— to grasp possibilities that have yet to be realized and seek to make real what initially seems to be only a possibility. Associated with each process are knowledge and praxis efforts.

Dancers have restricted world views.

For work we are interested in technical knowledge (skills) for production purposes; in language we seek interpretative knowledge (understanding); in steering we seek aesthetic knowledge about alternatives to the present and become "critical" of the present in order to produce a change that frees us from the present constraints (emancipation). These stages are ordered from technical to interpretative to aesthetic, and ballet dancers seek to pass through all these processes in becoming performers in elite companies. Dancers will differ at structurally defined points in their career in terms of being capable of moving on to the next level. Of course not all dancers achieve all three levels, and some will make relatively early arrivals at any given level.

In general, dancers constitute a group whose full professional consciousness and years of difficult, painful, and demanding mastery of technique intend an aesthetic praxis that is seen by most outsiders as having no practical value. As a profession that is socially devalued in critically significant ways by the larger society, dance must provide rewards not especially valued in the non-dance world. This reward is defined as the path of movement through the three stages described above, with the best dancers achieving all three systems of technical, interpretative, and aesthetic modes with the corresponding performance (praxis) associated with these demanding abilities. Dancers do not live by bread alone, although they could use more of it.

Notes

1. Reprinted with the permission of the author and the publisher from *Society* (vol. 14, 1976).

References

Becker, Howard S. 1974. "Art as Collective Action," *American Sociological Review* 39 (Dec.): 767–776.

Federico, Ronald C. 1968. "Ballet as an Occupation." Unpublished Ph.D. dissertation, Northwestern U.

Federico, Ronald C. 1974. "Recruitment, Training, and Performance: The Case of Ballet." Pp. 249–261 in Phyllis L. Steward & Muriel G. Cantor (eds.), *Varieties of Work Experience: The Social Control of Occupational Groups and Roles.* New York: John Wiley & Sons.

6

The Choice of Acting as a Profession[1]

EMANUEL LEVY

A brief examination of the literature of the sociology of occupations and professions reveals a concentration of efforts on the study of the traditional and established professions (medicine, law, clergy, the military), but few of the arts professions (Becker, 1961; Merton, 1957; Epstein, 1981; Fichter, 1961; Janowitz, 1960). Even the recent interest in dramaturgical analysis (Goffman, 1956) and in the analogy between social life and the theater has not led to many empirical studies of the performing arts. Indeed, there has not been any systematic study of acting, one of the most popular and most visible professions. This neglect by social scientists is odd because acting is historically one of the oldest professions and sociologically one of the most fascinating. This study examines some of the distinctive characteristics of the acting profession by focusing on the dynamics of occupational choice.

There are several analytic approaches to the study of occupational choice: the rational, the fortuitous, and the socio-cultural approach (Ginzberg, 1951; Super, 1957). The rational decision-making approach presumes that there are specific stages (or periods) of occupational interest which parallel stages in the life cycle. Thus, the emergence of occupational interests are related to the individual's process of emotional and psychological changes. The occupational choice is regarded as a purposive process consisting of several developmental periods (such as the fantasy period, the period of tentative choice, and the period of realistic choice). The fortuitous approach (Katz and Martin, 1962; Pavalko, 1971) regards occupational choice as less structured, less purposive, and less rational and conceptualizes it as a process of alternatives eliminated rather than a deliberate decision-making. The third approach examines a variety of socio-cultural variables, such as social class backgrounds, race, gender, and rural-urban contexts, and their impact on occupational choice. These parameters are viewed as external influences or constraints over which the perspective, using both the fortuitous and the socio-cultural approaches. The specific approach used is important because it determines to a large extent the

111

assumptions and concepts employed and the empirical questions asked. The occupational choice of actors is described in terms of four specific issues:

1. The social backgrounds of players: socio-economic status and rural-urban origins.
2. The nature and extent of direct occupational inheritance.
3. The availability and importance of occupational role models.
4. The impact of gender on career choices and patterns.

The research examines the occupational choice of all 564 players nominated for an Academy (Oscar) Award, conferred by the Academy of Motion Pictures Arts and Sciences in its entire history, from 1928 to 1982. This group includes the most accomplished actors: the Oscar is the most prestigious and influential award in the film world. Despite the fact that this category may not be statistically representative of all actors, its large size and the lengthy period of time studied, can shed some light on pertinent issues of the acting profession in general. Using a comparative-historical approach, the study makes three useful comparisons: the occupational choice of male and female, black and white, and American and foreign players. Thus, an attempt is made to assess the impact of gender, ethnicity, and nationality on the dynamics of occupational choice. These criteria divided the large group of Oscar winners and nominees into 285 actors and 279 actresses, 13 black and 551 white players, and 380 American and 184 foreign actors. The time dimension is also taken into an account: studying the career patterns of actors over half a century will show whether there have been significant changes in the process of occupational choice, and what are the causes and patterns of these changes.

The study draws on a variety of sources and data, both primary and secondary. It includes statistical analysis of the careers of 564 players (such as age at stage debut, age at film debut, etc.), analysis of biographies and autobiographies of actors, comparisons between actors and other professionals, archival documents of the Academy of Motion Pictures Arts and Sciences and the Screen Actors Guild. The major source of information is a detailed analysis of actors' life histories as documented by them (subjectively) and other sources (such as dictionaries, Current Biography, etc.).

Social Class Backgrounds: Upward Mobility

The social class context has a tremendous impact upon individuals' level of occupational expectations and achievements. By and large, the higher the social class (measured by the family's income or parental education and occupation) the more prestigious and rewarding the occupational positions individuals aspire to and attain (Sewell et. al., 1957). Furthermore, studies have shown a direct correlation between the family status and specific occupational fields. For instance, students of law and medicine tend to come from higher status backgrounds than students of engineering (Davis, 1964; Pavalko, 1971).

However, the acting profession differs from other professions because it attracts its members from divergent segments of the social structure: all social classes, from the upper-upper to the lower-lower, are represented in the sample. But despite a wide variety of social class origins, the choice of acting as a profession was a channel of upward mobility for over half of the players, many of whom came from extremely poor families. In this respect, acting differs from the more established professions: entry has always been open to all social classes. Indeed, because of its broad social class base, acting is one of the most democratic professions in modern industrial societies.

Upward mobility characterized many actors' careers but especially those of ethnic minorities: Hispanic, black, Jewish, and Italian-American. Most of the black players were reared in lower class milieus. Ethel Waters, for example, climbed up from a domestic servant at four dollars a week to singing in saloons for one dollar a night to becoming the highest paid black performer on Broadway. Cycley Tyson grew up in poverty in Harlem, where her father operated a pushcart. After the separation of her parents, she and her mother went on welfare and she earned extra money by selling shopping bags on the street. Furthermore, the occupational decision of the black actors was more conscious and deliberate and was based on artistic as well as political motives. James Earl Jones was born in Tate County Mississippi and reared by his maternal grandparents on a Michigan farm. He entered the University of Michigan as a pre-medical student and joined its dramatic club in an effort to find his own identity and overcome his feeling of being "big, shy, and ugly." He switched from medicine to acting and for a while thought of the army as a career. Although he had never been active in civil rights or the black movement, he has repeatedly said that if he had not become an actor he would have been a revolutionary. He found a great opportunity to make political statements about his race through the parts he plays on stage and film: "A lot of actors would prefer to ignore their Negroness, as if it were a limp that you hope people won't notice onstage. I don't want the audience to forget I'm a Negro. Acting is a visual art, and you want everything to count. . . . I ask an aesthetic response to my color." Indeed, the black actors were more concerned than the white with the functions of their screen roles and images for the plight of their ethnic group.

The Jewish actors also exemplified tremendous intergenerational mobility in their careers. John Garfield (born Julius Garfinkle) grew up in poverty in the Lower East Side of New York: his father, a Russian immigrant, was a tailor. A juvenile delinquent, he was sent to schools for problem children and, to round up the family income, peddled newspapers on street corners. Tony Curtis (born Bernard Schwartz) was reared in the Bronx, where his father worked as a tailor. He too grew up in poverty and at eleven was a member of a street gang. Walter Matthau (born Walter Matuschanskavasky), the son of an impoverished immigrant from Russia, started working in his early teens, first selling sodas in a Second Avenue Yiddish Theater, then playing bit parts for fifty cents a performance. All of the Jewish actors were highly aware of the opportunities for mobility that their profession provided. "My life's a "B" picture script," said Kirk Douglas (born Issur Danielovitch), "the kid who didn't have enough to eat, the parents who were Russian immigrants." Douglas had to teach his mother how to write her name: "It's like my parents came out of the Middle Ages and in one generation I jumped to here." He described his life as "an American life," because "the real American life, the typical one, is a "B" picture. Like mine—the kid who worked up from abject poverty to become a champion."

Many foreign actors came from the bottom of the social hierarchy, especially the British who grew up in a society where social class was far more important than in the U.S. Born in Bristol, Cary Grant (Archibald Alexander Leach) was the product of poverty-stricken environment; his father was employed by a clothing manufacturer, a lowly position on the economic scale. Richard Burton (born Richard Walter Jenkins), the twelfth of thirteen children of a coal miner, grew up in a small community in South Wales. Michael Caine (born Maurice Joseph Michlewhite) was born in Liverpool to a cockney fish market porter and a cleaning woman. His class-conscious parents expected him to become a fish porter, like his father, grandfather, and great grandfather, but he was determined to break out of "the caste system that traditionally limited the aspirations of people of my class. I always had what they call in those old English books ideas above my station, tastes above my means, and an intellect above my accent." He quit school at sixteen and got the "theater bug" when he served tea in a London theater. Peter O'Toole also quit a convent school at sixteen and aware that his Leeds slum backgrounds might narrow his opportunities he was determined to better his lot.

Indeed, what characterized most players was a sense of restlessness and unsettledness. Many were born in small towns where they felt stifled and wished to flee their economic and cultural stagnation. "I suppose I wanted to act in order to have a place in the sun," Richard Widmark explained his motive to become an actor, "I'd always lived in small towns and acting meant having some kind of identity." Laurence Harvey ran away from home to join the Royal South African Navy because, as he explained, "I was dissatisfied with my surroundings, and I had a growing curiosity about life." The same motive was instrumental in Valerie Perrine's occupational choice: "My parents were very strict, and I was tired of living in small towns. I wanted a little excitement in my life." Cultural mobility was therefore no less important than socio-economic mobility.

The mobility of actors on the economic echelon is not only remarkable but a rags to riches story. Barbara Stanwyck was orphaned in early childhood and was brought up by friends of the family. She quit school at thirteen and started to work at unskilled low-paying jobs, including a parcel wrapper in a department store. However, once she became a movie star she made tremendous amounts of money. In 1944, she was announced by the Internal Revenue Service as the highest-paid woman in the U.S.. Stanwyck's story is neither unique nor exceptional. Dustin Hoffman, a product of a California middle-class milieu, was paid only $17,000 for his first major film, *The Graduate* (1967). But it made him an instant star and two years later his salary for *Midnight Cowboy* jumped up to $400,000. In the 1970s, he commanded over a million dollar per picture and for *Tootsie* (1983), his first movie after his Oscar-winning role in *Kramer Vs. Kramer* (1979), he was paid no less than five million dollars!

Rural-Urban Origins: Geographic Mobility

Rural and urban environments tend to provide different opportunity structures concerning occupational ambitions and choices. Studies have found that urban youths have better opportunity to become familiar with a wider range of occupations than those reared in rural areas and small towns (Sewell and Orenstein, 1965). However, the penetration of the mass media (particularly television) into the most remote and provincial towns has diminished the differences between urban and rural youth in their awareness of the variety of occupational alternatives. Furthermore, acting has always been one of the most visible professions; actors are constantly in the public eye and get tremendous media exposure.

The study shows that the American players comprise a mix from all over the country: large cities as well as small towns. About one third of the actors came from big cities, especially New York (98 players or 26 percent) and Los Angeles (27 actors or 7 percent). These two have provided a large number of actors because cultural life in the U.S. has been quite concentrated: theater in New York and film and television in Los Angeles. In addition, because most film actors start their careers in the legitimate theater their geographic mobility follows one dominant pattern: they first move to New York, then to California.

The large number of players born or reared in New York City is disproportionate to both the percentage of actors from other big cities (Boston, Chicago, Philadelphia) and the percentage of the American population living in this city (about five percent), but it is no surprise. In the first place, one tenth of the players have parents in the same profession, which means that at one time or another they worked in New York. Secondly, it is plausible to assume that growing up in New York City, the center of theatrical activity, fostered an early interest in the theater. The exposure to and familiarity with the theater at an early age and the availability of dramatic education (there are many drama schools) are probably connected with their occupational choice; theater is really an integral part of the everyday life in the city. Thirdly, the overrepresentation of New Yorkers among the actors is also the result of the large number of Jewish actors, most of whom were born in this city; over half of the Jewish population in the United States resides in New York City.

The goal of players born in rural or small towns is to reach New York City or Los Angeles, usually upon graduation from high school. Actors' biographies and autobiographies are replete with detailed accounts of their laborious efforts to move to New York City. James Whitmore spent his last dollars to fly to N.Y. from New Hampshire, where he was working in summer stock, to take part in an audition. Upon graduation from college in La Jolla, Gregory Peck set out to N.Y. hoping to get a role in a Broadway production; he held an assortment of jobs, including a tour guide at Radio City, until he won a scholarship in a contest sponsored by the Neighborhood Playhouse. Maureen Stapleton arrived in N.Y. in 1943, when she was eighteen years old, with all her savings: a hundred dollars. Eileen Heckart managed to save 142 dollars before moving to the city, where she first worked in a department store. Patricia Neal moved from Illinois to N.Y. and worked as a cashier, doctor's assistant, clerk, and model. Kim Stanley was urged by a director from the California Pasadena Playhouse to become an actress. She arrived in the city in 1947 by bus, with only 21 dollars in her pocket but grand theatrical ambitions.

The foreign players born outside of their countrys' cultural centers also arrived in the big city in their late teens or early twenties. However, unlike the U.S., culture in these countries (theater, television, and film) is usually concentrated in the capital: London, Paris, Rome. James Mason arrived in London in 1931 penniless, after paying the railroad fare from the Midlands, where his company was touring. Peter O'Toole wandered around in England, after touring with a repertory company, until he was stranded in

Stratford; of the 30 shillings he had, he paid 23 for a ticket to see Michael Redgrave's *King Lear*. However, determined to become an actor, he hitch-hiked to London's Royal Academy of Dramatic Arts to get formal training.

Direct Occupational Inheritance

In modern industrial societies, occupational roles tend to be achieved rather than ascribed. However, studies have found that direct occupational inheritance, that is children stepping into their parents' occupations, pre-vails in some professions in greater proportions than one would expect on the basis of chance alone. Thus, several studies have shown that the per-centage of sons following in their fathers' footsteps was highest in the mil-itary (25 percent), followed by medicine (between 10 and 20), law (15 percent), and clergy (13 percent) (eg. Pavalko, 1971: 71). Compared with the proportion of male labor force in these occupations, those with fathers in the same occupation were overrepresented.

Direct occupational inheritance has also prevailed in the acting profes-sion. The study shows that about ten percent of the players had fathers or mothers who were actors and five percent had both parents in the same profession. However, there are differences between actors and actresses. The percentage of women whose mother was an actress is higher (twelve per-cent) than that of actors (seven percent), but there are no differences be-tween the percentage of men and women whose father was an actor. Indeed, unlike the traditional professions, in which it is usually the son who follows in his father's footsteps, in acting, the mother is more instrumental in the process of occupational choice. Furthermore, the proportion of players whose mother was in show business, not just in acting, was higher (four-teen percent), and there is a significant difference between the genders: eighteen percent of the women but only ten percent of the men had mothers in show business. Thus, mothers serve as occupational role models and play a more crucial role than fathers, especially for their daughters.

What are the mechanisms through which direct occupational inherit-ance operates? During the process of socialization, children tend to learn more about their parents' occupational world than about other occupations, and they learn by direct observation, which is denied to children born to parents in other occupations. The early exposure to and familiarity with their parents' profession (and lifestyle) give children a better idea of the occupation. At times, this influence is unintentional on the parents' part and subconscious or unconscious on the children's part. But even without their parents' overt planning or intervention, children grow up in distinctive subcultures which they get to know better than children brought up in other occupational subcultures. Moreover, acting, like other professions, involved a distinct lifestyle which extends beyond the work performed, but unlike other professions, acting seems to determine the entire lifestyle more extensively and pervasively.

Players whose parents were in the same profession were not only more knowledgeable about acting but also showed an earlier interest in the theater. More significantly, they chose acting and were committed to it at a much younger age than actors not born into such sub-cultures. For example, Paul Muni was reared in a theater trunk; his parents were strolling players who toured Europe and the U.S. with him and his two brothers. Shunning the financial hazards of acting, his parents hoped he would pursue a career as a violinist, but Muni was stagestruck and at thirteen became a regular member of his parents' company; he never learned acting in a school because there was no need for it. Mickey Rooney spent his infancy and early childhood backstage and on tour with his parents, both entertainers. He made his stage debut at fifteen months, appearing in a vaudeville act as a midget, wearing a tuxedo and a big rubber cigar. Jennifer Jones's parents were the owners, managers, and stars of the Isley Stock Company, a tent show which toured the Mid-West; she sold tickets and sodas and at ten made her acting debut with her family.

In some cases, direct occupational inheritance has prevailed for generations. There are theatrical families whose members have been players for three or more generations, such as the Barrymores (four generations: including John, Ethel, and Lionel Barrymore), the Powers (three generations: Tyrone Power's father and grandfather were actors), the Fondas (Henry, Jane, and Peter Fonda), the Redgraves (Michael Redgrave and his wife Rachel Kempson and all of their three children: Vanessa, Lynn, and Orin), the Robards (Jason Robards, his father, and his son).

The parents' influence on their children's occupational choice was neither overt nor intentional. When Gregory Peck was asked if he intended his children to follow in his footsteps, he said: "I won't pressure them in any way, but the idea of a son stepping into his fathers' boots is overdone in Hollywood" (Freedland, 1980: 247). However, Peck's three children pursued careers in show business and the film industry. Henry Fonda's father did not want him to become an actor, so he started to study journalism before switching to acting. His daughter Jane also considered alternate career lines before committing herself to acting, though it is unlikely that she would have become an actress had it not been for her father. She recalled that at the age of five, she and her brother Peter acted out Western stories similar to those her father played in the movies. She attended Vassar College and went to Paris for two years to study art. Upon return, she met Lee Strasberg of the Actors Studio and this meeting changed the course of her life: "I went to the Actors Studio and Lee Strasberg told me I had talent. Real talent. It was the first time that anyone, except my father—who had to say so—told me I was good. At anything. It was a turning point in my life. I went to bed thinking about acting. I woke up thinking about acting. It was like the roof had come off my life!"(Garcia, 1981:23).

Children whose parents were actors not only started their careers earlier but also moved with greater ease, using their first-hand knowledge and parents' connections. Jane Fonda's first performance was with her father in the Omaha Community Theater production of *The Country Girl*. Vanessa Redgrave made her first screen appearance in *Behind the Mask*, playing the onscreen daughter of her real-life father, Michael Redgrave. Ryan O'Neal, the son of a screenwriter and an actress, made his television debut as a stuntman at seventeen in a series in which his parents worked. Jeff Bridges, son of actor Lloyd Bridges, made his film debut in *Halls of Anger*, when he was twenty. He was guilt-ridden because he got the part due to his father's connections, when his friends were still struggling to get an agent.

But if connections are extremely instrumental in the initial phase, they cannot sustain careers for long if there is no recognition of talent by others (agents, producers, and directors). Furthermore, being a child of a famed player exerts tremendous pressures to live up to the parents' expectations and standards. "When I first started acting," Jane Fonda recalled, "I was genuinely afraid of not being very good. It's one thing to be mediocre if you're Jane Doe. It's quite another if you're Henry Fonda's daughter and have a lot to live up to!"(Garcia, 1981: 26).

Another distinctive characteristic of the acting profession is the high rate of endogamous marriages, that is marriages within the profession itself. The study shows that no fewer than 70 of the 564 players (12.4 percent) have been married to each other at one time or another. More significantly, over two thirds of the players have been (or are) married to other players or to persons working in show business and/or the film industry. There are no differences between the men and the women except that men tend to marry actresses whereas women tend to marry writers, producers, and directors—in addition to actors. Many of the actors have been married multiple times, though their spouses were almost invariably chosen from within the profession. Several factors account for the higher percentage of endogamous marriages, compared with other professions. First, for many acting is much more than a job or a profession; it is a way of life with no clear separation of work and leisure. Secondly, the nature of their work is such that there are long absences from home and family; the filming of a movie can last five or six months.

Furthermore, most players have met their prospective spouses while working on a play or film, and in some cases it was their screen leading man (or lady). Thus, Merle Oberon was married four times, three within the film industry. Her first husband was a producer, her second a cinematographer, and her fourth her co-star, Robert Walders, many years her junior whom she met in her comeback film *Interval*. Ironically, Wolders played in this film a handsome man falling in love with an aging woman. The adage that for many players life is art and art is life is not a cliche. Indeed, James Earl Jones met his prospective wife, actress Julienne Marie, when she played Desdemona to his Othello in the production of the New York Shakespeare Festival. The impact of this kind of marital selection on the durability of the marriage, career patterns, and other aspects of the lifestyle has yet to be examined.

Occupational Role Models

Role models fulfill many functions in the process of professional socialization but they are also instrumental in the process of occupational choice, particularly in acting. Acting is one of the most popular and most visible professions: actors enjoy tremendous media exposure. Indeed, most players were familiar with and exposed to acting at an early age: most children go to the theater and to the movies when they are very young. Many actors remember quite vividly their first visit to the theater. Peter O'Toole was six years old when he saw the operetta *Rose Marie* at the Leeds' Grand Theater, a show he considers a turning point because it made him think of acting as a career.

In addition, acting is one of the few professions one can practice as a child: in school amateur productions, dramatic clubs, etc. And because it involves acting out a wide variety of roles (in terms of age), it also provides an opportunity to practice at a very early age. Many of the players were extremely young when they made their stage debuts. Among the actors, George Kennedy was two, Walter Matthau and Jack Lemon each four, Clifton Webb seven, Sal Mineo ten, and Laurence Olivier eleven. Among the actresses, Bonita Granville was three, Mary Pickford and Helen Hayes each five, Hermione Baddeley six, Julie Andrews twelve, Anne Baxter and Ginger Rogers each thirteen, and Thelma Ritter fourteen.

Although most actors came from the legitimate theater, some started their careers as dancers, singers, radio performers, and models. Players of the older generation, such as Orson Welles, William Holden, Ed Begley, and Jane Wyman, embarked on a show business career via the radio. Others, such as Bing Crosby, Lew Ayres, Frank Sinatra, and Shirley Jones, began as singers. Previous dance experience was a characteristic channel of the women's careers: Leslie Caron, Shirley MacLaine, Deborah Kerr, and Audrey Hepburn studied ballet and intended to become dancers. Because attractive looks and appearances are important for a film career, especially for women, it is no surprise that many came to film via modeling, like Mary Astor, Jean Arthur, Susan Hayward, Janet Leigh and Sophia Loren. Some, like Nancy Kelly, Jeanne Crain, Tuesday Weld, and Jodie Foster were child models.

The great visibility of acting facilitates the choice of occupational role models, usually noted performers seen on stage and/or screen. The importance of role models is symbolic as well as pragmatic: they serve as exemplary professionals and guides for successful careers. They also serve as imaginary critics: actors tend to internalize their models' standards of excellence through emulation and direct observation.

Judith Anderson became interested in acting after she saw a performance of the noted Nellie Melba. Ruth Gordon's lifelong infatuation with the theater was heightened after seeing Hazel Dawn in the Boston production of *The Pink Lady.* Actress Pearl White became Barbara Stanwyck's idol after she saw her movies in her early teens and after acting out "my own version of Pearl White" (Smith, 1974: 1). Jennifer Jones's idol was stage actress Katharine Cornell, with whom she corresponded for professional advice. Teresa Wright saw a matinee performance of Helen Hayes in *Victoria Regina*, an event which "shaped my life." Anne Baxter's decision to become an actress was also related to a performance by Helen Hayes she saw when she was ten year old. Sandy Dennis decided that she wanted to be an actress after seeing Kim Stanley in a play in Washington D.C.

There are no differences between men and women in the significance they attribute to role models. John Gielgud studied at the Royal Academy of Dramatic Arts, where he met actor Claude Rains who affected his work immensely. French actor Charles Boyer made up his mind to become an actor when he was sixteen, after seeing Lucien Guitry in *Samson* on ten successive nights. Frederic March and Spencer Tracy were William Holden's "ideals": "I used them as a kind of goal for myself. I had enough of the extrovert in me to want that kind of recognition" (*The Films of William Holden*, 1980:14). Gene Hackman began to take acting seriously after meeting Marlon Brando whom he expected to be "a nine-foot tall and three-foot wide," but instead, "he was such a straight normal guy that I thought I could do it too." Gene Wilder saw Lee J. Cobb in Arthur Miller's *Death of a Salesman* when he was fourteen, a performance which turned him toward "more serious and more important form of acting." Bruce Dern was "profoundly affected" by James Dean's performance in *Rebel Without a Cause.* Ben Kingsley visited Stratford-upon-Avon when he was nineteen and was more than impressed by Ian Holm in *Richard III*: "I was so overcome that I fainted and they had to carry me out." He, like most actors, has no problem to identify his role models, Sir Ralph Richardson and Sir John Gielgud.

The Impact of Gender: Career Patterns of Men and Women

The fact that most women tend to have lower occupational aspirations and expectations is a direct result of the societal norms concerning sex roles. Some sociologists have suggested to develop a theory of occupational choice which specifically would apply to women because of the additional and unique considerations that affect their choices. However, despite some patterned differences between actors and actresses, this study does not call for such theory: Acting seems to provide equal opportunities for both men and women. Furthermore, it is one of the few professions which is considered to be typically female, along with teachers, nurses, and librarians. More significantly, it is a profession in which men are discriminated against because of cultural norms.

The study shows that women tend to make their film debuts at a much earlier age than men: one fourth of the actresses (23.7 percent), but only five percent of the actors, made their film debut before they were nineteen years old. And over half of the women (58.1 percent), but only one fifth of the men (21.4 percent), started their film careers prior to the age of twenty four. Indeed, the average age at film debut was 26.2 for the women and 30.3 for the men. But because the age range is extremely wide in both groups, the median age at film debut serves as a better measure: 24.1 for the women and 28.5 for the men. Thus, regardless of the measure used, there is at least four year difference between the film debut of actors and actresses.

It is noteworthy, that there were actors in every age group, ranging from those who made their debut as children to those who started their professional careers in their fifties and sixties. This is yet another distinctive feature of acting: because the nature of their work involves role playing (of characters in various ages), theoretically it is possible to make a film debut at any age. For instance, about one tenth of the players were late bloomers, that is made their first film appearance rather late. However, a relatively late start (over forty) was more common among the men (5 percent) than among the women (1.8 percent).

Most actresses evidenced a strong interest in the theater at an early age and decided to become professional actresses prior to or during high school. What distinguishes the women's careers is that most have made a deliberate and conscious decision to become actresses. Vivien Leigh made her first stage appearance at eight, in a school production of Shakespeare's *A Mid-summer Night Dream*. She loved the experience "because even then I wanted to be an actress. I can't remember when I didn't." Estelle Parsons joined the local community theater at Marblehead, Massachusetts when she was four and at ten played a lead: "I've always wanted to be an actress." Glenda Jackson spent most of her free time in her childhood at local movie theaters, watching Bette Davis and Joan Crawford, in all of their films. Ellen Burstyn was "hopelessly a movie-struck child," and wrote "my first Academy Award acceptance speech at the age of seven." Sally Field's mother was a starlet at Paramount and her stepfather a stuntman, which meant that "there was never a time when I didn't want to be an actress;" at the age of seven, she wrote and directed her own plays.

The women's decision to become actresses was usually supported by their families, especially their mothers. In many cases, mothers pushed their daughters into showbusiness careers and were instrumental in providing the necessary incentives for pursuing such careers. Bette Davis, a product of a broken home, was brought up by her mother, who functioned as stage mother in more senses than one: "My whole life was shaped by my mother." The child of vaudeville performers, Judy Garland made her stage debut at three, appearing with her two older sisters in the "Gumm Sisters Kiddie Act." She once described her extremely ambitious mother as "the real-life Wicked Witch of the West" (Gerold, 1975). Jane Wyman's mother took her when she was eight to Hollywood to display her dancing and singing talents. Nancy Kelly's early interest in acting was inspired by her mother, who "would tell me bedtime stories and then we would act them out together." She also pushed her into baby modeling and later motion picture career. Sophia Loren's mother was a frustrated actress who wanted her daughter to succeed; they started together as film extras in Italy when Loren was in her teens. Ann-Margret's mother encouraged her talents as singer-dancer from early childhood: "My mother was determined that I would have the singing, dancing and piano lessons she had always wanted but was too poor to have in Sweden." For Karen Black, movie stardom has been a goal from the time she was seven: "My mother wanted to be an actress, so she pushed me into acting." At her mother's insistence, Goldie Hawn studied tap dancing and ballet from the age of three, and jazz and modern dance from eleven; her father, a musician, gave her voice lessons. Jodie Foster's mother recognized her talent as a child and managed her career from the very beginning.

The actors' careers differ from the women's in several significant respects. First, many of the men did not intend to become actors and did not made a deliberate or rational choice to pursue an acting career; for many, it was a second choice. Second, many of the men became actors by accident, as a result of circumstances over which they had little or no control. A large number of the actors were drifters and dropouts, wandering from one city to another and from one job to another until they started acting and even then refused to commit themselves to acting as a profession. Third, the actors did not get the support of their families and peers once they decided to pursue an acting career. Moreover, many had to fight against societal stereotypes of acting as a frivolous, unserious, and unmanly profession.

Indeed, for many of the men acting was a second career after working in fields that had nothing to do with theater or film. Fredric March and Hugh Griffith worked as bank clerks, and Charles Laughton followed in his father's footsteps and worked as a hotel clerk. William Holden's father hoped he would follow a career in the natural sciences and put him to work in one of the family chemical laboratories. Paul Newman drifted into acting almost by default, when he joined the drama group at Kenyon College: "When I decided to go into acting I wasn't searching for my identity. I didn't have grease paint in my blood. I was just running away from the family retail business and from merchandizing. I just couldn't find any romance in it. Acting was a happy alternative to a way of life that meant nothing to me." (Quirk, 1971) Newman cut out of the family business, took his share and savings, and went off to the Yale School of Drama.

Many actors studied other professions before switching to acting. The "acting bug" hit Larry Parks while he was studying medicine at the University of Illinois and Gregory Peck was a pre-medical student at the University of California. James Stewart majored in architecture at Princeton University, which he never practiced. Jose Ferrer also abandoned his original plan to become an architect when he discovered dramatics at Princeton University. James Mason and Dan O'Herlihy also received degrees in architecture but neither practiced. Henry Fonda, George Scott, and Gene Hackman studied journalism before they became actors. The parents of Melvyn Douglas, Hume Cronyn, and Bruce Dern wished they would become lawyers and they all went to law schools.

Many of the older actors dropped out of high school and drifted for several years until they started to act, usually without making a conscious decision. Cary Grant ran away from home when he was thirteen and joined a traveling acrobatic troupe. Clark Gable left Cadiz, Ohio at fourteen to work in a tire factory in Akron, where he saw the first play in his life. David Niven dropped out of the Sandhurst military school and worked through itinerary jobs as lumberman, laundry messenger, bar tender, and promoter before he went to Hollywood as a film extra. Peter O'Toole quit school at fourteen and began working for the Yorkshire Evening Post in Leeds as a messenger and copy boy.

Drifting and wandering have always been—and still are—characteristic of actors, especially the American, perhaps because of the country's size and the opportunities it provides for both geographic and cultural mobility. Robert Mitchum wandered around the country, working at a variety of jobs, as an engine wiper on a freighter, a nightclub bouncer, and a promoter until he joined the Long Beach Theater Guild, under the influence of his sister. Gene Hackman, the son of a journeyman pressman in Danville, Illinois dropped out of school at sixteen to join the Marines. Upon release from service, he moved to New York City, where for two years he drifted from job to job, driving a truck, jerking sodas, and working as a doorman. He studied journalism and commercial drawing for a while, then moved across the country, holding an assortment of temporary jobs until he decided to settle down in N.Y. City and pursue a stage career.

Robert Redford accepted a baseball scholarship to the University of Colorado when he was eighteen, but was soon dissatisfied with sports and "the one-dimensional life of the athlete." He lost his scholarship, flunked out, and began what he described "a three-year-period when it seems I was drunk every other day." Redford drifted back and forth across the country, taking odd jobs to support himself and getting his "real education on the road." His drifting brought him to N.Y. City, then to Paris to study art. Upon return to the U.S., he enrolled at Pratt Institute, intending to become a painter. At a friend's suggestion, he enrolled at the American Academy of Dramatic Arts to study theatrical design; he thought it might be prudent to have a lucrative sideline to fall back on, until he established himself as a painter. He had no clear idea of becoming an actor because "I'd never been in a play in my life," and "acting seemed ludicrous to me."

But perhaps the most startling success story, a real rags to riches saga, is exemplified by Sylvester Stallone's career. A product of a poor broken home, he grew up in New York's Hell Kitchen, then in Silver Springs, Maryland, and in a Philadelphia slum. He spent years at homes of foster parents and was booted out of fourteen schools in eleven years. For a while, Stallone attended the drama department of the University of Miami, where his instructors discouraged him from pursuing a show business career. He subsequently tried his hand at a variety of jobs, including ushering at the Baronet Theater in N.Y. However, determined to become an actor, he managed to get some bit parts in films. When his career reached a dead end and he was nearly broken, with a pregnant wife, he decided to create his own opportunity and to write a screenplay for himself. The story of *Rocky*, whose first draft was completed in three days, is very similar to his own life: a down-and-out boxer triumphs against agreat odds; the rest is film history.

Unlike the women, most actors did not get the emotional and psychological support of their parents once they decided to pursue an acting career. On the contrary, their families, especially fathers, not only objected to their choice but also ridiculed it. In their opposition, they shared the common stereotypes and biases against the acting profession. Indeed, despite the fact that acting has historically evolved as a profession dominated by men, there has always been a stigma of effeminacy, with the profession considered more suitable and more appropriate for women. Among the long-enduring stereotypes of acting are the ideas that it is a frivolous, unuseful, parasytic, easy, unserious and therefore unmanly profession. The biases against acting probably derive from deep-rooted societal biases, such as the ideas that men should not dress up in fancy clothes and should not wear make-up and that the display of the body and good looks are normatively suitable for women, but not men. Acting has also been considered a romantic (thus feminine) profession because it is based on a world of dream and make-believe. For example, Clark Gable's father, an oil driller from Cadiz, Ohio, never approved of his son's profession. He believed that there were only two honest ways for men to make their living, as oil drillers or farmers. Appalled by Gable's career, he continued to despise him for the rest of his life. Even his son's popularity and success could not change his mind; the idea of a man putting on paint on his face was totally unacceptable to him. Gable spent a lifetime trying to prove it was a manly profession, by the "macho" screen roles he played and his manly leisure pursuits: shooting and hunting (Gabe, 1970; Tornabene, 1976).

The notion of acting as a female profession prevails in many countries, not just in the U.S. At the start of Edmund Gwenn's career, his father regarded the theater as "that sink of iniquity," and predicted that his son would inevitably end up in the gutter. He therefore urged his son to follow in his footsteps and become a civil servant. When stage-struck Gwenn was firm about his intentions, "in a scene without parallel in Victorian melodrama, my father quite literally showed me the door." Charles Laughton's parents were also disturbed by his yearnings to become an actor. Robert Morley was greeted with horror when he chose acting; his father was a Major in the British Army and expected him to follow a career in the diplomatic service. Indeed, to placate his family's protests, John Gielgud stipulated that if he were not a success by the age of twenty-five, he would abandon the theater and become an architect. John Hurt determined to become an actor when he was fifteen, but yielding to his parents' request he also trained for a second career and attended art school for four years. The biases against acting seem to have subsided over the years but they still persist among the lower and working classes. And because many actors are of such origins they have to fight against these stigmas.

Of Scottish working-class origins, Ian Charleson had to fight against his parental objection; his dad had told him that acting was full of frivolous people.

Conclusion

Because occupational choice is an important problem for the individual, the recruiting occupation, and the society at large, ideally, it should be examined from each of these perspectives. Furthermore, it is a complex issue that should be studied from an interdisciplinary approach, taking into account biologically conditioned skills, personality attributes, the individual's and society's value system, and the historical conditions of the economy (job market) and technology. This study examined occupational choice from the individual's point of view, focusing on the interplay between personal and occupational characteristics.

The study shows that there are significant differences between men and women: most actresses made a rational, deliberate decision to become actresses at an early age, while for most men this decision was less structured, less purposive, and less rational. Many men became actors by accident rather than by deliberate design: entry into acting was the product of drifting, or as many said, "it just happened." Furthermore, the choice of acting as a career was more of a continual crisis for the men than the women, probably because of the societal stereotypes of acting as a "female" profession. The actors tended to be much more defensive and to rationalize their occupational choice than the actresses.

However, for both men and women there were elements of spontaneity, of non-rational choice, influenced by situational pressures. Many of the players said they became actors because they happened to be "the right person at the right place in the right time." The importance of situational contingencies and often trivial bases of decision should not be underestimated. James Stewart, one of the most accomplished film actors, once summed up his career as: "If I hadn't been at some particular place at some particular time and some man hadn't happened to say so-and-so, and I hadn't answered this-and-that, I'd still be hunting a job in an architect's office."

More significantly, unlike other professions which require planning, because of the need for higher education and certification, many players first started to perform and only later decided to pursue an acting career and get a theatrical education. This was especially the case of the men, of players of the older generation (who started to act in the 1930s and 1940s), and of film rather than stage players. The fact that the actual experience preceded the decision to become actors derives from other distinctive features which set acting apart from other professions. It is one of the most readily entered (and readily left) professions; one can start acting on a professional basis at any age. In addition, as some sociologists suggested, occupational choice can be regarded as a compromise between its perceived rewards and expectations of access (Sherlock & Cohen, 1966). Acting was chosen by many because it was perceived as offering both great rewards (prestige, popularity, money, and power) and easy accessibility. Indeed, entry into acting requires little or no preparation by way of extensive formal training and educational prerequisites, which explains why many started to act at an early age and never made an explicit decision to become actors. Actual experience, "on the job" training, is still far more important than educational diplomas and formal training.

There has been a wide variety of training programs, ranging from college education and professional schools to private training. Considering the historical longevity of the profession, formal school training is a relatively recent phenomenon. The American Academy of Dramatic Arts (AADA), founded in New York City in 1884, is the oldest actors' training school in the English-speaking world; the Royal Academy of Dramatic Arts (RADA), established in London in 1904, is probably the most internationally recognizable acting school. Yet, the number of distinguished players who never studied acting in a formal or organized setting, is still very large, though it has been in decline in the last two decades. Moreover, there has always been a controversy over the necessity and importance of formal training: Many players are skeptical about what can be learned in a formal classroom. For instance, Paul Muni never liked to analyze his craft: "I have been in the business for years, but can't for the life of me tell what acting is or how it is done. I know I haven't tried to learn the 'art' of acting, whatever that may be." Robert Redford said he didn't learn how to act in school and does not believe "you can technicalize acting." However, he gives credit to school for "the space and opportunity to expand and form myself as an actor," and claims that the most important thing he learned was "not to be afraid to do things in front of people (Spada, 1977:18)." Others, like Glenn Close, hold that "there is a lot to be learned, but I don't know if it can be taught," and that "what you learn in school has very little to do with how you ultimately create a role." Even more important is the often-heard complaint that schools have not been adequate in preparing actors for auditions, "the bread and butter" of the profession. The fact that the entire career might depend on a five-minute-audition is frightening to most players, as Close said: "How can you in a single meeting show someone what you can do with a role?" (*Arts Weekly*, 1982: 25)

In conclusion, a high degree of generalized and theoretical knowledge is considered to be one of the distinctive characteristics of professions: expertise and skills, based on a systematic body of certified knowledge, serve as the practitioners' claim to professionalism and autonomy (Barber, 1963; Goode, 1960; Wilensky, 1964). However, it is impossible to define the optimal knowledge base to serve as a necessary foundation to actors' claim to expertise. In the first place, it is doubtful whether there is such systematic knowledge, though there are technical skills. Secondly, unlike the knowledge base of the established professions, "the knowledge" of the acting profession is neither cumulative nor codified. Thirdly, some believe that the "knowledge of acting" is inherent and that the major difference between professional actors and laymen is that the former are trained to develop their techniques and regard then as their specialized domain (Burns, 1972: 144–171). Finally, one of the inherent problems of the acting profession is how to define acting talent or acting skills. In acting, unlike many professions, the skills presumably indicating talent and necessary for professional achievement are neither specific nor clear. Furthermore, lay audiences as well as peers have the right and power to make judgments about acting talent, which is yet another distinctive attribute of the acting profession.

Notes

1. An earlier version of this article was presented at the 1984 annual meetings of Social Theory, Politics, and the Arts Conference, at Rutgers University, New Jersey. I would like to thank the members of the panel, and particularly Judith Blau, Hyman Enzer, and Robert Remley for their useful comments. Wellesley College has provided a small grant for completing the research. Unless otherwise indicated, quotations are from *Current Biography*.

References

1982. *Arts Weekly* (August): 18–25.

(Various dates). *Current Biography*. Atoka, OK: Wilson.

1980. *The Films of William Holden*. Secaucus: Citadel Press.

Barber, Bernard. 1963. "Some Problems in the Sociology of Professions," *Daedalus* 92: 669–688.

Becker, Howard S. et al. 1961. *Boys in White*. Chicago: U. of Chicago Press.

Blau, Peter, J. W. Gustad, R. Jessor, H. S. Parnes & R. C. Wilcock. 1956. "Occupational Choice: A Conceptual Framework," *Industrial and Labor Relations Review* 9 (July): 531–543.

Burns, Elizabeth. 1972. *Theatricality.* New York: Harper & Row.

Davis, James A. 1964. *Great Aspirations.* Chicago: Aldine.

Epstein, C. F. 1981, *Women in Law.* New York: Basic Books

Fichter, Joseph. 1961. *Religion as an Occupation.* South Bend: U. of Notre Dame Press.

Freedland, Michael. 1980. *Gregory Peck.* New York: William Morrow.

Gabe, Essoe. 1970. *The Films of Clark Gable.* Secaucus: Citadel Press.

Garcia, H. 1981. *The Films of Jane Fonda.* Secaucus: Citadel Press.

Gerold, Frank. 1975. *Judy.* New York: Harper & Row.

Ginzberg, Eli et al. 1951. *Occupational Choice.* New York: Columbia U. Press.

Goffman, Erving. 1956. *The Presentation of Self in Everyday Life.* Garden City: Doubleday.

Goode, William J. 1960. ''Encroachment, Charlatanism, and the Emerging Professions: Psychology, Sociology, and Medicine,'' *American Sociological Review* 25 (Dec.): 902–914.

Janowitz, Morris. 1960. *The Professional Soldier.* New York: The Free Press.

Katz, Fred E. & Harry W. Martin. 1962. ''Career Choice Processes,'' *Social Forces* 41 (Dec.): 149–154.

Merton, Robert K. et al. 1957. *The Student Physician.* Cambridge: Harvard U. Press.

Pavalko, Ronald M. 1971. *Sociology of Occupations and Professions.* Itasca: Peacock.

Quirk, Lawrence. 1971. *The Films of Paul Newman.* Secaucus: Citadel Press.

Sewell, William H., Archie O. Haller & Murray A. Strauss. 1957. ''Social Status and Educational and Occupational Aspiration,'' *American Sociological Review* 22 (Feb.): 67–73.

Sewell, William H. & Alan M. Orenstein. 1965. ''Community of Residence and Occupational Choice,'' *American Journal of Sociology* 70 (March): 551–563.

Sherlock, Basil & Alan Cohen. 1966. ''The Strategy of Occupational Choice: Recruitment to Dentistry,'' *Social Forces* 44 (March): 303–313.

Smith, Ella. 1974. *Starring Barbara Stanwyck.* New York: Crown Publishers.

Spada, J. 1977. *The Films of Robert Redford.* Secaucus: Citadel Press.

Super, Donald. 1957. *The Psychology of Careers.* New York: Harper & Row.

Tornabene, Lynn. 1976. *Long Live the King.* New York: Simon & Schuster.

Weis, Elizabeth, ed. 1981. *The Movie Star.* New York: Viking Press.

Wilensky, Harold L. 1964. ''The Professionalization of Everyone?'' *American Journal of Sociology* 70 (Sept.): 137–158.

$$\underline{\qquad} 7 \underline{\qquad}$$

Music and Its Audiences
Two Hundred Years Ago[1]

CHARLES W. HUGHES

Those who write of the response of the human organism to music are inclined to draw their materials from introspection or from a study of the reactions of a group of contemporary subjects. The historical record has been little studied from this point of view, and naturally so, since most musical records concern themselves with matters of more immediate practical interest than the question of how people listen to music. Nevertheless such writers as Romain Rolland and Michel Brenet have written shrewd and penetrating essays which throw much light on the focal point of the whole elaborate apparatus of music making, the moment of impact when organized musical sounds meet the receptive sensibility of the listener.

Needless to say the historical record must be studied with the utmost caution. These are witnesses whose testimony cannot be cross-examined, whose words, like those of our own contemporaries, are subject to a thousand distorting influences. But the glimpses they afford throw such a vivid and revealing light on the musical sensitivity of a whole period that the record, fragmentary and distorted though it may be, is well worth consulting.

In turning to Italy of the seventeenth and eighteenth centuries, the central fact that is revealed is the intense, almost overpowering response to music, a response so complete as to seem abnormal, even monstrous when we compare it to the decorously restrained response of the average concert-goer of the present day who smiles and strikes one palm gently against the other.

A priest of Genoa wrote of the singer Adriana Basile, "While she leaves us with our bodies on earth she wafts us to heaven with our sense of hearing." We are likely to dismiss the phrase as a piece of florid rhetoric and to assume that the writer was more interested in turning a phrase than in producing an accurate record. Less versimilitude and even greater indulgence in rhetoric appear in the words of Ridolphi who wrote of another singer, Baldassare Ferri, that "he had the spheres for his rivals and reduced himself to ecstasy and idleness."

If we turn, however, to the testimony of a few of the many foreigners who visited Italy, our impression of the extravagance of the emotions which music aroused in contemporary listeners is increased rather than diminished. The French Abbé Morellet wrote, "The people were swooning. One heard groans of: O benedetto, o che gusto, piacer di morir!" An Englishman who visited Italy somewhat more than twenty years later wrote, "The public remained with folded hands and eyes half closed, holding its breath: A young girl began to cry out from the middle of the parterra: O Dio! dove sono? Il piacere mi fa morire." Both of these visitors record explicitly traits which will reappear in our study—the identification of musical experience with fainting or even with death, the involuntary exclamation of pleasure, the intense absorption in the one faculty of hearing. So far our witnesses have dealt with operatic singing. Similar effects were recorded of church music which indeed, hardly differed from the music of the opera house at this period. We read that the performance of the great singer Vittori in the choir of Urban VIII so moved the congregation that auditors were compelled to loosen their clothes to keep from fainting. Those who could not gain entrance stood outside, hoping that they might at least hear some notes of the performance.

Finally, we summon our most professional witness, the music historian Burney, who wrote, "When the Italians admire a thing they seem on the point of dying of a pleasure too great for their senses." Here again is the same emphasis, the same traits observed and set down with the matter of factness of a professional critic.

The performer is the focal point of this strange world of music, and the most admired performers are the skilled singers, the fabulous virtuosi of that day. It was the interpreter and her power to sway and move an audience that was applauded. The worship of these virtuosi did not end with the applause of the audience, however. The satirist Adinari waxes indignant over the extravagance of the tribute rendered these singers. "Towns raise pompous trophies and fill the streets with flowers. A chain is drawn across the street so that no coach may disturb her sleep. Great ladies caress and kiss her." Yet even Adinari ends with a passage that seems less criticism than another contribution to the hymn of praise. "She makes her quivering notes vibrate, now joyous, now sad, and to her sweet voice she weds looks and gestures no less sweet, so that her whole body seems alive with music and her very hair, her cheeks, and her bosom seem to be singing like her lips."

Although it was the singer who enthralled the audience, the music of the period also bears the stamp of that smoldering and sinister passion which appears again and again in the music written for these empresses of song, in the dramatic recitative, in the arias, suave and lyric, glittering with fiorituri, or passionate and melancholy, portray the woes of Dido deserted by Aeneas, of Ariadne abandoned by Theseus. It was the lament, music of deprivation and anguish, which best typified the expressive power of this music. Whoever has heard and felt the power of Monteverdi's "Lasciatemi morire" realizes the power of a composer who could conceive a melody so sombrely alive and so tragic in its emotion. It was a moment of inspiration which crystallized into a formula, a type from which later composers were nevertheless able to develop moving scenes.

A measure of the difference between French and Italian music is the shock to which French ears were subjected when Italian music was introduced into France. The shock was long and painful, and a prolonged period of adjustment and of controversy, often of an extremely acrimonious sort, accompanied the acclimatization of Italian music.

Michel de Marolles, for example, writes (1657), "French music is indeed the equal of Italian music although it is not so noisy and though it has far more sweetness; but it seems that those are not qualities which make it worse." Similarly we find Rebel's "French sweetness" contrasted with the "frightful and monstrous leaps" of the Italians. Thus, it is easy to see that precisely the qualities of dramatic fire and of passionate musical speech, the characteristic qualities of Italian music, were repugnant to French taste. They seemed noisy, extravagant, lacking in balance and in good taste.

The French ideal was complex, as was the Italian, but its function was quite different. Nevertheless, it shared with Italian music the power of completely enthralling its listeners if we may credit the quaint account of René Francois, so vivid in its study of the attitudes and physiognomy of the attentive listener.

"He (the lute player) puts everyone in a transport and charms them with a gay melancholy, so that one lets his chin drop on his chest, another on his hand, one stretches out lazily at full length as if pulled by the ear, another has his eyes wide open or his mouth open as if his spirit were nailed to the strings. You would say that all are without consciousness save the sense of hearing, as if the spirit had abandoned all the other senses to retire to the tips of the ears to enjoy more at its ease this powerful harmony: But if, changing his style, he rouses his strings, he instantly calls back to life all the audience and, restoring to their bodies their spirits and faculties, reanimates them and thus does what he wills with men."

The sudden transformation of the audience at a change in the mood of music suggests the marvels so often told of the Greek musicians. The description of the attentive audience of the lutenist is, however, obviously drawn from nature, and is at once vividly descriptive and highly amusing.

Here again the emphasis is on the complete absorption of the audience in the sound of the lute. Nevertheless, though French ears shared this intense delight in music and the ability to lose themselves in it with the Italians, there were great differences in the music which moved them. These differences reflected the demands of French society on the musician. To appreciate these differences we shall again call up contemporary witnesses. French music of this period was of course of various kinds and was calculated to serve various purposes. This was also true of Italian music, but the concentration of interest on opera (and on its satellite forms, the aria and the cantata) was so intense that most contemporary accounts deal with them. In France we have the delightful chamber music for harpsichord of Chambonnières, of Couperin, of Rameau; the little songs which enlivened the leisure hours of the ladies and gentlemen of the court, drinking songs, pastorals, dance songs, and more serious airs. With Lully and with his predecessors the musical tragedy, which was the musical counterpart of the spoken drama of Corneille and Racine, appeared more spectacular (and sometimes less dramatic) by the incorporation of elements from the ballet de cour.

One of the abiding characteristics of French instrumental music is a certain reluctance to accept absolute instrumental music. "Sonate que veux tu de moi?" is far from being merely a witty quip at the expense of the serious composer. It represents a point of view which has remained relatively constant from Couperin to Ravel. Only two French symphonies have obtained worldwide success, the César Franck Symphony in D Minor and the Symphony in C Minor of Camille Saint-Saens. The list of symphonic poems and of operas is long indeed. The same preference for poetic delineation in music appears in the picturesque titles given to pieces for the harpsichord: "The Little Windmills," "The Amorous Nightingale," etc. Were they picturesque adornments to add external attractiveness to the composer's work, or was it the composer's intention actually to convey the images suggested by the title? The present bias toward absolute music would suggest the former solution, the available contemporary evidence the latter. In judging the aptness of a prospective pupil the clavinists of the period laid much stress on the manner in which he responded to the expressive intentions of the music. Saint Lambert is speaking to this point when he says, "They (the teachers) see whether, when they (the prospective pupils) hear fine music, they enter into all the moods (movements) which it attempts to inspire, whether they are moved by the tender passages, and rouse themselves at the gay passages." The ability to apply the suitable and fitting title to a composition was considered a proof of musical understanding. Michel Brenet gives an interesting example. When the violinist, Westhoff, played a solo before Louis XIV, that monarch gave a proof of his musical understanding by immediately christening it "La Guerre."

The little songs of the period were designed as a pleasant social recreation. But where the Italian fiercely embraced the emotions roused by the singer and claimed them as his own, the French demanded restraint, moderation, elegance. Each emotion must be kept within the limits of what was pleasurable. If one notes the qualities for which the Italian Doni praises French singers, one has a clear measure of the difference between the ideals of the countries.

"Where do they sing with so much charm and delicacy, and where does one hear every day so many new and agreeable songs even in the mouths of those who, without any artifice or study, make apparent both the beauty of their voices and the cultivation of their spirits: to a point where it seems that in other countries musicians are made only by study but that in France they become so by nature."

It is charm and delicacy which are praised, not vivid and passionate expression. Naturally the audience reacts in a more restrained fashion than these Italians who faint and call out in ecstasy. The French are titivated and pleasantly stirred. Thus Françion in the "Berger extravagant," by Sorel, "Then musicians came who sang many new airs, joining the sound of their lutes and their viols to that of the voices. 'Ah,' said Françion, resting his head against Laurette's breast, 'next to the sight of a beautiful woman there is no pleasure which enchants me like music. My heart bounds with each accent, I am no longer master of myself, my heart trembles delightfully with the trills of the voice.' "

La Pouplinière, a wealthy music lover of the period of Rameau, in a pregnant comparison showed both his love for music and that touch of grossness which was as characteristic of one side of the period as were the affected and dainty ardors of the précieuses of another. He had been travelling without being able to hear a note of music. Finally he reached a city and was able to hear several sonatas. They roused and comforted his spirits, said he, as a good consommé satisfies and comforts the stomach.

The desire to please, the will to charm had its appropriate expression in the music of the period, witty, dainty, elegant. With the great composers of the period the imposed limits do not prevent them from writing music which conforms to the narrow limits of form and the canons of good taste and moderation but at the same time possesses true grandeur of line. This is the exception. Most of the chamber music of the time provokes a pleased half smile. It charms as was its intention. With the weaker composers the desire to please led to an avoidance of the unusual which sometimes resulted in a deplorable weakness and monotony of style. Nowhere, I think, is this so amusingly confessed as in some prefatory remarks by Perrin. "I have always chosen my subjects from the tender passions and I have banished all serious reasoning and the darker passions—I have limited myself to the marvellous, to the amorous and the spirited—."

In the music of Lully's operas, however, the music of gallantry had to enlarge its scope to include the "darker passions." Yet the performance of a French opera had the dignity of a state function. The heroine suffered, but in the grand manner, much as the queen of France might be expected to behave in a similar situation. In spite of the pathos, the grandeur, and the truly moving quality of the best pages of Lully, the cold formalism of court etiquette and the ceremonial proprieties, which sometimes penetrate to the wrong side of the footlights, dull the sharp edge of tragedy and prevent the keen sense of the comic, the buffo spirit which is so evident in Lully's earlier work, from making its appearance.

In place of the raptures of the Italian audience interrupted by periods of noisy conversation, we find the musical abbés and the more studious music lovers conning their libretti by the light of the little wax tapers. The melodies of Lully diffused themselves, were played on every conceivable instrument, were sung not only with their original texts but to endless parodies and adaptations. But they aroused rapture less than admiration. His serious airs stirred but did not overwhelm the auditors. This was due in part to the character of the music, perhaps in even greater measure to the superior expressive magic of the Italian virtuous.

The same pompous ceremonial air characterized French church music of this period. La Fontaine emphasizes in a truly amusing fashion the pomp (and the noise) of the new concerted motets of Lalande for voices and orchestra which praised the glory and pomp of the French court quite as much as the glory of God.

> "Great in everything, he (Louis XIV) wishes to express
>   everything with grandeur
> War is his joy and his strongest passion
> His pleasures all have a warlike aspect
> His concerts of instruments have the noise of thunder
> And his vocal concerts are like the turmoil
> That the cries of soldiers make on the day of battle."

It is Mersenne, however, who has written the sentence which best sums up the French attitude towards music. "One must first assume that music, and as a result, that melodies are especially and chiefly composed to charm the mind and the ear, and to help us to pass our lives with a little pleasure among the misfortunes which one encounters . . . I would not deny that certain skillfully composed airs, well adjusted to the text, move one to pity, to compassion, to regret, and to the other passions, but only that this is not their chief end, but rather to rejoice or even to fill a cultivated audience with admiration."

We are not to suppose that Italian and French ears were different, but rather that they were molded to environments which were still sufficiently isolated to present marked differences. These were differences which were to diminish as the invading army of Italian singers, composers and librettists gradually extended their domination to England and over all of Europe. Composers in Italy as in France developed in a musical climate which moulded them and which limited and directed their development. The dukes and the princes of Italy, passionately devoted to singularly childish and inordinately expensive display in music as in all other forms of exterior pomp, passionate, unrestrained and uncontrolled themselves responded freely to the fiery ardors of their singers. Partly because music was ardently cultivated in so many centers, partly because it would appear that the crumbs from these musical banquets were more freely scattered to the crowd in Italy than in France, the whole nation acquired a natural disposition and a taste for music which was remarked by Burney as well as by many other travellers.

In France, on the other hand, we have a highly centralized musical bureaucracy. Never, perhaps, has one man so minutely and so completely regulated and controlled the musical life of a period as did Louis XIV. Musicians expressed not their own emotions but those of the king. His approval meant success, loss of his favor closed every door to advancement. Thus it was inevitable that the twin moods of elegant diversion and of pomp and ceremony should dominate in the music of the French court.

Notes

1. Reprinted with permission of the publisher from the *Journal of Aesthetics and Art Criticism* (vol. 2, 1943).

References

Adinari, n.d. *Contre le donne.*

Bobillier, Marie, n.d. *Musical Tour Through the Land of the Past and Present: Histoire du Concert en France.*

Francois, Rene. 1621. *Essai des Merveilles de Nature.* Rouen:

Rolland (pseud.), See Marie Bobillier.

8

Cultural Democracy in a Period of Cultural Expansion: The Social Composition of Arts Audiences in the United States[1]

PAUL DIMAGGIO
and
MICHAEL USEEM

The nature of the public for the arts in the United States has been a source of speculation and controversy for much of this country's history. Alexis de Tocqueville, the liberal French aristocrat who studied American democracy during the 1830s, noted then that America's Puritan simplicity and unbounded resources were more conducive to commerce than to culture. Nonetheless, he suggested, as the frontier closed and the Puritan legacy weakened, the natural tendencies of democracy might bring in unprecedented public involvement in the arts.

> Not only will the number of those who take an interest in the production
> of mind be greater, but the taste for intellectual enjoyment will descend,
> step by step, even to those who, in aristocratic societies, seem to have
> neither time nor ability to indulge in them (Tocqueville, 1956:162).

Tocqueville predicted the democratization of both the production and appreciation of art as the United States became more mature, but a half century later Thorstein Veblen (1899) could not see it. Having witnessed the rise of great fortunes that Tocqueville had not foreseen, Veblen feared that the arts (as well as most aspects of culture, learning and manners) had become the playthings of the rich—baubles and badges of social standing less respected for their beauty or intrinsic merit than for their rarity and expense. High culture, thought Veblen, would remain the preserve of the wealthy because only they had the leisure to attend to it and the power to define what, in fact, would be considered "art."

The opposing viewpoints of Tocqueville and Veblen have reappeared in debates throughout this century. In recent years, for instance, some writers have discerned a cultural "boom," asserting that the arts, while previously the monopoly of an elite, have become central to the lives of much of the American public. Alvin Toffler, perhaps the most optimistic spokesperson for this position, cites the rise of a massive middle-class constituency for the arts and contends that "millions of Americans have been attracted to the arts, changing the composition of the audience profoundly." While not all Americans are part of the culture boom, he argues, "a major step toward democratization has, indeed, been taken." As a result, the "rise of a mass public for the arts can, in its way, be compared with the rise of mass literacy in the eighteenth century in England" (Toffler, 1965:34; also see *Ms. Magazine*, 1977).

Others see just the opposite. For instance, Herbert Gans maintains that high culture remains the preserve of a small circle of *aficionados* and a diverse "user-oriented" public that includes art patrons, collectors, highly educated professionals and business executives. High culture continues to serve "a small public that prides itself on exclusiveness" (Gans, 1974:77). Similarly, Baumol and Bowen, in their major study of audiences for the performing arts in the mid-1960s, concluded that:

> If there has been a significant rise in the size of audiences in recent years, it has certainly not yet encompassed the general public. . . . Attempts to reach a wider and more representative audience, to interest the less educated or the less affluent, have so far had limited effects (1966:96).

The debate has gone on, in part, because of the lack of definitive evidence on the composition of arts audiences, and is only likely to intensify as more and more public money is put into the arts. Since 1966, the annual budget of the National Endowment for the Arts, the federal government's primary funding agency, has risen from $2.5 million to over $149 million. State contributions to the arts have grown from $1.7 million to over $55 million annually. State art agencies have increased from 18 to 55, and community arts councils from about one hundred to over twelve hundred (*Cultural Post*, 1976:16; National Committee for Cultural Resources, 1975:11; Netzer, 1978; National Endowment for the Arts, 1978). There has also been rapid expansion in the scale of arts activities. Between 1965 and 1975, the number of major professional dance companies rose from 10 to 51; resident, nonprofit professional theaters from 25 to 101; professional opera companies from 23 to 45; professional orchestras from 58 to 105; and touring dance companies from 27 to 86 (*Cultural Post*, 1976:16). The vast increase in the level of public support for the arts has, naturally, stimulated concern about the social composition of the expanding arts public (DiMaggio and Useem, 1978b). Policy makers and interest groups increasingly ask if government programs are underwriting an activity enjoyed by a large cross-section of the American public; or are they backing an activity that remains the special preserve of an exclusive social elite? Good baseline figures on audience social composition are clearly prerequisites if such policy questions are to be settled.

Comprehensive audience indicators are also important if we are to learn the extent to which cultural resources are inequitably distributed in the United States. Evidence suggests that the highly unequal distribution of cultural resources can be an important factor in maintaining class boundaries and in perpetuating social immobility from generation to generation. Exclusive social events surrounding the consumption of high culture provide valuable ritual occasions for the reaffirmation of elite solidarity. Familiarity with cultural matters and the possession of cultural credentials—initially bestowed by elite family socialization and later reinforced by involvement in cultural affairs—are important assets for ascent in the class hierarchy (Bourdieu, 1973; DiMaggio and Useem, 1978a). The extent to which cultural resources play a role in social class maintenance and reproduction depends on the degree of inequality in rates of cultural consumption. Thus, arts audience composition information is also important for understanding the extent to which the arts may help perpetuate class hierarchy.

Unfortunately, a comprehensive portrait of the American audience has not been available for resolution of these policy and analytic issues. Our primary purpose in this paper is to present major elements of such a portrait: our evidence will indicate the extent to which the major visual and performing arts are consumed by a cross-section of the public. A second purpose is to see if there has been any discernable trend toward broadening the arts audience over the past decade. The number of performing and visual arts organizations has expanded tremendously in recent years, the infusion of public money has been massive, but has there been a democratization of arts consumption, as some analysts claim? Our main efforts here will be devoted to establishing baseline data necessary if analytic efforts and policy debates are to go forward effectively, rather than to entering such analyses and debates more directly.

Until recently there were not enough studies of American arts audiences to make the present effort possible, but work in the past ten years has been sufficient to permit tentative identification of the extent of elite dominance of the arts audience and changes in audience social composition over time.[2] Although few have been published, many studies have been conducted, primarily of audiences for single art organizations. A single study provides little generalizable information, but the set of studies can provide a reasonably reliable and comprehensive portrait of the U.S. art audience. We have tried to assemble as many as possible of the arts-audience studies conducted since 1960 and to derive from them both overall compositional indicators and trends in composition during recent years.

The Audience Studies

Although audience surveys have been conducted for years, few have been published and many lost or buried in the organizations that conducted them. To obtain as complete as possible a set of audience studies, we first conducted an extensive bibliographic search to create a complete list of published studies conducted since 1960. A review of thirty-five standard indexes and bibliographic sources yielded approximately forty-five useful references. Twelve institutional libraries (e.g., those of the Massachusetts Council for the Arts and the Center for Arts Information in New York City) were consulted for additional references.

Next, it was necessary to approach those organizations that might have conducted the many unpublished studies. We compiled a list of more than 1200 arts organizations: museums, performing-arts organizations, regional, state and local arts councils, support organizations for specific art forms and foundations involved in arts funding. Museums and performing-arts organizations were selected from *The Art Museum Directory* and the *National Directory of Civic Centers and Performing Arts Organizations* on the basis of size, on the assumption that larger organizations are more apt to be able to conduct audience research. Included were all instrumental-music and theatrical organizations reporting budgets of over $100,000 annually, all other performing-arts organizations with budgets of over $50,000, and all museums reporting 100,000 or more visitors annually. (For comparative purposes, one hundred randomly selected smaller museums and performing-arts organizations were added to this list.) A brief form was addressed to the director or manager of each organization, inquiring whether the organization had ever conducted, commissioned or participated in an audience survey. If such a study had been conducted, we requested the name and address of the study's director and either a copy of the final report or information on how to obtain a copy. Respondents were also asked if they knew of any other organizations that had conducted audience studies. The response rate to this inquiry rose to slightly over 50 percent after one follow-up letter. In addition to the bibliographic search and mail survey, further efforts were made to acquire unpublished studies by contacting individuals known to be knowledgeable about arts research, and by placing queries in eight arts-related periodicals and newsletters (e.g., American Symphony Orchestra League *Newsletter, Musical America, New York Times Sunday Book Review*).

Materials were collected on 268 audience studies:[3] 14 of theater audiences; 44 of art-museum visitors; 32 of visitors to natural history, general, anthropology, and related museums and exhibits; 19 of science-museum or science-exhibit visitors; 16 of classical-music audiences; 14 of audiences for two or more kinds of art institutions; 12 of history-museum visitors; 11 of art-center visitors; 7 of opera audiences; and 6 of ballet and dance audiences. (Thirty-three were of population cross-sections which included both arts consumers and non-consumers.) Of the studies, more than 80 percent dated from 1972 or later and almost none were earlier than 1966.

The studies included surveys of visitors and audiences for institutions that cover the full range in size and function. Nonetheless, there is some bias in the data: nothing is known about the universe of all studies conducted; nor do we know about the representativeness of organizations that conduct audience studies in comparison to all museums of live performing-arts institutions. We cannot be sure how much our summary statistics might deviate from the actual composition of American audiences for museums and live performing arts. Although most of the studies eventually received were from medium and small-sized organizations, our inquiries had been mostly to large and medium-sized organizations. Thus the larger organizations are overrepresented in our data, in comparison to their number among all arts organizations, if not in comparison to the proportion of all annual visits and attendance for which they account. There is some reason to assume that the larger organizations in the larger cities draw a somewhat more affluent and well-educated public than do smaller or community-based organizations. On the other hand, since the technical quality of the studies was extremely uneven, since response rates and total numbers of respondents varied so greatly, and since some necessary data were not available, there was neither a powerful rationale for, nor the possibility of, weighting organizations by total attendance, size or location—in calculating overall audience-composition figures. The effect of granting data from small organizations equal weight with data from major organizations may countervail the tendency for the overrepresentation of major organizations' studies to inflate the audience percentages in high-status categories.

The audiences from which data have been drawn may be unrepresentative in several other ways. We do not know if audiences studied are systematically different from those not studied. Out of the universe of all audience studies that have been conducted, we would speculate that we

gathered a larger percentage of the published than of the unpublished studies, of recent than of less recent studies, of studies for which reports were
written than of studies yielding no formal reports, of major in-house or
academic studies than of proprietary studies, and of studies of organizations
with relatively low staff turnover than ones of organizations with relatively
greater staff turnover. Given the number and diversity of the studies from
which our conclusions are drawn, we believe such factors do not decisively
bias the findings one way or the other. Nonetheless, our statistics must be
seen as *estimates* rather than as rigorous descriptions of the public for museums and the live performing arts; they do represent the best figures ob-
tainable from data available now or in the near future.

The Composition of Arts Audiences

Of the many characteristics of audiences included in the studies we
reviewed, we decided to concentrate on only six of the most central social
features for which data were available in a number of studies: gender, age,
education, occupation, income and race. Since many of the 268 studies
assembled did not acquire information on all six, our summary statistics
must be based on subsets of the studies. In some cases a specific study
surveyed several distinct audiences, and these are counted as separate audiences in obtaining the overall compositional estimates. The estimates are
generally presented for museums and the performing arts separately and,
when possible, for specific types of each: art, science and history museums;
ballet and dance, theater, orchestra and opera in the performing arts. There
were too few studies of other art forms to allow estimates of their audience
composition.

Gender. Art, in this country, has been associated with femininity, and
it has often been suggested that women are disporportionately represented
in arts audiences. One theater trade association report complained that
theater-going "repudiates for many people the all-American red-blooded
image of what is supposed to be 'all-right' for a man to do and still be
considered 'all-man' " (Theater Communications Group, 1967:31). An
early study of a symphonic-music audience attributed the predominance of-
women to the fact that "women have greater esthetic appreciation for music, as they do for art and literature, than men, who place greater emphasis
on theoretical, economic, political, and practical-success values" (Beldo,
1956:15).

Our analysis of 72 studies of 112 audiences for which gender of respondents was reported indicates, however, that women are only slightly

overrepresented among arts attenders and that variation among audiences is enormous (see Table 1). While the percentage of men in the United States population is 49, the median percentage of men reported among museum visitors is 46 and in performing-arts audiences is 43. Sex composition varied among the art forms. Audiences for ballet and dance were most heavily female (a median 60 percent) while, among the performing arts, opera audiences drew the largest proportion of males (46 percent). Art museums drew large female percentages (median 57 percent) while history and science museums were slightly favored by men (52 percent). Composition varied extensively among audiences within an art form, with male percentages ranging from 30 to 71 percent in museums and from 31 to 58 percent for the performing arts. Men outnumbered women in a quarter of the performing-arts audiences and two-fifths of the museum visitors.

We should warn that response bias may significantly skew the observed proportions from the true population proportions. Baumol and Bowen (1966) suggest that husbands tend to fill out survey forms when the cooperation of only one spouse is requested. Book and Globerman (1975), in contrast, contend that men delegate the responsibility to women, creating a female bias. In two museum studies, men were found slightly more likely to volunteer if one person in a group was interviewed (Abbey and Cameron, 1960; New York State Education Department and Janus Museum Consultants, 1968). The extent and nature of gender bias thus depends upon the specific research design of a study and for this set of studies the overall effect cannot be estimated.

Finally, we should note that a substantial fraction of the wide variation observed from study to study may stem from factors such as survey time, performance or exhibit content and geographic variation. Since labor-force participation is greater among men than among women, more women are likely to attend on weekdays (Johnson, 1969; National Research Center of the Arts, 1976a, b, 1977). Sex ratios among ballet audiences and museum visitors are known to be affected by the particular program (Leo Burnett, U.S.A., 1975; National Research Center of the Arts, 1976c). Female arts-audience percentages vary from 51 percent in New York City to 62 percent in Washington State (National Research Center of the Arts, 1976a, b).

Age. Most of the studies with age data showed what percentage of the audience was in particular age categories. The categories were so variedthat we computed the median age for each audience (Table 2). Eighty-two studies had age data on 145 distinct audiences: the median age for performing-arts audience was 35, that for museum visitor populations was 31. Both figures are between the median age of the entire U.S. population (28) and the median age for the population sixteen and over (40). But ex-

TABLE 1
Percentage Men in Audience Studies, by Art Form

Art Form	Median Percentage	Percentage Range	Number of studies within percentage range								Total no. of studies
			27–32	32–37	37–42	42–47	47–52	52–57	57–62	62–72	
All museums	46.0	30–71	2	3	8	13	10	5	4	4	45
Art museums	43.0	30–59	2	3	8	10	6	—	1	—	30
History museums	48.5	44–53	—	—	—	2	1	1	—	—	4
Science museums	52.0	43–71	—	—	—	1	3	4	3	—	11
All perform. arts	42.5	31–58	1	15	14	21	6	8	2	—	67
Ballet and dance	40.0	31–50	1	5	3	2	2	—	—	—	13
Theater	42.5	32–58	—	8	7	11	3	3	1	—	33
Orchestra	44.5	33–54	—	2	3	4	1	2	—	—	12
Opera	46.1	41–58	—	—	1	4	—	3	1	—	9

TABLE 2
Median Age of Audiences, by Art Form

Art Form	Median of Medians	Range of Medians	Number of studies within age range								Total no. of studies
			19–22	23–26	27–30	31–34	35–38	39–42	43–46	47–50	
All museums	31	19–51	2	2	16	11	3	4	1	1	40
Art museums	31	26–51	—	1	6	6	2	2	1	1	19
History museums	33	28–42	—	—	2	1	1	1	—	—	5
Science museums	29	19–40	2	1	8	4	—	1	—	—	16
All performing arts	35	21–49	5	7	14	23	22	21	8	5	105
Ballet and dance	33	30–38	—	—	1	11	3	—	—	—	15
Theatre	34	21–48	5	6	12	9	13	10	3	2	60
Orchestra	40	24–49	—	1	1	2	3	8	3	2	20
Opera	41	33–40	—	—	—	1	3	3	2	1	10

tensive age variation was apparent both within and between art forms: the medians for performing-arts audiences ranged from 21 to 49; for museum-visitor populations, from 19 to 51. Typical arts audiences, then, had age profiles similar to that of the entire U.S. population, but specific audiences frequently diverged considerably from this central tendency.

Ballet and theater attracted the youngest audiences of the perform-ing arts, with medians of 33 and 34 respectively, while opera and sym-phony drew the oldest, with median ages of 41 and 40. The median age for science-museum visitor populations was two years lower than that for art-museum visitors (median age of 31) and four years lower than for history-museum visitors (median age of 33).

Most of the surveys analyzed had studied only people over a certain age. Surprisingly, however, there were no systematic differences between the findings of studies that restricted their sample populations and those that did not. We suspect that many studies either formally or in practice excluded young responders without reporting that they did so. Furthermore, it would appear that, except for science and history museums, individuals under the age of sixteen usually represent a negligible percentage of arts audiences.

Age composition appears to vary systematically by season, with younger visitors and attenders attracted during the summer, although this variation is not universal (National Research Center of the Arts, 1976b; O'Hare, 1974). Age composition may also vary by performance time: median ages for weekend evening performances were consistently lower than for matinees or weekday evenings (National Research Center of the Arts, 1976a, b, c). Finally the type of program also appears to have an impact on audience age (Moore, 1968; National Research Center of the Arts, 1976c).

Education. The studies used categories so different that we could not always calculate medians, so it was necessary to describe audience educa-tional compositions by reporting percentages of audiences in five categories of educational attainment. Findings for each category are based on some-what different sets of audiences.

Seventy-one studies reporting findings for 108 audiences and visitor groups indicate that the well educated are overrepresented with striking consistency in arts audiences, relative to their share of the U.S. population (Table 3). The proportion of college graduates reported for arts audiences exceeded the proportion of the adult population with college diplomas in all but one of ninety-seven audiences studied; the percentage of individuals who had not completed high school was below the national level in all but one of seventy-two audiences studied. (Both exceptions are attributable to sampling of large numbers of high-school students.) In seventy-eight of eighty-three audiences for which findings are available, the proportion of attenders with at least some college training was *twice* that for the general public.

Thirty percent of the typical audience had some graduate training; a median 54 percent had acquired at least a bachelor's degree, compared to 14 percent of the national adult population. Only 22 percent of the median audience had not attended any college, compared to 74 percent of the public as a whole, and only 5 percent were not high-school graduates, in contrast to 38 percent of the adult public. Educational attainment of performing-arts audiences was found to be somewhat higher than that of museum visitors. The median percentage reported for individuals with graduate training was 31 for the performing arts and 18 for museums. The median percentage of college graduates was similarly higher in the performing arts, 56 to 41. Museums also attracted more visitors with relatively little education than did the performing arts. The median percentage of non-high-school graduates was 9 for museums and 5 for the performing arts; for individuals with no schooling past high school the median percentages were 28 for museum-visitor populations and 21 for performing-arts audiences. Some, but not all, of the discrepancy is attributable to the greater representation of young people among museum visitors.

Among the performing arts, ballet and dance audiences included even larger proportions of well-educated attenders than did other forms; theater audiences included slightly lower porportions of the well educated. Among museums, art museums attracted a more well-educated public than did history, science and other museums, though still not so well educated as audiences for the performing arts.

It is evident, then, that visitors to museums and audiences for the live performing arts are considerably more well educated than is the public at large. Within the arts, museums appear to serve a somewhat broader public than do the performing arts; nonetheless, in educational attainment, museum visitors and performing-arts audiences are far more similar to one another than is either group to the general public.

There are several reasons why the arts audience has a very high proportion of the college-educated. First, understanding most works of art requires a certain amount of familiarity and background information to undertake the decoding that leads to appreciation. As Pierre Bourdieu notes, a work of art "only exists as such for a person who has the means to appropriate it" (Bourdieu, 1968:594). Higher education provides access to an environment where the means for appropriation can be readily acquired. Second, because higher education also offers exposure to an environment where the arts are valued, a college graduate has often experienced, at least for a period, peer pressure to attend arts events. Finally, a disporportionate

TABLE 3

Percentage of Audiences in Five Educational Categories, by Art Form

Educational level

Art form	Post-BA Training[A]			At least college graduate[B]			At least some college[C]			High school graduate or less[D]			Less than high school graduate[E]		
	M[1]	R	(N)	M	R	(N)	M	R	(N)	M	R	(N)	M	R	(N)
All museums	17.5	6–35	(13)	41.1	10–66	(23)	72.3	30–93	(18)	27.6	8–69	(18)	9.0	4–57	(23)
Art museums	22.0	18–35	(5)	48.0	41–66	(9)	83.5	75–90	(6)	17.0	10–25	(6)	5.5	4–16	(8)
Other museums[2]	13.5	6–20	(8)	34.4	10–53	(14)	59.6	30–93	(12)	40.4	8–69	(12)	13.1	7–57	(14)
All perform. arts[3]	32.0	9–66	(42)	61.8	23–67	(53)	83.0	62–95	(44)	17.0	5–38	(45)	4.0	1–19	(45)
Theater[3]	32.7	20–50	(24)	58.0	23–80	(27)	82.7	66–93	(25)	17.1	8–44	(26)	4.0	1–15	(21)
Classical music	37.5	21–36	(8)	63.0	46–87	(9)	83.4	63–95	(8)	14.6	5–37	(8)	1.7	1–19	(8)
Ballet and dance[4]	45.5	20–50	(5)	65.0	55–73	(10)	87.1	77–92	(5)	12.9	8–23	(5)	3.0	1–5	(10)
Opera	37.3	29–49	(5)	61.8	49–75	(7)	83.0	67–94	(6)	18.8	7–33	(6)	4.1	2–7	(6)

Museums and perform.
arts[5] 30.0 6–66 (73) 54.0 10–87 (97) 78.0 30–95 (83) 22.0 5–69 (84) 5.0 1–57 (72)

U.S. population over 24
years of age, 1975 n.a.   13.9   26.3   73.7   37.5

1. M = median percentage; R = range of percentages; N = number of studies.
2. Includes science, history, natural history, anthropology, and general museums.
3. Excludes audiences of outdoor dramas.
4. Dance audience percentages available only for two educational levels—at least college graduate and less than high school graduate.
5. Number of studies exceeds sum of other categories due to inclusion of regional studies reporting attendance of all, undifferentiated art forms.

   A. Includes those with at least some post-B.A. training.
   B. Includes those who are at least college graduates as well as those with post-B.A. training.
   C. Includes those who had at least some college as well as those who were college graduates and those who had post-B.A. training.
   D. Includes those who were high school graduates as well as those who were less than high school graduates.
   E. Includes only those who were less than high school graduates.

number of men and women who acquire a higher education have parents who are also well educated. Children of the well educated are more likely than others to have been exposed to the arts when they were young, and this early socialization persists into adulthood (Andreasen and Belk, 1978; Cober, 1977).

Occupation. As with educational attainment, occupational categories used in the studies varied widely and were often vague. We thus designed categories to be compatible with as many study findings as possible, and comparable to the classifications used by the U.S. Census. In some cases, categories were merged to fit our classificatory system; where study results could not be reliably altered to fit our system, they were omitted. Our findings for each occupational category, then, are based on somewhat different sets of audiences. Finally, because many studies reported occupation by percentages of total respondents, it was necessary to recompute the distributions and use employed respondents only.

Analysis of data from fifty-nine studies of ninety-six audiences indicates that arts audiences are dominated by individuals in high-status occupations. Professionals, who constituted 15 percent of the employed civilian labor force in 1975, composed a median 56 percent of employed persons in the arts audiences (Table 4). Conversely, blue-collar workers were conspicuous by their absence, a mere 4 percent of employed respondents in the arts audiences, as compared to 34 percent of the employed civilian labor force as a whole.

The marked overrepresentation of professionals was strikingly consistent throughout the studies. Professionals were present in percentages greater than their share of the population in every one of sixty-five arts audiences for which appropriate data were reported: in all but four of these, their share was twice their percentage of the work force; in 46 of 65, it was three times the national figure; and in more than a quarter of the audiences, they were overrepresented by a factor of four. (It is even possible that professionals, as defined by the United States Census, may have been underreported, since many studies provided residual "white-collar" categories in which some lower-status professionals may have included themselves rather than within the "professional" category itself.)

Proportions of professionals were significantly higher in audiences for performing arts than in attendance at museums (59 to 42 percent), primarily because of the relatively low medians of professionals attending non-art museums (Table 5). In six art-museum studies the median attendance by professionals was 59 percent, the same as for the performing arts, while in eleven studies of other museums the median attendance by professionalswas 42 percent. Aside from the non-art-museum category, findings were remarkably uniform among art forms, ranging from 56 percent for theater to 61 percent for classical music audiences.

TABLE 4
Occupational Distribution of Audiences

Occupation[1]	Percentage of employed labor force (1975)[2]	Median percentage of employed respondents in arts audience	
		%	(N)[3]
Professionals	15.0	55.9	(65)
Teachers	4.1	22.1	(22)
Artists, writers, entertainers	1.0	8.2	(8)
Managerial	10.5	14.9	(51)
Clerical/Sales	24.2	14.6	(41)
Service	14.1	3.7	(13)
Blue-Collar	33.6	3.7	(71)

	Percentage of US population aged 16 or over[2]	Median percentage of all respondents in arts audience	
		%	(N)
Homemakers	23.1	14.0	(78)
Students	5.5	18.0	(80)
Retired, unemployed	11.2	4.5	(65)

1. Census categories and audience categories are only approximately comparable due to varying classification schemes used in arts audience studies.
2. Source: U.S. Bureau of the Census, *Statistical Abstracts, 1976*. Washington, D.C.: U.S. Govt. Printing Office, 1976; U.S. Bureau of Labor Statistics, *Handbook of Labor Statistics, 1976*. Washington, D.C.: USGPO, 1976. Figures for U.S. population aged 16 or over excludes military personnel.
3. Number of audience studies reporting information for this category.

One group of professionals—teachers, including college and university faculty—constituted 21 percent of the twenty-two arts audiences for which findings were available, with a median 18 percent for performing arts and 23 percent for museums. This latter figure is more than five times the percentage of teachers in the employed civilian work force (4 percent).

Managers—defined to include respondents in 'business' and 'executive' categories used in some studies—composed 15 percent of employed respondents in the median of fifty-one audiences for which percentages were reported. In contrast, managers make up 11 percent of the employed work force. The median proportion of managers among performing-arts

TABLE 5
Occupational Distribution of Audiences, by Art Form

Occupation[1]

Art Form	Professional/ Managerial			Professional Only			Teachers			Managerial Only			Clerical & Sales		
	M	R	(N)	M	R	(N)	M	R	(N)	M	R	(N)	M	R	(N)
All museums	65.3	27–96	(32)	42.2	12–73	(17)	23.1	15–33	(6)	9.6	4–27	(14)	14.3	5–28	(23)
Art museums	77.1	56–96	(16)	59.2	31–74	(6)	23.1	15–33	(5)	9.0	4–27	(6)	14.3	4–22	(14)
Other museums	53.2	27–72	(16)	41.9	12–50	(11)	—	—	—	10.2	6–22	(8)	16.0	5–28	(9)
All perform. arts	70.9	49–95	(42)	59.1	24–80	(44)	17.9	6–33	(16)	15.6	4–27	(33)	18.0	8–33	(15)
Ballet and dance	74.6	61–88	(9)	59.6	55–73	(8)	—	—	—	15.2	7–22	(7)	—	—	—
Theater	69.5	49–95	(23)	56.3	23–70	(25)	17.9	6–33	(7)	16.0	4–27	(20)	19.7	8–29	(10)
Orchestra	75.5	64–87	(5)	61.1	50–80	(6)	—	—	—	—	—	—	—	—	—
Opera	—	—	—	58.3	50–70	(5)	—	—	—	—	—	—	—	—	—

Occupation

	Blue-Collar			Homemakers			Students			Retired & Unemployed		
	M	R	(N)	M	R	(N)	M	R	(N)	M	R	(N)
All museums	8.5	0–45	(35)	14.5	6–26	(24)	22.0	0–57	(25)	5.0	1–21	(21)
Art museums	3.1	0–12	(16)	13.0	7–22	(9)	22.5	0–40	(10)	8.0	3–21	(9)
Other museums	16.7	4–45	(19)	15.8	6–26	(15)	20.0	10–57	(15)	3.3	1–9	(12)
All perform. arts	2.8	0–27	(34)	14.0	5–52	(51)	17.1	5–63	(51)	3.9	0–16	(40)
Ballet and dance	2.7	1–7	(10)	11.1	6–32	(10)	15.0	9–34	(10)	3.0	1–5	(9)
Theater	2.9	0–27	(15)	14.0	5–52	(27)	18.9	5–63	(27)	4.2	0–16	(24)
Orchestra	—	—	—	19.0	5–26	(7)	18.0	7–31	(7)	—	—	—
Opera	2.8	1–13	(6)	16.2	8–40	(6)	10.7	7–23	(6)	—	—	—

1. The "professional/managerial" and "professional only" categories include teachers. The percentages for "homemakers," "students," and "retired/unemployed" are based on all respondents; the percentages for the other categories are based on employed respondents only. Percentages are not reported when fewer than five studies are available.

audiences (16) was higher than their representation among museum visitors (9 and 10 percent for art and other museums, respectively). The finding that managers are overrepresented in arts audiences to a far lesser degree than are professionals points toward the applicability in the United States of Bourdieu's thesis, developed with French data, that "cultural capital" (educational credentials and familiarity with elite culture) is of special value for the upward mobility strategies of professional groups (Bourdieu, 1973; Bourdieu *et al.*, 1974).

Since a number of research reports included professionals and managers in a single category, we also merged these categories in the other studies we assembled, to provide a more consistent, if rough, index of the representation of individuals in elite occupations among the audiences surveyed. Among employed respondents, the median percentage of professionals and managers in seventy-seven arts audiences for which data were available was 71 percent, more than two and a half times this group's share of the employed work force as a whole (26 percent). Their median percentages among audiences for the performing arts ranged from 70 percent for theater to 76 percent for classical music. The median managerial/professional percentage for art museums was 77 percent, higher than for any of the performing arts; the percentage for other museums was 53 percent, lower than for any of the performing arts.

If managers and professionals were present in numbers modestly higher than their share of the U.S. population, clerical and sales personnel composed a somewhat smaller percentage of audiences than their share of the work force. The median representation of clerks and salespeoples among employed respondents in the forty-one audiences for which data were available was 15 percent, while they constitute 24 percent of the employed civilian work force. Their median for attending the performing arts (18 percent) was higher than for visiting museums (14 percent).

As striking as the overrepresentation of professionals was the virtual absence of blue-collar workers from the audiences surveyed. In the seventy-one audiences for which data were available, blue-collar workers comprised a median 4 percent. That the median is even this high is due to the inclusion of nineteen studies of visitors to museums other than art museums, which reported a much higher median blue-collar participation of 17 percent. The median blue-collar share of performing-arts audiences was only 2.8 percent and blue-collar representation among art-museum visitors was a median 3.1 percent. Excluding visitors to non-art museums, the proportion of blue-collar workers in thirty-four of fifty-two arts audiences for which percentages were reported was *less than one tenth* of their share of the employed civilian work force. In only nine audiences was it as high as two fifths. Among art forms, blue-collar percentages were remarkably consistent: 2.7 percent for ballet and dance; 2.8 percent for opera; 2.9 percent for theater; and 3.1 percent for art museums.

The presence of three other groups—students, "homemakers," and retired and unemployed persons—was also analyzed. Homemakers constituted a median 14 percent of the seventy-eight audiences for which data were available, although they made up 23 percent of the over-sixteen civilian population in 1975. Students were sharply overrepresented: only 6 percent of the over-sixteen civilian population as a whole were students, but students constituted 18 percent of the median of eighty audiences with available data. Attendance of both groups varied greatly from audience to audience. Finally, the median percentage of retired and unemployed persons (usually reported as a single category) in sixty-five audiences for which appropriate data were available, was 5 percent, as compared to their 11 percent of the civilian over-sixteen population in 1975.

Occupations with the highest rates of attendance were also those with the highest educational attainment. Occupations may have a special influence on attendance because there are occupational and professional status-cultures in which familiarity with the arts is valued and encouraged (Parkin, 1974). That the relationship between occupation and attendance would be even more striking if finer occupational categories were available is indicated both by the findings for teachers in this study and by the work of Wilensky (1964), who found systematic differences in cultural taste between independent lawyers and those employed by law firms.

Income. Income data were available for eighty-eight audiences for museums and the performing arts. It proved possible to compare the various studies if we transformed categorical reports of audience percentages in different income ranges into median incomes for each audience, then used the consumer price index to transform all medians into constant mid-1976 dollars.

The median income for seventy performing-arts audiences was $18,983, approximately $4,500 above that of the public as a whole (Table 6). When audiences for eighteen outdoor dramas with patriotic and religious themes were omitted, the median income for the performing-arts audiences rose to $20,250. Among the performing arts, median incomes were lowest for theater audiences ($16,819 including outdoor dramas; $19,342 excluding them) and highest for opera audiences ($21,024). Excluding the eighteen outdoor-drama surveys, only three of fifty-three performing-arts audiences reported an income median below that of the general public.

The median income for museum visitors was $17,158, and ranged from $16,757 for history museums to $18,148 for art museums. Visitors to museums, then, appear to be significantly more affluent than the general public and significantly less affluent than performing-arts attenders. Among the

TABLE 6
Median Income[1] of Audiences, by Art Form

Art Form	Median of medians	Range of median	(N)
All museums	17,158	13,394–30,618	(18)
Art museums	18,148	14,016–30,618	(10)
History museums	16,757	13,394–29,005	(3)
Science museums	17,269	14,765–20,851	(5)
All performing arts	18,903	9,466–28,027	(70)
Ballet and dance	20,082	16,452–22,404	(10)
Theater			
Excluding outdoor drama	19,342	9,469–25,784	(27)
Including outdoor drama	16,819	9,466–25,784	(45)
Orchestra	20,825	18,221–28,027	(11)
Opera	21,024	19,017–27,245	(6)

Median family income, U.S. population

1960	10,778
1970	14,431
1975	14,476

1. In constand mid-1976 dollars.

many factors responsible for this finding, which was drawn from a small set of reports, are the generally lower admissions charged by museums and their greater appeal to students and young people, particulary parents with young children.

Racial and Ethnic Minorities. That there are usually few blacks and other racial and ethnic minorities in arts audiences has been commented on frequently and, indeed, has been a matter of some concern to the arts community. In 1972, the American Association of Museums called attention to the problem of making museums relevant and hospitable to inner-city and minority people, noting that the movement of many segments of the middle class to the suburbs and of lower-class blacks, Mexican-Americans and Puerto Ricans to the core city "have left the museum, an urban institution, to some extent a beached whale. . . . " (American Association of Museums, 1972:6). Museums have not been alone in recognizing this dilemma. Recently, the Kennedy Center for the Performing Arts formed a special committee to find out why so few of Washington's many black residents attend the Center's events.

Minorities were, indeed, underrepresented in most of the relatively few audiences for which data on race were acquired in the studies we reviewed. While blacks constituted 12.3 percent of the total urban population in 1970, they represented a median 3 percent of the fifteen arts audiences for which data were available. Minorities—blacks, orientals, and persons of Spanish origin—accounted for a median 7 percent of the 35 audiences for which figures were reported, although they are over 20 percent of the population as a whole. In a number of studies outside the west coast and southwest, individuals of Spanish origin were not separated from the white population, thus depressing the minority total. We surmise, however, from the few studies in these areas doing separate counts, that Hispanic people generally account for a very small percentage of the audience and that their exclusion depresses the minority median by no more than 1 percent.

The median minority percentage for thirteen audiences for the performing arts was 7, and for eleven sets of art-museum visitors it was 7 as well. As with other socioeconomic dimensions, visitor populations of museums other than art museums included a broader cross-section of the public; for eleven sets of visitors to such museums the median minority percentage is 11.

Such overall figures should be interpreted cautiously because of the small number of audiences studied, variation in the definition of minority and, above all, the large variation in the proportion of members of different minority groups in different locales. The set of studies reviewed here, for example, contains data from the Washington, D.C. area (where blacks composed 24.6 percent of the metropolitan population in 1970) and from Washington State (where only just over one in fifty persons was black). Similarly, persons of Spanish origin represent a substantial portion of the populations of Los Angeles and New York City (15.0 and 11.1 percent, respectively), but are a much less significant presence in such places as Boston or Montgomery, Alabama. For this reason, a selected comparison can be useful. For instance, in thirteen of the fourteen audiences for which there were data on black attenders and comparable census data, blacks were underrepresented relative to their numbers in the local population by ratios of up to eighteen-to-one. In five studies of museums in the San Francisco area, where blacks composed 10.6 percent of the metropolitan population in 1970, the highest black proportion was only 3 percent (Schwartz, 1971; Colvin, 1976; McElroy and Bellow, 1975; deYoung Memorial Museum, n.d.a., n.d.b.). In two New York City audiences, blacks represented 3 and 4 percent of attenders, in contrast to over 16 percent of the metropolitan population (National Research Center of the Arts, 1976c, 1977).

While the existing data do not permit a definitive assessment—for example, no surveys of museums or performing-arts companies appealing predominantly to minority-group members were available—it seems likely that blacks and other minorities are generally sharply underrepresented in performing-arts audiences and among museum visitors, relative to their share of the population. This is not in itself surprising, since a higher percentage of minorities than whites are very young, poor, without college educations, and/or employed in blue-collar or service occupations—all categories with disproportionately low participation in arts audiences. Although existing data do not permit an assessment, it is likely that poverty and lack of education, rather than cultural factors or minority exclusion, are largely responsible for the low level of minority arts attendance.

Audience Structure

Available evidence suggests that the arts audience has a core group who frequently attend a variety of events, and various peripheral groups who occasionally sample only a single art form. Those near the center constitute active arts social circles; friendship and acquaintanceship are formed around a shared interest in the arts, cultural events are central topics of informal discussion and exchange, and there is a strong expectation of high attendance at, and knowledge of, the arts. Several studies report that frequent attenders are more likely than infrequent visitors to hear about arts events through their social networks, to count cultural consumers among their friends and to indicate that arts attendance is fashionable in their social milieu (Beldo, 1956; David, 1977; National Research Center of the Arts, 1975a, b, c).

Those most often among the arts audience are also usually those with more education. Sixteen audience studies in our possession examined the relationship between frequency of attendance and education, and all sixteen found that regular visitors are more highly educated than irregular visitors for both museums and the performing arts. A cross-sectional study of California residents, for instance, found that of those who had not visited a museum during the past year, 7 percent held a college degree or more; of the infrequent museum visitors (one to five times), 18 percent were college educated; and of the frequent visitors (more than five times), 31 percent held college degrees. The corresponding figures for the performing arts are 7, 18 and 43 percent, respectively (National Research Center for the Arts, 1975b).

Those at the center of the arts audience also tend to have higher incomes than those at the periphery, though the evidence here is less clearcut than for education. Thirteen of seventeen studies with relevant data report higher incomes for frequent attenders than for infrequent attenders, but one study revealed no difference and three indicated the reverse (the three latter audiences were for ballet or dance.)

It is not clear whether frequency of attendance is associated with gender and age. Four studies reported that frequent attenders had a higher proportion of men, six a lower porportion of men, and two studies found no difference. Similarly, six studies concluded that frequent attenders were older than infrequent visitors, three found the opposite, and two reported no age difference.

To summarize the unambiguous trends: the social composition of the arts audience is far more elite than the general public, and the center of the audience is more elite than its periphery. Education and, to a lesser degree, income are good predictors not only of who consumes the arts but of the intensity of their consumption.

Trends Toward Democratization

Our overall findings clearly indicate that in this country the public for the visual and live performing arts is distinctly elite in level of education, occupation, income, and in race. The statistics we were able to summarize from the many studies reviewed show little indication of cultural democracy. But it seemed at least possible that the aggregation of all the studies might be disguising a trend toward greater involvement of poorly represented groups, as the "cultural boom" has continued in recent years. To see if such a trend is present, we have evaluated audience composition data at several different time periods between 1960 and 1976. Since relatively few of our studies were conducted during the 1960s, studies have been grouped into several-year spans so that each period includes at least six audience studies (with the exception of one period for the data on education). Few museum studies were available for some periods, so analysis is limited to the performing arts. It should be cautioned that the pre-1965 studies included a number conducted by Baumol and Bowen (1966). These studies yielded social profiles significantly more elite than those of other audience surveys undertaken at that time. Since relatively few other early studies are available, the Baumol and Bowen surveys (between eight and thirteen, depending on the social characteristic) dominate the mid- and early-1960s audience composition figures.

Gender. The proportion of men in the performing-arts audience evidences little change over time, though there is a slight drop in recent years (Table 7). Excluding the earliest period examined (pre-1966), the median

TABLE 7
Time Trends in the Gender, Age, Education, Occupation and Income Composition of Performing Arts Audiences

Social Character and Time Period	Median of medians	Range of median	(N)
Gender: percent men			
1960–65	56	45–58	(10)
1966–69	48	32–54	(7)
1970–71	42	36–51	(11)
1972–73	45	33–54	(11)
1974–75	37	35–43	(9)
1976	39	34–54	(13)
Age: median age			
1960–67	37	33–45	(9)
1968–70	36	24–46	(6)
1971–72	41	34–42	(8)
1973	30	21–35	(11)
1974	36	22–43	(8)
1975	38	29–48	(12)
1976	33	21–45	(18)
Education: percent with college degree or more			
1960–66	72	61–86	(14)
1967–72	47	21–66	(15)
1973	63	55–65	(6)
1974	67	54–74	(4)
1975	57	48–65	(7)
1976	65	34–78	(13)
Occupation: percent professional/technical			
1960–69	65	48–80	(11)
1970–74	67	50–63	(10)
1975–78	59	24–73	(20)
percent blue-collar worker			
1960–69	2.4	1–5	(8)
1970–74	2.8	0–5	(14)
1975–76	3.0	1–7	(11)
Income: 1976 dollars			
1960–67	23,407	19,342–28,027	(11)
1967–70	19,017	16,819–25,229	(10)
1971–73	19,684	9,466–27,245	(12)
1974–75	18,983	15,292–23,202	(7)
1976	20,004	14,003–21,004	(11)

percentages of men in the five successive periods between 1966 and 1976 are 46, 42, 45, 37 and 39. However, in all periods except one (1974–1975) the percentage of men varies from the low 30s to the low 50s, indicating that there is far more variation in gender composition from event to event than between time periods.

Age. There is no indication of any trend toward younger audiences. The median ages of audiences in six successive periods since 1967 are 36, 41, 30, 36, 38 and 33. Within the time periods, the median ages differed from study by 8 to 24 years.

Education. The proportion of the performing arts audience with at least a college education did not decline over time. The fourteen studies in the earliest time period (1960–1966) report a median figure of 72 percent for the college educated; the fifteen studies of the following period (1967–1972) indicate a median percentage of 47; and the surveys conducted in the next four one-year periods report median percentages of 63, 67, 57 and 65. While the education level appears to fluctuate considerably between the first three time periods, much if not most of the change reflects special features of the studies conducted during these periods. Thirteen of fourteen pre-1967 studies were executed by Baumol and Bowen, while seven of fifteen studies during the 1967–1972 period were conducted on audiences of university productions. (None of the post-1972 studies were of campus audiences.)

Occupation. Using two indices of the occupational composition of performing arts audiences—the percentages of professional/technical workers and blue-collar workers—it is evident that little change has occurred over the past seventeen years. Professionals and technicians constituted 65 percent of the audience in the 1960s, 57 percent during the 1970–1974 period, and 59 percent in 1975–1976; the blue-collar shares of the audience were 2.4, 2.8 and 3.0 percent, respectively.

Income. Income trends mirror those reported for the other social indicators. The median of the median audience income for the 1967–1970 period was $19,017 (in constant mid-1976 dollars). For the three following periods the median income stood at $19,684, $18,983 and $20,004, respectively. The average income for 1960–1967 was recorded at $23,407, but again this is almost entirely based on the Baumol and Bowen surveys of prominent performing-arts audiences. It is again notable that the median incomes reported for audience studies within a time period vary far more than do the averages between the periods.

Our data, then, do not reveal any striking changes in the composition of the audience over the past one and one-half decades. It should be cautioned, however, that the heterogeneity of the audience studies evaluated here may have concealed various subtler trends. For example, if audiences for one art form were becoming increasingly male while audiences for another were including greater percentages of women, such a change would not be discernable in our data. Similarly, if theater audiences in major cities were becoming more diverse, while theater audiences in smaller cities and suburbs were becoming less so, no change would be observed. Also, if pre-1960 data had been available, they might have revealed that, although the past one and one-half decades have seen little change, longer-range changes in audience composition have occurred. Finally, it should be remembered that while the overall composition appears static in recent years, important short-range trends could exist in other elements of audience structure. An increase in arts activity outside of major cities and the more frequent touring of arts organizations in outlying areas may mean, for instance, that the upper-middle and upper class in non-metropolitan areas now have more access to the arts than ever before.

Barriers to Democratization

The studies reviewed here consistently indicated that the audience for the visual and live performing arts are more well educated, of higher occupational standing, and more affluent than the general populace. The strong relationship between education and attendance, the extreme over-representation of professionals and managers, and the virtual absence of blue-collar workers was particularly striking. Moreover, cultural democratization (if defined as increasing representation of nonelites among visitors to museums and performing arts events) does not seem to be occurring, despite arguments to the contrary, outreach efforts of some arts administrators and a degree of pressure from those responsible for public funding of the arts (see DiMaggio and Useem, 1978b). The absence of discernable democratization suggests that there may be formidable barriers to any effort to open up the arts.

Although we cannot analyze these barriers here, we can suggest that they are related both to elite resistance to democratization and to entry problems facing nonelites. Elite resistance exists because, as Veblen perceived, arts events, aside from their aesthetic value, provide opportunities for reaffirmation of elite social and cultural cohesion. Participation in the world of the arts may be particularly crucial for the upper-middle class, the group whose status is most marginal to the elite, in that arts consumption provides this group with opportunity for symbolic identification with the upper class and may even yield socially useful contacts. Moreover, as Bourdieu has argued, cultural capital, both in formal education and in refined aesthetic taste, can serve as a useful medium for the transmission of elite position from generation to generation. By instilling cultivated aesthetic tastes and providing support for advanced university training, elite families endow their offspring with cultural capital that can be converted into social standing and economic position in later life (Bourdieu, 1973; Bourdieu *et al.*, 1974; Bourdieu and Boltanski, 1977; DiMaggio and Useem, 1978a). Thus, it is not surprising that some elites resist efforts to democratize the arts, for diversifying the audience can only undermine the social value of the arts for elite standing and cohesion.

At the same time, those outside the upper and upper-middle classes face important impediments to attendance, whatever the degree of opposition to their involvement by elites. These barriers include: lack of information about arts events and motivation to attend; relative lack of the training needed to ensure appreciation of and familiarity with the arts; relative unfamiliarity and often discomfort with the social conventions of the contexts in which the arts are presented; and lack of access to cultural brokers—artists, dealers and critics—who define changes in artistic taste and standards (DiMaggio and Useem, 1978a).

Whatever their precise forms, a topic itself deserving careful inquiry, the result of the existence of such barriers is that the cultural resources considered here are very inequitably distributed; and there is no clear evidence that they are becoming less so, despite the expansion of large-scale public support for cultural activities. For those concerned with the nature of the constituency served by arts organizations increasingly supported by public money, our findings imply that a highly unrepresentative constituency has been, and continues to be, the primary beneficiary. There are no signs that the democratization of arts funding is bringing a democratization of arts consumption. It is possible, of course, that more aggressive "outreach" programs, the allocation of additional monies to community-based and participatory-oriented arts activities, and greater attention to the arts in school programs may ultimately help broaden the arts public.

For those concerned with the broader role the arts may play in American society, dominance of arts audiences by members of the upper-middle and upper classes, evident in the overall portrait we were able to sketch here, clearly suggests that the arts play a significant role in defining class boundaries. Whatever the particular social barriers and differences in aesthetic taste involved in elite dominance may be, their existence (and persistence) also suggest that, like the education system, the arts are important in preserving class standing in the local community from generation to generation. Presently available evidence at least suggests that Veblen's predictions about the most probable relationship between art and democracy are still more accurate than those of Tocqueville.

Notes

1. We are grateful to Paula Brown for research assistance, to Jane Gallup for typing, administrative assistance, and editorial suggestions, to the National Endowment for the Arts for financial support, and to the Center for the Study of Public Policy for institutional support. We also want to thank Richard A. Peterson, Richard Scotch, and two anonymous reviewers for valuable comments on an earlier draft. This was a fully collaborative effort and the authors' names are in arbitrary order. The interpretations offered are the authors' and do not necessarily reflect the views of the individuals and organizations acknowledged. Reprinted with the permission of the authors and the publisher of Social Problems (vol. 26 (1978)

2. "Elite" is used here to refer to the upper class and upper-middle class. The upper class comprises those who own or manage large business firms, as well as families with substantial wealth. The upper-middle class primarily consists of those who are highly educated and whose work involves the manipulation of knowledge and information (e.g., lawyers, physicians, journalists, teachers, scientists). The concept of "cultural democracy" has also been ascribed to a specific and somewhat limited meaning in this paper. It refers here only to the social composition of those who visit museums and attend performing arts events. Issues involving control over the production of culture and the management of arts organizations, as well as the consumption of culture transmitted in other forms, are beyond the scope of the present paper.

3. A complete bibliography of the studies can be found in DiMaggio, Useem and Brown, 1978.

References

Abbey, D. S. and Duncan F. Cameron 1960. *The Museum Visitor: II—Survey Results.* Toronto: Royal Ontario Museum.

American Association of Museums 1972. *Museums: Their New Audience.* Washington, D.C.

Andreasen, Alan R. and Russell W. Belk 1978. "Consumer response to arts offerings: A study of theater and symphony in four southern cities." In David Cwi (ed.), *Research in the Arts.* Baltimore: Walters Art Gallery.

Baumol, William and William Bowen 1966. *The Performing Arts: The Economic Dilemma.* Cambridge: The M.I.T. Press.

Beldo, Les 1956. *A Report of Three Surveys: A State-wide Survey Conducted by the Minnesota Poll, Minneapolis Star and Tribune: An In-concert Survey and a Personal Interview Survey Both Conducted by Mid-Continent Surveys,* Minneapolis, Minnesota. March 12. Minneapolis: Campbell-Mithun.

Book, S. H. and S. Globerman 1975. *The Audience for the Performing Arts: A Study of Attendance Patterns in Ontario.* Toronto: Ontario Arts Council.

Bordieu, Pierre 1968. ''Outline of a sociological theory of art perception.'' *International Social Science Journal* 20(4):589–612.

——— 1973. ''Cultural reproduction and social reproduction.'' In Richard Brown (ed.), *Knowledge, Education, and Cultural Change.* London: Tavistock.

Bourdieu, Pierre and Luc Boltanski 1977. ''Changes in social structure and changes in the demand for education.'' Unpublished manuscript.

Bourdieu, Pierre, Luc Boltanski and Monique de Saint Martin 1974. ''Les strategies de reconversion.'' *Social Science Information* 12(5):61–113.

Brustein, Robert 1977. ''Whither the arts and humanities endowments'' *New York Times,* December 19.

Cober, Rodney L. 1977. ''A psychographic life style analysis of intergenerational continuity in the development of the rural theatre audience.'' Master's thesis, Pennsylvania State University.

Colvin, Clair 1976. *A Membership Study of the Fine Arts Museums of San Francisco and the Asian Art Museum.* San Francisco: Fine Arts Museums of San Francisco.

Cultural Post 1976. ''Estimated growth in selected cultural fields: 1965–1975.'' May/June: 16.

David, Deborah S. 1977. ''The ballet audience: One group or three?'' Unpublished manuscript.

deYoung, M. H., Memorial Museum n.d.a. *Acoustiguide Survey Final Talley.* San Francisco.

——— n.d.b *American Art: An Exhibition from the Collection of Mr. and Mrs. John D. Rockefeller 3rd.* San Francisco.

DiMaggio, Paul and Michael Useem 1978a. ''Social class and arts consumption: The origins and consequences of class differences in exposure to the arts in America.'' *Theory and Society* 5(March):141–161.

——— 1978b. ''Cultural property and public policy: Emerging tensions in government support for the arts.'' *Social Research* 45(Summer):356–389.

DiMaggio, Paul, Michael Useem and Paula Brown 1978. *Audience Studies of the Performing Arts and Museums: A Critical Review.* Washington, D.C.: Research Division, National Endowment for the Arts.

Gans, Herbert 1974. *Popular Culture and High Culture: An Analysis and Evaluation of Taste.* New York: Basic Books.

Johnson, David A. 1969. ''Museum attendance in the New York Metropolitan Region.'' *Curator* 12(3):201–230.

Leo Burnett. U.S.A. 1975. *The Art Institute Survey.* Chicago: Research Department, Leo Burnett U.S.A., November 5.

McElroy, Guy and Cleveland Bellow 1975. *Museum Audience Survey, 1974–75.* San Francisco: M. H. deYoung Memorial Museum.

Moore, Thomas Gale 1968. ''The audience.'' Chapter 5 in Thomas Gale Moore, *The Economics of the American Theater.* Durham, N.C.: Duke University Press.

Ms. Magazine 1977. ''How the arts boom will affect you.'' November. National Committee for Cultural Resources 1975. National Report on the Arts. New York.

National Endowment for the Arts 1978. *The State Arts Agencies in 1974: All Present and Accounted For.* Washington, D.C.: Research Division, National Endowment for the Arts.

National Research Center of the Arts 1975a. *Americans and the Arts: A Survey of Public Opinion.* New York: Associated Councils of the Arts.

———— 1975b. *Californians and the Arts: A Survey of Public Attitudes toward and Participation in the Arts and Culture in the State of California.* New York.

———— 1975c. *Anchorage, Alaska: Public Perspective on the Arts and Culture; Report on a Survey Conducted for Anchorage Arts Council.* New York.

———— 1976a. *A Study of Washingtonians' Attendance at Performing Arts Events and Museums.* New York.

———— 1976b. *The New York Cultural Consumer.* New York: New York Foundation for the Arts.

———— 1976c. *The Joffrey Ballet Audience: A Survey of the Spring 1976 Season at the City Center Theater.* New York.

———— 1977. *A Profile of Consumer Use and Evaluation: The American Museum of Natural History; Based on a Survey of Attendance July 1974–July 1975.* New York: American Museum of Natural History.

Netzer, Dick 1978. *The Subsidized Muse: Public Support for the Arts in the U.S.* New York: Cambridge University Press.

New York State Education Department and Janus Museums Consultants, Ltd. 1968. *The 1966 Audience of the New York State Museum: An Evaluation of the Museum's Visitors Program.* Albany: University of the State of New York, State Education Department, Division of Evaluation.

O'Hare, Michael 1974. ''The audience of the Museum of Fine Arts.'' *Curator* 17(2):126–159.

Parkin, Frank 1974. ''Strategies of social closure in class formation.'' In Frank Parkin (ed.), *The Social Analysis of Class Structure.* London: Tavistock.

Schwartz, Steve 1971. *Results of Survey of Oakland Museum Visitors.* Oakland: Oakland Museum.

Theatre Communications Group 1967. *Toward a New Audience: A Report on a Continuing Workshop in Audience Development.* New York.

Tocqueville, Alexis de 1956. *Democracy in America.* New York: New American Library.

Toffler, Alvin 1965. *The Culture Consumers.* Baltimore: Penguin Books.

Veblen, Thorstein 1899. *The Theory of the Leisure Class: An Economic Study in the Evaluation of Institutions.* New York: Macmillan.

Wilensky, Harold L. 1964. ''Mass society and mass culture: Interdependence or independence?'' *American Sociological Review* 29(2):173–197.

Part III

Patrons, Gatekeepers, and Critics

Historically, the connections between artists and a wealthy elite have made artistic development possible while at the same time have bestowed prestige on elites, thereby legitimizing their powerful roles. From the time of antiquity, whenever a group accumulates wealth, power and leisure, it demands outward symbols of its position (Read, 1966:70; Veblen, 1953). Art historians, including Berenson (1957), Gombrich (1956), and Male (1949), have emphasized how this relationship between artists and their patrons has helped to foster high standards, canons of good taste, and good art. This is undoubtedly true. But at the same time, patronage was—and in many respects, remains—a good investment.

Owning art or supporting the arts is what Bourdieu (1980; Bourdieu and Passeron, 1979) terms "cultural capital," for it is an investment that has profound symbolic significance for status and prestige. Cultural capital transforms the elementary power of wealth into acceptable forms of social dominance and class standing and lends legitimacy to economic, political, and social power. Moreover, an investment in art serves as a means of class cohesion, marking off members of those with economic resources (to amass art collections, commission buildings, or generously endow art institutions) from those without such resources. It is also a means of transmitting social rank from one generation to the next. Whether patronage has benefited the arts most, or has benefited the standing of the elites most, is a controversy that will probably never be settled. One would have to conclude that patronage, historically, benefited both, especially at times when great concentrations of wealth accompanied an emphasis on personal creation, as it did during the Renaissance and the Enlightenment. Yet, the patronage system by no means fostered a democratic art, as artists traditionally served an exclusive few. It is not, moreover, an exaggeration to argue that the popular and folk arts developed largely independently of the elite arts, except when they were promoted by ruling classes to appease the masses or divert revolutionary sentiments (for example, Roman circuses and Black field music).

Nevertheless, traditional patronage by nobles and the Church was gradually transformed and completely altered by the nineteenth century with the rise of capitalism and the development of new forms of production and dissemination for all products, including the arts. Complex markets developed that encompassed commercial producers, distributers, and outlets; economic agents took many forms, including entrepreneurships, corporations, and conglomerates. At the same time, technological developments, such as the radio, offset printing, and advances in the electronic and computer industries, empowered an already extraordinarily complex institutionalized base for the production and dissemination of the arts and altered significantly the nature of art consumption. These developments undermined to a considerable extent the significance of direct and simple patronage, helped some to democratize the elite arts, and broadened the appeal for the poplar and folk arts.

One consequence of these developments is that many artists now produce for an impersonal market that is governed by the laws of supply and demand. Intervening between patron or consumer and the arts are varieties of institutions and gatekeepers. For painters these include galleries, auction houses, curators, art journals, critics, and other artists, as analyzed in Chapter 9 by Bystryn and in Chapter 11 by Ridgeway. Counterparts for writers include agents, publishers, critics, and reviewers. The important role of the critic who mediates between the writer and the public is discussed by Lang (Chapter 10). Papers by DiMaggio and Useem (Chapter 8), Crane (Chapter 14), and Martorella (Chapter 17) provide useful comparisons with the articles in this section by Bystryn, Lang and Ridgeway. These various authors contribute to our understanding of how impersonal art markets and audiences tend to perpetuate the linkage between wealth (or inequalities in the social class structure) and culture. That is, they suggest that modern forms of patronage are not that dissimilar to traditional forms of elite patronage, and that art is anything but a democratic institution in contemporary society.

However, contrary to studies of markets and audiences—that is, studies of the demand for art—there is rather consistent evidence that the supply of art is supported by highly democratic forces (Blau, 1986; Blau et al., 1986). That is, cities that have relative social class equality with few extremes between the rich and the poor also tend to have a greater supply of cultural institutions of all kinds, including both commercial establishments (such as cinemas) and nonprofit institutions (such as symphony orchestras).

Generally speaking, government agencies tend to encourage democratization of the arts. Local arts councils, State art agencies, the National Endowment for the Arts all sponsor institutions that are handicapped in urban markets or overlooked by elite sponsors. Grass root policies that guided the WPA projects are also examples of this sort. Still, government

Lorenzo says you can hang them in his bank in October.

support in the United States has been erratic. With an initial budget of $2.5 million in 1976, the National Endowment for the Arts experienced considerable increases after 1970, reaching a proposed budget of $155 million in 1980, only to be halved during the Reagan administration. European governments have played a more active and direct role in the arts, through direct subsidies, purchases, and educational support. Clark (1977), for example, shows how this government role in France, accompanied with the proliferation of literacy societies and wide public support, contributes to the vitality of French literary life.

While the Bystryn and Ridgeway papers highlight the gatekeepers' roles in the visual arts, the paper by Lang provides a useful comparison for his interest in the gatekeeper's role in a commercial market. His discussion of the media and the publishing industry, of the problematic nature of the critic's identity, and of the relationship between the critic and the public can be usefully compared with the other chapters in this section, as well as with the papers by Hughes (Chapter 7), Stebbins (Chapter 12), and Kamin (Chapter 23). Taken together, these papers highlight major differences among art activities situated in commercial or popular sectors and those that are predominantly in the nonprofit sector.

References

Berenson, Bernard. 1957. *Italian Painters of the Renaissance*. Cleveland: World Publishing.

Blau, Judith R. 1986. "The Elite Arts—More or Less *de rigueur*." *Social Forces* 64:875–905.

Blau, Peter M., J. R. Blau, G. A. Quets, T. Tada. 1986. "Social Inequality and Art Institutions." *Sociological Forum* 1:561–85.

Bourdieu, Pierre. 1980. "The Artistocracy of Culture." *Media, Culture and Society* 2:225–254.

Bourdieu, Pierre and P. C. Passeron. 1979. *The Inheritors: French Students and Their Relation to Culture*. Chicago: University of Chicago Press.

Clark, Priscilla P. 1977. "Styles of Subsidy." *The French Review* 30:126–135.

Gombrich, E. H. 1966. *Norm and Form*. London: Phaidon.

Male, Emile. 1949. *Religious Art*. New York: Pantheon.

Read, Herbert. 1966. *Art and Society*. New York: Pantheon.

Veblen, Thorstein. 1953. [1899] *The Theory of the Leisure Class*. New York: Mentor.

9

Art Galleries as Gatekeepers: The Case of the Abstract Expressionists[1]

MARCIA BYSTRYN

The late 1940s and early 1950s marked the emergence of New York as the center of the international art world. There were two aspects to this development, both of which stemmed in part from the war's disruption of the European market. First, New York became the locus for those interested in buying and selling art. Second, the creation of avant-garde art shifted from Paris to New York. The first of these American avant-garde artists were the abstract expressionists. A great deal of mythologizing has gone on around the lives of these individuals. However, in order to understand their success one has to look at the market's gatekeepers, the art galleries. What was the relationship between gallery sponsorship and the development of this new style, and how was the decision made by certain galleries to promote these artists?

We can approach this question through an organizational analysis of the art market. One can conceptualize this market in terms of an industry system (Hirsch, 1972). This system is comprised of the organizations which filter the overflow of information and materials intended for the consumer, and it allows us to examine the process by which new products are filtered, on their way from producer to consumer. Implicit in this is the notion that there is an overabundance of supply. That is, there are far more artists painting than will ever be shown. As a result there is a continuing filtering-out process occurring in the through-put sector.

Innovation and Invention

Using the concept of organization set (Thompson, 1962), we can take as our focal organization the art gallery. The gallery's input sector is comprised of the community of artists striving to have their work shown. The output sector is made up of such gatekeepers as the critic and museum curator who are instrumental in this filtering process, and finally the consumer: the collector. This approach allows us to take into consideration processes which occur both within and between organizations. A basic assumption underlying this model is that uncertainty exists at both input and output ends of the organization set. Unlike the mass media, art galleries do not deploy a specialized group of contact personnel to either input or output boundaries. Attempts to stabilize the uncertain situation occur informally.

Finally, as we are interested in the market's sponsorship of the abstract expressionists, our major concern is with the manner in which this system deals with innovation and invention (see Mohr, 1969). Not only was it instrumental in bringing something new into existence (invention), through personal relationships with the artists who were developing the style of abstract expressionism, but it was also involved in bringing something new into use (innovation). That is, a market was being created for this style and for the contemporary painter.

What makes an organization conducive to innovation? Let's work with the hypothesis that this predisposition is a function of the interaction between motivation to innovate, the strength of the obstacles against innovation, and the availability of resources for overcoming these obstacles. Given this, we can ask certain questions about the organizations within the art market. Is there a motivation to innovate? We can take as indicators of motivation activism and ideology. Ideology can be measured in terms of where the organization sees its commitment. Is it to the avant-garde artist or to the patron? Does it see itself primarily as a cultural institution or an economic one? Activism refers to the extent to which the institution perceives its role as requiring interaction with others. These two factors interact with each other, and act as predictors of innovation only in conjunction with one another. An innovative ideology without activism could lead to little actual innovation, as there would be little exposure to invention. On the other hand, an organization could be high on activism but without a commitment to the avant-garde. In that case it also might never innovate.

Obstacles to innovation can occur within the organization or within its environment. An example of the former would be if the adoption of a new style were to require a new physical plant, as is true in the case of certain monumental sculpture. Obstacles in the environment would include an affluent clientele committed to a concept of collecting analogous to investing in blue-chip stocks. Resources for overcoming these obstacles, if the motivation exists, probably include size and capital. Both allow for diversification which minimizes the risks involved in innovation. When attempting to predict whether an organization is likely to innovate, all of these factors must be taken into consideration together. Lack of obstacles is not a predictor without the motivation to innovate.

One can divide the galleries involved in promoting the avant-garde American artists of the late 1940s and early 1950s into two types. These are ideal typical and differ in the following manner. Given the distinction between invention and innovation, the first type tends to foster invention in the artistic community. That is, it is more involved with the individual artist and bringing to fruition his creative potential. This includes the interchange of ideas on aesthetic questions and a dialogue over works in progress. The second type excells at innovation or rather bringing promising artists into the art market and promoting them successfully. In keeping with this, the first type tends to provide symbolic rewards to its artists while the latter type allocates out very distinct monetary rewards. One can make a distinction among galleries between those which conceive of themselves as primarily cultural institutions and those which conceive of themselves primarily as businesses. Our first type of gallery can be located within the first camp. It is concerned with fostering creativity among its artists. Our second type is more concerned with marketing a product. Individuals involved with the first type of gallery frequently are artists or would-be artists themselves, while the individuals who gravitate to the second type have business or law backgrounds and have usually had experience in promoting other products.

The two types of galleries constitute a division of labor. The first can perhaps be seen as serving a gatekeeping function for the second. This first type of gallery, through its connections with the artistic community, does an initial screening of potentially successful artists. The gallery usually gives them their first show, and provides for their initial media coverage. The relationship between the artist and dealer is usually close, and the dealer is respected for his or her artistic judgment. The second type of gallery assesses the potential marketability of the artists through exposure to the shows provided by this first type. From this set of artists, and not from the larger artistic community, those artists who are seen as having the most potential are drawn. They are then heavily promoted. As might be expected, the first type of gallery has closer ties with the artistic community while the latter has better connections with such institutions as museums.

The turnover in this first type of gallery is usually greater than in the second. New artists are continually being introduced, and it is not surprising that there is a higher percentage of artists who don't make it. The chance taken by the gallery therefore is greater. When an artist does become successful, however, he is usually more than happy to move over to a gallery of the second type, as it can be of greater help to him at this stage of his career. This second type of gallery generally has a more fixed stable. There has been a greater degree of screening before admitting an artist to the gallery, and therefore there is less chance of an artist being a financial failure. Furthermore, once an artist has made a contract with one of these galleries there is usually little reason for him to want to leave, unless there has been some sort of personal disagreement.

These two types can then be summarized in the following manner: Type one is characterized by its fostering of invention, allocation of symbolic rewards to the artist, personal ties with the artist, cultural goals, personnel who are artists themselves, and close connections with the artistic community. Type two is more involved with innovation than invention, rational economic goals, allocation of monetary rewards to the artist, business personnel, and close ties with the institutionalized art market. One can locate two galleries which serve as examples for each of these two ideal types during this crucial period for American art. Through an intensive analysis of the Betty Parsons and Sam Kootz galleries, we can get an idea of the role played by galleries in the promotion of abstract expressionism.

Betty Parsons*

A characteristic of our first type of gallery is a close personal relationship between dealer and artistic community. Betty Parsons is illustrative of this. Her relationship with art was not that of art historian, as we will see was the case with Sam Kootz. Rather her training was in studio. That is, her experience was as a practicing artist rather than as a theorizer about artists. From an old family, her education followed a predictable path. However, after attending the Chapin School and Miss Kendall McKeever's Finishing School, she was allowed to pursue an interest in art. In 1918–20 she studied sculpture in New York with Guston Borglum (the sculptor of Mount Rushmore). After a brief marriage to Schuyler Livingston Parsons, a wealthy, socially prominent New Yorker, she joined such expatriates as Man Ray, Gertrude Stein, Hart Crane, and Alexander Calder in Europe. She spent ten years there.

In 1933, she returned to the United States where she continued painting and studying. Because of financial problems brought about by the Depression, and because she could not live off her own work, she was forced to look for a job. This led her to selling art. From 1938 to 1946 she worked for a series of galleries including Midtown, Sullivan, Wakefield Bookshop, and Mortimer Brandt, and in 1946 she opened her own gallery. Both the

*Actual quotations in this section, unless noted, are from Parsons, n.d.; Parsons, 1969; Tompkins, 1975.

social contacts her background provided her and the contacts she had made with such people as Frank Crowinshield of *Vanity Fair*, a friend of a number of MOMA trustees, facilitated this move. She was able to get four backers, each putting up $1,000, and along with $1,500 of her own, she opened shop.

Not only was her experience that of an artist, but her introduction to artists was through other artists. Barnett Newman was to be the primary figure in making the introductions, among which was Pollock. She had met Newman at a dinner party at Adolph Gottlieb's in 1944, and the two had taken to each other immediately. As she says of him, "He was always a great help to me; he's such an intelligent man and he highly approved of everything I was doing and encouraged me." On another occasion, she says he was the greatest help, "Because I could discuss anything and everything with him, and he liked my point of view and never imposed on me." Newman was in close touch with most important artists of this time and in 1943 had published an article predicting that America would become the new center of Western art. Newman helped her organize the Northwest Coast Indian show which inaugurated her gallery and did the catalogue for the 1947 groundbreaking "Ideographic Picture."

Accounts suggest that not only was there camaraderie between the artists and the dealer but also between the artists themselves. The gallery became a meeting place for artists. The big four were Newman, Rothko, Still, and Pollock, or, as she called them, "The Four Men of the Apocalypse." In the beginning they were tremendously supportive of each other, and would help hang each other's pictures for shows. As she used to say, "I give them walls. They do the rest." The solidarity among the artists is understandable. The conditions of an avant-garde were present. These artists were consciously opposing the dominant direction of the New York art market and were facing strong opposition from the larger community.

Their drawing together was not surprising. What was interesting, though, was Parsons's relationship with this circle. She saw herself not as a promoter, outside the circle, but rather as a painter within it. She stressed that she belonged. Interestingly, it is in 1947 that she painted her first abstract picture. Recalling this moment, she explains that up until then she painted more or less "what [she] saw. . . . but after viewing a rodeo, I got so excited by it, by the color and movement, that I went back and did an abstract painting . . . I couldn't have conveyed that rodeo any other way. I just suddenly saw what to do and why and how to do it." Not only the change in style but the language in which it is described bespeak the influence of a group of artists on a fellow artist.

But there were inherent conflicts in a dealer conceiving of herself as, so to speak, one of the boys. The problem revolves around the competition which inevitably results. Furthermore, this strain tends to reinforce the emphasis on the cultural rather than the business goals which characterizes this type of gallery. An artist, Richard Tuttle, presently in her stable, suggests that a strain of competition seems to intrude into her relationship with "fully developed mature talents." "The gallery is unique because she has always thought an artist should mature slowly. She used to say she'd never show anybody under thirty-five. Betty won't push you—she cares primarily about your growth as an artist." Dorothy Miller, former Chief Curator at MOMA, seems to concur when she says, "Betty Parsons lost interest in an artist the moment he began selling at high prices."

Not surprisingly, Parsons herself was quite open about her emphasis on cultural goals: "The major idea [behind the gallery] is creative, is to find what's going on creatively in our day. That's the working principle." She was proud of the fact that she never used high-pressure advertising: "I didn't have the money to. . . . I just got around. . . . I have a great theory that artists liked the gallery, and I think artists make artists and also make galleries, if they like it." This concern with what is new and creative has attached to it certain mystical overtones. Quoting a line from her biography, she said at one point, "Another prophet shall arise and bring fresh fever from the skies. I'm after fresh fever and how." When asked what kind of painter she liked, she said "The painter [who] was trying to say something on his own and not lying back on all the props of the past and influences of the past. I was always interested in the courage of it you know. And then of course, I think I was born with a gift called love of the unfamiliar."

Although we have been stressing Parsons's emphasis on cultural goals, she was also running a business. What we will see characterized that business was a desire to provide exposure through exhibitions for her artists. Much less energy was utilized in actively promoting her artists to would-be collectors, museums, and critics. It would be fallacious, however, to suggest she totally recoiled from this. Parsons did know critics and museum curators and they did come to her gallery. When she opened in 1946, she claims that Barr and Dorothy Miller came to nearly every show. Apparently they liked a Rothko so much that they got Phillip Johnson to buy it and give it to the museum. However, the trustees hated it and they had to hide it for years from them.

In his flattering introduction to an exhibition publication commemorating the tenth anniversary of the gallery, Clement Greenberg writes: "I have seldom been able to bring her gallery into focus as part of the commercial apparatus of art (I'm not sneering at that apparatus); rather I think of it as belonging more to the studio and production side of art. In a sense, like a painter's painter, or a poet as a poet's poet, Mrs. Parsons's is an artist's—

and critic's—gallery; a place where art goes on and is not just shown and sold.'' (Greenberg, 1955).

This type of gallery is important in the early stages of an artist's career. It provides the sort of support necessary to withstand the usual critical onslaught made by the gatekeepers of the market. But it is also problematic for the artists who do get through the gates. They become desirous of the monetary rewards which come with being successful artists. Both dealer and artists then begin to feel used. In order to understand the dealer's position, it is necessary to understand the way a dealer conceives of the artist's obligation to him. A dealer invests a great deal of energy and money in any artist he handles. Frequently, money is lost on an artist. When an artist does succeed, however, the dealer feels that his effort should be rewarded.

Early in the 1950s, two things occurred which provided the necessary conditions for the financial success of a number of abstract expressionists. First, a number of these artists began to receive a sustained critical response. Furthermore, the conditions of the market in general improved. More money became available for art. New tax regulations permitted the donor of a work of art to a public collection to deduct up to thirty percent of its assessed value from his taxable income during the year of donation even if the donor retained custody of the work. Finally, although there was a tremendous demand for impressionist and post-impressionist work, the prices had skyrocketed. This resulted in many collectors beginning to appraise the investment value of the new American artists.

Parsons's artists were aware of the new possibilities. In 1951, Rothko, Newman, Pollock, and Still came to her with a proposal. What they wanted was for her to drop most of the other artists in the gallery and to concentrate on marketing them. ''They said they would make me the most famous dealer in the world,'' she recalled, ''and they were probably right. They were really paying me a great compliment. But I didn't want to do a thing like that. I told them that was my nature, I liked a bigger garden.'' It is at this point that many of her artists began to leave her for another type of gallery. Hofmann had already left her in 1947 and moved to Sam Kootz. The correspondence between the two and the reasons given are illuminating. Parsons heard about the move secondhand and wrote to Hofmann in Provincetown to express her shock and to tell him how upset she was. Hofmann responded that he was sorry, but ''It is my advanced age which dictates my acts—not business or hunger for fame. My work must be stronger promoted to avoid its larger destruction. You did the best for its recognition and I esteem you highly for it, but in the course of the events I could not help to feel uneasy that your effort brought not the prices wanted, more for the sake of the gallery as for my own.'' One can glean a bit more of Parsons's response, and the lure that Kootz used, from a letter of Parsons's to a Mrs. Wright Ludington: "I have had a very bad shock to find that I could no longer hold Hans Hofmann. Sam Kootz, the crocodile, has gobbled him as I was not able financially to hold him. Kootz intends to make it possible for Hofman to give up teaching, and as he is an old man that possibility is important."

Pollock and Rothko went to Sidney Janis in 1952, and in 1953 Still followed. Although her partings with the first two were relatively smooth, given the circumstances, the split with Still was vitriolic. Bickering began to be characteristic of the artists' relationship with each other. By 1952, Still wasn't speaking to any of the others and Newman was suing Ad Reinhardt for slander. At the same time, most of these artists had broken the barriers that kept them out of the market. Rothko, Pollock, and Still were included in the Museum of Modern Art's "Fifteen Americans" in 1952, and such collectors as Edward Rott, Duncan Phillips, Burton Tremaine, and Ben Heller were buying their works. It was apparent that money could be made and fame achieved. All that was needed was a dealer who could successfully promote them to their fullest potential.

Sam Kootz*

Kootz marks a shift from a concern with establishing a personal bond with the artist to a concern with a marketable product. This does not preclude intimate and sophisticated knowledge of that product. In fact, we will see that Kootz—and this can be generalized to other dealers of this type— had both an excellent knowledge of, and concern with, art history. Furthermore, he himself wrote on art as an historian. This type of activity has direct implications for the business, as it allows the dealer to write on his artists from an apparently objective position. It also allows him to define a style or movement and to locate it within the flow of history, thereby legitimating it.

Kootz was a Virginian, and his training was in law. His first acquaintance with art was during the 1920s when, as a student, he would come to New York and visit such oases of modern art as the Stieglitz and Daniel galleries. The international focus of these galleries and artists was to stay with him through the nationalistic fervor of the 1930s, and was to continue to be a factor in the orientation of his own gallery in the 'forties and 'fifties. This philosophy was first expressed in a book of his published in 1930 entitled *Modern American Painters*. This work was primarily a defense of the artists he had grown attached to in the 1920s: Marin, Sheeler, Dove,

*Unless noted, quotations in this section are from Kootz (1943, 1948, 1964).

Hartley, Weber, etc. The interest in these artists waned in the 'thirties in favor of such American scenists as Benton, Curry, and Marsh.

It was thirteen years before his next work came out. *New Frontiers in American Painting* continued this thrust, but at a more auspicious moment. By this time there had been a resurgence of interest in abstract art. Rather than try to defend the past, he attempted to predict the future in light of the developments of the previous decades. Kootz stressed that our past, or history, is international and denounced the regionalist painters. Furthermore, he attacked such institutions as museums and galleries for failing to understand this, for having no formal sensibilities and being concerned solely with questions of content. This book was a call for action. As he wrote, "Perhaps this book will play its own part in arousing the curiosity of its reader, in persuading him to seek out the work of the painters discussed, to appaise the current drive becoming part of our bid for important status in world culture."

Up until this point Kootz's own involvement with art must be characterized as an avocation rather than a vocation. From 1934 to 1940 he had been with a silk firm. During the 1940s he was an advertising executive, often for major film companies developing programs for public presentation of film spectaculars. Being an acute observer of artistic trends, as evidenced in *New Frontiers*, in 1945 he decided the moment was ripe for full-time involvement. This was preceded by a two-year warming-up period. In 1943, he had been appointed to the Advisory Board of the Museum of Modern Art. In 1944, he had become a dealer/patron with Baziotes and Motherwell as his first proteges. It was his plan "to buy the entire production of an artist during the 'perilous time of his development' and to enter into the usual percentage agreement once the artist's reputation was established."

Kootz was to apply the techniques he had learned in the advertising business to that of marketing his artists. Complaining about Stieglitz's attempts to determine whether a patron was worthy or not to buy a picture, he claimed to feel "that a gallery's attitude should be to keep the artist alive and not to interpose any objections to the purchase of a picture." One technique was to have art or literary critics write catalogue introductions. A classic example of this was an exhibition entitled "Women." The individual works were accompanied by pieces by writers on either the artist or his work. Included in these pairs were Tennessee Williams on Hans Hofmann, Jean-Paul Sartre on David Hare, Harold Rosenberg on William Baziotes, and Clement Greenberg on Fernand Leger. Furthermore, Kootz acted to define the group as a movement with a unifying theme. In 1949, he mounted a show entitled "Intra-Subjectives," where he defined the leaders of the new movement.

We have shown that Kootz was predisposed to innovate, as his writings indicate, and he exhibited activism vis-à-vis the other institutions within the market. His raids from Betty Parsons's stable are examples of this. However, we have suggested that motivation is not sufficient for innovation actually to occur. What obstacles stood in Kootz's way, and what resources did he have to overcome them? Until the mid-1950s, there was no serious market for these painters. True, an interest had been generated in them, but sales were few and prices were low. Kootz claims that he had a number of losses from his original stable. He remembers a de Kooning he sold in 1949 or 1950 which went for $1,700. In 1964, he estimated that the value at that time would be close to $25,000 or $30,000. His ability to remain in business and thus overcome these obstacles was to always remain in the market for established painters.

In the beginning this specifically meant handling Picasso. In 1947, he made what is generally considered a coup. Picasso's new works had not been seen because of the war, and every dealer in New York was fighting to represent him in the United States. Picasso was saying no to everyone. In December 1947, Kootz flew to Paris and came back with nine pictures, all of which had been sold at prices ranging from $3,500 to $20,000 before he landed in New York. Simultaneously MOMA mounted a show and Kootz held an exhibition. Kootz's approach with Picasso had apparently been to show him what he was doing for younger American artists. This move of Kootz's boosted him up to a respected position within the market. Furthermore, it acted as a tremendous draw to collectors. Hopefully, they would come in for a Picasso and go out with a Baziotes or a Motherwell. According to Kootz, he couldn't have existed in the 1940s without Picasso. In 1954 he took on Soulages and Mathieu, two contemporary French artists, in an attempt again to diversify in order to bring new people into his gallery.

This approach made sense, given the type of individual who collected from him. He claims that they were not only younger people but in many instances were larger collectors of impressionists and post-impressionists who no longer could buy pictures of the quality they had once bought and who were now willing for the first time to dip into more contemporary pictures. One might suggest that individuals were reassured by a dealer who had established himself in the European field. One problem facing Kootz, was the development of the large canvas. Collectors were reluctant to purchase a picture ten feet by seven feet. Where would they put it? In Kootz's statements on the development of the large canvas, one gets a sense of the technique he used: "It was because the painter was using his whole arm and body and that the large canvas gives more freedom for the stroke . . . it became imperative that in order to express himself more thoroughly and more consciously on the canvas, he needed that freedom of movement, that expansion.'' Here we can see the promotional use of an aesthetic theory based on the art as an expression of the personal subjectivity of the artist.

Kootz, as we have seen, was in business and concerned with marketing his art. Being quite astute, he was well aware of the importance of the gatekeeping functions of museums and critics. For instance, he would mount shows of artists selected by major critics. ''Talent 1950,'' a show running from April 25 to May 15 of that year, is an example of this sort of promotion. It focused on artists selected by Clement Greenberg and Meyer Schapiro. In 1955, Greenberg did a retrospective of Hofmann for Kootz. There was one painting priced at $150 done in 1940, which antedated Pollock's drip paintings of 1947. When Barr saw it he wanted to purchase it in order to demonstrate the ancestry of Pollock. When Kootz discovered this, he suggested to Hofmann that the price be pushed up to $15,000. Barr was horrified, but later secured a collector to put up the amount with the idea of presenting it at some time to MOMA.

He also understood the symbiotic relationship between the collector and the museum. Kootz claims that in a number of cases he helped collectors who said they wanted to give to a museum and didn't know which museum would accept a certain kind of painting. He had been able to point out the museums that needed the painting and hadn't the money to buy it. That is, he consciously acted as a liaison by pointing out that if he, a customer, had to get rid of a painting, giving it to a museum offered particular tax advantages.

The sort of knowledge Kootz possessed was important. A large collector could not affort to sell a collection because the tax bill on the capital gains which occurred, or the inheritance tax on the estate, would be crippling. The short-term benefit of this arrangement was that the dealer sold more paintings, but in the long run it takes a lot of works off the market, thereby creating a continual demand for the new. He was also aware of the museum's acceptance of a work in raising a collector's interest. MOMA was one of the first institutions to recognize Baziotes, Motherwell, and Gottlieb. As Kootz points out, Barr's enthusiasms influenced such individuals as the Rockefellers and other museum trustees who also happened to be collectors.

Summary

These two types of galleries were generally instrumental in the emergence of New York as an art capital, and specifically instrumental in fostering abstract expressionism. At both levels there was a division of labor. The artist-oriented type of gallery acted to foster artistic community in general and in particular a certain style. The market-oriented gallery acted to create a receptive institutional community and specifically a market for abstract expressionism.

This model does not only characterize the late 1940s and early 1950s, but it also continues to be useful in analyzing the contemporary market. I would speculate that the cooperative (artist-run) and alternative space galleries serve a similar function in today's market as the Betty Parsons Gallery did in an earlier one. They are both places where the emphasis is on fostering creative development. One might hypothesize that there is a greater impetus for this type of gallery to develop where there is an over-supply at the input end of the system. The rise of the cooperative movement at a time when there was a great influx of artists into a constricted market supports this view. Furthermore, also analogous to the early 'fifties, these co-ops appear to act as gatekeepers for the commercial galleries.

At the other end of the spectrum, the market-oriented galleries have grown more sophisticated. The more important ones have branch offices in Europe and have developed more complex internal structures. Furthermore, the acceptance of New York as the center of things for almost thirty years has resulted in more formalized relationships between the galleries and the rest of the institutional art world. The importance of studying the early 1950s is that it illustrates in embryonic form aspects of the contemporary market. The actual operations of this contemporary market require empirical research.

Notes

1. Reprinted with the permission of the author and the publisher from *Social Research* (vol. 45, 1978).

References

Greenberg, Clement. 1955. "Introduction." *Ten Years.* New York: Betty Parsons Gallery.

Hirsch, Paul M. 1972. "Processing Fads and Fashions." *American Journal of Sociology* 77:639–59.

Kootz, Samuel M. 1943. *New Frontiers in American Painting.* New York: Hasting House.

———. 1948. *Women.* New York: Samuel M. Kootz Editions.

———. 1964. "Interview by Dorothy Seckler, April 13." *Archives of American Art.*

Mohr, Lawrence B. 1969. "Determinants of Innovation in Organizations." *American Political Science Review* 63 (March): 111–126.

Parsons, Betty. n.d. "Betty Parsons's Papers." *Archives of American Art.*

———. 1969. "Interview by Paul Cummings, June 4." *Archives of American Art.*

Thompson, James. 1962. "Organizations and Output Transactions." *American Journal of Sociology* 68 (November): 309–324.

Tompkins, Calvin. 1975. "A Keeper of the Treasure." *New Yorker* 51 (June): 44–48.

—— 10 ——

Mass, Class, and the Reviewer[1]

KURT LANG

As reviewers or as the victims of reviewers many students of popular culture have rejoiced in Stephen Potter's broadsides on the art of review-manship. Yet little systematic evidence has been gathered to illuminate the roles of the reviewer whose criticism is regularly featured in the daily press and in weekly publications (see Dutscher, 1957; Siepmann, n.d.).

How influential is the reviewer? The theater critic continues to be credited most often with the crucial role of kingmaker or executioner in the world of legitimate theater. On the whole, however, many observers are inclined to discount the reviewer's influence altogether. Because critical ratings and audience ratings fail to jibe, one comes to deemphasize the impact which advertising and other mass media promotion usually have on public selections. This minimization, in turn, expresses an approach which views the consumer as being in the focal position within a network of mass and personal communication. Accordingly one studies how information and evaluations reach audiences. In terms of this frame of reference—most appropriate in assessing "effects"—daily and weekly reviews become merely one among the many promotional pressures which converge upon the potential consumers. And here it can be shown that a good part of the general informational flow actually reaches them not via the mass media but by word-of-mouth, i.e., by the kind of informal diffusion of evaluation which is characrteristic of every social circle (Handel, 1950: 88–90; Katz and Lazarsfeld, 1955; Herr, 1957).

To what extent the reviewer plays a decisive role in the determination of smash hits and best sellers constitutes an interesting question. In the small study which serves as the basis for this article, we have, however, taken the reviewer and not the consumer as the focus of observation. From this viewpoint, it is the reviewer who occupies a "central" position within mass entertainment world, standing between a potential or actual audience, on the one side, and the group of creators, managers, and distributors, en-

gaged in marketing the popular arts, on the other. The main point is just
how this intermediary position impinges on this role of the critic.

The Data

The writer undertook a systematic analysis of reviews over a six-week
period in the Fall of 1957. On the assumption that the role of the reviewer
would differ not only according to (a) medium under review, but also according to (b) schedule of publication (daily or weekly), and (c) the audience to whom the publication is directed. Reviews covered were those on
television, books, movies, and the legitimate theater printed in two New
York City newspapers—one a *mass* circulation publication, the other aimed
at a much narrower *class* market. Of the two weekly magazines included,
again, one was what we may broadly consider a *mass* magazine and the
other a *class* publication. These designations are not intended as invidious
terms. The two class publications were in a sense also mass offerings, except that they were aimed at a more specialized audience and at the higher
educational levels. The mass publications, on the other hand, are not by
definition low-brow and pulp publications. We simply selected a paper and
a mazine enjoying very wide circulation, fully recognizing that the national
magazine readership is what constitutes essentially a middle brow mass
market.

The number of reviews covered totals 462. Considered as reviews were
only those write-ups which, in the eyes of the publication, merited a head-
lined presentation. This definition eliminated a whole variety of book,
drama, movie, and TV "notes," which often are little more than announce-
ments, trade gossip, and news for an appropriate feature section. The mass
daily did not discuss books; therefore book reviews from the Sunday supplement of another were used.

Students in the writer's class on mass communications collected and
coded the reviews. Each code sheet was checked against the review at least
once either by the writer or by one of two volunteer helpers. The code
covered three areas:

I. The reviewer's *overall assessment* of the offering was rated along
afive-point scale.[2]
II. For each review we further checked whether the writer dealt with
any one or more of the following: (a) the *policy of the industry;*
placement of the offering in the context of the book world, theater, film, or television as signifying new styles, new talent, or
experimentation—in short, its *cultural significance;* (c) *public im-*

port, which entails some effort to evaluate (not merely interpret) the bearing of the content on contemporary social and political life; (d) estimating the *suitable audiences;* (e) estimation of its *public success.*

III. The allocation of space devoted exclusively to (a) description of *content* and manner of presentation, (b) background and history of the *production, and* (c) *personal data* unrelated to the production concerning the writers, producers, or actors. Because of low reliability concerning specific paragraphs, figures on the third set of categories are based on reviews, not on the space measure.

On all categories used, coder agreement was above 90 percent, often considerably above.

The Role of the Reviewer

Statistical and qualitative analysis of the reviews suggests that among the factors which must be considered in studying the role of the reviewer are his or her relations to the following: (a) the publication in which the reviews appear; (b) the medium with which the reviewer must be concerned; (c) industry pressures; (d) the image of the publication's audience (and the reviewer's image of his or her share of that audience); (e) professional self-conceptions of reviewers, i.e., how they conform to the commonly accepted role of reviewer; and finally, certain structural transformations which have altered the relationship among critics, producers, and their audiences. Through content analysis of the reviews, one may construct a preliminary definition of the reviewer's role.

The Relationship to the Publication

The reviewer's role is partially defined by his or her relation to the publication and to its publisher. By this we mean to indicate more than the usual reference to job-consciousness and security mindedness. Each publication has a slant to which every contributor adapts. As might be expected, there were noticeable differences among the four publications with regard to style as well as length of review. Also there were characteristic aspects of the reviews which distinguished them from those in other journals and could be explained by the general tone of the publications.

The mass daily, to begin with, contained more subjective reactions and also more general, overall, reactions which were not related to any specific content or element in the production. Thus these reviews can be thought of as generally more subjective but less inclined to "explain" the sources of the reviewer's subjective reactions. They recommend rather than evaluate.

In the two class publications, reviewers are more prone to dwell on specific aspects of the performance and to let these, however obliquely, carry the general evaluation. The reader's ability to form his or her own overall judgment is more likely to be taken for granted. A larger portion of each review consists of background information about the participating personalities, the history of the production, and its relation to other similar ones.

How the publication's tone carries over into the reviews is exemplified best by the mass weekly. The flippant style of its reviews, which are unsigned as is the rest of its copy, duplicates the jargon which distinguishes the publication in its entirety. In format a "critical," analytical magazine, it has developed a formula for mass appeal on the line of "We have no Gods except those we create." It singles out items, not necessarily central, to epitomize any topic. This deceptive tone permeates its sections on the popular arts and largely accounts for the generally severe ratings of its reviews. Books, drama, and movies are on the average rated lowest by this publication, while its evaluation of TV closely approximates the mean of the other journals. How simple flippancy may damn a production is illustrated by the anonymous reviewer's branding a movie " . . . a pretty good example of Stiff Upper Lipmanship, Jolly Good Show Division." After two sentences of rather lively description, the review concludes: "As usual in this sort of thing the Germans are all neck, the British all cheek, and the audience all ears for the next jeer at poor old jerry." This picture was well received by reviewers in other journals.

The Relationship to the Product

A review is not only a reflection of the image a publication creates of itself; some relation of the reviewer to the products of popular culture is also involved. The sheer availability of large amounts of material means that in taking note of an item, the reviewer (or editor) is already exercising some judgment concerning its significance or suitability for the readership. In not being notified about all offerings, the reader in effect receives information (or even explicit advice) about how to allocate time and money in order to satisfy personal inclinations.

In actuality, one medium more than another permits the reviewer leeway in exercising selective judgment. First, the variety of offerings in any medium is an important determinant of how this function is exercised. Only a small percentage of the many general book titles can be reviewed in the average publication. Among the 135 titles discussed in the four publications, only 13 were reviewed in three or more of them.[3] The average number of reviews per title was 1.5.

During the six-week period covered, there were significantly fewer plays than movie premieres, so that duplication might understandably be higher for the former. The reverse is the case. The observation of 2.3 reviews for the average drama and 2.9 for the average film suggests that the significance of many dramas is considered rather specialized in that they are not deemed worthy of general notice.

To offer a strictly comparable figure for television is not possible: a single program is often used to review and evaluate an entire series, and reviews of series may appear at different times. Yet duplication with respect to the series is extremely high: programs such as *Studio 1, Playhouse 90* or *Wide, Wide World* are subjected to discussion several times even in the same publication. On the other hand, the variety of programs available for viewing during a single week means the duplications in the strict sense are almost exclusively limited to the more spectacular programs thought to be of general significance.

Does the opportunity to select items affect the severity of criticism? An affirmative answer is indicated if, wherever selection is possible, only the "best" products are singled out for review. In the case of books, where reviews are least often duplicated, we did find the highest acclaim: 35 per cent of the books received the highest possible endorsement. In the case of drama, duplication was also low, and superlative ratings obtained in 27 per cent of the reviews, whereas movies, the medium most often discussed in more than one journal were also the ones reviewed most harshly. Forty-one per cent are noted unfavorably, and only 8 per cent got unqualified acclaim. Conversely, drama and book reviewers used the *least* favorable rating extremely sparingly (4 per cent of book reviews and 9 per cent of drama reviews), but use of this rating increases to 24 and 17 per cent respectively for movies and television. However, if selectivity were the major determinant of evaluation, weeklies which, because of space limitation, are able to give less coverage, should be more favorable than the daily newspapers. On the contrary, the weeklies are consistently more critical than the dailies, and the mass weekly, as well as the class weekly, is clearly more critical than its daily counterparts. These differences among publications remain even if only duplicate reviews are considered.

The observed rank-order of critical acclaim—books, drama, movies in 1–2–3 order—is reproduced in every one of the four publications, independent of whether the publication was directed at the class or mass market. Only the comparative rating of television productions varied according to the slant of the publications. Reviewers in the class journals rated video

Table 1[a]
Mean Ratings By Medium and Source

Publication	Books (N = 196)	Theater (N = 67)	Movies (N = 90)	TV (N = 109)	Total Rank[b]	Mean Order[c]
Mass Daily	1.8	2.3	2.8	2.1	2.3	1.3
Mass Weekly	2.7	3.2	3.3	3.0	3.0	3.8
Class Daily	1.7	2.5	3.0	3.1	2.5	2.5
Class Weekly	2.3	2.4	3.1	3.4	2.5	3.0
Total	(2.1)	(2.6)	(3.2)	(2.9)		

[a]The number "1" designates the most favorable ratings; "5" the least favorable.
[b]Mean rating for entire publication (all four media).
[c]Based on degree of favorableness of the publication for each medium.

lowest, but in the two mass publications the praise bestowed on TV production is second only to books. This class-mass differential concerning TV raises the question of whether, in contrast to the other arts, the acceptance of programs by reviewers might reflect the failure of TV criticism so far to congeal into widely practised conventions.

It was noted that TV reviews often do little more than articulate general attitudes concerning television, and radio in its heyday, while attracting mass enthusiasm, was met with similar reserve by the highbrow (Frost, 1937). Apparently, class publications judge television by their own "high" standards according to which it is grossly deficient. Mass publications utilize the standards of their readers who have already either seen the program under review or missed it irrevocably. The approach to the television product is "*Will* he, the reader, like it?" rather than "*Should* he like it?" The class journal, acting as a public conscience, seeks rather to influence people to reject what, by aesthetic standards, they should not like.

The Pressures of Publicity

Another factor deserving extensive study is the degree to which reviews are an extension of industry promotion. Notices of impending publications and announcement of production plans probably affect critical assessment in the reviews to an as yet undetermined degree. On the basis of the data, one can tentatively express doubt about a clear-cut relationship between rating and advertising. But the effect of industry publicity on the "independence" of the reviewer is more complicated.

Essentially the question is: how much do the public relations activities of the industry determine the selection of items? On the one hand, the reviewer is faced with the necessity of reporting events in the popular arts which at any moment are apt to attract wide attention, but the critic in him undoubtedly wants to bring to the readers' attention works of more permanent significance. This mixture of motives produces divergences between critical evaluation and editorial endorsement. It may also produce divergences between critical judgment and the decision to feature the review prominently. Especially in the weeklies, where the number of items reviewed is tailored to space, selection appears to hinge in good part on whether the item has received publicity. Consequently, while a selection by one of the major book clubs stands a greater chance of being reviewed, it does not necessarily receive greater approval.

That books are chosen for promotion through book clubs with some anticipation of their appeal does not exclude the possibility that reviewers contribute to the fulfillment of predicted appeal. They may do this not only by giving prominence to certain selections but by predicting wide appeal even for books about which they personally have little good to say. This possibility is suggested by three books, prominently featured in several of the publications, but which, nevertheless, received rather low evaluations. The prediction of wide sales was confirmed when all three subsequently made the bestseller list. The shock appeal of one author was duly noted in two reviews of his book. The third reviewer thought a season or two without a book by this author would only whet the public's literary appetite. Again—and this was not checked against a complete record of all releases and all openings—films at first-run theaters and Broadway plays (in contrast to those in smaller off-Broadway houses) appear (as judged by our sample) to have a better chance of being noted.

To gain more than routine notice for a newly launched enterprise, it seems almost necessary that the industry create an event of public significance. For example, in the case of a book by an unknown or virtually unknown author, all details of its production—the title, the make-up (including introductions by celebrities hailing the significance of the book), its very acceptance for publication—are in some measure conceived with an eye to promotional possibilities. Similarly, cinematic and dramatic productions must be launched as public events, but here the managers, since they are in a better position to choose their stars, create sensational publicity stunts, and determine the manner of release, are less dependent on favorable notice. Curiously enough, the television spectacular has had only very limited success in affecting or even upsetting entrenched viewing habits. But by dubbing this fare "an event of unusual interest," they have usually succeeded in drawing the attention of critics. Since editors have their eyes set on what is judged to be timely and significant for the public, the TV reviewer can rarely afford to overlook a "spectacular." And, in this sense, the TV reviewer, like the book reviewer, combines the functions of publicist and critic. In their selection of programs, reviewers are influenced as much by the ability of the industry to promote a feeling of public significance as they are by aesthetic criteria.

The Image of the Audience

Of course, the extent to which the reviews in any publication emerge as an adjunct to the communications industry varies. It is affected by whether the image which the publication has of its own audience (and presumably the critic's image of his own share of that audience) coincides with or diverges from the one at which the industry offering is aimed. Here the difference between *class* and *mass* publication appears significant.

To begin with, the reviews contained few attempts to depict and define the type of audience for whom any offering might be intended or for whom it might be suited. This was as true for books and television programs, which might be expected to appeal to widely different groups in the population, as it was for drama and movies which reach what is perhaps a more "homogeneous" audience. Where specific target audiences were mentioned, the most common referential categories are age-divisions, with an occasional allusion to the connoisseur vs. layman. And there were hints (percentagewise very few) that a book would make an ideal Christmas present, etc.

Many publications do recommend or point editorially to offerings expected to interest their readers. These take the form of "recommended" and "special interest" lists or of editorial "ratings." Also lists of best sellers, box office records, top audience ratings, etc. attract considerable attention.

How the image of the audience may affect reviewing policy comes out most clearly when we note that notwithstanding the amount of duplication between items selected for review, the reviewer for a *class* publication played a role different from a colleague writing for the *mass* journal. The mass reviewer, which often reviewed the whole bill at a movie theater (rather than a single film) focused on the star attraction. The class reviewer, too, gave prominence to the highly publicized feature but, at the same time, was more apt to note also out-of-the-way books, interesting Class B movies and documentaries, off-Broadway shows and limited engagement runs, as well as small-audience and limited-appeal programs which were not in any way launched as spectaculars. In such instances, the cultural significance of the offering was stressed, and the tendency of "class" reviewers to do so was markedly greater.

Reviewing as a Profession

Helping to structure the role of the reviewer, then, are certain relationships in which he participates—his position with respect to his publication, the product, industry promotion, his audience. Finally we must inquire about his professional definition of his function.

First, is the reviewer a newspaperman (or a journalist) who comes to specialize in reviews of the public or elite arts? Does he then think of himself as a newsman who is bound in his reviewing to seek out the newsworthy, to make use of public relations handouts, to go after the inside story of how a book came to be written, or how a play came to be produced even if that story has no critical relevance? Or is he a specialist in communications or literature or a student of society who, though a writer, thinks of his first job as criticism?

Second, is there a general convention among critics concerning how critical one should be? We observed earlier the rank-order of criticism. Can it be said, for example, that there is a tradition of just how hard one can be on the manuscripts which survive the screening-out process and make their way into the bindery? Do the same sort of conventions operate among theater critics and, in turn, movie reviewers? And may such conventions account in part for a rank order of acclaim independent of the reviewer's selectivity and of the audience for which he writes?

Third, such conventions are apt to reflect changes in the structural context of the popular arts, including the relationships between product and producer and the extent to which the critic thinks of himself as or is part of the industry which he is employed to evaluate. Criticism progressed in severity from books to theater, from theater to movies, and in the class magazines from movies to TV, as what once were private productions become more clearly corporate efforts. In this connection, a change in the structural context of the popular arts, the transmission from the older arts to what Seldes (1956; also see Lazarsfeld, 1948) has recently called the public arts, becomes important.

The Public Arts vs. the Elite Arts

At least since the beginning of the nineteenth century the traditional critic has been concerned primarily with an evaluation of his private experience. His was a self-created task of go-between between the creator and his select audience, seeking to clarify the artist's message, estimating his craftsmanship, and interpreting the psychological milieu in which the message was framed. Even as art diffused from its elite circles to become "mass culture," the emphasis of the reviewer was still on his highly private experience, culturally meaningful for the "happy few," rather than on the public significance of the art form being examined.

Among the reviewers of the popular arts, the theater critic, more than the others, appears to have retained this traditional function. He describes his feelings and gives his estimate of how well the meanings meant to be conveyed were conveyed. For example:

> Watching and hearing it [the play] I had the odd and uneasy feeling that I was a reluctant psychiatrist listening to the confidence of strangers. Since I did not know or particularly care for these strangers, I was uncomfortable.

While opening night is not exactly private, the critic does discuss experience which comes only to the select—experience which his interested readers may share with him, but whose public significance in terms of everyday life is apt to be minor. He writes about the special world of the theater, in terms of which his experience is interpreted, and there is little apprehension of any broader social significance. Twenty-seven per cent of all drama reviews contained references to the item's cultural significance, compared with 6 per cent of movie reviews and 10 per cent of TV reviews. While the theater reviewer indulged in considerable discussion of his special world and its personalities, he largely ignored *the* public, *the* theater as a vital part of American life. Only 7 per cent of the reviews alluded to industry policy and 13 per cent to the public or political import of the play under dissection.

While books—the other of the older, traditional arts—were most often reviewed in terms of their current public import, allusions to a book's cultural significance message were found as often here as in theater reviews. Still, the function of the book critic has metamorphosed with the changing times. He cannot assume that the book-reading public has the homogeneity of interests it once had. The reading public does not share a uniform conception of the importance of books, and this is due primarily to the variety of offerings. Nor can most of them be expected to have the time or inclination to live their lives within a world of books as does the full-time book reviewer.

As a consequence, the book reviewer cannot just report a personal reaction. Because he seems more impelled to document them, a much larger proportion of the total space is given over to mere outlining, even lengthy quotations, of the book contents. The book reviewer, like the drama critic, also fills in on the background and history of the title and its creator. But notification rather than assessment and evaluation appears to be the former's primary aim. His discussion usually fell upon the book and author whose views and actions have achieved some public notoriety or whose world appears "timely." Cultural significance is, however, duly noted.

In stark contrast to these two art forms, the reviewers of the public arts—movies and television—pay little attention to the cultural and creative significance of an offering. (Perhaps there is little of it, but certainly enough has been written about the film as art to belie this suggestion!) But this content analysis does not at all support the charge that TV reviewers devote the bulk of their comments to personality gossip. Indeed, a smaller percentage of the TV reviews than of other reviews indulged in extensive trade gossip. It is in the older arts that the personal lives of the producers become relevant to their productions. Gossip, on the other hand, may be the function of movie and TV fan magazines rather than movie and TV reviews, where it is not related to the content of an offering. It is also a common feature of movie and television *sections* in newspapers (mostly publicity handouts).

The theater critic seems much more a part of a world he shares with the creative people of the theater than the reviewer of the other art forms. This may go a long way toward explaining why drama criticism in "general interest" publications, even highly sophisticated drama criticism, is inclined to be favorable. The critic is impelled to give praise for effort and intent—even where he cannot approve the results. The book industry is a more impersonal business by comparison. Writers are more dispersed than in the highly centralized legitimate theater. And the relationship between reviewer and producer is more apt to revolve around a common interest in the subject matter of a book than in the trials and tribulations of production. Still, the interest in subject matter is apt to lead the reviewer who is often chosen because of this interest to put in a plug for the book. Hence book reviewing lends itself so well for promotion.

The reviewers of the cinema and of TV are far removed from the industry whose products are highly corporate creations. This is even more true of television than of the movies. Our analysis of reviews tends to confirm the charge that movie and TV reviewers show little awareness of the problems and techniques of production. Their reviews delve into the production background much less often than their counterparts who write about books and plays. Not always sharing a universe of discourse with the creators of broadcasting programs and films, the reviewers seem less apt to identify themselves with either the producers or creators. A movie ticket or a TV set constitutes sufficient qualification.

But there is a deeper sociological cause for this alienation of movie and TV reviewing from the production end. It is not only that many of these reviewers may come from the ranks of journalists. Moviegoing and televiewing are primarily habits. The reviewer of the public arts is in large measure the spokesman for his public vis-a-vis the industry. As such he is supposed to be "independent." For instance, when John Crosby appeared as narrator for *The Seven Lively Arts,* suspicion concerning his role as TV critic was aired in reviews falling within the period covered by our analysis. No dual allegiances were to be permitted. Much of the time the TV critic speaks *for* his audience, and, to the extent that he does, he speaks *to* it proportionately less of the time. He is inclined to deal with the public consequences of TV programming, to assess likes, effects, and to verbalize demands which cannot find expression in box office returns. Not every TV critic fills this role to the full. Penetrating analysis is often lacking, and the reviewer in the mass circulation daily is all too prone to worship the standards which a TV-hungry public has come to accept. Judged by our analysis, the TV reviews in the mass publications do indeed set a relatively lower standard of criticism for themselves than do their peers in the class publications. In any case, the TV reviewers identify themselves, it seems, much more with the perspectives of their readerships. It should be interesting to inquire to what extent their remarks are addressed to the industry which they evaluate rather than to the readership which they have come to represent.

This re-direction of attention to the industry and its policy follows to some degree from the fact that every viewer of a mass medium has his own special experience. Quite obviously, the television reviews are the only ones written *after* the prospective reader has presumably watched what is being reviewed. In a sense, each viewer is a part of the first-night audience. As part of such an elite, the viewer is his own expert. With the emergent tendency of the movie industry to release features directly to neighborhood houses, while giving extended runs in first-run houses with reserved seats at inflated prices, there may be a bifurcation in the movie audience and in movie reviewing as well. The function of reviews of these first-run showings may usher in a new era of reviewing the film as an elite art, while the function of reviewing the whole range of offerings directly available to moviegoers takes on more of the characteristics of TV reviewing.

Summary and Implications

On the basis of a content analysis of reviews, the writer has tried to outline some possible determinants of the role of the reviewer. The research is exploratory only; many problems are only touched upon. For instance, a more definite comparison of criticism contained in mass as compared to class publications had best seize upon a few works and examine in detail the range of elements singled out for review in *many* sources. Again, analysis of reviews of a work available in several forms, e.g., book, legitimate drama, and TV play (for example, Marquand's *Point of No Return*), would allow for a better evaluation of the content of the product (as opposed to medium and source) as a determinant of the reviewer's role.

Second, a more detailed picture of the place of reviews in the more general scheme of promotion would be desirable. The history of promoting a single product, the relationship of the release, advertising copy (White et al., 1957), and content of the product to the content of the review could give us a better picture of how reviewing may be influenced by promotion.

Finally, the whole question of the creation of public interest constitutes a fascinating area of research. For, what, after all, is the impact on consumption patterns of such "news services" as the publication in journals of best-seller lists, newsworthy TV shows, and the public institution of the *Hit Parade* on radio and TV? And how important is it that papers and magazines at intervals cite the "big ten" in television ratings and make a horse race out of Sullivan vs. Allen? In the last instance, criticism is no longer free; nor can it possibly be effective. The reviewer reports only on offerings produced for a special market dominated by monopolistic interests.

Notes

1. Reprinted with the permission of the author and the publisher, *Social Problems* (vol. 6, 1958).

2. The points in the scale were defined as follows: (1) enthusiastic and unsparing praise; (2) generally favorable, or favorable on most aspects, but not superlatively; (3) strictly qualified praise or balance between praise and criticism; (4) generally unfavorable, or on most aspects, with only some qualifications; (5) completely unfavorable and critical. A zero rating was used if the entire review was descriptive and it contained no evaluation.

3. The fact that books especially are not always reviewed at precisely the time they are published and the influence of different deadlines suggest that actual duplication is somewhat higher than observed duplication within a specified time period. We tried to track down some duplicate reviews even though they fell outside of the period covered in the analysis.

References

Dutscher, Alan. 1957. "The book business in America," Pp. 126–140 in B. Rosenberg and D. M. White (eds.), *Mass Culture: The Popular Arts in America.*- Glencoe, Ill.: Free Press.

Frost, S. E. Jr. 1937. *Is America Radio Democratic?* Chicago: University of Chicago Press.

Handel, Leo. 1950. *Hollywood Looks at Its Audience*. Urbana: University of Illinois Press.

Katz, Elihu and Paul F. Lazarsfeld. 1955. *Personal Influence*. Glencoe, Ill.: Free Press.

Herr, Walter, 1957. *Pieces at Eight*. New York: Simon & Schuster.

Lazarsfeld, Paul F. 1948. "The role of criticism in the management of the mass media." *Journalism Quarterly* 25 (June): 115–126.

Seldes, Gilbert. 1956. *The Public Arts*. New York: Simon and Schuster.

Siepmann, C. A. n.d. "Collection and analysis of prevailing criticisms of television programming."

White, David M., Robert S. Albert with R. Allan Seeger. 1957. "Hollywood's newspaper advertising. Pp. 443–450 in B. Rosenberg and D. M. White (eds.), *Mass Culture: The Popular Arts in America*. Glencoe, Ill.: Free Press.

───── 11 ─────

Artist Groups: Patrons and Gate-Keepers

SALLY RIDGEWAY

Style change in art is ongoing. Major changes result in new art movements and the stylistic paradigm of the new movement becomes the defining and directing mode by which artists approach their work during that particular period. While many factors contribute to the successful emergence of a new stylistic paradigm, traditionally we emphasize the importance of aesthetic factors, viewing the artist's role in a new movement as purely a creative one. However, the social role of the artist is as relevant to the process as the creative one and artistic innovation is as much a social process as an aesthetic one (Rosenblum, 1978).

Methodology and Data

Data for this paper were obtained from interviews with a group of twenty-eight artists, a gallery owner, and a museum curator. The artists were involved in the dominant avant-garde movement of the late sixties and seventies; the gallery owner showed the works of many of these artists; and the museum curator specialized in contemporary art. The artists, though at different career stages, had been prominent in galleries and generally accepted within the art world as members of the avant-garde. Interviews were largely open-ended. Additional data were obtained from secondary sources, including critical studies of this period, exhibition data, biographic and autobiographic writing. (Pincus-Whitten, 1969, 1971, 1972).

In the early phases of this movement, the artists were known as Minimalists, and later artists labeled as Conceptualists were included. Within this avant-garde paradigm, the primary goal was that art work should use forms and material not traditionally associated with art. Paint, materials and content were rejected because the salient intent became the confrontation, both radically and dramatically, of the prevailing concepts of art. These artists said anything could be art; nothing existed that was not potentially art. The early Minimal structures were often deliberately over-sized squares, rectangles or other geometric shapes. Continuation within this paradigm resulted in works that even further challenged the definition of art, as artists eliminated the object. Conceptual pieces consisted of performances and events. While the work of different artists varied, the basic premise remained central—that art could be whatever anyone wanted it to be (Hunter, 1974; Lippard, 1973).

Artist Interaction

Artists are frequently depicted as "solitary geniuses" by our cultural myths and popular literature (Geer, 1977). The solitude within which they work is believed an important aspect of the creative process. If the artist is a true genius, such myths imply, solitude will not prevent "discovery" and even the reverse, that the undiscovered artist is not a "genius." Like other mythologies, this one bears only partial resemblance to reality, and obscures much of the artist life style and career. Few artists are solitary and in isolation, but rather most are part of an art community composed of other artists, and of dealers, critics, collectors and the public. (Schucking, 1966; White and White, 1965; Simpson, 1981). Most artists do remain unknown to the public, since few relative to the many who aspire to artist careers ever succeed in achieving a successful or even a secure position. But those who are discovered are, with rare exceptions, active participants in the promotion of their careers and their art. Further, artists exist as one of several powers in the art community, playing a significant role in influencing the acceptance of stylistic ideas and artists they prefer. Though several factors, from stylistic imperatives to market factors, affect stylistic change, interaction between artists is a key, intrinsic element in both the achievement of personal success and the success of any new stylistic paradigm.

Focusing on the myths of "genius" and of artists' detachment from participation in their careers has obscured the role of artists in the process of stylistic change. In the interviews for this study, I found that artists exchange ideas with each other to shape and modify stylistic directions and provide support services to each other which facilitate economic survival and market entry. I will discuss two specific aspects of the interaction in which these patterns appear. First, artist groups composed of peers, with an occasional established artist, shared ideas and resources with each other during the time these artists were developing. Second, established artists, in the role of patrons and gate-keepers, provided new-comers with support and access to the market. The support from peers and the gate-keepers was closely tied to any artist's intellectual commitment to aesthetic goals within the avant-garde community.

Social Circles

Recent theoretical approaches to science and knowledge communities, employing social network concepts, such as that of social circles, have been useful for examining the patterns by which change is supported through member interaction. Social circles, as delineated by Crane (1973) and Kadushin (1966, 1976), are informal groups in which the member's intellectual interests are the primary basis of their interaction. The basis of the group is commitment to an overall, generalized body of knowledge of ideas relating to members' work. These groups are not part of any formal institutional structure and are characterized by loose rather than close interaction. Social circles may have a dense core or several cores, and members do not necessarily know or interact with every other member, though most are usually aware of others. The concept of social circles has contributed to our understanding of innovation and diffusion of ideas, in society, indicating the relationship of social structure to ideas in a society, or group.

Kadushin (1974) developed this concept in relation to art, suggesting a connection between specific kinds of interests, the form the group takes, and the effect of that form on ideas. He sees the movement circle characterizing artist communities of painting and sculpture, dance, theatre, and literature. Bonding of members follows from a sense of embattlement vis-a-vis established style. A movement circle facilitates the replacement of this established style with a new one. (Kadushin, 1974: 779–80). Interactions of members in these circles are seen as the major key to understanding the process of style change in art.

Using this conceptualization of movement circles I will describe how stylistic change was due to social interaction, indicating how artists' commitment to avant-garde goals and support systems became strengthened as artists became integrated within a movement circle.

Movement Circles

Creative Support

Support services from fellow artists are not immediately available for any artist. Rather such supports evolve out of relationships artists build as they work at their careers and find a place within the community. When artists arrive as newcomers to the place in which they intend to pursue their career they usually begin to form relationships with other artists. These groups are not, however, movement circles. The artists are not, at this point, focused on upsetting the status quo, or if they are, their program is not yet fully defined. At first, for newcomers friendship and personal compatibility take precedence over aesthetic goals. Organized commitment towards the prevailing stylistic paradigm emerges later.

Artists' groups first become the crucible for developing and maturing of an artist's work (Schucking, 1966: 49). Although, as noted, friendship and companionship may be the originating motive for early relationships, avant-garde goals become more important and increasingly define the nature of the relations. The young would-be artist soon learns that becoming part of the artist community includes participation where the exchange of ideas is more essential than social support. One artist stated this as follows:

> If you're going to be an artist you sort of surround yourself-enter into a group which may somehow be interested in the kind of thing you're doing. I mean, very few people in the world care about art anyway, of any kind. And if you want to have your paintings, your work exhibited, in any place besides your mother's living room, you've got to get into where the action is, where the ideas are, to exchange these ideas with other people. There are no fairy godmothers that come and say 'you're a great artist.'

During the early stages of group development, creativity is stimulated by the fact of interacting. The artists interviewed described the importance of their early group experiences. They talked about the exchange of ideas on art philosophies, techniques, materials and attitudes, discussing how ideas were modified and influenced by these exchanges. Innovative ideas developed as a result of the social and personal exchanges, as two remarks by artists illustrate:

> We talked a lot about technical problems. We talk about how you can do such and such with a certain kind of paint and what kind of brush does this, what ideas are you thinking about, or how do you feel about such and such a problem.

> In my own head, quite out of specific dialogues, I made certain kinds of changes. Like I said, we talked, we would meet together, then it would occur. Things would switch a little bit and for each of us, the steps were tentative.

Sharing and exploring these new aesthetic ideas gave all the artists a chance to clarify and solidify their work.

Work became more precisely individual while at the same time sustaining a continuity of concern with the prevailing aesthetic endorsed by group members. Stylistic change does not immediately occur with the introduction of a new idea, but these artists had focused on the establishment of a viable aesthetic position and had begun to formulate their definition of what the change would be.

Movement Circles and Support Services

At the same time that artists were influencing each other's art work, a second element of the interaction within these groups is also evident. Practical support services increasingly became part of the relationships in which these artists participated, and these supports rested on shared commitment to the expression of avant-garde goals.

Support services are crucial for artists. While aesthetic goals develop but artistic careers are not yet established, artists need some means of financial survival. Sometimes, parents and/or spouses are this source, but for the most part, artists must ultimately rely on their own resources. Some kind of income is necessary. However, particular kinds of economic supports are more desirable than others. Employment, though obviously one kind of support system, is not necessarily a solution. For example, earning a living through a nine-to-five job creates problems and this is least desirable. Jobs must meet several requirements other than that of money. First, a job should not interfere with working on art. As one artist mentioned:

> I tried to get jobs where I could learn something, but I shied away from things that would be too demanding, that would take away from my work.

Second, a job should not interfere with the ability to participate in the ongoing routines of the artist community. Such routines are an essential part of building up contacts that are the basis of a career. For example, aspiring artists want to be available to hang around bars in the evening to meet other artists. One artist described his system:

> My schedule was such that I'd sleep during the day and go to work around evening and it worked out well. I'd get back to New York around four AM, before the bars closed and maybe I'd run into DeKooning or Kline or someone late at night, at Dylan's drinking.

This artist would never have been able to stay out late every night, getting the chance to meet these and other artists, if he had held a day time job.

Being available during the day was also at least occasionally desirable. Artists frequented galleries during the week, meeting other artists also checking out the scene. During the week there was always the chance of getting into the back room of a gallery to share gossip with dealers and more successful friends. One artist, talking about his early years remembered how one of these friends who had a gallery would stop by to pick him up saying:

> Come on. Let's go up and drink some of Leo's (Castelli Gallery) whiskey,'' and none of us had any money, so why not get a free drink and see the world from the back room of a big gallery.

Such experiences were valuable both for contacts and for socialization into the established art world. Acceptable jobs, then had to be of very particular sorts. Artists prefer to have jobs that are flexible so that they can take a day off occasionally to visit galleries. The best jobs for meeting these requirements were usually unskilled and low paying. Also, artists like jobs which relate to art but not to making art. Commercial art employment was out because it was nine-to-five usually and one artist who held a job in such an office spoke of how it detracted from his own work. Lower-level museum and library work, teaching art, writing about art for art journals—all flexible jobs in terms of scheduling—were frequent choices among these artists. At one time, several of the guards at one museum were from among these artists. Many artists worked at manual labor jobs, including furniture moving, carpentry, construction. In at least two instances, these jobs were indirectly tied to art; one artist moved paintings and in the process met many well-known artists, while another made picture frames.

Access to the available information about job possibilities became a key element of survival. The artists ferreted out jobs, gave each other hints, passed on information when other jobs were known to be free, so that the possibility of getting the desirable work was most possible for those who were part of the community network.

While knowledge about jobs was a most important shared resource the young artists could help their peers with, other resources were also shared. However, no particular pattern predominated. Artists' help for each other developed as an intrinsic part of their relationships. They helped each other in whatever way possible, encouraged perhaps by Bohemian mythologies of shared life-styles. Meager financial assets were shared with those who had no money for the moment and needed supplies or other materials. The favor might be returned from the recipient, or from someone else. One artist talked of his first years in New York and how he lived:

> He wanted a place to stay and I said he could flop here. And then he moved. And then, I was kicked out because I lost my job and he said, "you can flop here," and I lived a year on the floor.

One young artist had a collection of early pieces by an established artist because they shared the youngers' working space, when the other was temporarily without his own space. Since the works are now worth high prices, the favor is probably considered repaid. Another artist related how after receiving an invitation to a major show in Switzerland, he scraped together the money from his dealer and other friends, "to fly off with the ticket paid for and four dollars extra to live on for a week."

Movement Circles and Style Change

The interaction of these artists was essential for the evolution and strengthening of stylistic ideas and for development of a new stylistic paradigm. In the early stages of this movement, these groups, composed primarily of young artists whose interaction was based on the exchange of ideas about stylistic goals reinforced their commitment to each other through sharing resources. The importance of these early support systems was that they allowed artists to survive as working artists before achieving some success and they provided the kind of life-style which fostered meeting others in casual settings. As the data presented here suggests, both the creative and the economic aspects of the interaction between artists are integrally related. Support mechanisms are an intrinsic rather than a subsidary part of the bonding mechanisms and economic support systems are clearly tied to stylistic boundary-maintenance. Artists' supports depended on stylistic commitment to avant-garde goals. They shared meagre assets with those whose aesthetic goals were compatible.

But for stylistic change to occur the shift into more goal-oriented and bonded movement circles is not sufficient alone to bring about a change. Many artists' groups within the art community are committed to stylistic change and developing art against an established paradigm is a goal for any avant-garde artist (Graña, 1967; Poggioli, 1968). Before change can occur, a group must develop links to the art market. These links are through other artists who act as gate-keepers, facilitating the exposure and acceptance of the avant-garde artists, and ultimately, the success of the movement circle.

Artists as Gate-keepers

Artists with established gallery connections and public reputations, occupy central and powerful positions within the art community. They are tied into the larger art community of artists, dealers, critics, journalists, collectors. Because of their position these artists can influence the acceptance of both artists and/or stylistic ideas. Thus, artists who have established reputations play a key role in style change by becoming gate-keepers within the community for a stylistic movement. (Hunter, 1974: 312).

Artists and Power

That artists have a great deal of power in the avant-garde art community is well-known and aspiring artists soon learn this fact. Two younger artists expressed this awareness quite cogently:

> I don't think any dealer walks into a studio and says "fabulous." I mean, I think the whole way it happens is underground reputations—artists recommending other artists.

> Artists run the art world and sooner or later the artists win out. A good artist can show anywhere and other artists know a good artist when they see one. It's reputation among fellow artists that counts.

These young artists perceived the necessity of extending contacts in order to achieve access to the critical centers of the art community and to the market, knowing such acceptance was a crucial link in the process of their own acceptance. The importance of developing an "underground" reputation was clear.

> Artists initiate styles. (Dealers) bring to the public guys who are already there. When the Minimalists, say Andre, Judd, LeWitt, you know—put Ryman there—they had been making art for a long time. By the time Virginia (Dwan Gallery) picked them up, they all had underground reputations. All of them.

That this power exists is amply supported by statements from members of the wider art market (Jervis and Schilds: 1979). Harold Rosenberg (1970: 395) writes:

> Yet the single most potent force in the art world is still, in the last analysis, the artist . . . It is to him that the dealers and the collectors, the curators and the art department heads turn for recommendations. It is his judgement of his colleagues that reviewers listen in on before committing themselves in their columns.

When asked how he brought artists into his gallery, the gallery owner interviewed for this study stated:

> You're asking how new talent is discovered. Mostly by looking at studios, listening to the advise of artists. It's mostly a subjective opinion. The artists are always visiting each other's studios and they really know what is going on, so the artists recommend other people.

Members of the market structure do not perceive themselves as having the specialized knowledge necessary to make critical judgements and since artists are presumed most knowledgeable about the work of other artists, they have been given power to make evaluations. This is supported by a comment made by a museum curator when discussing an artist-critic's review of the museum exhibition, which became the benchmark event for this group's movement, the "Primary Structures Show," held in June 1966 at the Jewish Museum.

> I could go the "Primary Structures" and of course I knew about Judd and Flavin. But there were many other people I couldn't have sorted out and obviously there were a lot of people. Mel really did know. He knew the ideas that were going on, you know, the validity of them.[1]

Konrad Fischer, a dealer with a gallery in Soho, the avant-garde gallery district in New York City, stated in a journal interview (see Jappe, 1971: 68):

> When I have no information of my own to go on, I rely on the judgments of my friends, especially the artists, There is no doubt that good artists respect other good artists.

Artists became, in this way as the experts and their power as gate-keepers is sustained and validated.

Any aspiring artist who believes the myth that the artist's ability rests on "genius" but that the artist is powerless, and who then acts on these beliefs would find it impossible to achieve a career as an artist, to find an audience or to become self-supporting through art and accepted as an artist.

Such reliance by outsiders on peers for judgment is common when the area of knowledge in question is so specialized or esoteric that outsiders can not make these distinctions themselves. Science is such an example (Merton, 1957: 558–9) where scientists act as authorities and legitimize the work of other scientists. As the avant-garde has become incresingly exotic and cerebral, it has also acquired informal means of social control over the values and goals that artists want to maintain and perpetuate.

Gate-Keeper Supports

Artistic Support

Established artists encourage and influence the ideas of younger, unestablished artists. Their work usually provides a visible sense of direction and stylistic coherence to the emerging ideas of young innovators. The Minimalists who in the early stage of their work had little knowledge of each other were first supported and helped by older artists. One artist talked about his participation in one of the seminal groups formed around an established elder:

> But at that time, he was not into making art so much as just kind of expounding about art. He was very anti-art scene at that time. He was a man who dealt with ideas, and I think, just his way of thinking about things, about his art—he was involved in the environment, he was involved in change, and he was searching for things—and that's what turned me on. Incredibly open. He never felt threatened by any new style that came along . . . To succeed with those guys, you had to be on your mettle. You couldn't bullshit them, you had to think things through clearly, if you were going to talk with them. It was very good. Whether I agreed with every thing they said is beside the point. I don't know. But to keep up with them, you had to be on your toes.

Thus, intellectual exchanges encouraged these artists to work in an innovative direction that became the basis of a stylistic paradigm.

Established artists also provide economic support which is usually much more substantial than support from peers. In effect, established artists become patrons. Morgan (1978: 12) has explored the concept of patron-artists among the Bloomsbury group in England and notes:

> Artists and writers as members of particular circles, schools or networks may provide shortterm patronage to newcomers or to each other, a patronage ranging from moral support to more direct financial or material aid.

According to the artists I interviewed about their early days, the financial support from artists was a frequent occurrence rather than an isolated event. One artist made the following comment:

> Nobody took (the art) seriously, except five or six people in the art world, one of which was Sol LeWitt who at that point had no money at all, and was always offering $25 or $30 for something if you wanted to do a project or needed something. The same for Carl, who was certainly one who somehow or other would call you the biggest prick, and you'd look down and see $10 in your pocket . . . I was never in isolation. I never had very much money so I was totally dependent on the art world to keep me afloat and I must say, many men, who were extremely generous, who seemed to understand what I was talking about—like Chamberlaine, who

is a seminal force everyone seems to forget. He was the first recognized person to accept, the first person who was a recognized superstar to accept Stella and Andre.

Such support was a means by which these established artists would help younger artists whose ideas excited them before a gallery owner expressed interest or before they were ready for a gallery. Often they accepted works of art in return from the younger artists, which had the double effect of providing financial support and indicating faith in future success.

Finally, the gate-keepers facilitated entrance into the market system itself by giving the younger artists introductions to collectors and a wider public visibility.

Market Supports

Introductions into the market itself through gate-keepers came in two ways in this period. Before major gallery interest in the work appeared, established artists often organized group shows at their own galleries. Second, they gave the young artists introductions to people who might help them obtain gallery support, and as interest in the movement grew, to gallery dealers and owners.

Group-Shows

One technique for creating interest in a new stylistic paradigm is to hold a group show. An historical precedent was the Salon des Refuses of the Impressionists. Sometimes these shows are put together by an interested dealer. But just as frequently the impetus for a group show is from the artists. A group show introduces new artists and also promulgates a point of view which coincides with the interests of the established artists. In order to generate interest in the new stylistic direction, the art world must see these. The first requirement for a group show is the existence of an activity engaged group or groups of artists working in this direction—the movement circle. Then galleries must indicate some interest in responding to these new possibilities. The gallery is a necessary, structural element in the formation of a new movement as it provides public exposure. Groups shows solve at least two problems: unknown artists are more acceptable in groups than in one-person shows; group shows diminish the risk of failure both for ideas and for individual artists.

Among the artists interviewed, most of the older ones started by being in a group show. One artist talked of his experiences with Ad Reinhardt, a major supportive figure for this movement:

> I met Ad Reinhardt, and he wanted to put on a show at Dwan called "Ten;" it was an important show and he asked Morris to help him out on this show, and he had meetings about it and everything, and got the ten artists together and put on the show.

For this artist, inclusion in the exhibition, which became one of the major shows during the life of this movement, provided the necessary boost to his career as he was invited to join the gallery after the show. He had met Reinhardt at a party and Reinhardt expressed interest in his work. Before this, the young artist was already part of a group of young artists who were gaining attention. The meeting with Reinhardt was a final step.

> I met Sol LeWitt and Dan Flavin up there, and it just seemed like a lot of people were coming out of different ranges and having something in common, but not similar ideologies and Ad Reinhardt brought a lot of people together with the "Ten" show, and that was very important for me in terms of meeting other artists, and as I was writing, I'd get calls from people.

Before 1966 and the "Primary Structures" exhibition, several group shows were held. Other group shows continued to be held after the acceptance of the new movement as artists developed variations and extensions of the original statement. One particular group used group shows alone instead of individual shows as the primary means of fostering their ideas. This group worked on one of their first shows for a year, as one artist relates:

> Because of the nature of a lot of our work we had to sit down with Seth and we had to figure out a way to present the information. All of the shows that materialized out of that were attempts at solving that problem.

Gallery Support

Gallery support was the goal of the newcomer since acceptance by the gallery usually assures some income as well as career legitimization. The established artists acting as gate-keepers shared contacts, giving younger artists introductions to their dealers and galleries. One artist talked of the continuous generosity of another artist in a typical way:

> . . . a very influential person—he's very generous in terms of talking about other artists. It's a very interesting trait in his personality. A couple of others were generous in those terms, pointing out new artists, new directions, so what happens is you have people like Fischer, Speroni (dealers) sponsoring these young American artists.

Few artists ever find their way into a major gallery without such an introduction. The majority of these artists attained their first gallery recommendation from other artists. One commented:

> I have been relatively lucky in that I've never had to approach a gallery, which was good because I didn't know how to do it. I have always had people who did it for me. It wasn't a heavy struggle for a gallery.

Those who attempted to solicit galleries on their own met with little success. One artist, who in 1960 went to Leo Castelli, one of the most prestigious avant-garde galleries, was rebuffed in what he felt seemed to be a standard format.

> Very polite—They were not rude. I'm sure he's never refused an artist. He said, "Next year, perhaps." And I never heard from him again.

Later this artist grew to understand the fruitlessness of appearing at a gallery without a recommendation from another experience. Visiting the same gallery with a friend, he witnessed the following scene:

> I remember Ivan Karp coming into the back room at Castelli with some slides from some poor son of a bitch, who'd brought slides to the front desk. He came in, dancing this silly jig as if we were going to see a big comedy show. And the slides were just ordinary sculpture of the day, and no better or no worse than the stuff Castelli was showing.

Another artist talked about the importance of contacts for gallery introductions:

> Well, I've always felt that the dealers, the gallery should come to me, that they should, of course, be aware of my work. But I wasn't going to say "I want to show." I felt it was their prerogative. After awhile, you meet people. You talk. They realize you're doing some work, and occasionally they want to see what you're doing.

As interest in the style and this artist's work evolved, he was approached because of his reputation among artists. Indeed, both artists just quoted here are among the most successful artists in the art world today.

Boundary-Maintenance and Gallery Introductions

As the new movement gains momentum, the final stage of the movement becomes visible, with membership in the movement circle more exclusive. While interest in the style was strong, established artists encouraged galleries and dealers to take on many of the increasing numbers of young artists who appeared on the scene and contributed to the definition of the new stylistic paradigm. But as the movement achieved public acclaim, numbers increased and ideas became diffused, so that competition developed for the gallery positions that were now becoming scarce. The tendency developed, according to some, to encourage younger artists who were relatively weak and who would not, presumably, threaten the artists who had achieved their success through the movement. One artist discussed the gallery situation which existed at the time of the interviews, comparing it to the decline of Abstract-Expressionism:

> You have this whole second generation of Abstract-Expressionists, who are encouraged, because they were alternately supporting the economic system of the artists and the dealer, who had come before them. If you have a group of artists who make certain kind of art, and they make art, then you have another group that comes along and they support the art. They, kind of, validate it in the history books, those other artists. And the dealers know second-rate people who keep up the names of the first-rate people and who perpetuate the art movement. It's changing a little bit, but not really. A lot of people are being shown, and I think it's damaging to them. They're young and they're being shown. It's a perfect example of someone who's being shown to validate other artists who came before them. Like—did the same pieces. He's very weak as an artist, and he's very foolish to allow himself to be used that way.

Thus, ultimately, the movement circle's exclusivity and competitiveness prevented new ideas and approaches, and this movement, as others before it, was weakened and superseded by new stylistic directions.

Conclusion

Stylistic change, a new direction in art, is not a result of mysterious aesthetic events nor the product of artistic geniuses working in solitude. It is like other innovations in ideas; they are grounded in the processes of society and in particular, in the organization of a particular occupation.

In examining artists we find certain patterns are the most important for the success of an art movement. It is crucial that there be an exchange of stylistic ideas within the context of the avant-garde paradigm so that the paradigm is expanded, developed, perfected. However, such exchanges are an ongoing facet of the art community, whether the stylistic direction changes or not. From analysis of this group, it seems clear that activities within the group around mutual support services are equally important, contributing to the encouragement of certain ideas about art over others.

As I have discussed, the nature of personal support varies with the capacities of the individual. In the beginning stages of the movement circle, support is expressed by the mutual exchange of available resources—jobs, apartments, working space and the critical support of ideas. This early support is characterized by co-operativeness. Once successful, competitiveness surfaces and most, if not all of the casual sharing, disappears.

Support from established artists falls into two categories: first, there is patronage, usually as monetary support; second, there are sponsor group shows or introductions to galleries and dealers. Since gallery acceptance is a key element in the public definition of a new movement, such introductions are important both to the individual artists and to the success of the stylistic paradigm which may become a major art movement.

Both interaction among artists and between artists and gate-keepers are essential for the success of stylistic change. Many young artists must be convinced of the workability and validity of an aesthetic ideal. Artists within the movement circle develop and support this direction. But without the intervention of older artists in the roles as patrons and gate-keepers, new ideas would not be "discovered." Thus, a new stylistic movement results from artists collectively developing ideas and providing support services rather than the solitary endeavors of any single artist.

Artists may have emerged within the open market system of the art world as the single most powerful element in determining the prevailing art style. This is because they control other artists' entry into the field, determine what is acceptable and not acceptable, advise gallery owners and often own galleries, and finally, because they are considered by others to be experts. Revolution in art occurs as a result of many factors, some of them are social and some of them are aesthetic. However, artists themselves play a major role in the shaping of art and the direction of stylistic change.

Notes

1. Mel is the art critic, Mel Bochner. See Bochner (1966).

References

Bochner, Mel. 1966. "Primary Structures." *Arts Magazine* 40: pp. 32–34.

Crane, Diane. 1973. *Invisible Colleges.* Chicago: The University of Chicago Press.

Geer, Josephine. 1977. *Masters and Servants.* New York and London: The Garland Press.

Graña, Cesar. 1969. *Modernity and its Discontents.* New York: Harper and Row, Publishers.

Hunter, Sam. 1974. *American Art of the Twentieth Century.* New York: Harry Abraham, Inc.

Jappe, Georg. 1971. "Georg Jappe Interviews Konrad Fisher." *Studio International* 181: p. 68.

Jervis, Nancy and Maureen Schilds. 1979. "Survey of NYC Galleries Finds Discrimination." *Artworkers News,* 8.8: 3,7–9.

Kadushin, Charles. 1966. "The Friends and Supporters of Psychotherapy: On Social Circles in Urban Life." *American Sociological Review,* 31: pp. 789–802.

Lippard, Lucy. 1973. *Six Years: The Dematerialization of the Art Object from 1966 to 1972.* New York: Praeger Press, 1.

Merton, Robert. 1957. *Social Theory and Social Structure,* Rev. and enlarged ed. Glencoe: The Free Press of Glencoe.

Morgan, David. 1978. "Patronage, Brokerage and Friendship—The Case of Bloomsbury." Paper presented at the British Sociological Association Annual Meeting.

Pincus-Whitten, Robert. 1969. "Richard Serra: Slow Information." *Art Forum* VIII (1) 34–39.

Poggioli, Renato. 1968. *The Theory of the Avant-garde.* Tran. Gerald Fitzgerald. New York: Harper and Row Publishers. Icon Editions.

Rosenberg, Harold. 1970. "The Art Establishment." pp. 338–395 in Mason, Griff, James Barnett and Milton Albrecht (eds.), *The Sociology of Art and Literature.* New York: Praeger Pub.

Schucking, Lewin. 1966. *The Sociology of Literary Taste.* Trans. Brian Battershaw. Chicago: The University of Chicago Press.

Simpson, Charles. 1981. *Soho: The Artist in the City,* Chicago & London: University of Chicago Press.

White, Cynthia and Harrison White. 1965. *Canvases and Careers.* New York: Wiley.

Part IV

Artists and Their Social Networks

Introduction

Social ties or networks are generally important for people. Friends, but particularly family members, provide individuals with social and emotional support. Through our linkages with a variety of other people, groups, and associations we obtain valued resources, including information, advice, critical feedback, and acknowledgement for a job "well done." Interpersonal ties provide in various ways the "glue" of the social order, as ties integrate members into groups and society and at the same time provide for their social, economic, and psychological needs.

Thus, social ties have universal significance for persons and for the integrity of any social system, but they have a special significance for particular groups whose members are scattered, that is, when members do not live and work in close proximity to one another. Notable among these groups are scientists who are working at the forefront of a rapidly developing field, as is pointed out by Crane in her discussion of scientific paradigms. Crane's comparison of scientists and artists is instructive, because artists too have special needs for linkages with other artists, though these needs have different origins compared to those of scientists. For example, artists must maintain contact with gate-keepers who are not artists (such as collectors, dealers, and museum curators in the case of painters) whereas scientists' networks include very few that are not scientists. Very often artists must work together, which means that their primary contacts are local, whereas scientists often collaborate over great distances. Yet while artists are less cosmopolitan in their working relations compared with scientists, their relations serve more diverse purposes than scientists' relations do. Artists' networks provide social support, recognition, justifications for ideological convictions, ideas about style and technique, and information about jobs, whereas scientists' networks are typically more narrowly focused on a specialized research agenda.

But we can say that the production of art, just like the production of science, is inexorably rooted in individuals' working relations, that is, a network of interpersonal contacts. The conventions, styles, and techniques of art depend on such networks. The authors of papers in this section focus on the significance of networks for artists and art conventions, but it is useful here to dissect the various types of interpersonal relations in which artists are involved, for this centers attention on different kinds of exchange patterns and forms of influence, and also helps to distinguish key features of a great many art activities.

The Mentor-Protege Relation

Apprenticeship has always been a method of teaching in the arts, and the mentor-protege relationship is critical for an understanding of the transmission of technique and style. Its importance is suggested in this volume for the dance (Sutherland), music (Stebbins, Peterson and White), and acting (Levy). In fields that are relatively new and highly innovative (for example, composition on electronic synthesizers), there exist only tenuous ties between teachers and students, with students seeking guidance from diverse specialists. In other fields, notably in those for which technique requires many years of training and in those for which the approach to the material changes only very slowly over time, such as in opera, the relationship between the teacher and student may be close and the teacher's influence will be longlasting in its effects on the student's career.

Informal Networks

The networks discussed by Crane and Stebbins are informal ones; they emerge more or less spontaneously around some common interest—to play music together, to criticize and evaluate one another's work, or to share information. Participation in such networks is largely voluntary and is not imposed by a division of labor, nor constrained by a bureaucratic organization. One incentive to participate voluntarily in networks stems from the fact that art deals with the nonroutine and is an uncertain task at best. Involvement in networks helps to legitimize artists' activities, to furnish social support, and to provide sources of validation (Meyer, 1967). Peterson and White's analysis of studio musicians and Ridgeway's conclusions about painters in Chapter 11 help to substantiate this interpretation. In addition these two papers suggest an additional function served by networks, specifically, they promote economic exchanges by providing members with information about jobs. Stebbins provides additional insights into the importance of musical instruments and the orientations of musicians as they shape interpersonal networks. In contrast, Crane's analysis highlights the signifi-

Be sure to watch "Sleuth" tonight at 8 o'clock. My painting will be over the couch where they find the body.

cance of an aesthetic ideology for networks of visual artists. In other words, some groups emerge in response to economic or practical needs of artists, other groups provide validation for an aesthetic approach or artistic innovation, whereas still others primarily provide members with mutual support and encouragement.

Collaboration and Co-operation

Informal networks largely involve voluntary participation. Other networks, including those that are based on collaboration and those that are based on co-operation, are more or less the social instrumentalities by which artistic work is accomplished. The analytic distinction being made here rests on the difference between interpersonal relations that develop among artists because they are engaged in the same activity (and although there is no division of labor, they must engage in it together) and interpersonal relations among artists whose work is governed by a division of labor. The first is termed, 'co-operation' and the second, 'collaboration.' Examples of co-operation include potters who share a kiln, a ballet corps, ballad singers, and folk dancers. Collaboration which grows out of some division of labor in an art activity is illustrated by rock groups that include instrumentalists and singers, specialized members of a film-making crew, an opera company, and a relationship between the lithographer and the printmaker. Of course, the line between these social arrangements of co-operation and collaboration is not always easy to draw, but collaboration, in contrast to co-operation, typically requires some form of organization and usually more rules and procedures. The analytical distinction is important, for it permits fuller exploration of the range of artists' networks and how collaborative relations between different types of artists are quite unlike those relations among artists who are engaged in the same art activity and must cooperate to do it.

According to Becker (Chapter 2), standing at the very core of art convention is collaboration: artistic collaboration is not possible without conventions and collaboration makes conventions possible. The history of the arts is rich with examples of collaboration: between the hardhewer and freestone mason, between the artist and the printmaker, between the singer and composer. Co-operation, too, is commonplace, but as Crane indicates, easily threatened when there are scarce economic resources that engender competition among artists. The conditions under which co-operative ties are likely to be established among amateur musicians are described by Stebbins. Those under which co-operation among professional artists emerges are spelled out by Peterson and White. They describe the situation of nearly perfect competition in the recording industry but one that encourages insiders to co-operate with one another, while collectively opposing outsiders through the control of communication and the manipulation of job information.

The readings in this section provide interesting contrasts with respect to the way that artists of different types draw boundaries that are inclusive of people with different social backgrounds, and also ones that are exclusive. Another comparison made is the degree to which networks foster quality and innovation and how they serve to maintain the status quo. Still another relates to the different ways that social networks influence the development of the criteria of merit and those of conformity with respect to art conventions. The distinctions made here between various types of social relations—those based on ties between the mentor and protege, relations in informal networks, the co-operative relationships between artists engaged in the same activity, and the relationships between artists whose specialized roles necessitate collaboration—may provide the reader with bases of comparison for readings in this section as well as for readings in the section on art organizations and the section on gatekeepers, critics and patrons.

References

Meyer, Leonard. 1967. *Music, the Arts and Ideas.* Chicago: University of Chicago Press.

—— 12 ——

Music Among Friends: The Social Networks of Amateur Musicians[1]

ROBERT A. STEBBINS

There is no more delightful way of introducing the reader to the theme of this paper than with Robert Haven Schauffler's (1911) fanciful plan:

> Never yet have I heard a passing stranger whistling anything worth-while; but I have my plans all laid for the event. The realization of that whistle will come with a shock like the one Childe Roland felt when something clicked in his brain, and he had actually found the dark tower. I hope I shall not be « a-dozing at the very nonce, after a life spent waiting for the » sound, and so lose my man among the passerby. When I hear him I shall chime in with the second violin or 'cello part perhaps, or, if he has stopped, I shall pipe up the answering melody. Of course he will be just as much on the alert as I have been, and will search eagerly for me in the crowd, and then we shall go away together, and be crony-hearts for-ever after. (p. 255)

The amateur classical musicians, on whom the following pages focus, are charmed by their leisure and by their friends and acquaintances.

The principal aim of this paper is to explore the relationships between certain antecedent musical identities and the development of the avocational side of the amateur's social network. Specifically, concentration is on how these identities are related to the morphological and interactional characteristics of that network. A later section considers two recent contradictory assertions about leisure participation, friendship formation, and social structure and the amateur's musical network as an example of how they can be reconciled.

For these purposes we are fortunate to have Clyde Mitchell's (1969) framework for describing and analyzing social networks. The musicians' networks are treated first in terms of their "morphological characteristics." The relationships and patterning of the links in a network to one another are revealed in its anchorage, reachability, density, and range. These networks are then examined with reference to their "interactional characteristics." Here attention is directed to the nature of the links; to the content, directedness, durability, intensity, and frequency of interaction within them.

The data upon which this paper is based come from over two-hundred biographic and autobiographic accounts, chiefly of or by North American amateur classical musicians. These constitute one main source of information about the amateur musical social network. Another is my personal experience as an amateur in this area. In this role I have played in fifteen enduring amateur music groups and scores of ephemeral ones over the past seventeen years in four communities in the United States and Canada.

Attention centers on the amateur instrumentalist in what is variously referred to as classical, art, or serious music. Achieving even amateur status in this field requires a moderate amount of good training, steady practice, serious playing experience, and native talent, besides equipment good enough to produce a sound that is acceptable to a schooled ear.

Definitions of Amateur

Before launching into the relationships between musical identities and the development of the amateur's avocational network, we must settle whom he or she is. The answer to this question its presented at length elsewhere (Stebbins, 1977; 1978) and need only be briefly paraphrased here. I point out that it is misleading to define an amateur, as compared with a professional, as one who pursues an activity on a part-time basis and who, at best, only supplements a principal source of income earned elsewhere. These two truisms provide us with useful operational definitions for certain research questions, but only because they relate both amateurs and professionals to the underlying theme of occupational *continuance* commitment— professional musicians are committed to music and amateur musicians to some livelihood outside it.

My research on amateurs in general and those in classical music in particular shows that the essence of amateurism lies in the social and attitudinal organization of it practitioners. Turning first to their social organization, the musical amateur may be defined as part of a professional-amateur-public (audience) or P-A-P system of functionally interdependent relationships. Seven ways are identified in which this type of amateur is functionally related to professionals, audiences, or both. (1) Amateurs perform before audiences, as professionals do, and at times the same ones. And, they are oriented by standards of excellence set and communicated by those professionals. (2) A monetary and organizational relationship is frequently established when professionals train, direct, advise, organize, and even perform with amateurs and when amateurs come to compose part of their audience. (3) There is an intellectual relationship among professionals, amateurs, and their audiences, which springs primarily from the amateurs. Having more time for such things, they can maintain a broader, and simultaneously less specialized, knowledge of music than can most professionals.

The amateur, as special member of the audience, knows better than run-of-the-mill members what constitutes a creditable performance. Consequently, he or she relates to both audience and professionals in three additional ways: (4) By restraining professionals from overemphasizing technique and other superficialities in lieu of a meaningful performance. (5) By insisting on the retention of good taste. (6) By furnishing professionals with the stimulus to give the audience the best they can.

The seventh functional relationship, this time among professionals and amateurs solely, concerns career. The professional who falls within this P-A-P system inevitably starts in amateur ranks and, unless he or she abandons the pursuit entirely or dies in this role, will return to those ranks at a later career stage.

Turning to attitudinal organization as a way of defining amateur, five attitudes were found that differentiate amateurs from professionals and differentiate both from their audiences, including such marginal participants as dabblers and novices. (1) Confidence is a prominent quality of experienced professionals, but less developed among amateurs. (2) A difference in perseverance distinguishes these two groups for, seasoned or green, the professionals know they must stick to their music when the going gets rough. (3) The greater perseverance of professionals is fostered, partly, by their greater continuance commitment (see Stebbins, 1970). They experience pressures to stay in music as a livelihood, which are rarely, or never, encountered by amateurs. (4) Professionals evince a degree of preparedness that is commonly lacking among amateurs. By ''preparedness'' is meant a readiness to play music to the best of one's ability at the appointed time and place. (5) Finally, professionals and amateurs have different self-conceptions; they conceive of themselves as either professional or amateur.

Musical Identities

The following social identities were extracted from the sources of data upon which this study is based. Every amateur musician is a member of at least two of them.

Orchestral identities
   1) Concertmaster
   2) Section principal
   3) Section member
Administrative identities
   1) President
   2) Treasurer
   3) Secretary
   4) Manager
   5) Librarian
   6) Other
Organizer identities
   1) Chamber music groups
   2) Orchestras
Instrumental identities
   1) String
   2) Reed
   3) Brass
   4) Percussion
   5) Piano or organ
Performance identities
   1) Orchestra
   2) Chamber music group
   3) Solo
Expert identities
   1) Instrumentalist
   2) Music theorist
   3) Music historian
   4) Music scene specialist

Some of these categories require explanation; others do not. So, the orchestral identities are standard and need no comment, while administrative identities in North America vary widely from one amateur orchestra to another. Those with administrative boards ordinarily have a president, treasurer, and secretary. With or without such boards there may also be a manager whose job may be limited to matters concerning the players or, if no other administrative officers exist, it may encompass the usual duties of president, treasurer, and secretary. Nearly every amateur orchestra appoints a librarian to look after the acquisition and maintenance of parts and their distribution to members. Among other possible administrative roles are publicity, fund raiser, and entertainment chairman.

The two organizer categories are both indistinctly held and infrequently encountered. The more common are the organizers of chamber music groups. It seems every community, no matter how small, has at least one votary who is willing to spend an hour or two on the telephone arranging for a convenient time and place to play quartets or trios. The orchestra organizer is rare and is more likely to be a conductor than an instrumentalist.

The instrumental identities need little explanation, outside the remark that listing by specific instrument is unnecessary for the aims of this paper. As for the performance identities of amateurs, many are either mainly orchestral players or mainly chamber music enthusiasts. A small number participate substantially in both forms. An even smaller number try their hand at solo performance, as a sideline to their primary commitment to orchestral or chamber music.

The expert is found in four relatively clear-cut forms. It may involve being an authority on a particular musical instrument; versed in its history, styles and methods of playing, ensemble and solo literature, and the like. Other amateurs, whether accomplished instrumentalists or not, establish themselves locally as music historians or theorists of sorts. The music scene specialists are conspicuous for their exceptional knowledge of the major contemporary orchestras around the world, their conductors, and their best-known recordings. Frequently, they can be counted upon for information about prominent world music festivals, special schools, and outstanding conservatories. In short, they are extraordinarily informed about the music scene of their day.

Social Networks

Social networks may be defined from two perspectives: objectively as a person's current set of social relationships for which there is no common boundary (Bott, 1957), and subjectively, as the orientation that develops from considering all or a portion of these relationships in the immediate situation (Stebbins, 1969). Both definitions apply in the following discussion, although only that part of the total network that is associated with music is examined.

Morphological Characteristics

The first of these morphological characteristics—anchorage—refers to the person or category of persons from whom the network is traced. Different anchorages spawn different social relationships, hence different networks. In amateur classical music anchorage could conceivably vary with every class of musical identity. Three are examined here: instrumental, orchestral, and administrative.

The very nature of art music encourages string players to associate with one another, reed players to associate with their kind, and similarly with brass players, percussionists, and pianists. Symphony orchestra musicians are grouped in this manner both in musical compositions and while performing them. Moreover, in playing a piece of music, each general type encounters special technical problems that are often solvable only through discussion with other instrumentalists. Chamber music is usually written for aggregates of musicians within each group and only infrequently for combinations drawn from two or more of them.

Of all these generic types, classical pianists have the greatest opportunity for developing social networks that span group boundaries. For, outside the small number of works written expressly for multiple pianos, only one of them is ever required in orchestral and chamber music compositions employing instruments from one or more of the other categories. However, a sizeable majority of these compositions omit piano altogether, which eventually forces many pianists into solitary music making wherein they provide both melody and accompaniment (possible only on piano, organ, and guitarlike instruments). Consequently, despite their exceptional opportunity for acquiring a heterogeneous network they often go through their avocational lives with a stunted set of contacts, typically composed of only the musician's teacher and maybe some of his pupils whom the musician has happened to meet.

Holding the orchestral position of concertmaster or section principal vis-a-vis that undifferentiated section member also affects network development. The first two positions lead their incumbents to a wider selection of contacts than the third. And, administrative roles, such as librarian or manager, tend to generate diverse ties, because they require frequent interaction with other musicians. Beyond these general sources of variation in anchorage are numerous particular sources. For instance, a violinist may find it convenient to ride to and from rehearsals with an oboist. Or they may gravitate toward each other through their vocational or other avocational interests, or these shared concerns may have preceded their entry into their music group (Phillips, 1974:58).

The second morphological characteristic is reachability, which denotes the number of intermediaries whom must be contacted in a personal network in order to reach certain others in the same network. Reachability is relatively great when few or no intermediaries are needed for this purpose versus when many are needed. Extensive reachability is characteristic of those in the orchestral, administrative, and organizer identities.

The concertmaster usually has the greatest reachability of any instrumentalist in a community orchestra because responsibilities bring him or her into direct contact with the majority of members. For example, the concertmaster may be simulataneously the assistant conductor, chief recruiter, and disciplinarian in addition to being the subleader of the orchestra. The responsibilities of principals also engender in those who lead large sections a degree of reachability that is normally lacking among the rank and file.

Owing to administrative assignments, it is possible that the third horn player in an amateur orchestra could have greater reachability than, say, the principal of the bass section. The person might be treasurer whose tasks include collecting the annual dues from each member. Finally, regardless of orchestral or administrative position a musician may emerge as an organizer of chamber music sessions, acquiring in the process numerous special, direct contacts and extensive network reachability.

For musicians with authority (e.g., concertmasters, principals) extensive reachability is crucial for their effective functioning in that role. It is difficult, to say the least, to urge better intonation, consistent punctuality at rehearsals, and more artistic playing from a player with whom one has no direct relationship.

Density, the third morphological characteristic of networks, refers to the extent to which links that could possibly exist among persons actually do. The denser ego's network, the larger the proportion of that persons' friends, relatives, and acquaintances who know one another.

Here, orchestral, administrative, and organizer identities as important antecedents join with a fourth: the identity of performance. On the one hand, a section cellist in an amateur orchestra who plays little chamber music or performs in no ephemeral groups (e.g., pit orchestras) has a dense network constituted largely, if not entirely, of the other cellists in his section. On the other hand, the concertmaster or president who knows nearly every member of the orchestra has a comparatively sparse network because many of those members have no direct interchange with each other. The same can be said for the local chamber session organizer. But, avid chamber musicians who meet regularly in an enduring ensemble have networks of greater density than those who play primarily in ad hoc sessions. So, the members of the reknowned Saturday Night Club, which met regularly to play chamber music in Baltimore from 1904 through 1950, likely had denser musical networks than do those who participate with different musicians today in such monthly open chamber sessions as the one held at the Hunterdon County Art Center, Clinton, New Jersey (Cheslock, 1961; Grueninger, 1957). Chamber musicians whose playing is largely restricted to Amateur Chamber Music Players (ACMP) contacts while away from home have diverse routine playing experiences.

Musicians who regularly organize chamber sessions or hold key playing or administrative positions in amateur orchestras are also apt to have a greater range range of contacts than others. Range, the fourth morphological characteristic, refers to the number of direct links in a network. Findings pertaining to the typical maximum number of interpersonal relationships people sustain are inconclusive, with estimates running from twelve to thirty (Jennings, 1950:309; Mitchell, 1969:20). Many amateur classical musicians appear to have network ranges closer to thirty than to twelve, while the ranges of such people as concertmasters and influential principals are probably far higher. A gregarious violinist, such as Leonard Strauss, founder of the ACMP, who made it a practice during his business trips to search for and perform with chamber music enthusiasts must exceed, by a wide margin, the hypothetical maximum of thirty (Antrim, 1956; *Life*, 1953).

Interactional Characteristics

The first interactional characteristic is content: the meanings ego attributes to his relationships with others in his network. There are, of course, a variety of meanings associated with particular relationships among amateur musicians as among other people; meanings of love, hate, respect, disrespect, envy, fear, and the like as they relate to such musical antecedents as playing ability and orchestral position. Though the common purpose that brings these people together is the making of music, the interpersonal ties that emerge come to mean much more than this. Sometimes these associations even break up over nonartistic issues as happened in an American string quartet that disbanded during World War II because three of its members grew intolerant of the pro-Hitler views of the fourth (Grueniger, 1957).

Like the morphological characteristic of anchorage, content varies with every music identity simply because each forces the incumbent into a peculiar relationship with other musicians. There is at least one general difference in the meanings attributed to musical relationships among amateurs that cuts across all the identities. It springs from the distinction between "devotee" and "participant." The devotee is highly dedicated to classical music, whereas the participant is only mildy interested, though significantly more so than the dabbler. The devotee and the participant are identified operationally by the amount of time they commit to practicing, rehearsing, performing, and studying in accordance with the accepted professional norms for classical music.

What I am suggesting is that the devotees, because of their deeper commitment to music, define their network of relationships differently from the participants. The former have invested significantly more time, energy, and money in music than the latter. They expect, therefore, a higher return in the form of self-enhancing or role supportive benefits. Network links are one of the principal ways these benefits reach the devotees. Hence, networks have special meaning or content for them when compared with the participants.

The movement of influence and information within a network is known as directedness or directionality; it is the second interactional characteristic. Directedness in a network link may be either symmetric or asymmetric. Amateur classical music, as its professional counterpart, has both informal and formal asymmetric relationships. The two major examples of the latter have already been mentioned several times: the concertmaster's authority over all members of the orchestra and the section principals' authority over their section members. To some extent, administrative position also contributes directedness to the networks of those who hold them. Information as well as influence flows through these formal channels.

One important type of informal asymmetric relationship is that between one of the respected music experts and those who seek their advice. The professionals who are hired near concert time by amateur groups to assist numerically or musically weak sections constitute a special case of this sort of asymmetry. These musicians frequently perform as undifferentiated section members, but their influence among the amateurs, assuming they are capable artists, is considerable.

Symmetric directedness in relationships, which occurs among peers in any identity, refers to the dissemination of information only, among ego and others in his network. Tidbits of all sorts are exchanged. A significant proportion of this information is of the gossip variety, pertaining to the lives and activities of mutual acquaintances (musical and nonmusical). Also transmited is information about new playing opportunities in chamber and orchestral music, technical advice about the playing of instruments, their repair, and the purchase of music (such may come even from equals); news about musical events; and instructions concerning the production of particular selections of music for the next concert. The norms of collective music making are often communicated in this symmetric fashion, such as by an admonition from a nearby player that rehearsing one's part while the conductor is speaking is bad musical manners.

Symmetric directedness is as significant as the asymmetric kind. Amateurs are rarely fully trained. Since many of them lack the time, money, or opportunity, or all three, for advanced instruction in music, they must pick up what they can when they can at gatherings with other musicians. This method of learning undoubtedly leads to the acquisition of some undesirable playing habits, but some improvement is also certain to be effected.

The interactional characteristic of durability refers to the degree of change that takes place in social networks. There is wide variation among amateur classical musicians on this dimension. Generally, this variation is associated with the type of performance identity, for orchestral music is

more likely to be made in permanent groups whereas chamber music is frequently performed in temporary ones. For instance, a violinist who has
played for several years in an enduring community or other type orchestra
has a more durable network than one who plays only chamber music with
the help of the ACMP Directory. The first occasionally loses a link in his
network or gains one as people leave or join the orchestra. But change in
this network is never matched by that in the network of the second who is
constantly meeting new musicians during travels away from home.

Yet, some musicians play in an enduring orchestra or chamber music
group while establishing new relationships through ephemeral orchestras
and chamber music sessions. In fact, it is the yearning to play chamber
music, a major artistic motive, that ultimately separates amateurs with
durable networks from those with less durable networks. In other words,
the yearning explains the variation in performance identities observed from
one amateur to another which, in turn, explains the variation in network
durability.

Why this yearning? Because chamber music is musicians' music. It is
performed with one player only for each part, thereby raising, significantly,
the visibility of individual playing. The musician may play, too, with
greater personal expression than is possible in an orchestra. The player thus
avoids the tension of overvisibility inherent in solo performance and the
dissatisfaction of undervisibility present in orchestral sectional work. It is
for their opportunities to play chamber music that professionals envy amateurs most.

The yearning to play chamber music is least often adulterated by such
dispositions as the desire to see old friends, the felt obligation to attend
rehearsals, the need to perfect a program for a concert, and the like, when
it is expressed through the medium of an ephemeral chamber music ensemble. Only the lure of the opportunity to play trios, quartets, or some other
chamber music arrangement draws the requisite numbers and kinds of players together for this purpose.

The commonest ways in which chamber music players make contacts
today is through the ACMP Directory; by extending to fellow members of
an orchestra invitations to play chamber music or by accepting such invitations (Brown, 1961:335) and by dropping hints while engaged with new
acquaintances in sociable conversation outside the sphere of music that one
is also a musician.

With respect to the next interactional characteristic, Mitchell states:
"The intensity of a link in a personal network refers to the degree to which
individuals are prepared to honour obligations, or feel free to exercise the
rights implied in their link to some other person" (Mitchell, 1969:27). Intensity is the *value* a relationship holds for an individual.

Intensity may be allowed to play a greater role in directing network interaction among amateurs than among professionals. That is, one aspect of the intensity of a relationship is the liking ego has for his partner. The amateur can avoid disliked activities and disliked people, while the professional has less choice in this regard. The professional must play for financial support, even if the music or musical associates are sometimes less than attractive.

Nevertheless, a relationship may be valued for different reasons. The orchestral, administrative, and organizer identities equip the musician with special perspectives on his or her artistic network and consequently with special evaluations of some of the relationships therein. The section principals prefer those who follow their advice to those who ignore it; the librarian appreciates the players who properly check out the music while scorning the ones who snub this procedure. Further, the chamber music devotee, as we have just seen, regards other devotees as a distinctive breed of musician. Beyond these, still other grounds exist for valuing a music relationship. For instance, it may provide ego with an exceptional opportunity to make new musical contacts, learn more about music, play the instrument better, or receive gossip.

The final interactional characteristic is frequency of contact among people in a personal network. As Mitchell (1969:29) cautioned, high frequency of contact does not necessarily imply high intensity in a social relationship. In amateur classical music frequency of contact is likely to be higher among those in authority (orchestral leaders and administrators), those who organize, and those who are sought for their advice (experts and administrators).

Frequency of contact is also associated with amount of collective music making. It is higher in the networks of musicians who rehearse weekly in an orchestra than in the networks of those who meet monthly in a chamber music group. It is lowest among chamber music players whose musical interchanges are fleeting and made in many different localities. It is highest among the amateurs in the institutional orchestras and chamber music ensembles found occasionally in prisons, mental hospitals, and homes for the aged. Music is perhaps the only meaningful activity available to these inmates who pursue it as often as possible, probably several times a week.

Leisure, Friendship, and Social Structure

The present analysis of the social networks of amateur classical musicians has an important bearing on the relationship between two contradictory assertions about leisure, friendship, and social structure in North

America. On the one hand, there are those who hold that coparticipants in avocational activities have similar occupational and social-class backgrounds. George Homans (1974) has taken this position most recently:

> First, the status of persons in all stratified societies, whether their status is inherited or achieved, is principally determined by their occupations, in the largest sense of that word, and by the incomes their occupations win for them . . . Second, the more nearly equal persons are in public status, the more apt they are to interact in the private field, the sphere of leisure, of after working hours, of "social" interaction: eating together, playing together, going to parties together (pp. 307–308)

On the other hand, studies of friendship and social networks indicate that these patterns often cut across major social boundaries in a society. Networks, Srinivas and Beteille (1964:167) argue, transcend the limits of corporate groups, institutions, and even whole communities, thereby articulating these with the wider social system.

What has been said so far about the networks of amateur classical musicians suggests a way in which the contradiction in these two propositions can be removed and their predictive strength increased. It is evident from my musical experience and from biographic and autobiographic accounts by amateurs that they come from diverse backgrounds. For example, the Chequamegon Symphonette in Ashland, Wisconsin, is composed of a college band director, several high school string and band teachers, several college and high school students, a number of housewives, a retired photographer, a retired clothing store salesman, and a college professor (Stycos, 1972: 16–17). At one time the Southern Illinois Symphony in Carbondale contained, in addition to college and high school students, housewives and teachers, a black woman bassoonist, and auto parts salesman, a building contractor, a physician, and several shop clerks (Hahesy, 1953:18–19). Max Kaplan (1957:210) reports an admixture of dentists, nurses, and business proprietors with beauty operators, house painters, printers, stenographers, and radio announcers in a community orchestra of a Colorado industrial town.

Tendencies toward such heterogeneity are noticeable in amateur orchestras in large cities, too, even though some groups there restrict entry to certain age, sex, occupational, and ethnic categories. This trend can also be found in lesser degree in amateur chamber music ensembles. Helen Rice (1959:129), Secretary of the ACMP, notes that its membership includes housewives, salesmen, streetcar conductors, and authors, along with the usual professionals (physicians, lawyers, professors, etc.).

Still, that a musician's community orchestra or ACMP Directory is filled with multifarious players is no assurance that his or her social network will reflect this situation. That partly depends on the anchorage and reachability of his network. Concertmasters, section principals, musician-administrators, and organizers of chamber music sessions are more likely to establish ties with players outside their occupational stations than those in the other musical identities. Moreover, even if the player's network tends to diversity, the content and intensity of its links could vary along the occupational or social-class dimension. Accordingly, it is possible that those of different external rank from ego also hold different meanings of amateur music; for instance, they are participants while ego is a devotee. Or, owing to a preference for performing music with someone of similar occupation (as happens in chamber music, inasmuch as it is often played in the home), the individual ascribes greater intensity to those network links that make this possible. The person is then inclined to interact more with people who share the same outlook on music and life.

In sum, friendships form in some amateur musicians' networks (because of the nature of the anchorage and reachability of those networks) that lead them across structural boundaries in the manner theorized by Suttles and denied by Homans. However, the tendency noted by Homans to interact at leisure with those of similar social rank or at least the preference to do so is also evident, and may be traced to the content and intensity these same musicians attribute to their bonds.

Summary and Conclusions

The aims of this paper have been twofold: to explore the relationships between certain antecedent musical identities and the development of the avocational side of the amateur classical musician's social network; and to present his network as an example of how to reconcile two contradictory assertions about leisure participation, friendship formation, and social structure. Amateurs were defined in terms of their social and attitudinal organization as members of a professional-amateur-public (audience) system of functionally interdependent relationships and as part-time practitioners who possess some of the same attitudes toward their selves and their activity as professionals do, but in significantly weaker or different form. Six types of amateur musical identities were also listed.

Turning to the morphological characteristics of amateurs' social networks, it was found that, conceivably, anchorage can vary with every type of musical identity. Extensive reachability in networks, however, was characteristic only of those in the orchestral, administrative, and organizer identities. These same identities were also shown to have the lowest network density and greatest range, although the performance identity was also discovered to be an antecedent where density is the focus.

Like the morphological characteristic of anchorage, the interactional characteristic of content varies with every musical identity. This was true of symmetric directedness as well. Asymmetric directedness, however, was limited to musicians in the expert, administrative, and orchestral identities. Variation in the durability of amateurs' networks was explained proximally by type of performance identity and distally by the presence of a powerful yearning to play chamber music. Network intensity, though it characterized all links irrespective of class of identity, was especially marked among those in the orchestral, administrative, and organizer identities. Frequency of network contact was likely to be highest in the orchestral, administrative, and expert categories and for those who engaged in the most collective music making.

In sum, it is clear that the administrative, orchestral, and organizer identities together account for the largest amount of variation in the characteristics of amateur classical musicians' avocational networks.

We concluded with a discussion of leisure, friendship, and social structure. Two contradictory statements were considered: that co-participants in avocational activities have similar occupational and social-class backgrounds and that friendships and social networks often cut across major social boundaries in a society. This analysis of amateur classical music suggests that friendships form in the networks of some people (because of the nature of the anchorage and reachability of those networks) that encourage them to cross structural boundaries. However, the tendency to interact at leisure with those of similar social rank, or at least the preference to do so, is also evident, and may be traced to the content and intensity these same musicians attribute to their bonds.

How typical these characteristics of the avocational network of the amateur classical musician are of the avocational networks in other areas of leisure remains to be seen. It should be noted, in closing, that there are conditions in classical music that greatly facilitate the crossing of social boundaries. One is that this music, by and large, is social. With the exceptions cited earlier, two or more players are required to constitute a melodic, rhythmic, and harmonic whole. Another is the supremacy of three values over all others, including attractiveness of network contacts. They are the values of artistic or creative ability, of musicianship or ability to play a musical instrument, and of commitment to classical music as an art form. A third condition is endemic to the amateur scene of North America: It is usually difficult to find enough musicians who have the artistic and musical sophistication to perform even moderately advanced orchestral or chamber music. Hence, when such a musician is found, that person's social background is unlikely to be considered as a criterion for recruitment. The second and third conditions indicate that to participate in classical music, is also to bracket the influence of external statuses in music settings.

Notes

1. Reprinted with the permission of the author and the publisher, *Revue International de Sociologie* (vol. 12, April/August 1976).

References

Antrim, Doron K. 1956. "They make music wherever they go." *The Etude* 72: 11, 61.

Bott, Elizabeth. 1957. *Family and Social Network*. London: Tavistock.

Brown, Jeffrey H. 1961. " 'Would you like to join my quartet?' " *The Strad* 71: 335, 337.

Cheslock, Louis. 1961. "Postlude." Pp. 207–205 in H. L. Mencken, *H. L. Mencken on Music*. New York: Alfred A. Knopf.

Grueninger, F. 1957. "Let's warm up on Hayden." *Dun's Review* 69: 58–60.

Hahesy, Ed. 1953. "Symphony in Illinois." *Music Journal* 11:18–19.

Homans, George C. 1974. *Social Behavior: Its Elementary Forms*, rev. ed. New York: Harcourt, Brace, Jovanovich.

Jennings, Helen H. 1950. *Leadership and Isolation*, 2nd. ed. New York: Longmans, Green.

Kaplan, Max. 1957. "Music in adult life." *Adult Leadership* 5: 210, 212.

Life Magazine. 1953. "Mr. Strauss has music wherever he goes." (May 18): 144–145.

Mitchell, J. Clyde. 1969. *Social Networks in Urban Situations*. Manchester: Manchester U. Press.

Phillips, Harvey. 1974. "The amateur virtuoso." *Physician's World* 2:51–52, 58.

Rice, Helen. 1959. "Potluck dates for amateur musicians." *Good Housekeeping* 148 (Feb.): 129.

Schauffler, Robert Haven. 1911. *The Musical Amateur*. Boston: Houghton, Mifflin.

Srinivas, M. M. & A. Betielle. 1964. "Networks in Indian social structure." *Man* 64: 165–180.

Stebbins, Robert A. 1969. "Social network as a subjective construct." *Canadian Review of Sociology and Anthropology* 6: 1–14.

Stebbins, Robert A. 1970. "On understanding the concept of commitment" *Social Forces* 48: 526–529.

Stebbins, Robert A. 1977. "The amateur: two sociological definitions." *Pacific Sociological Review* 20: 582–606.

Stebbins, Robert A. 1978. "Classical music amateurs." *Humboldt Journal of Social Relations* 5: 78–103.

Stycos, Roland. 1972. "How to grow symphonettes in cold weather." *Music Journal* 30: 16–17.

—— 13 ——

The Simplex Located in Art Worlds

RICHARD A. PETERSON
and
HOWARD G. WHITE

In 1976 there were 112 professional trumpet playing members of Nashville's Local 257 of the American Federation of Musicians. We judged approximately a dozen of these musicians competent to play the highly demanding and well-paid studio musicians jobs.[1] However, just four players, and not necessarily the most competent of the 112, garnered virtually all of this work, thus earning upward of $100,000 that year, while none outside the top five earned over $15,000 from professional trumpet playing.[2]

Such highly skewed reward structures are, of course, endemic in advanced industrial societies, but what drew our attention to the case of studio musicians is that they seem to work in a market economy of pure competition. All of the usual organizational and market supports of skewness are absent.

The session musician is ordinarily contracted to play for a three-hour engagement to augment the sounds of performers on phonograph records, TV and radio advertising jingles, and video or movie sound tracks. These studio musicians work anonymously and without public acclaim. Although the musicians' craft union has been able to increase wages and improve working conditions for recording session work, it does not restrict the number of competitors for this most desirable work. At the same time, high wages and job security are not guaranteed by long-term employment for a single organization. Thus, while a musician may make $100,000 a year, he/she does so in spite of being *fired* every three hours!

Without job tenure, without craft protection, without a star system, and without clearly being better than their rivals, how do a few trumpet players monopolize all the desirable work? With this question in mind, we interviewed numerous persons in, or knowledgeable about, the recording

243

industry. We reviewed our own field notes gathered from observing record ing sessions in New York, Los Angeles, Chicago, and Nashville intermit- tently for over a fourteen-year period. And author White brought to bear his knowledge of music gained as a professional musician and music teacher.

We found that trumpet players are not unique; other studio musician groups develop a form of self-protective interpersonal association very much like that discovered among trumpet players. Reviewing the literature, however, we found the *form* of these arrangements to be distinctly different from the other widely reported forms of collective art production. Since it had no name, we designated the form of interpersonal relations discovered among recording studio musicians as the *simplex*.[3]

Circles, Schools, and Simplexes

Art worlds exhibit a vast variety in shape, size, and duration (Wilson, 1964; Albrecht and Barnett, 1970; Kavolis, 1974; Peterson, 1979; Becker, 1982). But two forms, the *circle* and the *school*, have been found recur- rently across art forms, societies, and historical periods.

Schools develop where an academy can monopolize the definition of quality work,[4] and circles develop in a competitive avant-garde market to alter the definition of quality.[5] But studio musicians work in a oligopsonis- tic market (Scherer, 1970), one in which *many* musicians offer to sell their services to a *few* recording company buyers. This condition of near-perfect competition among sellers of artistic skills pitted against each other to fill jobs offered by a few buyers is found in some parts of the performing arts, and most of the commercial and media arts as well.

Craft associations often develop in such situations, and this case is no exception. The American Federation of Musicians operates to guarantee that record companies do not exploit the imbalance in bargaining power between the many sellers of services and the few buyers by bargaining for all professional musicians. The simplex, in turn, seems to operate to guar- antee that only a few union members earn a high and stable income.

Like movie or television production personnel (Powdermaker, 1950; Shanks, 1976; Faulkner, 1982), photographers (Rosenblum, 1973), and most workers in the performing arts as well (Becker, 1973, 1982; Martorella, 1974; Doll, 1974; Lyon, 1978), session musicians function as one among a number of linked crafts which combine their different talents in producing artistic works. And as in the case of these other sorts of linked craft ar- rangements, the diverse efforts are coordinated by a charismatic figure or entrepreneur who melds their work in ever-novel ways. Among orchestra musicians this is the conductor; in the theater and movies it is the director;

in the phonograph record industry and television it is the producer (Cantor, 1971; Peterson and Berger, 1971; Faulkner, 1971; Mukerji, 1976).

If the conditions of work and authority are distinctive among linked craftspersons, so is the way of defining success. Whereas the academic artist succeeds by working to match the traditional standard[6] and the avant-gardist succeeds by breaking with tradition,[7] the practitioner in the linked craft situation succeeds by foregoing tradition and self-expression to self-effacingly fit in with the efforts of the other craftsmen. This ability to fit in is the prime requisite for simplex membership, and so we turn now to focus on the several sorts of skills required to fit into the linked-craft job world of the studio musician.

Fitting In

Since session musicians are hired and fired every three hours, much of their effort is directed to maintaining the good opinion of hiring agents[8] and all others who might be able to help get them work. Musical ability is essential to secure employment, but it is only the first of several attributes necessary to fit in (Faulkner, 1971; Hensley, 1976). Six interrelated skills requisite for belonging to the simplex can be isolated.

First, the musician must show that he or she is *technically competent*. This means being able to play a wide range of musical styles at a moment's notice. The producer may ask for a Floyd Cramer piano style, a Sun echo, a Motown bass, or a melodic figure from any one of hundreds of songs. These are the sorts of elements from which arrangements are composed in the studio. So, for example, a player who may not read music must, nonetheless, be able to play any one of hundreds of solos carried in the collective memory of studio workers. The musicians must be able to change his/her part in the ensemble as arrangements are modified during the session, be able to play in a way that blends well with and does not show-up the other musicians, and be able to make the part he is asked to play sound right even when it has been scored in a way that does not "play." Though all-important, at the fine edge these skills are often quite subtle. For example, referring to a gifted and creative player, a producer said she was called primarily for less-demanding sessions because she did not hear and react to the other parts around her; he noted that she had to be told to raise her part an octave so as not to interfere with the solo guitar line, something a fully competent player would have done without being asked. Finally, having learned the complex and demanding arrangements, the musician must be able to forget them in order to be fresh and open for the next session with as little as one hour's break.

Second, the musician must be *socially reliable*. He or she must accept all calls for work and must not give priority to non-musical work or musical work that takes him away from the recording center. The only legitimate basis for declining work is that the player already has another record session. The musician must show up on time and be fit to play, free of alcohol and other drugs. In marked contrast to performing musicians who typically conform to the latest Bohemian style and present an exhibitionistic or cultivatedly withdrawn facade, studio musicians dress and deport themselves so as to look inconspicuous and reliable. The back-up female vocalists provide a conspicuous case in point, according to a veteran observer of the recording scene: "When that trio occasionally works behind [a performer] on the road, they wear very little and move everything they have, but here in the studio they look like three [inconspicuous] gray mice."[9]

Third, the musician must present a *craftsmanlike bearing*. This means *appearing* technically competent and socially reliable. The musician must bring all the appropriate instruments, accessories, and spares for those parts like strings and drumsticks that may break. Studio players standardly develop the fetishistic love of tools widely noted among craftsmen, and they go to great lengths to protect those parts of their body essential for smooth performance. Guitarists, for example, avoid all physical recreation that might hurt their hands. The social side of the craftsmanlike bearing is even more remarkable. The musician must appear interested in the recording process, and must not show contempt for the music, the lead performer, or others working in the situation, even when he or she considers them inferior. The session musician must also be willing to take and give musical suggestions without appearing egotistical or overbearing. Finally, a pose of noncommittal friendliness is essential in the casual social conversation on sessions. While any topic may be discussed, it cannot be pursued in a manner which suggests deep conviction.

Fourth, to keep the favor of hiring agents, the musician must be willing to do what is technically *illegal work*. The nature of the illegal work varies from instrument to instrument and from one recording center to another, but the most widespread practice is the technological manipulation of sound so that the work of a few musicians sounds like that of a full orchestra. The standard explanation for engaging in this illegal activity is "If I don't do it, they'll get someone else who will." Such illegal work not only saves money for the record makers, but it allows a few musicians to monopolize all of the available work, thus forestalling the entry of aspirants into the recording situation where their skills could be noted by hiring agents.

Fifth, the working musicians manage to do *all the available work*. This means that although they make incomes in the six-figure range, they do not take extended vacations, but remain available to take all recording sessions. When there is a temporary rush of work requiring more than the available members of the simplex, group members do not like to recommend aspiring studio musicians. Instead they invite musicians from other centers or competent part-time musicians who have well-paying non-music careers, two sorts of people who will not become full-time competitors for the available work. This tactic, together with the practice of doing illegal work, reduces, if it does not eliminate, the need for new recruits to studio work.

Finally, the set of behaviors and practices just described is sanctioned by the distinctive *occupational ideology of craftsmanship*. Studio musicians define creativity not in terms of the egoistic self-expression of genius (Becker, 1978), but as the ability to understand and deliver on demand exactly what is required. As a top-ranking New York session musician told Berger in 1965 (Peterson and Berger, 1971), "I don't have to believe in the music. If I don't like it, it's just three hours. It's a challenge to play my best just as you want it; it's being disciplined. I deal in a service. Like a bootblack who shines your shoes, he should give you a good shine; his reputation depends on it. I have the same attitude about [session work]. I play the producer's way, not my way. He will feel this attitude right away, that I am trying to co-operate, and the whole session goes better." Adler (1975:376–377) quotes a music teacher who tries to instill this selfless craftmanship: "If a kid tells me he 'just can't get into' a certain piece of music, I'll say, 'Tough shit' . . . They don't realize you have to go out and pay your dues to eat, do things you don't want to do, you don't believe in . . . What I really try to encourage in my students is a strong sense on nonentity!"

Simplex Structure

We had no great difficulty isolating the attributes necessary for a player to fit in as a session musician. Statements from our informants were continually affirmed by our own observations. Everyone recognized that there is a group of "first call" players of a given instrument which receives most of the work, and they generally agreed on the membership of this select group which we call the simplex. When we asked *why* some players and not others regularly get the work, however, we received two sorts of statements. Aspiring musicians said, "It's politics, it's contacts, it's who you know, it's getting in with the clique." The working musicians and the hiring agents said that "those who have proved themselves the best, and the most reliable, get the work."

These statements, which at first seemed to be self-serving rationalizations, have proved to reflect the two basic structuring principles of the simplex. First, simplex members in fact do help each other get work. Second, simplex members employ a wide range of tactics to insure that hiring agents believe that simplex members *alone* have the quality of musicianship and the ability to fit into the recording situation.

At least six sorts of activities faciliatate the dual simplex goals of boundary-maintaining co-operation and information control. The first four are discussed in this section.

RESTRICTING COMPETITION. Hiring agents are free to employ any union musician, but they are reluctant to take chances on persons they do not know, since recording sessions require the close co-operation of numerous craftsmen at the cost of hundreds of dollars a minute. Hiring agents prefer to employ those musicians they know will fit in, so they first call players who have performed adequately for them in the past. Musicians call these links to hiring agents their "accounts," and simplex members expect each other to respect an absolute taboo against raiding each other's accounts by criticizing another simplex member or promoting their own abilities to hiring agents. As we will detail below, account-raiding rivals receive the strongest possible sanctions.

Hiring agents are naturally interested in knowing the talent of other players, but they are prevented by strong industry customs from observing sessions where they are not directly involved. What is more, since all hiring agents are in competition with each other, they do not trust each other to give accurate recommendations for musicians. Thus, they tend to ask the players who they regularly hire to recommend additional players as they are needed. These various customs work together to put the evaluation of all musicians largely in the hands of the regularly employed studio musicians themselves.

RANKING. Evaluations resolve into a stable hierarchical ranking which includes all of those players of a given instrument who regularly engage in studio work in a given recording center. These ranked individuals comprise the simplex. They do not openly criticize each other's play, nor do they try to out-perform each other in public. Simplex members continually reaffirm the hierarchy and stress their *collective* excellence relative to nonmembers and to instrumentalists in rival recording centers around the world.

Evaluation has a public and a private face. Public rankings are elicited by asking, "who are the best players in town?" The list of rankings freely elicited in this way correlate almost perfectly with each other except at the lower end—the boundary of the simplex. Since the musician with the most accounts is in a position to give the most favors and tends to work most often, he is publicly ranked highest by the others. This public ranking does not necessarily correlate highly with *our* assessment of musical ability.

Rather, it correlates highly with income. As many respondents volunteered, "they must be the best, they get the work, right?"

In the strictest confidence, some players provide a different evaluation based primarily on the musician's *current* ability to play well. Each and every evidence of failure becomes a major topic of conversation among simplex members. High blood pressure, faltering musicianship, spouse trouble, irritability, the search for employment outside the studio situation, and so on are all noted as signs that the musician may be slipping.

FAVORS. Following the line of the ranking system, simplex members routinely recommend each other for jobs. This is the primary bonding mechanism of the simplex, but since studio musicians may also be songwriters, arrangers, copyists, live music band leaders, song publishers, teachers, clinic performers, and so on, the coinage of exchange is quite wide and diverse. The exchange of favors extends well beyond the simplex itself, and debts are remembered over extended periods of time. For example, a player told us that "by mistake, they erased my track while overdubbing. In a panic, the producer called to ask me to redo my part. I did it, and the producer prepared to pay the hundred dollars out of his own pocket. I said, 'Forget it.' He said, 'If you need a favor, just ask.' That was worth much more than the money."

SOCIAL ACTIVITIES. Simplex solidarity is reinforced through continuous socializing among members. Some of this activity, such as the creation of rehearsal bands, is job-related, but as often it involves leisure pursuits or joint ventures of one sort or another. Activities tend to be expensive and are engaged in faddishly. Not all simplex members may participate in a given fad such as tennis lessons, photography, hot tubs, psychic phenomena, or land speculation, but all become knowledgeable while the fad is in. Each of these activities provides occasions for demonstrating simplex solidarity and for reaffirming the internal hierarchy through the exchange of favors and flattery.

Such fads seem to be more important in New York and Los Angeles than in Nashville, but there it is important to be male, white, to come from the South-eastern states, and to demonstrate a casual nonchalance. In marked contrast, session musicians in New York and Los Angeles comes from remarkably divergent backgrounds. A simplex may include the son of a back-country black Louisiana share-cropper, a midwest Polish accountant's son, a San Francisco ex-flower child, and the Juilliard-trained son of a New Jersey Jewish merchant. The successive fads give them a common social experience to talk about, illustrating the pattern that Yancey et al. (1976) call "emergent ethnicity." Whether by shared consumption patterns or by ethnic homogeneity, simplex group members develop a distinct social vocabulary and come to share quite similar life-styles. As predicted by Bensman and Lilienfeld (1973), craft and not class is the basis of consciousness. The development of simplex culture not only helps members to play better together and get along off the job, but serves to exclude non-members who try to break into the recording scene. For example, an observer at a 1973 recording session in Los Angeles was the butt of extended jokes because he did not know the "power" of pyramids.

Patterns of Exclusion

Each month musicians come to the major recording centers seeking to find work in the prestigious and well-paying field of session work. Many do not have the ability, but some are excellent. All are a threat to the regular players because they have no formal right to the work. What is more, there is an age-old norm of fraternal co-operation among all musicians, so while simplex members try to exclude the outsider, they do so behind the facade of helpfulness.

Simplex members employ five strategies to actively discourage would-be session musicians. The first is by providing *discouraging advice*. The newcomer may be told that although there was a great deal of studio work earlier, currently it is very slow, that there are two or three very good newcomers in town who don't seem able to break in, and that one has just given up after six months. Recruits are advised that if they come, they should bring enough money to live for a year, and not expect to work regularly in the studio for several years, because it takes that long to become known as reliable by hiring agents. Finally, recruits are told stories of failed and successful break-ins. These demonstrate that you can't buck the power of the simplex and exemplify the deferential recruit strategy we will detail below as the "rookie." Simplex members present themselves as being helpful to the recruit in all possible ways so that they can best guide the newcomer's perception and experiences, and also discourage him from going directly to hiring agents. The pattern of advice not only guides the recruit's behavior, but it facilitates giving up. The musician can find that the prospects are slim, and that failure is due not to his musicianship but to circumstances beyond his control.

The second strategy of exclusion is *isolation*. After being advised to work through simplex members, the recruit may find that none respond after initial warm contacts are made. The telephone is the primary means of making contacts, and since studio musicians regularly use phone-answering devices, they often do not respond to the recruit's messages. Beyond this basic strategy, isolation takes a number of forms. The following is illustrative. During a brief period of high studio activity when simplex members could not perform all the work, a competent friend who wanted to break into the recording scene was flown into town, housed, fed, and entertained by simplex members for his entire stay. These acts of generosity meant that he left town without making a single contact on his own, and when hiring agents who like his work asked about him, they were told that he was good but not versatile and wanted to keep his secure music teaching job.

The third strategy of exclusion is to *shame* the recruit. To get studio work, the recruit must be heard. This is not difficult because musicians provide themselves with numerous informal occasions to practice and show their talents through rehearsal bands and jam sessions. Although sheet music may be used, and the tunes may be well known to the recruit, any aggregation develops a number of conventions of tone, phrasing, rhythm, and so on that are not written down. Behond these natural differences, the recruit's sheet music can be tampered with, simplex members may agree to change their play so that the recruit sounds shrill, ahead of the beat, or incompetent in any one of a number of ways. If the recruit does not react good-naturedly he is branded a sorehead as well as incompetent.

The fourth strategy of exclusion is to *verbally cut* the recruit. This is difficult if the recruit is obviously excellent or comes to the recording center highly recommended. In such cases, all quasi-errors exposed in the shaming process are bandied-about among musicians. The key word in such cutting evaluations is "inflexible." The musician can be lauded and at the same time excluded from studio work as the word gets out that he cannot fit in musically or interpersonally.

The final strategy of exclusion employed by simplex members is to *recommend* the newcomer for the sorts of playing jobs which render the recruit unavailable for studio work. Such jobs include work with touring aggregations and full-time pit orchestras playing live musical shows. Such work is attractive to the novice who wants to play and is short of money. Even if they do not take the musician out of the recording center, they are a musical Siberia for two reasons. First, they stigmatize the player as a hack musician or at least as a specialist, and second, they show that the novice is not continuously available and serious about making it in the studio.

Newcomer Strategies

Every instance is different, but the efforts of newcomers to become full-time studio musicians can be summarized into two distinct strategies which we designate the *rookie*, and the *rival*. These strategies tell us much about how simplexes operate to maintain their power over the allocation of studio work.

THE ROOKIE. The simplex expects newcomers to fit into the pattern we call the *rookie*. The rookie accepts the norm of the simplex and learns the means of getting and keeping work. He publicly reaffirms the hierarchical structure of the simplex, he never outplays a simplex member, and he makes no move to steal accounts even when he is substituting on a session for a simplex member. Even if he has no substantial favors to give simplex members, his willingness to take any job available and not challenge the status-quo is seen by simplex members as a legitimate form of exchange, and in some circles is explicitly called "paying dues." The competent and contrite rookies comprise a ready-reserve of the unemployed whose availability makes it less likely that hiring agents will look beyond the range of the simplex for studio musicians.

The rookie prospect is often taken in hand by a simplex member and taught the norms discussed above. This sponsor is usually an established player who wants to, or may be forced by failing ability to, get out of studio work. The sponsor gives favors in exchange for the rookie's acceptance of the status quo and his potential favors at a later time. Such sponsor-favors enjoy a great multiplier effect, for the few jobs he provides may make the critical difference in the rookie's breaking into a career of studio work.

Rookies often told us "You have to stick it out, wait your turn." They see the system as frustrating insofar as they are excluded, but rational and fair. As an aspiring percussionist said after reading a draft of this manuscript, "I am in favor of what you call the simplex, I'm not 'in' now, but I know I am getting there, and then I'll have it made." While the simplex members propagate this idea of a waiting line, and rookies seem to believe in it, it does *not* accurately describe how the system operates. For although most simplex members begin as rookies, most rookies do *not* become simplex members. The wait is too long for some, but others are passed-over by newer recruits who become regulars. Unsuccessful rookies leave the system questioning their own musical ability and/or embittered about the musical establishment which seems to play favorites, and does not reward their loyalty (Peterson and Ryan, 1983).

The alternative newcomer strategy relates to the simplex in the diametrically opposite way from that of the rookie. This other sort of newcomer challenges the simplex as its *rival*. The rival goes directly to hiring agents and is successful only if he can convince some of them that he is better than simplex members in creating at least some sorts of sound which are required in the studio situation. Once it is clear to simplex members that a newcomer does not accept the norms of the "accounts system," they do everything possible to discredit the budding rival by shaming and cutting. Since the rival is trying to establish his difference from the simplex players, this discrediting usually takes the form of showing that both the style of play and interpersonal manner of the rival are out of tune with the demands of the studio situation.

As the general norm is never to openly criticize another performer, the cutting language used by, and about, the rival is quite striking. To show his contempt for simplex members, one rival told us, "They are so lazy they sound like they are sucking their horns, not blowing them." Simplex members in turn said of this rival, "He can't blend his tone with others, can't play anything but too loud, can't read music well, can't hold his temper, and won't take the jobs he doesn't like." Short of saying he refuses to join the union, this is a perfect condemnation of a prospective studio musician. Some rivals learn their lessons and become contrite rookies. Most of the rest leave the major recording centers within months, but, surprising as it may seem, the rival can make it into the recording scene under certain conditions. These are best understood by describing how simplexes evolve over time.

Continuity and Succession

Simplexes do change over time, and while our observations are not fully documented because of the brief span of intensive observation, change seems to follow two patterns—one evolutionary and the other revolutionary (Ryan and Peterson, 1982). As long as there is no great change in the demand for studio musicians, simplex membership changes gradually by the process of replacement. When members leave for one reason or another, they are replaced by well-socialized rookies. But commercial music *is* continually changing to fit the fads of the moment (Peterson and Berger, 1975; Denisoff, 1975). If the change is gradual, most simplex members are able to adjust their personal styles of play, but this is not always possible. Under such conditions, simplex members go to great lengths to defend their way of playing. They try to educate hiring agents about what is good or even possible. They make non-conformists look bad, and they even see to it that music is written or arranged so they can easily perform it.

There is an unending stream of slightly different sounds which enjoy momentary success in commercial music, but on those few occasions when one becomes defined as a "new sound," hiring agents begin to actively seek out musicians who can regularly deliver this sound. This provides the opportunity for the kind of recruit we defined above as the rival and elsewhere has been called a rebel (Peterson and Ryan, 1983). For example, Glenn Campbell, Mike Post and several others were able to break into Los Angeles studio work in the early 1960s because they could play in the newly popular folk-country style. After breaking in, such rivals may teach their new techniques to established players, show their versatility, fit in socially, and become part of the gradually evolving simplexes. The string bass players in New York provide an excellent case in point. In the late 1960s, solid-body electric bass players schooled in rock and soul techniques began to displace the jazz-schooled acoustic-bass players. Some of the latter were forced out, but others acquired the new instrument and the techniques necessary to continue in studio work. Perhaps the classic example of the outsider turned simplex stalwart is Chet Atkins. In the late 1940s, he was fired from many guitar-playing jobs because his jazz-based sound did not fit with the country music of the time. By the mid-1950s, however, his technique had become the standard for country session-guitarists and he was at the center of the Nashville-based simplex as player and producer (Malone, 1968: 253; Atkins, 1974).

Most *new* sounds depend on the co-operative efforts of a number of studio musicians. In such situations, the individual rival stands no chance since the primary recording centers are controlled by overlapping sets of simplexes for each of the various instruments which together share an interest in playing in their conventional ways. Collectively, these other musicians can often make the newcomer look bad. For this reason, major new sounds ordinarily are created by *groups* of non-studio musicians or by studio players working in secondary recording centers such as Detroit, Memphis, Austin, Muscle Shoals, Bakersfield, or the Colorado Hills. Quite often they move together to the major recording centers. Rather than melding into the established simplex structures, these aggregations of rivals often form the nuclei of new simplex structures which first parallel and then succeed the older simplexes.

Reification and Reality

We have described a number of mechanisms which collectively serve to stabilize the job lives of workers exposed to conditions of near-perfect competition in a branch of the commercial music industry. For the sake of convenience, we have called this set of mechanisms the simplex. Doing so in a brief presentation such as this, there is a danger of reifying the term *simplex* and making it appear all-powerful. First of all, recall that the term is our invention, and what limited power is has derives in large part from *not* being recognized by hiring agents.

While simplexes are real in their consequences, if not always apparent, they are not always equally coherent or powerful. For example, when jobs in Nashville expanded rapidly in the early 1970s due to increasing recording work in this center, there was less need for the work-protecting strategies of the simplex, and newcomers were more often welcomed. The strength of the simplex also varies by instrument, being most strong when solid musicianship is required but when there is little scope to show inventiveness. Bass players and rhythm guitarists provide two cases in point. Finally, the strength of the simplex in any instrument group seems to vary by the number of players who are regularly employed. If only a few players get work, they are more able to form a stable simplex. When more than a dozen players of a given instrument are regularly involved in studio work, the simplex structure is less visible. What seems to happen in these larger networks is that the simplex bifurcates along lines of musical style, and the sub-groupings are joined only at the top by the few top-ranked superstar players.

The simplex blossoms in the world of diverse craftsmen linked by short-term contracts in a creative task. For studio musicians, the crafts include arrangers, studio engineers, sound mixers, and above all the musicians playing other instruments, who are themselves members of simplex groups. A fully developed picture of this art would need to trace the patterns of mutual aid exchanged across the boundary of instrument-specific simplex-groups which together form a matrix of simplexes.

Here we have seen the simplex as emerging in the job world of linked crafts, and we have contrasted this art-producing world with two other art worlds—the avant-garde market which generates circles, and the academic tradition which fosters schools. If the simplex described here contrasts with creative groups in other sorts of art worlds, of course, it is possible that simplical forms may be found in situations well beyond the world of art. Our preliminary review of the literature (Peterson and White, 1977) suggests that it may be located in quite diverse situations, and these speculations are expanded and formalized in our second joint article on the simplex (Peterson and White, 1981).

Notes

1. The judgement of competence was made independently by several knowledgeable observers who requested anonymity, and affirmed by Howard White, a skilled professional musician and long-time college music teacher.

2. In 1976, musicians received just over $100 for each three-hour master session, and they might receive double or triple scale for providing additional services on a session. Musicians may play several sessions a day, seven days a week. The gross income figures were taken from American Federation of Musicians records.

3. Following Peterson and White (1977), the term *simplex* is used to set off the focus of this research from *complex* or *formal* organization. We are aware that the term has other meanings in mathematics and statistics (Peterson, 1964). All the other possible terms—such as *primary* or *informal* organization, *circle, cliche,* or *cabal*—carry their own baggage of undesired connotations. On balance, the advan-

tage of denotation without a history of numerous connotations outweighed the disadvantage of creating a new word.

4. Research on the structure and dynamics of artistic schools and academies can be found in: Becker (1982); Boime (1971); Mukerji (1976); Pevsner (1940); and White and White (1965).

5. Research on artistic circles in a market context can be found in: Bystryn (1978); Kadushin (1976); Merrill (1970); Poggioli (1968); Ridgeway (1978); and Simpson (1982).

6. Research that shows that artistic schools define excellence with reference to a set of standards can be found in Adler (1978); Crane (1976); Becker (1982); and White and White (1965).

7. Research that shows how artistic circles thrive on breaking with established aesthetic standards can be found in Adler (1975); Rogers (1970); Rosenberg and Fliegel (1965); Shapiro (1976); and Zolberg (1978).

8. The synthetic term *hiring agent* is used here because, depending on the recording center and the specific situation, persons with a number of different designations are in charge of hiring session musicians. These include the producer (sometimes called a & r man), the contractor, leader, concertmaster, section agent, and arranger (Kirsch, 1974). Most often, however, the producer acts as hiring agent (Peterson and Berger, 1971).

9. This and all further attributed quotes are drawn from our informants.

References

Adler, J. 1978. *Artists in Offices.* New Brunswick, NJ: Transaction.

——— 1975. "Innovative art and obsolescent artists." *Social Research* 42 (Summer):360–378.

Albrecht, M. C. and J. H. Barnett, [eds.] 1970. *The Sociology of Art and Literature.* New York: Praeger.

Atkins, C. 1974. *Country Gentleman.* Chicago: Regnery.

Becker, G. 1978. *The Mad Genius Controversey: A Study in the Sociology of Deviance.* Beverly Hills, CA: Sage.

Becker, H. S. 1982. *Art Worlds.* Berkeley: University of California Press.

——— 1973. "Art as collective action." *Amer. Soc. Rev.* 39 (December): 767–776.

Bensman, J. and R. Lilienfeld (1973) *Craft and Consciousness.* New York: John Wiley.

Boime, A. 1971. *The Academy and French Painting in the Nineteenth Century.* London: Phaidon.

Bystryn, M. 1978. "Variation in artistic circles." Paper presented at the American Sociological Society meetings.

Cantor, M. G. 1971. *The Hollywood TV Producer: His Work and His Audience.* New York: Basic Books.

Crane, D. 1976. "Reward systems in art, science, and religion," pp. 57–73 in R. A. Peterson (ed.) *The Production of Culture.* Beverly Hills, CA: Sage.

———— 1972. *Invisible Colleges.* Chicago: Univ. of Chicago Press.

Denisoff, R. S. (1975) *Solid Gold.* Rutgers, NJ: Transaction.

Doll, W. 1974. "The management of creativity: the case of the professional theatre." Paper presented at the American Sociological Association meetings, Montreal.

Faulkner, R. R. 1983. *Music on Demand: Composers and Careers in the Hollywood Film Industry.* New Brunswick: Transaction Books.

———— 1971. *Hollywood Studio Musicians.* Chicago: Aldine.

Guerard, A. L. 1966. *Art for Art's Sake.* New York: Schocken.

Hensley, D. E. 1976. "Paul Yandell at the top of the Nashville studio scene." *Guitar Player* 10 (December):22, 60–66.

Kadushin, C. 1976. "Networks and circles in the production of culture," pp. 107–122 in R. A. Peterson (ed.) *The Production of Culture.* Beverly Hills, CA: Sage.

Kavolis, V. 1974. "Social and economic aspects of the arts," pp. 102–122 in *Encyclopaedia Britannica* (15th ed.). Chicago: Encyclopaedia Britannica.

Kirsch, B. 1974. "Studio contractor is disc's unsung hero." *Billboard* 4 (May): 1, 12.

Lyon, E. 1978. "Stages of theatrical rehearsal." Paper presented at the American Sociological Association meetings.

Malone, B. C. 1968. *Country Music U.S.A.* Austin: Univ. of Texas Press.

Martorella, R. 1974. "The performing artist as a member of an organization: a sociological study of opera." Ph.D. dissertation, New School for Social Research, New York.

Merrill, F. E. 1970. "Le groupe des Batagnolles: a study in the sociology of art," pp. 250–259 in T. Shibutani (ed.) *Human Nature and Collective Behavior.* Englewood Cliffs, NJ: Prentice-Hall.

Mukerji, D. 1976. "Having the authority to know." *Sociology of Work and Occupations* 3 (February).

Peterson, R. A. [ed.] 1976. *The Production of Culture*. Beverly Hills, CA: Sage.

———— 1964. "Simplex: a mathematical model for the analysis of social change." *Soc. Q.* 5 (Summer): 264–271.

———— and D. G. Berger 1975. "Cycles in symbol production: the case of popular music." *Amer. Soc. Rev.* 40 (April):158–173.

———— 1971. "Entrepreneurship in organizations: evidence from the popular music industry." *Admin. Sci. Q.* 16 (March):97–106.

———— and J. Ryan 1983. "Success, failure and anomie in art and craft work: breaking in to commercial country music songwriting." *Research in the Sociology of Work* 2:201–323.

———— and H. G. White 1981. "Elements of simplex structure." *Urban Life* 10: 3–24.

———— 1977. "Simplex: the form of informal organization." Paper presented at the American Sociological Association meetings, September.

Pevsner, N. 1940. *Academies of Art Past and Present*. Cambridge, MA: Cambridge Univ. Press.

Poggioli, R. 1968. *The Theory of the Avant-Garde*. Cambridge, MA: Belknap.

Powdermaker, H. 1950. *Hollywood: The Dream Factory*. Boston: Little, Brown.

Ridgeway, S. 1978. "Artist cliques, gate-keepers, and structural change." Paper presented at the American Sociological Association meetings.

Rogers, M. 1970. "The Batignolles group: creators of impressionism," pp. 194–220 in M. C. Albrecht, J. H. Barnett, and M. Griff (eds.) *The Sociology of Art and Literature*. New York: Praeger.

Rosenberg, B. and N. Fliegel 1965. *The Vanguard Artist: Portrait and Self-Portrait*. Chicago: Quadrangle.

Rosenblum, B. 1973. "Photographers." Ph.D. dissertation, Evanston, IL, Northwestern University.

Ryan, J. and R. A. Peterson 1982. "The product image: the fate of creativity in country music songwriting." *Sage Annual Reviews of Communication Research* 10:11–32.

Scherer, F. M. 1970. *Industrial Market Structure and Economic Performance*. Chicago: Rand-McNally.

Shanks, B. 1976. *The Cool Fire: How to Make It in Television*. New York: Vintage.

Shapiro, T. 1976. *Painters and Politics: The European Avant-Garde and Society, 1900–1925*. New York: Elsevier.

Simpson, C. R. 1981. *Soho: The Artist in the City*. Chicago: University of Chicago Press.

White, H. C. and C. A. White 1965. *Canvases and Careers: Institutional Change in the French Painting World.* New World: John Wiley.

Wilson, R. N. [ed.] 1964. *The Arts in Society.* Englewood Cliffs, NJ: Prentice-Hall.

Yancey, W. L., E. P. Eriksen, and R. N. Juliani 1976. "Emergent ethnicity: a review and reformulation." *Amer. Soc. Rev.* 41 (June):391–403.

Zolberg, V. L. 1978. "Why contemporary displayed art is innovative while performed music is not." Paper presented at the Southern Sociological Society meetings, New Orleans.

——— 14 ———

Reward Systems in Avant-Garde Art: Social Networks and Stylistic Change[1]

DIANA CRANE

Sociologists of science have shown that the nature of the social relationships among scientists affects the development of knowledge in scientific research areas. In fact, the development of research areas seems to require the existence of a social community. Innovations in basic science are developed by networks of scientists who share cognitive and technical norms (often called paradigms) about the nature of their innovations (Crane, 1972; Mulkay, 1975).

Does the process of innovation and cultural change in avant-garde art resemble that in basic science? Do these activities take place in social systems that have similar components and that function in similar ways? My aim is to identify the elements of these systems for producing cultural innovations and to see how these elements compare with one another. Each element, such as social community and paradigm, should exhibit a range of possibilities in different cultural institutions.

The following questions will be examined: Can communities of innovators be identified in avant-garde art? If so, what is the nature of the social relationships among members? Do members share something equivalent to a paradigm? How do the social and ideational (knowledge-based) components of such communities change over time?

Models of Cultural Change

In scientific research areas, networks of scientists go through distinct stages of growth. Changes in the intellectual aspects of the field parallel these stages of growth. In the first stage, there are only a few researchers who may or may not be in contact. Growth of the area is stimulated by intriguing findings or by a new and untested theoretical model. These ideas attract scientists to the research area. In the second stage, the group grows rapidly. A few highly productive scientists set priorities for research, recruit and train students and are in communication with other members of the area. In the third stage, as difficulties in further development of the ideas become increasingly evident, new scientists are less likely to enter the area and old members are more likely to drop out. The group may break up into sub-groups that disagree with one another. In the final stage, most scientists abandon the area because they perceive the major problems as solved or as unsolvable. Only a few diehards remain. In some cases, a new 'breakthrough' may start the process over again.

Kadushin (1976) has suggested a somewhat different model for the social aspects of the development of innovations in avant-garde painting and sculpture as well as in literature, drama and poetry. According to him, the first stage of an artistic movement is very inclusive; anyone who is 'on our side' may join. Fairly soon, however, members become more concerned with drawing boundaries around the group and they attempt to define the notion of 'membership'.[1] At the same time, they attempt to give the ideas greater artistic clarity.

In the second stage, the group has become an establishment with a core of central members and a periphery of marginal members. In the third stage, it is institutionalized with the development of journals and other organizations. At this stage, there is likely to be rebellion against its authority and the development of a new community.

The principal difference between the two models is in the degree to which communities of innovators are perceived as being open or closed. In the first model, a community is seen as remaining open to newcomers throughout its history. In the second model, such a community is seen as gradually becoming 'exclusive,' closed to would-be members. By implication, it would seem to be characterized by a high level of agreement among members of the in-group. The model also implies that the community has a high degree of control over the support structure, the organizations and material resources which make possible the production of innovations.

How well do these models fit the emergence of styles in avant-garde art? In the following pages, I will examine three recent styles in avant-garde art from this point of view. My information has been obtained in part from interviews with artists which I conducted in New York in 1977 and in part from books and articles that have been written about these styles.

The Development of Avant-Garde Art Movements

At the present time, a variety of movements exist simultaneously in the New York art world. Some are very small; others are large and successful. The three movements which I will discuss have been selected because they represent a range of different types of activity in terms of size and style: Abstract Expressionism, figurative painting, and Photo Realism.

Abstract Expressionism was the first indigenous American art movement. When it developed, the New York art world was very different from what it is today. The number of avant-garde artists was very small, perhaps 200 to 300. They had little prestige in American society and this was reflected in the low prices paid for their paintings. Abstract Expressionism dominated the New York art world for over a decade in a way that no single contemporary art movement could dominate the New York art world today. Of the first stage of the movement, Sandler says (1976: 79):

> After 1943, the New Yorkers who were venturing into automatist and bi-
> omorphic abstraction—among them, Baziotes, Gottlieb, Hofmann, Moth-
> erwell, Pollock and Rothko—became increasingly familiar with each
> other's work and often exhibited together. This resulted in a loose commu-
> nity based on mutual understanding and respect. Personal interactions
> were of great importance, for they gave rise to an aesthetic climate in
> which innovation and extreme positions were accepted and encouraged.

After the war, their works were shown primarily in a few galleries in New York City and a few critics—including Clement Greenberg—began to write about them. New magazines began to discuss their work but the group was generally ignored by the New York art world (Sandler, 1976: 211). However, in 1948, the 'underground movement' as Sandler calls it, began to surface. Members of the group started a school on Eighth Street; they gave public lectures; there were many exhibitions, books, magazine articles, museum shows and prizes. In 1949, they started a social club which became the focal point of Abstract Expressionist activities throughout the early fifties. Membership jumped quickly. By the summer of 1950, the original twenty had tripled. The movement was expanding rapidly. Sandler (1976: 214) reports:

> The Club became the core of a subculture whose purpose was as much
> social as it was intellectual. For artists venturing into untried areas in art,
> the need to exchange ideas was urgent . . . the incessant discussions
> forced each artist to renew his ideas constantly, to justify his painting to
> himself by justifying it to his colleagues.

Rosenberg and Fliegel (1965) who studied the same group during the fifties also found a high level of exchange of ideas. One of their informants said:

One has the feeling that everybody knows about everybody else's paintings and that there is a kind of running commentary going on within each work. This creates a very concentrated and electric ambience: the least inflection that an individual artist puts into it counts and has repercussions and echoes which other people can pick up and use.

By the early fifties, there were clearly leaders—primarily de Kooning and Kline—and followers. The followers included a second generation of painters. The group became less an association of equals and increasingly divided into camps surrounding the leaders of the movement. By the late fifties, the social group had disintegrated and was replaced by entirely new movements in the sixties.

The development of this movement fits the model of cultural change which has been observed in scientific research areas remarkably well. Due to the geographical concentration of its members, it was probably more tightly knit than many scientific communities although relatively intense relationships also occur among scientists, particularly when the group is developing ideas that are not accepted by members of neighboring specialties (Griffith and Mullins, 1972). The other two movements that I will discuss fit the model less well.

A movement which developed in reaction to Abstract Expressionism but which has never had as much influence as the latter is that of figurative art, a return to realism. During the sixties, a number of artists were working in a figurative style but they were in what Sidney Tillim (1969a: 32) calls "almost anarchic disagreement." It was a highly diversified group.

In 1968, an organization called the Alliance of Figurative Artists was formed in New York City. The first meeting was attended by a large number of artists, many of them young. Tillim (1969b: 45) described the organization as "an utterly disorganized, rancorous group." On the other hand, its lack of formal organization seemed to emulate the informality of the social circle (Kadushin, 1976). According to Kuh's (1971: 88) account:

there are no officers, no chairman, no dues, no obligations . . . a program committee . . . establishes loose guidelines in order to avoid repetitious hangups . . . The meetings take many forms, sometimes revolving around panels, sometimes turning into open forums where artists bring their own work, defend it, explain it, and then listen to the uninhibited comments of their colleagues.

As a result of bringing figurative painters into contact with one another, a number of artist-owned and artist-run co-operative galleries were formed to show figurative art, soon after the Alliance was organized. In its early years, the Alliance seems to have provided a valuable meeting ground for younger partists. One painter said:

> When we first started, everyone who painted figuratively needed to share with each other, because the scene was so unaccepting of that . . . While I was getting all my ideas together and teaching myself how to paint figuratively, the feedback I was getting there and the ideas were helping me tremendously . . .

A sculptor commented:

> To know that so many other artists were working in the figurative field was news to us. We had all considered ourselves kind of separate and isolated. When we all got together, we realized that maybe we weren't so isolated and that the thing we had to do was to continue to meet.

As in the case of Abstract Expressionism, older artists with different perspectives on figurative painting became the informal leaders of the group. Eventually, these different perspectives engendered increasing conflict and led to the formation of factions within the Alliance, composed of their students. Members became increasingly argumentative at meetings and some stopped attending altogether.

However, figurative painting as such has continued to expand. In 1976, several co-operative galleries sponsored a group exhibition of figurative art, including 122 painters and 21 sculptors (*Artists' Choice: Figurative Art in New York,* 1976). In a sense, this group appears to have gone through social changes not unlike those that occur in scientific communities but the ideational components remain incomplete. This issue will be discussed in the following section.

Toward the end of the sixties, a new group of realist painters emerged who, unlike the figurative painters, have evolved a distinct and readily identifiable style, working from photographs, which they reproduce precisely, rather than from life. The Photo Realists (also called Super-realists and Hyper-realists) do not seem to have developed a cohesive social group. They are not members of the Alliance of Figurative Artists and there tends to be antipathy between members of the two groups. Informants in New York indicated that they had been in contact at least superficially with each other and with several others working in the same style. One of these artists said:

> We all see each other's work. It's important to keep up with what others are doing.

Another said:

> If I see other paintings I like, I can be influenced to a certain extent. It
> can suggest things to me, technically, or it might give me ideas of other
> things to do.

Artists on the West Coast who paint in this style apparently had more
contact with one another. However, in response to a question posed by a
journalist, "Is there a Photo Realist movement?", four painters replied in
the negative and four were mildly positive. An art critic, Chase (1973: 7),
characterized the group as follows:

> Hyper-realism is not a movement in the formal sense . . . Many of the
> artists have never seen each other. They come from many parts of the
> United States but they have been subjected to the same influences and are
> pre-occupied in a similar manner by the problem of translating these in-
> fluences in painting. Perhaps one can speak of a common sensibility based
> on the relationship between the artist and his subject.

In this group, it appears that the ideational components are more developed than the social components. Other artists are often very negative
toward this style of art because the subject matter and some of the techniques are considered taboo. This may also explain why the group has remained very small. Around thirty artists are consistently identified with it
(Chase, 1975; 1976). By comparison, weekly attendance at the Alliance of
Figurative Artists was around two-hundred in the early seventies (Kuh,
1971).

Style and Paradigm

The development of research traditions in science is stimulated by paradigmatic achievements or exemplars that guide further research. They suggest relevant problems and appropriate ways of solving them. Analysis of
the literature discussing the nature of paradigms suggests that the paradigm
has two elements: (1) a way of seeing or a world view and (2) a set of
specific tools and procedures for dealing with reality—the latter is sometimes called a puzzle-solving device (Kuhn, 1972; Masterman, 1970). Do
art movements develop a unique world view and a set of techniques or
methods that go with it? Do artistic styles have a paradigmatic character?
Schapiro (1962: 300) has described style in art in a way that suggests
that it has aspects of both the broad and the narrow components of a
paradigm:

> Style, then, is the means of communication, a language not only as a system of devices for conveying a precise message by representing or symbolizing objects and actions but also as a qualitative whole which is capable of suggesting the diffuse connotations as well and intensifying the associated or intrinsic effects.

Associated with Abstract Expressionism were certain types of problems which the artists were trying to solve and goals they were trying to achieve. For example, Sandler (1976: 148) describes the color field painters within Abstract Expressionism as attempting to solve the problem of "the modulation of light and dark values to produce an illusion of mass in space . . . They aimed to create an abstract art suggestive of the sublime, of transcendence, of revelation."

At the same time, certain technical innovations—tools and procedures—were invented in and identified with the movement. Examples include the departure from easel painting and the development of so-called 'drip' techniques that were associated with the other main group of Abstract Expressionists, the gesture painters, specifically Jackson Pollock. He placed canvasses on the floor and threw or dribbled paint on them.

The world view of the Photo Realists is very different from that of the Abstract Expressionists. They paint extremely precise pictures but there is "a sense of detachment or noninvolvement with the melancholy or distasteful subject" (Karp, 1975: 24). They avoid self-expression. The key aspect of their work is the acceptance and objective treatment of subject matter that is very banal. One critic (Chase, 1975: 82–85) states that these artists are:

> extremely committed to (their) morality of impersonal observation and unsparing factuality . . . the Photo Realist replaces the artist's personal, interpretive vision with the recording of visual fact; he replaces the subjectivity of the artist's eye with the objectivity of the camera's lens. This subjectivity is the cherished value that Photo Realism requires its public to sacrifice.

At the same time, there is a set of techniques and procedures that are associated with the style. These artists work from photographs instead of models or the actual scene itself. Some of the painters work from slides or projections. One artist sets up still lifes which she photographs and then paints from the photograph. Some of the artists use an air brush, a novel technique often considered to represent an impersonal, technological style. By contrast, the work of the figurative artists is much more diverse. In 1969, Tillim commented (1969b: 47) that their style "has not developed either as a movement or with as much clarity of intention as movements generally imply."

Several years later, Kramer (1976:C14) described these painters as follows:

> Taken as a group, these artists have almost nothing in common except their interest in *not* painting abstract paintings. Theirs is a negative alliance.

However, members of the group do appear to share a world view in a very general sense that has been described by Nemser (1971–72:46) as follows:

> All are united by their desire to integrate the lessons of art history with the precepts of modernism in some new, meaningful way.

Tillim (1969b:43) argues that the differences among these artists stem from the fact that "everything depends on where an artist stood in relation to modernist art when he made his commitment to figuration . . . " There are a number of distinct styles within the group that are identified with senior figures and that are being developed in new directions by their students.

Reward Systems for Avant-Garde Art

Art movements exist within reward systems. Groups of painters set cognitive and technical goals but they function in a larger social system where they compete for symbolic and material rewards (Crane, 1976). They are linked to this reward system via the support structure which develops to facilitate the production of their art works. Critics who are often in close contact with the artists may specialize in writing about a particular group. Certain dealers show primarily painters who belong to a particular movement and play important roles in developing the careers of its members. Sometimes museum curators become interested in a particular style and, through their purchases, lend it prestige.

The financial success of its members and the impact of a movement as a whole depends upon the extent to which it can either develop a new support structure or co-opt members of the existing support structure. In the past, new support structures have tended to develop around new art movements (White and White, 1965). In the early years of Abstract Expressionism, a number of new galleries were formed, many of which ceased to exist when Abstract Expressionism went into decline. Critics emerged whose reputations were closely associated with it (for example, Clement Greenberg and Harold Rosenberg). Museum curators also played important roles in the development of this movement (Bystryn, 1977).

The development of figurative art and Photo Realism occurred in a different atmosphere. During the 1960's, American art increased enormously in value. The increasing power of the consumer was seen in the frantic production of innovations to attract his attention. While, in the 1950's, galleries had been cooperatives or were run by relatively modest dealers who followed the advice of their artists, the 1960's were characterized by (Downes, 1974–75:127):

> the development of an extensive, high-powered management of critics, impresarios, dealers, and curators whose idea appeared to be to stage a stylistic 'advance' for every season.

In this milieu, the Photo Realists won rapid acceptance while the figurative artists did not. Perhaps because from the very beginning they had a clearly identifiable style and one that contained elements that are 'unacceptable' to many avant-garde artists but appealing to some collectors, dealers to show their work, collectors to buy it, and museum curators to exhibit it were available very early in the development of the movement. By contrast, the figurative artists had to create a new support structure; they exhibited and sold their work primarily in small co-operative art galleries. In the early seventies, an economic recession led to a decline in prices for contemporary painting. However, Photo Realism continued to sell well while figurative art, on the whole, did not. Among the older generation, only three or four painters have achieved any real success. There is some indication that the younger generation is finding it easier to win acceptance in the art world.

Neither group succeeded in winning the support of 'establishment' critics. While figurative art has been largely ignored by the critics (with the exception of the work of three or four stars), Photo Realism developed in the face of a great deal of critical disapproval (Seitz, 1972: 72). In recent years, criticism has begun to be more favorable, but the figurative artists still attract little attention. One of the few critics who has continued over the years to write about figurative art is himself a figurative artist, Sidney Tillim.

What is the relationship between these trends in the reward system for avant-garde art and the characteristics of the art movements that were discussed earlier? At this point, one can only speculate that the unstable reward system for avant-garde art may have affected the development of these movements in such a way that neither developed entirely along the lines that have been observed in other fields. In one movement, the social aspects were affected; in the other, the conceptual aspects. For example, in Photo Realism, the immediate availability of a lucrative market for their paintings meant that there was less need for social solidarity among the artists in the early stages of the movement. In the case of the figurative artists, it is possible that the lack of even a minimal level of economic success affected the rate of conceptual development. In spite of its size, the ideational elements of the movement have evolved very slowly.

Conclusion

To summarize, an art movement is both a social and an ideational phenomenon. It involves a new world view, new techniques, a community of interacting artists and a support structure which consists of critics, dealers, collectors, and museum curators. A model of the development of an art movement was presented in which both the social and the ideational components change and develop over time. The development of one movement, Abstract Expressionism, fit this model very well. Two other movements, figurative art and Photo Realism, did not develop entirely as predicted. In the former, the social elements developed more rapidly than the ideational ones; in the latter, the ideational elements were more evident than the social ones. None of the groups seems to exhibit the characteristics of a tightly-knit establishment, excluding newcomers, perhaps because none succeeded in taking over the support structure for avant-garde art entirely (for an example of an art establishment, see White and White's description of the French Academy in the 19th century).

Like other groups of innovators, the boundaries of these groups are somewhat imprecise. It is not always easy to establish membership in a movement in an individual case. In addition, members of these groups are likely to be in contact with artists working in other styles. Such contacts develop in art schools, through galleries, or through geographical proximity in artists' neighborhoods (for example, SoHo in New York City). Exactly how much integration there is among members of various styles of avant-garde art would be an interesting subject for further study.

Notes

1. Paper presented at the Ninth World Congress of Sociology, Uppsala, Sweden, 1978. The research for this chapter was subsequently expanded and appears in Diana Crane's book, *The Transformation of the Avant-Garde* (University of Chicago Press, 1987).

References

Artists' Choice: Figurative Art in New York Catalogue, 1976.

Bystryn, M. 1977. *The Social Production of Artistic Identity.* Unpublished Ph.D. dissertation, New York University.

Chase, L. 1973. *Les hyperréalistes américains.* Paris: Filipacchi (EPI Editions).

Chase, L. 1975. "Existential vs. humanist realism." In G. Battcock (ed.) *Super Realism: A Critical Anthology.* New York: E. P. Dutton.

Chase, L. 1976. "Photo realism: post modernist illusionism." *Art International,* 20 (March-April): 14–27.

Crane, D. 1972. *Invisible Colleges: Diffusion of Knowledge in Scientific Communities.* Chicago: University of Chicago Press.

Crane, D. 1976. "Reward systems in art, science, and religion." *American Behavioral Scientist.* 19: 719–734.

Downes, R. 1974/75. "What the sixties meant to me." *Art Journal* 34: 125–131.

Griffith, B. C. and N. C. Mullins. 1972. "Coherent social groups in scientific change." *Science* 177 (September 15): 959–964.

Kadushin, C. 1976. "Networks and circles in the production of culture." *American Behavioral Scientist* 19: 769–784.

Karp, I. 1975. "Rent is the only reality, or the hotel instead of the hymns." In G. Battcock (ed.), *Super Realism.* New York: E. P. Dutton.

Kramer, H. 1976. "SoHo: figures at an exhibition." *New York Times* (December 10), p. C. 10.

Kuh, K. 1971. "Of, by and for artists." *Saturday Review* (January 23): 88–89.

Kuhn, T. S. 1972. *The Structure of Scientific Revolutions.* Rev. Ed. Chicago: University of Chicago Press.

Kultermann, U. 1972. *New Realism.* Greenwich, Conn.: New York Graphic Society.

Masterman, M. 1970. "The nature of a paradim." In I. Lakatos and A. E. Musgrave (eds.), *Criticism and the Growth of Knowledge.* Cambridge: Cambridge University Press.

Mulkay, M. et al., "Problem areas and research networks in science." *Sociology* 9:187–203.

Nemser, C. 1971/72. "Representational art in 1971." *Arts Magazine* 46 (December/January): 41–46.

Rosenberg, B. and N. Fliegel. 1965. *The Vanguard Artist.* Chicago: Quadrangle Books.

Sandler, I. 1976. *The Triumph of American Painting: A History of Abstract Expressionism.* New York: Harper & Row.

Schapiro, M. "Style." In S. Tax (ed.), *Anthropology Today.* Chicago: University of Chicago Press.

Seitz, W. C. 1972. "The real and the artificial." *Art in America* 60 (November/December): 59–72.

Tillim, S. 1969a. "The reception of figurative art." *Artforum* 7: 30–33.

Tillim, S. 1969b. "A variety of realisms." *Artforum* 7: 42–48.

White, H. and C. White. 1965. *Canvases and Careers.* New York: Wiley.

Part V

Art Organizations

Carrying out a set of interrelated activities that center on a very complex task, such as manufacturing automobiles, providing comprehensive medical services, or producing an opera, requires a large, bureaucratic organization. In his publication, *Wirtschaft and Gesellschaft,* Max Weber described the essential nature of bureaucratic organizations and provided a basic model that has been useful in the social sciences since its publication over sixty years ago. It has been helpful as a model to guide research and it has also served as a basis for criticism and hence, new directions of thinking about organizations.

Weber essentially argued that to achieve a certain end—one that involves a very complex task—with the fewest uncertainties possible, the overall task must be sub-divided into many narrower tasks that are, in turn, assigned to specialized and hierarchically arranged sub-units and to the positions within those sub-units. In theory, this strategy of organizing work leads to a formal structure that has certain advantages over alternative strategies: every person's specialized skills and talents can be maximized as their efforts are focused on a narrowly defined objective; each person and each subunit is accountable and responsible for a given operation; the specialized components of the organization relate in a precise and logical way to the overall objectives of the organization. This means, according to Weber, that supervision, workflow, and actual performance of work are all relatively unproblematic. Organizational complexity, or the individual specialization that complexity entails, is, according to Weber, what makes the formal organization uniquely suited to carrying out complex tasks in an effective and efficient way.

There is an initial problem here, however, and it is one that Weber recognized. The subdivision of the organization into departments, subunits, hierarchical levels, and positions creates problems of co-ordination. Weber posited that a set of organizational features solves these problems. Co-ordination within the organization would be achieved by the work of the clerical and administrative staff, regulations, formalized rules, and to some extent, by the career advancement of individuals who bring their experience from one job to the requirements of a new job. Were Weber living these days he would probably add office technology, including computers, to his list of mechanisms of co-ordination.

Social scientists have reformulated Weber's model to make it amenable to empirical testing, but they have also seriously questioned the main premises underlying the model. An early elaboration, which is useful for the examination of arts organizations, was suggested by Parsons (1947:59) in his translation of Weber's essays. Professional organizations, Parsons noted, are different from most other types of organizations owing to the skills, long training, and expectations for autonomy that professionals bring with them to organizational work. Professionals expect and are accorded latitude for the exercise of independent judgment. They use their discretion and require little direct supervision. Professional organizations, as a result, are based more on consensual decision-making and have little control from top management. Moreover, the formal lines of demarcation between subunits become blurred as professionals establish their own patterns of communication and co-ordination.

Critics have also pointed out that although Weber discussed the general historical conditions that were favorable to the development of bureaucratic organizations, he failed to deal systematically with the specific environments of organizations, such as markets for industrial firms, clients for service organizations (and, we would add, publics for art institutions and performers).

Efficiency and effectiveness were at the foremost of Weber's concerns as he chiefly was concerned with the agencies of the state and the economic organizations of the capitalistic economy. Our conception of the structures that promote these ends of efficiency and effectiveness must be radically revised when we consider organizations that are primarily oriented to providing high quality products and services, or are oriented to innovation and creativity. Whereas the traditional complex organization is capable of achieving its objective by routinizing and standardizing activities, the organization that is oriented to quality or innovation cannot so easily increase predictability by routinization, standardization and hierarchical control.

A final general problem that Weber did not consider are the problems created by inequalities—and these inequalities arise out of differences in power, in wealth, in information, and in a variety of other resources, that confound organizationally based inequalities. A Marxist conception of social structures, generally, and of organizations in particular draws special attention to this problem of inequalities. Here one could consider the monopolization of services or products by a given industry that creates opportunities of exploitation of consumers who depend on these services or products. Also, the dependence of an organization on wealthy patrons and commissioners creates problems for organizational autonomy and for the freedom of individual members. Within an organization, the concentration of power and resources in the hands of a few managers, creates problems of alienation and estrangement from work, particularly among professional employees.

The issues outlined here serve to illustrate some main issues in contemporary research and theory on organizations. Yet, most sociological investigations deal primarily with the same type of organizations with which Weber was concerned—public agencies and industries in the private sector—and the research that has been carried out on professional organizations has tended to focus on organizations that serve clients—law firms, hospitals, social service organizations, prisons—not publics. Art organizations and culture producing institutions (such as motion picture studios, publishers, and radio stations) are different. One main difference between them and other organizations is that they serve publics. By considering them, we cast a new light on substantive knowledge of organizations.

The particular combination of qualities that make culture producing organizations unique is also what makes them of interest in challenging conventional organizational theory. However, the extent to which they share the same problems that all organizations have—commitment of members, relating to an environment, co-ordinating work—indicates how organizational theory is relevant for understanding them. They are unique in that they serve publics, but they are unique in other respects as well.

Whereas many art organizations are professional in the sense that their members undergo long training, artists are not professional in the strict sense of the word. If we define a professional as someone who provides services for clients, most artists would not be considered professionals. Also, filmmaking, playing an instrument, designing a building, opera singing, and improvization in a jazz group involve activities that are closer to the traditions of craft work than to those of professional work.

The goals of efficiency and effectiveness become intermingled and often subordinated to other goals in any art organization. Producing a "product" of the highest quality is a prime objective in the performing arts, whereas an emphasis on uniqueness and creativity is dominant in the non-performing arts. Yet, it is not so clearcut as that. In many arts—popular and elite, commercial and non-commercial—innovation and excellence are at times coincident and at times in competition with one another. This tension is clearly evident in the performance of symphonic and operatic music and in the organizational activities of museums. Although each paper in this section addresses various aspects of this problem, Faulkner's analysis of orchestras is particularly important in this regard.

A major way in which traditional arts organizations have distinctive characteristics derives from their dependence on a wealthy elite who provide patronage, legitimacy, and political support. The fact of dependence has extraordinary consequences for limiting innovative repertories for opera companies, as Martorella indicates, and contributes, along with organizational imperatives, to the rationalization of orchestras, as discussed by Couch. Both the restrictions imposed by patronage and constraints of organizational imperatives, according to Couch, contribute to the proletarianization of orchestra members.

All cultural producing organizations face more different kinds of uncertainties than most economic enterprises. This is because the goals of originality and quality are difficult to define and always relative, because many of these organizations do not benefit from the economies of scale that other organizations are benefited by, and, finally, because they often have mixtures of personnel that are rarely found in organizations. Art organizations cope with uncertainties in various ways: operas and symphony orchestras rely on traditional classical pieces (Zolberg and Martorella); members of symphony orchestras develop informal networks to define and reinforce conventions about how to play well, and how to coordinate and collaborate in a performance (Faulkner); and, paradoxically art museums cope with uncertainties by providing diverse "products," whereas orchestras cope with uncertainties by providing uniform ones (Zolberg).

Two other issues can be raised that question the conventional wisdom in sociology, and these issues are interrelated. One tenet of organizational theory is that because of the principle of economy of scale, large organizations are more likely to have features that are conducive to innovation. Blau (1984) demonstrates that in architecture firms in which creative contributions are valued, it is an organizational structure that is "eccentric" that tends to promote innovation, not a structure that exhibits features that are "normal" and consistent with the premise of economy of scale. That is, innovation is most likely when an organization is structurally out of kilter. The comparative analysis by Zolberg pushes this anti-structural argument even further. The art product itself—be it music or the display of art— governs the structure of the organization and determines whether that organization is innovative or not.

What is suggested here is that there is a two way street in our thinking about organizations. Our conventional knowledge about art as a social product that involves social roles is furthered by an understanding of how artists collaborate in organizations and how organizations both provide opportunities and set constraints for artists. On the other hand, organizational analyses that are based on conventional types of organizations often neglect the components that are prominent in the sociology of the arts: style, innovation, quality, novelty, the tradition of elite patrons or the more impersonal "mass" markets of the popular arts. Consideration of these components enhances our understanding of all organizations—even those that do not produce art.

Students interested in pursuing these organizational issues further should certainly trace the important tradition known as 'the production of culture' approach. Important early landmarks in this tradition include Peterson's edited volume, *The Production of Culture,* and articles by Peterson and Berger (1975) and Hirsch (1972).

References

Blau, Judith R. 1984. *Architects and Firms.* Cambridge: M.I.T. Press.

Hirsch, Paul M. 1972. "Processing Fads and Fashions." *American Journal of Sociology* 77: 639–659.

Parsons, Talcott. 1947. "Introduction." In A. M. Henderson & T. Parsons, eds. *The Theory of Social and Economic Organization.* New York: Oxford U. Press.

Peterson, Richard A., ed. 1976. *The Production of Culture.* Beverly Hills: Sage.

Peterson, Richard A. & David G. Berger. 1975. "Cycles in Symbol Production." *American Sociological Review* 40: 158–173.

Sponsors are Arts in Parks, the City Arts and Recreation Office, the Village Band, the Arts and Crafts Club, the Group Therapy Association and the Clean-up and Recycle Committee.

——— 15 ———

Orchestra Interaction: Some Features of Communication and Authority in an Artistic Organization[1]

ROBERT R. FAULKNER

In his classic treatment of authority in organization, Barnard directs attention to the persistent, stable, and reproducible features of interaction in deliberately created social structures (Barnard, 1962). He focuses on the problematic features of compliance by organizational subordinates and, specifically, on the interpretive contexts in which directives from superiors are scrutinized, evaluated, and translated into appropriate behavior by members. In his formulation, communications are viewed as situated work contingencies: factors upon which the legitimation of authority depends. Following Weber, the probability that an authority will be given obedience is dependent in part upon the extent to which his communications are viewed as authoritative (Barnard, 1962; Weber, 1964; Silverman, 1970). In other words, authoritative directives are socially constructed and sustained (Berger and Luckmann, 1966; Rose, 1962; Blumer, 1969). This theoretical emphasis concerns itself with the perspectives of subordinates (Shibutani, 1955), their standards for what they construe as clear and understandable directives, the propriety and compatibility of communications with their beliefs, and their sense of achieved competence in being able to comply with these directives.

The description and analysis which follows focuses on symphony orchestra performers' perceptions of the problematics of making music and their interaction with conductors. These occupational members have organized their work experiences into procedures and perspectives for engaging in collective lines of action to accomplish their purposes, and for dealing with the exigencies of role performance. Making music together is a practical organizational achievement which rests on recognized and sanctioned ways of doing things. Conductors' directives, in rehearsals and final performances, build upon those features which enhance the spontaneous playing of the musicians and reduce areas of ambiguity and unpredictability for them. Players themselves claim considerable expertise in assessing the wisdom, interpretive powers, consistency, and controlled spontaneity of the man on the podium. Because the specific musical task has most likely been performed previously under other conductors, musicians have had a chance to develop generalized work standards for evaluating the ability of any one maestro to move a group of high-powered virtuosi to perform as he wishes. This special world of concerted action that emerges between performances and conductors reveals many features relevant to the sociological study of authority. This study analyzes the ways in which performers, as "lower-level participants" in artistic organizations (Etzioni, 1961), perceive and construct definitions of interaction with conductors and proceed to respond to situations created for them.

Methods and Organizational Setting

This study is based on seven months of observation and fifty interviews, each lasting from one to four hours, with members of one of the top fifteen symphony orchestras in the U.S. During the orchestra season, rehearsals were attended, and tape-recorded interviews were conducted, either after the morning's work or later in the performer's home. Some reinterviewing was done in order to generate more complete evaluations of the succession of maestros. Performers were queried in their own language and encouraged to talk about the various conductors and work experiences faced over the season, to express their own ideas of work contingencies which could make their job tough, unpleasant, and at times degrading. Musicians are frank respondents when it comes to the generalities of making music, but getting at their troubles with particular conductors was difficult and at times required subtle and indirect interviewing tactics. These consisted of beginning the questions about their work by asking the musicians to define the ideal conductor; once the interview was underway, respondents were asked to compare the merits of the conductors under whom they had worked during the season. This tactic put players in the position of describing specific work experiences which either approached or fell short of their own conception and image of the ideal. It also elicited detailed interpretations of those work situations in which the fracture between ideals and reality was most obvious, role-expectations were violated, and performer tensions and complaints were viewed as "caused" by certain forms of interaction between musician and conductor.

The symphony world today offers a number of organizational settings in which subordinates are frequently under the direction and command of guest conductors. Musicians in both the major league or "Big Five" orchestras (Cleveland, Chicago, New York, Boston, Philadelphia) and in the set of organizations a notch below these ranks are likely to experience high rates of conductor succession over the musical season. Peripatetic guest conductors travel from orchestra to orchestra, rehearsing a week or two, giving concerts, and then moving on to another setting. Their tours of duty put them before orchestras with different talent, technique, and temperament. Musicians hear a great deal about the reputation and style of these maestros and know something about their ability to handle an orchestra.

An occupational lore develops around performers' problems and work adventures with conductors. Performers may play under more than twenty or twenty-five conductors in succession over the concert season; some are recognized as skilled but not too inspiring, others are seen as extraordinary and even charismatic leaders of men; still others are viewed as mediocre or worse. Similar standards are applied to permanent conductors. Such structural instability may well affect an organization's performance. Variations in leadership, due to constant succession, should have an impact on subordinates' perceptions of authority and compliance. In fact, this variability offers the organizational theorist something of an extreme case in the dynamics of work, in that the positions or offices in the formal structure are stable, but the incumbency of superiors changes rapidly and their mastery of communicative efforts and competence is closely scrutinized by subordinates. The conductor is supposed to be a leader. That person sets the tempo, maintains proper ensemble and balances, and impresses a will over a group of virtuosi. Musicians agree that it takes about ten or fifteen minutes for an orchestra to determine whether a new maestro is a fake, a phony, a brilliant technician, a charismatic personality, or a poseur (see Schonberg, 1967). Between the orchestra and the conductor must lie respect, reciprocity, and trust.

The conductor is the focal participant in the ensemble's efforts, for the on-going musical experience is continually shared and sifted through members' evaluative standards and their stock of preconstituted knowledge about the particulars of concerted playing. When asked specifically what they look for in the person on the podium, it becomes clear that words and actions are closely attended to and scrutinized for their practical content. Communications and directives which are inadequate, incomprehensible, shallow, and incompatible with the purposive action of performers can carry little authoritativeness. A conductor must create respect. He or she is not accorded a fixed distribution of deference because of the position. From the moment a conductor steps on the podium a special world is in the process of being constructed. Performers respond to the person directly. They

develop interpretations into situational definitions, and project lines of concerted action on the basis of these constructions.

Making music is an act of collaboration and practical decision-making,
and not a routine to which performers merely accommodate themselves as
players. Moreover, musicians have ideas of the possibilities in any piece of
music, and beyond that, an idea of the maestro as an agent of their own
behavior. One of their major preoccupations and concerns is the authoritativeness, the controlling force, of the maestro directives as the orchestra
plays through them, not once but many times. In "playing through" a conductor's translation of musical symbols into meaningful sound, the effects
of interaction, such as shared meanings, become objectified (Berger and
Luckmann, 1967:34). A musical world of meaning is built up and sustained, for better or for worse, as players put it, "you're either making
music or just playing notes." They agree that each maestro reads the symbols differently. They also agree that those expressive signs that fail to communicate a sum total of information allowing members to engage in lines of
action and interaction can have little, if any, authoritativeness within the
orchestra. This is a process of defining the situation (Ball, 1977; Stebbins,
1969) in which communicative competence and wisdom are attributed to
the conductor's error-correcting ability, knowledge of the performance
problems faced by musicians, and in general, an interpretive skill in trans-
forming the occasion from one of merely playing notes and "experiencing
things" to a situation of genuinely creative cooperation and "having an
experience" (Dewey, 1958:35–37; 1926:382–391).

Defining Directives and Concerted Action

Turning to the situational definitions constructed out of the cues and
cognitions from the podium, the acts which spring from these constructions, and the standards to which they hold a conductor, we can ask what
given "communication problems" imply making music. In the interpretive
construction and maintenance of orchestral performances, two conditions
appear to be a recurrent topic among orchestra performers. First, these respondents stress the idea that meanings emerge from interaction and that
some directives are open to various interpretations and, especially, fail to
specify *in advance* the desired musical outcome produced by an individual
musician, a section of the orchestra, or the entire ensemble. In selectively
responding to cues, ambiguity of expressive signs results in uncertainty.
These conditions generate lowered expectancies for players sense of control
and mastery of performance while reducing their ability to forecast or adjust to what like-situated colleagues will in turn perform.

A second, and related, contingency is found under those conditions where directives are viewed as unpredictable, inconsistent, and which combine competing instructions for the players. Performers' depictions of the meanings of a conductor's actions stress the negative consequences of equivocation. They see behind a series of expressive signs an underlying pattern in which the conductor cannot make decisions. This is different from the maestro who either does not know what he or she wants from the orchestra or is incapable of communicating it to its members.

As the following interviews illustrate, what is specific to the responses of these players is not some type of absolute obedience toward the conductor. By virtue of what they identify as extraordinary qualities and directives, the conductor exercises not only a type of inspiration but also an exemplary persuasiveness in demonstrating to them that the interpretation is correct. By these features the conductor exercises a kind of domination over performers (Weber, 1964:324–328). This does not involve, as these excerpts demonstrate, some kind of automatic acquiescence of musicians to the director's views. Nor does it exclude the possibility that they disagree on musical interpretations, phrasing, and tempo. This is all the more relevant since the conductor, as innovator, at times challenges these expert performers' ways of thinking and playing music. Like all professionals, musicians jealously guard their prerogatives and "working prejudices" from outside interference (Becker, 1963:85–100).

As Weber reminds us, the crucial test of charisma and expertise can be found not only in communicative strength and persuasiveness, but also in the responses of organizational subordinates. Conductors call for new ways of thinking and playing; that performers are receptive to this is recognized in the recurring phrase, "He has to show us what he wants, he has to have that personality, then we'll follow him." Resistance to the demands of some conductors is a concrete indication of the perspectives and sentiments which can be found among every performer in the orchestra. Here are some examples of the scrutiny given to definitions of the situation and the standards to which they hold conductors.

Asked to compare several of the conductors he had worked with over the season, a middle-aged woodwind player responded as follows:

> R. is very good, this week has been enjoyable, but T. to my mind is second-rate. There are a lot of things a second-rate conductor doesn't even begin to realize. It's easy for a conductor to be a charlatan. The whole thing is based on his being a musician's musician. You see, the musician needs someone who has leadership, a sense of beauty, intelligence . . . but leadership is not enough, you just can't force us to play. You can have a bull up there on the podium but that isn't going to bring you anything of

beauty. He has to be more than that, R. knows what he wants and can convey it to us. A conductor has to have, well, ability, just technical ability with the stick, he must tell us what he wants with the stick. We have to have confidence in him because if he can't convince us with the stick, then he's lacking in his own convictions somewhere.

A percussionist with a penchant for musical particulars judged one of the less-talented conductors against these standards and interpreted him as displaying exceedingly vague directives which then led to some incompatibility between maestro and musician.

The conductor must know what he wants and then convince me, convince the orchestra, that he is right, now that's important. We all have our own ideas and it's difficult if he doesn't know himself. Now Y., he was with us last week, is horrible, just totally inadequate. He doesn't communicate with technique or with words. He sort of looks surprised when we play. That's when the troubles start, it lacks authority, his beat lacks it. He follows us and you can't follow somebody who is following you. He can't tell us, so what can we do? We were very depressed about the whole thing, we ended up sounding bad.

Not surprisingly, inadequately defined cues and cognitions not only lack authoritativeness, they are themselves generators or causes of subsequent conduct such as open disrespect, sullenness, deliberately lowered work effort, selective inattention, sarcasm, and in general the making and taking of role distance (Goffman, 1961:105–115). At other times players witness a transformation of rehearsals into muted character contests (see Goffman, 1967:239–258) in which musicians test the conductor's ear, integrity, and presented self. A young reed player who had started his career in the orchestra world a few years back was considerably more opinionated than his colleagues. He made several allusions to the above-mentioned conductor and then went on to discuss one other. He objected to a frozen communicative style, a constricted expressiveness, and limited understanding of the proper use of rehearsals. He was asked if there were differences between the conductors over the season.

Sure. A lot of them have a very small range of emotional expression, how shall I put it, they have two or three expressions and they use them all the time so they get up and huff and puff and it doesn't mean a thing. They don't communicate. They are of no use to us. And then maybe they're too distant, you can never tell whether you're doing it right or wrong, they never respond when you respond to them. I guess after a while you stop watching them, you stop paying attention to what they're doing, you start making subtle jokes, things like that. E., I shouldn't mention names, but he doesn't have anything to offer, he isn't saying anything up there, he just is beating time—nothing happens. You play and you play, it's just notes followed by his beating time. We resent this. Anyone can beat time, but you've got to communicate.

Inept orders result in a sensed lack of effective coordination as well as a decline, as Barnard puts it, in the next inducement for accepting conductor orders and directives as having authority (Barnard, 1962:166). Moreover, performers are highly skeptical of conductors who employ a kind of verbal overkill where expressions are vapid, do not define clearly the particularized role information necessary for compliance, and do not foster a continuity of shared meanings between musicians.

Q: What are some of the work problems you faced over the past weeks with W., T., and S.?

Well, take S., the other day we rehearsed this one work and his idea was to take it bar by bar and he never accomplished anything, no phrases, no understanding of the music, no nothing, it was a disappointing show. We all hate him. When he stops and makes comments, he gets nothing done. With W., this week, you do, he knows what to say, just the few words to say to us. Then he lets us play. But with S., it's words followed by. . . .

Q: . . . music?

No . . . words followed by notes, it didn't mean anything, just notes. He stops and I think he doesn't even know what to say to us, or maybe how to say it. I was talking with my stand partner yesterday at the break and he said that with S. or E. you could stop the music anywhere and put a cadence in at any bar and it wouldn't matter at all. You could end it in the last movement in the second bar, now that kind of conductor you don't need.

A brass player discussed some of the consequences of inadequate communications and the attentiveness of his colleagues to signs or proof of a conductor's exceptional leadership abilities as well as personal qualities. These excerpts from an interview which lasted over three hours suggest the inclination of members to view authority in personalistic terms.

I think W. has that personality, he has that quality. He knows exactly when he wants us to do and he conveys it, the concert last night was exciting, really. He has that charisma. It's just their personality, that's the mark of a good conductor. He can make you want to play as good as you can for him, he gives you that confidence. I think you can tell when a man gets up there whether or not he has it, they just have a certain personal mag-

> netism, it's hard to explain. Like T., he'll make you play, whether you want to or not. We can tell right away . . . And then I would put the other side of this by saying if there's not an outstanding personality up there, well, why knock yourself out? Sure . . . it's not worth the effort, the physical and mental effort of paying attention, of concentrating, of listening, of constantly adjusting, all of this is hard work. I think if the guy doesn't have it you play with indifference. If he can't tell you, forget it, then there's the efficient and inefficient way of doing a rehearsal, it's not unlimited time. So we feel that you might as well stop watching him closely, start dreaming or something.

The distinction between expertise and the person exercising it has for most of these musicians a reduced importance; it is not a clearcut dichotomy but rather a blending of imputed authority of competence, charismatic leadership, and performance effort. The content of their knowledge turns on several well-developed cliches and an immensely factual spectrum of conductor types, styles of leadership, and varieties of skill. Moreover, players, with the ease of seasoned veterans, claim to be able to compare and assess conductors. While there is some disagreement about just how quickly a musician can accurately assess and "psych-out" the expertise and "personality" of a conductor, it is generally agreed that authoritativeness and the more elusive ability to take command can be established within a few minutes. All claim to know, and know a great deal about, what to look for in terms of musical erudition, the meanings of expressive signs for their own role performances, and especially the meshing of a particular conductor's authority at his first rehearsal with their own reconstructions of past work experiences under others.

The following player is representative of many in emphasizing that his grasp of and control over his own performance is primarily commensurate with the conductor's expertise and leadership skills. Facial expressions, directives, and inflections are closely attended to and carefully scrutinized as he tunes into the podium performance and the directives given and given off by the conductor. He could tell right away:

> . . . what the man has. You know with the first downbeat. In other words, he's taking command. If he doesn't take command, then you know he'll heel back. But if he takes command and has that personality and that ability, you know, with the first beat, then you sit up and give your attention. He's got to be inspiring, he must convince us that his way, his concept, is the right one. If he does, we'll follow him, if he proves he can weld the players into a unit.

Here is a respondent who slides immediately from the problems of inadequate information to his ideas about unpredictability between performances and the trouble with contradictory expressive signs. He was talking about a conductor he especially enjoyed working with.

> When W. gets up there and conducts, he acts out the emotions of the piece at the time, you know exactly what it's supposed to sound like, and what exactly you're supposed to do. This is it. But some conductors don't communicate, they are very limited and can only act out one kind of emotion and they do that for every type of music. J. cannot give you a feeling of happiness or joy or gaiety. You see a big problem is that these guys can't convey it through the stick, facial expressions, the whole body. I'd say we're confronted with too many conductors who are too competent for their own mediocrity. T. is an excellent musician, he rarely makes a mistake in the score, but he just doesn't communicate to me. The standard joke is the conductor who goes 'faster, faster' he says, but his beat gets slower and slower—the guy who says one thing and does another or who can't communicate, who gives gestures of expression but they're not showing us his meaning. He is of no use. Uninspired conductors and uninspired performances—that's the problem . . . We get upset when this happens.

Musicians hold the conductor accountable for correcting errors and increasing the scope of collaborative consensus; work pressures build up under conditions where performance outcomes are doubtful. A brass player had this to say about rehearsals and sensed mastery over the part he had to play.

> I've played the same composition several times under different conductors, like the Hindemith we did last night, and sometimes it's very easy and sometimes it's very difficult. It all depends on the conductor—and this is the same music.

> Q: Could you give me some examples of this problem?

> It's their technique of the baton, that more than anything else. The baton doesn't make any sound but if you're really watching, it can confuse you. Like R., he can make it difficult for you to play. He can create pressure on you. If he's inadequate as far as his knowledge, and we see some like that, then what he does can make life miserable, awfully miserable. Most of the tension and pressure comes from poor rehearsal techniques, that's a problem. Some of them just don't seem to be able to budget their time, and quite frequently for the last rehearsal I feel that we don't know the piece of music that well. I don't know my part well enough, it's not properly rehearsed, the balances are unclear, tempos are not clear, the whole thing is poorly done. This is where the pressure always comes right back

to *me*. I don't like this, because if the guy on the podium did a better job of budgeting his time and clearly telling me what he wants, then we wouldn't have this last minute frenzy, this big panic. If he was better as a conductor and could show us what he wanted, we wouldn't have this and I wouldn't be suffering because of it.

Several of these musicians point to instances where conductors, under pressure of the concert, seriously affect the sum of information musicians receive from the podium. Moreover, persistent discrepancies appeared between what the performers anticipated on the basis of a conductor's gestural signs and imputed attributes, and what the unfolding events actually showed him to be. A player with quite opinionated views about the attributes required for suitable communication from the podium became unrestrained in his account of one particular maestro.

You expect certain kinds of things to happen, and when they don't, well, the tempo may be completely different than what has been rehearsed for five rehearsals. Some conductors fall apart during concerts, I'm thinking of one man who was so erratic, one day it's here, another rehearsal it's there, and then during the concert he's doing it entirely different. We don't know what to expect. . . . That's one of the troubles with T. From the first day he came here I called him one of the biggest fakers in the business. He had everything that a conductor's supposed to have. He looked like one, he knew how to work his frustrations out on the orchestra all week long. He was nastier than anybody you would want to have on the podium and he had a tremendous amount of showmanship. But when the chips were down on the night of the concert, he just couldn't deliver. He'd get lost, he would ride roughshod over things he'd worked on all week long. You can't respect a man like that. I would express my opinion to his face, I don't care. He was a faker.

Incompetence and charlatanism, abuse of players and excessive posturing are viewed in terms of imputed expertise and conductor character. Maestros who prevent the performer from successfully *predicting* behavioral outcomes—both the conductor's and those of his co-performers—and who abuse the mandate of position come in for some of the harshest appraisals to appear in the interviews. Ambiguous definitions of the situation and inconsistent directives not only decrease the player's expectations of being able to interpret collective action, but undermine the conditions under which he can comply with a directive. To the recipients of such communications, this increases their work pressures and heightens overall tension within the ensemble. As for the impact on making music and the attachment players experience in working for an indifferent or bad conductor, one player had this to say:

These guys make us sound bad, they make the orchestra angry, they make *me* sound bad, and then some of the more discontent and lazy players take over and you wonder after a few rehearsals of fighting with the man and the stick why the hell he's up there in the first place. You see the man must know what he's doing and be able to tell us how to do it, then we'll play.

As for trust as a condition for concerted action, a principal in the woodwind section had this to say:

With the conductor last week . . . like if I have a solo to play, I know I can play as expressively as I know how and I know he won't go off and leave me and he knows I won't go off and leave him. There's a component of faith in what happens between us and a conductor. If it's there the music is there . . . You learn to size a conductor up, to see what he can do, this takes a rehearsal before you know. You sort of get a feel for him. With some of these guys, you just stop listening, you just stop being attentive because there's no reward, I would say, in being especially attentive.

For these musicians, ambiguity and equivocation create discrepancies between the role mastery a player expects and the degree of control he or she achieves. Under inept conductors, communications and directives become, in effect, poor predictors of collective action by reducing the minimal standards for clarity in decision making and thereby resulting in a particular kind of alienation at work. Another problem is introduced by the above musician. Whereas ambiguity and equivocation can be seen as problems of inadequate communicative gestures and role prescriptions, there is a problem of what players view as illegitimate directives and role prescriptions, that is, unwarranted attempts by the maestro to extend influence and power into the performer's own sphere of professional expertise. In this instance, too much control, rather than not enough, is exerted. These communications are often defined as incompatible with a player's personal and professional interest as a whole. Of course, it is the ability of the conductor to convince the musicians that there is the correct interpretation. The conductor's authority therefore builds upon those features which simultaneously enhance the spontaneous playing of musicians and on the substantially reducing areas of unpredictability while, at the same time, as one put it, "inspiring confidence in your own playing of what *he* wants."

Conclusion

I have presented orchestra performers as organizational members who experience work problems with conductors to the degree that directives are vaguely defined, grossly incompatible with performers' standards, unconvincing as musical interpretations, and technically unsound as guides for the successful execution of the music. The system of authority in the orchestra, I have argued, is more than a pattern of static roles and statuses. It is a network of interacting human beings, each transmitting information to the other, sifting their transactions through an evaluative screen of beliefs and standards, and appraising the meaning and credibility of conductor directives. The orchestra, as the most complex musical instrument, is composed of performers who communicate with one another, establish definitions of the situation under successive maestros, and thereby affect each others' tacit and explicit understandings about music and music-making under various conductors.

This picture discloses certain ideas of general relevance for the study of organizational authority. In the first place, an organization like the symphony can be seen as a system of social control in which members bring to bear a set of interpretive schemes for sizing up and evaluating the "focal superior," the man on the podium. This creates an organizational climate and work setting in which communications and shared meanings of exemplary performances are the conditions under which the conductor legitimizes his authority.

Second, like professionals in other organizations, these performers resist illegitimate intrusions into their sphere of competence and feel maligned under imputed incompetence. Communications and conductors are accepted to the extent they help members achieve their purposes. In the performing arts, as in sports organizations, organizational success and effectiveness are closely tied to the efforts of the "team leader." But unlike the film director, field manager, or ballet master, the conductor is directly involved and implicated in the organizational execution of the performance. Thus, like a "crew leader," the role performance has an impact on members' culture markedly different from that exerted by expert supervisors in industry.

Finally, I have argued that the authoritativeness of communications in organizations is not only situationally approved, but socially created and maintained. To this end, I have focused on performers' definitions of the situation and what they construe as information which allows them to engage in lines of concerted action. This suggests the general proposition that part of the sum total of recognized musical knowledge is generated in on-going organizational action. In his perceptive piece on "Making Music Together," Alfred Schutz writes:

> . . . within this socially derived knowledge there stands out the knowledge transmitted from those upon whom the prestige of authenticity and

authority has been bestowed, that is, from the great masters among the composers and the acknowledged interpreters of their work. Musical knowledge transmitted by them is not only socially derived; it is also socially approved, being regarded as authentic and therefore more qualified to become a pattern for others than knowledge originating elsewhere (Schutz, 1964:168–169).

It is the validation and confirmation of this knowledge and expertise which are problematic within the transaction between conductor as interpreter and musicians as performers. And it is this imputed authenticity upon which the excellence of an orchestra depends as well as upon which the authoritativeness of communication and conductors rest.

Notes

1. Reprinted with permission of the author and the publisher, *The Sociological Quarterly* (vol. 14, Spring 1973).

References

Ball, Donald W. Forthcoming. "The definition of the situation: some theoretical and methodological consequences of taking W. I. Thomas seriously," in Jack D. Douglas and J. M. Johnson (eds.), *Existential Sociology.* New York: Cambridge Univ. Press.

Barnard, Chester I. 1962. *The Functions of The Executive.* Cambridge, Massachusetts: Harvard University Press.

Becker, Howard S. 1963. *Outsiders: Studies in the Sociology of Deviance.* New York: The Free Press.

Berger, Peter, and Thomas Luckmann. 1966. *The Social Construction of Reality.* Garden City: Doubleday.

Blumer, Herbert. 1969. *Symbolic Interactionism: Perspective and Method.* Englewood Cliffs: Prentice-Hall.

Dewey, John. 1958. *Art as Experience.* New York: Capricorn Books.

———. 1926. "The nature of aesthetic experience." *International Journal of Ethics,* 36:382–391.

Etzioni, Amitai. 1961. *A Comparative Analysis of Complex Organizations.* Glencoe, Illinois: The Free Press.

Goffman, Erving. 1967. *Interaction Ritual: Essays on Face-To-Face Behavior.* Chicago: Aldine.

———. 1961. *Encounters: Two Studies in the Sociology of Interaction.* Indianapolis: Bobbs-Merrill.

Rose, Arnold (ed.). 1962. *Human Behavior and Social Processes: An Interactionist Approach.* Boston: Houghton-Mifflin.

Schonberg, Harold C. 1967. *The Great Conductors.* New York: Simon and Schuster.

Schutz, Alfred. 1964. "Making music together." Pp. 159–178 in Arvid Broderson (ed.), *Collected Papers II: Studies in Social Theory.* The Hague: Martinus Nijhoff.

Shibutani, Tamotsu. 1955. "Reference groups as perspectives." *American Journal of Sociology,* 60 (May):562–569.

Silverman, David. 1970. *The Theory of Organizations.* London: Heinemann.

Stebbins, Robert A. 1969. "Studying the definition of the situation: theory and field research strategies." *Canadian Review of Sociology and Anthropology* 6 (November): 193–211.

Weber, Max. 1964. *The Theory of Social and Economic Organization.* New York: The Free Press.

———— 16 ————

The Orchestra as Factory: Interrelationships of Occupational Change, Social Structure and Musical Style[1]

STEPHEN R. COUCH

Introduction

Some students of occupations have characterized recent trends as showing an increased "professionalization" of work in our society (e.g., Parsons, 1970:205–08; Hall, 1969:71–72). Increasing educational levels and new job requirements calling for higher technical specialization as well as the development of new "professions" within or outside traditional professional areas are all cited as evidence in support of this contention. However, others have argued that the trend is not toward increasing job autonomy and other characteristics generally associated with "professionals," but toward the incorporation of professions—even of traditional ones—into large-scale organizations where autonomy and other professional attributes are minimized (Braverman, 1974:293–358, 403–09).

Interestingly enough, performing artists have not been considered in this debate. Reference to them has not been made in any major book dealing with "professions" or "semi-professions" (e.g., Friedson, 1973; Etzioni, 1969; Hall, 1969). And yet this occupational category provides an interesting case for study. While most orchestra musicians do not possess job autonomy or the financial remuneration which would make them seem fully "professional," they can be considered "professionals" in terms of their possession of specialized knowledge, years and mode of training, and in terms of the prestige and status performing artists generally are considered to enjoy (Mueller, 1951; Hodge et al, 1964; Hart, 1973; Moskow, 1969; Lowry, 1978; Faulkner, 1973).

Some sociological investigations have dealt with various aspects of performing artists' careers. Generally this research has dealt more with descriptions of artistic careers, career contingencies, the social psychology of artists, and the organization of the immediate work environment, and not with the structure of the occupation in relation to the larger society (Westby, 1960; Faulkner, 1971; Falk, 1975; Becker, 1951). Also, the relationships between occupational structures of artists and artistic style have been underinvestigated, although some work has begun to fill this lacuna (e.g., Becker, 1978; Rosenblum, 1978; Ridgeway, 1977; Zolberg, 1977).

This paper attempts to link the areas of occupational change, large-scale social structural change and artistic style by examining the historical development of the occupation of the symphony orchestra musician in the United States. Its main focus is the extent to which the symphony orchestra musician approaches or is moving toward an ideal typical definition of the "professional," or the extent to which the evolution of the orchestra musician can be seen to parallel the proletarianization of the factory worker. Also considered is the role that musical style plays in the development of this occupation.[2]

The Musician As "Professional"

First, to what extent can symphony orchestra musicians be considered to be similar to professionals? In an article contrasting professional musicians with amateurs, Robert Stebbins summarized the following as being characteristics of professionals:

> (1) They turn out an unstandardized product; (2) they hold wide knowledge of a specialized technique; (3) they have a sense of identity with their colleagues; (4) they have mastered a generalized cultural tradition; (5) they use institutionalized means of validating adequacy of training and competence of trained individuals; (6) they emphasize standards and service rather than material rewards; (7) they are recognized by their clients for their professional authority based on knowledge and technique. (1978:84).

Symphony orchestra musicians hold wide knowledge of a specialized technique, have a sense of identity with their colleagues, and have mastered a generalized cultural tradition. While there is no institutionalized licensing of musicians, there do exist means of validating adequacy of training and competence of trained individuals. For orchestra jobs, this is accomplished by audition. The audition, however, is a test of performance alone; decisions are not influenced by a musician's credentials, or training.[3] Yet being granted an audition in the first place is often at least as much a function of personal connections as of institutionalized criteria.

While a certain autonomy exists in musicians' interpretations of the music within the constraints imposed by the conductor, the musicians' product is very standardized, consisting of a conventional repertoire of early "classics." The musicians are unionized and the unions' emphasis has largely been on improving wages and working conditions rather than improving the quality and diversity of performances. And, if musicians' talents are recognized by the public, this does not mean they can exercise their authority within the workplace, where they face a highly authoritarian work structure and traditionally have had little or no say about the operation of the orchestra (Hart, 1973; Mueller, 1951; Shanet, 1975; Arian, 1971).

So overall, symphony orchestra musicians do not approach the ideal type of professional very closely. While ranking high on some criteria, they rank low on many others. Their occupation in this century has been full of contradictions and this is manifest in much alienation. As David L. Westby concludes on the basis of his interviews with musicians in a United States orchestra:

> Strong commitments to the values of art and of his chosen profession are often undermined by unhappy experiences centering about unmet demands for material and status rewards, and the felt instability of his position. Sensing that others pull the strings that may ultimately affect his destiny, many a symphony musician experiences a chronic anxiety concerning his life chances (1960:223).

How has this disjuncture between aspirations and values, and the objective conditions of the occupation, come to pass? A brief historical examination of the development of the symphony orchestra occupation in this country provides some of the answers.

The Musician As Worker[4]

While there was some orchestral music in the United States before the turn of the nineteenth century, the young country lacked the human and financial resources to support very much of it. It was during the nineteenth century that the orchestra gained a strong foothold and became institutionalized in various cities.

Throughout most of the nineteenth century, symphony orchestras gave only a few concerts a year. Most orchestras had both "professional" and "amateur" musicians, and no one expected to make much, if any, money through playing orchestral concerts.

Musicians were not full-time employees of any organization, but rather independent free-lancers who would be hired by a contractor for each job. The contractor, a musician himself, would provide the link between the musicians and the employer. The whole organization of musical performance was arranged much like the present-day building trades which, because of their need to assemble persons possessing particular skills which vary from job to job, and because the jobs themselves are sporadic and seasonal, require more flexibility than can be accommodated in a rational bureaucratic structure (Stinchcombe, 1959). For music, such an arrangement was a response to the fact that it was financially impossible to give musicians steady year-round employment. The free-lance system allowed both musicians and organizations the flexibility to adjust to unstable demand.

Such arrangements had advantages and disadvantages for the musicians. For most, employment was unstable and financial remuneration modest. But within financial constraints there was a good deal of individual freedom for the musician. He had the ability to work at many types of musical jobs and for many groups, and also was able to teach. He was not tied to one organization, with all the constraints such an association brings with it.

During the middle of the nineteenth century, massive German immigration provided the United States with many excellent orchestra musicians. It also brought to this country an audience anxious to hear orchestra music from their homeland. German composers had come to dominate the world of orchestral music just at the time their music was brought to the United States by German immigrants. German musical style, German immigrant musicians and German audiences combined to bring about the formation of symphony orchestras in numerous cities.

Several attempts were made to form professional orchestras at this time—orchestras that would stay together for a substantial period of time each year playing concerts and that would be staffed by highly trained musicians. These attempts failed, as there was insufficient wealth to support such orchestras.

Changes in the music being written for orchestras added to their financial problems and brought about changes in the organization of the orchestra itself. Music was being written which called for larger orchestras, in response to and in turn encouraging larger audiences, the members of which were increasingly middle class. To hire the additional musicians put even more financial pressure on orchestras. Also, and probably more importantly, the conductor became much more critical as the orchestra's musical leader. On the one hand, he was needed to control the expanded number of players, and on the other, his role in interpreting the music took on greater importance. Music was being written that contained many more directional markings and subtleties than previously and that required more work to produce a unified ensemble and sound to meet the composer's explicit wishes.

Of course, this had a direct effect on the nature of the orchestra as a workplace. As the conductor's authority grew, individual musicians became increasingly dominated by his wishes. Discipline was enhanced as the conductor took fuller control. The music had also become more difficult to play, requiring additional rehearsal time. And, as audiences became more sophisticated through increased exposure to orchestral music, the demand for high quality performances increased. All of this greatly increased pressures for musicians in rehearsals and concerts.

By the late nineteenth century, major changes in the structure of United States society had taken place which eventually would lead to the creation of the full-time occupation of orchestra musician. Monopoly capitalism had resulted in great and concentrated wealth. Orchestra concerts had been a way the wealthy could demonstrate their cultural knowledge and sensitivity for a number of years; now, the *nouveaux riches* justified their class position by partaking in "high" culture. On the one hand, this led to competition with the established elite, namely, those with claims to "old" wealth, and on the other, to collaboration and expansion of "high" cultural institutions on a scale never thought possible before.[5]

For the orchestra, this patronage revolution began in earnest in 1881, when the wealthy Henry Lee Higginson offered to cover all yearly operating deficits of the Boston Symphony Orchestra if the orchestra players would make the orchestra their primary commitment for a relatively lengthy season. This arrangement led to extremely important changes in orchestral performances and organization. It allowed the musicians to play together as one group for a substantial period of time under the primary leadership of one conductor, greatly improving performance quality (a fact that was noticed by residents of other cities when the orchestra went on tour, encouraging other American cities to use the Boston Symphony Orchestra as a model for their own.) Moreover, this arrangement gave the musician security of employment and a steady income from symphony work. Orchestral playing could finally become a musician's primary occupation.

At the same time, there were tradeoffs. Being tied to one organization limited the number and variety of performing jobs the musician could take. Stricter controls, exercised by the conductor during rehearsals and performances, and imposed by the management concerning organizational matters, limited the freedom of the musicians. In addition, the fact that one wealthy patron usually controlled the orchestra wrested any possibility of organizational control from the musicians.

The era when a single patron could support an orchestra did not last long. Changing economic factors, including the institution of the Federal Income Tax in 1913, made support by one patron less feasible. Also, as orchestras turned to employing musicians for longer periods of time and under tighter controls, union demands for higher salaries increased. The solution was to replace the single rich patron with a committee of rich patrons. Under this arrangement, the expansion of orchestras' seasons and the occupationalization of the musician proceeded apace.

Between the years 1900 and 1960, there was a great increase in the number of orchestras in the United States, almost all of them being built on the layboard organizational principle. The length of seasons expanded for most orchestras, but no board was able to provide full-year employment for its musicians. Also, the conductor's power continued to increase. As expansion put still greater financial stress on orchestras, the conductor evolved into a celebrity whose box office drawing power was essential, and whose power over musicians became, in many cases, virtually complete. This was aided by the development of a standard repertoire consisting primarily of the classics. Modern music became too strident for the ears of most orchestra audiences. Since the music which was played was familiar to most concert-goers, emphasis was placed on differing interpretations of standard works, rather than on hearing different works. This increased the importance of the conductor in that it was *his* interpretation that was heard and judged. He came to be regarded as playing his orchestra like a pianist plays his piano; the orchestra became a mere instrument through which the conductor expressed his musicianship.

Further specialization within the structure of the orchestra took place with the advent of the professional orchestra manager. Expansion and financial pressures created the need for efficient management, and the orchestra manager, along with the conductor and the board, became the triumverate responsible for the operation of the orchestra. The musicians had become merely hired labor.

While some musicians finally were able to develop their careers solely within an orchestra, they were grossly underpaid when compared with professionals or highly skilled laborers. We could use musicians, in fact, as illustrating the concept of status inconsistency—their status was high as perceived by themselves and by the general public, yet their income was extremely low.

And yet, overall, their wage demands through the 1950's as made by unions were very moderate. Perhaps their conception of themselves as highly trained professional artists worked against their active participation in labor unions. Surely the arguments made by boards of directors that orchestras were financially unstable non-profit institutions reduced the likelihood that musicians would press their demands. Also the fact that the musicians' union was organized primarily to represent the majority of its members who played "popular" music and whose problems differed greatly from members of orchestras, hindered effective union representation of orchestra musicians.

Thus, at the end of the 1950s, in many important respects, the professional symphony orchestra can be seen as being a musical factory. Run by a wealthy lay board of directors, employing bureaucratic management, hiring musicians who were tightly controlled in the workplace and had no say in the running of the organization, the orchestra turned out a standardized product over which the musicians had no control beyond the performance of their individual parts. Even here, constraints on individual interpretation were imposed by conductors, and the individual contributions of most players (especially those in sections in which many performers played the identical part) tended to be insignificant. While musicians tended to consider themselves gifted professional artists, an examination of their actual working conditions shows them to have been much more akin to the conditions of factory laborers than to the conditions in which professionals work. The process was not one of professionalization, but rather one which shows marked resemblance to the proletarianization of factory labor.

Developments Since 1960

During the last twenty years, the organization of United States professional orchestras has been modified in several ways. To some extent trends already outlined persisted and the patterns continue to fit the factory analogy; there are, however, trends in the opposite direction, toward a partial professionalization of the orchestra musician.

For one thing, the general prosperity of the 1960s coupled with the "culture boom," the militancy of various groups which had previously been passive, and the better general education musicians were receiving, produced an increase in musician militancy at the bargaining table. Between 1920 and 1957, there were only three strikes by United States orchestras; between 1957 and 1966, there were ten (Moskow, 1969:115); during the 1970s, there were over thirty (International Conference of Symphony and Opera Musicians, 1973–80).

Perhaps the most momentous outcome of this militancy was the introduction of the fifty-two week contract by a few orchestras in the mid-1960s.

For the first time, some United States orchestras employed their musicians year-round and at a livable minimum wage. Today, there are fifteen United States orchestras providing their musicians with year-round employment.

It is somewhat ironic that by calling for recognition, pay and a year-round contract that would be worthy of "professionals," the musicians succeeded in integrating themselves completely into the wage labor structure, losing more of their autonomy and freedom in the process. They had decent salaries and job security, to be sure, but many quickly came to realize that year-round employment for one organization involves tradeoffs. They had less time for teaching and for other performing opportunities that would relieve the monotony and pressure of orchestra work. In short, they had lost what was left of the control they had possessed over their working lives. Much collective bargaining since the institution of full-year contracts has centered around trying to resolve this contradiction.

Also since the 1960s, there has been an even greater emphasis on rationalization of the management of performing arts organization (Martorella, 1977). Major orchestras had become big businesses with budgets in the millions of dollars. Efficient management and active public relations and fund raising were absolutely essential. The beginning of direct government funding encouraged this trend, as it required a type of accountability which requires a different kind of expertise and additional personnel. Arts administration became an academic specialty. The numbers of managers and administrators increased and the complexity of their tasks grew. This continued specialization further isolated musicians from the decision-making process and they were unable to provide input into the overall policies and business affairs of the orchestra. In some cases, the power of the manager came to rival and even exceed that of the musical director.

At the same time, there are indications that the occupation of symphony orchestra musician is starting to move in the direction of professionalization in some areas. First, over the past two decades, the absolute rule of the conductor over the musicians has been modified in most professional orchestras.[6] Musicians have demanded and been given some say over the hiring of new members; constraints on the ability of conductors to fire players have been negotiated, and firing now often involves peer review; some orchestras have artistic advisory committees that are made up of musicians who meet with the conductor and/or the board of directors and give suggestions on artistic policy matters. All of these reforms can be seen as indicating an increased ability of musicians to demand and receive some recognition of their authority as "professionals." At the same time, their present role is still small. The final say in hiring is almost always the conductor's. Moreover, the role of musicians' artistic committees is invariably advisory. Some see their formation as cooptation of musicians by boards;

allowing such committees to exist may stave off the possibility of musicians gaining some real power over orchestra policy.

Two additional trends should be mentioned. One is the formation in 1961 of the International Conference of Symphony and Opera Musicians (ICSOM). Though affiliated with the union, ICSOM is actually a professional association of symphony and opera orchestra musicians. It was formed out of dissatisfaction with the union's representation of orchestra musicians, has been responsible for increasing the union's awareness of orchestra musicians' special problems, and has gained some real power for itself and for orchestra musicians in negotiating contract matters for themselves.

Finally, various factors have been to push the orchestra out of its traditional mold of playing large-scale nineteenth century symphonic works in a large concert hall for middle and upper class audiences. Because of economic realities and pressures from government and foundations, alternative types of performing formats are being attempted, including, for example: subdividing the orchestra into smaller groups that play chamber symphony, chamber, and ensemble pieces; playing in parks and schools; accompanying operas, and giving special concerts of contemporary music. All these variations break up the monotonous routine of orchestra work and have the potential of reducing musicians' alienation.[7]

Summary and Discussion

Until recently, the course of development of the occupation of the professional symphony orchestra musician has been predominately away from the ideal typical model of professionalization. Indeed, the process can be seen as quite analogous to proletarianization. Orchestras in the United States first used primarily amateur musicians; later they relied on professional musicians who played in the orchestra as a sideline; then they employed full-time professional musicians. Now, in many cases, musicians who are employed year-round by the orchestra are limited in the outside activities they can perform. The musician has been transformed from amateur, to free-lancer, to wage laborer. At the same time, the orchestra has changed from a small, relatively egalitarian and loosely structured group into a large, complex, and highly disciplined organization—one that is quite akin to a factory.

Viewed from a broader perspective, the development of this occupation can be seen to have followed a trend common to monopoly capitalism: an increasing integration of the working population into the wage labor structure. As Braverman argues:

> The complexities of the class structure of pre-monopoly capitalism arose from the fact that so large a proportion of the working population, being neither employed by capital or itself employing labor to any significant extent, fell outside the capital-labor polarity. The complexity of the class structure of modern monopoly capitalism arises from the very opposite consideration: namely, that *almost all of the population has been transformed into employees of capital.* (author's emphasis) (1974:404)

Braverman goes on to argue that this transformation has separated conception of tasks from their execution, resulting in the ability of management to exercise much greater control over the work force, with the result that workers have been alienated from the products of their labor. This argument can be applied to the historical development of orchestras as well.

Braverman maintains that the reason such transformations have occurred is the drive to secure profits. However, symphony orchestras are money-losing ventures. Instead of increasing profits, their expansion into year-round professional organizations has significantly increased their losses. How can such economically irrational behavior be explained?

At one level, simply enough, those who were responsible for expanding orchestras must have desired more and better quality performances of orchestral music, and desired this enough to pay handsomely for it. Why they desired more and better quality music is more complex and goes beyond the scope of this paper. Suffice it to say that musicians themselves had what seemed to them to be an obvious self-interest in increasing the size of orchestras, as it offered them longer seasons and better pay (although, as we have seen, the tradeoffs were not insignificant). Patrons' status was enhanced by supporting large-scale high quality orchestras. And, of course, better quality music is generally preferred to poor quality music by all who have the ability to tell the difference.

But why did orchestras come to resemble factories in so many ways? Here, two factors are paramount. The first is that even if profits are not being made, there is no reason to suppose that those in charge of an organization will not want to maximize control over its operation. Members of orchestra boards are generally capitalists or, at least, very wealthy, and the wage labor bureaucratic structure is not only effective, but to them it seems natural—the best, most efficient way to get the job done.

The other factor is the music itself, and it is here that we can see most clearly the importance of considering the relationship between the music and the occupational structure. As was mentioned above, during the nineteenth century, orchestral music became more difficult, making it harder for amateur musicians to give decent performances and encouraging the professionalization of the orchestra musician. It also became much more complex, placing increased emphasis on nuances of sound and tone color as well as rhythmic variation, and calling for larger numbers of players. These factors themselves can be seen as significant with regard to the orchestra's factory-like structure. The quality of this new music depended on a leader assuming responsibility for coordinating and balancing the sections of the orchestra and for creating a unified interpretation and sound. These musical factors combined with the box office benefits of an image of a flashy conductor, who is, moreover, a source of authoritarian control over the labor force.

What of the future development of the orchestra musician and of the musician's role within the orchestra? Recent trends indicating professional-ization of the occupation along some lines have been discussed, although because of the entrenched power structure in orchestras, it is unlikely that those trends increasing the musicians as professionals who exercise influence will go extremely far. Musicians are likely to get a share of power, but nothing approaching the lion's share. At the same time, the "proletarian-ization" of the musician is unlikely to proceed much further. There are definite limits on how far this can go, given the economic position of orchestras. For instance, only a limited number of orchestras can afford to fully integrate their musicians into the wage labor structure by giving them year-round employment. Also, while a case can be made that the string sections of orchestras provide undifferentiated labor power (another sign of "proletarianization"), this analogy can be pushed too far, for even though they play the same part, all second violins in major orchestras are highly skilled, and the market is not gutted with them. Still, however, if only because of the nature of the music being performed, the factory-like nature of the orchestra as a workplace undoubtedly will remain.

This study has implications for the study of occupations and profes-sions. Support seems to be given to those theorists who argue that a sort of macro-sociological "proletarianization," not "professionalization," has been taking place. But such support is equivocal, as recent trends in the case of orchestra musicians indicate the possibility of at least partial rever-sal. It would be interesting to do further study on this trend as well as on comparisons with other occupations which are making similar efforts to claim professional status and increase control over their work.

Finally, it would be interesting to compare the professional symphony orchestra musicians in the United States with their European counterparts. Musicians in Europe generally have much more influence over their work-ing lives; and, their professional authority carries a great deal of weight (see for preliminary comparisons, Dorian 1964; Taubman, 1970; Couch 1983). Perhaps some would say that this is because musicians in Europe have been of high status traditionally, and those in the U.S. have not. Yet what evi-dence, albeit imperfect, we do have suggests that orchestra musicians are given very high status by the general public in the United States (Hodge et al 1964). Perhaps there are factors which in this country mitigate against the possibility of musicians translating their high status into authority and power, or perhaps status has less to do with authority than is often supposed. Without question, a comparative study of this occupation would throw light on more general sociological questions dealing with occupational and organizational development.

Notes

1. Partial funding for research related to this paper was provided by a Chairman's Grant from the National Endowment for the Humanities (FT–10755–80–1625) and from the Faculty Scholarship Support Fund of The Pennsylvania State University. An earlier version of this paper was presented at the Annual Meetings of the American Sociological Association, Boston, MA, September 1979.

2. It is a difficult task to assess whether an orchestra musician is "really" a professional or a craftsperson since the differences between these two concepts have never been conceptualized adequately (see, for instance, Friedson, 1977; Hall, 1969: 206–18). For the purpose of this paper, the task would be pointless since the purpose is to explore the *directions* of the development of this occupation, not to fit it into one or another category.

3. To make certain that neither credentials nor ascribed traits of the auditioner influence the outcome, many orchestras separate the auditioner and the judges by a screen.

4. The historical and organizational material presented in this section relies especially on Raynor (1976); Couch (1983); Shanet (1975); Hart (1973); and Mueller (1951).

5. The story of the founding of the Metropolitan Opera provides an interesting case in point. Parvenu families were not allowed to subscribe to boxes at the exclusive Academy of Music for opera performances. They reacted by building their own opera house, the "Met," which proceeded to drive the Academy of Music's opera out of business.

6. In a way, changes in the nature of the conductor can be seen as an example of the application of "scientific management" to the orchestra. The more cordial, business-like conductor of today attempts to gain and keep control over the musicians more through tactful cajoling than tyrannical outbursts.

7. Although it is questionable how musically satisfying it can be to perform orchestra music in a high school gymnasium before hundreds of screaming children, such concerts are at least breaks in the highly pressured routine. And opportunities to perform chamber music under the orchestra's auspices do provide outlets for musical expression.

References

Arian, Edward. 1971. *Bach, Beethoven and Bureaucracy,* University: University of Alabama Press.

Baumol, William J. and William G. Bowen. 1966. *Performing Arts: An Economic Dilemma.* New York: Twentieth Century Fund.

Becker, Howard S. 1951. "The Professional Jazz Musician and His Audience." *American Journal of Sociology* 57:136–44.

Becker, Howard S. 1978. "Arts and Crafts." *American Journal of Sociology* 83: 862–89.

Braverman, Harry. 1974. *Labor and Monopoly Capital.* New York: Monthly Review Press.

Couch, Stephen R. 1983. "Patronage and Organizational Structure in Symphony Orchestra in London and New York." Pp. 109–121 in Jack B. Kamerman and Rosanne Martorella (eds.), *Performers and Performances: The Social Organization of Artistic Work.* South Hadley, MA: J. F. Bergin.

Dorian, Frederick. 1964. *Commitment to Culture.* Pittsburgh: University of Pittsburgh Press.

Etzioni, Aritai (ed.). 1969. *The Semi-Professions and Their Organization.* New York: The Free Press.

Falk, Gerhard. 1975. " 'Moral Density' and the Job of Symphony Conducting." *International Journal of Contemporary Sociology* 12:206–11.

Faulkner, Robert. 1971. *Hollywood Studio Musicians.* New York: Aldine-Atherton.

Faulkner, Robert. 1973. "Orchestra Interaction: Some Features of Communication and Authority in an Artistic Organization." *The Sociological Quarterly* 14:147–57.

Friedson, Eliot. 1977. "The Future of Professionalization." in M. Stacey, et. al., (eds.) *Health and the Division of Labor.* London: Croom, Helm.

Friedson, Eliot. ed. 1973. *The Professions and Their Prospects.* Beverly Hills: Sage Publications.

Hall, Richard H. 1969. *Occupations and the Social Structure.* Englewood Cliffs, N.J.: Prentice-Hall.

Hart, Philip. 1973. *Orpheus in the New World.* New York: W. W. Norton.

Hodge, Robert W., Paul M. Seigel and Peter H. Rossi. 1964. "Occupational Prestige in the United States, 1925–1963." *American Journal of Sociology* 70:286–302.

International Conference of Symphony and Opera Musicians, 1973–80. Senza Sordino. Chicago: M. Kallis.

Lowry, W. McNeil ed. 1978. *The Performing Arts and American Society.* Englewood Cliffs, N.J.: Prentice-Hall.

Martorella, Rosanne. 1977. "Art Administration in the Performing Arts." Paper presented at the Annual Meeting of the American Sociological Association, Chicago, Illinois.

Moskow, Michael H. 1969. *Labor Relations in the Performing Arts.* New York: Associated Councils of the Arts.

Mueller, John H. 1951. *The American Symphony Orchestra.* Bloomington: Indiana University Press.

Parsons, Talcott (with Winston White), 1970. "The Link Between Character and Society." Pp. 183–235 in T. Parsons (ed.), *Social Structure and Personality.* New York: The Free Press.

Raynor, Henry. 1978. *Music and Society Since 1815.* New York: Taplinger.

Ridgeway, Sally O. 1977. "The Social Dynamics of an Avant-Garde Art Movement." Paper presented at the Annual Meeting of the American Sociological Association, Chicago, Illinois.

Rosenblum, Barbara. 1978. "Style as Social Process." *American Sociological Review* 43:422–38.

Shanet, Howard. 1975. *Philharmonic: A History of New York's Orchestra.* Garden City, N.Y.: Doubleday.

Stebbins, Robert A. 1978. "Classical Music Amateurs: A Definitional Study." *Humboldt Journal of Social Relations* 5:78–103.

Stinchcombe, Arthur. 1959. "Bureaucratic and Craft Administration of Production: A Comparative Study." *Administrative Science Quarterly* 4:168–87.

Taubman, Howard. 1970. *The Symphony Orchestra Abroad.* Vienna, Va.: American Symphony Orchestra League.

Westby, David L. 1960. "The Career Experience of the Symphony Musician." *Social Forces* 38:223–30.

Zolberg, Vera L. 1977. "Displayed Art and Performed Music: Selective Innovation and the Structure of Artistic Media." Unpublished.

—— 17 ——

The Relationships Between Box Office and Repertoire: a Case Study of Opera[1]

ROSANNE MARTORELLA

The work milieu of artists—writers, painters and musicians—has been interpreted through various theoretical perspectives (Albrecht et al. 1970; Wilson, 1952; Hauser, 1951). One orientation, from a Marxist tradition, includes a description of market structures and relates them to artistic styles and careers. Albrecht (1973) integrates these various efforts, and offers some guidelines about marketing networks (from production, distribution, and consumption), which influence art products, artistic recruitment, and socialization.

Recently, sociologists interested in popular culture have analyzed it in terms of markets (see, for example, Hesbacher, 1975; Peterson and Berger, 1972, 1975; Denisoff, 1974; Tuchman, 1974; and Hirsch, 1969). Other studies have taken a slightly different orientation, through organizational analysis, and document the effect of client domination, for example, on music and film (Faulkner, 1976; Peterson and Berger, 1972; Powdermaker, 1950). But little attention has been given to the fine arts,[2] and opera, as an artistic organization, has not been studied.

This paper investigates the market dimension of opera production. The nature of this classical performing art activity—its nonprofit structure, and its reliance upon an organizational complex of support personnel—lends itself to an interpretation in terms of market constraints facilitated by a client-centeredness or a commercial-like milieu. Studying the consequences of production goals and values of opera, mediated by market conditions (including its system of patronage, mass orientation, and European traditions), will allow us to explore the relationship between the economics of opera and what is selected for presentation.[3]

The Structure of the Opera Market

Studies of the market for works of art have revealed that as social institutions became specialized and market relations changed, the social position of the artist, the nature of his role, and the cultural product also changed (Martindale, 1972; Huaco, 1965; Bensman and Gerver, 1958; Hauser, 1951). Using this framework, Martorella (1974) showed that the emergence and specialization of the various performing roles which comprise the modern operatic-symphonic structure were facilitated by changes in patronage and the musical taste of audiences. Musicians, favored by specific audiences, contributed in turn to the development of particular innovations, interpretations, and styles in music. The role of the castrati and solo singer of the seventeenth and eighteenth centuries giving rise to the "bel canto" tradition in singing, and the high position and prestige held by the virtuoso instrumentalist of the nineteenth century, reveals the importance of patronage systems upon performing roles and styles (Raynor, 1972:329–30; Pincherle, 1965:41–52; Bukofzer, 1947:408–11).

National distinctions—comprised of different patrons, audiences or sociopolitical situations—enabled opera to take varied forms. When opera in Germany, for example, began to attract the interest of the middle class, they opposed the aristocratic music of the "opera seria." Their love for the Singspiel, and their literary tradition, combined to create what Wagner later called "Gesumtkunstwerk"—a total art form integrating music, poetry, and drama. Dilletante instrumentalists and choral groups in Northern Europe extended their preferences for the composer-performer, while the aristocratic and Venetian families favored the singer's virtuosity (Lang 1941:378; Thomson, 1939; Rolland, 1915:229).

As the patronage of music shifted from the nobility and clergy to the middle class, music still functioned to grant status to its consumers. The baroque lifestyle and splendor of the court opera were transposed to the commercial opera house; with this change came a preference for superstars, especially in Italy and later in the United States. Lacking national traditions of its own, and possessing a cultural elite which discounted anything American, opera production in the United States has tried to incorporate as much as possible from Europe since the middle of the nineteenth century (Pleasants, 1973:73; Stone, 1957). Although the rise of urban centers and the influx of immigrant populations have secularized middle class music, opera has retained its strong European allegiances which, even to the present, have fostered a distrust of experimentation in the modern repertoire.

The history of the four leading opera companies in the United States (the Metropolitan Opera, Lyric Opera of Chicago, New York City Opera, and the San Francisco Opera), which comprise over half of the total budgets of all professional opera companies, reflect these structural changes. These changes have influenced artistic decisions and the nature of the organization. The relationship depends upon which segments of their audience these companies rely on for financial support. The Metropolitan Opera, having been transformed from a profit-making and prestigious enterprise in about 1880 to a nonprofit public association by 1932, specifically reflects these structural changes. In the beginning, it was manipulated by the rich who owned stock, received large interest returns and, more importantly, owned their much-sought-after box seats for the entire season. This transition has not concomitantly altered repertory trends, however. Unlike painting in France and Holland, or writing in England, artistic innovations (in American opera) have not occurred with increased middle class patronage. No indigenous operatic music, representative of the middle or upper classes, has developed, while anything avant-garde has been the product of composers hidden away in academic subcultures. For example, one could estimate that of the 463 different productions that were given over 10,000 performances from 1966 to 1972, over 90 percent were given by universities. Companies which have come to rely on subscribers and the more casual on-going opera audience simply cannot afford to risk producing works that are not insured of immediate popular response. In addition to the sheer size of the opera company, which is expensive, the changing nature of philanthropy and the inflationary trend reduces any economic stability. Powerful board members who share similar tastes with the majority of the opera audience aggravate such a situation and have acted to constrain repertory selection and inhibit innovation further.

In comparison, both the San Francisco Opera (Bloomfield, 1972:139) and the New York City Opera, until very recently, have not been as severely restricted and client controlled since they have much smaller budgets (approximately a $4 million annual expense as compared to the Metropolitan's $25 million) and are subsidized a bit more. Their respective directors, too, have been committed to presenting more experimental productions. Nevertheless, New York City Opera's move to Lincoln Center, with its concomitant rise in production costs and an expanding market, was soon followed by changes making it more responsive to box office demands and the star system. Increasingly, all opera companies have been affected by larger production and maintenance costs, union demands, 52-week seasons and inflationary economic trends. The economic dilemma in the arts, however, cannot be explained by inflation alone. The nature of the performing arts organization as "labor intensive," with a limited repertoire and a relatively small audience which can sustain only a minimal portion of the total costs of production, places it in debt. One attempt to control costs is to increase box office sales—a mechanism all to familiar in the commercial film and theatre industry. An investigation into the nature of the box office, in light of the institutional changes discussed, follows.

The Box Office, Patrons, and Client Control

The opera audience includes those who buy tickets once or twice a year, the private patron, the devoted opera buff, the subscriber, and the more recent contributors—foundations, corporations, and government. Repertory selection is made in response to these groups, and involves a long and complicated network of organizational stages of its internal resources and client control. The technical requirements of a composition (e.g., availability of vocal ranges, proper lighting and staging equipment, size of orchestra and chorus, money to offset new productions and rehearsal time, etc.) as well as the nature of its reception are serious considerations. Ultimately, however, the audience and patrons weigh heavily since they express their interest by purchasing tickets and making contributions.

The high rate of inflation in light of the overall economic structure of the arts in the United States makes the box office more consequential for the future of the arts in America (Baumol and Bowen, 1966; Ford Foundation, 1975, 1974; New York State Council of the Arts, 1973; Rockefeller Foundation, 1965). Box office income accounts for at least 60 percent of the total income for the Metropolitan and San Francisco operas, while it provides a little less than half for the Lyric Opera of Chicago. Private contributions, which accounts for the remaining income, have risen considerably and without them organizations could not survive. For example, in a ten-year study from 1965–1975, the Metropolitan reported that income had doubled while expenses had tripled. If contributions had not risen from $4.4 to $9 million during this period, bankruptcy would have resulted. The degree to which patrons create constraints on opera companies varies according to their representation within the total income. Private donors and guild members, therefore, are more influential as "clients" of the Chicago and the Metropolitan operas than they are of the San Francisco Opera and the New York City Opera. One manager expresses the notion that if donations are spent in a way preferred by the patron, future contributions are insured.

> If you are given a donation, you spend it. If you examine the records, we did very well. The public was excited; they sent checks (Krawitz, 1973).

Attendance at the Metropolitan during the sixties was consistently averaging about 95 percent of the house capacity through their subscription series; however, during the past few years, it has dropped considerably, with the 1975 season having a low of 86 percent. This decline both in daily ticket sales and subscription series has aggravated the situation. Companies have come to rely on box office favorites and are fearful of risky productions, since each percent of house capacity represents approximately $100,000 of income for a place like the Metropolitan. Rolf Lieberman, who achieved great success and acclaim as general manager of the Hamburg Opera, now leads the Paris Opera. Summarizing the Metropolitan's problem, he alludes to the relationship between box office and what is selected for presentation:

> The problem with the Metropolitan is that one is always dependent on the goodwill of the people who may or may not be willing to help, so that one can never plan on a really secure budget. That's one dangerous thing. The other is that if the budget is based on a 96 percent box office, then that excludes everything risky and anything modern (Heyworth, 1971).

Submission to box office demands insures greater financial security and has come to be justified because it means survival. Carol Fox, general manger of the Lyric Opera of Chicago, has gone even further in asserting that it may not be her job to produce repertoire which does not offer box office returns. Legitimating an ideology prevalent among service organizations, she claims:

> Our audience might take a lot of hearing to comprehend and enjoy them. And I don't know that it's our purpose to do all these things. The most important purpose is to content the public, to get them to come, and bit by bit to indoctrinate them to the new (Jenkins, 1972:14).

A "White Paper" published by the Metropolitan Opera admits to this inevitable and unfortunate consequence of organizations dependent on box office and compares opera houses abroad that have government support:

> It has also been said that subsidy means greater freedom and opportunity to experiment than dependence exclusively on box office allows. Where the government makes up the difference between box office income and expenses (about 70 percent in Germany and as high as 90 percent in Sweden), it is much easier to plan a more adventurous repertoire and not worry about selling tickets to works which are artistically worthwhile but have not yet had sufficient exposure to the public to be popular (Metropolitan, 1971:27).

If, as in the case of large companies which are caught in the financial squeeze, every opportunity to increase box office receipts is taken; popular operas will be selected for presentation and superstars will be cast in major roles. Although accurate prediction of the box office returns is not always

ROSANNE MARTORELLA

Table 1
Ten Highest Box Office Percentages: Metropolitan Opera
1972 and 1974

1972		1974	
Production	*%*	*Production*	*%*
Trovatore	99	Tristan	99
Norma	99	Gotterdamerung	98
Barber	99	Rosenkavalier	97
Aida	98	Hoffman	97
Carmen	98	Carman	97
La Fille	98	Trojans	95
Siegfried	97	Trovatore	95
Rosenkavalier	97	Otello	95
Walkure	96	Barber	95
Otello	95	Butterfly	94
Average	87	Average	92

Source: Metropolitan Opera Association, 1974.

possible, prudent management is well aware of the "winners" and what audiences buy. A rare or unfamiliar work by Verdi, Wagner, or Puccini is a sure hit, and this is enhanced when superstars are engaged for these new productions. One is reminded of a statement by Edward Johnson who, as manager of the Metropolitan from 1935 to 1950, remarked that "Opera depends for its prosperity on Verdi, Wagner and Puccini." When asked who contributes to the development of artistic standards, Francis Robinson, well known in the opera world and long affiliated with the Metropolitan, responded:

> The public. We put it as ABC, "Aida," "Boheme" and "Carmen." Sir Rudolph used to say, 'They know the masterpieces, and it's not just because they heard about it. They know and feel the difference immediately.' They demand and want the best.

Box office receipts reflect preferences for compositions from the Romantic Era, and Table 1 lists the only available data of the 10 highest box office percentages for the Metropolitan's 1972 and 1974 seasons. They include Verdi's "Aida," "Il Trovatore," and "Otello," Wagner's "Die Walküre," "Siegfried," "Gotterdamerung," and "Tristan and Isolde," Bizet's "Carmen" and Rossini's "Il Barbiere di Siviglia."

Table 2
Percent of Opera Productions Among Most Popular Composers:
Metropolitan Opera (1971 to 1976)

Season	Composer	Percent of Productions
1971–72	Verdi	29
	Donizetti	11
	Puccini	10
	Rossini	7
	Wagner	7
1972–73	Verdi	30
	Puccini	11
	Gounod	11
	Donizetti	8
	Wagner	4
1973–74	Verdi	28
	Puccini	16
	Rossini	9
	Wagner	8
	Donizetti	6
1974–75	Verdi	26
	Puccini	21
	Rossini	8
	Wagner	7
1975–76	Verdi	19
	Mozart	13
	Bellini	11
	Strauss	11

Source: Metropolitan Opera Schedules, 1971–76.

Table 2 outlines the most often produced composers for the Metropolitan from 1971 to 1975 seasons. The "box office" composers appear more often within the repertoire over the last five seasons. The Wagnerian productions, with exception, have a lower number of performances given their high cost of production.

An assistant manager, wanting to remain anonymous, alludes to the consequences of client-domination and refers to the Metropolitan as a "petrified and fossilized house'' because of the need to sell tickets. He included other institutions in his criticisms, but LaScala and Covent Garden, he thought, were not as rigid in programming because of the supplements they receive from their respective governments. He went on to blame the subscription system. ''Sure, income is needed, but it has led to a conservative, even reactionary repertory.''

Music organizations have come to rely more heavily on subscription performances to fill the house and, therefore, provide some minimal financial base.[4] Although opera subscribers remain the largest group of the total box office income, they are the most conservative and place specific ''constraints'' upon repertory selection. Their demands for superstars and preferences for Italian opera add to the fact that subscriptions limit repetition of repertoire. As a result, inhibitions occur regarding not only the specific content of the repertoire, but also the total number of productions, performances, and composers selected for each season. Maestro Kubelik, in summing up the irreversible set of circumstances involved in producing opera today, reveals the importance of the organizational structure. He specifically addresses the size and nature of the audience.

> I don't think the repertoire of the Met is so terrible. A big house, one cannot afford to risk too much. I wonder whether it is just to say that the City Opera does avant-garde things and so-and-so and the Met doesn't. Look, I don't want to fight them, but their budget and their possibilities are on a much smaller scale, and almost call for that 'little better.' They have the chance to try more because it doesn't cost so much money. The Met is the largest opera house in the world, and cannot afford to be too audacious, but, of course, it should improve on its repertory (Rubin, 1971).

These foregoing exigencies now become the basis for investigating how market conditions act to constrain and determine repertory trends among the leading opera producers in the United States.

The Standardization of Repertoire[5]

Table 3 presents the percentage distribution of standard (operas premiered before 1930) and contemporary operas and composers in the United States for a nine-year period, 1966–1975. Of the total number of operas performed during this period, 64 percent involved the compositions of approximately 31 percent of the standard composers. Contemporary composers, representing 69 percent of the total number of composers, received only

Table 3

Works Produced and Number of Performances in the United States: Standard* and Contemporary Repertoire (1966–1975)

	Number	Percent
Performances		
Standard	28,060	*64*
Contemporary	15,631	*36*
Total	43,691	*100*
Composers		
Standard	112	*31*
Contemporary	255	*69*
Total	367	*100*
Productions		
Standard	550	*46*
Contemporary	641	*54*
Total	1,191	*100*
Average number of performances by composer:		
Standard	250	
Contemporary	61	

*Operas premiered before 1930
Source: See Opera Repertory 1966–1972, Central Opera Service, 1972; and "United States Opera Survey 1974–1975," (Rich, 1975:40–3).

36 percent of the performances. Consequently, standard composers were produced four times more than contemporary composers, averaging 250 performances and 61 performances, respectively. The "standardization" of classical works and a resistance to change repertory trends appears due to the higher number of performances of the same works by standard composers. In comparison, more contemporary composers received fewer performances of their compositions, often two or three performances on a short-term commission basis, which accounts for the larger proportion of contemporary works produced during this period.

Table 4 confirms this trend further in revealing a lower percentage of productions in the standard category, which have less than 10 performances

Table 4
Annual Reappearance of Standard and Contemporary Repertoire
(1966–1972)

Total Repertoire		Less 10 Number	%	Reappearance Number	%
Standard	341	163	48	58	17
Contemporary	463	338	73	27	.06

Source: See Opera Repertory 1966–1972, Central Opera Service, 1972.

over the five-year period, 1966–1972, and have a higher percentage of seasonal reappearances (17 percent) than the contemporary works (.06 percent). If the annual averages of these compositions could be documented, standardization would be explicitly revealed. The data appear, however, to suggest this. The lower percentages of contemporary composers from the total number of performances indicates that higher fluctuating averages would result—that is, while contemporary operas may be produced, they are performed a few times during the year of their premiere and then never appear again. Classical works are more resistant to change.

We are able to observe from Table 5 that the four leading opera companies present a disproportionate number of compositions from the nineteenth century. Contemporary operas are often totally absent from seasons, and in an unprecedented year, they accounted for 12 percent of the Metropolitan's 1974–1975 season. The Lyric Opera of Chicago, have a similar board-management relationship and an audience that supports Italian repertoire, reveals the same repertory trends as the Metropolitan.

The history of these two houses, in fact, reveals a long standing commitment to the works of Wagner, Verdi, and Puccini with more recent interest in Donizetti and Rossini. Both have similar support from the upper class in their cities and long-time immigrant subscribers, who share European allegiances. San Francisco Opera and the New York City Opera remain contrasts. They are companies in which contemporary operas and more avant-garde productions are a regular event, as evidenced by their occurrence in all the seasons surveyed. In comparison, their public is younger, and from the beginning were made to expect something out of the ordinary from the directors of the companies. The minimal representation of contemporary works in the repertoire, however, indicates that such works are predominately presented by university workshops and small experimental theatre groups across the nation, who can afford to produce them because of their foundation and government subsidies.

Table 5 also confirms that larger companies are more inhibited in repertory selection. For example, the Metropolitan presents some contemporary compositions during alternating seasons, representing 3 percent in 1972–1973, and 12 percent in 1974–1975. We also can observe a general trend in the reduction of the total number of performances, from 281 in 1971 to 189 in 1975. On the other hand, the New York City Opera, making use of grants, seems to produce a more diversified repertoire in a shorter season. Although the move to Lincoln Center for the New York City Opera has expanded its market, other significant factors have inhibited its commit-

Table 5
Total Number of Performances and Contemporary Repertoire by Percentages: Metropolitan, New York City, Lyric Opera of Chicago, and San Francisco (1971–1976)

	Chicago	*Metropolitan*	*New York*	*San Francisco*
1971–1972				
Total number performances	44	281	67*	72
Percent contemporary	*0*	*0*	*24**	*19*
1972–1973				
Total number performances	47	223	163	64
Percent contemporary	*0*	*3*	*12*	*11*
1973–1974				
Total number performances	48	211	160	80
Percent contemporary	*0*	*0*	*9*	*10*
1974–1975				
Total number performances	47	210	156	76
Percent contemporary	*0*	*12*	*13*	*5*
1975–1976				
Total number performances	46	189	158	77
Percent contemporary	*0*	*0*	*9*	*5*

*Represents figures for the spring season only.

ment to the presentation of avant-garde works. After its initial growth and utilization of subsidies to offset the costs of new and experimental works, it was beset with a loss of grants and an audience which has come to rely on its own superstars and traditional repertoire. Daniel Rule, manager of the New York City Opera, remarked to the author that producing compositions which sell varies with the seriousness of the deficit.

> There are times when we plan something which is less secure than something else. The weight (of the decision) may fall on the side of something which is more secure from the standpoint of audience popularity.

It appears that the companies examined have reached peak levels of production which act to stabilize their budgets, and make maximum use of their minimal resources. Repertory trends from the 1960s show a more rapid growth and diversification, reflecting the overall proliferation of the arts in the United States during this past decade. Mounting deficits have caused companies to reduce their total number of productions and/or new productions. More performances of the same production and revivals offset the expenditures required by new productions and premieres, which involve astronomical costs and fees due to extra rehearsal time, new staging, casting, etc. For example, San Francisco Opera presented six new productions in 1966 at the expense of producing none the following year (Bloomfield, 1972:247). Specific documentation of repertoire would confirm this further.

Conclusion

In attempting to investigate the relationship between the market and opera, we have revealed a standardization of repertoire among the leading opera companies in the United States. This could best be understood in light of the goal of opera companies as service organizations which have been influenced dramatically by their economic structure. In analyzing an art form in terms of its organizational goals, we focused on opera houses as an ongoing organization responding to its external environment—in this case, repertoire became a measure of this relationship. Given the lack of diversity both in their number and content, the tendency is to rely more and more on the staples to offset the expenses of new productions for the season, and to curtail costs. What companies select for presentation depends on what the public buys—paradoxically, at times irrespective of its cost. For example, "Aida" is the most popular and yet the most expensive production; consequently, it receives the highest number of performances. Still, this too must be viewed in light of the precarious economic structure which needs some ideology to come to terms with the increasing rationalization within this artistic community. The standardization has forced the repeat of such expensive extravaganzas as "Aida" solely because of their popularity; at the same time, without accounting for the overall economic losses such productions create, managers can boast of the increase in box-office sales.

Music organizations have come to rely more heavily on subscription performances, which fill the house in more than half of the total number of opera performances. This group—predominantly of middle and upper-middle class sponsorship—has not caused either boldness in production or in the selection of operas. The long term trend has been a reliance on compositions of the nineteenth century. Given the time in which repertoire becomes firmly established and the complex institutional matrix to support it (including publishers, the recording industry, educational institutions, mass media, unions, etc.), repertoire is highly resistant to change. This raises doubt as to the aesthetic dimension of taste outside the content of economic contingencies. Long term and comparative trends would be helpful in addressing this question.

Although the importance of such client-centeredness has been made clear in terms of opera producers' responses to the box office, other questions must be raised as to its effect on artistic roles, recruitment, and its impact on operatic styles. This study, however, cannot go beyond presenting some guidelines for future research exploring some of these issues. For example, this set of circumstances has not been without its effect on operatic styles of performance and interpretation. The way operas are produced has become most important in attracting audiences and in establishing aesthetic norms which prevail today. All energy seems to go toward incorporating new developments in lighting and stage-craft and developing an experience for the audience. These innovations are not innovations in opera as a musical form; they are undertaken primarily with reference to the restaging and redesigning of nineteenth century compositions. This has, undoubtedly, had an impact on the meaning of interpretation as well as on the social position of the performer. We witness, for example, the rise and prestige of the stage director within the last decade. Creative work in the development of the opera is left to composers who are university-affiliated and heavily funded by government. This limits the development of opera that is creative in its essential forms. The conflict over the dominance of one of the various components of opera (orchestration, voice, drama, etc.) continues; but, unlike the past, the battle is resolved in terms of its being a reproduction or a re-creation. Aesthetically, this conflict has been extended to the more liberal interpretation of the score, to virtuoso production techniques or to the dominance of the conductor as the main interpreter of the score. Companies, consequently, boast of "new" productions—the reworking of old works and revivals—in terms of the new technology in theater and orchestration. Future research in this area will have to give serious attention to the impact of these factors upon aesthetic developments within the social organization of opera.

In attempting to investigate the relationship between box office and opera repertoire, I have revealed a standardization of repertoire among the leading opera houses in the United States. I hope to have contributed, also, to motivating future research relating nonprofit structures and client-centeredness to aesthetic norms.

Notes

1. The author thanks Joseph Bensman and Arthur Vidich for their continued interest and support, and is especially grateful for Robert Faulkner's insightful suggestions on an earlier draft of this paper. Reprinted with the permission of the author and of the publisher, *The Sociological Quarterly* 18 (Summer 1977): 354–366.

2. Economic and Institutional factors which have been documented and could be incorporated in such market analysis should include: an organizational study of the symphony orchestra (Arian, 1971); Faulkner, 1973; Mueller (1951), and various studies exploring the economics of the performing arts in America and within the state art councils (Baumol and Bowen, 1966; Ford Foundation, 1974; National Council of the Arts of New York, 1973a, 1973b; Rockefeller Foundation Report, 1965).

3. The description and analysis are based on taped interviews concluded from 1971–1973, annual budgets of opera companies, economic reports by Ford Foundation, the National Council of the Arts of New York State, and repertory schedules from 1962 to 1976.

4. In comparison, subscriptions fill the house in more than one-half of the total opera performances while covering about one-seventh of the tickets sold in theater and about one-sixth in dance (National Council of the Arts, 1973a).

5. The term "standardization" is borrowed from Mueller's study on the American Symphony Orchestra (1951) and represents repertoire which has undergone a competitive selection process over time and appears season after season. It also includes operas premiered before 1930.

References

Albrecht, Milton C. 1973. "The arts in market systems." A paper presented at the 68th annual meeting of the American Sociological Association, New York, 27 August.

Albrecht, Milton C., James H. Barnett and Mason Griff, eds. 1970. *The Sociology of Art and Literature.* New York: Praeger Publishing Co.

Arian, Edward 1971. *Bach, Beethoven and Bureaucracy: The Case of the Philadelphia Orchestra.* Alabama: University of Alabama Press.

Baumol, William J. and William G. Bowen. 1966. *The Performing Arts: The Economic Dilemma.* New York: Twentieth Century Fund.

Becker, Howard S. 1974. "Art as collective action." *American Sociological Review* 39:767–76.

Bensman, Joseph and Israel Gerver. 1958. "Art and mass society." *Social Problems* 6:4–10.

Bloomfield, Arthur. 1972. *Fifty Years of the San Francisco Opera.* California: San Francisco Book Co.

Bukofzer, Manfred. 1947. *Music in the Baroque Era: From Monteverdi to Bach.* New York: W. W. Norton & Co.

Denisoff, Serge R. 1974. *Solid Gold.* Rutgers, N.J.: Transaction Books.

Einstein, Alfred. 1954. *A Short History of Music.* New York: Knopf.

Etzkorn, Peter K., ed. 1973. *Music and Society: The Later Writings of Paul Honigsheim.* New York: Wiley.

Faulkner, Robert. 1973. "Orchestra interaction: some features of communications and authority in an artistic organization." *Sociological Quarterly* 14:147–57.

————. 1976. "Dilemmas in commercial work: Hollywood film composers and their clients." *Urban Life* 5:3–32.

Ford Foundation. 1974. *The Finances of the Performing Arts.* New York: Ford Foundation.

Grout, Donald. 1965. *A Brief History of Opera.* New York: Columbia University Press.

Hauser, Arnold. 1951. *The Social History of Art,* vol. 2. New York: Vintage Books.

Henderson, William J. 1921. *Early History of Singing.* New York: Amsterdam Press.

Hesbacher, Peter, Robert Downing and David G. Berger. 1975. "Record roulette: what makes it spin?" *Journal of Communication* 25:75–85.

Heyworth, Peter. 1971. "Will the Paris Opera become the greatest?" *New York Times,* 25 March.

Hirsch, Paul. 1969. *The Structure of the Popular Music Industry.* Ann Arbor: University of Michigan Press.

Huaco, George A. 1965. *The Sociology of Film Art.* New York: Basic Books.

Jenkins, Steven. 1972. "Carol and company." *Opera News* (November):14–9.

Kavolis, Vytautas. 1968. *Artistic Expression: A Sociological Analysis.* Ithaca, N.Y.: Cornell University Press.

Kolodin, Irving. 1966. *The Metropolitan Opera 1883–1966: A Candid History,* New York: Knopf.

Krawitz, Herman. 1973. Interview, New York City, 19 March.

Lang, Paul H. 1941. *Music in Western Civilization.* New York: W. W. Norton & Co.

Lowenthal, Leo. 1961. *Literature, Popular Culture and Society.* Englewood Cliffs, N.J.: Prentice-Hall.

Lyric Opera of Chicago. 1971–76. Program Schedules and Annual Reports. Chicago: Lyric Opera of Chicago.

Martindale, Andrew. 1972. *The Rise of the Artist in the Middle Ages and the Early Renaissance.* New York: McGraw Hill.

Martorella, Rosanne. 1974. The Performing Artist as a Member of an Organization: A Sociological Study of Opera Performers and The Economics of Opera Production. New School for Social Research. New York: Unpublished Ph.D. dissertation.

McPhee, William N. 1963. *Formal Theories of Mass Behavior.* New York: Free Press.

Metropolitan Opera Association. 1971–76. Annual Reports and Program Schedules. New York: Metropolitan Opera Association.

————. 1971. *White Paper.* New York: Metropolitan Opera Association.

Mueller, John H. 1951. *The American Symphony Orchestra: A Social History of Musical Taste.* Indianapolis: University of Indiana Press.

Nash, Dennison. 1952. "The Alienated composer." Pp. 41–56 in Robert Wilson, ed., *The Arts in Society.* Englewood Cliffs, N.J.: Prentice-Hall.

National Endowment for the Arts. 1974. *NEA Guide to Programs.* Washington, D.C.: Government Printing Office.

New York City Opera. 1971–76. Annual Program Schedules. New York: New York City Opera.

New York National Council of the Arts. 1973a. *Arts and the People.* New York: Cranford Wood, Inc.

————. 1973b. *A Study of the Nonprofit Arts and Cultural Industry in New York State.* New York: Cranford Wood, Inc.

Peterson, Richard and David G. Berger. 1972. "Three eras in the manufacture of popular music lyrics." Pp. 282–303 in Serge Denisoff and Richard Peterson, eds., *The Sounds of Social Change.* New York: Rand McNally & Co.

————. 1975. "Cycles in music production: the case of popular music." *American Sociological Review* 40:158–73.

Peyser, Ethel Rose and Marion Bauer. 1925. *How Opera Grew.* New York: G. P. Putnam.

Pincherle, Marc. 1963. *The World of the Virtuoso.* New York: W. W. Norton & Co.

Pleasants, Henry. 1970. *The Agony of Modern Music.* New York: Clarion Press.

————. 1966. *The Great Singers.* New York: Simon & Schuster.

Powdermaker, Hortense. 1950. *The Dream Factory.* Boston: Brown & Co.

Raynor, Henry. 1972. *A Social History of Music: From the Middle Ages to Beethoven.* New York: Schocken Books.

Rich, Maria F. 1966. *Opera Companies in the United States.* New York: Central Opera Service.

————. 1973. *Opera Repertory in the United States, 1966–1972.* New York: Central Opera Service.

————. 1974. "Arts, Money, Free Services." *Central Opera Service Bulletin* (Fall). New York: Central Opera Service.

————. "United States Opera Survey, 1974–75." *Opera News* 40(5):40–43.

Robinson, Francis. 1971. Interview. New York City, 3 December.

Rockefeller Foundation. 1965. *The Performing Arts: Problems and Prospects.* New York: McGraw Hill.

Rolland, Romain. 1915. *Some Musicians of Former Days.* New York: Books for Libraries Press.

Rubin, Stephen. 1971. "Kubelik: New conscience of the Met?" *New York Times,* 17 October.

————. 1974. *The Metropolitan in Profile.* New York: Macmillan.

Rule, Daniel. 1973. Interview. New York City, 6 March.

Rushmore, Robert. 1971. *The Singing Voice.* New York: Dodd, Mead & Co.

San Francisco Opera. 1971–76. Annual Reports and Program Schedules. San Francisco: San Francisco Opera Association.

Sargeant, Winthrop. 1973. *Divas.* New York: Coward, McCann & Geohegan.

Schonberg, Harold C. 1967. *The Great Conductors*. New York: Simon & Schuster.

Stone, H. H. 1957. "Mid Nineteenth Century Beliefs in the Social Values of Music." *Musical Quarterly* 43:38–49.

Thomson, Virgil. 1939. *The State of Music*. New York: St. Martin's Press.

Tuchman, Gaye, ed. 1974. *The TV Establishment: Programming for Power and Profit*. Englewood Cliffs, N.J.: Prentice-Hall.

White, Harrison C. and Cynthia A. White. 1965. *Canvasses and Careers: Institutional Changes in the French Painting World*. New York: Wiley.

—— 18 ——

Displayed Art and Performed Music: Selective Innovation and the Structure of Artistic Media[1]

VERA L. ZOLBERG

The arts are often treated as a single, homogeneous category in societal analysis (Parsons, 1960:46–47; Arnheim, 1966:7), but this view obscures more than it clarifies. It does not help us to understand, for instance, why American art museums are much more likely to exhibit innovative painting and sculpture than symphony orchestras and opera companies are to perform innovative music. I propose to show that these divergent patterns are due to differences peculiar to the media of expression of the arts themselves, and not to extrinsic factors, such as organizational structures or processes of production. I argue instead that structural features of art forms are relatively autonomous, and themselves either limit or facilitate the outcomes of arrangements for production and diffusion of these cultural products.

Already in the fifteenth century, before the development of artistic specialization, Leonardo da Vinci, who was both master painter and master musician, had noted that: "Painting is superior to music because, unlike unfortunate music, it does not have to die as soon as it is born . . . Music which is consumed in the very act of its birth is inferior to painting which the use of varnish has rendered eternal" (Benjamin, 1969:249). Without accepting his judgment of superiority (and despite the fragile nature of his own paintings), but by extending his insight into the inherent differences of the two media, I hope to cast light on how, even today, when recordings and reproductions make music as well as painting less ephemeral, the structural features of these media have diverse consequences with respect to innovation in the arts.

Other classes of causal variables may be adduced to explain differences in how art museums and symphony orchestras function, among them organizational-structure, patronage sources, and market factors. But as I shall show, despite the importance of other variables, they are not sufficient to explain the strikingly divergent outcomes for innovation. Indeed, in the realm of what has come to be called serious or academic art and music (Peterson, 1976:13) diffused in major loci of exhibit-performance, the media structures limit or enhance organizational structure and functioning, rates of innovation and, ultimately, aesthetics itself.

As a contribution to a sociology of the arts uniting organizational study and the humanities, this essay explores the relationship between art institutions and media, particular art forms. The analysis is based on a survey of the literature of arts organizations from across the nation but with most substantive examples taken from the cultural institutions of one city (Chicago) with particular attention to the Art Institute of Chicago and concert programs of the Chicago Symphony Orchestra from its founding in 1891 through the early 1970s.

My first task is to delineate possible forms of aesthetic innovation in serious art and music. Next, I will show that American cultural institutions (museums, orchestras, opera companies) share a number of organizational features, functions, goals and personnel, and exist in a similar environmental context. This will lead me to suggest that despite their extrinsic similarities, the important differences in innovation depend upon the structure of the media with which they are associated. The visual arts must be displayed, music must be performed; visual art is concrete, music is ephemeral. Finally, I will explore the consequences deriving from these imperatives: their effects upon costs, breadth and potential growth of donors and publics, and aesthetic innovation itself.

Innovation in Performing and Displaying Institutions

American cultural institutions such as symphony orchestras and art museums have as a central goal the preservation through performance and display of acknowledged masterworks. More recently, to their mission of enshrining works already recognized by others, they have added another goal—innovation. Ordinarily the term innovation refers to the creation of new works, even revolutionary ones. But as we shall see this characterization is inadequate to cover the meanings and processes of innovation in the arts: first, because innovation by artists is different from innovation by institutions; second, because of the varying importance of these cultural institutions to the arts associated with them; and third, because of the differences between the two media, visual art and music.

From the creative standpoint innovations stem from artists who go beyond the existing corpus either by stylistic or technical development, stylistic variation or revolutionary departure from existing canons or conventions (Poggioli, 1971). Creative innovations in this sense are related to institutional innovations to the extent that institutions discover and incorporate new works. But institutional innovation is also somewhat distinct from creative innovation in that institutions actually define the history of the art with which they are concerned. Not only do they acknowledge the value of new works, but they may include previously excluded work, or reject previously included works. In the course of these actions of accreditation, they alter the meaning of existing works, whether paintings or musical compositions by, among other things, providing elements and models to artists which further enhance creation. At the most formal level the same definition of innovation may be applied to the two media, but as I shall show below, the process of institutional innovation has very different implications in symphony orchestras and art museums.

Institutional innovation is evident when new works are introduced, but the introduction of new works may just as easily indicate conservatism and conventionality. For example, recently created works may include not only new forms or styles of art and music (such as earthworks, abstraction, serial or aleatory music), but also conventional styles in newly created works, such as paintings done in the style of nineteenth century Impressionism or music which ignores the existence of serial innovations or "new" sounds. Works of this kind may be new in date but are not innovative, because their content merely repeats well-known formulae. Indeed, revivals of older works which have disappeared from public view or hearing may constitute greater innovations than rehashing "safe" patterns (Kubler, 1976: Chapter 2).

In a different sense innovations in "meanings" assigned to works may elevate ordinary objects to the status of fine art. These include industrial products, decorative furnishings (of the S.S. Normandie at the Metropolitan Museum of Art), anonymous folk art or commercial music. Some of these are the successors to the crafts associated with the power, prestige and wealth of ancient civilizations already part of art museum collections. They now include works hitherto kept in ethnographic collections, such as primitive sculpture, but which have found their place in art museums (Rosenberg, 1965:36). In addition, the work of "maverick" or "naive" artists and composers may become integrated into collections and repertoires, though this is more likely to occur if their form can be structurally modified, or if the artists' total output includes "manageable" items (Becker,1976:46–49). The reverse may also occur when, for example, works previously considered legitimate art are "expelled" from collections. This was the fate, for example, of plaster casts of classical statues (Whitehill, 1970:Chapter 6; Zolberg, 1974:Chapter 5), and popular music from symphonic repertoires, such as medleys of marches, now banished to "pops" concerts.

The role of these institutions in defining what is or is not serious art or music may be compared to the relationship of science museums to science. As Kuhn has convincingly argued, in spite of certain similarities between them, the arts and the sciences have diverged in that while innovation for its own sake has come to be a central goal in the arts, particularly since the nineteenth century, this is not the case for science (Kuhn, 1977:350). Furthermore, when innovations of a revolutionary nature occur in science, older paradigms are discarded in favor of the new. Although a similar revolutionary pattern may arise in the arts, it is usual for old works to coexist with new without losing their stature. This coexistence is particularly striking if we compare the relationship of art museums to artists and science museums to scientists. As Kuhn has pointed out, while both institutions have a lay public as their target, art museums are useful to artists but science museums are of no consequence to practicing scientists (Kuhn, 1977:340–51).

Our tentative definition of innovation by cultural institutions may now be stated as the acknowledgement of contemporaneous works which go beyond the existing corpus. In the visual arts this includes newly created and innovative work, or existing but not generally acknowledged works. Similarly for music, it includes newly composed and innovative works or the rediscovery, retrieval or redefinition of existing music. In light of this definition, we may ask if orchestras and museums play similar roles in relation to their art form. As we shall see, they have significantly different records for innovation. On the whole, with few exceptions, American art museums have tended to be fairly open to new forms of art, some of which were previously considered outlandish or inappropriate. For example, the Art Institute of Chicago practiced openness to the new when it was one of the few museums (in the first two decades of this century) to exhibit works of the "Ashcan School" of painting, and the Armory Show (including Duchamps' "Nude Descending a Staircase," among other Cubist and Fauve works); in the 1930s when it included a number of then still unusual Impressionist and Post-Impressionist works, and primitive art; in the early 1950s (at about the same time as the Museum of Modern Art) when it included works of the New York Abstract Expressionists. Photographs and, more recently, even out-of-door works, such as Christos' "Canyon Curtain," have entered its permanent collection, at least in the form of drawings and photographs. Almost anything which can be displayed appears capable of incorporation.

The story is quite the opposite when we turn to symphonic performances. In the same city as the Art Institute, the Chicago Symphony Orchestra has not achieved a similar reputation for innovation, particularly in recent decades. Its programming suggests that innovation was more likely in the past. Theodore Thomas, the first conductor, was able to persuade his trustees to allow new music (Wagner, Debussy, Mahler); Frederick Stock, his successor and conductor until the mid-1940s, frequently devoted half of his yearly programming to post-1900 music (Mueller, 1973:1, liii). Since then, much depends upon the interest of the music director. In contrast to Fritz Reiner, who in the 1950s and early 1960s was likely to devote only one-third or less of a year's programs to "recent" (i.e., post-1900) works, in the 1960s Jean Martinon chose about half of his music from among recent compositions. Almost all other music directors have neglected the modern repertory, but premiered works, which totaled as much as 18 and 21 percent of annual programs in 1950 and 1964, consisted almost entirely of new works, to the neglect of older revivals.

In contrast to the tendency of art museums to view the whole world and all of time as a reservoir on which to draw for exhibitions and collections (Malraux, 1963), the prevailing pattern for orchestras is to limit both time and space as the source of music. The Chicago Symphony Orchestra, for example, is known as a "German" orchestra, a fair description if Austrian and peripheral national music such as Czech or Hungarian is included. To a lesser degree it gives some attention to Russian, French and English composers. American music, however, has little chance of being performed, and almost never fills as much as ten percent of yearly programming (Mueller, 1973:civ). Furthermore, American compositions have actually tended to decline since the 1950s, a period during which training of American musicians and composers has been increasing (Mueller, 1973:1). With some modifications, similar patterns have been found in most other orchestras (Mueller, 1951; and Arian, 1971).

In the analysis of what constitutes innovation in artistic products, dates of composition or life span of composers are only approximate indicators. Ideally, analysis should focus on form and style. In fact, this would make the conservatism of the symphony orchestra even more striking. Contemporary music selected for performance is never too "avant-garde." Rather, new music, as a highly placed orchestra administrator observed, is likely to be "calendar contemporary," recently composed, but in a style which does not rely too much upon modern dissonances, unusual forms and novel instrumentation.

From an aesthetic point of view the musical avant-garde since the introduction of serialism and its offshoots may be too *outré,* too "difficult" for the public to accept. Yet the avant-garde of the plastic arts is hardly less *outré* and still enters museums. Indeed, even patron-type museums, as Graña calls the Boston Museum of Fine Arts, have begun to acquire examples of "difficult" contemporary works (Graña, 1971; Whitehill, 1970:Vol.

2). Difficulty of new works cannot account for the fact that until recently many symphony orchestras (and opera companies) were more open to contemporary music but have become more closed, while many art museums have moved in the opposite direction, as will be shown below. The differences in innovative trends in these two types of institutions call for explanation. With this in mind, I turn next to a set of variables which may be summarized as societal and technical, extrinsic, and nonaesthetic. Subsumed in this type of explanation are, at the intermediate level, organizational structure, institutional ideology, personnel recruitment, and at a more general level, the economic context within which these variables operate.

Extrinsic Influences on Innovativeness

From an organizational standpoint most American orchestras and museums are structured similarly. Governed by boards of trustees drawn from the same stratum of society (mostly business men, but occasionally educators, and in recent years even representatives of ethnic or racial minorities), they are expected to donate money, art works, services, or merely be present as legitimating symbols. In many communities the same people sit on several cultural boards simultaneously or move from one to another. While some boards exercise their authority directly, most do so through their appointed administrators and artistic directors. Managerial administrators may move, as trustees do between cultural institutions and other philanthropies or institutions in their career trajectories. Although they may have a particular devotion to one kind of art, this is not a requirement. Trustees are expected to be amateurs, while administrators are expected to have general technical competence. Only artistic professionals confine themselves to one art form, in that curators may work in a museum or university, while conductors and musicians may move between or simultaneously work in orchestras and conservatories. Orchestral musicians have tended to become unionized, and curators are beginning to organize themselves into bodies which try to deal collectively with management about working conditions or aesthetic policy (K. Meyer, 1979:227–31).

Unlike European countries where cultural organizations are more often fully public (Moulin, 1976), many American ones are predominantly private. The major difference between public and private is that for public institutions a much greater share of financial support comes directly from public sources with private sources ancillary, while in private organizations individuals, businesses or foundations provide a larger share. Until recently in the United States public support was likely to take the form of indirect subsidies (freedom from real estate taxes, or tax deductions to donors for gifts) and grants given by public bodies for specific purposes, such as educational service to certain groups (public school children or ethnic minorities). Recently, direct governmental subsidies for general purposes have been increasing in the United States as well (Netzer, 1978).

Both public and private sources of support require justification, because they bestow advantages on the institutions and their donors which are denied to commercial organizations, defined as entertainment purveyors (Ulanov, 1965). In contrast to commercial organizations which display or perform, such as wax museums or commercial musical theater, art museums and symphony orchestras define themselves as non-profit, public service bodies which provide a highly valued good to the community, a product which is intrinsically important and is legitimated by its quasi-sacred nature. Cultural institutions, therefore, are not expected to support themselves through gate receipts. Rather, people should be led to them because the fine arts are "good" for them. In fact, the product should not be contaminated with pecuniary considerations and the practitioners of the art should be freed from the need to appeal to base interests in order to attract a following. In line with this ideology, an important function of American cultural institutions is to teach or indoctrinate as large a public as possible with the importance of the arts. Paradoxically this places requirements on the high arts similar to those of the commercial: entertainment enterprises require a large public in order to turn a profit, but high cultural institutions depend upon a large public whose presence legitimates the support they receive.

At a macro-societal level it has been argued that in the bourgeois epoch innovation "functions" to maintain the commodity structure of the artistic market place, but does so in different ways for the visual arts and music. According to this line of reasoning, paintings and sculpture represent concrete commodities or "goods," while music is essentially a "service." In music the labor-value of artists is rendered up in nonreproducible form. As a result, a problem of endemic deflation must be faced in the art market, but not in the music market. Thus a work of art may prove to be a poor investment if it loses value, whereas in music it is not the work but the performance which is purchased.

Furthermore, modern technology produces different consequences in the two art forms. Recording cannot replicate the experience of the musical performance, but in the visual arts photography has made realistic or representational art obsolete. In the case of commodity arts deflationary tendencies must be staved off by stressing identifiable styles and historical continuity, and these are best promoted by non-representational art styles.

While not denying the merit of this line of reasoning, I argue that closer examination reveals it to be less than wholly convincing. As is well known, until very recently innovations in the visual arts have not generally been welcomed by the public or its gatekeepers. In fact, because conventional styles provide more security to artists than innovative breakthroughs, it is not surprising that the majority of artists have oriented themselves away from experimentation and towards safety in convention, whether in commercial art or such crafts as portrait painting. It has further been argued that breakthroughs in photography made realistic representation undesirable and promoted non-representational art. Yet, in fact, photography has not eliminated representational art at all. Indeed artists have used photography to gain a better grasp of anatomy and motion in their work. Representational art has not died as a style, even at the present time (Andrew Wyeth, Philip Pearlstein, Andy Warhol, among many others) and continues to provide a viable aesthetic. It is true that much emphasis is placed on the artist's development of an "identifiable" style, a goal that has gained greater currency in the "bourgeois epoch," but identifiable styles seem to have emerged in a considerable number of artists even before the emergence of the epoch.

These qualifications aside, the macro historical and social context which this type of explanation invokes point to the importance of the relatively autonomous attributes of music and the plastic arts. It is these attributes and their interaction with non-aesthetic societal variables to which I turn next.

Display versus Performance: The Structure of Artistic Media

The two attributes of music central to its distinctiveness as an artistic medium, in contrast to visual or plastic art, are time and the absence of concrete objects embodying value. In the case of the plastic or visual arts, equivalent attributes are space and the existence of concrete objects of value. These attributes and their implications, outlined in Table 1, are reflected in the basic unit of music, the performance, while for painting and sculpture, it is the exhibition.

Without performance music does not "exist" as a social phenomenon. It is an art which requires the playing by a corps of performers under the direction of a leader, conventionally a conductor, on prearranged, rehearsed occasions, within the confines of a hall with limited seating (Silbermann, 1968). Because of these limitations, which have grown more stringent and demanding of coordination over the years, the numbers of works which may be performed in any time period are necessarily circumscribed. A museum, in contrast, is capable of exhibiting simultaneously a variety of works representing various styles, media, period of history, and taste. De-

Table 1
Media Attributes and Their Implications

	Plastic Arts	*Music*
Attributes	Space	Time
	Concrete Objects	Ephemeral Works
Presentation	Exhibition	Performance
Mode	Simultaneity of Works	Consecutive performance
	Custodial Care	Live musicians
		Numerous Professionals
Costs	Expensive	Extremely expensive
	Lower cost for new works	Higher costs for new works
Patronage	Unlimited Entry	Limited Seating
	Variety of Taste Publics	Limited Taste Publics
	Capital gain potential for Patrons	No private profits

spite occasional crowding, it is possible for a variety of publics to be accommodated, with visitors free to select for their attention works of schools of art, spending as much or as little time on each as they like, without necessarily infringing upon the access of others. Once works are arranged in an exhibition by a curator, only custodial care is required. Music, in contrast, requires a full complement of trained professionals even to be potentially available to a public in a live form. As a result of constraints imposed by time and the other exigencies of performance, it is to be expected that the number and variety of works which can be performed are limited. It follows, therefore, that live music is much less accessible to publics than is original art.

The other important sense in which the structure of the medium has effects on organizations is that while the plastic arts are usually concrete objects of permanence, the live performance of music is ephemeral. Thus not only does it take time to perform and hear music, but once performed, it no longer exists. Despite the advent of recording, performed music (and especially opera) is no more equivalent to recorded than original art is to reproductions. In spite of the fact that a recording under present conditions probably provides more of the total information of the original than does a visual reproduction, and that the quality of sound from a well-equipped record playing system may be better than a poorly placed seat in an auditorium, it cannot replace the live performance with its glamorous aura, extrinsic to music, but closely intertwined with it nevertheless, not to speak of the visual aspect of orchestra-conductor interaction.

Whether recordings and reproductions are valid art forms in their own right is a matter of sharp debate (Kramer, 1978; Elsen and Merryman,

1979), but in spite of technological perfection and perhaps even because of it, the "live" performance and the "original" art work are not necessarily, as Benjamin (1969) suggested, diminished. Indeed, contrary to his view, that because elite art is essentially a cult object whose reproduction cheapens it by shattering its aura (Benjamin, 1969:220), I argue that the opposite result is equally plausible. The elite arts are enhanced as symbolic representations from which copies draw their value, and to whose value a multiplicity of copies contributes. The increasing perfection or perfectability of recorded performances has an impact upon live performances in that audience expectations of technical perfection (because mistakes are edited out) are increased and standards of quality raised, with the further consequence of increasing costs of performance. Indeed, while all cultural institutions are faced with problems of rising costs, recent studies demonstrate that performed music, especially opera, is increasingly expensive to finance (Salem, 1976; Baumol and Bowen, 1968). Table 2 provides evidence for this phenomenon by viewing comparatively three major cultural institutions in Chicago.

As Table 2 indicates, the numbers accommodated by the organizations vary greatly, both per performance and per visit (or per seat). Admission charges do not reflect actual operating expenses. Indeed, it is difficult to determine how much entry fees (where they exist), actually cover. Admission to the Art Institute is free to those paying for annual membership, either for themselves or also for their families. The rough estimate arrived at suggests that costs per visitor were half that of the Symphony and less than a third that of the Opera. Symphony and Opera patrons pay according to their seat location, with a discount for subscribers. The Orchestra, Opera and Museum operate at deficits which are largely filled by contributors. When more people go to museums there is relatively little increase in costs, but for performances, increasing the numbers of presentations merely increases deficits beyond the ability or desire of donors to cover them.

Because live performed music is far more limited in availability, it is unlikely to be capable of enlarging audiences very far beyond present capacity, especially in Chicago, where the two performing institutions are among the most successful in the world in attracting audiences. Museums, however, are inherently more flexible because of the "cafeteria" which modern display favors. Much more freedom of choice is thus available to consumers of art than of music. Music audiences are more dependent upon the judgments of those who make aesthetic choices within the institution than are museum-goers, who have the possibility of ignoring what does not interest them while enjoying what they prefer at no extra outlay to themselves if they are already members. Because of this, the gatekeepers to innovation in music are far more vulnerable to subscriber taste and must be

Table 2
Publics, Budgets, Performances of Three Chicago Cultural
Organizations 1971–72 Season

Cultural Organization	Numbers Attending	Operating Expenditures (in $)	Numbers of Performances	Cost/seat or /visitor (in $)	Cost/day or /performance (in $)
Art Institute of Chicago[a]	1,669,119	10,219,119	364[d]	6.00	28,388
Chicago Symphony Orchestra[b]	300,000	3,499,201	104	11.67	33,653
Lyric Opera[c]	164,000	3,385,300	48	20.60	70,541[e]

[a]Art Institute of Chicago, *Annual Report 1971–72*, pp. 8, 54–5.

[b]Precise figures for attendance are unavailable, but the figure shown is estimated in the following manner: seating space in Orchestra Hall (2,566) times Number of Concerts in 9 subscription series (90) times percent seats subscribed (92 percent) equals 212,465. Added to these are 60,000 who attended 24 youth concerts. The total of 272,465 is too low, because it omits a few special concerts for associations, pension fund raising, and various other purposes. Nor does it include performances at the Ravinia Summer Festival where seating limitations are not a factor, out of town concerts and a European tour, but most of these are separately budgeted. If single ticket sales were to fill the hall to 100 percent capacity at the subscription concerts, then the figure of 291,005 would be attained. Based on Annual Report in the Orchestral Association Program, Nov. 29–30, Dec. 1, 1973, pp. 68–79.

[c]The figure of 163,687 in 1971 represents 99 percent of seats sold. The figure shown here is an estimate for 1972, approximately the reported sales of 102 percent of seats because of single seat resales, when subscribers return unused tickets as a donation.

[d]Open every day but one.

[e]This estimate is based upon computations from figures supplied by a member of the administrative staff. Another estimate offered a year later is $80,000. (Rob Cuscaden, "The Opera: A Curious Business," *Chicago Sun-Times*, Nov. 22, 1974:91)

highly sensitive to it for fear of losing patronage than are museum gatekeepers. Because both types of organizations must continually renew their claims to legitimacy through public service, they must attract a large following. Yet the costs of achieving this goal and the risks involved must necessarily be higher for music than for art.

This structural condition has further consequences for the different capacity of performance and display institutions to innovate. Performance organizations run a risk each time they play an unfamiliar work and must protect themselves either by selecting mainly "calendar contemporary" work, rather than unconventional music, or if they play a stylistically contemporary work, it is likely to be short (Mueller, 1973:xiv). Beyond that, there is a high probability that it was composed by someone close to the music director (a compatriot, relative, board member, patron or the conductor himself), its cost financed by a foundation or government grant, and hidden in the midst of a conventional concert as part of a regular subscription series. The consumer is given little choice, but has the pill sweetened with the sugar-coating of familiar pieces, perhaps one of the "fifty famous," whose ubiquity Thomson (1962:110) has long deplored.

In display organizations, in contrast, not only are there fewer risks of losing patrons, but there are rewards for innovation which are unavailable to performing organizations. Furthermore, these rewards come not only to the institution, which may gain a reputation for being adventuresome, priority in recognizing new works and talent, and for diffusing them to potentially large publics, but also to individuals involved in the process, such as curators, art historians, critics, donors, trustees, some of whom are collectors. Unlike live music which has no counterpart in a concrete form, and can only be collected as manuscripts, art objects have permanence. They acquire a market value through the various transactions in which they circulate. Thus a work which is exhibited at a museum or, even better, enters its permanent collection, either through purchase or as a gift, gains value which is diffused to the other works of the artist. Alternatively, a new style which enters a museum gains legitimacy for artists working in similar styles. Because old works are rare and costly, many collectors find it to their advantage, as do many museums, to take risks on unfamiliar works (Moulin, 1978). Collectors are easily persuaded, and sometimes even pressure museums to accept their art gifts to gain prestige and tax advantages on the (sometimes) inflated value of their works. This applies equally to rediscovered works as to new ones. There is, however, no "calendar contemporary" in museums. Contemporary work done in the style of what has come to be viewed as convention, such as that of Renoir (styles sold in large commercial galleries or available in the form of commissioned family portraits) is not defined as fine art, but as pastiche. Thus while novelty in creation has become a canon of contemporary art (Rosenberg, 1965; L. Meyer, 1967:87), only the visual arts institution is structured to reward it quickly, while the music institution provides little support and even blocks it.

The consequences of the ephemeral nature of music are far-reaching. While art museums may, by accepting art works, provide donors with lucrative tax advantages and validation of their collection, music organizations provide little incentive for prospective donors on an equivalent scale. Thus they are relatively less able to attract a constantly increasing pool of patrons. Consequently, while art museum donors have a stake in bringing contemporary works into museums, prospective donors to music organizations have little incentive to have contemporary music incorporated into repertoires.

Because of the expense of purchasing or soliciting donations of older works, art museums are attracted by less expensive and plentiful modern works. In contrast, orchestras have an interest in playing older music for several reasons: (1) there are no copyright restrictions; and (2) they fit in with the technical capabilities of the players without requiring re-tooling in modern modes, a procedure demanding unusually long rehearsal periods whose costs as a result of union requirements create financial strain. Given client conservatism and absentee music directors who find it more convenient to adhere to a repertoire that they know extremely well, there is little pay-off for anyone. The result is that it is far more difficult for performing organizations to play the dual role at which museums are growing more and more adept—preserving the old as well as incorporating the new.

It has been said that the goal of museums is to collect collectors (Seligman, 1961:223) and through them, collections. But what do orchestras collect? Conductors and players, but rarely composers. The symphony orchestra defines itself as a musical instrument which developed in conjunction with the compositions which were created to feed it (Mueller, 1951). Something like that may be said for museums which, in Europe, were the palaces of art suitable for the works over which a shrinking nobility had less and less exclusive control. Works were often created for museums through various academic systems (White and White, 1965). But with the expansion of middle-class viewers and collectors, particularly in recent American society, newer museums which could not aspire to owning rare old works were encouraged and even constrained to risk new directions in the visual arts, including even the "*art moyen*" of photography and its offshoots (Bourdieu, 1965; Moulin, 1978; Sontag, 1977), thus encouraging its redefinition as a fine art. Artists, even those who take an ideological stance opposed to the "established" art world with its capitalistic, undemocratic, and commercial connotations, and create works which are intended to run counter to suitability for "museumification," such as those creating earthworks, outdoor events, happenings, or conceptual art in its many forms, find their works acceptable in some form not only to galleries or temporary exhibitions, but to permanent collections. While music institutions followed a similar trend away from control by elites to a broadened base of middle-class patronage, the orchestra and opera have become relatively fixed vis-a-vis publics and, especially, composers.

Consequences for Artistic Innovators

Despite the complaints of many artists about what they take to be the inequities of museum selection processes, in which they see the not-so-invisible hand of favoritism, crass motives, and elite conspiracies, modern museums are far more open to innovation than one would expect of established organizations. The symphony orchestra tends to lag far beyond the open, if sometimes revolving-door pattern of museums. The results are apparent in light of the behavior of creative artists and their expectations. While visual artists are able to aspire to museum inclusion, composers have, on the whole, turned away in anger and despair from orchestras, opera companies and even live musicians (Schwartz and Childs, 1967:369). Composers are more and more likely to create works for small ensembles, electronic equipment, invent and build their own instruments and train dedicated followers to perform on them, thus by-passing the orchestra altogether. It is ironic that experimental music has a better chance of being performed in a museum than in an orthodox setting for music. (Harry Partch's work, for example, performed by his own trained group on instruments designed by himself, at the Whitney Museum in New York).

Until well into the twentieth century, museums tended to be viewed as dusty mausoleums of venerable taste, while symphony orchestras were lively contemporary performance vehicles. They seem now to have reversed roles. Observers of and participants in cultural organizations tend to draw analogies between them which suggest a greater degree of isomorphism than does my analysis. It has been suggested by a staff member of the Chicago Symphony Orchestra, for example, that an orchestra relies on a repertoire of "standard works equivalent to a museum's permanent collection" while "odd things are introduced in small doses, the equivalent of special shows." But the same person pointed out that "real innovations are made elsewhere . . . in universities, for example, which are equivalent to galleries." In a general way this is a fairly accurate statement of the incorporation process in cultural organizations. What it neglects, however, are the initiatives which cultural institutions themselves may take in introducing new art forms. Indeed, many new ideas in the arts find their way to established institutions via the corridor of related organizations. But museums have a strong interest in seeking out aesthetic innovations, while orchestras do not. To these differences the fundamental structure of the artistic media makes an important contribution.

Notes

1. An earlier version of this paper was presented at the annual meetings of the Midwest Sociological Society, Minneapolis (1977). I thank the colleagues whose helpful comments I have incorporated into this paper: Remi Clignet, Paul DiMaggio, K. Peter Etzkorn, Roger Masters, Richard A. Peterson, Michael Useem and Aristide R. Zolberg. I am indebted also to anonymous reviewers whose cogent arguments caused me to rethink a number of points. Reprinted with the permission of the author and the publisher. *The Sociological Quarterly* (vol. 21, Spring 1980).

References

Arian, Edward. 1971. *Bach, Beethoven and Bureaucracy.* Birmingham: University of Alabama Press.

Arnheim, Rudolph. 1966. *Toward a Psychology of Art.* Berkeley: University of California Press.

Art Institute of Chicago. 1971–72. *Annual Reports.*

Baumol, W. J. and W. G. Bowen. 1968. *Performing Arts: The Economic Dilemma.* A Twentieth Century Fund Study. Cambridge: MIT Press.

Becker, Howard S. 1976. "Art worlds and social types." Pp. 41–56 in Richard A. Peterson (ed.), *The Production of Culture.* Beverly Hills: Sage.

Benjamin, Walter. 1969. *Illuminations.* New York: Schocken.

Bourdieu, Pierre, Luc Boltanski, R. Castel and Jean-Claude Chamborderon. 1965. *Un Art moyen: Essai sur les Usages sociaux de la photographie.* Paris: Editions de Minuit.

Cuscaden, Rob. 1974. "The opera: a curious business." *Chicago Sun-Times,* Nov. 22.

Elsen, Albert and John Merryman. 1979. "Art replicas: a question of ethics." *Art News* 78 (February): 61.

Graña, César. 1971. "The private lives of public museums: can they be democratic?" Pp, 95–111 in *Fact and Symbol.* New York: Oxford University Press.

Kramer, Hilton. 1978. "Reproductions are all the rage, but are they art? *New York Times,* December 10, Arts and Leisure Section: 1.

Kubler, George. 1976. *The Shape of Time*. New Haven: Yale University Press.

Kuhn, Thomas S. 1977. *The Essential Tension*. Chicago: University of Chicago Press.

Malraux, André. 1963. *The Voices of Silence*. New York: Doubleday.

Meyer, Karl. 1979. *The Art Museum*. A Twentieth Century Fund Report. New York: William Morrow and Company.

Meyer, Leonard. 1967. *Music, Arts, and Ideas*. Chicago: University of Chicago Press.

Moulin, Raymonde. 1978. ''La Genèse de la rareté artistique.'' Paris: Centre Européen de Sociologie Historique, *Ethnologie Francaise*, no. 2–3.

————. 1976. *Le Marché de la peinture en France*. Paris: Editions de Minuit.

Mueller, John H. 1951. *The American Symphony Orchestra*. Bloomington: Indiana University Press.

Mueller, Kate H. 1973. *Twenty-Seven Major American Symphony Orchestras*. Bloomington: Indiana University Press.

Netzer, Dick. 1978. *The Subsidized Muse*. A Twentieth Century Fund Study. New York: Cambridge University Press.

Orchestral Association. 1973. Annual Report, in *Chicago Symphony Orchestra Program*, Nov. 29–30 through December 1.

Parsons, Talcott. 1960. *Structure and Process in Modern Society*. New York: Free Press.

Peterson, Richard A. 1976. ''The production of culture: a prolegomenon.'' Pp. 7–22 in Richard A. Peterson (ed.), *The Production of Culture*. Beverly Hills: Sage.

Poggiolli, Renato. 1971. *The Theory of Avant-Garde*. New York: Harper and Row.

Rosenberg, Harold. 1965. *The Tradition of the New*. New York: McGraw-Hill.

Salem, Mahmoud. 1976. *Organizational Survival in the Performing Arts*. New York: Holt, Rinehart and Winston.

Schwartz, Elliott and Barry Childs. 1967. *Contemporary Composers on Contemporary Music*. New York: Holt, Rinehart and Winston.

Seligman, Germain. 1961. *Merchants of Art*. New York: Appleton-Century-Crofts.

Sibermann, Alphonse. 1968. *Les Principes de la sociologie de la musique*. Geneva: Librarie Droz.

Sontag, Susan. 1977. *On Photography*. New York: Delta.

Thomson, Virgil. 1962. *The State of Music*. New York: Vintage.

Ulanov, Barry. 1985. *The Two Worlds of American Art*. New York: Macmillan.

White, Harrison C. and Cynthia A. White. 1985. *Canvases and Careers*. New York: Wiley.

Whitehill, Walter Muir. 1970. *Museum of Fine Arts Boston*. 2 vols. Cambridge: Belknap.

Winternitz, Emanuel. 1977. "Leonardo da Vinci as a musician." *Times Literary Supplement*, April 1: 411–12.

Zolberg, Vera L. 1974. "The art institute of Chicago." Unpublished Ph.D. dissertation, University of Chicago.

Part VI

Art and Society

The Influence of Art on Society

There are strikingly different notions about the relationship between society and art. In popular discourse it is often stated that "art mirrors society." But this is a vague idea and not very meaningful. Certainly, all conventions or styles of art do not consistently resemble or reflect specific aspects of society. For example, realistic paintings have been popular during revolutionary periods as well as during harmonious times. A different belief is that art presages social developments as is given in the argument that German film and drama of the 1920s anticipated the triumph of Nazism and World War II. The assumption is made that artists are seers who anticipate changes in society or that art styles reveal in some enigmatic way future developments in the social order. Here again, the connection between conventions or styles in art and aspects or processes of society are not specified in any concrete way.

It is also commonly believed that art influences society by shaping patterns of belief or meaning, although this, too, is difficult to establish. This notion—however difficult to prove scientifically—has been taken very seriously in some political circles. For example, at one time Marxist ideology in the Soviet Union was used to justify the policy that artists must work in the style called Socialist Realism (Tertz, 1960). This rested on the assumption that the arts—literature, poster art, film—are effective in educating and mobilizing the masses. At the same time, some members of the European Critical School claim that capitalism and industrialism produce so much alienation that there will be little chance for art to have impact or meaning until there are genuine social, economic, and political transformations.

It is undeniable that in capitalist societies (and in socialist ones also) art is used for the purpose of manipulation—to sell products—to implement political propaganda, to pacify the discontent, and to legitimate the status quo.

Thus, in specific historical situations we can see how art can influence people and how this very assumption is so effectively used by economic and political elites (Leith, 1965). However, in more general theoretical terms it is difficult to establish how art has a pervasive effect on society and its development. This is a major task for future sociologists.

The Influence of Society on the Arts

How social and cultural factors influence the arts is much easier to understand than how the arts influence society. At least it is a topic to which much more scholarly work has been devoted. The range of influences on art include religion (Harrison, 1913), the community (Martindale, 1960), the economy (Denisoff, 1986; Baumol & Bowen, 1966) and patrons (Clark & Clark, 1977). The bibliography contains references for many sources dealing with these and other societal influences. This is a literature to which critics, art and cultural historians, economists, anthropologists and sociologists have contributed.

To briefly illustrate, using what might appear to many readers to be a mundane example of societal influences on art, it can be shown that demographic factors play a role in shaping a society's art forms. Shifts in the ethnic balance affects the forms of art that are present in a society and people's preferences for them. A population with a disproportionate number of older people would support certain art forms—for example, crafts and traditional arts—whereas a population with relatively many younger people would probably support other art forms—for example, live music. It is very likely that rapid population growth would stimulate a great diversity of art.

Society and Art as Mutually Related

Although it may be useful for research purposes to treat art and society as dependent or independent factors, in the real world the two are inextricably entwined. It may be possible to view change in both art and society more clearly by focussing on the relationships between them.

The Papers

The first paper in this section illustrates the embeddedness of music in the broader culture. Cantometrics, a mode of measurement of the variety of ways in which music is organized in different cultures was developed by Alan Lomax. Through this mode of analysis he has demonstrated that the different models of the use and organization of music relate strongly to

other cultural factors. In this paper, the authors have expanded the canto-metric methodology to include measures of other cultural factors.

Parallels in the themes of Nazi songs and Christian hymns are unexpected. But if one reconsiders, it seems clear that both are appealing to human values and must do so to be effective. Can art influence society by developing social solidarity? Warren's evidence shows that a political party and a religious institution believe that it can.

Kavolis' uncovered two variables—"individual motivation" and the "commitment of social resources"—which must come together for a period of efflorescence in the arts to occur. Social resources are available only at certain periods of economic transformations. However, it is not the economic conditions alone which cause art to develop. Psychological and social tensions related to the economic conditions must also be taken into account.

"Sound and Censorship . . . "demonstrates how the film industry adjusted to the introduction of a new technology—the use of sound; and to an influence from the wider society—censorship. Like Crozier, Leue argues that cultural factors can produce structural change in the art institution. The artistic product, the film was also changed by the necessity to adapt to the larger social and the more immediate institutional changes that ensued.

The paper by Jonathan Kamin provides us with a good picture of cyclical change. He weds the development of two popular styles of music to patterns of social acceptance. The process of the development of publics are amazingly similar and the accompanying clash of values also parallel.

A major task of the sociologist is to test the assumptions held about society in order to check their accuracy. Judith Blau found that there was much less variation between the regions of the United States in the availability of high art forms if one measures the number of art institutions and art events in relationship to population size. Even such art forms as country music and opera companies, contrary to the stereotypes, show no variation between regions. However, there was regional variation in the availability of specialized museums, craft fairs and, where not expected, in the popular arts of cinemas, commercial bands, variety entertainment and dance halls.

References

Albrecht, Milton C., James H. Barnett & Mason Griff (eds.). 1970. *The Sociology of Art and Literature: a Reader.* New York: Praeger.

Baumol, William J. & William G. Bowen. 1966. *Performing Arts—The Economic Dilemma.* Cambridge: M.I.T. Press.

Clark, Priscilla P. & Terry Nichols Clark. 1977. "Patrons, publishers, and prizes; the writer's estate in France." Pp. 197–225 in Joseph Ben-David & Terry Nichols Clark, eds. *Culture and Its Creators.* Chicago: U of Chicago Press.

Denisoff, R. Serge. 1986. *Tarnished Gold.* New Brunswick: Transaction Press.

Harrison, Jane. 1913. *Ancient Art and Ritual.* New York: Henry Holt.

Leith, James A. 1965. *The Idea of Art as Propaganda in France, 1750–1799.* Toronto: U. of Toronto Press.

Martindale, Don. 1960. *American Society.* Princeton: Van Nostrand.

Tertz, Abram. 1960. *The Trial Begins* and *On Socialist Realism.* New York: Random House.

——— 19 ———

The Evolutionary Taxonomy of Culture[1]

ALAN LOMAX
and
NORMAN BERKOWITZ

The grand theme of anthropology is that man, to a far greater degree than the other animals, adapts to his environment by means of changes in socially transmitted, rather than biologically inherited, patterns of action and interaction. The ways of a people—its economic, affective, political, communicative and expressive systems—are learned and may be changed by each succeeding generation. Margaret Mead tells how the Manus, a Stone Age people, were so impressed by Western culture that they decided to get rid of their own and straightway threw much of it into the sea (Mead, 1956). This instance illustrates the malleability of culture. It is this flexibility of cultural, as compared to biological, systems that gave man an advantage over other species and enabled him, early in his history, to occupy every zone of the globe.

Since cultures consist of enormous complexes of customs, beliefs, institutions, and modes of communication, they could only be transmitted, before the invention of written language, by whole societies. An ideal cultural taxonomy should, therefore, discover a series of geographically continuous culture regions, each explicable as a pattern of adaptation that was carried from its zone of origin to others along feasible land or sea routes. The borders of a given culture region should be defined by physical barriers or by the limits of other such culture regions. Any breaks in the distribution of such a culture continuum should be explained by the intrusion of another, more productive and better adapted cultural system. It should be possible to arrange these geographically bounded cultural taxa in a developmental sequence that would account for their boundaries and their discontinuities. Thus, human subspeciation could be viewed as a continuum of cultural adaptions with several regional specializations.

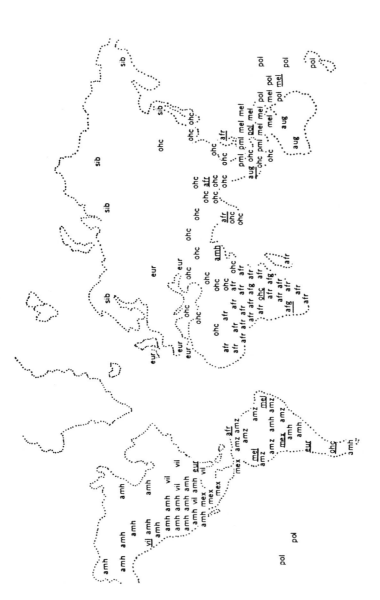

Fig. 1. Factor identification of 137 cultures located geographically (approximately) by the appropriate abbreviation. The following are abbreviations for the factors: afg, African Gatherers; afr, Black Africa; amh, American Hunters; amz, Amazonia; aug, Australian Gatherers; eur, Europe; pml, Proto-Malay; mel, Melanesia; mex, Mexico; ohc, Old High Culture; pol, Polynesia; sib, Siberia; vil, American Villagers. Underling indicates that the culture is an exception to the geographic continuity rule.

The factored culture taxonomy presented here meets those requirements. Its weak spots occur exactly in those places where it lacks data, which may, with further effort, be supplied. Otherwise, its inclusiveness and its parsimony recommend it. First, the scheme accounts for most of the variation in human cultures by a small number of discrete cultural zones (Fig. 1) organized into three large regional clusters (Fig. 2): (i) the simple producers; (ii) the tropical gardeners; and (iii) the Eurasian agriculturalists. Each of these regions represents a decisive adaptive development. Second, factor analysis clusters the measures of culture themselves around two main vectors: (i) economic and social control of the environment, and (ii) organization and integration of teams. Vector 1 orders the main zones of culture on a steadily rising curve of socioeconomic development. Vector 2 (which depicts the form of team organization each subsistence level requires) oscillates in a regular, wavelike fashion along the curve of progress as the species deploys, again and again, its limited repertory of organizational resources (Fig. 5). A third group of factors, which includes the organization of kin and family, shows no clear vectored relation to evolutionary development.

The data for this evolutionary taxonomy came from two sources—a comparative survey of world song styles and a similar survey of ethnography: namely, G. P. Murdock's *Ethnographic Atlas* (1967). Murdock encodes from the literature of ethnology the economic, social, and political features of more than 1000 societies. In some cases, these codes formed scales—for example, the one concerning the number of levels of political authority outside the local community, from 0 among hunters to 4 for Oriental empires. In other cases, Conrad Arensberg and I arranged the codes into scales in order to measure the relative frequency of certain kind of behaviors or features of culture, such as level of production or permanence of settlement. Combinations of these scales exhibited man's full range as a producer and as an inventor of new forms of social organization. However, factor analysis of a sample of world cultures, using these measures alone, did not produce the geographically discrete taxonomy required. This was not achieved until measures of human communication were added to the measures of social relations. This seems logical, since the most distinctive trait of *Homo sapiens* is his elaboration of symbolic systems, by means of which knowledge can be shared and preplanned activities with others can be carried out.

The data relating to the variance of human communication systems came from a somewhat novel source—a worldwide study of song performance style. Earlier areal classifications of cultures had incorporated linguistic identifications, but with minor taxonomic effect. There are two reasons for this. First, languages can be learned as systems and, as such, can move easily across cultural borders. Second, languages, as they have so far been described, seem not to vary in any regular ways across cultures. Perhaps this is because linguistic analysis has largely dealt with grammar, phonemic structure, and vocabulary, all of which are useful in formal instruction but, since they are the most arbitrary aspects of speech, they cannot be expected to have an orderly relation to the structure of societies.

The Cantometric study of song (Lomax, 1968), however, revealed strong statistical relations between song style and social norms—for instance, that the explicitness, or information load, of song varies with the level of economic productivity, that cohesiveness of performance is an indicator of the level of community solidarity, that multipart singing occurs in societies where the sexes have a complementary relationship, and that degree of ornamentation increases with increased social stratification. (Lomax, 1968) Thus song appears to function as a reinforcement of culture's social structure, and profiles of song performance can be used as indicators of culture pattern. Since the Cantometric measures report on how people use their voices or organize their choruses, they point to patterns of behavior transmitted as part of the cultural substructure. Moreover, main song performance patterns seem to be extremely stable (as well as very audible) aspects of regional cultures and, on the whole, do not migrate unless a whole people or culture also migrates.

These conclusions are based on the analysis and comparison of 4000 recorded song performances from about 400 different cultures, located in every world zone. It was this first panhuman study of communication that produced scaled data on norms of group organization and models of communication to match the species-wide scoring of socioeconomic patterns in the *Ethnographic Atlas*. The descriptive grid combining these two sets of measures was sizable and so was the number of societies required to represent the whole range of human culture. Norman Berkowitz devised a special adaptation of the varimax rotation multifactor analysis to classify these complex profiles. This computer procedure swiftly compares a large number of cultures on a long roster of scales, clusters the most similar cultures, and then picks out the distinctive profiles of each cluster. It has two different outputs—Q, factoring of cultures, and R, factoring of scales of culture measurement. The criteria I established to estimate the success of these operations are postulates of some importance to the comparative study of human behavior.

Taxonomic Criteria

The members of each of the culture factors should outline one continuous geographic zone through which a cultural pattern or style might have migrated or been transmitted from group to group. Any discontinuous geographic factor must have a clear historical explanation—for instance, the shattering of one cultural continuum by another, invading tradition. The "best" of several geographic factor runs is the one that satisfies these criteria, which together define the culture hypothesis—that most human behavior is determined by complex patterns of learned behavior transmitted through the centuries in the same territory.

The criterion for the success of the factoring of measures is that each cluster of measures should be conceptually pure—that is, capable of being given a label that characterizes all of its members. All members of such a factor can then be viewed as formalized manifestations of the same deep attribute or general characteristic of culture. It is here assumed that the principle of substitutability is applicable to culture as well as to communication: just as a series of gestures or statements can serve as interchangeable symbols for a thing or an idea, so a set of behavioral norms can interchangeably represent the same underlying cultural attribute. Thus one may account for the endless amplifications of human behavior in terms of the regrouping of a small number of deep attributes.

These two criteria—one for geographic continuity and the other for operational unity—were used to test the acceptability of the factor analyses. When a culture factor that was run through the computer did not meet the geographic criterion, we usually found that our sample was defective. For example, if too many neighbors of a given culture were missing, it might be grouped with similar, but inappropriately distant, cultures or remain unclassified. When a measure was inappropriately grouped, this usually pointed to defects in its structure, which might then be remedied. The input of culture profiles and measures was changed in run after run until both criteria were approximately satisfied. The simplicity of these tests and the flexibility of the computer procedure itself provide an excellent method for the objective comparison of the multimember, multifaceted phenomena called cultures.

The Geographic Taxa

In order to provide a balanced picture of the range of human culture, I used a subset of the Murdock standard test sample of culture, in which geographic neighbors and duplicates have presumably been eliminated. The subsample, for which there were data on both song performance and social structure, include 148 cultures from the 186 provinces in the Murdock sample. In the Q, or geographic phase of the factoring, the computer grouped over 90 percent of this sample into 13 clusters, or factors, which were either geographic or historical continuums, or both. Each of the 13 has a clear-cut and distinctive profile of traits (ten profiles are partially presented in Fig. 3). In other words, each of these 13 cultural factors can be viewed as a distinct subvariety or style of human culture, a historical-geographic continuum of one pattern of adaptation. The map in Fig. 1 presents the geography of these 13 culture styles; the distribution of each one can be traced by its abbreviation. Brief descriptions of these 13 cultural factors follow.

1) Siberia: A continuous zone of nomadic hunters, fishers, and reindeer herders, from European Lapland across Siberia to Kanchatka. Two paleo-Siberian cultures, the Yukaghir and the Ainu, are equal members of this and the Amerindian Hunters zone, thus indicating a common origin in early Siberia for both of these clusters.

2) Amerindian Hunters: A clustering of the hunters and fishers of the American Arctic and the Northern Plains with those of Mato Grosso, the Gran Chaco, and Patagonia. This clustering points to the existence of a continuous distribution of an ancient cultural substratum across both continents—a continuum broken by the rise of agricultural adaptations, represented by the following three clusters.

3) American Villagers: Corn farmers of the Eastern woodlands and prairie areas and the pueblo-dwelling, drywash irrigationists of the Southwest. These cultures would probably have formed an unbroken continuum if information from the Mississippi Valley cultures, such as the Natchez, had been available.

4) Amazonia: The forest-dwelling, seminomadic, root gardeners and riverine fishers of the Amazon and Orinoco basins.

5) Nuclear America: A somewhat flawed continuum (reaching from northern Mexico through middle America to Peru) of societies affected by the development of Amerindian civilizations.

6) Australian Gatherers: A cultural continuum on the subcontinent of Australia prior to the arrival of Europeans in the 18th century.

7) African Gatherers: Bushman and Pygmy groups occupied most of Africa south of the Sahara, before the coming of black herders and gardeners in the last two or three millennia.

8) Black Africa: A continuous distribution in Africa showing the spread of gardeners and herders through the southern half of the continent and, recently, into the Americas. Inclusion of tribal Indian culture in this cluster suggests that an old transoceanic continuum of tropical agriculture once connected Africa with lands to the east.

9) Melanesia: Includes the horticulturalists and pig farmers of New Guinea, Melanesia, and nearby Micronesia, along with two similar South American societies, the Timbira and the Bora Witoto.

10) Polynesia-Pacific: The seafaring cultures of the Pacific, including the Motu of southern New Guinea, the eastern Micronesians, and the Polynesians.

11) Proto-Malay: In spite of a weak sample, this factor outlines the spread of rice-growing Malay people (the so-called "bamboo culture") from the hills of Indochina to Borneo and the Philippines.

12) Old High Culture: Shows the spread of cities, empire, irrigation, and craft specialization from the Middle East, west through the Mediterranean, south with the Cushites into central Africa, and all the way east through India, Southeast Asia, and Indonesia into east and central Asia.

13) Europe: The hard-grain, plough, dairying agriculturalists of Europe and colonial America.

Four of the 148 cultures remained unattached and unique—the Miao Tipeto-Burmans, the Andean Aymara, the Zadruga Strpci of Yugoslavia, and the cattle-herding Mesakin of Kordofan. Five cultures were classified out of region: the Bedouin in factor 2, the Arauanians in factor 12, the Timbira and Bora in factor 9, and the Sajek of Formosa in factor 8. Thus, only 7 percent of the sample of 148 cultures remained outside of this system of regional cultural continuums. Otherwise, the classification fulfills the first of the two taxonomic criteria surprisingly well, considering the state of available data. A set of homogeneous and continuous regions of culture, each with a distinctive behavioral and adaptive profile, presents a coherent picture of human subspeciation.

The Behavioral Taxa

A number of other anthropologists have applied factor analysis to culture, most of them using the criteria in the *Ethnographic Atlas*. Their findings (Driver & Schuessler, 1957; Erickson, 1969; Goodman & Kruskal, 1963; Kaiser, 1958; Lomax & Erickson, 1968; Rummel, 1970; Sawyer & Levine, 1966) point in a similar direction to those presented here.

Multifactor analysis of our 71 measures of social and communicative structure clustered them into 14 factors and five single measures. Inspection of the display of these factors (see box) shows that most of them are conceptually pure and clearly represent some single tendency or deep attribute of culture. The four apparent exceptions to this rule all imply interesting hypotheses, which may produce further unities.

Factor 13, in which the availability of milk products is linked to vocal dynamics, suggests that this extra source of protein accounts for many cases of energetic vocalizing. In fact, loud and forceful singing does seem to be more common where protein is plentiful.

A summary of the factor analysis that grouped the 71 measures of social and per-formance norms into 14 clusters and 5 single factors. Each cluster consists of two or more measures. With a few exceptions, all measures in these clusters represent a single deep attribute of culture. A few measures are either attached with equal strength to two factors or also occurred as a unique or single factor.

1) *Differentiation*
   Productive range
   Intensity of agriculture
   Percent of animal husbandry
   Size of settlement
   Number of extra-local
      hierarchies
   Inheritance of land
   Degree of stratification
   Presence of metalworking
   Task differentiation by sex
   Percent of repeated text
   Percent of precise enunciation
   Interval size
   Degree of melodic variation
   Severity of premarital sex
      sanctions
   Games of skill versus games
      of strategy
   Rules for leadership
      succession (unique)
   Difficulty of wiving (unique)

2) *Caloric value of produce*
   Size of domestic animals
   Root versus grain agriculture
   Percent of fishing
   Importance of milking
   Presence and activity of gods
   Games of skill versus games
      of strategy
   Kinship system

3) *Sexual division of labor*
   In main productive activity
   In overall productive acts
   Percent collecting versus
      percent hunting, fishing

4) *Organization of groups*
   Importance of leaders versus
      group
   Unison versus multipart
      choruses

5) *Level of cohesiveness*
   In rhythm of vocal
      group
   In vocal blend
   In orchestra tonal blend
   In rhythm of orchestra
   Organization of vocal
      group rhythm orches-
      tral rhythmic type

6) *Noise and tension*
   Raspy vocalizing
   Nasal vocalizing
   Tight and narrow
      vocalizing
   Severity of premarital
      sex sanctions

7) *Ornamentation*
   Melisma
   Glissando
   Embellishment
   Glottal Shake
   Tremolo
   Degree of melodic
      variation

8) *Community type*
   Solidarity-index
   Unilineal-bilateral
   Solidary kin
      organizations
   Kinship system

9) *Matri-patri*
   Female-male inheri-
      tance of real property
   Female-male inheri-
      tance of movable
      property
   Marital residence rules
      (F-M)
   Matrilineal-patrilineal

10) *Size and type of
      statement*
    Number of phrases
    Litany, strophe,
       through-composed
    Symmetry of form
    Melodic range
    Presence and activity of
       gods

11) *Orchestral model*
    Social organization of
       the orchestra
    Unison versus multipart
       in the orchestra
    Organization of orches-
       tral group rhythm
    Relations of orchestra to
       vocal part orchestral
       rhythmic type

12) *Vocal rhythm*
    Vocal rhythmic type
       (regular to irregular)
    Tempo
    Phrase length

13) *Dynamics*
    Soft-loud vocalizing
    Lax-forceful vocal
       accents
    Low-high register
    Importance of milking

14) *Part organization*
    Type of polyphony
    Social organization of
       chorus

15) *Type of family*
16) *Size of family*
17) *Segregation of boys*
18) *Female dominance in
      pottery, weaving,
      leatherwork*
19) *Position of final note in
      songs*

Factor 6, which clusters the measure of sexual sanctions with vocal noise, relates to a finding, fully established in earlier research (Lomax, 1968: 194–195), that degree of voice tension varies directly with the severity of sexual mores. Factor 3 properly includes collecting versus hunting with sexual division of labor, since gathering is largely a female, and hunting largely a male, activity.

The composition of factor 2 suggests a number of interesting ideas. First, games of strategy, like checkers, grow popular after the management of herds of milk-producing animals becomes a central cultural theme. Second, the incorporation in the produce factor (factor 2) of the scale dealing with beliefs about the presence and potency of high gods is fascinating. Swanson's pioneer work (1960) indicated that the development of religious belief, from animism, through polytheism, to monotheism, paralleled the rise and centralization of political authority, from the acephalous tribal council, through the feudal confederacies, to centralized monarchy. The connection of monotheism to milking, implied in the structure of factor 2, suggests, moreover, that the spiritual authority of powerful divinities represents the control of the triad of essential foods—namely, grain plus meat and milk—on which the members of specialized agricultural and pastoral societies came increasingly to depend. In fact, belief in one, authoritarian, male god does seem to have originated in the patriarchal cultures of the Middle East, where control of the herds and land rested in the hands of the male head of the patriline.

It thus appears that the 71 measures, which reduced the variety of human culture to a small number of homogeneous culture regions, represent no more than 19 attributes. If the geographic taxonomy of culture presented earlier (Fig. 1) is judged to be fairly satisfactory, then a compact set of terms such as these 19 may be sufficient to describe and classify human culture and, insofar as behavior is cultural, human behavior itself. Actually I shall try to show that a successful taxonomy of culture and an acceptable account of cultural evolution can be achieved with only 5 of the 19 factors. Moreover, these five may be lumped into two vectors, the interplay of which has shaped the development of culture and the emergence of the subspecies of man.

A Tree of Culture

Factor 1 puts the scales of economic productivity, increase of population, stability of settlements, and centralization of political and social controls together with measures of the amount of information the performance carries, as indicated by the importance of small intervals, precise enunciation, and nonrepeated text. It has been established elsewhere that the explicitness, or information load, in song performance increases directly with the productivity of the subsistence system and with other features of the social economy (Lomax, 1968). Indeed, there appears to be a lawful relation between the explicitness of communication performance and increased productivity and political centralization. Therefore, postponing further discussion of the relations among these variables (Fig. 3), I shall consider that all of these measures together represent the effect of one powerful cultural attribute—man's concern with differential control of his environment. Change here affects the whole social, economic, and communicative structure. In a word, human culture evolves as its differentiative capacity increases.

The tree diagram (Fig. 2) offers a cursory view of this evolutionary principle. Here the 13 culture zones presented earlier are arranged on a vertical scale of increasing differentiation. The numbers along the vertical axis are calculations of the weighted average of the 13 on the differentiation factor. The scale rises from 1 and 2 for Australian and African gatherers to 8 + for agriculturalists of Europe and Asia. The effect of industry was not considered here because reliable ratings of industrialized cultures were not available.

The branches of this evolutionary tree are formed by the residual bonds of similarity that link the 13 culture types. These linking bonds were also derived by the computer, which, once it had established independent geographic factors, then calculated the residual similarity between these cultural taxa. The two highest bonds for each of the 13 are drawn between them to complete the tree diagram and to show how the taxa are interrelated along its branches. Note, for instance, that Melanesia is linked by its highest bonds to its closest geographic and historical congeners—to Australia by .25 similarity and to Polynesia-Micronesia by .27 similarity. Interlinking establishes interesting families, such as a circum-Pacific region of simple producers. Black Africa's highest bonds tie it to Polynesia and Melanesia, shaping a world family of tropical gardeners. However, the ancient cultural link of Black Africa to the Middle East shows up in the bond of 14 between the Old High Culture and the African factor.

Indeed, this purely numerical operation arranges human cultural families in a highly provocative way. The known historical relationships among the 13 areas are reaffirmed, with the one exception of Malaysia, where the sample is weak. The diagram points to the ongoing tie between European and classical Oriental civilization, Polynesia and Melanesia, primitive America and its Siberian roots, and to the separate branching out of Indian cultures in the Americas. The intercontinental affiliations of the African

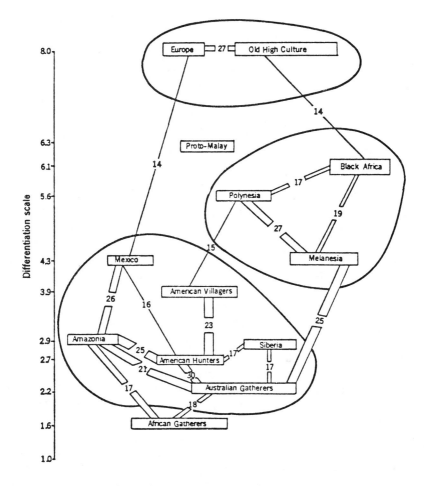

Fig. 2. Numerical scores for each of the 13 main geographic factors were calculated on the differentiation factor. The vertical axis shows the resultant scale, with a point for each of the 13 main geographic factors. Connections between the boxes represent the residual bonds, or levels of similarity, between the geographic taxa. Each of the taxa is limited to its two highest bonds. The differential strength of the bonds is indicated by the width of the connecting lines. No bond lower than the mean of 13 for the whole field was allowed.

and Australian gatherers suggest that these two clusters represent the earliest and most generally distributed culture types of which we have a living record. Although hunting is practiced by both, it is clearly a secondary, although valued, source of food. These facts suggest that gathering, rather than hunting, was the first major subsistence activity of human beings. This finding, if true, overturns the now popular view of early man as a bloodthirsty caveman, whose adaptive success was due to his interest in weaponry combined with a calculated ferocity. Like our nearest relatives, the great apes, and like present-day gatherers, early human societies were probably nonaggressive, highly intrasupportive teams of foraging amateur botanists, quarterbacked by women and guarded by males.

Beyond the gatherers, three grand regions of culture, ringed by circles in the diagram, can be seen in the clusters of interbonded factors. Two of the regions are known—the Eurasian and the circum-Pacific. The latter embraces all of the primitive producers of the Pacific rim, from Australia, through Melanesia and Siberia, and into Amerindia. The clear emergence of an Afro-Oceanic region supports the hypothesis that a continuous ring of gardening cultures once linked Oceania to Africa in the tropical latitudes. Only traces of this ancient human distribution seem to have survived the incursion of higher cultures in Malaysia, Indonesia, and Southeast Asia. However, in main features of social interaction, and especially in song and dance style, the peoples of Black Africa and the maritime Pacific affirm an ancient cultural allegiance. Their shared patterns include a complementary relation between the sexes; emphasis upon fertility as a central social value; and social solidarity manifested in massed choirs of rhythmically unified performers and workers, in sensual hip-swinging, polyrhythmic dancing, in polyrhythmic orchestras, and in open-throated, polyvoiced choruses. All these habits are highly functional in a solidary, village, gardening economy without a complex technology.

The computer weighed a mountain of evidence to produce the numbers that point to the existence of this tropical factor. If this arrangement of cultures proves acceptable, one can take very seriously the following grand scheme of human cultural evolution.

Stage 1, African Gatherers: Less than 2 for differentiation score, low productivity, nomadic bands, acephalous, egalitarian, complementary social relationships, cohesive and highly integrated singing organization, and polyrhythmic, flowing, sensuous dance style. These are found among the Bushmen and Pygmies of Africa, with traces in refuge areas on every continent.

Stage 2, Circum-Pacific simple producers: About 3 for differentiation score, seminomadic, basically acephalous, males dominate productive and social relations, hunting, fishing, or slash-burn agriculture without animal husbandry, individualized and unison singing organization, and a linear dance style. This culture type presumably spread from a hunting origin in Siberia, around the perimeter of the Pacific, and flowered in the Americas.

Stage 3, Tropical, gardeners: about 5.5 for differentiation score, full agriculture with animal husbandry, settled villages, confederacies, a two-class system, complementary productive and social relationships, great solidarity in community life, cohesive and polyvoiced singing, and highly erotic synchronous, and polyrhythmic dance style. An early continuous distribution is indicated—from Melanesia, through Southeast and southern Asia to East Africa and the Sudan, later spreading into sub-Saharan Africa, east to Polynesia, and west into the New World.

Stage 4, Eurasian plow agriculture: 8 for differentiation score, large towns, centralized government, complex stratification, male dominance of productive and social system, and emphasis on virtuosic soloists in performance, with elaborate and drilled participation of chorus and orchestra.

The advantage of such an overview is not only that it summed up much of the evidence of comparative ethnology, but it also permits one to see the main events in cultural history in terms of the growth and encounter of a small number of traditions. Though not isolated, the three main traditions clearly developed in different zones of the world around distinctive adaptive and communicative patterns. Each gave rise to sets of regional and areal subtraditions, all of whose members share some of the distinctive traits of one parental stem, most markedly in their expressive behavior.

All of this argues for the direct relation of cultural evolution to the regional development of differentiative capacity. Figure 3 summarizes the stepwise emergence of the differentiative components through time. The evolutionary scale of culture types is used as the horizontal axis, from African Gatherers on the left to Old High Culture on the right. The entries in the column above each evolutionary stage are those, and only those, traits that became statistically distinctive at that level.

Column 1: Among the acephalous, nomadic, freely associating African Gatherers, most familiar traits of social control are absent, just as their performances are empty of explicit and group-controlling content.

Column 2: Emergent traits for Australian aboriginal societies outline a masculine gerontocracy, in which elder male clan heads control the sexual, economic, and ritual life of their people. Note an accompanying rise of narrow intervals and of voice tension indicators, as well as an accompanying drop in performance cohesiveness.

Column 3: Men become the principal producers in the diffusely bonded hunting-fishing economies of America and Siberia, and this masculine productive dominance is symbolized by the importance of male solo performances and male choruses singing in rough unison.

	1 African Gatherers (1.6)	2 Australian Gatherers (2.2)	3 American Hunters (2.7)	4 Amazonia (2.9)	5 American Villagers (3.9)	6 Melanesia (4.3)	7 Polynesia (5.6)	8 Black Africa (6.1)	9 Europe (8.0)	10 Old High Culture (8.0)
Differentiation										
Succession of leader	Absent	Hereditary							Formal	
Milking	None								Present	
High gods	None	None		None	Otiose			Otiose	Involved	
Games	PS & C	None	Physical skill and chance					Strategy		
Metal	None							Present		
Stratification *	None						2	3 to 4		5 to 7
Land inheritance	None						Present			
Size of animals	None					Pigs		Cattle, sheep and goats		
Animal husbandry	None					10 to 20%			30 to 40%	
Permanence of settlement	Bands		Seminomadic			Villages or nuclear				
Extra-local government	None				2	None	2	1	3	
Size of settlement	Fewer than 49				200 to 400				50,000	5 to 50,000
Roots versus grains	None			Roots	Grains	Roots		Grains		
Intensity of agriculture	None			Extensive			Horticulture	Extensive	Intensive	Irrigation
Production scale	Extracting			Incipient		Gardening			Plow	Irrigation
Fishing	10%	20 to 30%	40% plus	20 to 30%			40% plus		10%	
Collecting/game	Collecting		Game	Less than 10% of either						
Communication										
Embellishment	Little			Little	Some	Little				Much
Leader/Group	Group	L/G			L/G	G/L	L/G	Group	Solo	
Variation	Little		Little		Little			Much		Much
Interval size	Wide	Narrow	Wide			Mid			Mid	Narrow
Enunciation	Slurred				Mid	Slurred	Precise	Slurred	Precise	
Wordy/Nonsense	Nonsense		Nonsense / wordy			Nonsense	Wordy/nons	Mid	Wordy	
Integration										
Division of labor †	Female		Male	Female					Male	
Solidarity index	Nonsolidary				Solidary				Nonsolidary	
Community organization	None	Clan	None		Clan		Ramage	Clan	None	
Tonal blend	Good	Medium	Poor		Good		Good			Med-poor
Vocal organization	Integrated	Diffuse	Unison			Integrated				Solo
Vocal width	Very wide	Narrow	Mid		Wide					Narrow
Rasp	Little	Great				Little		Great	Mid	Great

Fig. 3. The emergent traits of the differential control factor. All entries correspond to scale steps used in the factor analysis; no entry is made in any location unless it is statistically distinctive and different from the entry in the column to its left. For example, the distinctive scores for the first stage, African Gatherers, are largely zeros in the societal rows, whereas the scores for group organization and performance point to high levels of performance integration. The zero scores of the Australian Gatherers in most of the same columns are indicated by their inclusion in the same bars. Exceptions point to hereditary clan leaders and a tense-voiced, diffuse performance style. In the same way, all entries in any succeeding stage record only significant changes from the previous stage—that is, changes that are statistically distinctive and thus can be considered truly emergent. Blanks occur where no clear and distinctive trait was found in a column or culture zone. Dashed lines serve only to make the diagram easier to read. Numbers in parentheses under each of the column heads indicate their numerical standing on the differentiative factor. (*Number of levels. †The sex contributing more than 50 percent to the main productive task.)

Column 4: In the Amazon-Orinoco Basin, loosely bonded, bisexual teams carry out a rudimentary agriculture, and song performances are notable for diffuseness and multipartedness.

Column 5: Among aboriginal North Americans, corn farming fosters larger communities, tribal confederacies, and clan-based community organizations whose solidarity and complementarity are reflected in the unity and frequent bisexuality of singing and dancing groups.

Columns 6, 7, and 8: In Melanesia, Polynesia, and Black Africa, the need for highly synchronous male-female work teams to carry out the monotonous routines of year-round agriculture emerges in the usually cohesive, multipart, male-female dancing choruses of the tropical gardeners. Here the extra nourishment resources of horticulture and animal husbandry give rise to stable settlements, systems of land inheritance, and social stratification. In Black Africa, sheep, goat, and cattle culture, grains, and metallurgy give rise to further social stratification, kingdoms and empires, and a passion for games of strategy resembling chess.

Column 9: In Europe, intensive plow agriculture, and an increase in animal husbandry and dairy products stimulates the growth of cities, where centralized governments replace local, kin-based organizations in authority. An authoritarian monotheism arises, males take over the main roles in the productive system, and highly explicit song style becomes the rule.

Column 10: The centralization of economic and political control, essential in large riverine irrigation systems, leads to further centralization and stratification in much of the Orient. The musical specialist appears, addressing the center with long, complex, highly embellished songs, loaded with the tension of an alienating and authoritarian social system.

These seem to be the main stepwise developments in the evolution of cultures as outlined in the present factor analysis. A steady buildup in subsistence productivity is at first accompanied by changes in male-female division of labor and in lineage organization, and then (from the middle of the scale on) by mounting stratification and political centralization. Ever more highly articulated societal entities are mirrored in more and more explicit performance style (Lomax, 1968: 194–199). All of these developments contribute to a steadily rising curve of differentiation. Some important aspects of social and performance organization, however, do not conform to this curve of progress. Figure 3 shows that women dominate in gathering and gardening subsistence systems, while males dominate in hunting and intensive agriculture, and that cohesive, noise-free, highly integrated, rather than leader-dominated, performance peaks among African Gatherers and among gardeners. This contrast confirms the finding that a highly integrated style of performance is typical of complementary and solidary communities, whereas noisy, tense-voiced, solo, unison, or diffuse

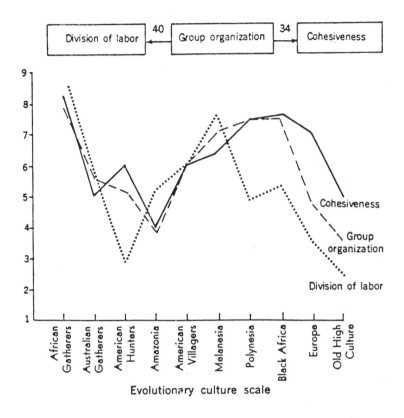

Fig. 4. The weighted means of three R factors are plotted along the evolutionary culture scale: division of labor by sex, organization of groups, and level of cohesiveness.

performance occurs in male-dominated, loosely bonded, network-like societies (Lomax, 1968: 130–148). It seems, therefore, that the prevalent performance style of a culture reflects and reinforces not only the degree of differentiative control, but the degree and kind of group integration that is appropriate and necessary to the culture's adaptive structure. There is, in other words, a parallel between the way cultures synchronize activity in productive efforts and in expressive performances.

Supporting evidence of this hypothesis comes from S. H. Udy's cross-cultural study (1959) of how work is organized. I have extracted from Udy's study pertinent data on the structure of tasks and teams in a hundred cultures, from gatherers to irrigators. The percentage of stable work teams by region is as follows: African Gatherers, no score; Australian Gatherers,

33; American Hunters, 20; Amazonians, 0; American Villagers, 95; Melanesia, no score; Polynesia, 91; Black Africa, 85; Europe, 25; Old High Culture, 44.

It appears that stable teams occur most frequently where choral solidarity is highest—among the gardeners. The personnel of hunting and fishing parties may vary with each venture, and here performance is generally individualized. The teams of complex agriculture are also likely to be loosely textured, since farming is often done by individuals, small family units (as in Western Europe), or under exploitative conditions of forced labor or peonage, as in much of the ancient world. Thus, at the level of complex agriculture, strong social forces militate against the social solidarity that apparently leads to unforced, synchronous choralizing. An exception that proves this rule is the complementary, village-based dance and song groups that once enlivened the work bees of Eastern Europe.

The Main Evolutionary Factors

An earlier study (Lomax, 1968) established a strong correlation between the cohesiveness of a culture's performance style and both the stability of its teams and the level of its community solidarity. I feel justified in regarding the variance of Factor 5, the level of cohesiveness (in song), as standing for the general adaptive importance of highly unified behavior. The way this factor varies along the evolutionary scale is shown in Fig. 4. This figure also shows the variance in the part played by women in the principal subsistence activity at each level of culture and the degree to which groups are integrated in organization at each level. These three curves follow more or less the same regular, wavelike path along the evolutionary scale. Moreover, all three represent factors that are interlinked by the strongest residual bonds in the factor analysis of the measures (Fig. 4, top). These three factors seem to represent a single deep attribute of culture—the integrative tendency, which can best be observed by combining its three indicators.

Figure 5 shows how the combined weighted mean of integration varies in a clear, wavelike fashion along the evolutionary series and how this mean is related to the steadily mounting curve of differentiation. As I have already suggested, an intimate, though not direct, relation exists between these two general cultural characterizers. It has been pointed out that group teams are needed for many gardening tasks, while individualized teams are more suitable for hunting, fishing, and intensive agriculture. The sexual makeup of teams also changes with the main subsistence base of culture. Most gathering and gardening is relatively light work and takes place in moderate or warm climates; therefore, it can be performed by women, even

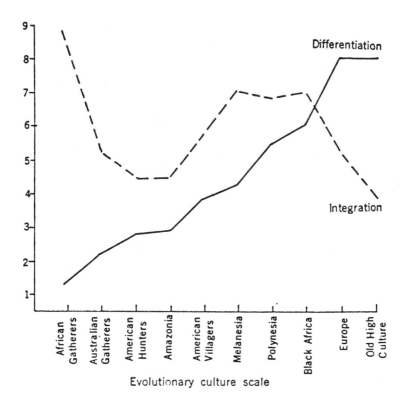

Fig. 5. The weighted means of the differentiative factor (solid line) and the integrative composite factor (broken line) are plotted along the evolutionary culture scale. These are the main factors from the 71 measures that were factored over the sample of 148 world cultures.

if accompanied by their children. Extractive activities, except in the case of river and shoreline fishing, are often strenuous and hazardous operations, and are normally carried out by men—especially since, as main subsistence activities, they are usually confined to cold climates, where women must stay home to keep the children alive (Lee & DeVore, 1968). A good deal of intensive agriculture, such as plowing with large draft animals, is heavy work for which male strength is usually required.

Although this is a sketchy account of a vast and important subject, it serves to show that the character and the sexual makeup of productive teams, as well as performing groups, change according to the requirements of the subsistence system. All the components of the integration factor shift together as subsistence teams of different sexual character, kind of organization, and type of leadership are fielded. These ongoing, diurnal demands profoundly affect the whole social fabric. For example, Barry, Child, and Bacon (1959) have shown that child-rearing aims and practices change with the requirements of the subsistence system. Initiative is useful in the hunt, and therefore hunters cultivate independence in their sons, while farmers train their children in obedience. Moreover, it seems logical to suggest that family structure should vary in relation to child-rearing needs and thus only indirectly in relation to societal evolution.

Many basic structural features of social and communication systems, however, do vary with the differentiation-integration pair. When the variance of all the factors of culture measurement is plotted along the evolutionary scale, the factors fall into three groups: (i) those that essentially go along with the differentiation factor, (ii) those whose variance follows the wavelike movement of the integration curve, and (iii) a miscellaneous group, whose even or indeterminate movements indicate that they play no clear part in the overall course of cultural evolution [Factors 6, 9 through 12, 14, and 6 through 19 (see box)]. It is notable that measures concerning the character of the family and the dimensions and structures of the kin group seem not to have a decisive relation to the overall course of species development as outlined in the evolutionary scale of culture. If this is not an expected result, it may be a logical one. Family and kin are human psychobiological constants, essential to all societies for ensuring the nurture of children and the emotional stability of adults. These institutions are, of course, subject to change, but only within a small range—perhaps because they are too fundamental to emotional security to vary in such drastic ways as the features of the integration factor. It appears, therefore, that those social scientists who have sought to chart the course of social evolution by studying changes in family and kin structure have been looking in the wrong direction.

In fact, two deep attributes (differentiation and integration) may be all that are needed to produce an evolutionary taxonomy of culture. The comparative study of world dance styles supports this supposition. When multifactor analysis was performed on 50 measures of movement style against a world sample of dance, only two factors emerged which varied in a unique and meaningful way along the evolutionary rank. (Five factors out of the remaining seven varied in a random way; two minor factors varied in the same way as the first of the two main factors.)

The first of these two factors clusters the differentiating, or manipulative aspects of movement, and the second encompasses the erotic, feminine, in-gathering aspects of movement. The manipulative factor involves frequent peripheral movement, varied movement, three-dimensional movement, light movement, and hand and foot synchrony. The sinuous factor involves frequent multipart trunk movement, trunk synchrony, successive-ness, a flowing quality, trunk presentation, high synchrony, and curving movement.

Not only does this pair of factors correspond in many ways to the differentiation-integration pair, but they shift along the evolutionary rank order in a similar way (Fig. 6). The mean level of the manipulative factor rises in three stages along the evolutionary rank. These stages reflect an increase in light, varied, three-dimensional movement of the extremities of the body in dance, as manifested, for example, in the toe-dancing of Europe and the elaborate handplay of the Oriental dance. This body style symbol-izes a complex and varied approach to the environment. As a matter of fact, all of the measures in the manipulative factor are highly correlated to ele-ments in the differentiation factor.

The wavelike factor in Fig. 6, I term "sinuous" because it traces the mean level of scales that measure fluid, curvaceous movement, often in-volving the central body (pelvis, breasts, shoulders). All of these features, taken together symbolize the feminine and the sexual. They are visible among African Gatherers and among Polynesians and Black Africans, where women are prime producers and where a feminine esthetic is domi-nant. The members of such cultures fall easily into synchrony with each other at a level that other cultures can scarcely achieve by intensive drill, probably because the sinuous movement style maintains a network of erotic signals that keeps interpersonal awareness high. It is, therefore, quite un-derstandable that these qualities of movement should be prominent in those cultures in which people dance, sing, talk, and work together with a great deal of "natural and spontaneous" coordination. A high level of coordi-nation has an adaptive function in these culture zones, as I have already argued.

It will be noted that this sinuous factor moves across the evolutionary rank in a wavelike path which resembles that of the integration curve. In fact, the two have highs and lows at most of the same points. That the behav-ior of these pairs of factors—differentiation-integration and manipulative-sinuous—should so closely resemble each other is all the more striking since the systems involved in measuring songs, dances, and societies are based upon different sets of concepts, each set derived from the data being measured. Therefore, it is highly probable that these two pairs of factors measure the same pair of deep attributes of culture—two forces that shape all human behavior—practical, interactional, and expressive. The main events in human evolution can be explained in terms of the interplay of these two attributes—the differentiative and integrative-erotic, both equally important in social and communication systems.

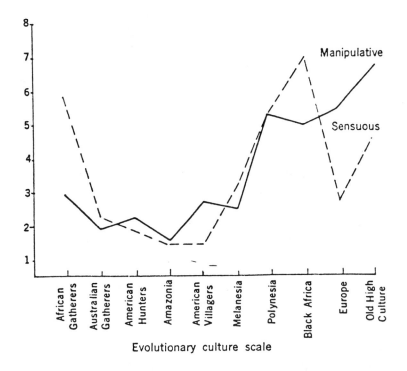

Fig. 6. The two main factors of the multifactor analysis of dance style are plotted.

Modern Evolutionary Trends

I now go beyond the data of ethnology, considered so far, beyond the stage of peasant agriculture and irrigation empire, and employ the evolutionary frame and the paired factors to illuminate some of the main features of industrial societies. In the first place, the differentiative factors continue their ascent (Fig. 5) as science and machinery multiply man's economic range. An expanding economy and growing population are accompanied by the rise of a monstrous administrative bureaucracy, along with an increase in the range, capacity, speed, and precision of communications media. The solo bards and the Salomes who entertained at court remain, becoming entertainment stars adored by millions. All this is familiar.

Less noticed is the fact that the coming of industry involves organizational changes that are reflected in an upward swing of the integration factor. In the stage of plow agriculture, women stayed largely in the harem, the home, or the garden, going out only in the company of chaperoning relatives or neighbors. Modern city life tends to break these ties or loosen their restraints. Factories and offices bring women back into public productive function, not at first as equals, but in an ever more complementary relation to men. Concomitantly, performance style grows steadily more multivoiced as musicians experiment with polyphony, accept African polyrhythms in jazz and rock, and, nowadays, habitually utilize multichannel recording. Certain forms of rock combine and integrate more independent musical levels than any other form of music analyzed by Cantometrics.

It is notorious that industrial production and distribution depend, above all, upon the synchronous meshing of many systems. A symbolic parallel can be found in the ordered sections of the great 19th- and 20th-century symphony orchestra, which spread from Europe, across America, and into Japan, Australia, and now China, along with the industrial-managerial system which it reinforces. Not only the symphony, however, but marching bands, football, the ballet, and other massive demonstrations of multileveled coordination fascinate the people of industrial economies.

This recent trend in human evolution thus seems to indicate that culture is moving into a stage where a peak for integration will match an unparalleled high in differentiation. A somewhat similar situation prevailed once before in man's cultural evolution—in one of its earliest stages (Turnbull, 1961). The Mbuti Pygmies have apparently lived for many millennia in remarkable balance with their environment. The climate in their high jungle is moderate, mild, and healthful. Disease is rare, food is plentiful, and Mbuti society is permissive, egalitarian, supportive, fun-loving, and sharing. Their music is a kind of perfectly blended, joyous vocal counterpoint—the sound of a Golden Age that has somehow survived into the present. We moderns may now have a similar possibility, as predicted by these curves of the evolutionary process. After twenty millennia of blood, sweat, and tears, we have a technology that can reduce environmental pressures up to a minimum, if it is administered properly. Man might again, like his remote African ancestors, live in balance with his environment, with all his needs provided for in a genuinely egalitarian, sharing society.

But let us return to the known, to some of the general conclusions that can be drawn from this comparative survey of the behavior of the human species. First of all, the record of living cultures demonstrates that, at the beginning of the evolutionary series, *Homo sapiens* lived mainly by gathering fruits, nuts, seeds, honey, tubers, grubs, rodents, and so on, rather than principally by hunting large animals. Thus it was not aggressiveness, but an understanding of the food resources of the terrain, and especially plant lore, that powered the nonauthoritarian, pacifist, collecting cultures. Recent studies of man's closest relatives among the great apes show that ape societies, too, are peaceful, highly intrasupportive communities that subsist principally by gathering. Therefore, the thesis that man began as a bloodthirsty carnivore and an expert killer is a wish-fulfillment legend of armchair scientists that can go on the shelf with *Tarzan and the Apes.*

Indeed, if we can believe the evidence available from contemporary gathering societies, the earliest cultures flourished not because of superior aggressiveness, but because of the accumulation of economic and, especially, communicative know-how (Lee & DeVore, 1968; Downs, 1966; Marshall, n.d.). African Pygmies and Bushmen are famed wits and accomplished vocal polyphonists, their songs reflecting the harmonious internal balance of cultures that have endured since the dawn of human society. However, not only were the beginning of culture rooted in cooperation and communications, but cultural progress has been marked, at every stage, by further development of technical, administrative, and, especially verbal skills. I reemphasize the importance of vocal agility in human evolution since, before it was found to be an indicator of change, the very fact of cultural evolution remained in doubt. It is not yet clear whether languages can be arranged in a progressive series, but there can be no doubt of a rapid evolutionary development in systems for handling symbols. In fact, the close parallel between the manipulative and the differentiative factors suggests that every major human advance has been made possible by an increase in manipulative finesse. In sum, the progress of human culture is plainly reflected in the degree of differential control man brings to bear upon the whole spectrum of his activities.

Some people argue that advances in armaments have been the spur in evolution, but weapons are merely one of many kinds of tools. Other pessimists, looking back over the period of empire, from the days of Egypt to the end of the Chinese Empire, maintain that history is a sorry circle of the same greedy mistakes. but these writers confuse the history of one stage of human evolution, that of Old High Culture, with all of human history, which consists of at least ten main phases. In fact, the rise and fall of empire in classic times can be best viewed as the utilization of the resources of the Old High Culture phase by one people after another. Indeed, the rich possibilities of this stage of culture have only recently been exhausted. This interpretation permits us to turn our backs on the gloomy view of man's history that has haunted us from the time of Gibbon and Hegel.

It seems clear that human culture has progressed in one positive respect. However, the process has been multilineal, as well as multileveled. Several branches of the human family have flowered in their own theaters of development, each producing an independent series of brilliant civilizations. Moreover, most of the 19 factors discovered in this analysis do not increase with the differentiation factor. More than half of them—those that concern family and marriage, melody and rhythm, for instance—seem to have only an indirect relation to cultural evolution. Other factors, having to do with male-female, face-to-face relationships in teams, move in response to the progressive differentiative factor, but along a contrary path. This important integrative factor, it will be recalled, draws together sexual division of labor, organization of groups, level of coordination, and sinuous and synchronous movement.

The interplay of the relatively independent factors with those bound directly and indirectly to technical progress gives human evolution a special, nondeterministic character. Each stage of technological development produces a syndrome of communication and organization that is, in its setting, a unique and ideal adaptive pattern. Each new combination of the basic structural factors with the other less determined, factors gives rise to a new life-style. Each of these life-styles, both past and emergent, is a human universe, with its own logic and its own endless and unpredictable possibilities. Man, the most social of the animals, keeps on inventing cultures, each one capable of caring for people from infancy to old age. Each of these emerging patterns brings forth fresh human solutions and ideas of lasting value. Man's greatest achievement is here—in the sum of his cultural, his communicative know-how.

Only part of this know-how is encompassed in the differentiative factor, which has thus far been the spur to cultural evolution. In planning for the future of the entire human species, for the children of the more than 13 cultural subspecies, we must work with all aspects of culture, especially the much-neglected integrative factor, and we must also draw upon the full range of human solutions. Man's total heritage of life-styles can contribute to the future, without giving precedence any longer to the European social and esthetic practices that accompanied the rise of industry. The varied styles of industrial society emerging today in China, Japan, Yugoslavia, the U.S.S.R., India, and Sweden only hint at the cultural variety that the future can bring forth as the character of cultural evolution is more generally understood. For almost a century, the intellectual atmosphere of the world has been poisoned by a false Darwinism that judged human social development as the survival of the fittest—that is, of the most successfully aggressive individuals and the societies. This view can now be corrected.

Notes

1. Reprinted with permission of the author and publisher from *Science* (vol. 177, 1972).

2. I thank Columbia University for sponsorship and the National Institute of Mental Health, National Endowment for the Humanities, The Wenner Gren Foundation, and the Rockefeller and Ford Foundations for support of this research. I also thank Victor Grauer, coinventor of Cantometrics, and Roswell Rudd, musicologist, for the musical ratings; Edwin Erickson for his statistical guidance, Irmgaard Bartinieff and Forrestine Paulay, coinventors with me of choreometrics for the movement data; and especially Conrad Arensberg, close collaborator, mentor, and codirector of the research. This article may be identified as reprint article A-661 of the Bureau of Applied Social Research, Columbia University.

References

Barry, H., I. L. Child & M. K. Bacon. 1959. *American Anthropologist.* 61:51.

Downs, J. F. 1966. *The Two Worlds of the Washo.* New York: Holt, Rinehart & Winston.

Driver, H. E. & K. F. Scheussler. 1957. *American Anthropologist* 59:655.

Erickson, E. E. 1969. Thesis. New York: Columbia U.

Goodman, L. A. & W. H. Kruskal. 1963. *Journal of the American Statistical Association* 58:310.

Kaiser, H. F. 1958. *Psychometrika* 23:187.

Lee, R. B. & I. DeVore. 1968. *Man the Hunter.* Chicago: Aldine.

Lomax, A., ed. 1968. *Folk Song Style and Culture.* Washington: AAAS.

Lomax, A. & E. E. Erickson. 1968. In A. Lomax, ed. *Folk Song Style and Culture.* Washington: AAAS, pp. 75–110.

Marshall, S. L. nd. *Africa* 31:231.

Mead, M. 1956. *New Lives for Old.* New York: Dell.

Murdock, G. P. 1967. *Ethnographic Atlas.* Pittsburgh: U. of Pittsburgh Press.

Rummel, R. J. 1970. *Applied Factor Analysis.* Evanston: Northwestern U. Press.

Sawyer, J. & R. J. LeVine. 1966. *American Anthropologist* 68:708.

Swanson, G. E. 1960. *The Birth of the Gods.* Ann Arbor: U. of Michigan Press.

Turnbull, C. M. 1961. *The Forest People.* New York: Simon and Schuster.

Udy, S. H. 1959. *The Organization of Work.* New York: Human Relations Area File Press.

20

German Parteilieder *and Christian Hymns as Instruments of Social Control*[1]

ROLAND L. WARREN

National Socialism as a movement has depended from the beginning on the sustained emotional appeal of a crisis psychology. Stirring speeches, repetition of emotionally toned slogans, breath-taking visual displays, mass meetings, press propaganda, and the appeal to German history, tradition, and legend have all been exploited as instruments for maintaining the necessary morale to support the movement. An important source of emotional support is also furnished by group singing, a fact which has received little attention in the United States, perhaps because group singing in this country does not play as important a role as it does in Germany.

In times of war crisis, it is true, songwriters rise to the occasion by contributing their bit to national defense. There are many significant differences, however, between the fighting songs of the United States and those of National Socialist Germany. Perhaps the greatest difference is that most of the American songs are rag-time or jazz, designed for dancing as well as singing. The National Socialist songs, on the other hand, are designed to be sung, rather than to be listened to or danced to. Many are designed to be sung without accompaniment, and resemble the simplicity of the folk song.

Further, American "morale songs" arise generally during limited emergencies. So it was with the World War I songs, most popular of which was probably George M. Cohan's "Over There," so it was with depression songs such as "Marching along Together," and so, more recently, with the host of morale songs which stemmed from the success of "God Bless America." A counterpart for "The White Cliffs of Dover" and "Remember Pearl Harbor" cannot be found in the National Socialist songs. The first is too manifestly sentimental, the second too "football-ish." "My Buddy" and "Ich hatt einen Kameraden," both popular in World War days, point the contrast. The former was composed during the war, was a dance tune, and was designed to meet the current market for sentimental

375

war numbers. The latter went back for its tune to 1825, and for its words to Ludwig Uhland, a famous German poet who composed them in 1809. It is more rigorous, and, although equally sentimental, it is almost "marchable" and tells a story.

Indeed, the National Socialist songs are more comparable to Christian church hymns than they are to American war songs. They occupy a place of permanence in the national life, they depend upon the same psychological mechanisms of mass singing, they are highly symbolic, and are inspired by a similar prerogative of eternity. The "Horst Wessel" song is in many respects more similar to "Onward, Christian Soldiers" than it is to "Marching along Together." The last-mentioned shows the characteristic football derivation of most American marching songs, while the first two have in common their broader, slower rhythm, their implications of eternity, their appeal to dead heroes, their reference to "the foe," and their urging on to victory.

The National Socialist and Christian hymns have a double purpose. Their *primary* function is to arouse the emotions of the singers to a point where they are more sensitive to the impact of the words (sermon, political address) of the speaker. But they also fulfill the *derivative* function of exercising a lasting influence over the attitude of the individual participants after they leave the group.

Interstimulation is the key process which transforms a mere group of people in close physical proximity into a crowd. Psychologists have analyzed the techniques employed by religious leaders in furthering this process. The use of symbols encrusted with emotional meaning, the performance of hallowed rituals, the group recitation of the creed, the singing of hymns—all help in the primary function of breaking down resistances which inhibit the desired responsive attitude in the members of the fold.

Seashore (1938:142) has emphasized the "feeling of freedom, luxury, and expanse" created by the rhythmic qualities of music, tending to neutralize inhibitions and make the individual feel "as if one could lift oneself by one's bootstraps." Pratt (1921:172ff) has reported the increase in suggestibility brought about by group singing of hymns. The individual, as he re- peats the words borne up by the compelling urge of the melody, affirms his faith, and that in a loud voice. Through singing he can say things which it would embarrass him to repeat in his more inhibited moments. And, hearing his own uninhibited confession on the lips of those surrounding him, he is led to an even deeper affirmation of faith in what he is reciting. It was this insight which led William James to speak of "faith in someone else's faith." Common affirmation of faith, supported by rhythm and melody, is an important factor in "whipping up a crowd," as any evangelist will testify.

The derivative function of hymns is that of conditioning attitudes which will remain with the individual after the group has dispersed. As such, their verbal content can be analyzed in terms of "the control of opinion by significant symbols," as Lasswell (1927:9) has succinctly put it, and consequently many of the better known propaganda techniques apply to these hymns as well as to other instruments of controlled attitude formation. Propaganda must be considered in its context. To be successful, it must meet the level of interests and prejudices of those whom it is to influence, as well as adjust its appeal to their degree of emotional excitement. Religious leaders have sensed this condition, as evidenced by the care which they use in selecting hymns appropriate to the main theme of the sermon or to the festival which the church is celebrating. The Nazi hymns are also selected according to the "message" to be implanted and the state to which the emotions of the singers are expected to be aroused.

A careful analysis of the hymns included in the National Socialist party songbook indicates that certain clearly discernible appeals occur with unusual frequency (1939). The appeals most frequently employed are to the following motives: loyalty, eternity, dead heroes, self-sacrifice, the leader, freedom, chief symbols, the fatherland, nearness of victory, "everybody's doing it," not too much questioning of goal, enemies, youth, and "all together in the cause." It will be shown below that the Christian church hymns are replete with substantially the same type of leading motives.

The National Socialist songs are an excellent example of the efficient adaptation of means to ends in the formation of group sentiment. This is not to imply that in every case a song fulfilling certain definite functions as made to order for the Party. Indeed, some of the songs antedate the National Socialist movement. Three generalizations would appear to be warranted, however: (1) The songs which were either "pushed" by the Party or came more naturally to popularity were those which, as a matter of fact, had high functional value in strengthening the National Socialist cause. (2) The songs which were purposely written to bolster Party solidarity employed, as a matter of fact, those techniques of appeal which were already apparent in the movement and which were potentially effective in the social milieu from which the songs arose. (3) As a result, the songs, partly by deliberation, partly by accident, became an integral part of the total propaganda effort on the home front.

Typical quotations from the party songs are given below under the heading of the leading motive of the appeal. Accompanying each set of quotations are corresponding quotations from a representative Christian hymn book (A HYMNAL . . . ; 1916). The comparison serves to illustrate the similarity of appeal, and affords another interesting example of aremarkable correspondence between certain appeals used by the Church and the National Socialist Party (Warren, 1941).

Under each topic, quotations from National Socialist songs will be given first, and underneath them quotations from Christian hymns. Seventy-six National Socialist songs were examined for this study. The number in parentheses after each topic refers to the frequency with which the topical motive is employed. The number in parentheses after the quotations from the Christian songs refers to the number of the hymn.

Loyalty: (17) Though all should grow disloyal, we shall still remain true . . . Defiantly waved their flags as they lowered him into the grave, and they swore eternal loyalty for the Hitler-comrade. . . .

Am I a soldier of the cross, a follower of the Lamb? And shall I fear to own His cause, or blush to speak His name? (488) I bind this day to me for ever, by power of faith, Christ's Incarnation . . . (525)

Eternity: (17) . . . Germany, the proud manor, carries thy countenance, carries thy spirit into all eternities. We shall hold thee, flag . . . high over death's rule into eternity.

Breathe on me, Breath of God, so shall I never die; but live with Thee the perfect life of Thine eternity. (380) . . . To Him that overcometh, a crown of life shall be; He with the King of glory shall reign eternally. (538)

Dead Heroes: (15) . . . Marching on before us, with battle-scarred flags, are the dead heroes of the young nation . . . Comrades shot by Red Front and Reaction march in spirit with us in our rows.

For all the saints, who from their labours rest, who Thee by faith before the world confessed, Thy Name, O Jesus, be for ever blessed. Alleluia. (195) The martyr first, whose eagle eye could pierce beyond the grave; who saw his Master in the sky, and called on Him to save . . . Who follows in his train? (85)

Self-sacrifice: (23) . . . We are faithfully devoted to Hitler, faithful unto death . . . Heart that has loved only Germany, heart which in battle never degenerated, heart which gives itself to the people.

Fight on, my soul, till death shall bring thee to thy God . . . (118) Yea, let Thy cross be borne each day by me; mind not how heavy, if but with Thee. (163)

The leader . . . we come like a storm, the *Führer* has called. Soon Hitler flags will flutter over every street, the oppression will last only a little while longer.

Jesus calls us; o'er the tumult of our life's wild restless sea, day by day His sweet voice soundeth, saying, "Christian, follow Me." (168) Jesus shall reign where'er the sun doth his successive journeys run; His kingdom stretch from shore to shore, till moons shall wax and wane no more. (480)

Freedom: (14) . . . the day of freedom and bread is dawning . . . Father, in life and death help us to win freedom. . . .

(Such quotations as "Lord make us free!" could be given. No word, however, seems to be the counterpart. Rather, a variety of words and ideas would correspond:)

"Salvation, glory, honour!" I heard the song arise . . . (542)

Chief symbols: (40) Leader, carry the flag before us into clouds and sun . . . The flag stretched high, the rows formed close together, S. A. marches with a quiet firm step. . . .

Onward Christian soldiers, marching as to war, with the Cross of Jesus going on before . . . Forward into battle see his banners go. (530)

The fatherland: (26) . . . Germany, in flowering beauty you ever rise up anew. Germany, Germany above everything, above everything in the world. . . .

Jerusalem! high tower thy glorious walls . . . (543) Glorious things of thee are spoken, Sion, city of our God . . . (468)

Nearness of victory: (11) Soon Hitler flags will flutter over every street, the oppression will last only a little while longer . . . One day shall come the day of revenge, one day we shall be free. . . .

What rush of alleluias fills all the earth and sky! What ringing of a thousand harps bespeaks the triumph nigh! (541) At last the march shall end; the wearied ones shall rest; the pilgrims find their Father's house, Jerusalem the blest. (537)

"*Everybody's doing it*": (6) . . . Millions are already looking to the swastika full of hope . . . no one can stand idle along the way, everyone must come along with us. . . .

Onward, then, ye people! Join our happy throng! Blend with ours your voices in the triumph song! (530) Come, labour on. Who dares stand idle on the harvest plain . . . (497)

Not too much questioning of goal: (2) . . . and no-one is here who in cowardice despairs or tiring, questions the way . . . How stupid to ask, how small to ask why we are marching!

I do not ask to see the distant scene; one step enough for me. (244) How blest are they who have not seen and yet whose faith has constant been . . . (555)

Enemies: (18) . . . Day and night let us guard the flag against all enemies . . . Judah appears, to win over the Reich . . .

Principalities and power, mustering their unseen array, wait for thy unguarded hours . . . (128) Christian! dost thou see them on the holy ground, how the power of darkness rage thy steps around? (126) (Indeed, the Jews come in here, too, for hostile reference in one hymn:) Have we no tears to shed for Him while soldiers scoff and Jews deride? (153)

Youth: (10) . . . We (youths) are the glory of our times . . . We youths stride through the German land full of faith facing the sun; we are a sacred Spring . . .

O thou Whose feet have climbed life's hill, and trod the path of youth . . . Thy Name, proclaimed on every lip, the Master of our schools. (365) . . . In every tongue and nation she (the Church) calls her sons to pray . . . (352)

"All together in the cause": (12) . . . Youth and aged, man for man, embrace the swastika banner . . . Brothers of spade, desk, and hammer silently shake each other's hand.

Bright youth and snow-crowned age, strong men and maidens meek . . . (537) Brother clasps the hand of brother, stepping fearless thro' the night. (539)

The Church hymns come closer to being the American counterpart of the Party hymns than any other group of songs in America. This is not only because they are the only sizable body of songs built around a cause familiar to great numbers of Americans, but because they use a similar technique in their emotional appeal. The similarity can be overemphasized, however. First, although they employ similar psychological means, their ideological ends are vastly dissimilar. Secondly, and more important for this study, they make appeals on a social psychological level which are employed to a certain degree by all social movements: the appeal to enemies to solidify the in-group, the appeal to dead heroes, the sanction of eternity, the employment of symbols, the imminence of victory as a bolster to morale, the rallying around a leader, etc. Thirdly, although the theme has not been fully exploited in this paper, the Party songs, despite their employment of the sanction of eternity, emphasize deeds and this-worldliness, while the Church hymns emphasize faith and the world to come.

Notes

1. Reprinted with permission of the author and publisher from the *Journal of Abnormal and Social Psychology* (vol. 38, 1943).

References

———— . 1916. *A Hymnal: as Authorized and Approved for Use by the General Convention of the Protestant Episcopal Church in the United States of America in the Year of Our Lord 1916.* New York: Gray.

———— . 1939. *Liederbuch der Nationalsozialistischen Deutschen Arbeiterpartei* München: Franz Eher nachfolger.

Lasswell, Harold D. 1927. *Propaganda Technique in the World War.* New York: Knopf.

Pratt, James B. 1921. *The Religious Consciousness: A Psychological Study.* New York: Macmillan.

Seashore, Carl E. 1938. *Psychology of Music.* New York: McGraw-Hill.

Warren, Roland L. 1941. "Fascism and the Church," *American Sociological Review* 7:45–51.

—— 21 ——

Economic Correlates of Artistic Creativity[1]

VYTAUTAS KAVOLIS

Studies of the relationship between economic conditions and artistic creativity have generally been based on somewhat imprecise historical data from the urban cultures of classical and modern Europe. They suggest the presence of a direct relationship between economic achievement and artistic creativity (Clough, 1961). It may be argued, however, that the virtual exclusion of the data from preliterate cultures, together with inadequate attention to intervening variables, have frequently resulted in generalizations about the economic backgrounds of artistic creativity which lack both universality and theoretical significance.

In the present survey, a tentative attempt will be made to deal with this relationship in a somewhat wider perspective, and to formulate a conception of the mechanisms responsible for the observed associations between economic and artistic conditions. The processes to be related to artistic creativity will be conceptualized within an interpretive framework derived from the sociological theory of the phase cycles (Bales, 1953; Parsons and Smelser, 1956).

The Phase-Cycles Theory

A general statement of the phase-cycles theory may be formulated in the following manner:

1. All social systems have a number of basic functional problems to solve. Among these, instrumental *adaptation* to the external environment, organization of the legal-institutional machinery for *goal attainment*, internal social-emotional *integration*, and *tension reduction* (and latent pattern maintenance) are of paramount importance.

2. Social systems produce only limited amounts of social resources (such as wealth, administrative power, disposable time, and popular interest) and, in addition, may be able to mobilize only a part of the resources for problem-solving action. Furthermore, specialization with regard to any particular system problem tends to some extent to circumscribe, even if resources are available, the possibility of action oriented toward the solution of any other problem. For example, when the emphasis is on tension reduction, some of the potential resources for creative action are likely to be unproductively dissipated, by virtue of the negative effects of a prevalent "latent tension-management and pattern-maintenance" orientation on the readiness to commit resources to purposive action.

3. For these reasons, basic system problems tend to be dealt with in a cyclical manner. Major emphasis is placed on one type of problem, to the relative neglect of others, at any particular time. As a functional problem is being successfully resolved, resources are increasingly recommitted to previously neglected tasks which the solution of this problem has made salient. The process can be conceptualized in terms of several typical phase sequences which can be directly observed in small-group studies and also abstracted from complex historical events. In problem-solving processes, the normal phase sequence is as indicated under statement 1.

In terms of this theory, it is hypothesized that artistic creativity will tend to be stimulated in the phase of social-emotional integration (Parsons, Bales, and Shils, 1953) and relatively inhibited in the other phases of any type of large-scale social process. The main body of the present paper consists of an application of this theory to two types of economy-related processes. First, however, to demonstrate the need for such a theory, it must be shown that artistic creativity cannot be explained, even in part, as a natural product or a symbolic expression of concentrated wealth (or of comfortable general prosperity), as some of the existing theories implicitly suggest.

The Degree of Economic Achievement

To indicate the dependence of artistic creativity on economic capacity, evidence can be cited to show that an advance in prosperity or the attainment of economic dominance in a culture area is frequently associated with increases in artistic creativity (Clough, 1961; Hauser, 1957; Kroeber, 1949; Edmundson, 1922; Clark, 1957). Contrariwise, a long-range decline in economic activity or prosperity does appear to be associated with a lowering of artistic creativity (Gimpel, 1961; Ettinghausen, 1962; Oliver and Fage, 1962; Clough, 1960).

However, these kinds of data may merely mean that changes in economic prosperity are correlated with variations in artistic creativity. No absolute level of prosperity can be identified as necessary for artistic excellence. The cave art of the European Paleclithic hunters, the rock art of South Africa, and the powerful image-making of the Australian natives are all associated with quite limited material resources. "In Oceania . . . life is often very precarious indeed," especially "in the swampy areas of New Guinea or in the very inhospitable coral islands," yet it is "these areas in particular" which "have yielded some of the finest works in the whole of primitive art" (Buehler et al., 1962).

As Redfield (1958: 18) has observed, "such a contrast as that between the Haida and the Paiute Indians reminds us that generally speaking a people desperately concerned with getting a living cannot develop a rich moral or aesthetic life." This generalization, however, points to the artistically adverse effects *not* of a low-attainment economy, but of a near-total preoccupation with economically instrumental action. Such a preoccupation may be a consequence of a low-attainment economy in areas with difficult access to natural resources, as in the American Plains before the introduction of the horse. But where a low-attainment economy is combined with more easily accessible natural resources, as in many parts of Oceania (and on the Northwest Coast of America), economic backwardness may coexist with high-level artistic creativity. On comparable levels of economic development, a cultural emphasis on the accumulation of wealth appears likely to preclude an adequate commitment of social resources to artistic pursuits, as a comparison of the Tchambuli, the artistic headhunters, with the Kapauku, the capitalist businessmen of New Guinea suggests (Mead, 1950).

Our illustrative comparisons imply that it is not the level of economic achievement, but the proportion of social resources which is allocated to non-instrumental pursuits that is causally related to artistic creativity. Artistic achievement is not proportional to the amount of wealth accumulated; nor is it impossible in the absence of a considerable economic surplus. Art *creation* is hence not primarily a symbolic projection of material prosperity (though self-conscious art *collecting* may serve this purpose) (See Veblen, 1931; Clark, 1961).

The Effects of Economic Advancement

While, in a static cross-cultural comparison, prosperity is not a prerequisite of artistic creativity, the latter seems to be stimulated by *recently attained* prosperity. The accumulation of urban wealth in Europe, beginning in the eleventh century, is followed in the twelfth and thirteenth centuries—an age of "magnificent prosperity"—by the period of Gothic cathedral-building (Gimpel, 1961: 38–42). The creation of the great fortunes in America during the nineteenth century is succeeded in the twentieth by the first original American contributions to visual art.

In general, "the flourishing periods of fine art do not come in the periods when a rising upper class is building up its wealth and power, but afterward" (Tomars, 1940: 171). One linkage between the recent achievement of prosperity and artistic creativity is the leisure which the former makes possible, as in Athens in the classic period and Florence during the Renaissance. In this context, artistic creativity could be regarded either as the product of recommitment of resources from instrumental to expressive activity, or what may be only a special case of the former more general tendency, as a means of symbolic legitimation of recently acquired socioeconomic dominance. It does not, however, seem possible to account for this linkage by assuming that, in urban as contrasted with preliterate cultures, artistic creativity is generally a consequence of the accumulation of wealth and might be regarded as a response to the demand for luxury goods, which great wealth presumably generates (at least in non-puritanic cultures).

In some cases, "refined luxury" coincides indeed with "creative spontaneity" in the arts, as in the Warrring States and in the late Shang periods of Chinese history. At other times, by stimulating a demand for luxury goods great wealth merely increases the capacity to afford, but not the ability to create, works of artistic value. "The four centuries of the Han *Pax Sinica*, like the four centuries of the Mediterranean *Pax Romana* . . . encouraged the development of a rich material civilization. In both cases the period of creative spontaneity—in the Mediterranean world the apogee of Athens and Alexandria, in China the 'Warring States'—had ended. Civilization passed through a stagnant and apparently happy period in which the luxury arts, on both sides, played a considerable role" (Grousset, 1959). "Luxury art," observes an art historian, "has a deadening effect. The most obvious example is the art of eighteenth-century France" (Clark, 1961: 77).

The comparison of the effects of recently attained prosperity and of stabilized great wealth on artistic creativity implies that artistic efflorescences are indeed, to a significant degree, the result of spontaneous recommitment of social resources from instrumental to expressive pursuits, which the achievement of what is felt as *relative* prosperity makes psychologically possible (and perhaps even necessary). Social resources may be committed to expressive action, as in Melanesia, where economic achievement is low, provided that, within the context of the prevalent cultural aspirations, it is felt to be relatively satisfying. However, within more dynamic economies the successful accomplishment of a significant economic advance apparently makes the diversion of social resources to artistic creativity more probable. But it seems to be only in the earlier (and less "luxurious") stages of such diversion that artistic creativity is maximally stimulated. To explain the frequently evident reduction of artistic creativity in the later stages of economic advancement (marked by greater "luxury"), the dynamics of the achievement drive must be considered (Sorokin, 1947).

The Dynamics of Achievement Motivation: Some Psychological Evidence

Evidence of a change in the patterning of individual motivation with increasing prosperity is implicit in a series of psychological analyses of fantasy-production samples from four historical societies. On the basis of literary and graphic evidence, Berlew and Aronson have demonstrated the need for achievement to have been strongest during the "growth" stage of classical Greek culture (900–475 B.C.), to have declined during the "climax" (475–362 B.C.), and to have been still further reduced in the "decline" phase (362–100 B.C.) (McClelland, 1961: 119, 125). In Spain, the climax in painting can perhaps be placed (if El Greco is to be included) in the period from 1580 to 1660; and four different types of literary indexes of the need for achievement show it to have been declining from 1200 to 1730 (McClelland, 1963: 131). However, the first significant growth of modern English painting, in the eighteenth century, coincided with a period of increasing need for achievement—which McClelland (1961: 134, 145–149) attributes to the Wesleyan revival. In their analysis of American children's literature, de Charms and Moeller have demonstrated an increase in the frequency of achievement imagery up to 1890 and a continuing decline in every decade since 1900 (cited in McClelland, 1961: 156). In three cases out of four, the attainment of economic prosperity has been associated with a lowering of achievement motivation (and it might have been in England as well, if not for the unpredictably intrusive factor of the Methodist movement). Presumably, in those cases, the level of prosperity attained has been felt to be sufficiently gratifying to legitimate the diversion of some motivational energy toward other kinds of activities, including those of the expressive kind. The decline in achievement motivation is roughly linked with increasing artistic creativity.

However, the Greek and Spanish data suggest that it is in the transitional period of *declining* achievement motivation that artistic creativity may be most stimulated. An extremely low level of achievement motivation, after a period of continuous decline, appears to be associated with a demand for material luxury, but also with a reduction in artistic creativity. This suggests that artistic creativity may in general be linked with changing patterns of motivation, (Kavolis, 1963) and that, consequently, high-quality art may have socially integrative and psychologically stabilizing functions to perform (which luxury in itself, presumably, does not).

These inferences are borne out by the observations of an economic historian on Renaissance Italy. "After the first decades of the thirteenth century and in the first half of the fourteenth . . . the urban economy of medieval Italy may be said to have entered its prime." but "by the fifteenth century," toward the culmination of the Renaissance, "Italy no longer occupied the same place in the economy of Europe as in the two preceding centuries . . . the old power of expansion was enfeebled," partly because of what seems to be a reduced achievement drive: "the new aristocracy of money" tended by now "to withdraw their capital from industry and trade and invest it, from motives of security and social prestige, in town and country properties." This was, however, a period of continued prosperity, and "during the fifteenth century court life in Italy attained its highest point of splendour (Luzzatto, 1961: 85, 142, 146, 143). The forfeiture of artistic leadership by the Italians after the High Renaissance may be associated with a hypothetical further decline in achievement motivation.

The evidence presented in this section suggests the general interpretation that increasing prosperity tends to reduce the motivation for achievement and to strengthen that for expressive action; and that it is in the extended moment when the two types of motivation are, in some at present not precisely definable manner, balanced in strength that highest-level artistic achievements are most probable. The theoretical justification of this expectation lies in the natural dependency of creative attainment in art upon the presence, in a strongly developed form, of *both* types of motivation.

With further increase in economic prosperity, however, achievement motivation tends further to decline and expressive motivation to become still stronger. This may be sufficient, on the one hand, to terminate economic advancement (and even to reduce abundance per capita) and, on the other hand, to cause the further growth of a self-conscious interest in art works, as objects of luxury to which no profound emotional significance need be attached. But, in this stage, achievement motivation would seem to become inadequate to sustain creative achievements of the highest order, even in the sphere of artistic expression. Indeed, once this stage is reached, an *increase* in achievement motivation may stimulate the capacity to create great art.

Economic Activity and Artistic Creativity

It is possible to conceive the data surveyed in the previous section in terms of an extremely long-range psychoeconomic phase cycle. Within this framework, the historical observations of the achievement-motive school suggest that artistic creativity tends to be inhibited in both the adaptive (pre-prosperity, high-achievement motivation) phase and in that of socioeconomic latency (stabilized wealth, low-achievement motivation). Conversely, it is stimulated in what may be regarded as the integrative phase, following immediately upon the attainment of relative prosperity (when achievement motivation is comparatively balanced against the drive for self-expression).

As contrasted with this psychoeconomic cycle, defined by the motivational accompaniments of economic achievement, a *socioeconomic* phase cycle may be conceptualized on the basis of changes over time in the commitment of social resources to economic action. While the nature of the relationship between the two types of cycles may be viewed as problematic, the phase-cycles model seems applicable, with appropriate modifications, to both types. As will be seen, however, it provides more useful information when applied to the socioeconomic data to be reviewed in this section.

Our theory predicts that the adaptive phase, indicated by sharply increased activity oriented to adaption to the external environment, should be inversely associated with artistic creativity. Two strategic cases will be considered. The decline of the earliest great artistic tradition, that of the European Stone Age, appears to be due, at least in part, to the new need for readaptation to the post-glacial environment, which must have absorbed the social resources of the population. In principle, this case is comparable to the sharply increased need for re-adaptation effected by the Industrial Revolution, both in the West and in the developing non-Western societies; and its (possibly transitional) anti-artistic effects (Bandi et al., 1960; Smith, 1924) are explicable as the product of a radical movement, in the socioeconomic process, into the adaptive phase.

If this is valid reasoning, the period of the industrial transformation in which economic growth proceeds at the most rapid rate should be marked by reduced artistic creativity. Such periods were 1819–48 in Great Britain, 1868–93 in the United States, and 1928–40 in Russia (Rostow, 1962). When the dates of artistic debuts of the most prominent painters of the period are considered, the expectation is borne out for the two European societies, and, possibly though not certainly, for the American as well (Digeon, 1955).

While the most intensive concentration on economic action appears to inhibit artistic creativity, there are indications that the gradual *beginning* of an economic transformation, before it gets into full gear, may have an artistically stimulating effect. Rostow (1962: 38) has placed the dates of the "takeoffs" to industrialization at 1783–1802 in Great Britain, 1830–?? in France, 1843–60 in the United States, 1850–73 in Germany, and 1890–1914 in Russia. In each case (with the possible exception of Germany), the beginning of a modern artistic efflorescence follows closely upon the take-off. However, the artistically stimulating effect of the disturbance of relative socioeconomic latency by the beginning of a phase of intensive adaptive action tends later to be weakened by a more extreme commitment of social resources to adaptive action.

A second, and major, revival of artistic creativity should follow the transition from the adaptive (and goal-attainment) into the integrative phase of the total social process. Two sets of data will be used for identifying such transitions: (1) the beginning of contraction in the area, value, or amount of foreign trade, and (2) the beginning of a long-range decline in the number of discoveries (in the case of Greece and Rome) or (in all other cases) in the percentage of the sum total of important inventions and dis-coveries made in a particular nation. The latter index is only a tangential indicator of the degree of commitment of social resources to economically relevant adaptive activity, and consequently, so far as the present theory is concerned, it should be a less precise predictor of periods of artistic creativity.

On the assumption that artistic creativity is maximally stimulated in the phase of integration after intensive action, *before* this phase passes over into that of social latency, it is hypothesized, for the purpose of facilitating measurement, that the maxima of artistic creativity will occur within one hundred (plus or minus fifty) years after the beginning of a long-range de-cline in the commitment of social resources to economic action, as defined by the two previously cited indexes. The first set of data, then gives the following *predicted* maxima of artistic creativity: Greece, 550–450 B.C.; Spain, 1560–1660; England, 1634–1734. The second set gives the following maxima: Greece, 300–200 B.C.; Rome, A.D. 100–200; Spain, 1450–1550; Germany, 1100–1200, 1525–1625, and 1875–1975; France, 1200–1300 and 1825–1925; Italy, 1350–1450; Holland, 1551–1651 (or 1675–1775); En-gland, 1100–1200 (or 1250–1350), and 1800–1900.

To provide a rough test of this hypothesis, the "artistic climaxes," as judged by Sorokin, of the respective nations will be listed, first for sculp-ture and then for painting: Greece, 559–350 B.C. and 450–300 B.C.; Rome, 30 B.C.–A.D. 100 and A.D. 50–110; Germany, 1120–1260, 1400–1550, and 1450–1560, 1800–1900 (?); France, 1140–1325, 1450–1550, 1850–1910, and 1620–70, 1760–1880 (?); Italy, 1420–1600 and 1420–1600; England, 1220–50, 1758–87, and 1715–1850 (Sorokin, 1947: 549–551). The periods of greatest artistic creativity in Holland and Spain may be set at approximately 1580–1660. While there are artistic peaks which do not seem, at least in this rough comparison, to be associated with the eco-nomic variables used here, there is apparently a very consistent tendency for periods of incipient decline in the commitment of social resources to

economic action to coincide or overlap with significant artistic efflorescences. This correspondence is the more remarkable in view of the impre-
cision of the data, which have not been collected for the purpose at hand.
As has been expected, the first index seems to be a somewhat better predictor of artistic peaks, except in the case of England where the Puritan
Revolution may have "postponed" an otherwise expectable artistic efflorescence (although even in this case it overlaps with the predicted period).

The hypothesis that artistic creativity is associated with the passage
from the adaptive into the integrative phase can apparently also be supported, though with less certainty, by prehistoric data. The important artistic tradition of the European Paleolithic hunters was created by an
"advanced hunter culture" which had reached a "dead end along a particular path of development," while "two other types of economic activity,
hoeing of the soil and pasturing cattle . . . in combination led to settled
agriculture," without producing, during this period, art of comparable
value (Bandi et al., 1961). It was this materially adequate, yet no longer
progressing, change that was responsible for "the birth of art." A parallel
association of relative economic backwardness with artistic creativity presents itself in the case of rock engravings so profusely carved, in several
areas, in the period of transition from the Stone to the Metal Age (Anati,
1961; Bataille, 1955).

Other variables being at all comparable, the lack of economic progress
in one society, while other societies under similar circumstance are advancing, implies relative satisfaction with the level attained. This suggests an
ori- entation to the integrative rather than the adaptive exigencies in the
social system of the Stone Age hunters who created the greatest art of their
age.

Summarizing the materials presented in this section, it can be said that
artistic creativity tends to be stimulated (a) in the period of initial response
to the beginning of economic transformations and (b) in the phase of social-
emotional reintegration following successful adaptive action in the economic sphere. It is adversely affected (a) in the phase of most intensive
adaptive action in the economy and (b) in the phase of economic latency—
which has been here identified as the condition of relative equilibrium preceding the beginning of a basic transformation of the socioeconomic
system.

Clearly, artistic creativity does not arise from a state of relatively stable social integration, but from a felt need to achieve reintegration. Objectively viewed, the need exists during all stages of an economic transition,
but the requisite resources are made available only in its very early stages
(when they are not yet primarily committed to economic action) and in its
relatively late stages (when the results of economic action are felt to be

sufficiently satisfying to justify an increasing release of resources for sym-
bolically expressive activities, and before the need for reintroduction is felt
to have been adequately resolved).

Conclusion

In the course of this survey, an extremely general sociological theory
of artistic creativity has emerged. That economic data have been used as
indexes of measurement is, in the most basic sense, incidental to the theory.
The interpretations presented should have made clear that what is regarded
as causally related to artistic creativity is not economic processes or
achievements as such, but certain psychological and sociological conditions
which can be empirically correlated with economic as well as, presumably,
with other kinds of social processes.

The *psychological* factor favoring artistic creativity has been identified
as a relatively balanced tension, in the personality system, between the
drives toward achievement and toward expression. There is a very real
problem, which our data do no help much in resolving, whether, in a highly
differentiated society, this type of motivation must be present only in the
personality systems of creative minorities, or whether it must be more generally prevalent to make possible an artistic efflorescence. It is assumed
that this personality characteristic constitutes the patterning of individual
motivation which is most conducive to artistic attainment.

The *sociological* factor which the data suggests to be an important
causal agent in artistic efflorescences is a widely felt need for reintegration
of the social system. While this need has been treated here as a theoretical
construct to account for the pattern of data, its existence has been experi-
mentally demonstrated in small-group research, from which the conceptual
model of this investigation has been derived. The collective perception of
this need is viewed as the cause of an increased demand for art and consequently of a tendency to commit social resources to the action of artistic
creation. It is not assumed, however, that the social demand for art is
caused only by the integrative need.

The relationship between the two basic variables—the patterning of
individual motivation and the commitment of social resources—must be regarded as intrinsically problematic. If the kind of motivation which is most
conducive to artistic attainment has not been developed in the personality
system, a widespread social demand for art will probably be insufficient to
cause an artistic efflorescence. It is only by exploring the historically variable relationship between the two variables that a systematic sociological
theory of artistic creativity can be developed.

Regarded by itself, no economic or any other social process can be expected always to have the theoretically predicted effect on artistic creativity. First, a tradition of high art must be present for any social factor to have a significant artistically stimulating effect, and such traditions cannot be taken for granted. Second, the artistically propitious phases of one type of cycle may overlap with, and in their effects be offset by, unpropitious phases of other partly differentiated cycles (political, religious, communal), or vice versa. Third, any historically real cycle movement may be interrupted by the beginning of a new cycle before the former has reached the integrative phase, in which its artistic effects should be most strongly felt.

In spite of the blurring effect which the complexities of historical data have on any theoretically conceived pattern, the evidence presented tends to indicate that the theory of phase cycles constitutes a useful approach to the study of artistic creativity, certainly one of the areas to which the authors of the theory have least intended to apply it.

Notes

1. Reprinted with permission of the author and publisher from the *American Journal of Sociology* (vol. 70, 1964).

References

Anati, Emmanuel. 1961. *Camonica Valley.* New York: Knoph.

Bales, Robert F. 1953. "The Equilibrium Problem in Small Groups." In Talcott Parsons, Robert F. Bales & Edward A. Shils, *Working Papers in the Theory of Action.* Glencoe: The Free Press.

Bandi, Hans-Georg, Henri Breuil, Lilo Berger-Kirchner, Henri Lhote, Erik Holm & Andreas Lommel. 1961. *The Art of the Stone Age.* No publisher listed.

Bataille, Georges. 1955. *Laxcaux; or, the Birth of Art: Prehistoric Painting.* Lausanne: Skira.

Buehler, Alfred, Terry Barrow and Charles P. Mountford. 1962. *The Art of the South Sea Islands.* New York: Greystone Press.

Clark, G. N. 1957. *The Seventeenth Century* (2nd ed.). Oxford: Oxford University Press.

Clark, Kenneth. 1961. "Art and Society." *Harper's Magazine* (August): 77–78.

Clough, Shephard B. 1960. *Basic Values of Western Civilization.* New York: Greenwood.

Clough, Shephard B. 1961. *The Rise and Fall of Civilization: An Inquiry into the Relationship Between Economic Development and Civilization.* New York: Greenwood.

Digeon, Aurelien. 1955. *The English School of Painting.* Paris: Didier.

Edmundson, George. 1922. *History of Holland.* Cambridge: University of Cambridge Press.

Ettinghausen, Richard. 1962. *Arab Painting.* Lausanne: Wittenborn.

Gimpel, Jean. 1961. *The Cathedral Builders.* New York: Harper & Row.

Grousset, Rene. 1959. *Chinese Art and Culture.* New York: Pion.

Hauser, Arnold. 1957. *The Social History of Art.* 2 vols. New York: Random House.

Kavolis, Vytautas. 1963. "A Role Theory of Artistic Interest." *Journal of Social Psychology* 60: 31–37.

Kroeber, A. L. 1949. *Configurations of Culture Growth.* Berkeley: University of California Press.

Luzzatto, Gino. 1961. *An Economic History of Italy from the Fall of the Roman Empire to the Beginning of the Sixteenth Century.* Milan: Bank of Italy.

McClelland, David C. 1961. *The Achieving Society.* Princeton: Princeton University Press.

Mead, Margaret. 1950. *Sex and Temperament in Three Primitive Societies.* New York: Morrow.

Oliver, Roland, and J. D. Fage. 1962. *A Short History of Africa.* Baltimore: Penguin Books.

Parsons, Talcott, Robert F. Bales and Edward A. Shils. 1953. "Phase Movement in Relation to Motivation, Symbol Formation, and Role Structure." In Talcott Parsons, Robert F. Bales and Edward A. Shils, *Working Papers in the Theory of Action.* Glencoe: The Free Press.

Parsons, Talcott and Neil J. Smelser. 1956. *Economy and Society: A Study in the Integration of Economic and Social Theory.* Glencoe: The Free Press.

Redfield, Robert. 1958. *The Primitive World and Its Transformations.* Ithaca: Cornell University Press.

Rostow, W. W. 1962. *The Stages of Economic Growth: A Non-Communist Manifesto.* Cambridge: Cambridge University Press.

Smith, Hubert Llewellyn. 1924. *The Economic Laws of Art Production: An Essay Towards the Construction of a Missing Chapter of Economics.* London: P. S. King.

Sorokin, Pitirim A. 1937. *Social and Cultural Dynamics.* Englewood Cliffs, N.J.: Bedminster.

Sorokin, Pitirim A. 1947. *Society, Culture and Personality: Their Structure and Dynamics.* New York: Cooper.

Tomars, Adolph Siegfried. 1940. *Introduction to the Sociology of Art.* Mexico City: privately printed.

Veblen, Thorstein. 1931. *The Theory of the Leisure Class.* New York: American Library.

22

Sound and Censorship: Two Crises in the Motion Picture Industry

LINDA B. LEUE

The formal organization of an industry cannot be understood without an examination of that industry's interaction with the institutions, ideologies, and technology of the larger society. Pressures from the consumer of a product, and pressures arising from the introduction of new techniques into the production process may initiate a process of change in industrial organization. If these pressures are perceived by producers to have reached 'crisis' proportions, we might expect the enterprise to become involved in an intensive search for new organizational forms.

This paper will examine two incidents of the search for new organizational forms in the American film industry. Each occurred during a relatively short time span, primarily the decade of the nineteen-twenties. Each was initiated by pressure from consumers of the Hollywood product: the mass audience. One search was necessitated by a change in technology, the other by an intensification of public opinion concerning the content of films. The introduction of sound technology and the response to the censorship battle shaped industrial organization for decades past the time of these crises.

I. Organizational Crisis: A Functional Analysis of Technological Impact

Industrial organization can be viewed as a function of the relationship between the enterprise and the technology, institutions, and ideologies existant in the society. An organization must be examined as it interacts with new technical procedures, value patterns, and major structural organizations of the social order; it cannot isolate itself from the changes which occur in the social structure, nor can it ignore, except at its own peril, demands placed upon it by that structure. It is involved in a system of functional interdependence, and must be capable of following a reorganizational process when external conditions demand change.

Robert Merton's (1967) discussion of the concept of function sets a framework for understanding that these demands for organizational change may have positive or negative consequences. Merton suggested that a refinement of the concept of function was in order for two reasons. Previous discussions had both overstressed positive consequences and confused motive with function.

To combat the over-emphasis on positive consequences, Merton defines function as 'the observed consequences which make for an adaptation or adjustment of a given system.' He reserves the concept of dysfunction for those 'observed consequences which lessen the adaptation or adjustment of a given system.' An item may have multiple consequences; thus, an assessment of the net balance of functional and dysfunctional consequences is also in order.

To combat the confusion between motive and function, Merton suggests a further conceptual refinement which includes both manifest and latent aspects. Manifest functions are "the objective consequences . . . which are intended and recognized by participants," while latent functions are "those which are neither intended nor recognized." This dimension may also be used to characterize negative consequences (dysfunctions).

This paradigm may be used in an assessment of the range of sub-units in an organization for which a given item has consequences. That is, what is functional for one organizational sub-unit may be dysfunctional for another, and any item may have unanticipated latent consequences for a sub-unit or an entire system.

Merton also points out that unanticipated consequences are inherent in social action. Decisions and action oriented toward the future are functions of the state of knowledge in the present. There is always the risk that ignorance and error, parts of an uncertain cognitive system, will have latent impacts on an organization.

The stress on net values of positive and negative consequences, and on the inevitable unanticipated consequences of action, makes the Mertonian conceptualization of function a particularly useful tool in the analysis of the impact of change on organizational structure. The consequences of external pressure for internal change may fall into any or all of the categories of Merton's typology. The differential and unanticipated impacts of technological and social change necessitate organizational flexibility.

Bureaucratic structures, however, are often inflexible when faced with a discrepancy between the organization and the demands of the larger social structure. Crozier (1964; 227) characterizes bureaucracy as a social system which is incapable of taking into account its own errors in a process of self-correction. The feedback process of *error-information-correction* does not work well. Stabilization of patterns, such as the impersonality of rules and the centralization of decision-making, tends to reinforce the structure of the enterprise even in the face of error.

When organizational structure is threatened by conditions of uncertainty in the market place, conformity and rigidity, rather than adaptation, may be the result. However, if that uncertainty intensifies into a crisis which threatens the continuation of the enterprise, some adjustment to new demands will be made.

Because of this enterprise-shaking nature of crisis Crozier argues that they are a necessary and distinctive element of bureaucratic systems. "A bureaucratic system will resist change as long as it can; it will only move when serious dysfunctions develop." (1964: 190). In Crozier's view, manifest dysfunctions are latently functional, in that it is only through response to them that systems can adapt to change.

Crozier also examines cultural aspects which influence the form of dysfunctional consequences. Although bureaucratic organization is a cross-cultural phenomenon, it does not follow a universal pattern. Dysfunctions are tied to larger cultural influences.

The American pattern of organization emphasizes the sub-unit and its rights and responsibilities in the enterprise. Specialization of sub-units is stressed. Due process assures the sub-unit's exercise of power. Centralization of power is unlikely; rather, sub-units have carefully delineated amounts of power in various situations. Crozier suggests that the lack of centralization of power may be related to American values for egalitarianism and status by achievement.

Lack of centralization may insure greater participation in decision-making, but it is also the basis for crisis. American bureaucratic dysfunctions "emerge from the innumerable conflicts that develop between different centers of decision-making." (Crozier, 1964: 234). Dysfunctions grow from disagreement concerning the ability of a sub-unit to make competent decisions for the organization. Each of the parts of an organization can be expected to preserve, and even enlarge, decision areas over which it has discretion. Crisis occurs when there is serious question concerning which part of the organization has jurisdiction and/or competence in a problem area.

II. Crisis in the Motion Picture Industry

In the American motion picture industry of the 1920's, two problem areas took on the dimensions of crises. Bureaucratic studio organization was forced, in each case, to redefine the sub-unit which had power over aspects of the finished film product. The first of these crisis areas was the introduction of sound technology into the film industry. Although sound was a technological change which seemed to promise a great market for films, it did not have unequivocally good results. The second crisis was more directly linked to the relationship between film producers and their public. The censorship issue, which was as old as the film itself, took on the dimensions of a crisis by 1922, and was not settled until 1934.

Within both these areas of "maximum uncertainty," the industry attempted to control dysfunctions by introducing new sub-units into studio organization and delegating decision-making power to them. We shall see that in each case the creation of these new decision-making units contained, rather than settled, the crisis.

III. The Introduction of Sound

A satisfactory method of adding sound to motion-pictures was sought from the earliest years of production. As early as 1914, 'vocal pictures,' which were reproductions of musical numbers with records, were exhibited. In 1921, D. W. Griffith inserted an experimental sound sequence into *Dream Street*. The problem with early experiments in sound was one of amplification.

It was possible to synchronize sound with image, but not possible to amplify the sound so that audiences in large theaters could hear it. Major studio and theater owners were aware of the large capital investment which would be necessary to perfect and install adequate amplification systems. They were unwilling to take such a large risk for what they believed would be only a fad.

Industrial mergers, however, created a situation in which a minor studio inevitably considered the introduction of sound as a survival tactic. In the twenties, major studios continued their previous practice of forming large combinations which assured their ability to control the largest number of theaters, and thus provide a secure market for their product. This practice was typified by the creation of Metro-Goldwyn-Mayer in 1924. MGM was formed from three already existing and powerful companies: Metro Pictures Corp., Goldwyn Pictures Corp., (both producing companies), and Loews, Inc., (a distribution company which owned a large proportion of the available theaters). The vertical integration of companies such as MGM insured a market for all the films it produced.

In the face of the production and marketing power of such companies, smaller production companies lost their competitive ability. By 1926, one of these smaller studios, Warner Brothers, was about to go completely out of business. That year, however, it purchased the rights to the "Vitaphone," an amplification system which had been developed by Bell Telephone. Sound was about to become a crisis for the industry.

Audience response to *The Jazz Singer* (1927) was so intensely favorable that immediate production of more sound films began. Scarcely anyone (other than Warner Bros.) was prepared for this change. Hastily finished sound scenes were added to silent films before their release, but the problem of integrating sound and film was yet to be resolved.

For the first year of the sound film, it seemed that audiences would see any film that "talked." When audience attendance dropped by 20 percent in the early part of 1929, however, film producers had to reexamine their product.

Sound had almost obliterated the techniques of the silent film. Knight has written that, "In no time at all, the techniques and artistry that directors had acquired through years of silent films were cast aside and forgotten in the shadow of the microphone. (Knight, 1957: 148) In effect, sound undermined the motion of the motion picture.

It did this for three reasons:

Camera Movement. Because the noise of the camera could be picked up by the sound system, the camera had to be encased in a large heavy soundproof box. The box completely limited the kind of shot the camera could handle. Tracking or panning shots were now impossible; the camera had to be stationary.

Editing. Editing had to be kept to a minimum because a complex series of images could not have a sound track synchronized to it. Films had very long, uninterrupted sequences which contributed to a stage-like quality.

Acting. Microphones had to be hidden on the set (in telephones, flower vases, etc.). The actors could never stray from the microphones, and often appeared rather odd as they stood speaking into a vase of flowers. Again, cinematic possibilities were lessened as actors had to be stationary.

Immediate industrial response to the sound problem only intensified the staginess of the sound film. The three important changes which were made in film production further curtailed the moving screen image until the audience, bored with the new toy, showed its displeasure through reduced attendance.

The first studio response was to set up a new, powerful sub-unit of production. The "sound experts" moved into film production, and although as "staff personnel" they were nominally less powerful than directors, who were "line" personnel they were able to impose their demands because of their special expertise. Soon, the sound engineers were actually directing, by making decisions concerning the positioning of cameras and actors. The demands of the new technology paralyzed many directors, and made it possible for technical experts, limited in their knowledge of the moving camera, to take power in the production process.

The industry's second response was to seek personnel in the theater. By 1929, the New York stage had been raided by Hollywood for both actors and directors. Plays were transferred identically onto film. The camera had regressed to being a simple recorder.

Actions which are suited to the stage must be changed if they are to be suited to film. Acting which projects in the live theater often appears over-done and stagey on the more intimate screen. Directing which concentrates on movement on the procenium stage is not easily adapted to the greater possibilities of space in the film. Often, cinematic adaptations of style were not made by imported theater personnel.

The third industrial response took the notion of the film as a filmed stage play and extended it even further. Plans were made to acquire theaters where movies could be tried out on the stage. In 1930, Paramount Pictures began buying theaters for play productions.

These theaters were expected to serve as laboratories where producers would be able to gauge audience reaction to properties before they were filmed. A director and cast would be chosen from the motion picture indus-try. If the play proved successful, they would repeat their actions in front of the camera. If not, undesirable properties could be eliminated before they were financed for the screen. The laboratory would also serve to train film personnel, and allow time for revision of properties which met with less than extravagant audience approval.

This experiment was doomed to failure. The response of a theater au-dience could not be expected to predict the response of a film audience; the composition of the audiences is socially disparate rather than similar. Also, the disparity between the forms of film and theater made it likely that a property which captured favorable audience response as a play might be a dreadful film. The experiment in laboratory theater was abandoned within two years.

These three responses to the crisis of sound had dysfunctional conse-quences for the industry's marketing problem. Films from 1927 to 1930 were more and more motionless; the effect of audience displeasure was in-tensified by the displeasure. Attendance continued to drop.

It was not until directors regained control over the finished product that the crisis of sound was solved. The latent functions of sound technol-ogy in film production became clear when some directors devised tech-niques which allowed them to supercede the demands of sound experts.

Ernst Lubitsch, in *The Love Parade* (1929) and *Monte Carlo* (1930) used silent sequences to free the camera from the confining microphone;

sound was added later by post-synchronization. Rouben Mammoulian liberated the camera from its box in *Applause* (1929). In the same film, he overcame the predominant belief that the audience would not understand sound if its source was not shown by introducing the sound flashback (previously spoken dialogue heard as a voice-over in a later scene).

It was through the work of these and other directors that the trend for sound films to become increasingly like stage plays was reversed. When audiences responded favorably to these new techniques, the ideas of sound technicians and studio bureaucrats ceased to guide film production. In the early thirties, films regained the cinematic techniques that the silent film had perfected, while adding those made possible by sound. The crisis, born by technology and fostered by the sound experts and those who saw films as filmed stage plays, was over.

IV. The Battle Over Censorship

A full-fledged movie censorship battle in the United States is a national phenomenon; a sociological convulsion. (Schumach, 1964: 4)

The sound crisis was relatively short-lived, but the problems of film censorship were born and grew up with the industry. The first censorship demands were raised by an indignant public in a response to a nickelodeon sequence depicting ''The Kiss'' from *The Widow Jones* (1896). Subsequently, political and civic organizations called repeatedly for control over the content of films.

In 1907, a *Chicago Tribune* editorial said that the nickelodeon was without a redeeming feature to warrant its existence (Ramsaye, 1926: 414). The censorship issue raised by the newspaper resulted that year in the first direct censorship legislation, when Chicago police were given the power to grant ''picture permits'' to those films which passed their review.

In 1909, the mayor of New York City closed down all motion picture theaters. The ban was lifted when the People's Institute (a bureau of social research) and the Motion Picture Patents Company (a conglomerate of the industry) agreed to form the National Board of Censorship of Motion Pictures (1909). This board agreed to exercise prior restraint on films by reviewing and cutting them before they were publicly shown. In 1914, funds from the movie industry completely replaced those of the People's Institute. The board was reconstituted as the National Board of Review, and became a rubber-stamping organization.

Civic and religious organizations which sought to control film content fought their battle politically. Laws which granted power to censor films were passed in Pennsylvania (1911), Ohio and Kansas (1913), Maryland (1916), New York (1921), and Virginia (1922). In addition, censorship bills were introduced into 36 state legislatures in 1921, and into Congress in 1915 and 1920. A lecturer demanded that motion pictures be rescued from the hands of the Devil and 500 Jews. (Schumach, 1964: 16)

The film industry sought to circumvent censorship demands by forming the National Board of Review. It was evident, however, that local organizations were becoming more powerful in their ability to alter film content. A particular threat was posed by this control. As censorship procedures were imposed just prior to consumption of the product, and differential judgemental criteria were used in different locales, the industry was losing any assurance of the form of the final product. It could no longer be sure that the film it distributed would reach the public in a uniform condition. Censorship imposed by communities would be dysfunctional for the distribution of films.

Censorship was still being circumvented by the industry. Films portrayed lurid details of divorce, adultery, and drug use, and then neatly condemned these activities in the last few hurried scenes. The ''marriage comedies'' of Cecil B. DeMille (1919–1922) are examples of how Hollywood managed to combine maximum sin and minimum retribution in its films.

Censorship reached crisis proportions in conjunction with the public reaction to a series of well-publicized scandalous incidents. Scandals concerning Pickford (1920), Reid (1921), Arbuckle (1921) and Taylor (1922), added to Hollywood's reputation as ''Sin City'', attracting much public attention and inspiring the renewed efforts of censorship groups. Schumach suggests that these scandals were much more offensive to audiences that anything contained within films. (Schumach 1964: 22) Audiences were all too willing to mistake the private activities of film stars for their film performances.

It was after the Taylor murder that the industry began to mount a serious campaign to convince the public that it was interested in self-regulation. The Motion Pictures Producers and Distributors of America, Inc. was formed, originally as a public relations group which would hear complaints from censorship interests. This group soon became known informally as the Hays Office.

Thus, when the censorship issue reached crisis proportions, the film industry responded by complicating the power structure and creating a sub-unit which would eventually come into conflict with film producers. For the next decade, the Hays Office came to have increasing power over the film product, for Will Hays did not run it as a rubber-stamping operation.

By 1926, the Hays Office had formed an advisory board with representation from each studio which was a member of the MPPDA. The following year, it completed a survey of pro-censorship groups and produced a list of 11 "don'ts" and 27 "be carefuls" for film content. By 1929, this organization had the power to advise on stories and deletions before production, and it also published a review journal, *Motion Picture Monthly*. (It is interesting to note that during these years DeMille began producing his Bible epics: there is still a maximum of sin in these, but there is also a maximum of retribution.)

There was a subtle relationship between the introduction of sound technology into film production and the increasing regulation of content during these years. Sound added a new dimension to censorable material in films—dialogue and inflection could add layers of meaning to the image. Film became a more potent transmitter of information and values, perceived as more threatening by censors.

In 1930, the Hays Office introduced the Production Code. Based on its list of "don'ts and be carefuls," the code restricted the treatment of eleven subjects, ranging from depiction of sexual activities to scenes involving cruelty to animals. The treatment of questionnable areas that the code suggested was to pave the way for a new balance of sin and retribution. Now films would show maximum retribution for what often seemed to be minimum sin.

The bureaucratic regulations which enforced the Code were completed in 1934. Enforcement was necessary in response to threats of film boycott which had been made by the Roman Catholic League of Decency. In what seemed to be a recurrent pattern of public reaction to films, these threats were precipitated by a well-publicized scandal.

At this time, the Hays Office was given complete prior restraint over film production. No distribution prints could be made until this office had granted a production code seal. Although some small studios which were not members of the MPPDA attempted to exhibit films which had not been granted a seal, they soon found public pressure intolerable.

Powdermaker, in her anthropological study of Hollywood, discusses the introduction of the Production Code:

> The real reason behind Hollywood taking on its moral "false face" is a double-edged fear: of the political power of organized religion and civic groups to get restrictive legislation passed, and of their power in the community to boycott theatres showing condemned films. (Powdermaker, 1950: 69)

Powdermaker calls the code a "false face" because she notes that it distorted the cinematic portrayl of human life by tabooing a wide range of human activities and circumstances. According to the code, one could not even show an infant with a wet diaper.

The code had complete control over film content until 1953, when *The Moon Is Blue* was released without a seal. The seal had been denied because the balance of sin and retribution seemed to favor sin. Previous films had been given a seal even though they outwitted the code through the use of symbols or subterfuge to present condemned material (for instance, the many westerns in which dance-hall girls were thinly-disguised prostitutes).

The interdependence of the film industry with the institutional and ideological demands of the larger society is exemplified by the censorship crisis. Religious and civic organizations, convinced that the content of films represented a threat to the moral order of the community, pressured the industry to limit that content.

An organized response to censorship demands could not be made while the film industry was characterized by intense rivalry and competition. When the uncertainty attached to film reception threatened to have a serious dysfunctional impact, a response to censorship demands was necessitated. During the twenties, this response could be made through the MPPDA.

A containment policy was followed with the creation of a public relations sub-unit. Gradually, this sub-unit created and enforced a set of complex requirements for control.

V. The Impact of Technological and Ideological Crisis on Organizational Change

Merton's (1967) multi-dimensional conceptualization of function presents a framework for the analysis of the impact of the sound and censorship crises in the film industry. Each of these problems affected the industry in a number of stages of intensity.

In its introductory stage, sound had a manifest functional effect on film production; box office demands rose to reflect the demands of the curious. Subsequently, the necessities of sound technology had unanticipated dysfunctions for film production, and in turn, for box office receipts. Finally, during a resolution phase, the latent consequences of new technology became evident as new technological forms were added to the cinematic repertoire.

The stages of the censorship crisis were somewhat different. There was no clear introductory phase, but rather a series of critical peaks and valleys which culminated in the creation of the Hays Office. This seemed to be a manifestly functional resolution of the crisis, but it soon had latent dysfunctional consequences for the Hollywood film.

The responses of the film industry to the crises of sound and censorship also illustrate Crozier's discussion of the function of crisis in organizational change. It was not until public pressure, in the form of declining attendance, or increased political activity, seriously threatened the reception of films, that organizational change occurred.

Each of these situations also illustrates the complications that sub-unit power struggles introduce into organizational structure. Disagreement between sound experts, producers, and directors impeded an immediate solution to the sound crisis; it was not until the early thirties that sound and cinema were integrated. The power struggle between the industry and its public resulted in the rigid codification of a regulatory sub-unit in the enterprise; the proliferation of organizational structure which the Hays Office represented proved to have dysfunctional effects on film content and image.

These particular incidents in the history of American film support Merton's discussion of the concept of function in organizational impact and also indicate the utility of Crozier's linkage of cultural with structural forms.

References

Crozier, Michel. 1964. *The Bureaucratic Phenomenon*. Chicago: University of Chicago Press.

Knight, Arthur. 1957. *The Liveliest Art*. New York: New American Library.

Merton, Robert. 1967. "Manifest and Latent Functions." Chapter III, pp. 73–136 in his *On Theoretical Sociology*, New York: The Free Press.

Powdermaker, Hortense. 1950. *Hollywood: The Dream Factory*. Boston: Little, Brown and Co.

Ramsaye, Terry. 1926. *A Million and One Nights*. New York: Simon and Schuster.

Schumach, Murray. 1964. *The Face on the Cutting Room Floor*. New York: William Morris and Co.

23

Parallels in the Social Reactions to Jazz and Rock[1]

JONATHAN KAMIN

The popularization and dilution of rhythm & blues as it became rock may be seen in part as a series of responses to societal pressures. At the same time, this historical process has many close parallels to the popularization and dilution of jazz in the form of swing. Models for understanding the development and acceptance of jazz have been developed by Morroe Berger, (1947) Neil Leonard (1960) and Richard Peterson. (1972a; 1972b). Since Leonard elaborated Berger's work, the emphasis here will be on the application of Leonard's and Peterson's models to the development of rock, with the hope that the result will shed some light on the history of rock as well as on the generality of the models. While Leonard provides a model for "the reception of esthetic novelty" in his discussion of the transition from jazz to swing, his use of the Hegelian dialectic as the main organizing principle makes it more of a descriptive than an explanatory model. However, since the parallels are so close, and since Leonard's work contains a wealth of well-organized descriptive data, I will follow his organization.

I. Traditionalist Opposition

Leonard begins his argument with a summary of the historical basis of support for, and opposition to, traditional academic music. Opposition to jazz, he found, went hand in hand with support for traditional academic music and "traditional values."

> Upheld chiefly by Protestant, middle-class Americans of Anglo-Saxon ancestry, traditional values demanded among other things belief in moral and metaphysical idealism, confidence in the individual's capacity for self-directed growth toward intelligence and high purpose, and faith in

the progress of civilization. For some time traditionalists were becoming increasingly alarmed at the threats to their values posed by relative norms that were fast making inroads into American society. After the [World War I] Armistice, traditionalists were fully aroused for a militant counter-attack on what they saw as a rising tide of degeneration. Many of them regarded jazz, along with intemperance and unconventional sexual behav-ior, as a sign or a cause of the advancing degeneration and assailed the new music as a major vice. (Leonard, 1960: 30).

There are both similarities and differences in the setting into which rock 'n' roll was to thrust itself. Rock 'n' roll also appeared in a period of postwar reaction—1953–56 were the years immediately following the Ko-rean war. The ascendancy of traditional values might be symbolized by the presence of General Eisenhower in the White House in the years 1953–60. However, as in the twenties, there were also major currents of social change beneath the surface.

Part of the reason for the public's unreadiness was the historical uniqueness of rock 'n' roll as a social phenomenon. Tom Wolfe points out,

> Practically every style in art history is the result of the same thing— a lot of attention to form, plus the money to make monuments to it . . . But throughout history, everywhere this kind of thing took place; China, Egypt, France under the Bourbons, everyplace; it has been something the aristocracy has been responsible for. What has happened in the United States since World War II, however, has broken that pattern. The war created money. It made massive infusions of money into every level of society. Suddenly classes of people whose styles of life had been practi-cally invisible had the money to build monuments to their own styles. (Wolfe, 1965: xiv)

Rock 'n' roll was one such "monument" to previously invisible lifestyles. That cultured observers should have failed to accord rock 'n' roll the atten-tion its importance deserved should not be surprising, however. Such peo-ple, by virtue of their training and habits of thought, are inclined to look elsewhere to "an ancient, aristocratic esthetic" for innovations. As we shall see, such attitudes helped to slow down the acceptance of rock 'n' roll. Among the groups which acquired money after World War II, if not for the first time, were working-class Negroes.

Also among those acquiring new wealth were working- and middle-class teenagers, for whom the postwar prosperity brought larger allowances, as well as increased opportunities for part-time and summer jobs. Teenagers also were a larger proportion of the population than at any other time in the twentieth century.

This generation, unlike its parents, had never known anything but prosperity. Thus there developed, for the first time in the early fifties, a large group of relatively economically secure young people with money to spend but with no clear sense of direction or identity. This group was clearly different from the older, more established pop music audience. Furthermore, being young, they simply had not heard as much music as their elders, and were therefore in a better position than their elders to absorb a new music, since they had fewer preconceptions as to how music ought to sound. Moreover, the young had always been a dancing audience, and while the swing of the thirties had degenerated into the bland pop of the fifties, the new jazz that developed from the same source was much too musically advanced to win a mass audience. Thus, there was also a demand for an exciting, danceable music.

While the effects of wartime changes in the status of many groups parallel the events following World War I, as does the loosening of morals that accompanies war, there are additional facts to be considered. Most importantly, at the time of the advent of rock 'n' roll, the changes the traditionalists were resisting after World War I had already occurred. Thus the barriers which rock 'n' roll would have to cross were much lower than those which jazz faced. In addition, on the purely musical level, jazz, at least in its diluted forms as swing and Dixieland, were already part of the cultural vocabulary of most whites, who thus would probably find borrowings from black music less unfamiliar than their ancestors did when jazz first appeared.

In addition to those whose opposition to jazz stemmed from a fear that its acceptance would accelerate the erosion of traditional values, Leonard notes that two other groups also opposed jazz: those who had commitments to traditional academic music either for esthetic or for economic reasons. (Leonard, 1960: 31; also see Stearns, 1970). In the case of rock 'n' roll, the opposition from these quarters was somewhat weaker. They had already fought and lost a battle to prevent the acceptance of jazz, but had nonetheless survived. Accordingly, we find fewer well-known composers and conductors among the ranks of the opponents of rock 'n' roll than there were among those opposed to jazz. Among music educators, dance teachers, and their ilk, however, opposition was much more pronounced and vocal, as the music posed a more immediate threat to the control of the sensibilities of their charges.

Given the changes in American society and American taste, however, there were two other groups involved in the opposition to the new sound. These groups comprised those with either esthetic or economic commitments to what was by then traditional popular music.

Ironically, among the musical traditionalists by this time were many members of the newly respectable jazz community. Jazz musicians had only recently won the right to describe themselves publicly as artists. Thus along with the guardians of public manners and morals, rock 'n' roll faced the opposition of not one, but three musical establishments. We will deal with each of these groups in turn.

Guardians of Public Manners and Morals

Leonard gives an excellent summary of the background behind the arguments raised against jazz by guardians of public manners and morals. These arguments seem to be, in sum, that jazz is sensual rather than spiritual, and consequently is a cause or consequence of the downfall of our society. This argument was augmented by open or thinly-veiled racist arguments based on assumptions that other races were inferior to the white race and that maintenance of white civilization required racial purity. Consequently, jazz, a music of black people, was a corrupting influence in civilization. Furthermore, its appeal to the young was an additional cause for alarm, since they would lack the necessary defenses to protect themselves from its influence.

Similar arguments, in a somewhat attenuated form, were made against rock 'n' roll (or at least against what the moralists thought was rock 'n' roll—they were not, on the whole, very discriminating). While the arguments to the effect that music ought to have purpose in the life of the soul were missing, there were many complaints about the sensuality of the music, the vulgarity of the lyrics, and the appeal to the baser emotions. In general, the music itself was, like jazz, unequivocally condemned for its primitiveness and sensuality, and was suspected of returning us to barbarism and savagery. The dancing which accompanied the music was also thought to provide sure evidence of the degenerative trend.

The most common target of moralist invective was the lyrics to the songs. The open sexuality common to rhythm & blues lyrics disturbed many white critics, especially in view of the youth of the audience. In many cities, the police power was invoked to halt the spread of rock 'n' roll. This was, however, more often aimed at the behavior of the audiences than the songs themselves. (*Time*, 1956)

Since the attack on moral grounds failed to eliminate completely the perceived threat, other tactics were used. As with jazz, there were frequent pronouncements that the music was dying. An editorial in 1957 in *Musical America* described rock 'n' roll as a "passing fad." Paul Cunningham, president of ASCAP, reported after a European tour that rock 'n' roll was not popular there and was dying in the U.S. The entertainment trade journal *Variety* was among the most active and vocal opponents of rock 'n' roll; it used all these approaches, citing every possible piece of evidence that rock 'n' roll was immoral, ludicrous, or dying.

Ridicule was another approach, as it had been with jazz. (In the 1920s, the *New York Times* ran articles such as "Jazz Frightens Bears" and "Cornetist to Queen Victoria Drops Dead on Hearing Coney Island Jazz Band.") Many publications quoted disk jockeys who shared their point of view. *Variety* headlines were especially exaggerated; "Baptist Minister's Sermon vs Elvis; He'll Hit the Skids," was the headline of a story about a sermon in which Rev. Edward J. Hales described Presley's music as a reflection of troubled times, and suggested that, as with so many things, his popularity would eventually fade. (*Variety*, 1956: 1)

Those Dependent Upon Popular Music

Probably the most outspoken critics of the new music, however, were those most directly threatened by it. Disk jockeys, composers, recording artists, and record company executives involved in the older style of popular music spoke out strongly against rock 'n' roll, using all the approaches indicated above. This should not surprise us. The sociology of knowledge tells us that a person's ideas and beliefs reflect his social background. We should not be at all surprised if his tastes behaved the same way. (Johnstone and Katz, 1957; Schuessler, 1948). Still less should we be surprised if a man who makes his living by virtue of his tastes rejects styles which do not conform to his canons of taste.

Thus, from the moralist standpoint, we find such sentiments as, "All rhythm & blues records are dirty and as bad for kids as dope," voiced by West Coast disk jockey, Peter Potter, or the following from Frank Sinatra:

> Rock 'n' roll music smells phony and false. It is sung, played and written for the most part by cretinous goons and by means of its almost imbecilic reiteration and sly, lewd, in plain fact, dirty lyrics . . . it manages to be the martial music of every sideburned delinquent on the face of the earth. (*Time*, 1957: 48)

Concerning musical characteristics, there were statements from Abel Green, editor of *Variety*, that "the 'style' includes a broken voice treatment not unlike an uncouth burp or an impolite clearing of the throat," and from composer Richard Rodgers, "I like Presley—he makes me sound better." (*Variety*, 1955a: 51)

Those Dependent Upon Jazz

Thus rock 'n' roll received criticism from many of the same quarters that saw in jazz a threat to traditional culture thirty-five years earlier. In addition, however, this time there was also a great outcry in the jazz world. Jazz had only recently become respectable as "America's only native art form," and people in the jazz world were guarding their new-found respectability jealously. Great pains were taken to differentiate jazz from rock 'n' roll and to disclaim any relationship. In the jazz press as elsewhere, there were many articles linking rock 'n' roll to juvenile delinquency and gloatingly describing riots at rock 'n' roll concerts, as if anything discrediting rock would redound favorably to jazz. Underlying this tendency, I suspect, were fears not only that the now-good name of jazz might be besmirched, but also that jazz would lose some of its audience to the new music. (That actually happened in the long run, but only after extensive changes in both types of music, changes that made jazz more intellectually and emotionally difficult and rock more sophisticated.)

Strategies of Opposition

When rock 'n' roll failed to disappear after these attacks, both the moralists and the marketers combined forces and adopted two strategies that, as Richard Peterson (1972: a) points out, had been used thirty years earlier in the war against jazz. The first was a policy of containment, which was not pursued as actively as it was in the case of jazz. It was argued that rock 'n' roll's sort of lyric was acceptable in its place, i.e., juke boxes in late-night spots and in the Negro community, but that it didn't belong in the mainstream. In many cases, radio stations, prodded by local pressure from newspaper columnists and religious organizations, set up their own censorship boards to screen the offending lyrics. (See Variety 1955b; 1955c)

The dominant feeling among disk jockeys and pop music people in general seems to have been that rhythm & blues was "crude" and "in bad taste," sentiments that had also been expressed thirty years earlier about jazz. (Variety 1955a) Disk jockey Bill Randle correctly predicted that the ultimate acceptance of rhythm & blues would come through a watering-down with pop elements, with the eventual absorption of enough r&b to be a new pop style, leaving the "crudity" to the black specialty market, where, presumably, it belonged. He saw pop "cover" versions of r&b songs as a way of taking what was viable in r&b but eliminating the crudeness. (Variety, 1954; Kamin, 1973; Denisoff, 1974).

Defense of Rock 'n' Roll

Unlike jazz, however, rock 'n' roll had many defenders. Although few besides disk jockey Alan Freed went so far as to praise the music, many pleaded at least for tolerance and felt that the campaign against the music was misguided and unnecessary. Not surprisingly, many of those were within the jazz community. Remembering their own struggles for acceptance, they were unhappy to see another group of musicians suffering the same fate. Benny Goodman and Sammy Kaye, along with Freed, called on parents to remember their own teenage years and the public reaction to their own musical idols.

There were defenders in the trade press as well. *Cashbox* argued that the smut was in the ears of the critics, and *Billboard* consistently ran articles and editorials congratulating r&b performers for their successes and criticizing as rigid and backward the disk jockeys who fought the trend.

Al Jarvis, a Hollywood disk jockey who played r&b, agreed, noting that " . . . youngsters have taken to rhythm and blues in much the same manner that the youngsters of a generation ago took to swing, the Lindy hop, and swooning to Frank Sinatra." He also argued that what was obscene was not the music but the adult concept of the teenager. Jarvis found it not only presumptuous but financially unrewarding to try to dictate taste to the public, noting presciently that no one sound had to appeal to everybody. (Billboard, 1955)

Adaptations in the Music

The direct consequence of all the moral and social pressure was a change in the character of the music that reached the audience, as it had been with jazz. Since so many of the rhythm & blues records had been banned by local authorities or radio stations, the pop cover versions had the field to themselves for a period of time, along with a series of "teenage" pop songs. In a short time, however, many of the r&b labels learned to produce a product that was more acceptable to the authorities and had considerable success in the pop field. At the same time, many young whites began to perform the music, not only avoiding at least the racial aspects of the moral opposition, but also performing in a style more acceptable to white audiences.

By the time these changes had taken place, the controversy had, to all intents and purposes, died down. By 1958, both factions had moderated their voices, and rock and roll music was accepted as a harmless, if irritating, fixture of the teen scene. We should note that rock and roll of 1958 was not the same music as rhythm & blues of 1954 or rock 'n' roll of 1956. Most of the features of the originally offensive music had been eliminated in stylistic changes that paralleled the name changes, a process that will be discussed in the next section. It is worth noting that similar changes occurred in jazz, even to the change of name, from "jazz" to "experiments in modern music" à la Paul Whiteman, to "swing," and that the significance of the changes was the same.

In Leonard's terms, these phases can be fitted into a Hegelian dialectic. First, an esthetic innovation (rhythm & blues) appears, which is supported by modernists and opposed by traditionalists. Eventually, some people from the modernist camp blend elements of traditional music with the new innovation (rock 'n' roll). This paves the way for people from the traditionalist camp to form a more moderate synthesis (rock and roll) which is generally accepted, and there is a falling away of both extremes.

It is important to consider two other factors. First, the various stages form an acculturative continuum (Gray, 1961), not only for the music but for the audiences. Thus, at the beginning, rhythm & blues was a black music for black audiences. As elements of the white audience became interested in it, it was modified to suit their tastes. Those who first took an interest might well be modernists in Leonard's terms. As this happened, it became acceptable to the more adventurous in a less avant-garde group. Each stage reaches a larger audience through the same process. But each larger audience has less awareness of, or commitment to, the original innovation than the previous one, and so will accept the more diluted form. Learning takes energy. If a new product is blended with the familiar, less learning is necessary and more people can accept it.

Second, as I suggested above, a principal factor in the changes was pressure from the music industry, motivated by economic considerations. Rhythm & blues was a product the major record companies couldn't control; it had unpredictable performers and markets. A major impetus for the changes was the industry's aim of reaching the widest possible audience with the most controllable product. To achieve this aim, the industry purged the music of both its offensive and its most foreign elements. Thus, it changed the lyrics. However, another important element that was lost in translation was the rhythmic organization that had made the original r&b so exciting. The only elements that passed into white culture were those which were not offensive, not too hard to duplicate, and not too foreign to white cultural preconceptions. In a sense, only surface elements of r&b got through. The real innovation was never accepted. This will be expanded in the next section.

Summary and Conclusions

To summarize the parallels with jazz: the moralist objections to jazz were fourfold—the music provokes man's lower nature, infects the minds of children, leads to race-mixing, and is associated with sex, dope and alcohol. These objections were also raised against rhythm & blues when it first appeared in the pop market. However, in keeping with the changing times, many observers viewed its effect as a spur to racial integration positively rather than negatively.

The esthetic objections to jazz took two forms. First, there were objections to the musicians themselves: they did not come from the idealist tradition prized by traditionalists, they were not properly trained, and their music detracted from interest in proper musical style. These lines of argument were uncommon with r&b and rock 'n' roll. Apparently after all the years of jazz, nobody expected them to be properly trained. The only ones who seemed to be possessed by fears of this type were music teachers, who did fear the influence of the new music on the development of their students.

The second form of esthetic objection was to the music itself. Besides the usual complaints about lyrics, jazz was offensive to traditional ears because it contained improvisation, because it was not restrained, and because it contained weird noises thought not proper to music. Rhythm & blues, also a black music, contained some of the same elements from the same sources. Given the constant vocal reference in black instrumental music, the use of sounds thought not proper to an instrument was quite common. There was some improvisation in r&b. But jazz was touted by some critics as America's only true native art form and improvisation was considered one of its saving graces. A by-product of jazz becoming an art form, however, was that it no longer fulfilled its former social functions in the black community. Where early jazz and blues could be a blood ritual in the black community, (Jones, 1963; Keil, 1966) and later jazz could still fulfill those functions simultaneously serving as pop music for the mass audience and art for the avant-garde, after the bop revolution, jazz lost its following in the black community as a whole and maintained virtually no popular following, becoming an art form for the avant-garde intellectuals and hipsters of both races. (Peterson, 1972b: 145)

In that context, rhythm & blues could be seen as embodying the social functions that jazz had in the black community before it became "art." Since those elements in jazz which were offensive to traditional whites fulfilled esthetic and social needs in the black lower-class community, (Keil, 1966), a new place had to be found for them. That place was rhythm & blues, which functioned as a dance music, as personal expression, and as a stylistic form for elements of black musical culture no longer fully acceptable in jazz. Thus, at least some of the opposition to rhythm & blues and rock 'n' roll was similar to that of jazz. Many differences can be accounted for by the amount of musical acculturation that occurred between 1920 and 1954. It is worth noting that many elements which did not cross over with jazz or rock 'n' roll have finally crept into rock in the late sixties. However, as of 1974 there still seem to be very few white musicians in rock and related fields, and still fewer bands, who have learned to think like blacks from a rhythmic point of view, while many blacks who do not use black rhythmic organization create pop hits using all the elements that did cross over.

Finally, the tactics that were used to contain the "menace" were similar. The first attack consisted of ignoring the music publicly, calling it a dying fad, and trying to ban it. All of these were also used against rhythm & blues and rock 'n' roll. When these attacks failed, policies of containment and musical compromise were pursued successfully in both cases. The fact that jazz had cracked the concert hall barrier by 1938, however, made it harder to contain rock in the long run, even though many municipalities have recently banned rock festivals.

What Leonard does not mention specifically is that underlying the foofaraw about jazz was the fact that a previously submerged ethnic subculture was emerging into public visibility, possessing different esthetic standards at a time when cultural relativism was not yet fashionable among the powers that be and esthetics were assumed to be ruled by natural laws. (Meyer, 1967: 146–149) The popularization of rhythm & blues represented something similar, but changes both in the social-political climate and in the distribution of wealth considerably weakened the opposition, although it took a similar stance.

II. Acceptance of Rock 'n' Roll in the Fifties

As Leonard points out, there were connections between the social and moral values and the musical attitudes of both those who opposed and those who accepted jazz. This is also true of early rock 'n' roll music. As with jazz, those who accepted rock 'n' roll often rejected traditional standards. The single most important group of those who accepted jazz, in terms of sheer numbers, were "adolescents revolting against convention." It has also been argued that jazz appeals to those with an adolescent psychology, those "seeking liberation and individuality." (Esman, 1951: 225). Just as after World War I, a widespread breakdown in traditional standards of behavior and a change in the distribution of wealth led many adolescents to reject the behavioral standards of their parents. This situation helped to create an appealfor rock 'n' roll after World War II just as it had for jazz after World War I.

First and most obviously, rock 'n' roll served as a weapon in the generational war. It has been said that one reason for the music's great popularity among teenagers was that parents could neither stand nor understand it. If this is true, it is also true that the youth of the fifties differed from their parents in less superficial ways than other generations. As we have noted, World War II pumped vast quantities of money into all segments of the American population. The youth of the fifties were the first generation to grow up in relative affluence. Their parents, on the other hand, were the survivors of the Great Depression, an experience which impressed an entire generation with the importance of acquiring material wealth and the security and respectability it brings, a concern which their children on generous allowances could not be expected to share.

The wealth brought about by World War II had similar consequences for the lower classes. Many of the newly prosperous were from unassimilated ethnic groups, which did not share the dominant WASP standards to any great degree. Many were also black, and with the burgeoning race pride engendered by the freedom rides, the sit-ins, and the African independence movement, they were anxious to support their own music. At the same time, the Beat movement brought to a head discontents within some segments of the WASP-oriented bourgeoisie itself. What happened, in sum, was that these groups in the population had become prosperous enough to have their own music made publicly available for the first time.

The newness of this phenomenon was more apparent than real. Groups with other standards had previously existed in the population. Not having access to the channels of mass communication, however, they remained largely submerged and invisible on the cultural level. Moreover, as Leonard demonstrates, part of the significance of jazz was that it was just such a breakthrough from a submerged culture. But in the form in which it received general acceptance, jazz was already quite far from the subculture which gave it birth. In the fifties, though, at least some of these previously submerged groups had access to the media in a way they never had before. Significant changes in the music business had helped to bring about these new conditions. These changes included the formation of BMI (Jablonski, 1961: 343–349; Spaeth, 1948: 526–527), which decentralized music publishing; the parallel decentralization of the record industry (Gillett, 1970: 7–8; Charters, 1959: 232–234), and the rise of television, whose effects are discussed below.

The result of these changes was that a vast new body of music was available to those who would seek it out. Louis Armstrong noted that in the 1920s: "the people who liked jazz bands best and followed them, were the people who didn't know much about the older music, mostly the young people in the high schools and colleges." (Armstrong, 1936: 76) A similar phenomenon occurred during the swing era when songs were made popular primarily through late-night broadcasts by dance bands. "The people who 'made' the hits were the older teenagers and young couples in their early twenties who went dancing where these bands played—and bought their records." (Wilson, 1956: 28)

The first significant, large-scale crossover of r&b into the pop market, however, occurred in the summer of 1954, in the form of "beach records" for dancing at beach parties. The phenomenon was at first restricted to the South, where, as Jerry Wexler points out, black and white cultures are closer than elsewhere. Given the availability of the music, many high school and college-age youth began listening to black radio stations. Parents tended to disapprove, but when this occurred in college and prep school dorm rooms, little could be done.

As the music was picked up by whites in other parts of the country, it was generally the most rebellious and unconventional youth who were the first to adopt it. Thus, the apparent correlation between rock 'n' roll and juvenile delinquency may not be entirely specious, although it seems as if the music functioned more as a symbol of rebelliousness than a cause.

Among the young whites of an earlier era who had supported jazz were the Bohemian intellectuals, including the young white musicians, who were the most rebellious of all. Given the notoriety of jazz it would appear that one would have had to be committed to alternate values to take it seriously. Moreover, as Peterson points out, the campaign against jazz virtually forced a deviant life style on jazz musicians by cutting off all access to social respectability. (Peterson, 1972: 239–240) But the same did not seem to be true with early rock 'n' roll or rhythm & blues. As noted, rhythm & blues was an integral part of lower and working class black culture, as jazz had been a half century earlier. Its practitioners were members of the community and fulfilled a known social role. (Keil, 1966).

There were very few white performers of the music in the early days, and when they did come along, they tended to be teenagers themselves. However, they seemed to come from the juvenile delinquency end of the working-class culture. Such Bohemians and intellectuals as were concerned with this sort of thing still seemed to be very much committed to jazz. Indeed, this might be one reason why rhythm & blues, and later rock 'n' roll, were so much more popular with the young than jazz in the fifties. Jazz had become an adult art music and thus was no longer an effective means of expressing adolescent rebelliousness.

As the crossover trend that began in the South with beach records gathered steam, new sources of support appeared, especially within the music industry. Many pop disk jockeys began to program rhythm & blues on their pop radio shows. The new listeners they attracted were primarily young and, as with early jazz, most were not as committed to the music as the hard core of avid enthusiasts and not as likely to distinguish between the real r&b or rock 'n' roll and its commercial imitations.

III. The Breakthrough of Commercial Rock and Roll:
Shifts Toward Traditional Standards

Leonard notes that in the twenties, as jazz gained some general acceptance in spite of opposition, the jazz which was most common was "commercial jazz" rather than the real thing. This came in two varieties, "refined jazz," which usually was a form of traditional music with jazz elements added, and "nut jazz," which made use of the most extreme elements of jazz style but burlesqued them.

Similar phenomena occurred as rhythm & blues broke into the pop market as rock 'n' roll. As previously noted, for a period of time cover versions of rhythm & blues songs received the most attention in the pop market. One variety of covers, made by Coral and to some extent by Mercury Records, seems to present a close parallel with refined jazz. The arrangements were characteristically pop arrangements using a swing band sound and using only enough elements of the original rhythm & blues to identify the song.

Moreover many of the first r&b records to cross over in their original versions were closely akin to what Leonard terms "nut jazz." As disk jockey Joe Bostic noted, "strange singing groups" were the principal means by which r&b reached the pop audience. (*Variety*, 1955a).

The second type of pop cover record, exemplified by those made by Dot Records, also has a parallel in swing of the thirties. These were note-for-note copies of hits by black groups with slight changes in style. Benny Goodman's version of Fletcher Henderson's "Don't Be That Way" is an example from the earlier period. Unlike the records made by swing musicians, however, the cover records by companies like Dot preserved little of the character of the music. While they used *all* the separable elements of the rhythm & blues arrangements they copied, they generally had none of the spirit of rhythm & blues. The hierarchical rhythmic structure, which generated so much of that spirit, was lost in the analytic process.

A more exact parallel with the swing popularization, that is, of applying traditional devices to a basically jazz concept, is what Gillett calls "uptown rhythm & blues," the style that was developed by the r&b record companies after it was clear that r&b would sell in the pop market if it were not so outrageous as to provoke the censors. They tended to stick close to pop song forms and lyrics, to keep their lead singers from using extreme gospel styles, and to use complete string sections as part of their backup orchestras.

Two other changes which affected the spread of both jazz and rock 'n' roll were changes in technology and concomitant changes in the economic structure of the music industry. In the case of jazz, the use of the music on the radio and in films led to explicit requests that the music be restructured to suit the tastes of mass audiences. Among other things this pressure led to the use of larger ensembles, the substitution of popular songs for blues and other songs of black origin, and fuller, more carefully worked out arrangements. These changes, in effect, made possible the swing era. (Leonard, 1960: 90–107) In the transition from rhythm & blues, the major technological change involved was the advent of television. Its effects were indirect. By 1958, television had virtually taken over the mass audience from radio. In order to fill the void left by the demise of the mass-audience radio programs, stations began to program for specialized audiences. This gave rhythm & blues a widespread radio outlet and led to the development of black-oriented radio stations.

The other important technological change was the development of the 45 rpm plastic record, which could be manufactured much more cheaply than the old shellac 78s, yet sold at the same price. This made economically feasible the growth of the independent record companies, which were prepared to meet the demand for material suitable for specialty programing. (Peterson and Berger, 1972).

IV. The Beginnings of General Acceptance

There was a general growth in the popularity of the various styles of music known as rock and roll throughout the fifties, although at different rates in different regions and social groups. This process was fostered equally by the major record companies and the independents, because new styles of songs had to be found once the novelty tunes were exhausted and because a style had to be developed which would please the teenagers who wanted "the beat," yet not offend parents and radio station managers. (Gillett, 1970; Hirsch, 1969).

In order to keep the product flowing, the industry turned not only to new sources of songs but to new types of singers, who would be more amenable to studio direction. Among the sources of new singers were the ranks of as-yet-unknown crooners and country singers, who could be persuaded to change their style and sing "rock and roll' material. Other singers were drawn from film and television. These singers had little connection with r&b or even with rock 'n' roll, and generally did what they were told by their producers. (Gillett, 1970)

While these changes had helped to spread the popularity of rock and roll (a somewhat less wild name for a somewhat less wild product), a major breakthrough came in 1962 with the twist. This dance was adopted by the international "jet set," who, by patronizing the discotheques where the twist flourished, helped to make both the dance and the nightclubs fashionable. Thus, it was the first form of rock and roll to be given a social cachet. The dance was widely taught by dance instructors and became quite acceptable to the suburban middle class, although not without an initial flurry of controversy.

In the years following the twist, a number of changes took place in the music and in the performers, changes which had profound effects on the reaction of the public. While many people, performers and otherwise, were involved in these changes, they may be aptly symbolized by the work of the Beatles and Bob Dylan.

There were many things about the work of these artists that were different from previous rock and roll, and these differences were symbolized by a new name, rock. Since both were of the generation that grew up on rock 'n' roll and its heirs, they could assume their audience's familiarity with its basic material, and thus were in a position to achieve a much greater degree of complexity in their work than had previously been the norm.

This change made it possible for critics to begin to take the music seriously. It was not long before articles began to appear noting "echoes of Renaissance harmonies" in the works of the Beatles, while others hailed Dylan as the "folk poet for a new age." (Eisen, 1969)

The fact that the Beatles, as well as a number of other groups involved in the new development, were British was also a factor in the spread of general acceptance. Americans, especially those committed to traditional standards, have always been suspicious of their own popular culture. Acceptance by Europeans is one means by which it can become respectable. If one of our forms of popular culture has received attention in Europe, then American traditionalists can safely pay attention to it without fearing loss of status. As Leonard (1960: 133–52) notes, the attention of European classical musicians and critics helped to pave the way for critical acceptance of jazz in America and to break the "concert hall barrier" that had been erected in the 1920s. Something similar may have happened through the British acceptance of rock (see Peterson, 1972b).

V. Rock as "Fine Art": Parallels Between Rock and Bop

Both musically and socially there are many parallels between the development of rock from its predecessors and the development of bop in jazz. These parallels seem to be the result of internal dynamics in the development of the respective styles and undoubtedly had some effect on the type of acceptance the music was accorded. Bop and rock represented mu-

sic made by a second generation in their respective traditions. Each was
made by people who had grown up on its ancestors and consequently had
achieved a relatively high degree of internalized redundancy. Thus, they
were able to create compositions and performances that were considerably
longer and more complex, rhythmically, harmonically and melodically, and
in the case of rock, lyrically, than earlier examples. Groups such as Cream,
the Jimi Hendrix Experience, and the Grateful Dead evolved extended im-
provisational structures. Albums became "concepts" instead of collections
of singles, epitomized by the Beatles' *Sergeant Pepper's Lonely Hearts
Club Band*. As rock composers gained self-confidence, they learned to use
complex orchestral textures for something other than a "class" sound, bor-
rowing compositional techniques from classical music and coloristic devices
from almost everywhere. Lyrics attempted to embody transcendent experiences, political and emotional realities, and drug trips, instead of teenage
romance and fast cars.

These musical changes had three important social consequences. First,
since the results made sense in terms of traditional artistic canons, it became possible for critics to take the music seriously. (It is no accident that
it was with the advent of bop that the cry was heard that "jazz is America's
only true native art form.") While the early ancestors of rock might have
been acceptable as folk art, and the later developments were dismissed as
kitsch, there was an extent to which both rock and bop could be considered
"fine art." Of course this implies that the music is acceptable only in so far
as it conforms to traditional canons of structure and style which are fairly
far from the original intent of the music.

This leads to our second consequence. While a generation may have
grown up which could accept the more complex products of second-
generation musicians, there is no reason to believe that the masses would
be able to do so. (The fact that the Beatles lost their youngest audience by
their middle period is evidence.) Thus, a void was left in the mass market,
which the new products were too complex to fill. The development of bop,
therefore, left the way clear for both the development of rhythm & blues as
a separate genre and also for traditional pop, both of which filled the void
left by the demise of swing. The complexity of rock led to the conscious
creation by the music industry of "bubblegum music," a simple pop-
oriented rock and roll aimed primarily at pre-teen-age whites.

The third consequence was a change in the behavior of the performers.
They began to conceptualize their role differently. Traditional black jazz
musicians had tended to see themselves as craftsmen who made a living
from their craft. They had an established place in the community. White
musicians, on the other hand, had to drop out of their social community to
play jazz, and developed for themselves the role of the Bohemian artist. By

the fifties, serious jazz musicians, both white and black, tended to conceive of themselves as artists with all the rights and privileges pertaining to that role. They began to dress like Bohemian intellectuals, were known to eschew the entertainers' postures that had been associated with jazz, and to declare, "I don't care if you listen to my music or not," sometimes playing with their backs to the audience and refusing to acknowledge applause.

Rock, since it was by the middle sixties largely a white music, did not have to surmount the same racial barriers. It was rare that rock performers attempted to appeal on the basis of dignity, although the New York Rock and Roll Ensemble was a notable exception. Generally, rock performers felt free to engage in wild stage antics and elaborate settings to insure access to mass audiences even while increasing the complexity of their music. While the newer rock may have lost the youngest element of the audience, it has maintained its hold on those slightly older by appealing to the sophistication they had acquired through extended television viewing, thereby insuring attendance at concerts almost in spite of the music.

A model that seems adequate to comprehend the changes is provided by Peterson. (1972b). The process begins with three factors. The first is the exhaustion of a style. This sets the stage musically for the emergence of a new style. A second is the social ferment of the time. The third is the breakdown of oligopolistic control of the music industry. In the post-World War I era, this was brought on by the popularization of the 78 rpm phonograph record and the radio. The pertinent changes in the post-World War II era have already been discussed. These are preconditions necessary for the birth of a "vital fad" involving a fusion of folk and pop elements. The fad ended when the conditions changed; the possibilities of the original musical innovation had been explored, the social ferment subsided, and the music industry was reoligopolized.

Once these things happened, the mass popular interest in the original jazz died out. Jazz survived only in specialized locales and in a very attenuated form as swing, a form of popular music. As this started to fade, it gave birth to two new directions, revivalism and the "vital cult," a new creative movement, in this case bop, resembling other fine art media in its ideology, institutional underpinnings and audience response.

Applying this model to rock, it is easy to see rock 'n' roll as a vital fad, rock and roll as a popular music similar to swing, and rock as an equivalent to the vital cult of bop in some respects. More specifically, there are parallels between the bop scene of the forties and the San Francisco psychedelic scene of the sixties, which nurtured some of the most creative trends in rock. The new emphasis on soloists and virtuosity and the rise of the rock critic are other fine-art characteristics that have emerged, along with serious academic consideration of the medium.

VI. Summary and Conclusion

Leonard has presented a model for the reception of esthetic novelty. Specifically, he has developed a social process model for the acceptance of jazz, showing the sources of social opposition and social support for the esthetic innovation it represented, as well as the modifications resulting from the social conflict surrounding the innovation.

Peterson has developed a process model for the esthetic stages in the development of jazz. These two models are complementary: the esthetic phases outlined by Peterson are, at least in part, the results of the social pressures outlined by Leonard.

I have attempted to give some indication of the generality of these models by demonstrating their application to the evolution of rock from roots in rhythm and blues, as well as to jazz. The commonalities suggest that the models have application beyond jazz. However, jazz and rhythm and blues are similar social phenomena in that they are both folk-oriented musical traditions originating in black American culture. The fact that they both come from the sub-culture of an oppressed minority striving for recognition may have a great deal to do with the social responses to the music and the responses to social pressure on the part of musicians and fans. Further applications of these models to "esthetic novelties" stemming from other social sources would be necessary to verify this hypothesis.

Notes

1. Grateful acknowledgement is made to David O. Arnold, who assisted in the preparation of an earlier draft of this paper and made many helpful suggestions. Thanks are also due to Barbara Fittery and Cheryl Maynard, who assisted in the preparation of the manuscript. Reprinted with permission of the publisher, *Journal of Jazz Studies* (vol. 2, no. 1, December 1974).

References

Armstrong, Louis. 1936. *Swing That Music*. New York: Longmans, Green.

Berger, Morroe. 1947. "Jazz: Resistance to the Diffusion of a Culture Pattern," *Journal of Negro History* 33 (Oct.): 461–494.

Billboard 1955. "If They Want Want R&B, Play It." (Jan 29):58, 69.

Charters, Samuel B. 1958. *The Country Blues*. New York: Rinehart.

Denisoff, R. Serge. 1974. "The Vinyl Crap Game: The Pop Record Industry," *Journal of Jazz Studies* 1, no. 2 (June): 3–26.

Eisen, Janathan, ed. 1969. *The Age of Rock*. New York: Random House.

Esman, Aaron H. 1951. "Jazz—A Study in Cultural Conflict," *American Imago* 8: 225.

Gillett, Charles. 1970. *The Sound of the City*. New York: Outerbridge and Dienstfrey.

Gray, Ed. 1961. "An Acculturative Continuum for Negro Folk Song in the U.S.," *Ethnomusicology* 5, no. 1: 10–15.

Hirsch, Paul. 1969. *The Structure of the Popular Music Industry*. Ann Arbor: Institute for Social Research, U. of Michigan.

Jablonski, Edward. 1961. "Supplement:" Pp. 343–344 in Isaac Goldberg, *Tin Pan Alley: A Chronicle of American Popular Music*. New York: Unger.

Johnstone, John & Elihu Katz. 1957. "Youth and Popular Music: A Study in the Sociology of Taste," *American Journal of Sociology* 62 (May): 563–568.

Jones, LeRoi. 1963. *Blues People*. New York: Morrow.

Kamin, Jonathan. 1973. "Taking the Roll Out of Rock "n" Roll: Reverse Acculturation," *Popular Music and Society* 2, no. 1 (Fall): 1–14.

Keil, Charles. 1966. *Urban Blues*. Chicago: U. of Chicago Press.

Leonard, Neil. 1960. *Jazz and the White Americans*. Chicago: U. of Chicago Press.

Meyer, Leonard. 1967. *Music, the Arts and Ideas*. Chicago: U. of Chicago Press.

Musical America. 1957. "Passing Fad." (March): 4

Peterson, Richard A. 1972a. "Market and Moralist Censors of a Black Art Form: Jazz." Pp. 236–245 in R. Serge Denisoff and Richard A. Peterson (eds.), *The Sounds of Social Change*. New York: Rand McNally.

Peterson, Richard A. 1972b. "A Process Model of the Folk, Pop, and Fine Art Phases of Jazz." Pp. 135–151 in Charles Nanry (ed.), *American Music*. New Brunswick: Transaction Books.

Peterson, Richard A. & David G. Berger. 1972. "Three Eras in the Manufacture of Popular Music Lyrics." Pp. 293–296 in R. Serge Denisoff and Richard A. Peterson (eds.), *The Sounds of Social Change*. New York: Rand McNally.

Schuessler, Karl. 1948. "Social Background and Musical Taste," *American Sociological Review* 13 (June): 330–335.

Spaeth, Sigmund. 1948. *A History of Popular Music in America*. New York: Random House.

Stearns, Marshall. 1970. *The Story of Jazz*. New York: Oxford Univ. Press.

Time. 1956. "Rock 'n' Roll." (July 23): 33.

———— . 1957. "The Rock is Solid." (November 4): 48.

Variety. 1955. "Houston's 'Wash-out-the-air' Committee Knocks 26 & B Tunes Out of Box." (August 24): 51.

———— . 1955b. "Negro DJ Raps Spread of 'Filth' Via R&B Disks." (March 23): 1.

———— . 1955C. "Juve Gets Jock Support in Drive to Kayo Leeric Platters." (July 20): 47.

———— . 1955d "WINS Sez Teenagers 'Hate' Haymes for His WCBS Pan of R&B Music," (March 9): 49.

———— . 1956. "Baptist Minister's Sermon vs Elvis; He Hit the Skids." (October 17): 1.

Wilson, John S. 1956. "What Makes 'Pop' Music Popular: Answer is the Adolescents." *New York Times Magazine* 107 (April 20): 28.

Wolfe, Tom. 1965. *The Kandy-Kolored Tangerine-Flake Streamline Baby.* New York: Pocket Books.

———— 24 ————

High Culture as Mass Culture

JUDITH R. BLAU

Commercially produced popular culture is presumed to pervade American society and to be distributed—in various forms, such as cinema and rock music—more or less uniformly from one region of the country to another, from one city to another. By relying on universal conventions and prevailing taste, commercial supporters of popular culture are perceived to be very successful in reaching audiences throughout the country. At the same time, it is assumed that most forms of institutionalized high culture, such as opera houses, museums, and art galleries, are concentrated in a few large eastern cities, such as New York, Boston, Washington, and Philadelphia. Although some midwestern and western cities, notably San Francisco and Chicago, have fostered important high culture institutions, and, more recently, southern cities, such as Dallas and Houston, have intensified their efforts to establish their cultural worth, the undisputed centers for the visual arts, symphonic music, opera, chamber music, and the theater are considered to be cities on the eastern seaboard. The American cultural landscape is perceived to be one in which the elite arts are highly concentrated while the popular arts are pervasive. The presumed merits of this view and the extent to which it is shared is clearly illustrated by our common understanding of what the New Yorker or the Bostonian means when she or he refers to a place as a "cultural wasteland."

The cultural landscape for the folk arts is assumed to be a bit more complex than that for either the popular or elite arts. Sociologists maintain that crafts as well as live country music, bluegrass music, and jazz are concentrated in particular cities or rural areas as they are closely tied to local traditions, styles of life, or subcultures. Often they have commercial potential in which case they are produced for national markets, and particular forms of a folk art, such as jazz, are incorporated into high culture.

Elite View of Mass Society

What became known as the theory of mass society in the 1950s continued to be widely accepted during the 1960s. And, stripped of its polemical and moralistic tone, it still informs social scientists' interpretation of culture. A premise of mass society theory is that commercially produced culture has deleterious consequences for the integrity of American arts, if not for the moral fabric of the society. It was argued that because popular culture panders to mass demands for entertainment and amusement, it corrupts the standards of the traditional, elite arts and debases the conventions governing "good" art (van den Haag, 1957; Shils, 1961; 1963). This version of mass society theory asserts that because of their low symbolic content, the popular commercial arts divert audiences from reality, narcotize the public, and render the masses vulnerable to totalitarian rule. The emphasis in the sociology of culture changed during the 1970s, largely as the results of writings by Herbert Gans (1974) and Richard Peterson (1976) who stressed that high culture is not intrinsically superior nor popular culture intrinsically inferior. While recognizing that the commercial arts are organized on a profit-making basis and high culture is not. Gans and Peterson indicated that the line between them may be blurred for other reasons: the popular and traditional arts borrow styles from one another: because their respective audiences overlap they do not have distinctive followings; and, the commercially supported arts are often more dynamic than the elite arts, as a comparison of popular music and symphonic music illustrates.

One legacy of mass society theory persists and informs our current understanding of culture: popular culture is geographically ubiquitous whereas high culture is entrenched in certain sections of the country and folk culture is highly localized. Film, popular music, television, night club entertainment, and disco or breakdancing, it is assumed, are the staples of amusement throughout the United States. Not everyone is expert at breakdancing, goes to the cinema, or even watches television, but our conception is that these forms of popular arts pervade American society and are universally available for those interested. At the same time, we assume that most, if not all, forms of high culture are concentrated in a few prominent centers. This legacy of mass society theory is eminently plausible. Profitable enterprises seek as large a market as possible, and there is no apriori reason to believe that cost factors discourage commercial ventures for the popular arts: cinemas, nightclubs, and variety entertainment establishments do not involve high capital investments. There are historical reasons to support our belief that east coast cities are dominant in high culture. Simply put, they had an early start. The concentration of individual wealth in Philadelphia, Boston, and New York in the nineteenth century facilitated patronage of the arts and culture building. The commercial ties of these eastern cities with Europe promoted intellectual and artistic ties as well, which helped to foster a taste for the arts. These cities early achieved a strong economic base that encouraged public figures and families of means to turn to symbolic ways of expressing their economic prominence, social worth, and good taste.

Specialization in Places

While a plausible argument can be made that the elite arts are concentrated in a few cities and the popular arts are uniformly distributed throughout the country, some research and social science theory suggest a far more complex pattern, minimizing the significance of geographical differences and emphasizing that cities specialize in particular forms of culture. To establish symbols of distinctiveness and to attract tourists, urban planners and policymakers capitalize on their cities' economic resources and their potential for corporate investment. Both high culture and popular culture have benefited from alliances between wealthy families or corporations and municipalities, as illustrated by the examples of the city of Rochester and Eastman Kodak. Pittsburgh and the Mellon family, and Los Angeles and the Disney Corporation. A city can also turn local traditions to good account to amplify its cultural standing. New Orleans's Mardi Gras, Louisville's Kentucky Derby, and Nashville's Grand Ole Opry are instances of the success of cities institutionalizing local traditions to make them important tourist activities. These are distinctive types of cultural activities, founded on unusual local traditions, but they suggest that there may be great variation among urban places with respect to the kinds of culture they support.

Economists and sociologists have examined the quality of life in urban places, using indicators from the United States census of population and other sources that pertain to health, crime, housing conditions, cost of living, income, and employment. Very few have attempted to incorporate indicators of culture in these comparisons of cities. An interesting exception is Ben-Chieh Liu's (1976) study of 243 metropolitan areas. It includes over 120 indicators, three of which pertain to cultural activities. Whereas the sources for the health, crime, and other indicators are official government documents and subject to relatively little error, the source for the cultural indicators is a questionnaire completed by Chamber of Commerce representatives from each metropolitan area. Liu recognizes that biases may result from relying on individuals whose job it is to publicize their cities' cultural contributions and who also may have to rely on estimates in the absence of official records. Nevertheless, this is an important study for it is probably the first to systematically examine cultural indicators as well as those traditionally used in quality-of-life research. Liu reports that the variation among urban places with respect to fairs and festivals, forms of popular culture, is far greater than one would expect; while the variation among them with respect to dance, drama, and music events is much less. These patterns are contrary to those described by mass society theory.

Social indicator research, illustrated by the Liu study, examines the supply of cultural activities and facilities for them. Those who have studied the demand for culture, that is, audience interest and participation, report marked regional differences. Raymond Gastil (1975) and Marsden and his colleagues (1982) indicate that southerners are less likely than people from other regions of the country to attend cultural events of all kinds and are less likely to engage in artistic activities. Although the relationship between demand and supply, especially for culture, is not a perfect one, these audience studies suggest that the South has fewer cultural institutions compared with other regions.

These different conclusions for variation among cities and among regions are based on empirical studies, but there are also theoretical reasons to suppose that urban places are differentiated from one another and that a dimension of this differentiation relates to culture and art. The rational choice model of urban growth and development posits that at the city's highest political and economic levels as well as at the local neighborhood, or vernacular, level decisions are made; they accumulate and become embodied in institutional forms (see Rapoport, 1976). Thus, a city's cultural, social and economic patterns emerge from a highly localized process. Another theory explaining locational patterning of organizations posits that there are economic interdependencies among subsystems of a local market, and, therefore, that related firms and industries tend to develop together as the result of explicit transactions in a given locale. The film industry in California, as Faulkner (1973) describes it depends on close relations among occupational groups (scriptwriters, musicians, filmmakers, designers) and among industries (studios, orchestras, schools of acting). Although the rational choice model and the organizational model rest on quite different assumptions, the conclusion is the same: because transactions of all kinds emerge as an orderly process at the local level, there will be marked differences among urban places, including differences with respect to the kinds of art and culture they support. This conclusion is consistent with the observation of Gunter Barth (1980) a cultural historian, who notes that the unique historical experiences of America, compared with Europe, gave rise to a set of cultural institutions that rest on local taste, traditions, and values. The result, according to Barth, is that America has a variegated cultural landscape rather than a uniform one.

Considering Cultural Variety

Information on a great variety of forms of high and popular culture has been collected that helps to answer the following questions: To what extent are urban places specialized or not? Is there disproportionately much elite art in east coast cities? Are the popular arts uniformly distributed among urban places and among different regions? Is there coherence among related forms of elite or popular art so that, for example, urban places that have relatively many museums also have relatively many art galleries? Diverse sources of information are used for the purpose of comparison for the largest 125 standard metropolitan statistical areas (SMSAs). The U.S. Bureau of the Census defines an SMSA as a central city with a population of at least 50,000 and its surrounding built-up area. The largest 125 SMSAs include about 73 percent of the American population. There are advantages in using the SMSA as the geographical unit because the area of which it is comprised is considered to be a socially, economically and politically inter-related whole. It is the area that defines the limits for most routine trips, whether these be commuting to work, going to a baseball game, or attending an opera.

Ernest van den Haag (1957: 508) wrote, "As society becomes fully industrialized, popular culture becomes the most universally shared type of culture and colors most aspects of individual and social life. High and folk culture retain only marginal influence on private and social life. They become islands lapped at and often swamped by popular culture." He added that high and folk culture "are isolated and dry up in institutions or regions cut off from social development." If this were true we would expect great regional differences in forms of high culture, such as operatic companies and orchestras, and in forms of craft and folk culture, such as crafts fairs and country music festivals. We would also expect that popular culture, such as cinemas and live rock concerts, would exhibit little regional variation.

I consider the following forms of elite culture: art museums; art galleries; antique and other special interest galleries; opera companies; opera workshops and festivals; professional, non-profit theaters; theater premiers; symphony orchestras; ballet and dance companies; contemporary chamber ensemble companies; and legitimate theaters. Culture with broad popular appeal includes the following: live popular music concerts; general interest museums including natural history, science, and space museums; and cinemas, commercial bands, dance halls, and variety entertainment establishments. Also, two forms of folk culture were included: country music festivals and crafts fairs.

Because the largest SMSAs will naturally have many more cultural

events and cultural institutions than the smallest SMSAs—the range is between 11 million for the New York City SMSA and about 248,000 for the
Salinas-Monterey SMSA—the appropriate base of comparison for metropolitan places is the number of institutions or events per 100,000 population. The regional comparisons made here are based on the means for all of
the SMSAs in the four geographical regions—Northeast, South, North Central, and West.

Based on the number of institutions and events per 100,000 people for
each region's SMSAs, the following are cultural forms for which there is no
regional variation—that is, the metropolitan places in the four regions do
not significantly differ from one another with respect to their numbers of art
museums, galleries, or opera companies, or any of the other cultural establishments listed relative to their population size. On a per capita basis, we
could say, SMSAs in the South, Northeast, West, and North Central have
about the same number of art museums, of ballet companies, and of chamber ensemble groups that play avant-garde music.

- Art Museums
- Art Galleries
- Specialized Galleries (including galleries for antiques, religious ob-
  jects, and primitive art)
- Opera Companies
- Opera Workshops and Festivals
- Non-profit Theaters
- Commercial Legitimate Theaters
- Theater Premieres
- Major Orchestras (those with annual income greater than two million
  dollars)
- Non-major Orchestras (including municipal, college, community, and
  children's orchestras)
- Ballet Companies
- Non-ballet Companies (including modern, historical, and solo dance
  companies)
- Contemporary Chamber Ensemble Companies
- Country Music Festivals
- Popular Music Concerts

The following are those cultural forms for which there is regional variation:
some region's metropolitan places have an excess of a particular form while
others have a deficit. Those regions in which metropolitan places have high
concentrations of a given type of culture are indicated.

- Specialized Museums (including space, science, children's, and natural history museums)—Northeast
- Cinemas, commercial—South and West
- Bands, commercial—West
- Variety Entertainment Establishments (nightclubs and bars with live performances)—West
- Dance Halls—South and West
- Crafts Fairs—Northeast

My sources for data on the cultural forms are: *International Directory of Arts*, volumes 1 and 2; *Opera Directory: Opera Companies and Workshops in U.S. and Canada; Theater Profiles 4; Census of Selected Service Industries; Notable Names in the Theater; Symphony Magazine; Dance Magazine Annual; Contemporary Music Performance Directory; The Festival Sourcebook; Rolling Stone Magazine;* and *Craft Horizons.*

Contrary to the assertions of van den Haag and other mass society theorists, and also probably contrary to our own impressions of the American cultural landscape, every type of high culture considered is nearly uniformly distributed throughout all regions of the country on a per capita basis. Conventional wisdom notwithstanding, there is not a large concentration on art museums, art galleries, operas, ballet companies, or any other form of elite art in the Northwest. Nor are the South, West, and North Central regions of the country impoverished in high culture. Of the two forms of folk culture considered, the one considered to have strong roots in the rural South and North Central regions of the country—country music festivals that feature old-time and bluegrass music—does not vary in relative numbers from one region to another. These patterns provide strong evidence that weighs against the contention that folk culture and, especially, high culture have become isolated islands that are confined to a few regions of the country where people appreciate them. On the contrary, all forms of high culture considered and one form of folk culture are widely distributed throughout all regions of the United States.

Nearly all forms of art with reputed wide popular appeal, including science and natural history museums, cinemas, commercial bands, variety entertainment (such as clubs and bars with live entertainment), and dance halls are concentrated in one or two regions of the United States. For example, there are more cinemas per capita in SMSAs in the South and West. While art museums—repositories for traditional, elite art—are distributed uniformly throughout the four regions; science and natural history museums—mandated to serve the broadest possible public—are concentrated in the Northeast. Of all the popular arts considered, only live rock concerts exhibit no marked regional variation; like forms of elite culture, they are generally ubiquitous. The second form of folk art considered here are the craft fairs. They, unlike country music festivals, exhibit pronounced regional variation with disproportionately many of them held in the Northeast.

With the one exception of live rock concerts, the contrast between the locational patterns for high culture and those for popular culture is marked and consistent. Elite art is widely dispersed throughout the nation whereas each of the popular forms of art is more heavily concentrated in certain areas of the country and less widely available in other areas. Before advancing an explanation for these patterns, I examine how urban places themselves vary.

Our pre-conceptions about the cultural resources of particular urban places do not take into account the sheer numbers of people that reside in them. Moreover, our pre-conceptions involving which cities are the cultural giants and which cities are deficient in cultural resources are probably most shaped by the reputations of a few cultural institutions and not by the number of institutions. The numbers of institutions and events per 100,000 population for each of the 125 metropolitan areas is instructive. They show, for example, that some of our pre-conceptions are correct. The New York metropolitan area ranks high in terms of professional nonprofit theaters; Washington D.C. is in the top ten percent for the number of specialized museums and in the top twenty-six percent for the number of art museums. Both Nashville and Atlanta are major centers for live popular concerts, even on a per capita basis.

There are many surprises when we consider the supply of culture relative to the population base. For example, Augusta, Georgia, has about the same number of professional nonprofit theaters per capita as New York, and both the Baton Rouge and the Springfield SMSAs outrank Washington D.C. in terms of their relative numbers of art museums. To be specific, Washington D.C.'s thirteen art museums are available to a population of nearly three million people, whereas Springfield's six art museums serve approximately 500,000 people. If we also take into account that Washington's museums undoubtedly attract far more tourists than Springfield's, the conclusion is that the number of local residents that can benefit from Springfield's (or Baton Rouge's) art collections is probably greater than that of Washington's local population. This comparison does not take into account the relative sizes of the collections nor the differences in prestige; no museum in Springfield has the scope of the Smithsonian's comprehensive collection nor the quality of the relatively specialized exhibit at the Hirshhorn. The urban place that ranks the highest on most indicators of elite culture is Tucson; it is in the top ten percent for art museums, art galleries, orchestras, and nonprofit professional theaters.

Such observations suggest that the traditionally dominant cities—New York, Philadelphia, Boston, and Washington D.C.—have narrowly focused their economic resources by emphasizing the symbolic importance of a relatively small number of elite institutions; other metropolitan places have not placed great stake in the cultural reputations of one or a few institutions but have encouraged the proliferation of many, albeit small ones, devoted to high culture. The regional differences for popular culture are apparent in the urban comparisons as well. There are more cinemas per capita in many southern SMSAs—Charlotte and Greenville, for example—and also in many western SMSAs—Corpus Christi, Salinas-Monterey, and Albuquerque. Orlando, Richmond, Austin, and Tulsa are major centers for dance hall establishments, whereas most places in the Northeast and North Central region provide their residents with relatively few dance halls and apparently few opportunities to go out dancing.

There are three general patterns worth noting. First, although a few metropolises—such as Atlanta—appear to exhibit a taste for all forms of popular culture, most SMSAs tend to specialize in one or two forms of popular culture, just as they tend to specialize in only one or two forms of elite culture. Second, popular and elite arts are not substitutes for one another, and all configurations are represented. For example, Tulsa and Tucson rank exceptionally high on practically all forms of culture, whereas Youngstown and Jersey City rank low on both elite and popular forms. Some metropolitan places are particularly strong on most forms of high culture and weak on most forms of popular culture. Jackson and Santa Barbara are examples of this particular configuration. There are also major centers for the popular arts that have relatively little highbrow art. Notable examples of this particular pattern are Atlanta and Charlotte. The concerns of the mass society theorists that the "bad" (that is, commercial, popular culture) would drive out the "good" (that is, traditional, elite culture) appear to be unfounded. There is a great deal of variation among urban places with respect to their cultural strengths and weaknesses; that variation is not systematic with respect to the distinction between elite and popular culture.

Without question New York City is the dominant leader in the visual arts, as trends and prices are set by its galleries, auction houses, and museum acquisition decisions, and as it attracts the most ambitious and promising young artists. So are, without question, the leading symphonies in the United States located in New York, Philadelphia, Cleveland, San Francisco, Chicago, and Boston. Yet the art world in New York involves a tiny proportion of New York residents and it has relatively few museums considering the size of its population and the fact that a substantial number of museum visitors are not New Yorkers. The symphonies in New York, Philadelphia, Cleveland, San Francisco, Chicago, and Boston serve a small fraction of their populations. High culture is far more democratic and widely accessible now than it was previously, and forms of high culture flourish in many metropolitan centers that have no longstanding traditions of high culture. That there are more orchestras relative to total population in Albuquerque than there are in Boston means that there are greater opportunities for residents of Albuquerque to attend a symphony than for those in Boston (assuming that the seating capacities of halls and the length of the season are approximately the same). Perhaps no symphony in Albuquerque can match the standards of the Boston Symphony, but the ones in Albuquerque are more accessible to a larger proportion of its population.

High culture is widely disseminated throughout the United States; there are no regional enclaves as there are for popular culture. On the other hand, there are patterns of specialization with regard to high culture, with some places having, for example, much theater but relatively few art collections. While there is also considerable specialization of the popular arts in urban places—with, for example, some having many cinemas per capita but few establishments with live bands or cabarets—popular culture exhibits strong regional patterns. How can it be that popular culture that has commercial backing and, presumably, universal appeal is not uniformly distributed throughout the United States while the many forms of traditional elite culture are?

The historian James Sloan Allen (1983) provides one answer, high culture has symbolic value for places and it also has great commercial value. For these reasons it has been dislodged from conventional enclaves and widely disseminated throughout the United States. Whatever the traditions or the tastes of the local community, considerations of commerce and symbolic worth carry economic and political decision makers into the activities of culture-building. As F. D. Klingender (1970: 62) wrote of the capitalist, "Buying art is an indication of making it." The same could be said of any growing city. On the other hand, forms of popular culture rest most on free market principles. Competition among firms within a given locale will set an equilibrium based on what the market will bear, and market research is carried out with an eye to local demand and taste. The demographic and lifestyle differences that exist between the Sunbelt cities of the South and West compared with the older industrial cities in the Northeast and North Central region are probably a major factor that explains the prevalence of forms of popular culture in the South and West. Paradoxical as it may seem, high culture has become more popular than what we call "popular culture." Although high culture has not continued to flourish in those places where it originated and was once entrenched, high culture has become quite ordinary elsewhere.

Notes

1. Reprinted with permission of the publisher, *Society* (vol. 23, May/June 1986).

References

Allen, James Sloan. 1983. *The Romance of Commerce and Culture*. Chicago: University of Chicago Press.

Barth, Gunter. 1980. *City People: The Rise of Modern City Culture in the 19th Century City*. Oxford: Oxford University Press.

Faulkner, Robert. 1983. *Music on Demand*. New Brunswick: Transaction.

Gans, Herbert J. 1974. *Popular Culture and High Culture*. New York: Basic Books.

Gastil, Raymond. 1975. *Cultural Regions of the United States*. Seattle: University of Washington Press.

Klingender, Francis D. 1970. *Art and the Industrial Revolution*. Ed. and rev. Arthur Elton. New York: Schocken.

Liu, Ben-Chieh. 1976. *Quality of Life Indicators in the U.S.* New York: Praeger.

Marsden, P. V., J. S. Reed, M. D. Kennedy, and K. M. Stinson. 1982. "American Regional Culture and Differences in Leisure Time Activities." *Social Forces* 60: 1023–49.

Peterson, Richard A. 1976. "A Prolegomenmon." Pp. 7–22 in Richard A. Peterson (ed.), *The Production of Culture*. Beverly Hills: Sage.

Rapoport, Amos, ed. 1976. *Mutual Interaction of People and Their Environment*. The Hague: Mouton.

Shils, Edward. 1961. "Mass Society and Its Cultures." Pp. 1–27 in Norman Jacobs (ed.), *Culture for the Millions?* New York: Van Nostrand.

Shils, Edward. 1963. "The Theory of Mass Society." Pp. 30–50 in Philip Olson (ed.), *America as a Mass Society*. Glencoe, Ill: Free Press.

van den Haag, Ernest. 1957. "Of Happiness and Despair We Have No Measure." Pp. 504–36 in Bernard Rosenberg and David Manning White (eds.), *Mass Culture*. Glencoe: Free Press.

Bibliography

Books

General

Albrecht, M. C., James H. Barnett & Mason Griff, eds. 1970. The Sociology of Art and Literature: A Reader. New York: Praeger.

Allen, J. S. 1983. The Romance of Commerce and Culture. Chicago: U. of Chicago Press.

Allen, P. M. 1956. The Sociology of Art in America. Ann Arbor: University Microfilms.

American Council for the Arts. 1981. Americans and their Arts. New York: ACA.

American Council for the Arts in Education. 1973. Arts and the People. New York: Publishing Center for Cultural Resources.

Arts Council of Great Britain. Annually. Annual Reports. London: Arts Coucil of Great Britain.

Associated Councils of the Arts. 1975. Americans and their Arts, A Survey of Public Opinion. New York: Associated Councils of the Arts.

Balfe, J. H. & M. J. Wyszomirski, eds. 1985. Art, Ideology, and Politics. New York: Praeger.

Becker, H. S. 1982. Art Worlds. Berkeley: U. of California Press.

Benjamin, W. 1968. Illuminations. New York: Schocken Books. [Also 1970. London: Jonathan Cape].

Blau, J. R. 1989. The Shape of Culture. Cambridge: Cambridge U. Press.

Bourdieu, P. 1984. Distinction. Cambridge: Harvard U. Press.

Carrier, D. 1987. Artwriting. Amherst: U. of Massachusetts Press.

Congressional Quarterly. 1985. After Hours: Arts & Leisure in America. Washington: Congressional Quarterly.

Creedy, J., ed. 1970. The Social Context of Art. London: Tavistock.

Duvignaud, J. 1967. The Sociology of Art. New York: Harper & Row. [also London: Paladin, 1972].

Finkelstein, S. 1947. Art and Society. New York: International Publishers.

Gotshalk, D. W. 1962. Art and the Social Order, 2nd ed. New York: Dover Publications.

Gowans, A. 1970. The Unchanging Arts: New Forms for the Traditional Functions of Art in Society. Philadelphia: J. B. Lippincott.

Graña, C. 1971. Fact and Symbol: Essays in the Sociology of Art and Literature. New York: Oxford U. Press.

Hall, J. B. & B. Ulanov. 1972. Modern Culture and the Arts, 2nd ed. New York: McGraw-Hill.

Hauser, A. 1982. The Sociology of Art. Chicago: U. of Chicago Press.

Manfredi, J. 1982. The Social Limits of Art. Amherst: U. of Massachusetts Press.

Miller, J. & P. D. Herring, eds. 1967. The Arts and the Public. Chicago: U. of Chicago Press.

National Endowment for the Arts. 1978. Minorities and Women in the Arts: 1970, Research Division Report no. 7. Washington: National Endowment for the Arts.

National Research Center of the Arts. 1972. A Study of the Non-Profit Arts and Cultural Industry of New York State. New York: National Research Center of the Arts.

Nikolov, E., ed. 1983. Contributions to the Sociology of the Arts [Reports from the 10th World Congress of Sociology]. Sofia: Research Institute for Culture.

Poggioli, R. 1968. The Theory of the Avant-Garde. Cambridge: Belknap Press of Harvard U. Press.

Robinson, J. P., ed. 1985. Social Science and the Arts 1984. Lanham: U. Press of America.

Tomars, A. S. 1940. Introduction to the Sociology of Art. Mexico City: privately printed.

Williams, R. 1982. The Sociology of Culture. New York: Schocken Books.

Wilson, R. N., ed. 1964. The Arts in Society. Englewood Cliffs: Prentice-Hall.

Wilson, R. N. 1973. The Sociology and Psychology of Art. Morristown: General Learning Press.

The Publishing Center for Cultural Resources (625 Broadway, New York, New York 10012) has a list of monographs sponsored by the National Endowment for the Arts.

Social Theories of Art

Adorno, T. W. 1976. Introduction to the Sociology of Music. New York: Seabury Press.

Apresyan, Z. 1968. Freedom and the Artist. Moscow: Progress Publishers.

Baxandall, L. & S. Morawski. 1977. Marx and Engels on Literature and Art. New York: International General.

Burns, E. 1972. Theatricality: A Study of Convention in the Theatre and in Social Life. New York: Harper & Row. [Also London: Longman].

Duncan, H. D. 1962. Communication and Social Order. New York: Bedminster Press.

Fischer, E. 1963. The Necessity of Art. Baltimore: Penguin Books.

Frisby, D. 1986. Fragments of Modernity: Theories of Modernity in the Work of Simmel, Kracauer and Benjamin. Cambridge: MIT Press.

Gans, H. 1974. Popular Culture and High Culture. New York: Basic Books.

Hadjinicolaou, N. 1978. Art History and Class Struggle. London: Pluto Press.

Harap. L. 1949. Social Roots of the Arts. New York: International Publishers.

Harrison, J. 1978. Ancient Art and Ritual. Bradford-on-Avon: Moonraker Press.

Herek, L. & D. Rupel, eds. 1985. Alienation and Participation in Culture. Ljubljana: U. Edvard Kardelj.

Kubler, G. 1962. The Shape of Time: Remarks on the History of Things. New Haven: Yale U. Press.

Lang, B. & F. Williams, eds. 1972. Marxism and Art. New York: David McKay.

Lynes, R. 1980. The Tastemakers: The Shaping of American Popular Taste. New York: Dover.

Martindale, D. 1984. The Scope of Social Theory: Essays and Sketches, vol. II. Houston: Cap & Gown Press.

Marx, K. & F. Engels. 1978. On Literature and Art. Moscow: Progress Publishers.

Morawski, S. 1974. Inquiries into the Fundamentals of Aesthetics. Cambridge: MIT Press.

Ortega y Gasset, J. 1950. [1932] The Revolt of the Masses. New York: Mentor.

Perris, A. 1985. Music as Propaganda. Westport: Greenwood Press.

Peterson, R. A., ed. 1976. The Production of Culture. Beverly Hills: Sage.

Phillipson, M. 1985. Painting, Language & Modernity. London: Routledge & Kegan Paul.

Plekhanov, G. 1936. Art and Society: A Marxist Analysis. New York: Critics Group.

Ross, R. 1962. Symbols and Civilization. New York: Harcourt, Brace & World (Harbinger).

Simmel, G. 1968. The Conflict in Modern Culture and Other Essays, tr. by K. Peter Etzkorn. New York: Teachers College Press.

Sorokin, P. 1937. Social and Cultural Dynamics, Vol. I: Fluctuations of Forms of Art. New York: American Book.

Weber, M. 1958. The Rational and Social Foundations of Music. Carbondale: Southern Illinois U. Press.

Wolff, J. 1975. Hermeneutic Philosophy and the Sociology of Art. London: Routledge & Kegan Paul.

Wolff, J. 1981. The Social Production of Art. New York: St. Martin's Press.

Aesthetics, Philosophy and Social History

Adorno, T. W. 1973. Philosophy of Modern Music. New York: Seabury Press.

Allen, B. S. 1959. Tides in English Taste, new ed. 2 vols. New York.

Antal, F. 1948. Florentine Painting and Its Social Background. London: Routledge.

Baxandall, M., ed. 1972. Radical Perspectives in the Arts. Harmondsworth: Penguin Books.

Baxandall, M. 1985. Patterns of Intention. New Haven: Yale U. Press.

Benjamin, W. 1969. Illuminations. New York: Schocken Books.

Bosanquet, B. 1904. A History of Aesthetics, 2nd ed. New York: MacMillan.

Bradbrook, M. C. 1962. The Rise of the Common Player. Cambridge: Harvard U. Press.

Broude, N. & M. D. Gerrard, eds. 1982. Feminism and Art History. New York: Harper & Row.

Brown, R. H. 1977. A Poetic for Sociology. Cambridge: Cambridge U. Press.

Burt, N. 1977. Palaces for the People: A Social History of the American Art Museum. Boston: Little, Brown.

Chambers, F. P. 1932. The History of Taste. New York: Columbia U. Press.

Collingwood, R. G. 1958. The Principles of Art. London: Oxford U. Press.

Daiches, David. 1938. Literature and Society. London: Gollancz.

Danto, A. 1981. The Transfiguration of the Commonplace. Cambridge: Harvard U. Press.

Dewey, J. 1934. Art as Experience. New York: G. P. Putnam's Sons (Capricorn).

Dickie, G. 1974. Art and the Aesthetic: An Institutional Analysis. Ithaca: Cornell U. Press.

Eco, U. 1986. Art and Beauty in the Middle Ages. New Haven: Yale U. Press.

Egbert, D. D. 1970. Social Radicalism and the Arts. New York: Alfred A. Knopf.

Ehrlich, C. 1985. The Music Profession in Britain since the Eighteenth Century. Oxford: Clarendon Press.

Ewen, D. 1961. History of Popular Music. New York: Barnes & Noble.

Feather, L. 1961. The Book of Jazz. New York: Paperback Library.

Forcucci, S. L. 1984. A Folk Song History of America. Englewood Cliffs: Prentice-Hall.

Foster, H., ed. 1987. Discussions in Contemporary Culture, Number One. Seattle: Bay Press.

Gimpel, J. 1969. The Cult of Art: Against Art and Artists. London: Weidenfeld & Nicolson.

Gombrich, E. H. 1963. Meditations of a Hobby Horse and Other Essays in the Theory of Art. London: Phaidon Press.

Griswold, W. 1986. Renaissance Revivals. Chicago: U. of Chicago Press.

Guilbaut, S. 1983. How New York Stole the Idea of Modern Art. Chicago: U. of Chicago Press.

Hall, P. D. 1984. The Organization of American Culture, 1700–1900. New York: New York U. Press.

Harker, D. 1985. Fakesong. London: Open U. Press.

Harris, N. 1966. The Artist in American Society: The Formative Years 1790–1860. New York: Simon & Shuster (Clarion).

Hart, J. D. 1961. The Popular Book: A History of America's Literary Taste. Berkeley: U. of California Press.

Haskell, F. 1980. Patrons and Painters: Art and Society in Baroque Italy. New Haven: Yale U. Press.

Hauser, A. 1951. The Social History of Art [2 vols.]. London: Routledge & Kegan Paul.

Katz, R. 1986. Divining the Powers of Music: Aesthetic Theory and the Origins of Opera. New York: Pendragon Press.

Kavolis, V. 1972. History on Art's Side. Ithaca: Cornell U. Press.

Klingender, F. D. 1970. Art and Industrial Revolution. New York: Schocken Books.

Kohansky, M. 1984. The Disreputable Profession: The Actor in Society. Westport: Greenwood Press.

König, R. 1973. A La Mode. New York: Seabury Press.

Laing, D. 1978. The Marxist Theory of Art. Sussex: Harvester Press.

Langer, S. K. 1942. Philosophy in a New Key. New York: Penguin Books.

Leith, J. A. 1965. The Idea of Art as Propaganda in France 1750–1799. Toronto: U. of Toronto Press.

Leith, J. A. 1968. Media and Revolution. Toronto: CBC Publishers.

Lloyd, A. L. 1967. Folk Song in England. New York: International Publishers.

Lucie-Smith, E. 1981. The Story of Craft: The Craftsman's Role in Society. Ithaca: Cornell U. Press.

Mackerness, E. D. 1976. A Social History of English Music. Westport: Greenwood Press.

Martindale, A. 1972. The Rise of the Artist. New York: McGraw-Hill.

Miller, E. H. 1959. The Professional Writer in Elizabethan England. Cambridge: Harvard U. Press.

Montias, J. M. 1982. Artists and Artisans in Delft: A Socio-Economic Study of the Seventeenth Century. Princeton: Princeton U. Press.

Neil, J. M. 1975. Toward a National Taste. Honolulu: U. Press of Hawaii.

Nettel, R. 1969. A Social History of Traditional Song. New York: Augustus M. Kelley.

Oakley, G. 1983. The Devil's Music, rev. ed. London: BBC (Ariel).

Oliver, P. 1969. The Story of the Blues. Radnor: Chilton.

Pelles, G. 1963. Art, Artists and Society. Englewood Cliffs: Prentice-Hall.

Pevsner, H. 1940. Academies of Art, Past and Present. Cambridge: Cambridge U. Press.

Rader, M., ed. 1964. A Modern Book of Esthetics: An Anthology, 3rd ed. New York: Holt, Rinehart & Winston.

Raynor, H. 1976. Music and Society Since 1815. New York: Schocken Books.

Raynor, H. 1972. A Social History of Music from the Middle Ages to Beethoven. London: Barrie & Jenkins.

Read, H. 1967. Art and Alienation. New York: Viking Press.

Reid, L. A. 1969. Meaning in the Arts. London: George Allen & Unwin.

Salmen, Walter, ed. 1983. The Social Status of the Professional Musician from the Middle Ages to the 19th Century. New York: Pendragon Press.

Shapiro, T. 1976. Painters and Politics. New York: Elsevier

Solomon, M., ed. 1974. Marxism and Art. New York: Random House (Vintage).

Spector, J. J. 1972. The Aesthetics of Freud. New York: McGraw-Hill.

Swingewood, A. 1987. Sociological Poetics and Aesthetic Theory. New York: St. Martins Press.

Taylor, J. C. 1976. America As Art. New York: Harper & Row.

Wackernagel, M. 1981. The World of the Florentine Renaissance Artist: Projects and Patrons, Workshop and Art Market. Princeton: Princeton U. Press.

Watt, I. 1965. The Rise of the Novel. Berkeley: U. of California Press.

Westrup, J. 1955. An Introduction to Musical History. London: Hutchinson.

White, H. C. & C. A. White. 1965. Canvasses and Careers: Institutional Change in the French Painting World. New York: John Wiley & Sons.

Williams, R. 1961. The Long Revolution. New York: Columbia U. Press.

Wold, M. & E. Cykler. 1959. Music and Art in the Western World. Dubuque: Wm. C. Brown.

Wolff, J. 1983. Aesthetics and the Sociology of Art. London: George Allen & Unwin.

Worringer, W. 1957. Form in Gothic. New York: Schocken Books.

Zeitler, R. ed. 1972. Proceedings of the Sixth International Congress of Aesthetics: Uppsala, 1968. Uppsala: Uppsala U.

Anthropology

Adam, L. 1949. Primitive Art (rev. ed.). Harmondsworth: Penguin Books.

Alland, A., Jr. 1977. The Artistic Animal. Garden City: Doubleday (Anchor).

Biebuyck, D., ed. 1969. Tradition and Creativity in Tribal Art. Berkeley: U. of California Press.

Blacking, J. 1973. How Musical is Man? Seattle: U. of Washington Press.

Boas, F. 1955. Primitive Art. New York: Dover Press.

Bowra, C. M. 1962. Primitive Song. New York: World, 1962. [Also 1963. New York: New American Library-Mentor].

Burland, C. A. & J. T. Hooper. 1953. The Art of Primitive Peoples. London: Fountain Press.

Clifford, J. 1988. The Predicament of Culture: Twentieth-Century Ethnography, Literature, and Art. Cambridge: Harvard U. Press.

d'Azevedo, W. L., ed. 1973. The Traditional Artist in African Societies. Bloomington: Indiana U. Press.

Fraser, D. 1962. Primitive Art. Garden City: Doubleday.

Fraser, D., ed. 1966. The Many Faces of Primitive Art. Englewood Cliffs: Prentice-Hall.

Gerbrands, A. A. 1957. Art As an Element of Culture. Leiden: Rijksmuseum voor Volkenkunde.

Graburn, N. H. H., ed. 1976. Ethnic and Tourist Arts. Berkeley: U. of California Press.

Hanna, J. L. 1987. To Dance is Human: A Theory of Non-verbal Communication. Chicago: U. of Chicago Press.

Hatcher, E. P. 1985. Art as Culture: An Introduction to the Anthropology of Art. Lanham: U. Press of America.

Helm, J., ed. 1967. Essays on the Verbal and Visual Arts. Seattle: U. of Washington Press.

Hopkins, P. 1986. Aural Thinking in Norway. New York: Human Sciences Press.

Jules-Rosette, B. 1984. The Messages of Tourist Art. New York: Plenum Press.

Kingsbury, H. 1988. Music, Talent, and Performance. Philadelphia: Temple U. Press.

Kroeber, A. L. 1957. Style and Civilization. Ithaca: Cornell U. Press.

Lange, R. 1976. The Nature of Dance—an Anthropological Perspective. New York: International Publications.

Layton, R. 1981. The Anthropology of Art. New York: Columbia U. Press.

Lomax, A. 1968. Folk Song Style and Culture. New Brunswick: Transaction Books.

Maquet, J. 1986. The Aesthetic Experience. New Haven: Yale U. Press.

Merriam., A. P. 1964. The Anthropology of Music. Evanston: Northwestern U. Press.

Minihan, J. 1977. The Nationalization of Culture. New York: New York U. Press.

Nettl, B. 1976. Folk Music in the United States. Detroit: Wayne State U. Press.

Nettl, B. 1983. The Study of Ethnomusicology. Champaign: U. of Illinois Press.

Otten, C., ed. 1971. Anthropology and Art: Readings in Cross-Cultural Aesthetics. Garden City: Natural History Press.

Powdermaker, H. 1950. Hollywood: The Dream Factory. Boston: Little, Brown.

Royce, A. P. 1977. The Anthropology of Dance. Bloomington: Indiana U. Press.

Wingert, P. S. 1962. Primitive Art. New York: Oxford U. Press.

Visual Arts

Adler, J. E. 1979. Artists in Offices. New Brunswick: Transaction Press.

Antal, F. 1947. Florentine Painting and Its Social Background. London: Kegan, Paul.

Barrell, J. 1983. The Dark Side of the Landscape. New York: Cambridge U. Press.

Barron, F. 1972. Artists in the Making. New York: Seminar Press.

Baxandall, M. 1972. Painting and Experience in Fifteenth-Century Italy. London: Oxford U. Press.

Boris, E. 1986. Art and Labor: Ruskin, Morris, and the Craftsman Ideal in America. Philadelphia: Temple U. Press.

Burnham, J. 1968. Beyond Modern Sculpture: the Effects of Science and Technology on the Sculpture of This Century. New York: George Braziller.

Burt, C. 1977. Palaces for the People: A Social History of the American Art Museum. Boston: Little, Brown.

Cassou, J. et al. 1968. Art and Confrontation: The Arts in an Age of Change. Greenwich: New York Graphic Society.

Castriota, D., ed. 1986. Artist Strategy and the Rhetoric of Power: Political Uses of Art from Antiquity to the Present. Carbondale: Southern Illinois U. Press.

Clignet, R. 1985. The Structure of Artistic Revolutions. Philadelphia: U. of Pennsylvania Press.

Crane, D. 1987. The Transformation of the Avant-Garde. Chicago: U. of Chicago Press.

Estrow, M. 1973. The Art Stealers, rev. ed. New York: Macmillan.

Katz, H. & M. Katz. 1965. Museums, USA. Garden City: Doubleday.

Kavolis, V. 1968. Artistic Expression—A Sociological Analysis. Ithaca: Cornell U. Press.

McMullen, R. 1968. Art, Affluence and Alienation. New York: Frederick A. Praeger.

Meyer, K. E. 1979. The Art Museum: Power, Money, Ethics. New York: William Morrow.

Perlman, B. B. 1962. The Immortal Eight. New York: Exposition Press.

Riemer, J. W. & N. A. Brooks. 1982. Framing the Artist. Washington: U. Press of America.

Rodman, S. 1961. Conversations With Artists. New York: Capricorn Books.

Rosenberg, B. & N. Fliegel. 1965. The Vanguard Artist. Chicago: Quadrangle.

Rosenberg, H. 1964. The Anxious Object. New York: New American Library (Anchor).

Rosenblum, B. 1978. Photographers at Work. New York: Holmes & Meier.

Simpson, C. R. 1981. SoHo: The Artist in the City. Chicago: U. of Chicago Press.

Performing Arts and Their Publics

Arian, E. 1971. Bach, Beethoven, and Bureaucracy: The Case of the Philadelphia Orchestra. University: U. of Alabama Press.

American Symphony Orchestra League. Annually. Compiled Annual Reports. Vienna: American Symphony Orchestra League.

Barzun, J. 1958. Music in American Life. New York: Doubleday.

Blacking, J. & J. W. Kealinohomoko, eds. 1979. The Performing Arts: Music & Dance. The Hague: Mouton.

Boas, F. 1972. The Function of Dance in Human Society. New York: Dance Horizons.

Bogue, D. J. 1973. The Radio Audience for Classical Music. Chicago: CFSC Communications Laboratory.

Elson, A. 1976. Woman's Work in Music. Portland: Longwood Press.

Etzkorn, K. P, ed. 1973. Music and Society: The Later Writings of Paul Honigsheim. New York: John Wiley & Sons.

Farnsworth, P. R. 1958. The Social Psychology of Music. New York: Dryden.

Faulkner, R. R. 1971. Hollywood Studio Musicians. Chicago: Aldine-Atherton.

Faulkner, R. R. 1983. Music on Demand. New Brunswick: Transaction Books.

Finkelstein, S. 1975. Jazz, a People's Music. New York: DaCapo Press [1948. New York: The Citadel Press].

Fulcher, J. 1987. The Nation's Image: French Grand Opera as Politics and Politicized Art. Cambridge: Cambridge U. Press.

Goldfarb, J. C. 1980. The Persistence of Freedom: The Sociological Implications of Polish Student Theater. Boulder: Westview Press.

Greenway, J. 1976. Ethno-musicology. Minneapolis: Burgess.

Hampton, W. 1986. Guerrilla Minstrels. Knoxville: U. of Tennessee Press.

Hanna, J. L. 1988. Dance, Sex and Gender. Chicago: U. of Chicago Press.

Hanna, J. L. 1983. The Performer-Audience Connection: Emotion to Metaphor in Dance and Society. Austin: U. of Texas Press.

Kamerman, J. B. & R. Martorella, eds. 1983. Performers and Performances. South Hadley: J. F. Bergin. [New York: Praeger].

Katz, R. 1986. Divining the Powers of Music: Aesthetic Theory and the Origins of Opera. New York: Pendragon Press.

Kingsbury, H. 1988. Music, Talent & Performance: A Conservatory Cultural System. Philadelphia: Temple U. Press.

Leppert, R. & S. McClary, eds. 1987. Music and Society: The Politics of Composition, Performance and Reception. Cambridge: Cambridge U. Press.

Lowry, W. M., ed. 1978. The Performing Arts and American Society. Englewood Cliffs: Prentice-Hall.

Lynes, R. 1985. The Lively Audience. New York: Harper & Row.

Martorella, R. 1982. The Sociology of Opera. South Hadley: J. F. Bergin.

Moore, M. S. 1985. Yankee Blues: Musical Culture and American Identity. Bloomington: Indiana U. Press.

Mueller, J. H. 1951. The American Symphony Orchestra. Bloomington: Indiana U. Press.

Mueller, K. H. 1973. Twenty-Seven Major Symphony Orchestras. Bloomington: Indiana U. Press.

Nettl, B., ed. 1978. Eight Urban Musical Cultures. Champaign: U. of Illinois Press.

Preston, K. K. 1987. John Prosperi and Friends: A Study of Professional Musicians in Washington, 1877–1900. Stuyvesant: Pendragon Press.

Rosenberg, D. & B. Rosenberg. 1979. The Music Makers. New York: Columbia U. Press.

Schuessler, K. F. 1980. Musical Taste and Socio-Economic Background. New York: Arno Press.

Shepherd, J., P. Virden, G. Vulliamy & T. Wishart. 1977. Whose Music? New Brunswick: Transaction Books.

Silbermann, A. 1963. The Sociology of Music. London: Routledge & Kegan Paul.

Spencer, P. 1985. Society and the Dance. Cambridge: Cambridge U. Press.

Stebbins, R. A. 1979. Amateurs. Beverly Hills: Sage.

Supicic, I., ed. 1987. Music in Society: A Guide to the Sociology of Music, Revised in English. Stuyvesant: Pendragon Press.

Thomson, V. 1962. The State of Music, 2nd ed. New York: Random House (Vintage).

Weber, W. 1975. Music and the Middle Class. New York: Holmes & Meier.

Woodworth, G. W. 1964. The World of Music. Cambridge: Belknap Press of Harvard U. Press.

Zaimont, J. L., C. Overhauser & J. Gottlieb, eds. 1984 The Musical Woman: An International Perspective. Westport: Greenwood Press.

Popular and Folk Arts

Abel, R. H. 1963. The Funnies. London: Collier, Macmillan.

Bailey, P., ed. 1987. Music Hall. London: Open U. Press.

Ball-Rokeach, S. J. & M. G. Cantor, eds. 1986. Media, Audience, and Social Structure. Newbury Park: Sage.

Barnett, A. W. 1984. Community Murals: The People's Art. New York: Associated U. Presses.

Barthes, R. 1983. The Fashion System. New York: Hill & Wang.

Bennett, H. S. 1980. On Becoming a Rock Musician. Amherst: U. of Massachusetts Press.

Bennett, T. C. Mercer & J. Woollcott. 1986. Popular Culture and Social Relations. London: Open U. Press.

Berger, A. A. 1974. The Comic-Stripped American. Baltimore: Penguin Books.

Blumer, H. 1933. Movies and Conduct. New York: Macmillan.

Brand, O. 1962. The Ballad Mongers. New York: Funk & Wagnalls (Minerva).

Bratton, J. S. & P. Bailey. ed. 1987. Music Hall. London: Open U. Press.

Braun, D. D. 1969. The Sociology and History of American Music and Dance 1920–1968. Ann Arbor: Ann Arbor Publishers.

Cantor, M. G. 1971. The Hollywood TV Producer. New York: Basic Books.

Chambers, I. 1985. Urban Rhythms. New York: St. Martin's Press.

Chambers, I. 1986. Popular Culture: The Metropolitan Experience. London: Methuen.

Christgau, R. 1973. Any Old Way You Choose It. Baltimore: Penguin Books.

Dachs, David. 1964. Anything Goes: The World of Popular Music. Indianapolis: Bobbs-Merrill.

Davies, P. & B. Neve, eds. 1981. Cinema, Politics and Society in America. New York: St. Martin's Press.

Davison, P., R. Meyersohn & E. Shils, eds. 1978. Literary Taste, Culture and Mass Communication. Teaneck: Somerset House.

Denisoff, R. S. 1973. Great Day Coming. Baltimore: Penguin Books.

Denisoff, R. S. 1975. Solid Gold. Rutgers: Transaction Books.

Denisoff, R. S. 1983. Sing a Song of Social Significance. Bowling Green: Bowling Green State U. Popular Press.

Denisoff, R. S. 1986. Tarnished Gold: The Record Industry Revisited. New Brunswick: Transaction Books.

Denisoff, R. S. & R. A. Peterson, eds. 1972. The Sounds of Social Change. Chicago: Rand McNally.

Denney, R. 1957. The Astonished Muse. Chicago: U. of Chicago Press. [1969. New York: Grosset & Dunlap].

De Turk, D. A. & A. Poulin, Jr., eds. 1967. The American Folk Scene: Dimensions of the Folksong Revival. New York: Dell (Laurel).

Eisen, J., ed. 1969. The Age of Rock: Sounds of the American Cultural Revolution. New York: Random House (Vintage).

Ewen, S. & E. Ewen. 1982. Channels of Desire. New York: McGraw-Hill.

Frith, S. 1983. Sound Effects: Youth, Leisure, and the Politics of Rock 'n' Roll. London: Constable.

Hall, S. & P. Whannel. 1964. The Popular Arts. Boston: Beacon Press.

Hammel, W. M., ed. 1972. The Popular Arts in America: A Reader. New York: Harcourt, Brace, Jovanovich.

Haralambos, M. 1979. Right On: From Blues to Soul in Black America. New York: DaCapo Press.

Harker, D. 1985. Fakesong. London: Open U. Press.

Hebdige, D. 1987. Cut 'n' Mix: Culture, Identity and Caribbean Music. London: Methuen.

Heilbut, T. 1975. The Gospel Sound. Garden City: Doubleday (Anchor).

Hirsch, P. 1969. The Structure of the Popular Music Industry. Ann Arbor: Institute for Social Research.

Hoggart, R. 1957. The Uses of Literacy: Changing Patterns in English Mass Culture. Boston: Beacon Press.

Huaco, G. A. 1965. The Sociology of Film Art. New York: Basic Books.

Jacobs, N., ed. 1964. Culture for the Millions? Boston: Beacon Press.

Jarvie, I. C. 1970. Movies and Society. New York: Basic Books.

Kaplan, S. 1984. Understanding Popular Culture. Berlin: Mouton.

Katz, E. & M. Gurevitch. 1976. The Secularization of Leisure. Cambridge: Harvard U. Press.

Keil, C. 1966. Urban Blues. Chicago: U. of Chicago Press.

Kofsky, F. 1970. Black Nationalism and the Revolution in Music. New York: Pathfinder Press.

Kracauer, S. 1947. From Caligari to Hitler. Princeton: Princeton U. Press.

Levy, E. 1988. And the Winner is. . . . New York: Ungar.

Lewis, G. H., ed. 1972. Side-Saddle on the Golden Calf: Social Structure and Popular Culture in America. Pacific Palisades: Goodyear.

Lull, J., ed. 1987. Popular Music and Communication. Beverly Hills: Sage.

Malone, B. C. 1968. Country Music, U.S.A. Austin: U. of Texas Press.

May, L. 1980. Screening Out the Past. New York: Oxford U. Press.

Mayer, J. P. 1979. Sociology of Film. London: Faber & Faber.

Nanry, C., ed. 1972. American Music: From Storyville to Woodstock. New Brunswick: Transaction Press.

Newton, F. [E. Hobsbaum]. 1975. The Jazz Scene. New York: DaCapo Press.

Orman, J. 1984. The Politics of Rock Music. Chicago: Nelson-Hall.

Palmer, R. 1981. Deep Blues. New York: Viking Press.

Pye, M. 1979. The Movie Brats. Boston: Faber & Faber.

Rodntizky, J. L. 1976. Minstrels of the Dawn: The Folk-Protest Singer as a Cultural Hero. Chicago: Nelson-Hall.

Rust. F. 1969. Dance in Society. London: Routledge & Kegan Paul.

Spencer, P. 1985. Society and the Dance. Cambridge: Cambridge U. Press.

Street, J. 1986. Rebel Rock: The Politics of Popular Music. Oxford: Basil Blackwell.

Swingewood, A. 1977. The Myth of Mass Culture. London: Macmillan.

Tawa, N. 1984. A Music for the Millions. New York: Pendragon Press.

Whitcomb, I. 1974. After the Ball: Pop Music from Rag to Rock. Baltimore: Penguin Books.

Sociology of Literature

Abbe, D. M. van. 1964. Image of a People. Modern German Writing In Its Social Context, New York:

Altick, R. D. 1957. The English Common Reader. Cambridge: Cambridge U. Press.

Barnett, J. H. 1939. Divorce and the American Divorce Novel, 1858–1937: A Study in Literary Reflections of Social Influences. Philadelphia: privately printed U. of Pennsylvania thesis.

Berger, M. 1977. Real and Imagined Worlds: The Novel and Social Science. Cambridge: Harvard U. Press.

Bradbury, M. 1971. The Social Context of Modern English Literature, London:

Burke, K. 1945. A Grammar of Motives. New York: Prentice-Hall.

Burns, E. & T. Burns, eds. 1973. Sociology of Literature and Drama. Harmondsworth: Penguin Books.

Cowley, M. 1954. The Literary Situation. New York: Viking.

Dudek, L. 1960. Literature and the Press. Toronto: Ryerson.

Duncan, H. D. 1953. Language and Literature in Society. New York: Bedminster Press.

Ennis, P. H. 1965. Adult Book Reading in the United States, Report #105. Chicago: National Opinion Research Center.

Escarpit, R. 1961. The Sociology of Literature. London: Frank Cass.

Gold, B., ed. 1982. Literary and Artistic Patronage in Ancient Rome. Austin: U. of Texas Press.

Graña, C. 1964. Bohemian Versus Bourgeois. New York: Basic Books.

Guerard, A. 1935. Literature and Society. Boston: Lothrop, Lee & Shepard.

Hall, J. 1979. The Sociology of Literature. London: Longman.

Kingston, P. W. & J. R. Cole. 1986. The Wages of Writing: Per Word, Per Piece or Perhaps. New York: Columbia U. Press.

Laurenson, D. T. & A. Swingewood. 1972. The Sociology of Literature. New York: Schocken Books.

Long, E. 1985. The American Dream and the Popular Novel. Boston: Routledge & Kegan Paul.

Lowenthal, L. 1961. Literature, Popular Culture, and Society. Englewood Cliffs: Prentice-Hall (Spectrum).

Lowenthal, L. 1986. Literature and the Image of Man, new & expanded. New Brunswick: Transaction Books.

Orr, J. 1977. Tragic Realism and Modern Society. London: Macmillan.

Radway, J. A. 1984. Reading the Romance: Women, Patriarchy, and Popular Literature. Chapel Hill: U. of North Carolina Press.

Routh, J. & J. Wolff, eds. 1977. The Sociology of Literature: Theoretical Approaches. Keele: U. of Keele.

Schücking, L. L. 1944. The Sociology of Literary Taste. London: Kegan Paul.

Spearman, D. 1966. The Novel and Society. New York: Barnes & Noble.

Strelka, J. P., ed. 1973. Literary Criticism and Sociology. University Park: Pennsylvania State U. Press.

Thompson, A. 1979. Social Roles for the Artist. Liverpool: Art, Politics and Society Group.

Unseld, S. 1980. The Author and His Publisher. Chicago: U. of Chicago Press.

Watt, I. 1965. The Rise of the Novel. Berkeley: U. of California Press.

Wilson, R. N. 1986. Experiencing Creativity. New Brunswick: Transaction Books.

Funding and Control: Economics and Policy

Arts Council of Great Britain. 1952+ Annual Reports. London: Arts Council of Great Britain.

Banfield, E. 1984. The Democratic Muse: Visual Arts and the Public Interest. New York: Basic Books.

Baumol, W. J. & W. G. Bowen. 1966. Performing Arts—The Economic Dilemma. Cambridge: MIT Press.

Blau, J. R. 1984. Architects and Firms. Cambridge: MIT Press.

Blaug, M., ed. 1976. The Economics of the Arts. Boulder: Westview Press.

Brody, J. J. 1971. Indian Painters and White Patrons. Albuquerque: U. of New Mexico Press.

Coser, L. A., C. Kadushin & W. W. Powell. 1982. Books: The Culture and Commerce of Publishing. New York: Basic Books.

Cox, A. 1982. Art-as-Politics: The Abstract Expressionist Avant-Garde and Society. Ann Arbor: UMI Research Press.

DiMaggio, P. ed., 1986. Non-profit Enterprise in the Arts. New York: Oxford U. Press.

Dorian, F. 1964. Commitment to Culture: Art Patronage in Europe, Its Significance for America. Pittsburgh: U. of Pittsburgh Press.

Dubin, S. C. 1987. Bureaucratizing the Muse: Public Funds and the Cultural Worker. Chicago: U. of Chicago Press.

Feld, A. L., M. O'Hare & J. M. D. Schuster. 1983. Patrons Despite Themselves: Taxpayers and Arts Policy. New York: New York U. Press.

Ford Foundation. 1974. The Finances of the Performing Arts, 2 vols. New York:

Gibans, N. F. 1982. The Community Arts Council Movement: History, Opinions, Issues. New York: Praeger.

Harris, J. S. 1970. Government Patronage of the Arts in Great Britain. Chicago: U. of Chicago Press.

Hendon, W. S., J. L. Shanahan & A. J. MacDonald, eds. 1980. Economic Policy for the Arts. Cambridge: Abt Books.

Keen, G. 1971. Money and Art. New York: G. P. Putnam's Sons.

Lowry, W. M., ed. 1984. The Arts and Public Policy in the United States. Englewood Cliffs: Prentice-Hall.

Moore, T. G. 1968. The Economics of the American Theater. Durham: Duke U. Press.

Moulin, R. 1987. The French Art Market: A Sociological View. New Brunswick: Rutgers U. Press.

Netzer, D. 1978. The Subsidized Muse. Cambridge: Cambridge U. Press.

Rockefeller Brothers Fund. 1965. The Performing Arts: Problems and Prospects. New York: McGraw-Hill.

Ryan, J. 1985. The Production of Culture in the Music Industry: The ASCAP-BMI Controversy. Lanham: U. Press of America.

Schuman, W. & R. Stevens. 1979. Economic Pressures and the Future of the Arts. New York: New York U. Press.

Taylor, F. & A. L. Barresi. 1984. The Arts at a New Frontier: The National Endowment for the Arts. New York: Plenum Press.

Toffler, A. 1965. The Culture Consumers. Baltimore: Penguin Books.

Articles

General

Abrams, M. H. 1985. "Art-as-such." Bulletin of the American Academy of Arts and Science 38: 8–33.

Ackerman, J. S. 1969. "The demise of the avant-garde: Notes on the sociology of recent American art." Comparative Studies in Society and History II: 371–384.

Albrecht, M. C. 1968. "Art as an institution." American Sociological Review 33: 383–397.

Anderson, C. H. 1967. "Kitsch and the academic." Sociology and Social Research 51: 445–452.

Bensman, J. & I. Gerver. 1958. "Art and mass society," Social Problems 6: 4–10.

Barnett, J. H. 1958. "Research areas in the sociology of art." Sociology and Social Research 42: 401–405.

Barnett, J. H. 1959. "The sociology of art." Pp. 197–214 in R. K. Merton, L. Broom & L. S. Cottrell, Jr., eds. Sociology Today. New York: Basic Books, 1959.

Bloch, H. A. 1943. "Towards the development of a sociology of literary and art forms" American Sociological Review 8: 313–20.

Brodbeck, A. J. 1964. "Placing aesthetic developments in social context: a program of value analysis." The Journal of Social Issues 20: 8–25.

Chalmers, F. G. 1974. "Aesthetic experience and social status." Arts in Society 11: 300–306.

Child, I. L. 1972. "The experts and the bridge of judgment that crosses every cultural gap," in Change: Readings in Society and Human Behavior, Del Mar: CRM Books.

DiMaggio, P. 1987. "Classification in art," American Sociological Review 52: 440–455.

DiMaggio, P. & P. Hirsch. 1976. "Production organizations in the arts." American Behavioral Scientist 19: 735–752.

DiMaggio, P. & M. Useem. 1978a. "Cultural democracy in a period of cultural expansion: the social composition of arts audiences in the United States." Social Problems 26: 179–197.

DiMaggio, P. & M. Useem. 1978b. "Social class and arts consumption." Theory and Society 5: 141–161.

Duncan, H. D. 1957. "Sociology of art, literature, and music," in H. P. Becker & A. Boskoff, eds., Modern Social Theory. New York: Dryden Press.

Etzkorn, K. P. 1966. "Non-rational elements in the sociology of arts." Indian Sociological Bulletin 3: 279–285.

Etzkorn, K. P. 1975. "Social validity of art and social change." Revue Internationale de Sociologie 11: 38–48.

Farnsworth, P. R. 1960. "The effects of role-taking on artistic achievement." Journal of Aesthetics and Art Criticism 18: 345–349.

Ferrarotti, F. 1969. "The sociological perspective in studies of art and literature." La Critica Sociologica 9: 30–32.

Ferrucci, C. 1971. "Methodological considerations on the sociology of literature." La Critica Sociologica 18: 164–68.

Haacke, H. 1978. "The Good Will Umbrella," Qualitative Sociology 1: 108–21.

Halley, J. & H. Etzkowitz. 1981. "Visual sociology, the sociology of art and the sociology of culture: A common approach and organizing strategy." In T. J. Curry, ed. Whither Visual Sociology. Columbus: State University Visual Research Laboratory Report.

Henning, E. B. 1960. "Patronage and style in the arts: a suggestion concerning their relations." Journal of Aesthetics and Art Criticism 18: 264–271.

Hertzler, J. O. 1961. "Art institutions." in his American Social Institutions. Boston: Allyn & Bacon.

Jones, D. 1942. "Quantitative analysis of motion picture content." Public Opinion Quarterly 6: 411–428.

Kadushin, C. 1976. "Networks and circles in the production of culture." In R. A. Peterson, ed. The Production of Culture. Beverly Hills: Sage, pp. 107–122.

Lehman, H. C. 1947. "National differences in creativity." American Journal of Sociology 52: 475–488.

Levy, E. 1980. "Youth, generations and artistic change." Youth and Society 12: 142–172.

Martindale, D. 1960. "The sociology of art: art and the community." In his American Society. Princeton: D. Van Nostrand, pp. 496–510.

Meadows, P. & M. Meadows. 1942. "Social determination of art." Sociology and Social Research 26: 310–313.

Merrill, F. E. 1968. "Art and the self." Sociology and Social Research 52: 185–194.

Morawski, S. 1973. "Politicians versus artists." Arts in Society 10: 8–18.

Morris, R. E. 1958. "What is the sociology of art?" American Catholic Sociological Review 4: 310–321.

Moulin R. 1986. "Introduction," sociologie de l'art, proceedings of the colloque international Marseille. Paris: La Documentation Française, pp. XIff.

Mueller, J. H. 1935. "Is art the product of its age?" Social Forces 13: 367–376.

Mueller, J. H. 1945. "Methods of measurement of aesthetic folkways." American Journal of Sociology 51: 276–282.

Mueller, J. H. 1965. "The arts and the individual." Music Educator's Journal 52: 48–50.

Mukerji, C. 1978. "Artwork." American Journal of Sociology 84: 348–365.

Nochlin, L. 1967. "The invention of the avant-garde. In T. B. Hess & J. Ashberry, eds. Avant-garde Art. London: Collier, pp. 1–24.

Peterson, R. A. & D. G. Berger. 1975. "Cycles in symbol production." American Sociological Review 40: 158–173.

Rosengren, K. I. 1984. "Cultural indicators for the comparative study of culture." In G. Melischek, K. E. Rosengren, & J. Stappers, eds. Cultural Indicators. Vienna: Osterreichischen Akad. Wissenschaften.

Roucek, J. S. & R. P. Mohan. 1972. "An essay on the developments in and implications for the sociology of art." International Journal of Contemporary Sociology 9: 214–230.

Strauss, A. 1986. "Three related frameworks for studying artistic production." Sociologie de l'art; Proceedings of the Colloque international Marseilles, 1985, Paris: La documentation Française, pp. 183–190.

Sydie, R. A. 1981. "The state of the art: Sociology of art in the Canadian context." Canadian Review of Sociology and Anthropology 18: 14–29.

Thorndike, E. L. & E. Woodyard. 1943. "The relation between the aesthetic status of a community and its status in other respects." American Journal of Sociology 49: 59.

Toffler, A. 1967. "The art of measuring the arts." The Annals of the Academy of Social Science 373: 141–155.

Truzzi, M. 1978. "Toward a general sociology of the folk, popular, and elite arts." Research in Sociology of Knowledge, Sciences and Art 1: 279–289.

Tumin, M. 1971. "The arts in a technological environment." Arts in Society 8: 483–493.

Virgilio, C. 1971. "Notes toward a sociological analysis of artistic phenomena." Sociologia 5: 165–204.

White, D. 1978. "Art and the social scientists." New Society 45: 617–619.

Society and the Arts: Research, Theories, Models, Hypotheses,

Adorno, T. W. 1978. "On the social situation of music." Telos 35: 128–164.

Balfe, J. H. 1986. "Moving toward a new paradigm." In J. P. Robinson, ed. Social Science and the Arts: Lanham: U. Press of America. pp. 5–17.

Becker, H. S. 1974. "Art as Collective Action." American Sociological Review 39: 767–76.

Benjamin, W. 1960. "The work of art in the epoch of mechanical reproduction." Studies on the Left 1: 28–46.

Bergesen, A. 1984. "The semantic equation: A theory of the social origins of art styles." Sociological Theory 2: 187–221.

Blau, J. R. 1980. "A framework of meaning in architecture." In G. Broadbent, R. Bunt & C. Jencks, eds. Signs, Symbols and Architecture. New York: John Wiley, pp. 333–368.

Blau, J. R. 1986a. "High culture as mass culture." Society 23: 65–69.

Blau, J. R. 1986b. "The elite arts, more or less *de rigueur*. A comparative analysis of metropolitan culture." Social Forces 64: 875–905.

Blau, J. R., P. M. Blau & R. M. Golden. 1985. "Social inequality and the arts." American Journal of Sociology 91: 309–331.

Blau, J. R. & R. H. Hall. 1986. "The supply of performing arts in metropolitan places." Urban Affairs Quarterly 22: 42–65.

Blau, P. M., J. R. Blau, G. A. Quets & T. Tada. 1986. "Social inequality and art institutions." Sociological Forum 1: 561–585.

Blizek, W. 1974. "An institutional theory of art," British Journal of Aesthetics 14: 142–50.

Bourdieu, P. 1968. "Outline of a sociological theory of art perception." International Social Science Journal 20: 589–612.

Burke, P. 1971. "Pierre Francastel and the sociology of art." European Journal of Sociology 12: 141–154.

Burnham, J. 1970. "Systems and art." Arts in Society 6: 195–204.

Burton, B. 1985. "A cultural study of music: Suggestions for a contemporary framework." Critical Social Research 1: 67–85.

Cameron, W. B. 1963. "Is jazz a folk-art?" In his Informal Sociology. New York: Random House, pp. 109–117.

Clignet, R. 1979. "The variability of paradigms in the production of culture." American Sociological Review 44: 392–409.

Crane, D. 1976. "Reward systems in art, science and religion," American Behavioral Scientist.

Duncan, H. D. 1957. "Sociology of art, literature, and music." In H. P. Becker & A. Boskoff, eds. Modern Social Theory. New York: Dryden, pp. 482–497.

D'Azevedo, W. L. 1958. "A structural approach to esthetics: Towards a definition of art in anthropology." American Anthropologist 60: 702–14.

Etzkorn, K. P. 1964. "Georg Simmel and the sociology of music," Social Forces 43: 101–107.

Etzkorn, K. P. 1974. "On music, social structures and sociology." International Review of the Aesthetics and Sociology of Music 5: 43–49.

Fernandez, J. W. 1966. "Principles of opposition and vitality in Fang aesthetics." Journal of Aesthetics and Art Criticism 25: 53–64.

Fernandez, J. W. 1969. "The exposition and imposition of order: Artistic expression in Fang culture." In W. L. d'Azevedo, ed. The Traditional Artist in African Societies. Bloomington: Indiana U. Press, pp. 194–220.

Fischer, J. L. 1961. "Art style as cultural cognitive maps," American Anthropologist 63: 79–93.

Foster, A. W. 1976. "The slow radical: Restrictions on the artist as a change agent." British Journal of Aesthetics 16: 161–169.

Foster, A. W. 1979. "Dominant themes in interpreting the arts." European Journal of Sociology 20: 301–332.

Gaertner, J. A. 1955. "Art as the function of an audience." Daedalus 86: 80–93.

Goldfarb, J. C. 1980. "The repressive context of art work." Theory and Society 9: 623–632.

Grohs, G. 1970. "Problems of a sociology of the fine arts." European Journal of Sociology 11: 155–176.

Hamblen, K. A. 1983. "Motivational theories of art evaluated according to cross-cultural and sociological criteria." International Journal of Contemporary Sociology 20: 3–4.

Hamblen, K. A. 1986. "Bases of study for the sociology of art." International Journal of Contemporary Sociology 23: 41–67.

Herskovits, M. J. 1959. "Art and value." In R. Goldwater, ed. Aspects of Primitive Art. New York: Museum of Primitive Art, pp. 41–68.

Horowitz, I. L. & C. Nanry. 1975. "Ideologies and theories about American jazz." Journal of Jazz Studies 2: 24–41.

Jaspers, J. M. 1984. "Art and audiences: Do politics matter?" Berkeley Journal of Sociology 29: 153–180.

Kaplan, M. 1960. "Art as leisure." In his Leisure in America: A Social Inquiry. New York: John Wiley.

Karbusicky, V. "The interaction between 'reality-work of art-society'." International Social Science Journal 20: 644–655.

Lucie-Smith, E. 1970. "Manifestations of current social trends in contemporary art." In J. Creedy, ed. The Social Context of Art. London: Tavistock, pp. 27–44.

Malraux, A. 1951. "Art, popular art, and the illusion of the folk." Partisan Review 18: 487–495.

Mannheim, K. 1952. "Weltanschauung: its mode of presentation." In his Essays on the Sociology of Knowledge. London: Routledge & Kegan Paul, pp. 83–133.

Martindale, D. 1978. "Aesthetic theory and the sociology of art: The social foundations of classicism and romanticism." Research in Sociology of Knowledge, Sciences and Art 1: 259–277.

Messinger, J. 1958. "Reflections on aesthetic talent." Basic College Quarterly 4: 20–24.

Morawski, S. 1971. "Three functions of art." Arts in Society 8: 290–305.

Mueller, J. H. 1938. "The folkway of art: An analysis of the social theories of art." American Journal of Sociology 44: 222–238.

Mueller, J. H. 1956. "The social nature of musical taste." Journal of Research in Music Education 4: 113–122.

Mueller, J. H. 1958. "Social nature of musical taste." In T. Madison, ed. Basic Concepts in Music Education. n.p.: National Society for the Study of Education, pp. 99–105.

Mukerjee, R. 1944. "Art as social science." Sociological Review 36: 60–66.

Mukerjee, R. 1945a. "Social disguise as the principle of art." Sociology and Social Research 30: 3–10.

Mukerjee, R. 1945b. "The sociological approach to art." Sociology and Social Research 30: 177–184.

Mukerjee, R. 1945c. "The meaning and evolution of art in society." American Sociological Review 10: 496–503.

Mumford, L. 1957. "The role of the creative arts in contemporary society." The Virginia Quarterly Review 33: 522–538.

Munro, T. 1955. "Do the arts progress?" Journal of Aesthetics and Art Criticism 14: 175–190.

Munro, T. 1961. "Do the arts evolve? Some recent conflicting answers." Journal of Aesthetics and Art Criticism 19: 407–418.

Munro, T. 1962. "What causes creative epochs in the arts?" Journal of Aesthetics and Art Criticism 21: 35–48.

Parsons, T. 1951. "The role of the artist." In his The Social System. Glencoe: The Free Press, pp. 408–414.

Peterson, R. A. 1978. "The production of cultural change." Social Research 45: 292–314.

Peterson, R. A. 1979. "Revitalizing the culture concept." Annual Review of Sociology 4: 137–166.

Ross, E. A. 1897. "Social control, VIII." American Journal of Sociology 3: 64–78.

Sapir, E. 1924. "Culture: genuine or spurious." American Journal of Sociology 29: 401–429.

Silbermann, A. 1968. "Introduction, a definition of the sociology of art." International Social Science Journal 20: 467–588.

Silver, H. R. 1979. "Rethinking arts and crafts: a comment on Becker." American Journal of Sociology 84: 1452–1456.

Smith, T. S. 1974. "Aestheticism and social structure." American Sociological Review 39: 725–743.

Sorokin, P. A. 1966. "Sociology of aesthetic systems." In his Sociological Theories of Today. New York: Harper & Row.

Steiner, R. L. & J. Weiss. 1951. "Veblen revised in the light of counter-snobbery." Journal of Aesthetics and Art Criticism 9: 263–268.

Tomars, A. S. 1964. "Class systems and the arts." In W. J. Cahnman & A. Boskoff, eds. Sociology and History. Glencoe: The Free Press, pp. 472–483.

Wolfe, A. W. 1969. "Social structural bases of art." Current Anthropology 10: 3–44.

Wright, D. F. 1975. "Musical meaning and its social determinants." Sociology 9: 419–435.

Aesthetics and Philosophy

Becker, S. & J. Walton "Social science and the world of Hans Haacke." In H. Haacke. Framing and Being Framed. Halifax: Nova Scotia College of Art and Design, pp. 145–53.

Child, I. L. 1968. "Aesthetics." In G. Lindzey & E. Aronson, eds. Handbook of Social Psychology, Vol. III. Reading: Addison-Wesley, pp. 853–916.

Child, I. L. 1968. "The experts and the bridge of judgment that crosses every cultural gap." In Change: Readings in Society and Human Behavior. Del Mar: CRM Books, pp. 16–21.

Crowley, D. J. 1968. "Aesthetic judgment and cultural relativism." Journal of Aesthetics and Art Criticism 17: 187–193.

Danto, A. 1964. "The artworld," Journal of Philosophy 41: 571–84.

Dark, P. J. C. 1967. "The study of ethno-aesthetics: The visual arts." In J. Helm, ed. Essays on the Verbal and Visual Arts." Seattle: U. of Washington Press, pp. 131–148.

Davydov, Y. 1970. "Aesthetics and sociology," Society and Leisure 2: 5–27.

D'Azevedo, W. L. 1958. "A structural approach to aesthetics: Toward a definition of art in anthropology." American Anthropologist 60: 702–714.

Flores, T. 1985. "The anthropology of aesthetics. Dialectical Anthropology 10: 27–41.

Gombrich, E. H. 1968. "Style." In D. L. Sills, ed. International Encyclopedia of the Social Sciences, Vol. 15. New York: Macmillan, pp. 352–363.

Hafner, E. M. 1969. "The new reality in art and science." Comparative Studies in Society and History 11: 385–397.

Ianni, L. A. 1969. "Science and art as forms of communication." Arts in Society 6: 165–175.

Iwao, S. & I. L. Child. 1966. "Comparison of aesthetic judgments by American experts and by Japanese potters." Journal of Social Psychology 68: 27–33.

Jamieson, J. W. 1984. "Anthropology and the philosophy of art." Mankind Quarterly 25: 145–162.

Kaelin, E. 1969. "Between scientist and humanist." Arts in Society 6: 215–227.

Kaelin, E. 1972. "The social uses of art: A plea for the institution." Arts in Society 9: 371–386.

Leach, E. R. 1954. "Aesthetics." In E. E. Evans-Pritchard et al, eds. The Institutions of Primitive Society. Glencoe: The Free Press.

Marcuse, H. 1970. "Art as a form of reality." In E. Fry, ed. On the Future of Art. New York: Viking Press, pp. 123–134.

Marcuse, H. 1972. "Art and revolution." In his Counter-Revolution and Revolt. Boston: Beacon Press.

Martin, B. 1984. "The arts as languages: A sociological comment." Journal of Aesthetic Education 18: 59–81.

Mead, G. H. 1926. "The nature of aesthetic experience." International Journal of Ethics. 36: 382–393.

Mendoza de Arce, D. 1976. "The concept of musical meaning in some modern sociological theories." Revue Internationale de Sociologie 12: 19–34.

Redfield, R. 1959. "Art and icon." In R. Goldwater, ed. Aspects of Primitive Art. New York: Museum of Primitive Art, pp. 11–40.

Schapiro, M. 1953. "Style." In A. L. Kroeber et al, eds. Anthropology Today. Chicago: U. of Chicago Press, pp. 287–312.

Virden, P. 1972. "The social determinants of aesthetic styles." British Journal of Aesthetics 12: 175–185.

Wolin, R. 1984. "Modernism vs Postmodernism." Telos 62: 9–29.

Historical Analyses

Ackerman, J. S. 1969. "The demise of the avant garde." Comparative Studies in Society and History 11: 371–384.

Andrews, P. 1977. "The birth of the talkies." Saturday Review 5: 40, 42–43.

Bell, V. G. H. 1986. "The idea of art for art's sake: Intellectual origins, social conditions, and poetic doctrine." Science and Society 50: 415–439.

Bell, Q. 1961. "Conformity and non-conformity in the fine arts." In S. M. Lipset & L. Lowenthal, eds. Culture and Social Character. New York: Free Press of Glencoe, pp. 389–403.

Benedict, P. 1985. "Towards the comparative study of the popular market for art: The ownership of paintings in Seventeenth-Century Metz." Past and Present 109: 100–117.

Caswell, A. B. 1977. "Social and moral music." In G. McCue, ed. Music in American Society, 1776–1976. New Brunswick: Transaction Books, pp. 47–72.

Crane, D. 1986. "Avant-garde art and social change: the New York art world and the transformation of the reward system 1940–1980." Sociologie de l'art, Proceedings of the Colloque international Marseille, 1985. Paris: La documentation Française. pp. 69–82.

DiMaggio, P. 1982. "Cultural entrepreneurship in nineteenth century Boston." Media, Culture and Society 4: 33–50.

Dowd, D. L. 1951. "Art as national propaganda in the French Revolution." Public Opinion Quarterly 15: 532–546.

Egbert, D. D. 1967. "The idea of 'avant-garde' in art and politics." American Historical Review 73: 339–366.

Goddard, W. Z. 1936. "Literary taste and democracy." Sociological Review 28: 423–437.

Goranov, K. 1981. "History and the sociology of art." International Social Science Journal 33: 611–623.

Greenfeld, L. 1981. "The social context of artistic style: Impressionism in France and Critical Realism in Russia." Knowledge and Society: Studies in the Sociology of Culture Past and Present. 3: 217–255.

Halfpenny, E. 1943. "The influence of timbre and technique on musical aesthetic: a study of music and sociology." Music Review 4: 250–265.

Hammond, P. E. & S. N. Hammond. 1979. "The internal logic of dance: A Weberian perspective on the history of ballet." Journal of Social History 12: 591–608.

Haskell, F. 1968. "Art and society." International Encyclopedia of the Social Sciences. New York: Crowell-Collier & Macmillan.

Isherwood, R. M. 1978. "Popular musical entertainment in eighteenth-century Paris." International Review of the Aesthetics and Sociology of Music 9: 295–309.

Josephs, W. & G. S. Snyderman. 1939. "Bohemia: The underworld of art." Social Forces 18: 187–199.

Kasdan, L. & J. H. Kasdan. 1970. "Tradition and change: The case of music." Comparative Studies in Society and History 12: 50–58.

Kavolis, V. 1979. "Social evolution of the artistic enterprise." Research in Sociology of Knowledge, Sciences and Art 2: 155–188.

Keppel, F. P. 1933. "The arts in social life." In President's Research Committee on Social Trends. Recent Social Trends, Vol. II. New York: McGraw-Hill.

Kofsky, R. 1979. "Afro-American innovation and the folk treatment in jazz: Their historical significance." Journal of Ethnic Studies 7: 1–12.

Kolodin, I. 1977. "Edison's baby: From tinfoil to tape." Saturday Review (July 23): 20–22.

Larson, C. 1939. "The cultural products of the WPA." Public Opinion Quarterly 3: 491–496.

Lowenthal, L. 1950. "Historical perspectives of popular culture." American Journal of Sociology 55: 323–332.

Lowenthal, L. & M. Fiske. 1957. "The debate over art and popular culture in eighteenth century England." In M. Komarovsky, ed. Common Frontiers of the Social Sciences. Glencoe: The Free Press, pp. 33–112 & 413–418.

Lowenthal, L. & I. Lawson. 1963. "The debate on cultural standards in nineteenth century England." Social Research 30: 417–433.

Marshak, M. 1944. "German fiction today: State control and public demand." American Journal of Sociology 49: 356–360.

Martin, W. "The life of the Dutch artist in the 17th century." The Burlington Magazine 7: 125–133 & 416–419.

Martorella, R. 1979. "Occupational specialization and aesthetic change in opera: Some historical inquiries." International Review of the Aesthetics and Sociology of Music 10: 9.

Means, R. L. & B. Doleman. 1968. "Notes on negro jazz: 1920–1950; The use of biographical materials in sociology." Sociological Quarterly 9: 332–342.

Pleasants, H. 1975. "America's impact on the arts: Music." Saturday Review 3: 88–93.

Rogers, M. 1959. "The Batignolles group: Creators of Impressionism." Autonomous Groups 14, nos. 3 & 4. [Reprinted 1970 in M. C. Albrecht, J. H. Barnett & M. Griff, eds. The Sociology of Art and Literature: A Reader. New York: Praeger, pp.194–220].

Schlesinger, A., Jr. 1977. "America at the movies." Saturday Review 5: 36–37.

Sieber, R. 1962. "The arts and their changing social function." Annals of the New York Academy of Sciences 96: 653–658.

Smith, C. S. 1970. "Art, technology and science: Notes on their historical interaction." Technology and Culture 11: 493–549.

Waltz, M. 1967. "Methodological reflections suggested by the study of groups of limited complexity: Outline of a sociology of medieval love poetry." International Social Science Journal 19: 599–613.

White, C. & H. C. White. 1964. "Institutional change in the French painting world." In R. N. Wilson, ed The Arts in Society. New York: Prentice-Hall, pp. 253–270.

Zolberg, V. L. 1980. "Displayed art and performed music." Sociological Quarterly 21: 219–231.

Anthropology of Art

Adams, M. J. 1973. "Structural aspects of a village art." American Anthropologist 75: 265–279.

Belo, J. 1955. "Balinese children's drawing." In M. Mead & M. Wolfenstein, eds. Childhood in Contemporary Cultures. Chicago: [Also in Jane Belo, ed. 1970. Traditional Balinese Culture. New York: Columbia U. Press].

Bohannan, P. 1961. "Artist and critic in tribal society." In M. W. Smith, ed. The Artist in Tribal Society. New York: Free Press of Glencoe.

Child, I. L. & L. Siroto. 1965. "Bakwele and American esthetic evaluations compared." Ethnology 4: 349–60.

Claerhout, G. H. 1965. "The concept of primitive applied to art," Current Anthropology 6: 432–38.

Etzkorn, K. P. 1973. "Reflections on ethnographic data." In W. L. d'Azevedo, ed. The Traditional Artist in African Societies. Bloomington: Indiana U. Press, pp. 343–78.

Firth, R. 1951. "The social framework of primitive art." In his Elements of Social Organization, New York: Philosophical Library, pp. 155–82. [Reprinted in D. Fraser, ed. 1966. The Many Faces of Primitive Art. Englewood Cliffs: Prentice-Hall, pp. 12–33].

Fischer, J. L. 1961. "Art style as cultural cognitive maps." American Anthropologist 63: 79–93.

Geertz, C. 1976. "Art as a cultural system." Modern Language Notes 91: 1473–1499.

Gerbrands, A. A. 1969. "The concept of style in non-western art.: In D. P. Biebuyck, ed. Tradition and Creativity in Tribal Art. Berkeley: U. of California Press, pp. 58–70.

Graburn, N. 1967. "The Eskimos and 'airport art'." Transaction: 28–33.

Graburn, N. 1984. "The evolution of tourist arts." Annals of Tourist Arts 11: 393–419.

Haag, W. G. 1960. "The artist as a reflection of his culture." In G. E. Dole & R. L. Carneiro, eds. Essays in the Science of Culture. New York: Thomas Y. Crowell.

Hanna, J. L. & W. J. Hanna. 1971. "The social significance of dance in black Africa." Civilizations 21: 238–242.

Herskovits, M. J. 1959. "Art and value." In R. Goldwater, ed. Aspects of Primitive Art. New York: The Museum of Primitive Art, pp. 41–68.

Himmelheber, H. 1963. "Personality and technique of African sculptors." In Technique and Personality in Primitive Art. New York: Museum of Primitive Art, pp. 79–110.

Leach, E. R. 1964. "Art in cultural context." In P. B. Hammond, ed. Cultural and Social Anthropology: Selected Readings. New York: Macmillan, pp. 344–350.

Leach, E. R. 1973. "Levels of communication and problems of taboo in the appreciation of primitive art." In A. Forge. Primitive Art and Society. London: Oxford U. Press, pp. 221–234.

Levine, M. H. 1957. "Prehistoric art and ideology." American Anthropologist 59: 949–962.

Linton, R. 1933. "Primitive art." The American Magazine of Art: 17–24.

Linton, R. 1941. "Primitive art." Kenyon Review 3: 34–51.

Lomax, A. 1959. "Folk song style." American Anthropologist 61: 927–954.

Lomax, A. 1960. "Saga of a folksong hunter." HiFi/Stereo: 38–46.

Lowie, R. H. 1921. "A note on aesthetics." American Anthropologist 23: 170–174.

Mead, M. 1959. "Creativity in cross-cultural perspective." In H. H. Anderson, ed. Creativity and It Cultivation. New York: Harpers.

Merriam, A. P. 1955a. "The use of music in the study of a problem of acculturation." American Anthropologist 57: 28–34.

Merriam, A. P. 1955b. "Music in American culture." American Anthropologist 57: 1173–1181.

Merriam, A. P. 1964. "The arts and anthropology." In S. Tax, ed. Horizons of Anthropology. Chicago: Aldine, pp. 224–236.

Mills, G. T. 1955. "Social anthropology and the art museum." American Anthropologist 57: 1002–1010.

Mills, G. T. 1957. "Art: an introduction to qualitative anthropology." Journal of Aesthetics and Art Criticism 16: 1–17.

Radin, P. 1955. "The literature of primitive peoples." Diogenes 12: 1–28.

Roe, P. G. 1979. "Marginal men: male artists among the Shipibo Indians of Peru." Anthropologila 21: 189–221.

Taylor, D. 1959. "Anthropologists on art." In M. H. Fried, ed. Readings in Anthropology II. New York: Crowell, pp. 478–490.

Whitten, N. E., Jr. 1968. "Personal networks and musical contexts in the Pacific lowlands of Columbia and Ecuador." Man 3: 50–63.

Wingert, P. S. 1950. "The cultural motivations of an artist." College Art Journal 9: 308–316.

Wolfe, A. W. 1967. "The complementarity of statistics and feeling in the study of art.: In J. Helm, ed. Essays on the Verbal and Visual Arts. Seattle: U. of Washington Press, pp. 149–159.

Visual Arts

Adler, J. 1975. "Innovative art and obsolescent artists." Social Research 42: 360–378.

Adler, J. 1976. "Revolutionary art and the art of revolution." Theory and Society 3: 417–435.

Amaya, M. 1979. "Victorians in Brooklyn." Art in America 67: 126–131.

Balfe, J. H. 1981. "Social mobility and modern art: Abstract Expressionism and its generative audience." Research in Social Movements, Conflicts and Change 4: 235–251.

Balfe, J. H. 1985. "Art style as political actor: social realism and its alternatives." Sociologia Internationalis 23: 3–26.

Becker, H. S. 1979. "Arts and crafts." American Journal of Sociology 83: 862–889.

Bergler, E. 1948. "The relation of the artist to society." American Imago 5: 247–58.

Bower, R. T. & L. M. Sharp. 1956. "The use of art in international communication: A case study." Public Opinion Quarterly 20: 221–229.

Bystryn, M. 1978. "Art galleries as gatekeepers." Social Research 45: 390–408.

Eye, A. 1918. "Women and the world of art." Arts and Decoration 10: 86–87.

Foster, A. W. 1986. "The many themes of alienation: Focus on the artist." In L. Herek & D. Rupel, ed. Alienation and Participation in Culture. Ljubljana: U. Edvard Kardelj, pp. 145–153.

Frumkin, R. M. 1961. "Social class, religion, values and dogmatism as factors in painting preferences." Indiana Journal of Social Research 2: 45–58.

Fyfe, G. J. 1986. "Art exhibitions and power during the Nineteenth Century." Sociological Review Monograph 32: 20–45.

Getzels, S. W. & M. Csikszentmihalyi. 1968. "On the roles, values and performance of future artists: A conceptual and empirical exploration." Sociological Quarterly 9: 516–530.

Graña, C. 1964. "French Impressionism as an urban art." Journal of Social Issues 20: 37–48.

Greenfeld, L. 1984. "The role of the public in the success of artistic styles." European Journal of Sociology 25: 83–98.

Griff, M. 1964a. "The recruitment of the artist." In R. N. Wilson, ed. The Arts in Society. Englewood Cliffs: Prentice-Hall, pp. 61–94.

Griff, M. 1964b. "Conflicts of the artist in mass society." Diogenes 46: 54–68.

Griff, M. 1968. "The recruitment and socialization of artists." International Encyclopedia of the Social Sciences V. New York: Crowell-Collier & Macmillan.

Halley, J. 1983. "Dada and its ideological practices: Resistance to rationalization." In E. Nikolov, ed. Contribution to the Sociology of the Arts: Reports from the 10th World Congress of Sociology, Mexico City, 1981, Sofia: Research Institute for Culture and the International Sociological Association Research Committee 37, pp. 336–347.

Halley, J. 1982. "The politics of style: Dada and the radical work of art," Art Workers News 11: 4.

Halley, J. 1986. "The sociology of reception: The alienation and recovery of Dada." In L. Herek & D. Rupel, eds. Alienation and Participation in Culture. Ljubljana: U. Edvard Kardelj, pp. 93–106.

Henning, E. B. 1960. "Patronage and style in the arts: A suggestion concerning their relations." Journal of Aesthetics and Art Criticism 18: 464–471.

Holmes, J. C. 1899. "Women as painters," Dome 3: 6.

Johnson, S. K. 1971. "Sociology of Christmas Cards," Transaction 8: 27–29.

Kavolis, V. 1963a. "A role theory of artistic interest." Journal of Social Psychology 60: 31–37.

Kavolis, V. 1963b. "Abstract Expressionism and Puritanism." Journal of Aesthetics and Art Criticism 21: 315–319.

Kavolis, V. 1963c. "Economic conditions and art styles," Journal of Aesthetics and Art Criticism 22: 437ff.

Kavolis, V. 1964a. "Economic correlates of artistic creativity." American Journal of Sociology 70: 332–341.

Kavolis, V. 1964b. "Collective anxiety as artistic inspiration.: Journal of Human Relations." 12: 459–465.

Kavolis, V. 1964c. "Art and content and social involvement." Social Forces 42: 467–472.

Kavolis, V. 1965a. "Artistic preferences of urban social classes." Pacific Sociological Review 8: 43–51.

Kavolis, V. 1965b. "Art content and economic reality." American Journal of Economics and Sociology 24: 321–328.

Kavolis, V. 1965c. "Political dynamics and artistic creativity." Sociology and Social Research 49: 412–424.

Kavolis, V. 1965d. "Art syle and social stratification." The Wisconsin Sociologist 4: 1–7.

Kavolis, V. 1970a. "The possibilities of an American artistic efflorescence." Journal of Aesthetic Education. 4: 21–36.

Kavolis, V. 1970b. "On the crises of creativity in contemporary art." Arts in Society 7: 205–207.

Kavolis, V. 1972. "Social uses of the notion of art." Arts in Society 9: 363–370.

Knapp, R. H., J. Brimner & M. White. 1959. "Educational level, class status and aesthetic preference." Journal of Social Psychology 50: 277–284.

Knapp, R. H. & S. M. Green. 1959. "Personality correlates of preference for abstract painting." American Psychology 14: 392.

Knapp, R. H. & S. M. Green. 1960. "Preferences for styles of abstract art and their personality correlates." Journal of Projective Techniques 24: 396–402.

Kolaja, J. & R. H. Wilson. 1954. "The theme of social isolation in American painting and poetry." Journal of Aesthetics and Art Criticism 13: 37–45.

Lang, G. & K. Lang. 1985. "The building and survival of artistic reputation: The case of the 'disappearing' lady etchers." Social Science Newsletter 70: 3–7.

Lawler, M. 1955. "Cultural influences on preferences for designs." Journal of Abnormal and Social Psychology 61: 690–692.

Levine, E. M. 1972. "Chicago's art world." Urban Life and Culture 1: 293–322.

Lipman, A. 1970. "Architectural education and the social comment of contemporary British architecture." Sociological Review 18: 5–27.

Luhmann, N. 1985. "The work of art and the self-reproduction of art." Thesis Eleven 12: 4–27.

Martinius, W. O. 1986. "Questions of style and taste—Art museums and national monuments." Netherlands Journal of Sociology 22: 18–35.

McCall, M. 1977. "Art without a market: Creating artistic value in a provincial art world." Symbolic Interaction 1: 32–43.

McCall, M. 1978. "The sociology of female artists." Studies in Symbolic Interaction 1: 289–318.

Mulkay, M. & E. Chaplin. 1982. "Aesthetics and the artistic career: A study of anomie in fine-art painting." Sociological Quarterly 23: 117–138.

Munsterberg, E. & P. H. Mussen. 1953. "The personality structures of art students." Journal of Personality 21: 457–466.

Neapolitan, J. & M. Ethridge. 1985. "An empirical examination of the existence of art, art/craft, and craft segment among craft media workers." Mid-American Review of Sociology 10: 45–64.

Nemser, Cindy. 1972. "Art Criticism and the gender prejudice," Arts Magazine 42–46.

Nelson, R. 1974. "Inner reality of women." Arts in Society 44–54.

Plessner, H. 1962. "Sociological observations on modern painting." Social Research 29: 190–200.

Porter, F. 1962. "Class content in American abstract painting." Art News 61: 24.

Rosenberg, H. 1965. "The art establishment." Esquire 62: 43–46, 114.

Rosenberg, H. 1971. "The artist as perceiver of social realities: The post-art artist." Arts in Society 8: 501–507.

Rosenblum, B. 1978. "Style as social process." American Sociological Review 43: 422–438.

Rosenblum, B. 1986. "Artists, alienation and the market," Sociologie de l'art; Colloque international Marseille. Paris: La documentation Française, pp. 173–182.

Schipiro, M. 1964. "On the relation of patron and artist." American Journal of Sociology 70: 363–369.

Schwartz, D. 1986. "Camera clubs and fine art photography: The social construction of an elite code." Urban Life 15: 165–195.

Sharon, B. 1979. "Artist-run galleries—a contemporary institutional change in the visual arts." Qualitative Sociology 2: 3–28.

Taylor, M. L. & R. C. Francis. 1961. "Human relations and the visual arts." Indian Journal of Social Research 2: 69–75.

Valentine, C. 1982. "The everyday life of art: Variation in the valuation of art works in a community art museum." Symbolic Interaction 5: 37–47.

Wayne, J. 1974. "The male artist as stereotypical female." Arts in Society 11: 107–113.

Wayte, G. 1986. "Stories of genius—Some notes on the socialisation of fine art students." Studies in Sexual Politics. 13–14: 132–144.

Wilkenson, D. Y. 1969. "The sociological orientation to artistic creations." Indian Journal of Social Research 10: 39–47.

Wynyard, R. N. 1986. "Painting and technological society." British Journal of Aesthetics 26: 57–61.

Zolberg, V. L. 1981. "Conflicting visions in American art museums." Theory and Society 10: 103–125.

Zolberg, V. L. 1984. "American art museums: Sanctuary or free-for-all." Social Forces 63: 377–392.

Zucker, W. M. 1969. "The artist as rebel." Journal of Aesthetics and Art Criticism 27: 389–397.

Performing Arts and Their Publics

Andreassen, A. R. & R. W. Belk. 1980. "Predictors of attendance at the performing arts." Journal of Consumer Research 7: 112–120.

Barbu, Z. 1967. "The sociology of drama." New Society 9: 161–164.

Becker, H. S. 1951. "The professional dance musician and his audience." American Journal of Sociology 57: 136–44.

Becker, H. S. 1953. "Some contingencies of the professional dance musician's career." Human Organization 12: 22–26.

Belafonte, H. 1974. "Concerns and outlooks: A performing artist views the contours of contemporary American culture." Arts in Society 11: 453–461.

Bensman, J. 1967. "Classical music and the status game." Transaction 4: 54–59.

Berger, B. M. 1971. "Audiences, art and power." Transaction 8: 26–30.

Berger, D. G. "Status attribution and self perception among music specialities." Sociological Quarterly 12: 259–65.

Berger, M. 1947. "Jazz: Resistance to the diffusion of a culture pattern." Journal of Negro History 32: 461–94.

Berger, M. 1957. "The new popularity of jazz." In B. Rosenberg & D. M. White, eds. Mass Culture: Glencoe: Free Press, pp. 404–407.

Björn, L. 1981. "The mass society and group action theories of cultural production: The case of stylistic innovation in jazz." Social Forces 60: 377–394.

Blau, J. R. 1988. "Music as social circumstance." Social Forces 66: 883–902.

Bogardus, E. 1949. "Social distance in Greek drama." Sociology and Social Research 33: 291–95.

Bunzel, J. H. 1970. "The theatre as a social institution." Indian Sociological Bulletin 7: 107–12.

Bunzel, J. H. 1970. "The theatre as a social institution." Indian Sociological Bulletin 7: 107–112.

Cameron, C. M. 1985. "Fighting with words: American composers' commentary on their work." Comparative Studies in Society and History 27: 430–460.

Cameron, W. B. 1963. "Sociological notes on the jam session." In his Informal Sociology. New York: Random House. pp. 118–130.

Cazden, N. 1945. "Musical consonance and dissonance: a cultural criterion," Journal of Aesthetics 4: 3–11.

Cerulo, K. A. 1984. "Social disruption and its effects on music: An empirical analysis." Social Forces 62: 885–904.

Chinoy, H. K. 1976. "The emergence of the director." In T. Cole & H. K. Chinoy, eds. Directors on Directing. Indianapolis: Bobbs-Merrill, pp. 1–78.

Conyers, J. E. 1963. "An exploratory study of musical tastes and interests of college students." Sociological Inquiry 33: 58–66.

Couch, S. R. 1983. "Patronage and organizational structure in symphony orchestras in London and New York." In J. B. Kamerman & R. Martorella, eds. Performers and Performances. South Hadley: Bergin & Garvey, pp. 109–122.

Couch, S. R. 1985. "Alienation and orchestra musicians in the United States." In L. Herek & D. Rupel, eds. Alienation and Participation in Culture. Ljubljana: U. Edvard Kardelj, pp. 107–113.

Dasilva, F. B. & D. R. Dees. 1976. "The social realms of music." Revue Internationale de Sociologie 12: 35–51.

Davis, F. 1986. "Nostalgic experience, art and the audience." Sociologie de l'art: Colloque international Marseille. Paris: La documentation Française, pp. 415–24.

Davis, R. L. 1966. "The glorious pauper: The financing of America's opera." Arts in Society 3: 25–31.

Denisoff, R. S. 1966. "Songs of persuasion: A sociological analysis of urban propaganda songs," Journal of American Folklore 79: 581–89.

Denisoff, R. S. 1968. "Protest movements: Class consciousness and the propaganda song," Sociological Quarterly 9: 228–47.

DiMaggio, P. & K. Stenberg. 1985. "Conformity and diversity in American resident theaters. In J. H. Balfe & M. J. Wyszomirski, eds. Art, Ideology and Politics. New York: Praeger, pp. 116–139.

Eaton, J. 1977. "The exhilarating adventure of new music in the U.S.A. since 1950." In G. McCue, ed. Music in American Society, 1776–1976. New Brunswick: Transaction Books, pp. 145–160.

Elson, J. 1985. "The social role of the theatre critic." Contemporary Review 246: 259–63.

Etzkorn, K. P. 1982. "On the sociology of musical practice and social groups," International Social Science Journal 34: 555–68.

Falk, G. 1975. " 'Moral density' and the job of symphony conducting." International Journal of Contemporary Sociology 12: 206–211.

Farnsworth, P. R., J. C. Trembley & C. E. Dutton. 1951. "Masculinity and feminity of musical phenomena." Journal of Aesthetics and Art Criticism 9: 257–262.

Faulkner, R. 1973a. "Orchestra interaction: Some features of communication and authority in an artistic organization." Sociological Quarterly 14: 147–57.

Faulkner, R. 1973b. "Career concerns and mobility motivation of orchestra musicians." Sociological Quarterly 14: 334–349.

Faulkner, R. 1974. "Making us sound bad: Performer compliance and interaction in the symphony orchestra.: In P. L. Stewart & M. G. Cantor, eds. Varieties of Work Experience: The Social Control of Occupational Groups and Roles. New York: John Wiley.

Federico, R. C. 1974. "Recruitment, training, and performance: The case of ballet." In Ph. L. Stewart & M. G. Cantor, eds. Varieties of Work Experience: The Social Control of Occupational Groups and Roles. New York: John Wiley, pp. 249–261.

Forsyth, S. & P. M. Kolenda. 1966. "Competition, co-operation, and group cohesion in the ballet company." Psychiatry 29: 123–145.

Fox, W. & M. H. Wince. 1975. "Musical taste cultures and taste publics." Youth and Society 7: 198–224.

Freiova, E. 1969. "The cultural orientation of Czechoslovak youth." European Journal of Sociology 10: 259–270.

Gatty, R. 1917. "The musical public and its opinions." Musical Quarterly 3: 517–538.

Goldfarb, J. C. 1976. "Student theatre in Poland." Survey 99: 155–178.

Goldfarb, J. C. 1978. "Social bases of independent public expression in Communist societies." American Journal of Sociology 83: 920–939.

Hall, G. A. 1977. "Workshop for a ballerina: An exercise in professional socialization." Urban Life and Culture 3: 193–220.

Halmos, P. 1952. "The decline of the choral dance." In his Solitude and Privacy. London: Routledge & Kegan Paul.

Hansen, C. C. 1960. "Social influences of jazz style: Chicago, 1920–1930." American Quarterly 12: 493–509.

Harris, H. J. 1915. "The occupation of the musician in the U.S." Musical Quarterly 1: 299–311.

Harvey, E. 1967. "Social change and the jazz musician." Social Forces 46: 34–42.

Henry, W. E. & J. H. Sims. 1970. "Actor's search for a self." Transaction 7: 57–62.

Kaplan, M. 1954. "The social role of the amateur." Music Educator's Journal: 26–28.

Kaplan, M. 1955. "Telopractice: A symphony orchestra as it prepares for a concert." Social Forces 33: 352–355.

Kracauer, S. 1949. "National types as Hollywood presents them." Public Opinion Quarterly 13: 53–72.

Lange, M., J. Bullard, W. Luksetich & P. Jacobs. 1985. "Cost functions for symphony orchestras." Journal of Cultural Economics 9: 71–85.

Lastrucci, C. L. 1941. "The professional dance musician." Journal of Musicology 3: 168–172.

Layder, D. 1984. "Sources and levels of commitment in actor careers." Work & Occupations 11: 147–163.

Levy, E. 1979. "The role of the critic: Theater in Israel, 1918–1968." Journal of Communication 29: 175–183.

Lipton, J. P. 1987. "Stereotypes concerning musicians within symphony orchestras." Journal of Psychology 121: 85–93.

Malhotra, V. A. 1981. "The social accomplishment of music in a symphony orchestra: A phenomenological analysis." Qualitative Sociology 4: 102–125.

Mann, P. H. 1967. "Surveying a theatre audience: Findings." British Journal of Sociology 18: 75–90.

Martorella, R. 1975. "The structure of the market and musical style." International Review of the Aesthetics and Sociology of Music 6: 241–253.

McGranahan, D. V. & I. Wayne. 1948. "German and American traits reflected in popular drama." Human Relations 1: 429–455.

Merriam, A. P. & R. W. Mack. 1960. "The jazz community." Social Forces 38: 211–222.

Mueller, J. H. 1963. "A sociological approach to musical behavior." Ethnomusicology 6: 216–220.

Mulligan, R. A. & J. C. Dinkins. 1956. "Socioeconomic background and theatrical preference." Sociology and Social Research 40: 325–328.

Nash, D. 1955. "Challenge and response in the American composer's career." Journal of Aesthetics and Art Criticism 14: 116–122.

Nash, D. 1957. "The socialization of an artist: The American composer." Social Forces, 35: 307–13.

Peters, A. K. 1974. "Aspiring Hollywood actresses: A sociological perspective." In P. L. Stewart & M. G. Cantor, eds. Varieties of Work Experience: The Social Control of Occupational Groups and Roles. New York: John Wiley, pp. 39–48.

Peterson, R. A. 1967. "Market and moralist censors of a rising art form: Jazz." Art in Society 4: 253–264.

Peterson, R. A. 1986. "The role of formal accountability in the shift from impresario to arts administrator." Sociologie de l'art, Proceedings of the Colloque international Marseille. Paris: la documentation Française. pp. 111–34.

Rees, V. D. D. 1970. "The creative process in the music composition: a cross-cultural study." Human Mosaic 4: 25–38.

Riedel, J. 1962. "The sociology of music." Music Educators Journal 49: 39–42.

Riggins, S. 1985. "Institutional change in Nineteenth-Century French music." Current Perspectives in Social Theory 6: 243–260.

Rubin, S. E. 1973. "Music and publicity." Stereo Review 30: 67–73.

Ryser, C. P. 1964. "The student dancer." In R. N. Wilson, ed. The Arts in Society. Englewood Cliffs: Prentice-Hall, pp. 97–121.

Scheff, T. J. 1976. "Audience awareness and catharsis in drama." Psychoanalytic Review 63: 529–554.

Schuessler, K. F. 1948. "Social background and musical taste." American Sociological Review 13: 330–335.

Seeger, C. 1957. "Music and class structure in the United States." American Quarterly 9: 281–294.

Shepherd, J. C. 1979. "Music and social control: An essay on the sociology of musical knowledge." Catalyst 13: 1–54.

Silber, I. 1951. "Racism, chauvinism keynote U.S. music." Sing Out 2: 6–7, 10.

Silber, I. 1953. "Male supremacy and the folk song." Sing Out 3: 4–5, 11.

Stebbins, R. A. 1966. "Class, status, and power among jazz and commercial musicians." Sociological Quarterly 7: 197–213.

Stebbins, R. A. 1968. "A theory of the jazz community." Sociological Quarterly 9: 318–331.

Stebbins, R. A. 1969. "Role distance, role distance behavior and jazz musicians." British Journal of Sociology 20: 406–415.

Stebbins, R. A. 1976. "Music among friends." Revue Internationale de Sociologie 12: 52–73.

Stebbins, R. A. 1978. "Classical music amateurs: A definitional study." Humboldt Journal of Social Relations 5: 78–103.

Sussmann, L. 1986. "The work of making dances." Sociologie de l'art; Proceedings of the Colloque international Marseilles, 1985, Paris: La documentation Française, pp. 203–212.

Szwed, J. F. 1966. "Musical style and racial conflict." Phylon 27: 358–366.

Vahemetsa, A. 1970. "A typology of the recipients of artistic films." Society and Leisure 2: 87–101.

Westby, D. L. 1960. "The career experience of the symphony musician." Social Forces 38: 223–230.

Mass Culture: Popular and Folk Arts

Adorno, T. W. 1941. "On popular music." Studies in Philosophy and Social Science 9: 17–48.

Anderson, B., P. Hesbacher, K. P. Etzkorn & R. S. Denisoff. 1980. "Hit record trends, 1940–1977." Journal of Communication 30: 31–43.

Arya, S. P. 1961. "Folk songs and social structure." Indian Journal of Social Research 2: 45–50.

Belz, C. I. 1967. "Popular music and the folk tradition." Journal of American Folklore 80: 130–43.

Bensman, J. & I. Gerver. 1958. "Art and the mass society." Social Problems 6: 4–10.

Bontinck, I. 1984. "Mass media and youth music," International Review of the Aesthetics and Sociology of Music 15: 39–51.

Brown, R. 1968. "The creative process in the popular arts." International Social Science Journal 20: 613–624.

Denisoff, R. S. 1969a. "The proletarian renascence: The folkness of the ideological folk." Journal of American Folklore 82: 51–65.

Denisoff, R. S. 1969b. ''Folk music and the American left: A generational-ideological comparison.'' British Journal of Sociology 20: 427–442.

Denisoff, R. S. & J. Bridges. 1982. ''Popular music: Who are the recording artists?'' Journal of Communication 32: 132–142.

Denisoff, R. S. & M. H. Levine. 1972. ''Youth and popular music.'' Youth and Society 4: 237–255.

Elkin, F. 1954. ''The value implications of popular films.'' Sociology and Social Research 38: 320–322.

Etzkorn, K. P. 1963. ''Social context of songwriting in the United States.'' Ethnomusicology 7: 96–106.

Etzkorn, K. P. 1964. ''The relationship between musical and social patterns in American popular music.'' Journal of Research in Music Education 12: 279–286.

Etzkorn, K. P. 1969. ''The vulnerability of occupations and social change: The example of the composer of popular hits.'' Kölner Zeitschrift für Soziologie und Sozial-Psychologie 21: 329–342.

Faulkner, R. R. & A. B. Anderson. 1987. ''Short-term projects and emergent careers: Evidence from Hollywood.'' American Journal of Sociology 92: 879–909.

Flores, T. 1986. ''Art, folklore, bureaucracy and ideology.'' Dialectical Anthropology 10: 249–264.

Gans, H. J. 1957. ''The creator-audience relationship in the mass media: An analysis of movie making.'' In B. Rosenberg & D. M. White, eds. Mass Culture. Glencoe: Free Press, pp. 315–324.

Gans, H. J. 1964. ''The rise of the problem-film: An analysis of changes in Hollywood films and the American audience.'' Social Problems 9: 327–336.

Gans, H. J. 1966. ''Popular culture in America: Social problem in a mass society or social asset in a pluralist society.'' In H. S. Becker, ed. Social Problems: A Modern Approach. New York: John Wiley, pp. 549–620.

Gans, H. J. 1985. ''American popular culture and high culture in a changing class structure.'' In J. Salzman, ed. Prospects: An Annual of American Cultural Studies, 10. Cambridge: Cambridge U. Press.

Gillespie, D. F. 1972. ''Sociology of popular culture: The other side of a definition.'' Journal of Popular Culture 6: 292–299.

Gottdiener, M. 1985. ''Hegemony and mass culture.'' American Journal of Sociology 90: 979–1001.

Griff, M. 1960. "The commercial artist: A study in changing and consistent identities." In M. Stein, A. Vidich & D. M. White, eds. Identity and Anxiety. Glencoe: Free Press.

Grossberg, L. 1987. "The politics of music: American images and British articulations." Canadian Journal of Political and Social Theory 11: 144–151.

Hayakawa, S. I. 1955. "Popular songs vs. the facts of life." ETC 12: 83–95.

Hennion, A. & C. Meadel. 1986. "Programming music: Radio as mediator." Media, Culture and Society 8: 281–303.

Henny, L. 1976. "The role of filmmakers in revolutionary social change." Praxis 1: 157–175.

Hirsch, P. M. 1971. "Sociological approaches to the pop music phenomenon." American Behavioral Scientist 14: 371–388.

Horkheimer, M. 1941. "Art and mass culture." Studies in Philosophy and Social Science 9: 290–304.

Jarvie, I. C. 1969. "Film and the communication of values." European Journal of Sociology 10: 205–219.

Johnstone, J. & E. Katz. 1957. "Youth and popular music: a study in the sociology of taste." American Journal of Sociology 62: 563–568.

Josipovic, I. 1984. "The mass media and musical culture." International Review of the Aesthetics and Sociology of Music 15: 39–51.

Kamin, J. 1975. "Musical culture and perceptual learning in the popularization of Black music." Journal of Jazz Studies 5: 54–65.

Kaplan, A. 1955. "Folksinging in a mass society." Sociologus 5: 14–28.

Kealy, E. 1979. "From craft to art: The case of sound mixers and popular music." Sociology of Work and Occupations 6: 3–29.

Larson, M. & S. Cavan. 1972. "Hollywood dream factory." Society 9: 68–70.

Lewis, J. M. 1985. "Social class origins of Academy Award winners, 1940–1982." Free Inquiry in Creative Sociology 13: 80–82.

Lund, J. & R. S. Denisoff. 1971. "The folk music revival and the counter culture: Contributions and contradictions." Journal of American Folklore 84: 394–405.

MacDonald, D. 1953. "A theory of mass culture." Diogenes 3: 1–17.

MacColl, E. 1964. "The singer and the audience." Sing Out 14: 16–20.

Marrus, M. R. 1976. "Modernization and dancing in rural France: From la bourree to le fox-trot." Dance Research Journal 8: 1–9.

Marsden, P. V., J. S. Reed, M. K. Kennedy & K. M. Stinson. 1982. "American regional cultures and differences in leisure time activities." Social Forces 60: 1023–1049.

Martel, M. & G. McCall. 1964. "Reality orientation and the pleasure principle: A study of American mass periodical fiction, 1890–1955." In L. A. Dexter & D. M. White, eds. People, Society and Mass Communications. New York: Free Press of Glencoe.

McCormack, T. 1969. "Folk culture and the mass media." European Journal of Sociology 10: 220–237.

Meyersohn, R. & E. Katz, 1957. "Notes on a natural history of fads." American Journal of Sociology 62: 594–601.

Peters, A. K. & M. G. Cantor. 1982. "Screen acting as work." In J. S. Ettema & D. C. Whitney, eds. Individuals as Mass Media Organizations. Beverly Hills: Sage, pp. 53–68.

Peterson, R. A. & D. G. Berger. 1971. "Entrepreneurship in organizations: Evidence from the popular music industry." Administrative Science Quarterly 16: 97–106

Powdermaker, H. 1947. "An anthropologist looks at the movies." Annals of the American Academy of Political and Social Science 254: 80–86.

Reed, S. 1970. "The film maker and the audience." In J. Creedy, ed. The Social Context of Art. London: Tavistock, pp. 127–146.

Riesman, D. 1950. "Listening to popular music." American Quarterly 2: 359–371.

Schechter, H. 1979. "Focus on myth and American popular art." Journal of American Culture 2: 210–216.

Shils, E. 1957. "Daydreams and nightmares: Reflections on the criticism of mass culture." Sewanee Review 45: 587–608.

Shils, E. 1964. "The high culture of the age." In R. N. Wilson, ed. The Arts in Society. New York: Prentice-Hall, pp. 317–362.

Shils, E. 1978. "Mass society and its culture." In P. Davison, R. Meyerson & E. Shils, eds. Literary Taste, Culture, and Mass Communication. Teaneck: Somerset House, pp. 200–229.

Skipper. J. K. 1975. "Musical tastes of Canadian and American college students: An examination of the massification and Americanization theses." Canadian Journal of Sociology 1: 49–59.

Taylor, M. L. 1960. "Participation in the art world by town and country people." Journal of Home Economics 52: 421–424.

Vignolle, J. P. 1980. "Mixing genres and reaching the public: The production of popular music." Social Science Information 19: 79–105.

Wang, B. 1934. "Folk songs as a means of social control." Sociology and Social Research 19: 64–69.

Wilensky, H. L. 1964. "Mass society and mass culture." American Sociological Review 29: 173–197.

Williams, R. 1974. "On high and popular culture." The New Republic (Nov. 23): 13–16.

Wilson, R. N. 1968. "High culture and popular culture in a business society." In I. Berg, ed. The Business of America. New York: Harcourt Brace & World.

Sociology of Literature

Albrecht, M. C. 1954. "The relationship of literature and society." American Journal of Sociology 59: 425–436.

Albrecht, M. C. 1956. "Does literature reflect common values?" American Sociological Review 21: 722–729.

Altick, R. D. 1953. "English publishing and the mass audience in 1852." Studies in Bibliography 6: 3–24.

Altick R. D. 1962. "The sociology of authorship: The social origins, education and occupations of 1,100 British writers, 1800–1935." The Bulletin of the New York Public Library 66: 389–404.

Arnold, A. 1958. "Why structure in fiction: a note to social scientists." American Quarterly 10: 325–37.

Asheim, L. 1949. "Portrait of the book reader as depicted in current research." In B. Berelson, ed. The Library's Public. New York: Columbia U. Press, pp. 19–50.

Bain, R. 1927. "Poetry and social research." Sociology and Social Research 12: 35–49.

Barbu, Z. 1970. "Sociological perspectives in art and literature." In J. Creedy, ed. The Social Context of Art. London: Tavistock, pp. 9–25.

Barnett, J. H. & R. Gruen. 1948. "Recent American divorce novels, 1938–1945: A study in the sociology of literature." Social Forces 26: 322–327.

Barrett, W. 1951. "American fiction and American values." Partisan Review (Nov.- –Dec., 1951):

Bellamy, R. F. 1956. "Art and literature." In J. S. Roucek, ed. Social Control. New York: D. Van Nostrand, pp. 240–59.

Berelson, B. 1957. "Who reads what books and why." In B. Rosenberg & D. M. White, eds. Mass Culture. Glencoe: The Free Press, pp. 119–25.

Berelson, B. & P. J. Salter. 1957. "Majority and minority Americans: An analysis of magazine fiction." Public Opinion Quarterly 10: 168–197.

Bloch, H. A. 1944. "Towards the development of a sociology of literary and art forms." American Sociological Review 8: 313–320.

Bloore, S. 1955. "Literature and human relations." Journal of Educational Sociology 28: 389–395.

Bogardus, E. S. 1933. "Social distance in Shakespeare." Sociology and Social Research 18: 67–73.

Bogardus, E. S. 1951. "Social distance in poetry." Sociology and Social Research 36: 40–47.

Bowron, B., L. Marx & A. Rose. 1957. "Literature and covert culture." American Quarterly 9: 377–86.

Boys, R. C. 1947. "Literary censorship and the public morals." Michigan Alumnus Quarterly Review 53: 323–30.

Brablikora, H. 1969. "On the tasks of the sociology of literature." Sociologicky Casopis 5: 213–17.

Burger, P. 1985. "The institution of 'art' as a category in the sociology of literature." Cultural Critique 2: 5–33.

Calverton, V. F. 1931. "The Puritan myth: A challenge to the theory that the Puritans are responsible for the inferiority of our literature and culture." Scribner's Magazine 89: 251–57.

Chartier, B. 1950. "The social role of the literary elite." Social Forces 29: 179–186.

Chase, R. 1957. "Radicalism in the American novel." Commentary 23: 65–71.

Chase, R. 1957. "Neo-conservatism and American literature." Commentary 23: 254–261.

Clark, P. P. 1977a. "Patrons, publishers, and prizes: The writer's estate in France." In J. Ben-David & T. N. Clark, eds. Culture and Its Creators. Chicago: U. of Chicago Press, pp. 197–225.

Clark, P. P. 1978. "The sociology of literature: An historical introduction." Research in Sociology of Knowledge, Science and Art 1: 237–58.

Clark, P. P. & T. N. Clark. 1969. "Writers, literature, and student movements in France." Sociology of Education 42: 293ff.

Cousins, A. N. 1961. "The sociology of the war novel." Indian Journal of Social Research 2: 83–90.

Cousins, A. N. 1976. "Creative literature and social change." International Journal of Contemporary Sociology 13: 239–248.

Cowley, M. 1950. "How the writer lives." In B. Bliven, ed. Twentieth Century Unlimited. Philadelphia: Lippincott.

Cowley, M. 1954. "How writers earn their livings." Saturday Review of Literature (Sept. 25) 9–10 & 36ff.

Escarpit, R. 1968. "The sociology of literature." In W. Kolb & J. Gould, eds. International Encyclopaedia of the Social Sciences. New York: Macmillan.

Gamberg, H. 1958. "The modern literary ethos." Social Forces 37: 7–14.

Griswold, W. 1987. "The fabrication of meaning: Literary interpretation in the United States, Great Britain, and the West Indies." American Journal of Sociology 92: 1077–1118.

Hallen, G. C. 1966. "The sociology of literature." Social Science 41: 12–18.

Kotok, A. B. 1971. "Foreign nationals and minority Americans in magazine fiction 1946–1968." In B. Rosenberg & D. M. White, eds. Mass Culture Revisited. New York: Van Nostrand, Reinhold, pp. 249–265.

Krieger, S. 1984. "Fiction and social science." Studies in Symbolic Interaction 5: 269–287.

Larsen, C. E. 1954. "The race problem in contemporary American negro poetry." Sociology and Social Research 38: 162–167.

Lash, J. S. 1961. "Sociological aspects of the Negro novel in Amerrican literature." Indian Journal of Social Research 2:76–82.

Laurenson, D. T. 1969. "A sociological study of authorship." British Journal of Sociology 20: 311–325.

Laurenson, D. T. 1978. "Current research in the sociology of literature: Introduction." Sociological Review Monograph 26: 1–14.

Le Col, J. P. 1946. "Dynamic social forces of literature: Some stages in its history." International Social Science Journal 19: 517–533.

Lengyel, P. 1967. "Sociology of literary creativity." International Social Science Journal 19: 489–613.

Lerner, M. & E. Mims, Jr. 1937. "Literature." In Encyclopedia of the Social Sciences V. New York: Macmillan, pp. 523–543.

Levin, H. 1946. "Literature as an institution." Accent no. 1 6: 159–168.

Lowenthal, L. 1953. "Sociology of literature." In W. Schramm, ed. Communications in Modern Society. Urbana: U. of Illinois Press.

Mannheim, K. 1963. "A review of Georg Lukac's Theory of the Novel." Studies on the Left 3: 50–53. [Also 1920. Logos 9: 298–302.]

McKenzie, V. 1941. "Treatment of war themes in magazine fiction." Public Opinion Quarterly 1: 227–232.

Merrill, F. E. 1967. "The sociology of literature." Social Research 34: 648–659.

Middleton, R. 1960. "Fertility values in American magazine fiction." Public Opinion Quarterly 24: 130–143.

Pospelov, G. N. 1967. "Literature and sociology." International Social Science Journal 19: 534–549.

Punke, H. H. 1937. "Cultural change and change in popular literature." Social Forces 15: 359–370.

Roucek, J. S. 1961. "The sociology of literature." Indian Journal of Social Research 2: 22–30.

Sayre, R. 1980. "Lowenthal, Goldman and the sociology of literature." Telos 45: 150–160.

Segal, A. 1971. "Portnoy's Complaint and the sociology of literature." British Journal of Sociology 22: 257–268.

Valentine, J. 1970. "The role of class in the social determination of thought: The relevance of Lucien Goldmann's sociology of literature." Sociological Analysis 1: 20–40.

Vincent, M. 1936. "Regionalism and fiction." Social Forces 14 335–340.

Ward, J. P. 1986. "Poetry and sociology." Human Studies 9: 323–345.

Washington, R. 1977. "The function of Black American literature as a cultural institution." Cornell Journal of Social Relations 2: 183–205.

Wilkinson, H. 1918. "Social thought in American fiction (1909–1917)." Studies in Sociology 3: 1–17.

Williams, R. 1958. "Literature and rural society." The Listener 78: 630.

Wilson, R. N. 1952. "Literature, society and personality." Journal of Aesthetics and Art Criticism 11: 297–309.

Wilson, R. N. 1964. "The poet in American society." In his The Arts in Society. New York: Prentice Hall, pp. 3–34.

Witte, W. 1941. "The sociological approach to literature." Social Forces 36: 860–894.

Funding and Control—Economics and Policy

Baro, G. 1967. "Patronage for Britain's art." Art in America 55: 40–43.

Becker, H. S. 1984. "Should the government pay for art?" Contemporary Sociology 13: 549–51.

Berry, R. 1970. "Patronage." In J. Creedy, ed. The Social Context of Art. London: Tavistock, pp. 83–107.

Blau, J. R. & W. McKinley. 1979. "Ideas, complexity and innovation." Administrative Science Quarterly 24: 200–219.

Blau, J. R., L. Newman & J. E. Schwartz. 1986. "Internal economics of scale in performing arts organizations." Journal of Cultural Economics 10: 63–76.

Cheyne, C. 1986. "The state and the arts: The state of the art." New Zealand Sociology 1: 113–120.

DiMaggio, P. 1978. "Cultural property and public policy: Emerging tensions in government support for the arts." Social Research 45: 356–89.

DiMaggio, P. 1982. "Cultural capital and schools success." American Sociological Review 47: 189ff.

DiMaggio, P. 1987. "Non-profit organizations in the production and distribution of culture." In W. W. Powell, ed. The Non-profit Sector. New Haven: Yale U. Press, pp. 195–220.

DiMaggio, P. & M. Useem. 1978. "Cultural property and public policy: Emerging tensions in government support for the arts." Social Research 45: 356–389.

Dubin, S. C. 1985. "The politics of public art." Urban Life 14: 274–299.

Dubin, S. C. 1986. "Artistic production and social control." Social Forces 64: 667–85.

Eells, R. 1968. "Business for art's sake: The case for corporate support of the arts." In Evar Berg, ed. The Business of America. New York: Harcourt, Brace & World.

Elkoff, M. 1965. "The American painter as a blue chip." Esquire 62: 37–42 & 114. [Reprinted in M. C. Albrecht, J. H. Barnett & M. Griff, eds. 1970. The Sociology of Art and Literature: A Reader. New York: Praeger, pp. 311–322].

Frow, J. 1986. "Class and culture: Funding the arts." Meanjin 45: 118–128.

Goldwater, R. 1950. "Government and art: A symposium." Magazine of Art 43: 243–259.

Grosser, M. 1951. "Art and economics." In his The Painters Eye. New York: New American Library (Mentor), pp. 154–167.

Harris, J. S. 1973. "The government and arts patronage." Public Administration Review 33: 407–414.

Hart, K. C. 1984. "Changing public attitudes toward funding of the arts." The Annals of the American Academy of Political and Social Science 471 (1984), 45–56.

Hayes, P. 1973. "The arts in America—Our new national product." The Annals of the American Academy of Political and Social Science 405: 131–136.

Heilbrun, J. 1984. "Keynes and the economics of the arts." Journal of Cultural Economics 8: 37–50.

Himmelstein, J. L. 1984. "American conservatism and government funding of the social sciences and the arts." Sociological Inquiry 54: 171–87.

Hodsoll, F. 1985. "The National Endowment for the Arts and cultural economics." In C. R. Watts, W. S. Hendon & H. Horowitz, eds. Governments and Culture, Col. II. Proceedings of the International Conference on Cultural Economics and Planning. Akron: U. of Akron, pp. 3–11.

Joyce, M. S. 1984. "Government funding of culture: What price the arts?" The Annals of the American Academy of Political and Social Sciences 471: 27–33.

Kaplan, M. 1975. "A Macrocosmic scheme of cultural analysis: Implication for arts policy." Arts in Society 12: 203–214.

Martorella, R. 1976. "The structure of the market and the social organization of opera: Some inquiries." Revue Internationale de Sociologie 12: 74–90.

Martorella, R. 1986. "Government and corporate ideologies in support of the arts." Sociologie de l'art: Colloque international Marseille, 1985. Paris: La documentation Française, pp. 31–46.

O'Hare, M. & A. L. Feld 1984. "Indirect aid to the arts." The Annals of the American Academy of Political and Social Science 471: 132–43.

Ridlay, F. F. "State patronage of the arts in Britain: The political culture of cultural politics." Social Science Information 17: 449–486.

Zukin, S. 1982. "Art in the arms of power." Theory and Society 11: 423–451.

Contributors

Howard S. Becker is Professor of Sociology at Northwestern University. In addition to his position as one of the leaders in the sociology of the arts, he has published widely about deviance, the professionalization of medical students, teachers, jazz musicians, research methodology and writing for sociologists. His book, *Art Worlds,* provides a full introduction to and analysis of the social nature of arts activity. As a teacher, he has sponsored the dissertations of many prominent sociologists currently working in cultural sociology.

Norman Berkowitz is a computer programmer in New York City.

Judith R. Blau is Professor of Sociology at The University of North Carolina at Chapel Hill. She earned her BA and MA from the University of Chicago and her PhD from Northwestern University. Her other publications include *Architects and Firms* (MIT Press, 1984, 1987), *The Shape of Culture* (Rose Monograph Series, Cambridge University Press, 1989), and with Gail A. Quets, *Cultural Life in City and Region* (University of Akron, 1989). She has also worked in the areas of sociology of science and organizational sociology.

Marcia H. Bystryn is Acting Director of the Twentieth Century Fund, a public policy foundation. Her scholarly interests are in the sociology of art and culture.

Stephen R. Couch is Associate Professor of Sociology, Pennsylvania State University, and Director of Penn State's Science, Technology and Society Consortium of Northeastern Pennsylvania. His scholarly interests include the sociology and social history of the symphony orchestra, and the relationship of technological development to the arts.

Diana Crane is Professor of Sociology at the University of Pennsylvania. Her fields of interest are the sociology of science, the arts, and popular culture. Her most recent book is *The Transformation of the Avant-Garde: The New York Art World, 1940–1985* (1987).

491

Paul J. DiMaggio is Associate Professor of Sociology at Yale University. He has written widely on sociological aspects of culture and the arts and is author of *Managers of the Arts* (1987), editor of *Nonprofit Enterprise in the Arts: Studies in Mission and Constraint* (1986), and co-editor (with Sharon Zukin) of *Structures of Capital: The Social Organization of Economic Life* (1990).

Robert R. Faulkner is Professor of Sociology, University of Massachusetts, Amherst, and author of *Hollywood Studio Musicians* (1971, 1985), *Music on Demand: Composers and Careers in the Hollywood Film Industry* (1983), and articles on orchestra players and jazz ensembles. His current work focuses on the interorganizational market relations between corporations and advertising agencies. He is the sociology editor of *Empirical Studies of the Arts*.

Arnold W. Foster is Associate Professor at the State University of New York at Albany. His papers on the sociology of the arts have appeared in journals in several countries and he is presently Secretary of Research Council #37 (Sociology of the Arts) of the International Sociological Association.

Charles W. Hughes is a musicologist and organist. He taught at Hunter College and Lehman College. His publications include *The Human Side of Music* (1948) and *American Hymns, Old and New* (1980).

Alicja Iwanska, Professor Emerita of the State University of New York at Albany and presently Professor of Sociology of the Polish University of London [England] is presently working on a book about the philosopher and aesthetician, J. M. Guyau.

Jonathan Kamin, a sociologist with a strong interest in popular culture, has performed professionally with rock bands.

Vytautas Kavolis is Charles A. Dana Professor of Comparative Civilizations and Professor of Sociology at Dickinson College. He is the author of *Artistic Expression—A Sociological Analysis* (1968) and *History on Art's Side: Social Dynamics in Artistic Efflorescences* (1972), editor of *Designs of Selfhood* (1984) and co-editor of *Comparative Civilizations Review.*

Kurt Lang is Professor of Sociology and Communications, University of Washington. He is author or co-author of *Collective Dynamics* (1961),

Television and Politics (1968), *Military Institutions and the Sociology of War* (1972), *The Battle for Public Opinion: The President, the Press, and the Polls during Watergate* (1983) and of *Etched in Memory: The Survival of Artistic Reputation* (forthcoming).

Linda B. Leue is currently Social Services Disability Analyst for the New York State Department of Social Services. Her MA and further work in sociology is from the State University of New York at Albany. Her main interests are in the sociology of film and popular culture.

Emanuel Levy is Associate Professor of Sociology and Film at Wellesley College and a Visiting Professor at Columbia University. He is the author of *And the Winner Is: The History and Politics of the Oscar Award* (1987), *John Wayne: Prophet of the American Way of Life* (1988), and *John Doe and Peggy Sue: Images of Small-Town America in Popular Culture* (in press).

Alan Lomax, head of the Columbia Cross-Cultural Survey of Expressive Style at Columbia, pioneered the technology of field recording and media use of folklore, and has recently developed computer-based, numerical taxonomies of song, dance and speech styles.

Rosanne Martorella is Professor of Sociology at William Paterson College, and author of several books and articles on performers, arts organizations, and corporate support to the arts (including *The Sociology of Opera,* and *Corporate Art Collecting*). She resides in Nyack, New York, with her husband and two children.

Dennison Nash, who is Professor of Anthropology and Sociology at the University of Connecticut, has drifted away from studies of composers in various cultures to a consideration of the ways of expatriates, including tourists. His most recent work is *A Little Anthropology* (Prentice Hall, 1989).

Richard A. Peterson is Professor of Sociology at Vanderbilt University, and past Chair of the Culture Section of the American Sociological Association. He has published widely in the sociology of art, culture, and music. He edited the seminal *Production of Culture* (1976).

Sally Ridgeway is Associate Professor in the Department of Sociology and Associate Dean, Office of Academic Attainment at Adelphi University.

Her scholarly interests are in the Sociology of Art and she has been an active participant in the annual Conference on Social Theory, Politics and the Arts since its beginnings.

Charles R. Simpson is Associate Professor of Sociology, State University of New York at Plattsburgh. He is the author of *SoHo: The Artist in the City* (1981) and contributor to the *International Journal of Politics, Culture and Society.*

Robert A. Stebbins is Professor in the Department of Sociology at the University of Calgary and President (1988–1989) of the Canadian Sociology and Anthropology Association. Among his research interests is the study of amateurs and professionals in art, science, sport, and entertainment. His publications on the fine and popular arts include *Amateurs: On the Margin between Work and Leisure* (1979), *The Magician: Career, Culture, and Social Psychology in a Variety Art* (1984), and *The Laugh Makers: Stand-Up Comedy as Art, Business, and Life-Style* (1989) as well as numerous articles. Dr. Stebbins is also the principal bassist with the Calgary Civic Orchestra.

David Earl Sutherland is a sociologist presently in the Department of Management Systems of the College of Business Administration at Ohio University. He retains his interest in the sociology of the arts, especially in dance.

Michael Useem is Professor of Sociology at Boston University and author of *The Inner Circle: Large Corporation and the Rise of Business Political Activity in the U.S. and U.K.* (1984) and *Liberal Education and the Corporation: The Hiring and Advancement of College Graduates* (1989). He is a co-author of *Audience Studies of the Performing Arts and Museums* (1978), prepared for the National Endowment for the Arts, and he has authored articles on corporate giving to culture and the arts. He is a member of the Research Advisory Committee of the American Council for the Arts.

Roland L. Warren is Professor Emeritus at the Heller School, Brandeis University. He is a widely known authority in the field of community, and the author of *Studying Your Community, The Community in America, Truth, Love, and Social Change, The Structure of Urban Reform* (with Stephen M. Rose and Ann F. Burgunder) *Social Change and Human Purpose* and some 70 articles in professional journals. Dr. Warren is the past chairman of the Community Section of the American Sociological Association and of the Committee on Community Research and Development of the Society for the Study of Social Problems. He is a former Guggenheim Fellow and recipient of a research scientist award from the National Institute of Mental Health.

Vera L. Zolberg is Senior Lecturer in the Department of Sociology and Committee on Liberal Studies of the Graduate Faculty, New School for Social Research. She has completed a book on the sociology of art, and is studying avant garde movements, cultural policy, and museums as texts.

Author Index

Subject Index